Practical Silverlight Programming

Advanced Graphics and User Interface Development With Silverlight 2

Practical Silverlight Programming

Advanced Graphics and User Interface Development with Silverlight 2

Jack Xu, Ph.D

UniCAD Publishing

Practical Silverlight Programming

Printed and bound in the United States of America 9 8 7 6 5 4 3 2 1UC

Editor: Anna Hsu

The publisher offers excellent discounts on this book when ordered in quantity for bulk purchases or special sales, which may include electronic versions and /or custom covers and content particular to your business, training goals, marketing focus, and branding interests. For more information, please contact:

sales@drxudotnet.com
Visit us on the website: www.drxudotnet.com

Published by UniCAD Publishing.
Phoenix, USA
ISBN-13: 978-0-9793725-2-0
ISBN-10: 0-9793725-2-6

Publisher's Cataloging-in-Publication Data

Xu, Jack
Practical Silverlight Programming – Advanced Graphics and User Interface Development with Silverlight 2/
Jack Xu – 1st ed.
p.cm.
ISBN 978-0-9793725-2-0

1. Silverlight. 2. User Interface. 3. XAML. 4. Windows Presentation Foundation. 5. Graphics Programming.
6. .NET Applications.
I. Title. II. Title III Title: Practical Silverlight Programming

For my wonderful family

Contents

Introduction

Overview

In the Internet age, web developers continue to push the boundaries of the browsing platform, yet remain locked in a world limited by HTML-based web development tools.

Silverlight aims to change this situation by bringing a new paradigm of web development to the table, providing developers with more powerful tools for their web development arsenals, while simultaneously allowing them to leverage existing development skills.

Silverlight enables the development of next-generation Microsoft .NET-based media experiences and rich interactive applications (RIAs) for the Web. Silverlight is delivered as a cross-platform and cross-browser plug-in that exposes a programming framework and features from a subset of the .NET Framework. With Silverlight, your Web development experience will much more closely resemble the development of desktop applications using the Windows Presentation Foundation (WPF). Ultimately, the goal of Silverlight is to create Web applications that are indistinguishable from desktop applications.

Silverlight 2.0 is based on the .NET Framework and is a subset of WPF, allowing you to use procedural programming languages such as C# or Visual Basic to develop RIAs for Web applications.

Practical Silverlight Programming will provide the programming techniques necessary for developing interactive web applications using Microsoft Silverlight and C# based on the .NET framework. I believe this book will be useful for Silverlight and C# programmers of all skill levels.

As a C# programmer, you are probably already familiar with WPF and the .NET 3.5 framework. Silverlight, as a lightweight version of WPF, takes advantage of WPF's advanced graphical features. Silverlight completely revolutionizes the landscape of Web application development based on conventional HTML techniques. At first, you may think that Silverlight is just another way to create Web pages and Web controls such as menus, dialogs, and custom controls. However, Silverlight has much more to offer than any other Web programming framework does. It integrates three basic Windows elements – text, controls, and graphics – into one single programming model, and puts these three elements into the same element tree in the same manner.

Without Silverlight, developing a Web application with interactive graphics objects and animations might involve a number of different technologies ranging from Flash to GIF animations. Silverlight, on the other hand, is designed as a single model for interactive Web application development, providing seamless integration between such services within an application. Similar constructs can be used for creating animations, data binding, and graphics models.

To take further advantage of new powerful graphics hardware technologies, Silverlight, like WPF, implements a vector-based graphics model. This allows for graphics to be scaled based on screen-specific resolution without loss of image quality, something nearly impossible with fixed-size raster graphics.

With Silverlight, graphics elements can be easily integrated into any part of your Web applications. For example, Silverlight provides 2D shape elements that can be involved in the user interface (UI) tree like other elements can. You are free to mix these shapes with any other kind of element, such as with a button control.

As you may have noticed, there already are a few Silverlight programming books available in bookstores. The vast majority of these books are general-purpose user guides and tutorials explaining the basics of Silverlight and how to implement simple Silverlight applications. To take full advantage of Silverlight's advanced features, however, there is need for a book that provides an in-depth introduction specifically for Silverlight programming for real-world Web applications.

This book is written with the intention of providing you with a complete and comprehensive explanation of Silverlight's capability in graphics and user interfaces, and pays special attention to code implementation details, which will be useful when you create your own real-world interactive Web applications. This book includes many ready-to-run code examples which cover a broad array of topics on Silverlight programming. Much of this book contains original work based on my own programming experience developing Web applications. Without Silverlight and the .NET framework, developing interactive Web applications with advanced graphics and user interfaces is a difficult and time-consuming task. To add even simple charts or animations to your Web applications, you often have to waste effort creating a chart and animation program, or buy commercial chart and animation add-on packages.

Practical Silverlight Programming provides everything you need to create advanced graphics and user interfaces in your Web applications using Silverlight. It shows you how to create a variety of graphics and user interfaces ranging from simple 2D shapes to complex custom user controls. Even though Silverlight doesn't contain a built-in 3D model, I'll show you how to create your own 3D graphics objects and how to interact with these 3D models. I'll try my best to introduce you to practical Silverlight programming in a simple way – simple enough to be easily followed by a beginner who only has basic .NET programming experience. From this book, you can learn how to create a full range of RIA Web applications and how to implement custom user controls that can be reused in your Silverlight projects.

What this Book Includes

This book and its sample code listings, which are available for download at my website at www.drxudotnet.com, provide you with:

- A complete, in-depth instruction on practical Silverlight programming. After reading this book and running the example programs, you will be able to add various sophisticated graphics and interactive user interfaces to your Web applications.

- About 100 ready-to-run example programs that allow you to explore the graphics techniques described in the book. These examples can be used to better understand how graphics algorithms work. You can modify the code examples or add new features to them to form the basis of your own projects. Some of the example code listings provided in this book are already sophisticated graphics packages that can be used directly in your own real-world Silverlight applications.
- Many classes in the sample code listings that you will find useful in your Silverlight programming. These classes contain matrix manipulation, coordinate transformation, color maps, and other useful utility classes. You can extract these classes and plug them into your own applications.

Is This Book for You?

You don't have to be an experienced Silverlight developer or an expert to use this book. I designed this book to be useful to people of all levels of Silverlight programming experience. In fact, I believe that if you have some experience with C#, Windows Forms, HTML, and the .NET framework, you will be able to sit down in front of your computer, start up Microsoft Visual Studio 2008 and Silverlight 2.0 Beta 2, follow the examples provided in this book, and quickly become familiar with Silverlight programming. For those of you who are already experienced Silverlight developers, I believe this book has much to offer as well. There is a great deal of information about Silverlight programming in this book not available in other Silverlight tutorial and reference books. In addition, most of the example programs in this book can be used directly in your own real-world Web application development. This book will provide you with a level of detail, explanation, instruction, and sample program code that will enable you to do just about anything Silverlight graphics and user interface related.

The majority of the example programs in this book can be used routinely by Silverlight developers and technical professionals. Throughout the book, I'll emphasize the *usefulness* of Silverlight programming in real-world Web applications. If you follow the instructions presented in this book closely, you'll be able to develop various practical Silverlight Web applications, from 2D graphics and charts to sophisticated 3D model and custom user controls. At the same time, I won't spend too much time discussing programming style, execution speed, and code optimization because there are a plethora of books out there that already deal with such topics. Most of the example programs you'll find in this book omit error handlings. This makes the code easier to understand by focusing only on the key concepts and practical applications.

What Do You Need to Use This Book?

You won't need any special equipment to make the best use of this book or to understand the algorithms. To run and modify the sample programs, you'll need a computer that is capable of running either Windows Vista or Windows XP. The software installed on your computer should include Visual Studio 2008 and Silverlight 2.0 Beta 2 or later. Please note that Silverlight 2.0 Beta 2 will not run applications that target Silverlight 2.0 Beta 1 since a number of API changes were made between Beta 1 and Beta 2. Therefore, if you have a browser with Silverlight 2.0 Beta 1 installed and visit a site that hosts a Silverlight 2.0 Beta 2 application, you will be prompted to upgrade to the newer Beta version of Silverlight. Once you do this you won't be able to run Beta 1 applications without uninstalling Beta 2. This means that if you have published a running sample on the Web built with Silverlight 2.0 Beta 1, you'll probably need to update it to Beta 2 soon.

If you have Visual Studio 2005 and Silverlight 2.0 Beta 1 installed, you can still run most of the sample code with few modifications. Please remember, however, that this book is intended for Visual Studio 2008 and Silverlight 2.0 Beta 2 or later, and that all of the example programs were created and tested on this platform, so it is best to run the sample code on the same platform.

How the Book Is Organized

This book is organized into fourteen chapters, each of which covers a different topic of Silverlight programming. The following summaries of each chapter should give you an overview of the book's content:

Chapter 1, *Overview of Silverlight Programming*

This chapter introduces the basics of Silverlight and reviews some of the general aspects of Silverlight programming, including XAML files used to define user interfaces.

Chapter 2, Graphics Basics in Silverlight

This chapter reviews some fundamental concepts of the 2D graphics and the 2D drawing model in Silverlight. It introduces coordinate systems and basic 2D shapes.

Chapter 3, 2D *Transformations*

This chapter covers the mathematical basics for 2D graphics programming. 2D vectors, matrices, and transformations in the homogeneous coordinate system, including translation, scaling, reflection, and rotation, are discussed. These 2D matrices and transformations allow Silverlight applications to perform a wide variety of graphical operations on graphics objects in a simple and consistent manner.

Chapter 4, *Geometry and 2D Drawing*

This chapter introduces Silverlight's Geometry classes and demonstrates why you need them to create complex 2D graphics objects. It also shows you how to create interactive 2D drawing programs.

Chapter 5, *Colors and Brushes*

This chapter covers the color system and brushes that Silverlight uses to paint graphics objects. It introduces a variety of brushes and their transformations. You'll learn how to create exotic visual effects using different brushes, such as the gradient and image brushes.

Chapter 6, *Animation*

This chapter describes Silverlight's animation facilities, which allow most of the properties and transformations of graphics objects (such as position, size, translation, rotation, etc.) to be animated. It also describes how to create a custom animation class that can be used in physics-based animation.

Chapter 7, *Physics and Games in Silverlight*

This chapter covers topics related to real-world Silverlight applications. You'll learn how to create and simulate physics models by solving ordinary differential equations with the Runge-Kutta method, and how to incorporate physics models into real-world games in Silverlight. This chapter discusses several physics models and games, including a pendulum, a coupled spring system, a golf ball (projectiles), and ball collision.

Chapter 8, *Charts in Silverlight*

This chapter contains instructions on creating 2D line charts in Silverlight. It introduces basic chart elements including the chart canvas, text canvas, axes, title, labels, ticks, and legend.

Chapter 9, *3D Transformations*

This chapter extends the concepts described in Chapter 3 into the third dimension. It explains how to define 3D graphics objects and how to translate, scale, reflect, and rotate these 3D objects. It also describes transformation matrices that represent projection and transformations, which allow you to view 3D graphics objects on a 2D screen. You'll also learn how to define 3D vectors, matrices, and projections.

Chapter 10, *3D Objects in Silverlight*

Silverlight does not provide 3D support, but this chapter shows you how to create your own 3D objects in Silverlight.

Chapter 11, *Silverlight Built-in Controls*

This chapter provides an introduction to the basic built-in controls in Silverlight and demonstrates how to use these controls in your Silverlight applications.

Chapter 12, *Styles, Templates, and Data Binding*

This chapter explains the Silverlight style and template system, which shows how you can apply a set of common property values to a group of controls and how you can give any Silverlight control a dramatic new look by applying a customized template. This chapter also introduces Silverlight data binding.

Chapter 13, *Expression Blend*

This chapter provides an overview of Microsoft's Expression Blend, which is a visual tool for developing complex Silverlight applications.

Chapter 14, *Custom Controls*

This chapter explains how you can extend the existing Silverlight controls and create your own custom controls. You'll learn how to create custom controls using three different approaches.

Using Code Examples

You may use the code in this book in your applications and documentation. You don't need to contact the author for permission unless you are reproducing a significant portion of the code. For example, writing a program that uses several chunks of code from this book doesn't require permission. Selling or distributing the example code listings does require permission. Incorporating a significant amount of example code from this book into your applications and documentation also requires permission. Integrating the example code from this book into commercial products isn't allowed without the written permission of the author.

Customer Support

I am always interested in hearing from readers, and would like to hear your thoughts on this book. You can send me comments by e-mail to `jxu@drxudotnet.com`. I also provide updates, bug fixes, and ongoing support via my website: `www.drxudotnet.com`.

You can also obtain the complete source code for all of examples in this book from the above website.

Note that this website was developed using Silverlight. In order to view the site, you'll be prompted to install Silverlight to your browser.

Chapter 1
Overview of Silverlight Programming

Silverlight is a cross-browser, cross-platform client technology that helps you design, develop, and deliver media-enabled experiences and rich interactive applications on the Web. It allows you to create interactive Web applications using .NET languages such as C# and Visual Basic. You can build Silverlight applications in the same manner that you create WPF desktop applications based on the Visual Studio 2008 and Expression Blend framework.

Silverlight 2 includes a compatible subset of the WPF-based graphics framework, which makes building rich Web applications much easier. It includes a powerful graphics and animation engine, as well as rich support for higher-level UI capabilities like controls, layout management, data-binding, styles, and template skinning. Silverlight enables developers to re-use skills, controls, code and content to build both web applications and desktop Windows applications.

As in the case of WPF, Silverlight 2 also includes a rich set of built-in controls, which can be used directly in creating your Web applications. These controls contain the standard WPF core form controls, including TextBox, CheckBox, RadioButton, etc.; built-in layout panels, including StackPanel, Grid, Canvas, etc.; common functionality controls, including Slider, ScrollViewer, Calendar, etc.; and data manipulation controls, including DataGrid, ListBox, etc. These built-in controls support a rich control templating model, which enables you to build sophisticated interactive Web applications.

Like WPF, Silverlight also includes a 2D vector graphics model. It allows graphics to scale according to screen-specific resolution without losing image quality, which is impossible to do with fixed-size raster graphics.

To easily represent UI and user interaction, Silverlight, like WPF, introduces a new XML based language, called XAML. XAML allows applications to dynamically parse and manipulate user interface elements at either design-time or runtime. It uses the code-behind model, similar to ASP.NET programming, allowing designers and developers to work in parallel and to seamlessly combine their work to create a compelling user experience. Of course, Silverlight also provides you with the option to not use XAML files when you develop Silverlight applications, meaning that you can develop your applications entirely in code such as C# or Visual Basic.

Silverlight is also based on a dynamic layout. This means that a UI element arranges itself on the Web page according to its content, its parent layout container, and the available screen area. Dynamic layout facilitates localization by automatically adjusting the size and position of UI elements when the strings they contain change length.

Silverlight 2 has a rich built-in networking support and a powerful base class library. It supports cross domain network access, enabling Silverlight clients to directly access resources and data from resources on the Web. It also includes LINQ and LINQ to XML library support, enabling easy transformation and querying of data.

Silverlight is designed to be a unified solution for Web application development, providing a seamless integration of different technologies. With Silverlight, you can easily create vector graphics or complex animations and incorporate media into your Web applications.

XAML basics

As mentioned previously, you can use XAML to create Silverlight applications. In this section, I'll present an introduction to XAML and consider its structure and syntax. Once you understand the basics of XAML, you can use it to easily create UI and layouts in Silverlight applications.

Why Is XAML Needed?

Since Silverlight applications can be developed entirely in code, you may ask a perfectly natural question – why do you need XAML in the first place? The reason can be traced back to the question of efficiently implementing complex, graphically rich applications. A long time ago, developers realized that the most efficient way to develop these kinds of applications was to separate the graphics and UI layout portions from the underlying code. In this way, the designers could work on the UI and graphics, while the developers could work on the code behind the UI graphics. Both parts could be designed and refined separately, without any versioning headaches.

The XAML technology introduced in WPF and Silverlight resolves these issues. When you develop a Silverlight application using Visual Studio 2008, the UI and graphics you are creating are not translated into code. Instead, they are serialized into a set of XAML tags. When you run the application, these tags are used to generate the objects that compose the UI.

XAML isn't a must for developing Silverlight applications. You can implement your Silverlight applications entirely in code. However, the pages and controls created in code will be locked into the Visual Studio environment and available only to programmers; there is no way to separate the UI and graphics portion from the code.

In orther words, Silverlight doesn't require XAML. However, XAML opens up a world of possibilities for collaboration, because many design tools understand the XAML format.

Creating XAML Files

There are some standard rules for creating a XAML file. First, every element in a XAML file must relate to an instance of a .NET class. The name of the element must match the name of the class exactly. For example, <TextBlock> tells WPF to create a TextBlock object.

In a XAML file, you can nest one element inside another. In this way, you can place an element as a child of another element. For example, if you have a Button inside a Canvas, this means that your UI contains a Canvas that has a Button as its child. You can also set the properties of each element through attributes.

Let's look at a simple XAML structure:

```
<UserControl x:Class="Example01_0.Page"
    xmlns="http://schemas.microsoft.com/client/2007"
    xmlns:x="http://schemas.microsoft.com/winfx/2006/xaml"
    Width="400" Height="300">
    <Grid x:Name="LayoutRoot" Background="LightBlue">
        <TextBlock>Hello, Silverlight!</TextBlock>
    </Grid>
</UserControl>
```

This file includes three elements: the top-level UserControl element, which represents the entire page; the Grid; and a TextBlock that is placed inside the Grid as a child. Silverlight also involves an Application file that defines application resources and startup settings. If you start with a new Silverlight project, Visual Studio will automatically generate an Application file called App.xaml

The starting tag for the page element includes a class name and two XML namespaces. The xmlns attribute is a specialized attribute in XML which is reserved for declaring namespaces. The two namespaces in the above XAML file will appear in every Silverlight XAML file. You only need to know that these namespaces simply allow the XAML parser to find the right classes. You can also see two properties within the tag: Height and Width. Each attribute corresponds to a property of the UserControl class. These attributes create a fixed 300 x 300 Silverlight application. This will become apparent if you expand your browser. If you remove the Height and Width attributes from the root control, the Silverlight application will automatically flow and resize with the browser, exactly like an HTML page would.

Inside the UserControl tag, there is a Grid control which in turn contains a TextBlock with its Text property setting to "Hello, Silverlight!". You can create the same TextBlock using the following snippet:

```
<TextBlock Text="Hello, Silverlight!"/>
```

Code-Behind Files

As mentioned previously, XAML is used to layout the UI and graphics elements for your Silverlight application, but in order to make the application functioning, you need to attach event handlers to the UI. XAML makes this easy using the Class attribute:

```
<UserControl x:Class="Example01_0.Page"... >
```

The x namespace prefix places the Class attribute in the XAML namespace, which means that this is a more general part of the XAML language. This example creates a new class named Example01_0.Page, which derives from the base UserControl class.

When you create a Silverlight application, Visual Studio will automatically create a partial class where you can place your event handling code. In the previous example, you created a Silverlight application named Example01-1 (the project name) which contained a default page called Page. Visual Studio will automatically generate the following code-behind file called Page.xaml.cs:

```
using System;
using System.Collections.Generic;
using System.Linq;
using System.Windows;
using System.Windows.Controls;
using System.Windows.Documents;
using System.Windows.Input;
```

```
using System.Windows.Media;
using System.Windows.Media.Animation;
using System.Windows.Shapes;

namespace Example01_0
{
    public partial class Page : UserControl
    {
        public Page()
        {
            InitializeComponent();
        }
    }
}
```

When you compile this application, XAML is translated into a CLR type declaration which is merged with the logic in the code-behind class file (Page.xaml.cs in this example) to form one single unit.

The above code-behind file only contains a default constructor, which calls the InitializeComponent method when you create an instance of the class. This is similar to the C# class in Windows Forms.

Your First Silverlight Program

Let's consider a simple Silverlight example. Open Visual Studio 2008, select File – New Project, and use the New Project dialog to create a Silverlight Application, as shown in Figure 1-1. Name the project Example01-1. Click the OK button to bring up an additional "Add Silverlight Application" dialog box, as shown in Figure 1-2. This dialog allows you to choose a method for hosting your Silverlight application. There are two hosting methods you can choose from:

- Choose "Add a new Web to the solution for hosting the control" if you want to add a separate ASP.NET-based Web site to your solution. If you choose this option, you will also need to specify the Project Type and Name in the Options group box.
- Choose "Generate an HTML test page to host Silverlight within this project" if you want Visual Studio to add a single HTML test page to host your Silverlight application to your project.

Here we choose the "Generate an HTML test page" method to host our Silverlight application. Click the OK button to generate the solution. The generated Silverlight application project contains several code files to build the following classes:

- Page – The Page class is used to create the main application user interface. Page derives from the UserControl base class and is implemented using a combination of one file for XAML markup (page.xaml) and one file for code-behind (page.xaml.cs).
- App – The App class is generated to be the application class, which is required by every Silverlight application in order to run an application and to show the main application UI. This class is subsequently instantiated by the Silverlight plug-in control directly after the application package (.xap file) is downloaded. App is also implemented using a combination of XAML (app.xaml) and a code-behind file (app.xaml.cs)

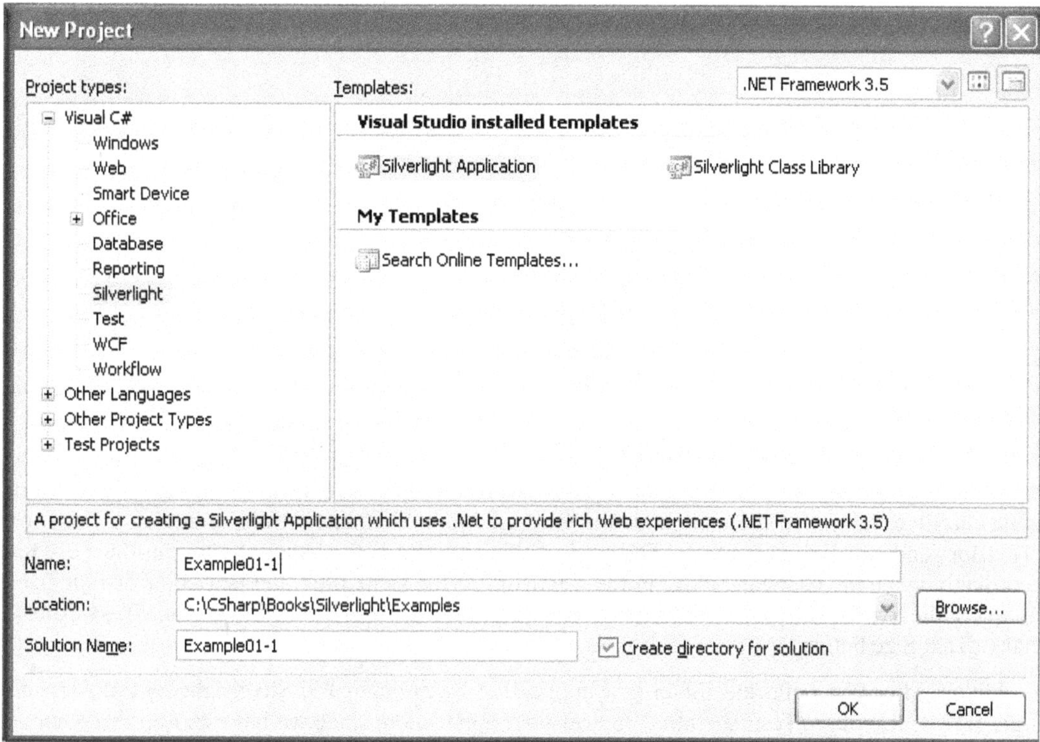

Figure 1-1 "New Project" Dialog window.

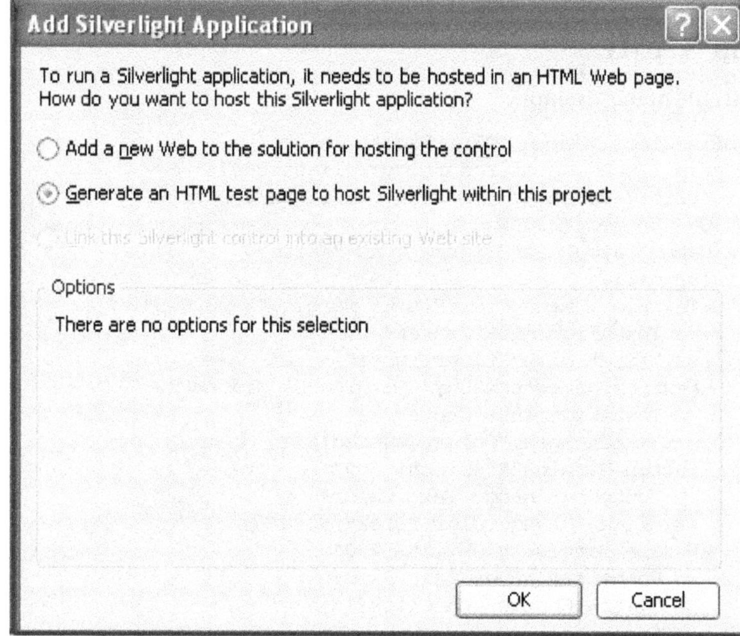

Figure 1-2 "Add Silverlight Application" Dialog.

The output from the application we want to create here is shown in Figure 1-3.

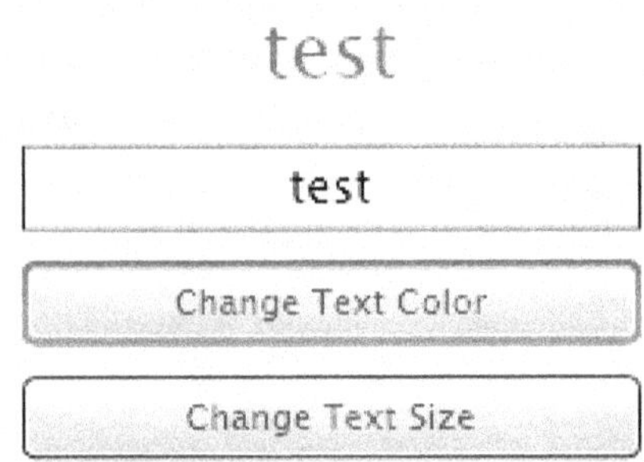

Figure 1-3 Your first Silverlight application example

This example includes several controls: a Grid, which is the most common control for arranging layouts in Silverlight; a StackPanel inside the Grid used to hold other controls, including a TextBlock; a TextBox; and two Button controls. The goal of this example is to change the text in the TextBlock accordingly when the user enters text in the TextBox. At the same time, the text color or font size of the text in the TextBlock control can be also changed when the user clicks the Change Text Color or Change Text Size button.

In addition, after you build the Silverlight application by pressing F5, Silverlight will also create a single HTML test page (TestPage.html) to host your application, since we have chosen the "Generate an HTML test page to host Silverlight within this project" option on the "Add Silverlight Application" dialog window. The TestPage.html file is located at the ~/Example01-1/ClientBin directory.

Properties in XAML

Here is the XAML file of this example:

```
<UserControl x:Class="Example01_1.Page"
    xmlns="http://schemas.microsoft.com/client/2007"
    xmlns:x="http://schemas.microsoft.com/winfx/2006/xaml"
    Width="300" Height="200">
    <Grid x:Name="LayoutRoot" Background="White">
        <StackPanel>
            <TextBlock Name="textBlock" Margin="5 20,5,5"
                TextAlignment="Center"
                Text="Hello Silverlight!"/>
            <TextBox Name="textBox" Margin="5" Width="200"
                TextAlignment="Center"
                TextChanged="OnTextChanged"/>
            <Button Margin="5" Width="200"
                Content="Change Text Color"
                Click="ChangeColor_Click"/>
            <Button Margin="5" Width="200"
                Content="Change Text Size"
                Click="ChangeSize_Click"/>
        </StackPanel>
    </Grid>
```

```
</UserControl>
```

You can see that the attributes of an element set properties of the corresponding object. For example, the TextBlock control in the above XAML file configures the name, margin, text alignment, and text:

```
<TextBlock Name="textBlock" Margin="5 20,5,5"
    TextAlignment="Center"
    Text="Hello Silverlight!"/>
```

In order for this to work, the TextBlock class in Silverlight must provide corresponding properties. You specify various properties for other controls that affect your layout and UI in a similar fashion.

To achieve the goal of this example, you need to have the ability to manipulate the TextBlock, TextBox and Button controls programmatically in the code-behind file. First, you need to name the TextBlock and TextBox controls in your XAML file. In this example, these controls are named textBlock and textBox. Remember that in a traditional Windows Forms application, every control must have a name. However, in a Silverlight or WPF application, you only need to name the elements that you want to manipulate programmatically. Here, you don't need to name the StackPanel and Button controls, for example.

Event Handlers in Code-Behind Files

In the previous section, you learned how to map attributes to their corresponding properties. However, to make controls functioning, sometimes you need to attach attributes with event handlers. In the above XAML file, you must attach an OnTextChanged event handler to the TextChanged property of the TextBox. You must also define the Click property of the two buttons using two click event handlers, ChangeColor_Click and ChangeSize_Click.

This assumes that there should be methods associated with the names OnTextChanged, ChangeColor_Click, and ChangeSize_Click in the code-behind file. Here is the corresponding code-behind file of this example:

```
using System;
using System.Windows;
using System.Windows.Controls;
using System.Windows.Media;
using System.Windows.Media.Animation;
using System.Windows.Shapes;

namespace Example01_1
{
    public partial class Page : UserControl
    {
        public Page()
        {
            InitializeComponent();
        }

        private void OnTextChanged(object sender, TextChangedEventArgs e)
        {
            textBlock.Text = textBox.Text;
        }
```

```
        private void ChangeColor_Click(object sender, RoutedEventArgs e)
        {
            SolidColorBrush brush =(SolidColorBrush)textBlock.Foreground;

            if (brush.Color==Color.FromArgb(255,0,0,0))
                textBlock.Foreground =
                    new SolidColorBrush(Color.FromArgb(255, 255, 0, 0));
            else
                textBlock.Foreground =
                    new SolidColorBrush(Color.FromArgb(255, 0, 0, 0));
        }

        private void ChangeSize_Click(object sender, RoutedEventArgs e)
        {
            if (textBlock.FontSize == 11)
                textBlock.FontSize = 24;
            else
                textBlock.FontSize = 11;
        }
    }
}
```

Note that the event handlers must have the correct signature. The event model in Silverlight and WPF is slightly different than that in earlier versions of .NET. Silverlight supports a new model based on event routing. The rest of the above code-behind file is very similar to that used in Windows Forms applications, which you should already be familiar with.

Running this example produces the results shown in Figure 1-3. If you type any text in the text box field, the text in the text block will change correspondingly. In addition, the color or font size will be changed depending on which button is clicked.

Code-Only Example

As mentioned previously, XAML isn't a must in order to create a Silverlight application. Silverlight fully supports code-only implementation, even though the use of this kind of implementation is less common. There are some pros and cons with the code-only approach. The advantage is that the code-only method gives you full control over customization. For example, when you want to conditionally add or substitute controls depending on the user's input, you can easily implement a condition logic in code. By contrast, this is hard to do with XAML because controls in XAML are embedded in your assembly as fixed unchanging resources. The disadvantage is that since Silverlight controls don't include parametric constructors, developing a code-only application in Silverlight is sometimes tedious. Even adding a simple control, such as a button, to your application takes several lines of code.

In the following example, we'll convert the previous example into a code-only application. Start a new Silverlight project and name it Example01-2. Silverlight automatically generates the Page.xaml and Page.xaml.cs files. Here, we just use the default Page.xaml file, which contains a Grid control called LayoutRoot. Next, we'll create all of the other controls in Figure 1-3 using a C# code-behind file. The following code listing will reproduce the same results shown in Figure 1-3:

```
using System;
using System.Windows;
using System.Windows.Controls;
using System.Windows.Media;
```

```
using System.Windows.Media.Animation;
using System.Windows.Shapes;

namespace Example01_2
{
    public partial class Page : UserControl
    {
        private TextBlock textBlock;
        private TextBox textBox;

        public Page()
        {
            InitializeComponent();
            Initialization();
        }

        private void Initialization()
        {
            // Configure the Page size:
            this.Height = 200;
            this.Width = 300;

            // StackPanel add it to the LayoutRoot Grid:
            StackPanel stackPanel = new StackPanel();
            LayoutRoot.Children.Add(stackPanel);

            // Add a text block to stackPanel:
            textBlock = new TextBlock();
            textBlock.Margin = new Thickness(5, 20, 5, 5);
            textBlock.Height = 30;
            textBlock.TextAlignment = TextAlignment.Center;
            textBlock.Text = "Hello Silverlight!";
            stackPanel.Children.Add(textBlock);

            // Add a text box to stackPanel:
            textBox = new TextBox();
            textBox.Margin = new Thickness(5);
            textBox.Width = 200;
            textBox.TextAlignment = TextAlignment.Center;
            textBox.TextChanged += OnTextChanged;
            stackPanel.Children.Add(textBox);

            // Add button to stackPanel used to change text color:
            Button btnColor = new Button();
            btnColor.Margin = new Thickness(5);
            btnColor.Width = 200;
            btnColor.Content = "Change Text Color";
            btnColor.Click += ChangeColor_Click;
            stackPanel.Children.Add(btnColor);

            // Add button to stackPanel used to change text font size:
            Button btnSize = new Button();
            btnSize.Margin = new Thickness(5);
            btnSize.Width = 200;
            btnSize.Content = "Change Text Color";
```

```
            btnSize.Click += ChangeSize_Click;
            stackPanel.Children.Add(btnSize);
        }

        private void OnTextChanged(object sender, TextChangedEventArgs e)
        {
            textBlock.Text = textBox.Text;
        }

        private void ChangeColor_Click(object sender, RoutedEventArgs e)
        {
            SolidColorBrush brush = (SolidColorBrush)textBlock.Foreground;

            if (brush.Color == Color.FromArgb(255, 0, 0, 0))
                textBlock.Foreground =
                    new SolidColorBrush(Color.FromArgb(255, 255, 0, 0));
            else
                textBlock.Foreground =
                    new SolidColorBrush(Color.FromArgb(255, 0, 0, 0));
        }

        private void ChangeSize_Click(object sender, RoutedEventArgs e)
        {
            if (textBlock.FontSize == 11)
                textBlock.FontSize = 24;
            else
                textBlock.FontSize = 11;
        }

    }
}
```

You can see that the code-behind class is similar to a form class in a traditional Windows Forms application. It derives from the base UserControl class and adds private member variables for TextBlock and TextBox. Pay close attention to how controls are added to their parents and how event handlers are attached.

From the above discussion, you learned how to create the same Silverlight application using both XAML+code and code-only techniques. The standard approach for developing Silverlight applications is to use XAML for a code-based application. Namely, you use XAML to lay out your UI, and use code to implement event handlers and business logic. For applications with a dynamic UI, you may want to go with the code-only method.

However, for simple static applications, it is also possible to use a XAML-only file without writing any C# code. You should remember that unlike WPF, Silverlight doesn't support EventTriggers nor UI to UI data binding. This means that for example, you can't trigger a Button's Click event in XAML, and you can't bind a TextBlock's Text property to a TextBox's Text property in XAML either. Therefore, any meaningful Silverlight application usually involves code-behind files.

Hosting Silverlight Controls

Silverlight 2 implemented a new packaging model for managed code applications. While you can still use the loose file (XAML + JavaScript) methods for JavaScript applications in Silverlight 2, you must use the so-called xap packaging model for managed applications. When you built your managed Silverlight application, Silverlight generates an application package with the Silverlight application name and .xap extension. This package is a compressed file that uses the standard .zip compression algorithm to minimize client download size. This single xap file model makes Web deployment easier and cleaner.

The xap packaging file contains your application DLLs, any assets you have packaged, and the AppManifest.xaml manifest file. The manifest file sets the starting point and lists all the components that make up your Silverlight applications.

Now, you can embed and configure the Silverlight control (xap package) directly into your HTML page using the <OBJECT> tag, which works in cross-browser scenarios. As mentioned previously, Silverlight created an HTML test page in Example01-1. Here is the content of this test page (TestPage.html):

```
<!DOCTYPE html PUBLIC "-//W3C//DTD XHTML 1.0 Transitional//EN"
                      "http://www.w3.org/TR/xhtml1/DTD/xhtml1-transitional.dtd">
<html xmlns="http://www.w3.org/1999/xhtml" >
<!-- saved from url=(0014)about:internet -->
<head>
    <title>Silverlight Project Test Page </title>

    <style type="text/css">
    html, body {
        height: 100%;
        overflow: auto;
    }
    body {
        padding: 0;
        margin: 0;
    }
    #silverlightControlHost {
        height: 100%;
    }
    </style>

    <script type="text/javascript">
        function onSilverlightError(sender, args) {

            var appSource = "";
            if (sender != null && sender != 0) {
                appSource = sender.getHost().Source;
            }
            var errorType = args.ErrorType;
            var iErrorCode = args.ErrorCode;

            var errMsg = "Unhandled Error in Silverlight 2 Application " +
                          appSource + "\n" ;

            errMsg += "Code: "+ iErrorCode + "    \n";
            errMsg += "Category: " + errorType + "       \n";
            errMsg += "Message: " + args.ErrorMessage + "     \n";

            if (errorType == "ParserError")
            {
```

```
                errMsg += "File: " + args.xamlFile + "     \n";
                errMsg += "Line: " + args.lineNumber + "     \n";
                errMsg += "Position: " + args.charPosition + "     \n";
            }
            else if (errorType == "RuntimeError")
            {
                if (args.lineNumber != 0)
                {
                    errMsg += "Line: " + args.lineNumber + "     \n";
                    errMsg += "Position: " +  args.charPosition + "     \n";
                }
                errMsg += "MethodName: " + args.methodName + "     \n";
            }

            throw new Error(errMsg);
        }
    </script>
</head>

<body>
    <!-- Runtime errors from Silverlight will be displayed here.
         This will contain debugging information and should be removed or hidden
         when debugging is completed -->
    <div id='errorLocation' style="font-size: small;color: Gray;"></div>

    <div id="silverlightControlHost">
            <object data="data:application/x-silverlight,"
                    type="application/x-silverlight-2-b2"
                    width="100%" height="100%">
                    <param name="source" value="Example01-1.xap"/>
                    <param name="onerror" value="onSilverlightError" />
                    <param name="background" value="white" />

                    <a href="http://go2.microsoft.com/fwlink/?LinkID=115261"
                       style="text-decoration: none;">
                            <img
src="http://go2.microsoft.com/fwlink/?LinkId=108181"
alt="Get Microsoft Silverlight" style="border-style: none"/>
                    </a>
            </object>
            <iframe
style='visibility:hidden;height:0;width:0;border:0px'></iframe>
    </div>
</body>
</html>
```

In the above HTML file, the Silverlight object model is exposed through the Silverlight plug-in (Example01-1.xap), which you create as a plug-in instance on a Web page. Silverlight uses the ActiveX plug-in for Internet explorer and uses the Netscape API plug-in for other browsers.

There are several mandatory and optional <OBJECT> tag attributes and parameters required for Silverlight applications:

id – provides a name for the plug-in instance within the HTML Document Object Model (DOM).

data – Streamlines the instantiation process. This attribute is required and its value should be specified as the Silverlight application MIME type – data:application/silverlight.

type – The MIME type that determines which version of the Silverlight plug-in control should be loaded.

height – Sets the height of the plug-in.

width – Sets the width of the plug-in.

Source – A URI containing the location of the Silverlight package file (e.g., Example01-1.xap).

The Silverlight plug-in also exposes two mandatory named events as parameters in the <OBECT> tag that can be set to specify an unmanaged JavaScript handler for the relevant event. You define this handler in JavaScript within the scope of the HTML DOM that contains the plug-in instance.

onError – Invoked when an error is generated in the Silverlight run-time components.

onResize – Invoked when the ActualHeight or ActualWidth property of the Silverlight control changes.

There are some other optional parameters you can specify for the Silverlight control, such as Background.

In a practical Web application, you can embed as many as Silverlight plug-in controls as needed in a single HTML page. The better way to do this is to create a SilverlightApp folder and put all of your Silverlight packaging (.xap) files into this folder. Then you use the <OBJECT> tag in your HTML page to embed different Silverlight controls in the different locations.

There may be an issue in some browsers associated with the <OBJECT> tag plug-in. Namely, the Silverlight plug-in needs to be clicked by the user before it can be interacted with. The plug-in content will be dispayed, including any animations and sounds, but it will not be able to interact with the user's mouse. Typically, the browser will display a tooltip when the plug-in is hovered, telling the user "Click to activate and use this control". One work-around is to modify the content within the <OBJECT> tag using the JavaScript:

```
<script type="text/javascript">
    var objscript = '<object data="data:application/x-silverlight,"
            type="application/x-silverlight-2-b2" width="850px" height="190px">';
        objscript += '<param name="source" value="silverlight_app/Header.xap"/>'
        objscript += '<param name="onError" value="onErrorHandler" />'
        objscript += '<param name="OnResize" value="OnResizeHandler"/>'
        objscript += '<a href=http://go2.microsoft.com/fwlink/?LinkID=108182
            style="text-decoration: none;">'
        objscript += '<img src=http://go2.microsoft.com/fwlink/?LinkId=108181
            alt="Get Microsoft Silverlight" style="border-style: none"/>';
        objscript += '</a>';
        objscript += '</object>';
</script>
<script type="text/javascript" src="docWrite.js"></script>
```

Here the docWrite.js is a separate JaveScript file and only contains one line of code:

```
document.write(objscript);
```

In this way, you can avoid having the “Click to activate and use this control” tooltip appear in any browser.

Here, we only discussed how to embed and configure the Silverlight plug-in into your HTML age using the <OBJECT> tag. There are other ways to place the Silverlight plug-in into your HTML page. For example, Silverlight SDK provides a JavaScript helper file called Silverlight.js. You can call functions defined in this file to initialize Silverlight plug-in instances on a Web page. Please refer to the Silverlight documentation for details.

Chapter 2
Graphics Basics in Silverlight

As mentioned in the previous chapter, Silverlight provides a unified graphics platform that allows you to easily create a variety of user interfaces and graphics objects in Web applications. This chapter begins by describing graphics coordinate systems used in Silverlight, and shows you several different coordinate systems that you can use to make graphics programming easier. Then it shows you how to create basic 2D shapes in Web applications.

2D Coordinate Systems in Silverlight

When you create a graphics object in Silverlight, you must determine where the graphics object or drawing will be displayed. To do this, you need to understand how Silverlight measures graphics object coordinates. Each point on a Silverlight page has an X and Y coordinate. In the following sections, we'll discuss various coordinate systems and their relationships.

Default Coordinates

For 2D graphics, the Silverlight coordinate system places the origin in the upper left hand corner of the rendering area. In the 2D space, the positive X-axis points to the right, and the positive Y-axis points downward, as shown in Figure 2-1.

All coordinates and sizes in the default Silverlight system are measured in units of 96 dots per inch (DPI), called device-independent pixels. In this system, you can create adaptive layouts to deal with different resolutions, making sure your controls and graphics objects stretch accordingly when the window is stretched.

The rendering area in Silverlight can be defined using layout elements, including Canvas, Grid, StackPanel, etc. However, it is also possible to use a custom layout component as the rendering area by overriding the default behavior of any of these layout elements.

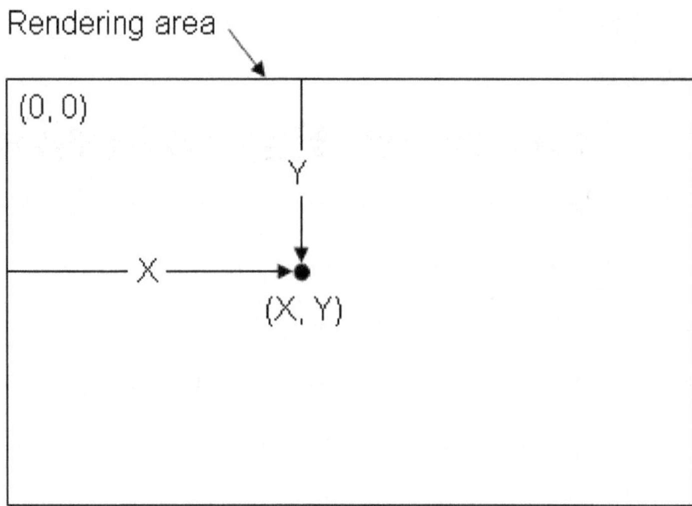

Figure 2-1 Default coordinate system in Silverlight.

Let's look at an example and see how this can be achieved . Open Microsoft Visual Studio 2008, create a new Silverlight project, and name it Example02-1. Add a Border control to the Grid in Page.xaml. The border will be the boundary of the drawing area. Then, add a Canvas element to the border. The canvas is particularly useful when you need to place graphics and other drawing elements at absolute positions. What's interesting is that Canvas elements can be nested. Namely, you can prepare part of a drawing in a canvas, then insert that entire drawing as a single element into another canvas. You can also apply various transformations, such as scaling or rotation, directly to the canvas.

Now you can draw a line from Point (0, 0) to Point (100, 100) on the canvas with the default units of device-independent pixels using the following XAML file:

```
<UserControl x:Class="Example02_1.Page"
    xmlns="http://schemas.microsoft.com/client/2007"
    xmlns:x="http://schemas.microsoft.com/winfx/2006/xaml"
    Width="300" Height="300">
    <Grid x:Name="LayoutRoot" Background="White">
        <Border BorderBrush="Gray" BorderThickness="1" Width="200" Height="200">
            <Canvas Height="200" Width="200">
                <Line X1="0" Y1="0" X2="100" Y2="100"
                      Stroke="Black" StrokeThickness="2"/>
            </Canvas>
        </Border>
    </Grid>
</UserControl>
```

Figure 2-2 shows the results of running this example.

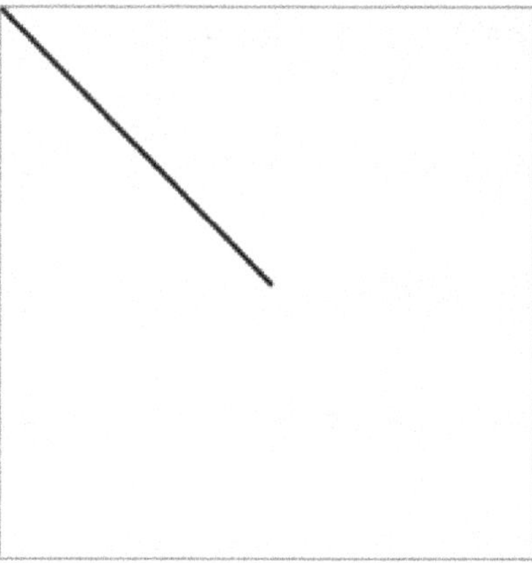

Figure 2-2 Draw a line from (0, 0) to (100, 100) on the canvas.

Custom Coordinates

In addition to the default coordinate system discussed in the previous section, a Silverlight application can define its own coordinate system. For example, 2D charting applications usually use a coordinate system in which the Y-axis points from bottom to top, as illustrated in Figure 2-3.

This system can be easily created in Silverlight by directly performing corresponding transformations to the canvas. Let's consider an example. Create a new Silverlight project and name it Example02-2. Here is the XAML file of this example:

```
<UserControl x:Class="Example02_2.Page"
    xmlns="http://schemas.microsoft.com/client/2007"
    xmlns:x="http://schemas.microsoft.com/winfx/2006/xaml"
    Width="300" Height="300">
    <Grid x:Name="LayoutRoot" Background="White">
        <Border BorderBrush="Black" BorderThickness="1"
                Height="200" Width="200">
            <Canvas Height="200" Width="200">
                <Canvas.RenderTransform>
                    <TransformGroup>
                        <ScaleTransform ScaleY="-1" />
                        <TranslateTransform Y="200" />
                    </TransformGroup>
                </Canvas.RenderTransform>
                <Line X1="0" Y1="0" X2="100" Y2="100"
                      Stroke="Black" StrokeThickness="2" />
            </Canvas>
        </Border>
    </Grid>
</UserControl>
```

In this example, you perform two successive transforms on the canvas: a scale transform, which reverses the Y axis; and a translation transform, which translates 200px (the height of the canvas) in the Y direction. These transforms move the origin from the top-left corner to the bottom-left corner of the canvas.

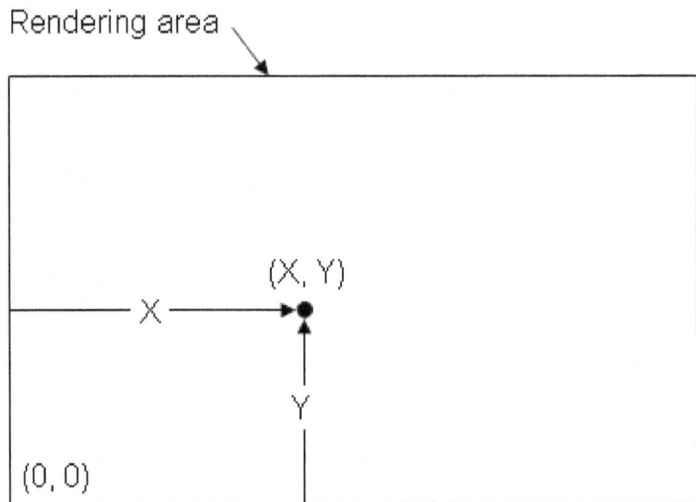

Figure 2-3 A custom coordinate system.

Figure 2-4 shows the result of this example. The line from (0, 0) to (100, 100) is now measured relative to the origin of the new custom coordinate system. You can compare this line with that drawn in the default system of Figure 2-2.

You may notice that there is an issue with this custom coordinate system: everything inside the Canvas will be transformed the same way that the canvas is. For instance, when you add a button control and a text block to the canvas, using the following XAML code,

```
<Button Canvas.Top="50" Canvas.Left="80" FontSize="15" Foreground="Red"
        Name="Button1" Content="My Button"/>
<TextBlock Canvas.Top="120" Canvas.Left="20" FontSize="16" FontWeight="Bold"
           Foreground="Blue" Text="My Text Block"/>
```

the content of the button and the text block will be up-side down, as shown in Figure 2-5.

In order to view the text content normally in this custom coordinate system, you have to perform a reflective transform on the corresponding controls separately.

You can change the apparent size and location of the graphics objects and user controls on the screen using this custom coordinate system. This technique is known as "Zooming" and "Panning". Zooming and Panning can be achieved using scaling and translation transforms.

Let's consider another example. Create a new Silverlight application and name it Example02-3. Add a StackPanel to the application, add a slider control and a border control to the content of the StackPanel, and add a canvas to the border control. Finally create a line and a rectangle object on the canvas control. The XAML file of this example is listed below:

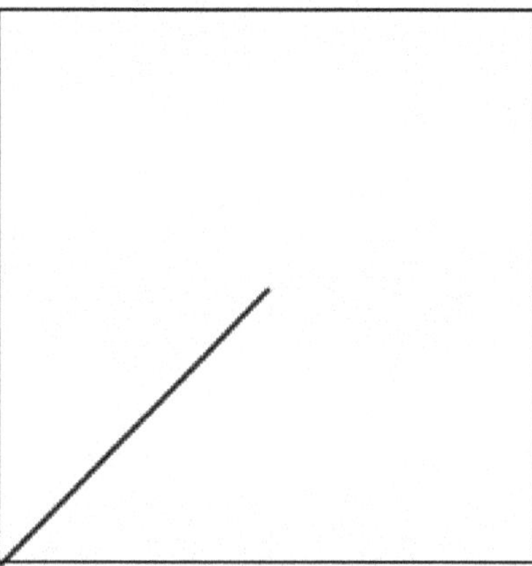

Figure 2-4 Draw a line from (0, 0) to (100, 100) in the custom coordinate system.

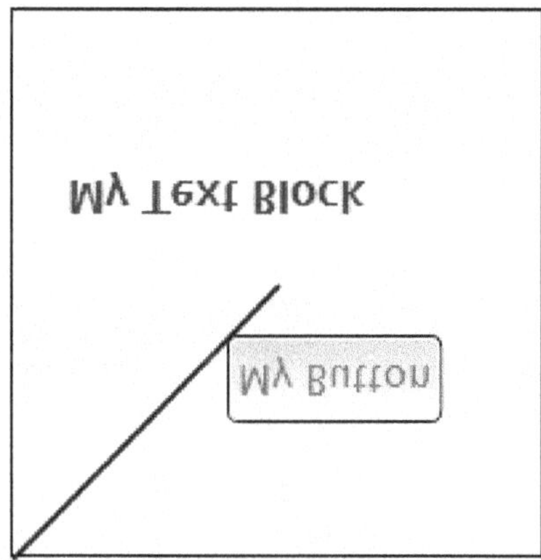

Figure 2-5 The button and text block are up-side down in the custom coordinate system.

```
<UserControl x:Class="Example02_3.Page"
    xmlns="http://schemas.microsoft.com/client/2007"
    xmlns:x="http://schemas.microsoft.com/winfx/2006/xaml"
    Width="300" Height="300">
    <StackPanel Height="280" Width="250" Background="White">
        <Border BorderBrush="Black" BorderThickness="1"
                Height="200" Width="200" Margin="20">
            <Canvas Height="200" Width="200">
                <Canvas.RenderTransform>
                    <TransformGroup>
                        <ScaleTransform ScaleY="-1" />
                        <TranslateTransform Y="200" />
                    </TransformGroup>
                </Canvas.RenderTransform>

                <Line X1="0" Y1="0" X2="80" Y2="80"
                  Stroke="Black" StrokeThickness="2">
                    <Line.RenderTransform>
                        <ScaleTransform x:Name="lineScale"/>
```

```
                    </Line.RenderTransform>
                </Line>

                <Rectangle Canvas.Top="100" Canvas.Left="30"
                           Width="80" Height="40"
                           Stroke="DarkRed"
                           StrokeThickness="3">
                    <Rectangle.RenderTransform>
                        <ScaleTransform x:Name="rectScale"/>
                    </Rectangle.RenderTransform>
                </Rectangle>
            </Canvas>
        </Border>
        <Slider x:Name="slider" Minimum="0" Maximum="3"
                ValueChanged="slider_ValueChanged"/>
    </StackPanel>
</UserControl>
```

The scale transform for the Line and Rectangle is related to the Slider's Value property through the Slider's ValueChanged event handler in the code-behind file:

```
using System;
using System.Windows;
using System.Windows.Controls;
using System.Windows.Media;
using System.Windows.Media.Animation;
using System.Windows.Shapes;

namespace Example02_3
{
    public partial class Page : UserControl
    {
        public Page()
        {
            InitializeComponent();
            Slider.Value = 1;
        }

        private void slider_ValueChanged(object sender,
            RoutedPropertyChangedEventArgs<double> e)
        {
            lineScale.ScaleX = slider.Value;
            lineScale.ScaleY = slider.Value;
            rectScale.ScaleX = slider.Value;
            rectScale.ScaleY = slider.Value;
        }
    }
}
```

The value of the slider varies from 0 to 3, meaning that the scaling factor for both the line and rectangle changes in the range of [0, 3]. When the user moves the slider with the mouse, the dimensions of the line and rectangle will change accordingly.

Figure 2-6 shows the results of running this example. You can zoom in or zoom out by moving the slider with your mouse. When you increase the scaling factor further, however, you might obtain unexpected results like the one shown in the figure. Namely, the graphics objects are extended outside of the drawing Canvas control specified by the black border line.

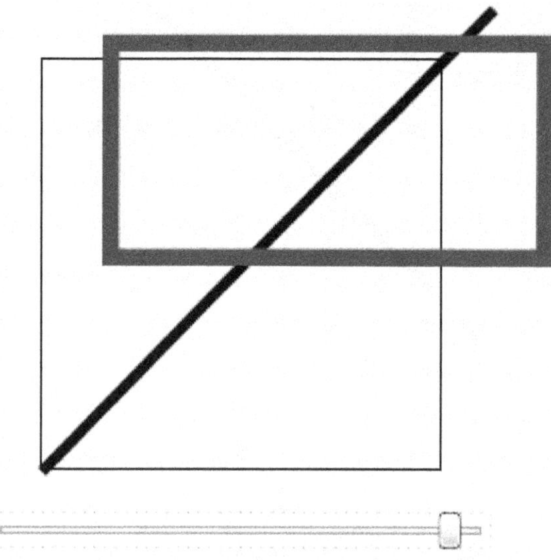

Figure 2-6 The line and rectangle objects are scaled.

In WPF, this can easily be fixed by specifying the ClipToBounds property of the Canvas to true:

```
<Canvas Height="200" Width="200" ClipToBounds="True">
```

However, the Canvas in Silverlight doesn't have the ClipToBounds property. You can get around this issue by using the Clip property in combination with a RectangleGeometry the same size as the drawing Canvas:

```
<Canvas.Clip>
    <RectangleGeometry Rect="0 0 200 200"/>
</Canvas.Clip>
```

This will produce the results shown in Figure 2-7. You can clearly see the difference between Figure 2-6 and Figure 2-7.

There are still issues associated with this custom coordinate system. First, the scaling affects not only the shape of the graphics objects, but also the StrokeThickness, which is undesirable for some applications. For example, for charting applications, you may want only the shape of the graphics or the line length to vary with the scaling factor, but not the StrokeThickness itself.

Another issue is the unit of measurement used in the coordinate system, where the default units are used. In practical applications, real-world units are usually used. For example, it is impossible to draw a line with a length of 100 miles on the screen in the current coordinate system. In the following section, we'll develop a new custom coordinate system that can be used in 2D charting applications.

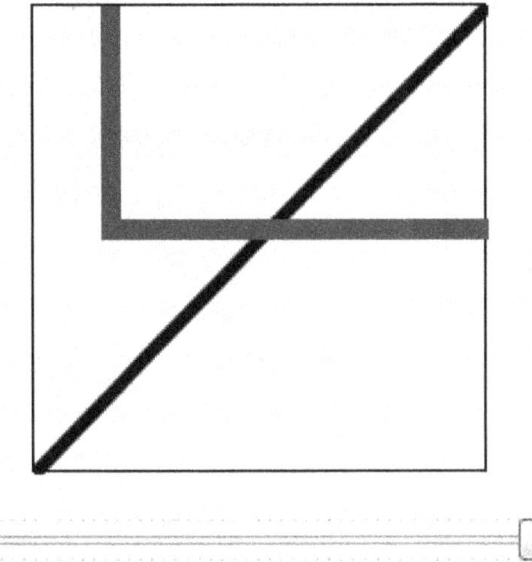

Figure 2-7 The line and rectangle objects are always drawn inside of the canvas control.

Custom Coordinates for 2D Charts

The custom coordinate system used in 2D charting applications must satisfy the following conditions: it must be independent of the unit of the real-world graphics objects, and its Y-axis must point from bottom to top as it does in most charting applications. This custom coordinate system is illustrated in Figure 2-8.

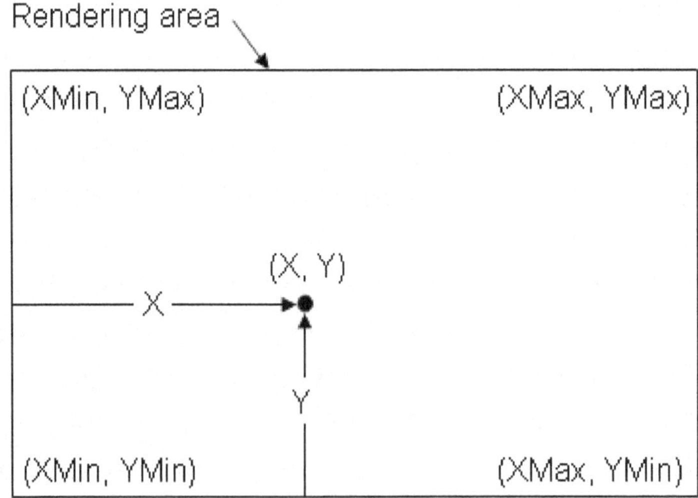

Figure 2-8 Custom Coordinate system for 2D charting applications.

The real-world X-Y coordinate system is defined within the rendering area. You can create such a coordinate system using a custom panel control by overriding the MeasureOverride and ArrangeOverride methods. Each method returns the size data that is needed to position and render child elements. This is a standard method used to create custom coordinate systems. Instead of creating a custom panel control, here we'll construct this coordinate system using another approach based on direct coding.

Start with a new Silverlight project and name it Example02-4. The following is the XAML file of this example:

```
<UserControl x:Class="Example02_4.Page"
    xmlns="http://schemas.microsoft.com/client/2007"
    xmlns:x="http://schemas.microsoft.com/winfx/2006/xaml"
    Width="360" Height="450">
    <Grid x:Name="LayoutRoot" Background="White">
        <StackPanel Height="450" Width="360">
            <Canvas x:Name="plotCanvas" Width="300" Height="250"
                    Margin="30,30,30,30">
                <Canvas.Clip>
                    <RectangleGeometry Rect="0,0,300,250"/>
                </Canvas.Clip>
                <Rectangle x:Name="plotArea" Width="300" Height="250"
                           Stroke="Black" StrokeThickness="1"/>
            </Canvas>
            <StackPanel Orientation="Horizontal">
                <TextBlock  Margin="45,5,10,5">XMin</TextBlock>
                <TextBox Name="tbXMin" TextAlignment="Center" Text="0"
                         Width="70" Height="25"/>
                <TextBlock Margin="25,5,10,5">XMax</TextBlock>
                <TextBox Name="tbXMax" TextAlignment="Center" Text="10"
                         Width="70" Height="25"/>
            </StackPanel>
            <StackPanel Orientation="Horizontal">
                <TextBlock  Margin="45,5,10,5">YMin</TextBlock>
                <TextBox Name="tbYMin" TextAlignment="Center" Text="0"
                         Width="70" Height="25"/>
                <TextBlock Margin="25,5,10,5">YMax</TextBlock>
                <TextBox Name="tbYMax" TextAlignment="Center" Text="10"
                         Width="70" Height="25"/>
            </StackPanel>
            <Button Click="Apply_Click" Margin="45,20,20,0" Height="25"
                    Width="100" Content="Apply" />
        </StackPanel>
    </Grid>
</UserControl>
```

The graphics objects or drawings will be created on the Canvas control, called plotCanvas. The rectangle, named plotArea, serves as the border of the rendering area. You can also use the Border control to perform the same function as it did in the previous example. The other UI elements will be used to control the appearance of the graphics.

The corresponding C# code of the code-behind file is listed below:

```
using System;
using System.Windows;
using System.Windows.Controls;
using System.Windows.Media;
using System.Windows.Media.Animation;
using System.Windows.Shapes;
```

```
namespace Example02_4
{
    public partial class Page : UserControl
    {
        private double xMin = 0.0;
        private double xMax = 10.0;
        private double yMin = 0.0;
        private double yMax = 10.0;
        private Line line1;
        private Polyline polyline1;

        public Page()
        {
            InitializeComponent();
            AddGraphics();
        }

        private void AddGraphics()
        {
            line1 = new Line();
            line1.X1 = XNormalize(2.0);
            line1.Y1 = YNormalize(4.0);
            line1.X2 = XNormalize(8.0);
            line1.Y2 = YNormalize(10.0);
            line1.Stroke = new SolidColorBrush(Color.FromArgb(255, 0, 0, 255));
            line1.StrokeThickness = 2;
            plotCanvas.Children.Add(line1);

            polyline1 = new Polyline();
            polyline1.Points.Add(new Point(XNormalize(8),
                YNormalize(8)));
            polyline1.Points.Add(new Point(XNormalize(6),
                YNormalize(6)));
            polyline1.Points.Add(new Point(XNormalize(6),
                YNormalize(4)));
            polyline1.Points.Add(new Point(XNormalize(4),
                YNormalize(4)));
            polyline1.Points.Add(new Point(XNormalize(4),
                YNormalize(6)));
            polyline1.Points.Add(new Point(XNormalize(6),
                YNormalize(6)));
            polyline1.Stroke =
                new SolidColorBrush(Color.FromArgb(255, 255, 0, 0));
            polyline1.StrokeThickness = 5;
            plotCanvas.Children.Add(polyline1);
        }

        private double XNormalize(double x)
        {
            double result = (x - xMin) *
                    plotCanvas.Width / (xMax - xMin);
            return result;
        }

        private double YNormalize(double y)
```

```
        {
            double result = plotCanvas.Height - (y - yMin) *
                plotCanvas.Height / (yMax - yMin);
            return result;
        }

        private void Apply_Click(object sender, EventArgs e)
        {
            xMin = Convert.ToDouble(tbXMin.Text);
            xMax = Convert.ToDouble(tbXMax.Text);
            yMin = Convert.ToDouble(tbXMin.Text);
            yMax = Convert.ToDouble(tbYMax.Text);
            plotCanvas.Children.Remove(line1);
            plotCanvas.Children.Remove(polyline1);
            AddGraphics();
        }
    }
}
```

In this code-behind file, we begin by defining private members to hold the minimum and maximum values of the custom coordinate axes. Note that by changing the values of xMin, xMax, yMin, and yMax, you can define the rendering area to be any size required by your applications. Make sure that the units of these qualtities are in real-world units defined in the real-world coordinate system.

You may notice that there is an issue concerning drawing graphics objects inside the rendering area, which should be independent of the units of the world coordinate system. Here we use the XNormalize and YNormalize methods to convert the X and Y coordinates in the real-world coordinate system to the default device-independent coordinate system. After this conversion, the units for all graphics objects are in device-independent pixels. This can be easily done by passing the X and Y coordinates of any unit in the world coordinate system to the XNormalize and YNormalize methods, which will perform the unit conversion automatically and always return the X and Y coordinates in device-independent pixels in the default Silverlight coordinate system.

Let's examine what we did inside the XNormalize method. We convert the X coordinate in the real-world coordinate system using the following formula:

```
double result = (x - xMin) * plotCanvas.Width / (xMax - xMin);
```

Here, we simply perform a scaling operation. Both (x – xMin) and (xMax – xMin) have the same unit in the world coordinate system, which is cancelled out by division. This means that the unit of this scaling term is determined solely by the unit of plotCanvas.Width, whose unit is in device-independent pixels. You can easily see that the above conversion provides not only the correct unit, but also the correct position in the default coordinate system.

For the Y coordinate conversion, the situation is a bit different. You need to not only perform the scaling operation, but also reverse the Y axis in the default coordinate system. The following formula is used for the Y coordinate conversion:

```
double result = plotCanvas.Height - (y - yMin) *
                plotCanvas.Height / (yMax - yMin);
```

Next, we add a straight line (line1) and a polyline (polyline1) to the plotCanvas using the AddGraphics method. We draw the straight line from point (2, 4) to point (8, 10). The endpoints of this line are in the unit (which can be any unit!) defined in the world coordinate system. These points aren't directly used in drawing the line, but their converted X and Y coordinates are used instead. The same procedure is used to create the polyline object.

The click event of the "Apply" button allows you to redraw the straight line and polyline using new values for the axis limits specified in corresponding TextBox elements. Notice that the statements inside the "Apply" button's event handler

```
plotCanvas.Children.Remove(line1);
plotCanvas.Children.Remove(polyline1);
```

are required. Otherwise, both the original and newly created graphics objects will remain on the screen. The above statements ensure that original objects are removed when new graphics objects are created.

Figure 2-9 shows the result of running this example. From this window, you can change the appearance of the graphics objects by changing the values of xMin, XMax, Ymin, and yMax, and clicking the "Apply" button.

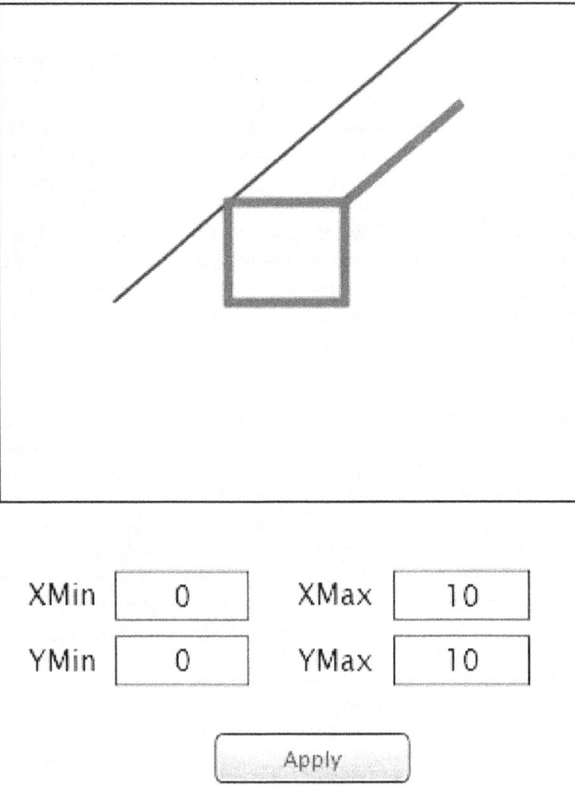

Figure 2-9 Draw a line and a polyline in the custom coordinate system.

2D Viewport

A graphics object can be considered to be defined in its own coordinate system, which is some abstract place with boundaries. For example, suppose you want to create a simple X-Y chart that plots Y-values from 50 to 100 over an X-data range from 0 to 10. You can work in a coordinate system space with $0 \leq X \leq 10$ and $50 \leq Y \leq 100$. This space is called the world coordinate system.

In practice, you usually aren't interested in the entire graphic, but only a portion of it. Thus, you can define the portion of interest as a specific area in the world coordinate system. This area of interest is called the "Window". In order to draw graphics objects on the screen, you need to map this "Window" to the default Silverlight coordinate system. We call this mapped "Window" in the default coordinate system a 2D viewport. The concept of the window and viewport in 2D space is illustrated in Figure 2-10.

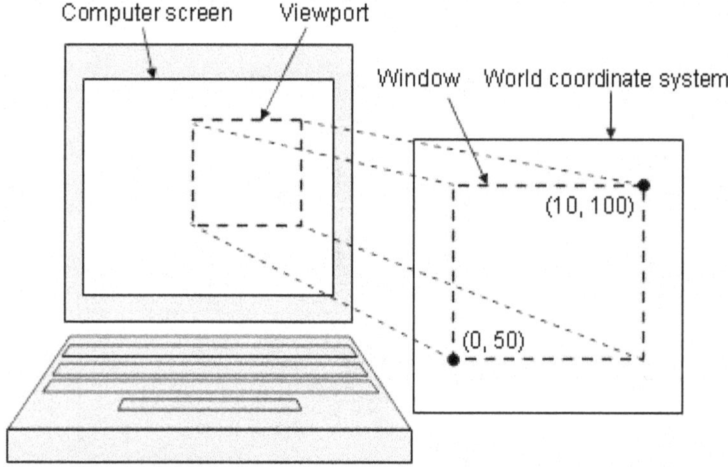

Figure 2-10 Window and viewport in 2D space.

In the previous section, we defined the default limits for the X and Y axes in the custom (world) coordinate system. For example:

```
private double xMin = 0.0;
private double xMax = 10.0;
private double yMin = 0.0;
private double yMax = 10.0;
```

This defines a portion of interest in the custom coordinate system. This area of interest is called the "Window". Once you know what you want to display, you need to decide where on the computer screen to display it. In the previous example, we defined a rendering area (plotCanvas) in the default Silverlight coordinate system, which creates a screen area to display the graphics objects. This rendering area is called the viewport.

You can use this viewport to change the apparent size and location of the graphics objects on the screen. Changing the viewport affects the display of the graphics objects on the screen. These effects are called "Zooming" and "Panning".

Zooming and Panning

The size and position of the "Window" determine which part of the graphics object is drawn. The relative size of the Window and the Viewport determine the scale at which the graphics object is displayed on the screen. For a given viewport or rendering area, a relatively large Window produces a small graphics object, because you are drawing a large piece of the custom coordinate space into a small viewport (rendering area). On the other hand, a relatively small Window produces a large graphics object. Therefore, you can increase the size of the Window (specified by the X and Y axis limits) to see the "zooming out" effect, which can be done by changing the values of the parameters, such as xMin, xMax, yMin, and yMax in the previous example discussed in the previous section. For instance, setting

```
xMin = -10;
xMax = 20;
yMin = 0;
yMax = 20;
```

and clicking the "Apply" button will generate the results shown in Figure 2-11.

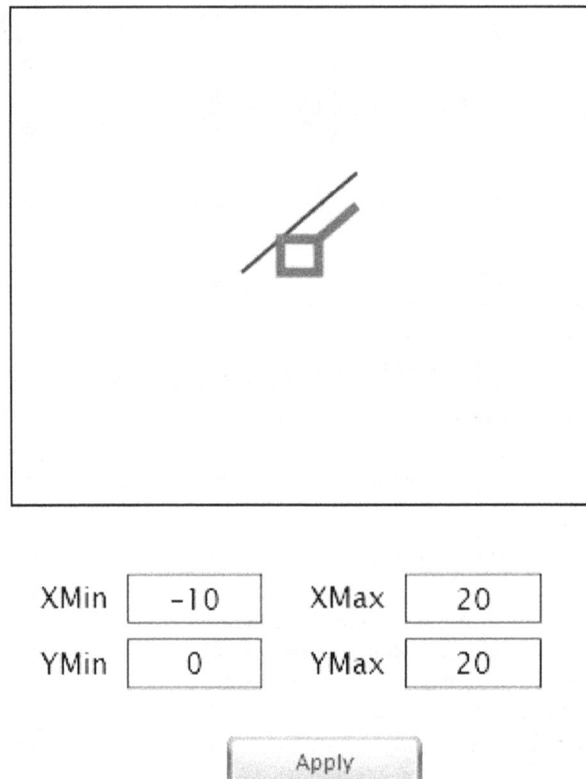

Figure 2-11 Both the size and location of the graphics objects are changed by increasing the size of the Window: "Zoom out".

On the other hand, if you decrease the Window size, the objects will appear larger on the screen; you would then have a "zoom in" effect. Change the parameters of your axis limits to the following:

```
xMin = 2;
xMax = 7;
yMin = 2;
yMax = 7;
```

You will get the following result by clicking the "Apply" button, as shown in Figure 2-12.

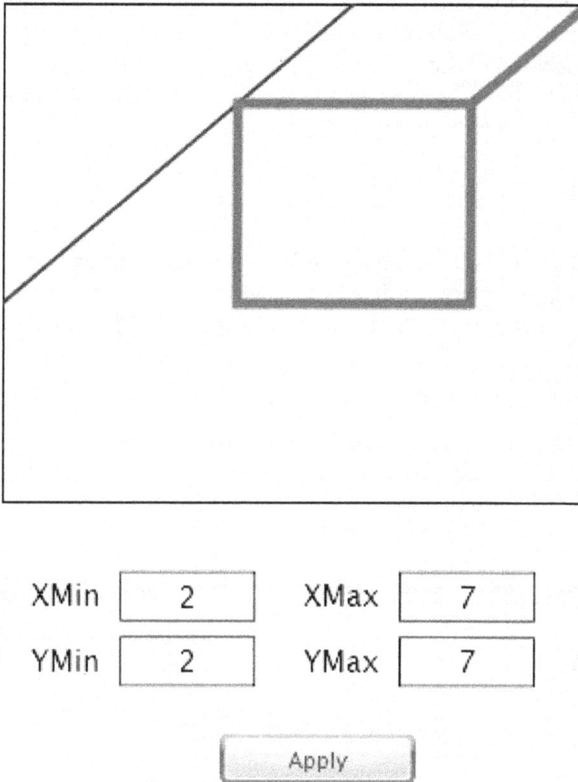

Figure 2-12 Both the size and location of the graphics objects are changed by decreasing the size of the Window: "Zoom in".

Panning is defined as the moving of all graphics objects in the scene by shifting the Window. In a panning process, the Window size is kept unchanged. For example, you can move the Window to the left by changing the following parameters:

```
xMin = -3;
xMax = 7;
yMin = 0;
yMax = 10;
```

This is equivalent to moving graphics objects toward the right side of the rendering area.

Please note that when you increase or decrease the size of graphics objects by zooming in or zooming out, the stroke thickness remains unchanged, which is different from when you directly scale the plotCanvas, where both the shape and stroke thickness change correspondingly with the scaling factor. In 2D charting applications, you usually want to change the size of the graphics only, and keep the stroke thickness unchanged.

Basic 2D Graphics Shapes

The simplest way to create 2D graphics objects in a Silverlight application is to use the Shape class, which represents a number of ready-to-use graphics shape objects. Available shape objects in Silverlight include the Line, Polyline, Path, Rectangle, and Ellipse. These shapes are drawing primitives. You can combine these basic shapes to generate more complex graphics. In the following sections, we'll consider these basic Silverlight shapes.

Lines

The Line class in Silverlight is used to create straight lines between two endpoints. The X1 and Y1 properties specify the starting point, and the X2 and Y2 properties represent the endpoint. The following XAML code snippet creates a blue line from point (30, 30) to point (180, 30):

```
<Line X1="30" Y1="30" X2 ="180" Y2="30"
      Stroke="Blue" StrokeThickness="2"/>
```

This code snippet produces a solid line. However, lines can have many different styles. For example, you can draw a dashed line with line caps, as shown in Figure 2-13. This means that a line has three parts: the line body, the starting cap, and the ending cap.

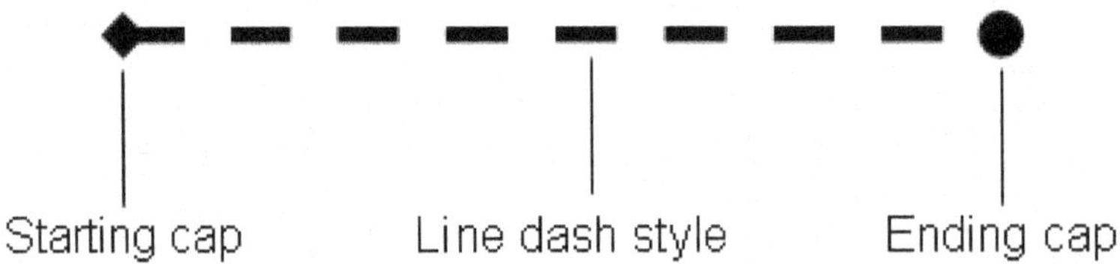

Figure 2-13 A line with starting cap, ending cap, and dash style.

The starting and ending caps can be specified by the StrokeStartLineCap and StrokeEndLineCap properties, respectively. Both the StrokeStartLineCap and StrokeEndLineCap get or set a PenLineCap enumeration value that describes the shape at the ends of a line. Available values in the PenLineCap enumeration include Flat, Round, Square, and Triangle. Unfortunately, the size of the line cap is the same as the StrokeThickness of the line. Thus, these caps aren't very useful in practical applications. If you want to create a line with an end anchor or an arrowhead, you have to create a custom shape by your own.

The dash style of a line is specified by the StrokeDashArray property, which gets or sets a collection of double variables that specify the pattern of dashes and gaps of the line. Consider the following code snippet:

```
<Line X1="30" Y1="50" X2 ="250" Y2="50"
      Stroke="Blue" StrokeThickness="2"
      StrokeDashArray="5,3" />
```

The above code creates a dashed line, which is shown in Figure 2-14.

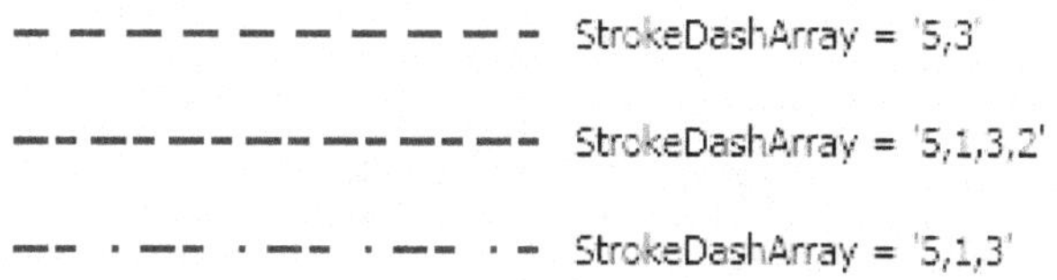

Figure 2-14 Dash Lines with different patterns.

The first line in the figure is a dashed line that is specified by the StrokeDashArray="5,3". These values means that it has a line value of 5 and a gap of 3, interpreted relative to the StrokeThickness of the line. So if your line is 2 units thick (as it is in this example), the solid portion is 5 x 2 = 10 units, followed by a gap portion of 3 x 2 = 6 units. The line then repeats this pattern for its entire length.

You can create a line with more complex dash pattern by varying the values of the StrokeDashArray. For example, you can specify the StrokeDashArray as the following:

```
StrokeDashArray="5,1,3,2"
```

This creates a line with a more complex sequence: a solid portion that is 10 units length, then a 1 x 2 = 2 unit break, followed by a solid portion of 3 x 2 = 6 units, and another gap of 2 x 2 = 4 units. At the end of this sequence, the line repeats the pattern from the beginning.

A funny thing happens if you use an odd number of values for the StrokeDashArray. Take this one, for example:

```
StrokeDashArray="5,1,3"
```

When you draw this line, you begin with a 10 unit solid line, followed by a 2 unit gap, followed by a 6 unit line. But when it repeats the pattern it starts with a gap, indicating you get a 10 units space, followed by a 2 units line, and so on. The dash line simply alternates its pattern between solid portions and gaps, as shown in Figure 2-14.

The second line has a Round starting cap and a Triangle ending cap. If you reduce the StrokeThickness, it is difficult to see the line caps, making them not very useful in real-world applications

Rectangles and Ellipses

The rectangle and the ellipse are the two simplest shapes. To create either one, set the Height and Width properties to define the size of the shape, then set the Fill and Stroke properties to make the shape visible.

The Rectangle class has two extra properties: RadiusX and RadiusY. When set to nonzero values, these two properties allow you to create rectangles with rounded corners.

Let's consider an example that shows how to create rectangles in Silverlight. Create a new Silverlight application project and name it Example02-5. Here is the XAML file of this example:

```
<UserControl x:Class="Example02_5.Page"
    xmlns="http://schemas.microsoft.com/client/2007"
    xmlns:x="http://schemas.microsoft.com/winfx/2006/xaml"
    Width="250" Height="340">
    <Grid x:Name="LayoutRoot" Background="White">
        <StackPanel>
            <TextBlock Text="RadiusX = 0, RadiusY = 0:"
                       Margin="10 10 10 5"/>
            <Rectangle Width="150" Height="70"
                       Fill="LightGray" Stroke="Black"/>
            <TextBlock Text="RadiusX = 20, RadiusY = 10:"
                       Margin="10 10 10 5"/>
            <Rectangle Width="150" Height="70"
                       RadiusX="20" RadiusY="10"
                       Fill="LightGray" Stroke="Black"/>
            <TextBlock Text="RadiusX = 75, RadiusY = 35:"
                       Margin="10 10 10 5"/>
            <Rectangle Width="150" Height="70"
                       RadiusX="75" RadiusY="35"
                       Fill="LightGray" Stroke="Black"/>
        </StackPanel>
    </Grid>
</UserControl>
```

Figure 2-15 shows the results of running this example.

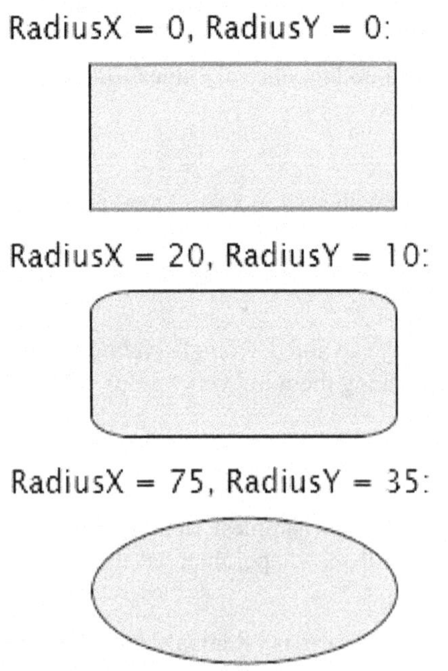

Figure 2-15 Rectangles in Silverlight.

You can easily create rectangles with rounded corners by specifying RadiusX and RadiusY properties with nonzero values. You can see that you can even create an ellipse by setting the RadiusX and RadiusY to large values (larger than half of the respective side length).

You can create an ellipse shape using properties similar to those used in creating rectangles. You can also create a circle by setting RadiusX = RadiusY.

Let's consider another example and name it Example02-6, which shows you how to create Ellipses. Here is the XAML file of this example:

```
<UserControl x:Class="Example02_6.Page"
    xmlns="http://schemas.microsoft.com/client/2007"
    xmlns:x="http://schemas.microsoft.com/winfx/2006/xaml"
    Width="200" Height="280">
    <Grid x:Name="LayoutRoot" Background="White">
        <StackPanel>
            <TextBlock Text="Ellipse:" Margin="10 10 10 5"/>
            <Ellipse Width="150" Height="70"
                     Fill="LightGray" Stroke="Black"/>
            <TextBlock Text="Circle:" Margin="10 10 10 5"/>
            <Ellipse Width="100" Height="100"
                     Fill="LightGray" Stroke="Black"/>
        </StackPanel>
    </Grid>
</UserControl>
```

This example produces the results shown in Figure 2-16.

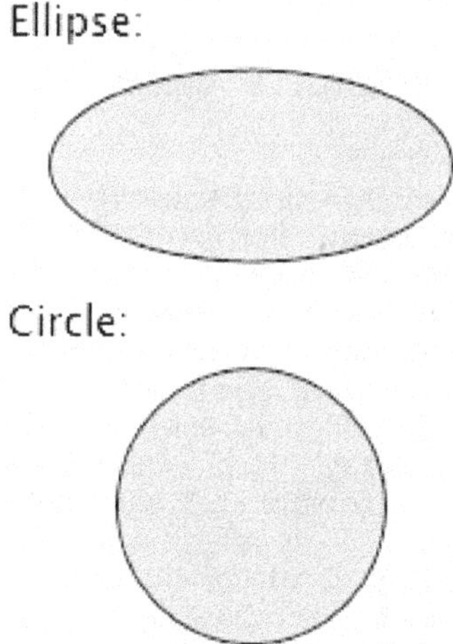

Figure 2-16 Ellipses in Silverlight.

Both the rectangle and ellipse have the ability to resize themselves to fill the available space. If the Height and Width properties aren't specified, the shape is sized based on its container. The sizing behavior of a shape depends on the value of its stretch property. The default value is set to Fill, which stretches a shape to fill its container if an explicit size is not specified.

Let's consider another example that illustrates how to place and resize rectangles and ellipses in Grid cells. Create a new Silverlight project and name it Example02-7. Here is the markup of this example:

```
<UserControl x:Class="Example02_7.Page"
    xmlns="http://schemas.microsoft.com/client/2007"
    xmlns:x="http://schemas.microsoft.com/winfx/2006/xaml"
    Width="420" Height="300">
    <Grid x:Name="LayoutRoot" Background="White" ShowGridLines="True">
        <Grid.RowDefinitions>
            <RowDefinition Height="Auto"/>
            <RowDefinition/>
            <RowDefinition/>
        </Grid.RowDefinitions>
        <Grid.ColumnDefinitions>
            <ColumnDefinition Width="Auto"/>
            <ColumnDefinition/>
            <ColumnDefinition/>
            <ColumnDefinition/>
        </Grid.ColumnDefinitions>

        <TextBlock Grid.Column="0" Grid.Row="1"
                   Text="Rectagle" Margin="5"/>
        <TextBlock Grid.Column="0" Grid.Row="2"
                   Text="Ellipse" Margin="5"/>
        <TextBlock Grid.Column="1" Grid.Row="0" Text="Fill"
                   TextAlignment="Center" Margin="5"/>
        <TextBlock Grid.Column="2" Grid.Row="0" Text="Uniform"
                   TextAlignment="Center" Margin="5"/>
        <TextBlock Grid.Column="3" Grid.Row="0"
                   Text="UniformToFill" TextAlignment="Center"
                   Margin="5"/>

        <Rectangle Grid.Column="1" Grid.Row="1"
                   Fill="LightGray" Stroke="Black"
                   Stretch="Fill" Margin="5"/>
        <Rectangle Grid.Column="2" Grid.Row="1"
                   Fill="LightGray" Stroke="Black"
                   Stretch="Uniform" Margin="5"/>
        <Rectangle Grid.Column="3" Grid.Row="1"
                   Fill="LightGray" Stroke="Black"
                   Stretch="UniformToFill" Margin="5"/>

        <Ellipse Grid.Column="1" Grid.Row="2" Fill="LightGray"
                 Stroke="Black" Stretch="Fill" Margin="5"/>
        <Ellipse Grid.Column="2" Grid.Row="2" Fill="LightGray"
                 Stroke="Black" Stretch="Uniform" Margin="5"/>
        <Ellipse Grid.Column="3" Grid.Row="2" Fill="LightGray"
                 Stroke="Black" Stretch="UniformToFill"
                 Margin="5"/>
    </Grid>
</UserControl>
```

In this example, you create three rectangles and three ellipses, each with a different Stretch property. Figure 2-17 shows the result of running this application. You can see how the different Stretch properties affect the appearances of the shapes.

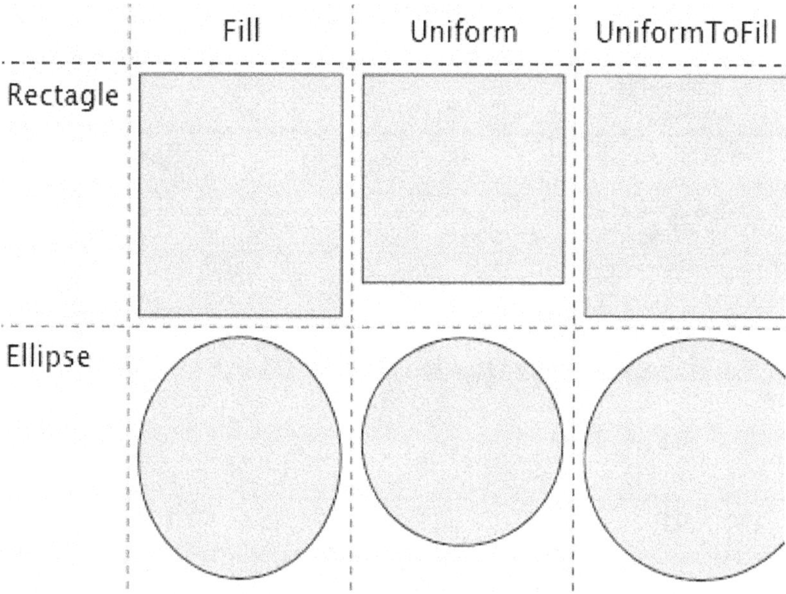

Figure 2-17 Shapes with different Stretch properties.

Polylines

The Polyline class allows you to draw a series of connected straight lines. You simply provide a list of points using its Points property. The Points property requires a PointCollection object if you create a polyline using code. However, you can fill this collection in XAML by simply using a lean string-based syntax.

Let's consider an example that shows you how to create a simple polyline, a closed polyline, and a Sine curve in code. Create a new Silverlight application project and name it Example02-8. Here is the XAML file of this example:

```
<UserControl x:Class="Example02_8.Page"
    xmlns="http://schemas.microsoft.com/client/2007"
    xmlns:x="http://schemas.microsoft.com/winfx/2006/xaml"
    Width="250" Height="340">
    <Grid x:Name="LayoutRoot" Background="White">
        <StackPanel Name="stackPanel1" Margin="10">
            <TextBlock Text="Polyline:"/>
            <Polyline Stroke="Black" StrokeThickness="3"
                Points="0 70,60 10,110 60,160 10,210 70"/>
            <TextBlock Text="Closed polyline:"
                       Margin="0 10 0 0"/>
            <Polyline Stroke="Black" StrokeThickness="3"
              Points="0 70,60 10,110 60,160 10,210 70, 0 70"/>
            <TextBlock Text="Sine curve:" Margin="0 10 0 0"/>
            <Polyline Name="polyline1" Stroke="Red"
                      StrokeThickness="2"/>
        </StackPanel>
    </Grid>
</UserControl>
```

Here you create two polylines directly in the XAML file. You also define another polyline called polyline1 that represents a Sine curve and needs to be created in code. Here is the code-behind file used to generate the Sine curve:

```
using System;
using System.Windows;
using System.Windows.Controls;
using System.Windows.Media;
using System.Windows.Media.Animation;
using System.Windows.Shapes;

namespace Example02_8
{
    public partial class Page : UserControl
    {
        public Page()
        {
            InitializeComponent();
            for (int i = 0; i < 70; i++)
            {
                double x = i * Math.PI;
                double y = 40 + 30 * Math.Sin(x / 10);
                polyline1.Points.Add(new Point(x, y));
            }
        }
    }
}
```

Here, you simply add points to polyline1's Points collection using a Sine function with a for-loop. Running this application produces the results shown in Figure 2-18.

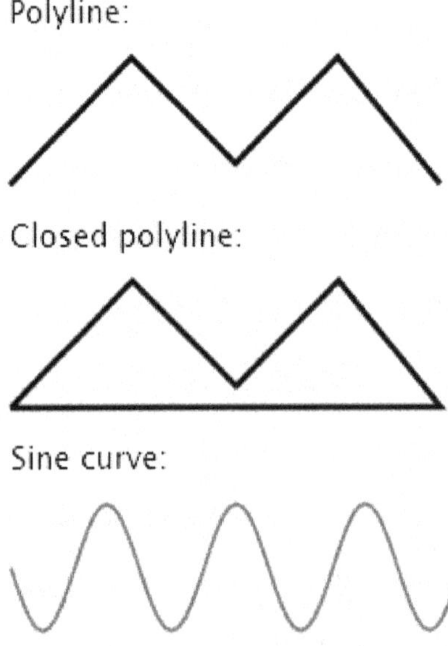

Figure 2-18 Polylines in Silverlight.

Polygons

The polygon is very similar to the polyline. Like the Polyline class, the Polygon class has a Points collection that takes a list of X and Y coordinates. The only difference is that the Polygon adds a final line segment that connects the final point to the starting point. You can fill the interior of this shape using the Fill property.

Create a new Silverlight project and name it Example02-9. This example fills the polylines in the previous example with a light gray color. Here is the XAML file of this example:

```
<UserControl x:Class="Example02_9.Page"
    xmlns="http://schemas.microsoft.com/client/2007"
    xmlns:x="http://schemas.microsoft.com/winfx/2006/xaml"
    Width="400" Height="300">
    <Grid x:Name="LayoutRoot" Background="White">
        <StackPanel Name="stackPanel1" Margin="10">
            <TextBlock Text="Polygon:"/>
            <Polygon Stroke="Black" StrokeThickness="3"
                     Fill="LightGray"
                    Points="0 70,60 10,110 60,160 10,210 70"/>
            <TextBlock Text="Filled sine curve:"
                       Margin="0 10 0 0"/>
            <Polygon Name="polygon1" Stroke="Red"
                StrokeThickness="2" Fill="LightCoral"/>
        </StackPanel>
    </Grid>
</UserControl>
```

The polygon1 is created using a Sine function in the code-behind file:

```
using System;
using System.Windows;
using System.Windows.Controls;
using System.Windows.Media;
using System.Windows.Media.Animation;
using System.Windows.Shapes;

namespace Example02_9
{
    public partial class Page : UserControl
    {
        public Page()
        {
            InitializeComponent();
            for (int i = 0; i < 71; i++)
            {
                double x = i * Math.PI;
                double y = 40 + 30 * Math.Sin(x / 10);
                polygon1.Points.Add(new Point(x, y));
            }
        }
    }
}
```

Running this application produces the results shown in Figure 2-19.

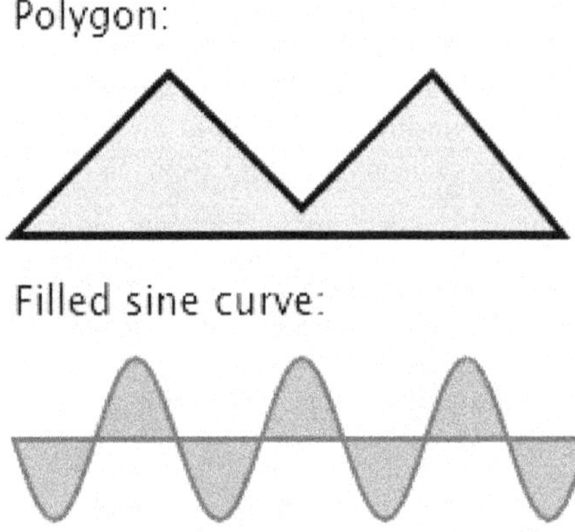

Figure 2-19 Polygons in Silverlight.

In a simple shape where the lines never cross, it is easy to fill the interior. However, sometimes, you'll have a more complex polygon where it isn't necessarily obvious which portions should be filled and which portions should not.

Let's consider an example which shows a line that crosses more than one other line, leaving an irregular region at the center that you may or may not want to fill. Create a new Silverlight project and name it Example02-10. Here is the XAML file of this example:

```
<UserControl x:Class="Example02_10.Page"
    xmlns="http://schemas.microsoft.com/client/2007"
    xmlns:x="http://schemas.microsoft.com/winfx/2006/xaml"
    Width="200" Height="600">
    <Grid x:Name="LayoutRoot" Background="White">
        <StackPanel Margin="10">
            <TextBlock Text="FileRule = EvenOdd:"
                       Margin="0 0 0 5"/>
            <Polygon Stroke="Black" Fill="LightGray"
                     FillRule="EvenOdd"
                     Points="0 0,0 150,100 150,100 50,
                             50 50,50 100,150 100,150 0"/>
            <TextBlock Text="FileRule = NonZero:"
                       Margin="0 10 0 5"/>
            <Polygon Stroke="Black" Fill="LightGray"
                     FillRule="Nonzero"
                     Points="0 0,0 150,100 150,100 50,50 50,
                             50 100,150 100,150 0"/>
            <TextBlock Text="FileRule = NonZero:"
                       Margin="0 10 0 5"/>
            <Polygon Stroke="Black" Fill="LightGray"
                     FillRule="Nonzero"
                     Points="0 0,0 150,100 150,100 100,50 100,
                         50 50,100 50,100 100,150 100,150 0"/>
        </StackPanel>
    </Grid>
</UserControl>
```

Here, you use the FillRule property to control the filled regions. Every polygon has a FillRule property that allows you to choose between two different methods for filling in regions, EvenOdd (the default value) or NonZero. In the EvenOdd case, in order to determine which region will be filled, Silverlight counts the number of lines that must be crossed to reach the outside of the shape. If this number is odd, the region is filled; if it is even, the region isn't filled, as shown in Figure 2-20.

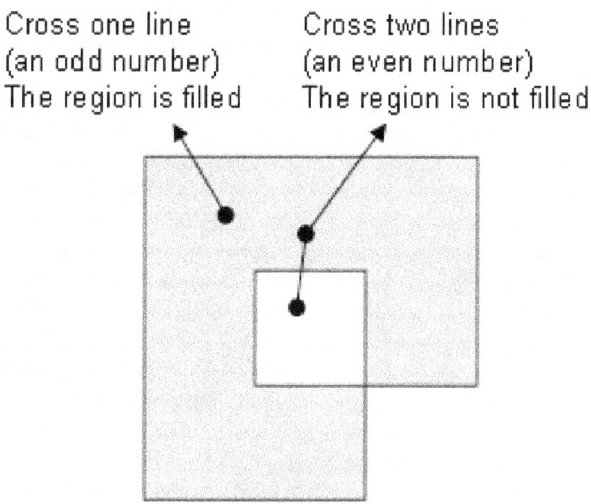

Figure 2-20 Determining filled regions when FillRule is set to EvenOdd.

When FillRule is set to NonZero, determining which region will be filled becomes tricky. In this case, Silverlight follows the same line-counting process as EvenOdd, but takes into account the line direction. If the number of lines going in one direction is equal to the number of lines going in the opposite direction, the region isn't filled. If the difference between these two counts isn't zero, the region is filled.

Figure 2-21 shows the results of running this example.

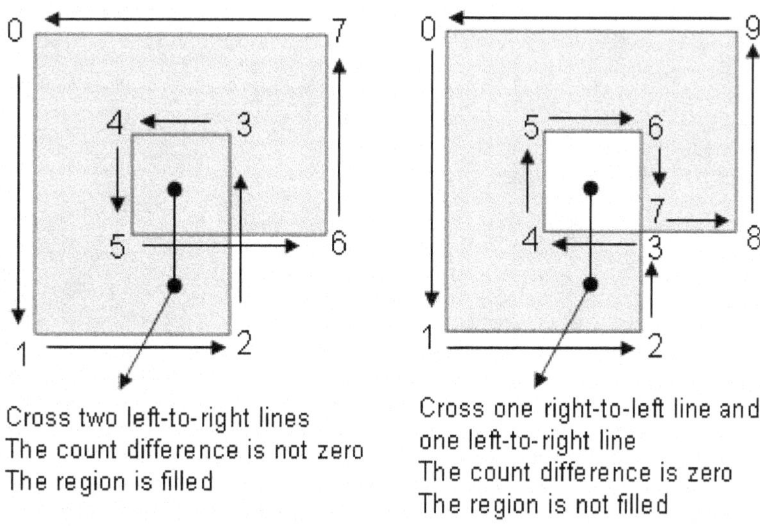

Figure 2-21 Determining filled regions when FillRule is set to NonZero.

The difference between the two shapes in the figure is that the order of points in the Points collection is different, leading to different line directions. This means that in the NonZero case, whether a region is filled or not depends on how you draw the shape, not what the shape itself looks like. Figure 2-21 clearly demonstrates this conclusion.

Chapter 3
2D Transformations

In the previous chapter, you learned about coordinate systems and basic shapes in Silverlight. To create complex shapes in real-world Silverlight applications, you need to understand transform operations on graphics objects.

In a graphics application, operations can be performed in different coordinate systems. Moving from one coordinate space to another requires the use of transformation matrices. In this chapter, we review the mathematic basis of vectors, matrices, and transforms in 2D space. Here we acknowledge the importance of matrices and transforms in graphics applications by presenting you with a more formal exposition of their properties. We concern ourselves with linear transformations among different coordinate systems. Such transforms include simple scaling, reflection, translation, and rotations. You'll learn how to perform matrix operations and graphics object transforms in Silverlight.

Basics of Matrices and Transforms

Vectors and matrices play an important role in the transformation process. Silverlight uses a row-major definition for matrices. Thus, a vector is a row array and a matrix is a multi-dimensional array in Silverlight. This section explains the basics of 2D matrices and 2D transforms. As we discussed in the previous chapter, by changing the coordinates of a graphics object in the world coordinate system, such as by zooming or panning, you can easily move the graphics object to another part of a viewport. However, if the graphic contains more than one object, you may want to move one of the objects without moving the others. In this case, you can't use simple zooming and panning to move the object because these approaches would move the other objects as well.

Instead, you can apply a transform to the object you want to move. Here we'll discuss transforms that scale, rotate, and translate an object.

Scaling

To scale or stretch an object in the X direction, you simply need to multiply the X coordinates of each of the object's points by the scaling factor s_x. Similarly, you can also scale an object in the Y direction. The scaling process can be described by the following equation:

$$(x1 \quad y1) = (x \quad y)\begin{pmatrix} s_x & 0 \\ 0 & s_y \end{pmatrix} = (s_x x \quad s_y y) \tag{3.1}$$

For example, a scaling matrix that shrinks x and y uniformly by a factor of two and a matrix that halves in the y direction and increases by three-halves in the x direction, are given below respectively:

$$\begin{pmatrix} 0.5 & 0 \\ 0 & 0.5 \end{pmatrix} \text{ and } \begin{pmatrix} 1.5 & 0 \\ 0 & 0.5 \end{pmatrix}$$

The above two scaling matrix operations have very different effects on objects, as shown in Figure 3-1.

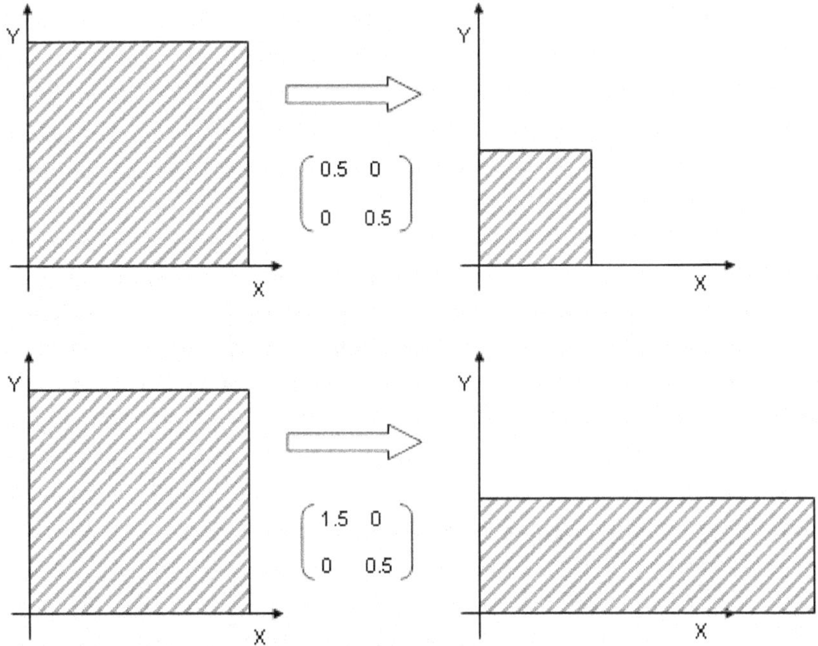

Figure 3-1 Uniform scaling by half in the x and y directions (top) and non-uniform scaling in the x and y directions (bottom).

Reflection

By reflecting an object across the X and Y axes, you can create a mirror image of the object. Reflecting an object across an axis is equivalent to scaling it with a negative scaling factor. The transform matrices across either of the coordinate axes can be written in the following forms:

Reflect across the x axis: $\begin{pmatrix} -1 & 0 \\ 0 & 1 \end{pmatrix}$

Reflect across the y axis: $\begin{pmatrix} 1 & 0 \\ 0 & -1 \end{pmatrix}$

As you might expect, a matrix with -1 in both elements of the diagonal is a reflection that is simply a rotation by 180 degrees.

Rotation

Suppose you want to rotate an object by an angle θ counter-clockwise. First, suppose you have a point (x1, y1) that you want to rotate by an angle θ to get to the point (x2, y2), as shown in Figure 3-2.

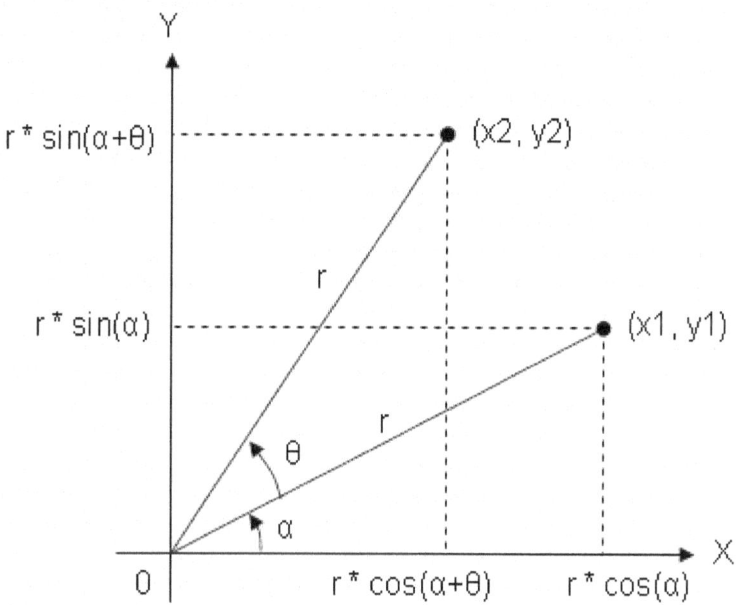

Figure 3-2 Rotation from point (x1, y1) to (x2, y2).

The distance from the point to the origin is assumed to be r. Then, we have the following relations:

$$x1 = r\cos\alpha$$
$$y1 = r\sin\alpha$$

The point (*x2, y2*) is the same point rotated by an additional angle of θ. Since this point also has a distance *r* from the origin, its coordinates are given by:

$$x2 = r\cos(\alpha+\theta) = r\cos\alpha\cos\theta - r\sin\alpha\sin\theta$$
$$y2 = r\sin(\alpha+\theta) = r\sin\alpha\cos\theta + r\cos\alpha\sin\theta$$

Substituting the components of x1 = rcosα and y1 = rsinα into the above equations gives

$$x2 = x1\cos\theta - y1\sin\theta$$
$$y2 = x1\sin\theta + y1\cos\theta$$

In matrix form, the equivalent rotation transform that takes point (x1, y1) to (x2, y2) is given by the following rotation matrix:

$$R(\theta) = \begin{pmatrix} \cos\theta & \sin\theta \\ -\sin\theta & \cos\theta \end{pmatrix} \tag{3.2}$$

Translation

To translate an object, you simply add an offset to the original X and Y coordinates of the points that make up the object

$$\begin{aligned} x1 &= x + dx \\ y1 &= y + dy \end{aligned} \tag{3.3}$$

Although translations look very simple, they can't be expressed in terms of a transform matrix. It would be feasible to keep track of scales, reflections, and rotations as matrices, while keeping track of translations separately. However, doing so would involve fairly painful bookkeeping, particularly if your application includes many different transforms. Instead, you can use a technique to move the computation into a higher dimension. This technique allows you to treat the different transforms in a uniform or homogeneous way. This approach, called homogeneous coordinates, has become standard in almost every graphics program. In the following section, we'll introduce homogeneous coordinates which allow you to manipulate all of these transforms with matrices.

Homogeneous Coordinates

We expect that all transforms in 2D space, including scaling, reflection, rotation, and translation, can be treated equally if points are expressed in homogeneous coordinates. Homogeneous coordinates were first introduced in geometry and have been applied subsequently to graphics.

In homogeneous coordinates, you add a third coordinate to a point. Instead of being represented by a pair of (X, Y) numbers, each point is represented by a triple (X, Y, W). If the W coordinate is nonzero, you can divide through by it: (X, Y, W) represents the same point as (X/W, Y/W, 1). When W is nonzero, you normally perform this division, and the numbers X/W and Y/W are usually called the point coordinates in the homogeneous coordinate system. The points where W = 0 are called points at infinity.

Since vectors and points in 2D space are now three-element row arrays, transform matrices, which multiply a vector to produce another vector, should be 3 x 3.

Translation in Homogeneous Coordinates

In homogeneous coordinates, a translation can be expressed in the form:

$$\begin{pmatrix} x1 & y1 & 1 \end{pmatrix} = \begin{pmatrix} x & y & 1 \end{pmatrix} \begin{pmatrix} 1 & 0 & 0 \\ 0 & 1 & 0 \\ dx & dy & 1 \end{pmatrix} \tag{3.4}$$

The above transform can be expressed differently as

$$P_1 = P \cdot T(dx, dy) \tag{3.5}$$

Here P and P_1 represent point (x, y) and point (x1, y1) respectively, and T(dx, dy) is the translation matrix:

$$T(dx, dy) = \begin{pmatrix} 1 & 0 & 0 \\ 0 & 1 & 0 \\ dx & dy & 1 \end{pmatrix} \tag{3.6}$$

What happens if a point P is translated by T(dx1, dy1) to P_1; and then translated by T(dx2, dy2) to P_2? The result, you might intuitively expect, is a net translation of T(dx1 + dx2, dy1+ dy2). This can be confirmed by the definitions:

$$P_1 = P \cdot T(dx1, dy1)$$
$$P_2 = P_1 \cdot T(dx2, dy2)$$

From the above equations we have:

$$P_2 = P \cdot T(dx1, dy1) \cdot T(dx2, dy2)$$

The matrix product T(dx1, dy1) T(dx2, dy2) is

$$\begin{pmatrix} 1 & 0 & 0 \\ 0 & 1 & 0 \\ dx1 & dy1 & 1 \end{pmatrix} \begin{pmatrix} 1 & 0 & 0 \\ 0 & 1 & 0 \\ dx2 & dy2 & 1 \end{pmatrix} = \begin{pmatrix} 1 & 0 & 0 \\ 0 & 1 & 0 \\ dx1 + dx2 & dy1 + dy2 & 1 \end{pmatrix} \tag{3.7}$$

The net translation is indeed T(dx1 + dx2, dy1 + dy2).

Scaling in Homogeneous Coordinates

Similarly, the scaling equation (3.1) can be represented in matrix form in homogeneous coordinates as:

$$\begin{pmatrix} x1 & y1 & 1 \end{pmatrix} = \begin{pmatrix} x & y & 1 \end{pmatrix} \begin{pmatrix} s_x & 0 & 0 \\ 0 & s_y & 0 \\ 0 & 0 & 1 \end{pmatrix}$$

It can also be expressed in the form:

$$P_1 = P \cdot S(s_x, s_y) \tag{3.9}$$

Just as successive translations are additive, we expect that successive scalings should be multiplicative. Given

$$P_1 = P \cdot S(s_{x1}, s_{y1}) \tag{3.10}$$

$$P_2 = P_1 \cdot S(s_{x2}, s_{y2}) \tag{3.11}$$

Substituting Eq.(3.10) into Eq.(3.11) obtains

$$P_2 = (P \cdot S(s_{x1}, s_{y1})) \cdot S(s_{x2}, s_{y2}) = P \cdot (S(s_{x1}, s_{y1}) \cdot S(s_{x2}, s_{y2}))$$

The matrix product in the above equation is

$$\begin{pmatrix} s_{x1} & 0 & 0 \\ 0 & s_{y1} & 0 \\ 0 & 0 & 1 \end{pmatrix}\begin{pmatrix} s_{x2} & 0 & 0 \\ 0 & s_{y2} & 0 \\ 0 & 0 & 1 \end{pmatrix} = \begin{pmatrix} s_{x1}s_{x2} & 0 & 0 \\ 0 & s_{y1}s_{y2} & 0 \\ 0 & 0 & 1 \end{pmatrix}$$

Thus, scalings are indeed multiplicative.

Reflection is a special case of scaling with a scaling factor of -1. You can represent a reflection in the same way as scaling.

Rotation in Homogeneous Coordinates

A rotation in homogeneous coordinates can be represented as

$$\begin{pmatrix} x1 & y1 & 1 \end{pmatrix} = \begin{pmatrix} x & y & 1 \end{pmatrix}\begin{pmatrix} \cos\theta & \sin\theta & 0 \\ -\sin\theta & \cos\theta & 0 \\ 0 & 0 & 1 \end{pmatrix} \tag{3.12}$$

It can be also written as

$$P_1 = P \cdot R(\theta)$$

Where R(θ) is the rotation matrix in homogeneous coordinates. You would expect that two successive rotations should be additive. Given

$$P_1 = P \cdot R(\theta_1) \tag{3.13}$$

$$P_2 = P_1 \cdot R(\theta_2) \tag{3.14}$$

Substituting Eq. (3.13) into Eq. (3.14) gets

$$P_2 = (P \cdot R(\theta_1)) \cdot R(\theta_2) = P \cdot (R(\theta_1) \cdot R(\theta_2))$$

The matrix product $R(\theta_1)$ $R(\theta_2)$ is

$$\begin{pmatrix} \cos\theta_1 & \sin\theta_1 & 0 \\ -\sin\theta_1 & \cos\theta_1 & 0 \\ 0 & 0 & 1 \end{pmatrix}\begin{pmatrix} \cos\theta_2 & \sin\theta_2 & 0 \\ -\sin\theta_2 & \cos\theta_2 & 0 \\ 0 & 0 & 1 \end{pmatrix}$$

$$= \begin{pmatrix} \cos\theta_1\cos\theta_2 - \sin\theta_1\sin\theta_2 & \cos\theta_1\sin\theta_2 + \sin\theta_1\cos\theta_2 & 0 \\ -\sin\theta_1\cos\theta_2 - \cos\theta_1\sin\theta_2 & \cos\theta_1\cos\theta_2 - \sin\theta_1\sin\theta_2 & 0 \\ 0 & 0 & 1 \end{pmatrix}$$

$$= \begin{pmatrix} \cos(\theta_1+\theta_2) & \sin(\theta_1+\theta_2) & 0 \\ -\sin(\theta_1+\theta_2) & \cos(\theta_1+\theta_2) & 0 \\ 0 & 0 & 1 \end{pmatrix}$$

Thus, rotations are indeed additive.

Combining Transforms

It is common for graphics applications to apply more than one transform to a graphics object. For example, you might want to first apply a scaling transform S, and then a rotation transform R. You can combine the fundamental S, T, and R matrices to produce desired general transform results. The basic purpose of combining transforms is to gain efficiency by applying a single composed transform to a point, rather than applying a series of transforms one after the other.

Consider the rotation of an object about some arbitrary point P1. Since you only know how to rotate about the origin, you need to convert the original problem into several separate problems. Thus, to rotate about P1, you need to perform a sequence of several fundamental transformations:

- Translate it so that the point is at the origin
- Rotate it to the desired angle
- Translate so that the point at the origin returns back to P1.

This sequence is illustrated in Figure 3-3, in which a rectangle is rotated about P1 (x1, y1).

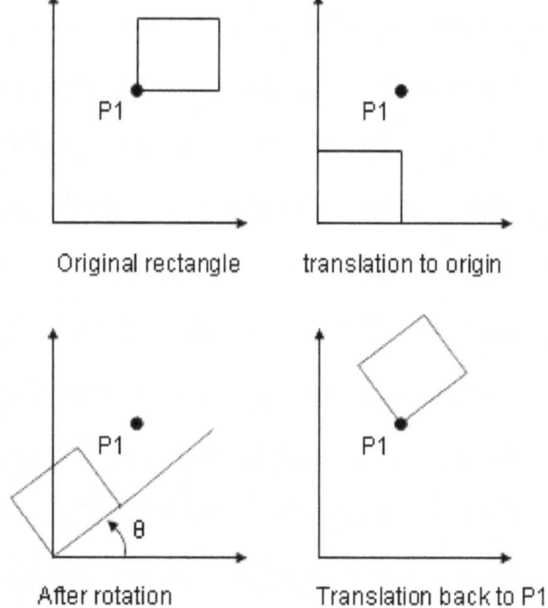

Figure 3-3 Rotation of a rectangle about a point P1.

The first translation is by (-x1,-y1), whereas the latter translation is by the inverse (x1, y1). The result is quite different from that of applying just the rotation. The net transformation is

$$T(-x1,-y1)\cdot R(\theta)\cdot T(x1,y1)=\begin{pmatrix}1 & 0 & 0\\ 0 & 1 & 0\\ -x1 & -y1 & 1\end{pmatrix}\begin{pmatrix}\cos\theta & \sin\theta & 0\\ -\sin\theta & \cos\theta & 0\\ 0 & 0 & 1\end{pmatrix}\begin{pmatrix}1 & 0 & 0\\ 0 & 1 & 0\\ x1 & y1 & 1\end{pmatrix}$$

$$= \begin{pmatrix} \cos\theta & -\sin\theta & 0 \\ \sin\theta & \cos\theta & 0 \\ x1\cdot(1-\cos\theta)+y1\cdot\sin\theta & y1\cdot(1-\cos\theta)-x1\cdot\sin\theta & 1 \end{pmatrix}$$

Vectors and Matrices in Silverlight

Silverlight implements a Matrix structure in homogeneous coordinates in 2D space. However, it doesn't contain a Vector definition. You'll find that the Vector structure or class is necessary for some graphics object operations. Here, I'll show you how to define your own Vector class in Silverlight.

The Matrix structure in Silverlight uses a convention of pre-multiplying matrices by row vectors. A point or a vector in homogeneous coordinates is defined using three double values (X, Y, 1). In Silverlight, it can also be expressed in terms of two doubles (X, Y) since the third double is always equal to one.

Vector Class

In this section, we'll define a vector class in 2D space. This vector class is specifically designed for transformation operations on various framework and user interface elements in Silverlight. Start with a new Silverlight project and name it Example03-1. Add a new public Vector class to the project and rename its namespace XuMath. This class will be part of the general Math library and can be used in different projects. Here, you need appropriate constructors which should be able to create an initialized 2D vector, a vector converted from a given double array, Point, or difference between two Points. To deal with these aspects, we first write:

```
using System;
using System.Windows;
using System.Windows.Media;

namespace XuMath
{
    public class Vector
    {
        public double[] vector;

        #region Constructor:
        public Vector()
        {
            this.vector = new double[2] { 0, 0 };
        }

        public Vector(double[] double2d)
        {
            if (double2d.Length == 2)
                this.vector = double2d;
        }

        public Vector(Point pt)
        {
            this.vector = new double[2] { pt.X, pt.Y };
```

```
        }

        public Vector(Point pt1, Point pt2)
        {
            this.vector = new double[2] { pt1.X - pt2.X, pt1.Y - pt2.Y };
        }
        #endregion
    }
}
```

The first constructor takes no parameter. It creates a 2D vector, whose elements are initialized to zero. The second constructor creates a vector to hold a given double precision float-point 2D array. The size of the vector is the same as the length of the array. The third constructor creates a vector from a 2D point object. The X and Y components of the vector correspond exactly to the components of the Point. The final constructor creates a 2D vector from the difference between two points, which is very useful in some graphics operations in Silverlight.

Basic Definition

Now, we need to define a number of operators and public methods. First, here is the indexing operation, which can be written as:

```
public double this[int n]
{
    get
    {
        if (n < 0 || n > 2)
        {
            throw new ArgumentOutOfRangeException(
             "n", n, "n is out of range!");
        }
        return vector[n];
    }
    set { vector[n] = value; }
}
```

This indexing operation allows you to access the nth element of the vector. For a vector v, you can simply use v[n] to access the nth element of v, which is very close to ordinary mathematical notations.

In condition statements, we need to know if two vectors are equal or not. The System.Object type offers a virtual method, named Equals. It will return true if two objects have the same "value".

In order to compare two vectors, we need to implement the Equals method in the Vector class using the following code snippet:

```
public override bool Equals(object obj)
{
    return (obj is Vector) && this.Equals((Vector)obj);
}

public bool Equals(Vector v)
{
    return vector == v.vector;
}
```

```
public override int GetHashCode()
{
    return vector.GetHashCode();
}

public static bool operator ==(Vector v1, Vector v2)
{
    return v1.Equals(v2);
}

public static bool operator !=(Vector v1, Vector v2)
{
    return !v1.Equals(v2);
}
```

You can examine the above Equals methods using the following code snippet:

```
double[] a1 = new double[2]{1.0, 2.0};
double[] a2 = new double[2]{4.0, 5.0};
Vector v1 = new Vector(a1);
Vector v2 = new Vector(a2);
    bool b = v1 == v2;
```

The result of b will be False.

Then there are the unary plus and minus operators:

```
public static Vector operator +(Vector v)
{
    return v;
}

public static Vector operator -(Vector v)
{
    double[] result = new double[v.GetSize()];
    for(int i=0; i < 2; i++)
    {
        result[i] = -v[i];
    }
    return new Vector(result);
}
```

Next, we define the norm and unit vectors:

```
public double GetNorm()
{
    double result = vector[0] * vector[0] + vector[1] * vector[1];
    return Math.Sqrt(result);
}

public double GetNormSquare()
{
    return vector[0] * vector[0] + vector[1] * vector[1];
}

public Vector GetUnitVector()
{
    Vector result = new Vector(vector);
```

```
        result.Normalize();
        return result;
    }

    public void Normalize()
    {
        double norm = GetNorm();
        if (norm == 0)
        {
            throw new DivideByZeroException("Normalize
                  a vector with norm of zero!");
        }
        for (int i = 0; i < 2; i++)
        {
            vector[i] /= norm;
        }
    }
```

For example, you can compute the norm for a vector using the following code snippet:

```
Vector v = new Vector();
for(int i = 0; i < 2; i++)
{
    v[i] = 0.5 * (i + 1);
}
double result = v.GetNorm();
```

This gives the result = 4.472.

Mathematical Operators

It is easy to implement various mathematical operations of vectors in C#:

```
public static Vector operator +(Vector v)
{
    return v;
}

public static Vector operator -(Vector v)
{
    double[] result = new double[2];
    for (int i = 0; i < 2; i++)
    {
        result[i] = -v[i];
    }
    return new Vector(result);
}

public static Vector operator +(Vector v1, Vector v2)
{
    Vector result = new Vector();
    for (int i = 0; i < 2; i++)
    {
        result[i] = v1[i] + v2[i];
    }
    return result;
```

```
    }

    public static Vector operator +(Vector v, double d)
    {
        Vector result = new Vector();
        for (int i = 0; i < 2; i++)
        {
            result[i] = v[i] + d;
        }
        return result;
    }

    public static Vector operator +(double d, Vector v)
    {
        Vector result = new Vector();
        for (int i = 0; i < 2; i++)
        {
            result[i] = v[i] + d;
        }
        return result;
    }

    public static Vector operator +(Vector v, Point pt)
    {
        Vector result = new Vector();
        result[0] = v[0] + pt.X;
        result[1] = v[1] + pt.Y;
        return result;
    }

    public static Vector operator -(Vector v1, Vector v2)
    {
        Vector result = new Vector();
        for (int i = 0; i < 2; i++)
        {
            result[i] = v1[i] - v2[i];
        }
        return result;
    }

    public static Vector operator -(Vector v, double d)
    {
        Vector result = new Vector();
        for (int i = 0; i < 2; i++)
        {
            result[i] = v[i] - d;
        }
        return result;
    }

    public static Vector operator -(double d, Vector v)
    {
        Vector result = new Vector();
        for (int i = 0; i < 2; i++)
        {
```

```
            result[i] = d - v[i];
        }
        return result;
    }

    public static Vector operator *(Vector v, double d)
    {
        Vector result = new Vector();
        for (int i = 0; i < 2; i++)
        {
            result[i] = v[i] * d;
        }
        return result;
    }

    public static Vector operator *(double d, Vector v)
    {
        Vector result = new Vector();
        for (int i = 0; i < 2; i++)
        {
            result[i] = d * v[i];
        }
        return result;
    }

    public static Vector operator *(Vector v, Matrix m)
    {
        Vector result = new Vector();
        result[0] = v[0] * m.M11 + v[1] * m.M21;
        result[1] = v[0] * m.M12 + v[1] * m.M22;
        return result;
    }

    public static Vector operator /(Vector v, double d)
    {
        Vector result = new Vector();
        for (int i = 0; i < 2; i++)
        {
            result[i] = v[i] / d;
        }
        return result;
    }

    public static Vector operator /(double d, Vector v)
    {
        Vector result = new Vector();
        for (int i = 0; i < 2; i++)
        {
            result[i] = d / v[i];
        }
        return result;
    }
```

Here, the standard vector addition, subtraction, multiplication, and division are performed using the above methods. Please note that the multiplication and division operations in the above methods are not for two-vector operations, but for a vector scaled by a scalar number. One important operation is the vector multiplied by a matrix, which represents a matrix operation on a vector.

We also implement a public method, DotProduct:

```
public static double DotProduct(Vector v1, Vector v2)
{
    double result = 0.0;
    for (int i = 0; i < 2; i++)
    {
        result += v1[i] * v2[i];
    }
    return result;
}
```

The dot product of two vectors in the above method produces a scalar quantity. You can view the complete source code by opening the Vector.cs class.

Matrix Structure

We have demonstrated that the transform matrices in homogeneous coordinates always have a last column of (0 0 1). It can be shown that any combined transform matrix using these fundamental transforms has the same last column. Based on this fact, Silverlight defines the transform in terms of a 3x2 matrix. Namely, the matrix structure in Silverlight takes 6 elements arranged in 3 rows by 2 columns. In methods and properties, the Matrix object is usually specified as a vector with six members, as follows: (M11, M12, M21, M22, OffsetX, OffsetY). The OffsetX and OffsetY represent translation values.

For example, the default identity matrix constructed by the default constructor has a value of (1, 0, 0, 1, 0, 0). In matrix representation, this means:

$$\begin{pmatrix} 1 & 0 \\ 0 & 1 \\ 0 & 0 \end{pmatrix}\text{. This is a simplification of } \begin{pmatrix} 1 & 0 & 0 \\ 0 & 1 & 0 \\ 0 & 0 & 1 \end{pmatrix}\text{. The last column is always } \begin{pmatrix} 0 \\ 0 \\ 1 \end{pmatrix}.$$

Thus a translation of of 3 units in the X direction and 2 units in the Y direction would be represented as (1, 0, 0, 1, 3, 2). In matrix form, we should have:

$$\begin{pmatrix} 1 & 0 \\ 0 & 1 \\ 3 & 2 \end{pmatrix}\text{. This is a simplification of } \begin{pmatrix} 1 & 0 & 0 \\ 0 & 1 & 0 \\ 3 & 2 & 1 \end{pmatrix}.$$

You can create a matrix object in Silverlight by using overloaded constructors, which take an array of double values (which hold the matrix items) as arguments. Please note that before you use the matrix class in your applications, you need to add a reference to the System.Windows.Media namespace. The following code snippet creates three matrix objects for translation, scaling, and rotation in code:

```
double dx = 3;
double dy = 2;
double sx = 0.5;
```

```
double sy = 1.5;
double theta = Math.PI / 4;
double sin = Math.Sin(theta);
double cos = Math.Cos(theta);
Matrix tm = new Matrix(1, 0, 0, 1, dx, dy);
Matrix sm = new Matrix(sx, 0, 0, sy, 0, 0);
Matrix rm = new Matrix(cos, sin, -sin, cos, 0, 0);
```

The matrix tm is a translation matrix that moves an object by 3 units in the x direction and by 2 units in the y direction. The scaling matrix sm scales an object by a factor of 0.5 in the x direction and by a factor of 1.5 in the y direction. The other matrix rm is a rotation matrix that rotates an object by 45 degrees about the origin.

In addition to the properties of these six matrix elements, there are two more public properties associated with a matrix, which are the static Identity property, which gets the Identity matrix, and the IsIdentity property, which gets a value indicating whether the Matrix structure is an identity matrix.

I should point out here that unlike WPF, Silverlight has no public method associated with the Matrix operations, such as Invert, Multiply, Scale, Rotate, etc. Therefore, you can't directly perform matrix operations in Silverlight.

Creating Perpendicular Lines

In implementing the Vector class in the previous section, we defined the matrix operation on a vector. In this section, I'll use an example to demonstrate how to use this matrix operation in a Silverlight application. The example application is very simple. As shown in Figure 3-4, for a given line segment (the solid line) specified by two end points, (x1, y1) and (x2, y2), we want to find a perpendicular line segment (the dashed line) at one end (for example, at Point(x2, y2)) of the original line segment.

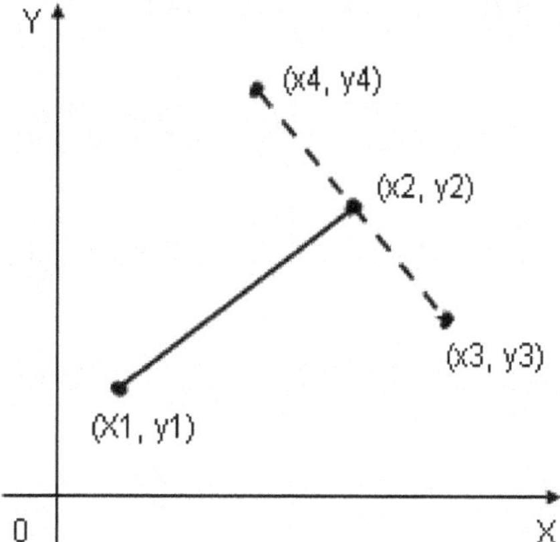

Figure 3-4 Creating a perpendicular line for a given line segment.

We can build the application in Project Example03-1. Create a user interface using the following XAML code for Page.xaml file:

```
<UserControl x:Class="Example03_1.Page"
    xmlns="http://schemas.microsoft.com/client/2007"
    xmlns:x="http://schemas.microsoft.com/winfx/2006/xaml"
    Width="450" Height="300">
    <Grid x:Name="LayoutRoot" Background="White" Width="430" Height="300"
        HorizontalAlignment="Left" VerticalAlignment="Top">
        <Grid.ColumnDefinitions>
            <ColumnDefinition Width="120" />
            <ColumnDefinition Width="320" />
        </Grid.ColumnDefinitions>
        <Grid Width="110" Height="300" Margin="5,10,5,5">
            <Grid.ColumnDefinitions>
                <ColumnDefinition Width="40" />
                <ColumnDefinition Width="70" />
            </Grid.ColumnDefinitions>
            <Grid.RowDefinitions>
                <RowDefinition Height="Auto" />
                <RowDefinition Height="Auto" />
                <RowDefinition Height="Auto" />
                <RowDefinition Height="Auto" />
                <RowDefinition Height="Auto" />
                <RowDefinition Height="Auto" />
            </Grid.RowDefinitions>

            <TextBlock HorizontalAlignment="Right" Grid.Column="0" Grid.Row="0"
                       Margin="5,5,10,5">X1</TextBlock>
            <TextBox Name="tbX1" Grid.Column="1" Grid.Row="0" Height="25"
                       TextAlignment="Center" Text="20"/>
            <TextBlock HorizontalAlignment="Right" Grid.Column="0" Grid.Row="1"
                       Margin="5,5,10,5">Y1</TextBlock>
            <TextBox Name="tbY1" Grid.Column="1" Grid.Row="1" Height="25"
                       TextAlignment="Center" Text="200"/>
            <TextBlock HorizontalAlignment="Right" Grid.Column="0" Grid.Row="2"
                       Margin="5,5,10,5">X2</TextBlock>
            <TextBox Name="tbX2" Grid.Column="1" Grid.Row="2" Height="25"
                       TextAlignment="Center" Text="130"/>
            <TextBlock HorizontalAlignment="Right" Grid.Column="0" Grid.Row="3"
                     Margin="5,5,10,5">Y2</TextBlock>
            <TextBox Name="tbY2" Grid.Column="1" Grid.Row="3" Height="25"
                       TextAlignment="Center" Text="100"/>

            <Button Click="Apply_Click" Margin="25,20,5,5" Grid.Row="4"
                    Height="25" Grid.ColumnSpan="2" Grid.Column="0"
                    Content="Apply"/>
        </Grid>

        <Border Width="270" Height="280" BorderBrush="Gray" BorderThickness="1"
               Grid.Column="1" Margin="10">
            <Canvas Name="canvas1" Width="270" Height="280">
                <Canvas.Clip>
                    <RectangleGeometry Rect="0,0,270,280"/>
                </Canvas.Clip>

                <TextBlock Name="tbPoint1" FontSize="12" Canvas.ZIndex="1"
                           Canvas.Top="10">Point1</TextBlock>
```

```
            <TextBlock Name="tbPoint2" FontSize="12" Canvas.ZIndex="1"
                       Canvas.Top="25">Point2</TextBlock>
            <TextBlock Name="tbPoint3" FontSize="12" Canvas.ZIndex="1"
                       Canvas.Top="40">Point3</TextBlock>
            <TextBlock Name="tbPoint4" FontSize="12" Canvas.ZIndex="1"
                       Canvas.Top="55">Point4</TextBlock>
         </Canvas>
      </Border>
   </Grid>
</UserControl>
```

This XAML code creates a user interface that allows you to specify the end-points of the line. The corresponding code-behind file of this example is given below:

```
using System;
using System.Windows;
using System.Windows.Controls;
using System.Windows.Media;
using System.Windows.Shapes;
using XuMath;

namespace Example03_1
{
    public partial class Page : UserControl
    {
        private Line line1;
        private Line line2;

        public Page()
        {
            InitializeComponent();
            line1 = new Line();
            line2 = new Line();
            AddLines();
        }


        private void AddLines()
        {
            Point pt1 = new Point();
            Point pt2 = new Point();

            pt1.X = Convert.ToDouble(tbX1.Text);
            pt1.Y = Convert.ToDouble(tbY1.Text);
            pt2.X = Convert.ToDouble(tbX2.Text);
            pt2.Y = Convert.ToDouble(tbY2.Text);
            double length = 0.5 * Math.Sqrt((pt2.X - pt1.X) * (pt2.X - pt1.X) +
                            (pt2.Y - pt1.Y) * (pt2.Y - pt1.Y));

            line1 = new Line();
            line1.X1 = pt1.X;
            line1.Y1 = pt1.Y;
            line1.X2 = pt2.X;
            line1.Y2 = pt2.Y;
            line1.Stroke =
                  new SolidColorBrush(Color.FromArgb(255, 200, 200, 200));
```

```
        line1.StrokeThickness = 4;
        canvas1.Children.Add(line1);
        Canvas.SetLeft(tbPoint1, pt1.X);
        Canvas.SetTop(tbPoint1, pt1.Y);
        Canvas.SetLeft(tbPoint2, pt2.X);
        Canvas.SetTop(tbPoint2, pt2.Y);
        tbPoint1.Text = "Pt1(" + pt1.ToString() + ")";
        tbPoint2.Text = "Pt2(" + pt2.ToString() + ")";

        Vector v1 = new Vector(pt1, pt2);
        Matrix m1 = new Matrix();
        Point pt3 = new Point();
        Point pt4 = new Point();
        m1.M11 = 0;
        m1.M12 = -1;
        m1.M21 = 1;
        m1.M22 = 0;
        v1.Normalize();
        v1 *= length;
        line2 = new Line();
        line2.Stroke =
              new SolidColorBrush(Color.FromArgb(255, 200, 200, 200));
        line2.StrokeThickness = 4;
        DoubleCollection dc = new DoubleCollection();
        dc.Add(3);
        dc.Add(1);
        line2.StrokeDashArray = dc;
        Vector v = v1 * m1;
        pt3 = new Point(pt2.X + v[0], pt2.Y + v[1]);
        m1 = new Matrix();
        m1.M11 = 0;
        m1.M12 = 1;
        m1.M21 = -1;
        m1.M22 = 0;
        v = v1 * m1;
        pt4 = new Point(pt2.X + v[0], pt2.Y + v[1]);
        line2.X1 = pt3.X;
        line2.Y1 = pt3.Y;
        line2.X2 = pt4.X;
        line2.Y2 = pt4.Y;
        canvas1.Children.Add(line2);
        Canvas.SetLeft(tbPoint3, pt3.X);
        Canvas.SetTop(tbPoint3, pt3.Y);
        Canvas.SetLeft(tbPoint4, pt4.X);
        Canvas.SetTop(tbPoint4, pt4.Y);
        pt3.X = Math.Round(pt3.X, 0);
        pt3.Y = Math.Round(pt3.Y, 0);
        pt4.X = Math.Round(pt4.X, 0);
        pt4.Y = Math.Round(pt4.Y, 0);
        tbPoint3.Text = "Pt3(" + pt3.ToString() + ")";
        tbPoint4.Text = "Pt4(" + pt4.ToString() + ")";
    }

    private void Apply_Click(object sender, RoutedEventArgs e)
    {
```

```
                if (line1 != null)
                    canvas1.Children.Remove(line1);
                if (line2 != null)
                    canvas1.Children.Remove(line2);
                AddLines();
            }
        }
    }
```

Here, we first create a Line segment (line1) using two endpoints specified by the user, then create a vector using these two endpoints:

```
Vector v1 = new Vector(pt1, pt2);
```

This gives the direction of line1. The perpendicular line you want to create will have the same length as the original line. We want the vector to have the same length as the perpendicular line (line2), so we use the following statements:

```
v1.Normalize();
v1 *= length;
```

This vector is first normalized to a unit vector, then multiplied by the length of the perpendicular line. Now the vector has the proper length and direction along Point(x2, y2) to Point(x1, y1). If we rotate this vector by 90 or -90 degrees at Point(x2, y2), we'll obtain a perpendicular line. This can be achieved using the code snippet:

```
Matrix m1 = new Matrix();
Point pt3 = new Point();
Point pt4 = new Point();
m1.M11 = 0;
m1.M12 = -1;
m1.M21 = 1;
m1.M22 = 0;
Vector v = v1 * m1;
pt3 = new Point(pt2.X + v[0], pt2.Y + v[1]);
m1 = new Matrix();
m1.M11 = 0;
m1.M12 = 1;
m1.M21 = -1;
m1.M22 = 0;
v = v1 * m1;
pt4 = new Point(pt2.X + v[0], pt2.Y + v[1]);
```

Here a rotation matrix m1 is used to rotate the vector by 90 or -90 degrees to find two endpoints pt3 and pt4 which define the perpendicular line.

Executing this project produces the results shown in Figure 3-5. The user interface allows you to specify arbitrary points, and the program automatically draws the perpendicular line on the screen.

If you change the rotation angle and make some modifications to the program, you can easily create a line with an arrowhead.

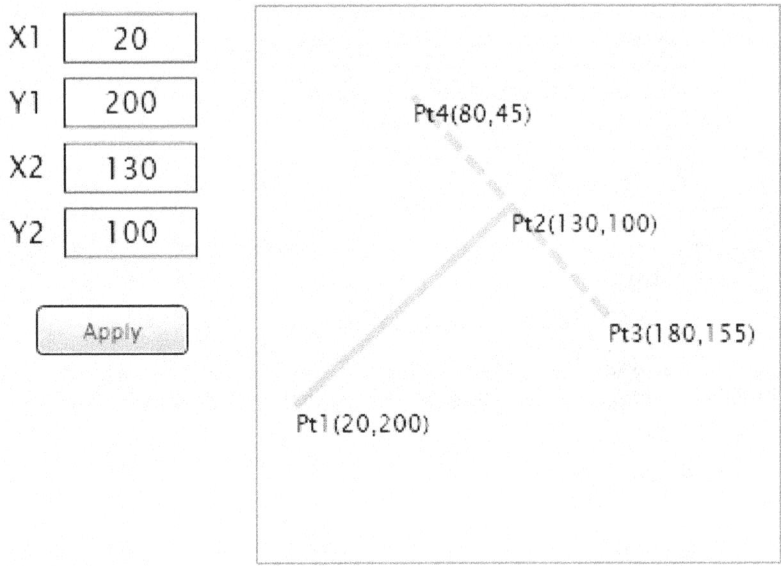

Figure 3-5 A perpendicular line in Silverlight.

Object Transforms in Silverlight

In the previous sections, we discussed the Vector and Matrix structures, as well as their operations in Silverlight. The Matrix structure can be applied to a Point or a Vector object. However, if you want to apply 2D transforms to objects or coordinate systems, you need to use the Transform classes. In Silverlight, there are five derived classes that can be used to perform specific transforms on objects:

- ScaleTransform – Scales an object in both the X and Y directions. The ScaleX property specifies how much to stretch or shrink an object along the X direction, and the ScaleY property specifies how much to stretch or shrink an object along the Y direction. Scale operations are centered on the point specified by the CenterX and CenterY properties.
- TranslateTransform – Defines a translation along the X and Y directions. The amount the object translated is specified using the X and Y properties.
- RotateTransform – Rotates an object in 2D space by specifying an angle using the Angle property and a center point specified by the CenterX and CenterY properties.
- SkewTransform – Defines a 2D skew that stretches the coordinate space in a non-uniform manner. Uses the CenterX and CenterY properties to specify the center point for the transform. Uses the AngleX and AngleY properties to specify the skew angle along the X and Y directions.
- MatrixTransform – Creates an affine matrix transform to manipulate an object in 2D space using a custom transform that isn't provided by the other Transform classes. Affine transform matrices can be multiplied to form any number of linear transforms, such as rotation and skew, followed by translation.

The structure of the TransformMatrix is the same as that of the Matrix structure in Silverlight. In the homogeneous coordinate system, the TransformMatrix always has a last column of (0, 0, 1). Based on this fact, Silverlight defines the TransformMatrix in terms of a 3x2 matrix. Namely, the

TransformMatrix classes in Silverlight take 6 elements arranged in 3 rows by 2 columns. In methods and properties, the transform matrix is usually specified as a vector with six members, as follows: (M11, M12, M21, M22, OffsetX, OffsetY). The OffsetX and OffsetY represent translation values.

By directly manipulating matrix values using the MatrixTransform class, you can rotate, scale, skew, and move an object. For example, if you change the value in the first column of the third row (the OffsetX value) to 100, you can use it to move an object 100 units along the X-axis. If you change the value in the second column of the second row to 3, you can use it to stretch an object to three times its current height. If you change both values, you move the object 100 units along the x-axis and stretch its height by a factor of 3. Since Silverlight only supports affine transforms in 2D, the values in the third column are always (0, 0, 1).

Although Silverlight allows you to directly manipulate matrix values in the MatrixTransform class, it also provides several Transform classes that enable you to transform an object without knowing how the underlying matrix structure is configured. For example, the ScaleTransform class enables you to scale an object by setting its ScaleX and ScaleY properties, instead of manipulating a transform matrix. Likewise, the RotateTransfrom class enables you to rotate an object simply by setting its Angle property. Silverlight will use the underlying structure of the TransformMatrix to perform the corresponding operation on the object. For instance, when you specify a RotateTransform by an angle of 45 degrees, the corresponding underlying TransformMatrix takes the following form:

$$\begin{pmatrix} \cos\theta & \sin\theta & 0 \\ -\sin\theta & \cos\theta & 0 \\ 0 & 0 & 1 \end{pmatrix} = \begin{pmatrix} 1 & 1 & 0 \\ -1 & 1 & 0 \\ 0 & 0 & 1 \end{pmatrix}$$

One way to transform an object is to declare the appropriate Transform type and apply it to the RenderTransform property of the object.

When you transform an object, you don't simply transform the object itself. You also transform the coordinate space in which that object exists. By default, a transform is centered at the origin of the target object's coordinate system: (0, 0). You can change the transform center by specifying the CenterX and CenterY properties of the transform matrix. The only exception is the TranslateTransform class. A TranslateTransform object has no center properties to set because the translation effect is the same regardless of where it is centered.

In the following few sections, you will apply various transforms to a Rectangle shape, a type of FrameworkElement that derives from the UIElement class.

MatrixTransform Class

You can create a custom transform using the MatrixTransform class. The custom transform can be applied to any FrameworkElement or UIElement objects, including graphics shapes, user controls, panels, etc.

Here I'll use an example to show you how to perform transforms on a Rectangle shape using the MatrixTransform class. Start with a new Silverlight application project and name it Example03-2. This application will allow the user to enter matrix elements for the transform matrix and to view the transformed Rectangle shape on the screen interactively. The XAML file of this example is listed below:

```
<UserControl x:Class="Example03_2.Page"
    xmlns="http://schemas.microsoft.com/client/2007"
    xmlns:x="http://schemas.microsoft.com/winfx/2006/xaml"
    Width="440" Height="310">
    <Grid x:Name="LayoutRoot" Background="White" Width="430" Height="300"
       HorizontalAlignment="Left" VerticalAlignment="Top">
            <Grid.ColumnDefinitions>
                <ColumnDefinition Width="150"/>
                <ColumnDefinition Width="280"/>
            </Grid.ColumnDefinitions>
            <Grid Width="140" Height="300" Margin="5,10,5,5">
                <Grid.ColumnDefinitions>
                    <ColumnDefinition Width="60"/>
                    <ColumnDefinition Width="70"/>
                </Grid.ColumnDefinitions>
                <Grid.RowDefinitions>
                    <RowDefinition Height="Auto"/>
                    <RowDefinition Height="Auto"/>
                    <RowDefinition Height="Auto"/>
                    <RowDefinition Height="Auto"/>
                    <RowDefinition Height="Auto"/>
                    <RowDefinition Height="Auto"/>
                    <RowDefinition Height="Auto"/>
                    <RowDefinition Height="Auto"/>
                </Grid.RowDefinitions>

                <TextBlock HorizontalAlignment="Right" FontSize="12"
                           Grid.Column="0" Grid.Row="0"
                           Margin="5,5,10,5">M11</TextBlock>
                <TextBox Name="tbM11" Grid.Column="1" FontSize="12" Grid.Row="0"
                         TextAlignment="Center" Text="1" Height="25"/>
                <TextBlock HorizontalAlignment="Right" Grid.Column="0"
                           Grid.Row="1"  FontSize="12"
                           Margin="5,5,10,5">M12</TextBlock>
                <TextBox Name="tbM12" Grid.Column="1" FontSize="12" Grid.Row="1"
                         TextAlignment="Center" Text="0" Height="25"/>
                <TextBlock HorizontalAlignment="Right" FontSize="12"
                           Grid.Column="0" Grid.Row="2"
                           Margin="5,5,10,5">M21</TextBlock>
                <TextBox Name="tbM21" Grid.Column="1" FontSize="12" Grid.Row="2"
                         TextAlignment="Center" Text="0" Height="25"/>
                <TextBlock HorizontalAlignment="Right" FontSize="12"
                           Grid.Column="0" Grid.Row="3"
                           Margin="5,5,10,5">M22</TextBlock>
                <TextBox Name="tbM22" Grid.Column="1" FontSize="12" Grid.Row="3"
                         TextAlignment="Center" Text="1" Height="25"/>
                <TextBlock HorizontalAlignment="Right" FontSize="12"
                           Grid.Column="0" Grid.Row="4"
                           Margin="5,5,10,5">OffsetX</TextBlock>
                <TextBox Name="tbOffsetX" Grid.Column="1" FontSize="12"
                         Grid.Row="4" TextAlignment="Center"
                         Text="0" Height="25"/>
                <TextBlock HorizontalAlignment="Right" FontSize="12"
                           Grid.Column="0" Grid.Row="5"
                           Margin="5,5,10,5">OffsetY</TextBlock>
```

```
                <TextBox Name="tbOffsetY" Grid.Column="1" FontSize="12"
                         Grid.Row="5" TextAlignment="Center"
                         Text="0" Height="25"/>
                <Button Click="Apply_Click" Margin="15,20,15,5" Grid.Row="6"
                        Height="25" Grid.ColumnSpan="2" Grid.Column="0"
                        Content="Apply"/>
            </Grid>

            <Border Margin="0,10,10,10" Grid.Column="1" BorderBrush="Black"
                    BorderThickness="1" HorizontalAlignment="Left">
                <Canvas Name="canvas1" Grid.Column="1" Width="270" Height="280">
                <Canvas.Clip>
                    <RectangleGeometry Rect="0,0,270,280"/>
                </Canvas.Clip>
                    <TextBlock Canvas.Top="53" Canvas.Left="90" FontSize="10">
                               Original shape</TextBlock>
                    <Rectangle Canvas.Top="70" Canvas.Left="100" Width="50"
                               Height="70" Stroke="Black"
                               StrokeThickness="2" StrokeDashArray="3,1"/>
                    <Rectangle Name="rect" Canvas.Top="70" Canvas.Left="100"
                               Width="50" Height="70"
                               Fill="LightCoral" Opacity="0.5" Stroke="Black"
                               StrokeThickness="2">
                        <Rectangle.RenderTransform>
                            <MatrixTransform x:Name="matrixTransform"/>
                        </Rectangle.RenderTransform>
                    </Rectangle>
                </Canvas>
            </Border>
        </Grid>
</UserControl>
```

This markup creates a user interface that contains TextBoxes, Buttons, and a Canvas, which allow you to interactively manipulate the elements of the TransformMatrix and display the transformed Rectangle shape on your screen. The transform on the rectangle is specified by the following XAML snippet:

```
<Rectangle.RenderTransform>
    <MatrixTransform x:Name="matrixTransform"/>
</Rectangle.RenderTransform>
```

From this snippet, you can see that to apply transforms to a FrameworkElement, you need to create a Transform matrix and apply it to the RenderTransform properties of the rectangle.

The following is the corresponding C# code that is responsible for the event handlers:

```
using System;
using System.Windows;
using System.Windows.Controls;
using System.Windows.Media;
using System.Windows.Media.Animation;
using System.Windows.Shapes;

namespace Example03_2
{
    public partial class Page : UserControl
```

```
        {
            public Page()
            {
                InitializeComponent();
            }

            public void Apply_Click(object sender, EventArgs e)
            {
                Matrix m = new Matrix();
                m.M11 = Double.Parse(tbM11.Text);
                m.M12 = Double.Parse(tbM12.Text);
                m.M21 = Double.Parse(tbM21.Text);
                m.M22 = Double.Parse(tbM22.Text);
                m.OffsetX = Double.Parse(tbOffsetX.Text);
                m.OffsetY = Double.Parse(tbOffsetY.Text);
                matrixTransform.Matrix = m;
            }
        }
    }
```

The main part of this code-behind file is the Apply button's click event handler. We create a new Matrix instance m, and specify its elements using the text content of the corresponding TextBoxes. Then the matrix m is passed to the transform matrix named matrixTransform, which is defined in the XAML file.

Building and running this project produces the output shown in Figure 3-6. On the left pane, you can change all six elements of a custom transform matrix by entering values of the double type in the TextBoxes. The entered values take effect after you click the Apply button. The original location of the Rectangle is obtained by an identical matrix (1, 0, 0, 1, 0, 0) in homogeneous coordinates. The results shown in Figure 3-6 are obtained by using the matrix (1, 0.5, 0.5, 1, 50, 100), which is a combination of a skew and a translation.

By changing the other elements, you can obtain a variety of transforms, including translations, scales, rotations, and skews.

ScaleTransform Class

In the previous section, we discussed how to perform transforms on UIElement or FrameworkElement objects by directly manipulating transform matrix values. However, Silverlight also provides several Transform classes that allow you to transform an object without knowing how the underlying matrix structure is configured. For example, the ScaleTransform class enables you to scale an object by setting its ScaleX and ScaleY properties instead of directly manipulating a transform matrix.

Let's look at an example. Start with a new Silverlight project and name it Example03-3. In this example, you create two Canvas panels. The left Canvas is used for animating the scale transform on a rectangle shape, while the right Canvas is used for an interactive transform that allows you to change the ScaleX and ScaleY on the screen. The animation gives you a real feeling of how the scale transform works. I'll discuss the animation process in Chapter 6. The following is the XAML file of this example:

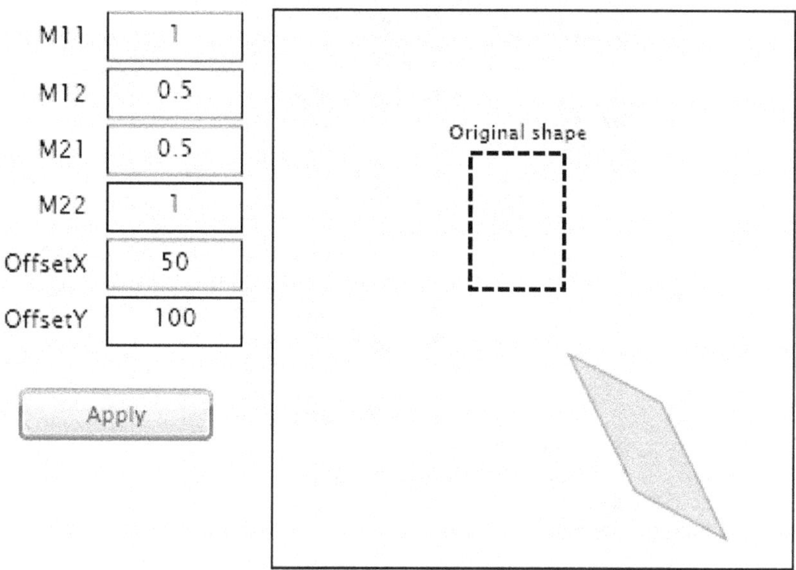

Figure 3-6 Transform on a rectangle using MatrixTransform class.

```
<UserControl x:Class="Example03_3.Page"
    xmlns="http://schemas.microsoft.com/client/2007"
    xmlns:x="http://schemas.microsoft.com/winfx/2006/xaml"
    Width="540" Height="400" Loaded="Page_Loaded">

    <UserControl.Resources>
        <Storyboard x:Name="storyboardRect" RepeatBehavior="Forever"
                    AutoReverse="True">
            <DoubleAnimation
                     Storyboard.TargetName="rectScale"
                     Storyboard.TargetProperty="ScaleX"
                     From="0" To="3" Duration="0:0:5"/>
            <DoubleAnimation
                     Storyboard.TargetName="rectScale"
                     Storyboard.TargetProperty="ScaleY"
                     From="0" To="3" Duration="0:0:5"/>
        </Storyboard>
    </UserControl.Resources>

<Grid x:Name="LayoutRoot" Background="White" Width="525" Height="330"
      HorizontalAlignment="Left" VerticalAlignment="Top"
      ShowGridLines="True" Margin="10">
            <Grid.ColumnDefinitions>
                <ColumnDefinition Width="260" />
                <ColumnDefinition Width="260" />
            </Grid.ColumnDefinitions>

            <StackPanel Grid.Column="0">
                <TextBlock HorizontalAlignment="Center" Margin="10,10,10,0"
                           TextWrapping="Wrap" FontSize="14" FontWeight="Bold"
```

```
                Text="Scaling Animation"/>
    <TextBlock Margin="10,10,10,0" TextWrapping="Wrap" FontSize="12"
                Text="The scaling parameters ScaleX and
                      ScaleY are animated from 0 to 3."/>
    <Border Margin="10" BorderBrush="Black" BorderThickness="1">
        <Canvas Width="240" Height="230">
            <Canvas.Clip>
                <RectangleGeometry Rect="0,0,240,250"/>
            </Canvas.Clip>
            <Rectangle Canvas.Left="100" Canvas.Top="80" Width="50"
                       Height="70" Fill="LightCoral" Opacity="0.5"
                       Stroke="Black" StrokeThickness="2">
                <Rectangle.RenderTransform>
                    <ScaleTransform x:Name="rectScale" CenterX="25"
                                    CenterY="35" />
                </Rectangle.RenderTransform>
            </Rectangle>
        </Canvas>
    </Border>
</StackPanel>

<StackPanel Grid.Column="1">
    <TextBlock  HorizontalAlignment="Center" Margin="10,10,10,10"
                TextWrapping="Wrap" FontSize="14" FontWeight="Bold"
                Text="Interactive Scaling"/>
    <Grid Width="260" Height="26" HorizontalAlignment="Left"
          VerticalAlignment="Top">
        <Grid.ColumnDefinitions>
            <ColumnDefinition Width="50" />
            <ColumnDefinition Width="40" />
            <ColumnDefinition Width="50" />
            <ColumnDefinition Width="40" />
            <ColumnDefinition Width="70" />
        </Grid.ColumnDefinitions>

        <TextBlock Margin="5,5,5,2" TextAlignment="Right"
                   Text="ScaleX" FontSize="11"/>
        <TextBox Name="tbScaleX" Width="40" Height="20"
                 Grid.Column="1" FontSize="11"
                 TextAlignment="Center" Text="1"/>
        <TextBlock Margin="2,5,5,2" Grid.Column="2"
                   TextAlignment="Right" Text="ScaleY"
                   FontSize="11"/>
        <TextBox Name="tbScaleY" Width="40" Height="20"
                 Grid.Column="3" FontSize="11"
                 TextAlignment="Center" Text="1"/>
        <Button Click="Apply_Click" Width="50" Height="20"
                Grid.Column="4" Content="Apply" Margin="10,0,0,0"/>
    </Grid>

    <Border Margin="10,20,0,0" BorderBrush="Black"
            BorderThickness="1" HorizontalAlignment="Left">
        <Canvas Width="240" Height="230">
            <Canvas.Clip>
                <RectangleGeometry Rect="0,0,240,250"/>
```

```
                    </Canvas.Clip>
                    <TextBlock Canvas.Left="90" Canvas.Top="63"
                               Text="Original shape" FontSize="10"/>
                    <Rectangle Canvas.Top="80" Canvas.Left="100" Width="50"
                               Height="70" Stroke="Black"
                               StrokeThickness="1" StrokeDashArray="3,1"/>

                    <Rectangle Canvas.Top="80" Canvas.Left="100" Width="50"
                               Height="70" Fill="LightCoral" Opacity="0.5"
                               Stroke="Black" StrokeThickness="2">
                         <!-- Set interactive scale: -->
                        <Rectangle.RenderTransform>
                            <ScaleTransform x:Name="interactiveScale"
                                            CenterX="25" CenterY="35"/>
                      </Rectangle.RenderTransform>
                    </Rectangle>
                </Canvas>
            </Border>
        </StackPanel>
    </Grid>
</UserControl>
```

This XAML file creates the user interface layout and a Storyboard animation in the UserControl.Resources. The code-behind file will start the animation and deal with the button click event handler:

```
using System;
using System.Windows;
using System.Windows.Controls;
using System.Windows.Media;
using System.Windows.Media.Animation;
using System.Windows.Shapes;

namespace Example03_3
{
    public partial class Page : UserControl
    {
        public Page()
        {
            InitializeComponent();
        }

        private void Page_Loaded(object sender, RoutedEventArgs e)
        {
            storyboardRect.Begin();
        }

        private void Apply_Click(object sender, RoutedEventArgs e)
        {
            interactiveScale.ScaleX = double.Parse(tbScaleX.Text);
            interactiveScale.ScaleY = double.Parse(tbScaleY.Text);
        }
    }
}
```

You start the animation for the rectangle object by varying its ScaleX and ScaleY dependency properties from 0 to 3. The details of Silverlight animations will be covered in Chapter 6.

For the interactive scale transform on the rectangle in the right pane, the ScaleX and ScaleY in the TextBox fields will be used to specify the ScaleTransform named interactiveScale. These properties can be specified by the user's input in the corresponding TextBoxes. The user's input parameters will take effect when he clicks the Apply button. This allows you to interactively examine the scaling transform directly on the screen. Figure 3-7 shows a snapshot of this example.

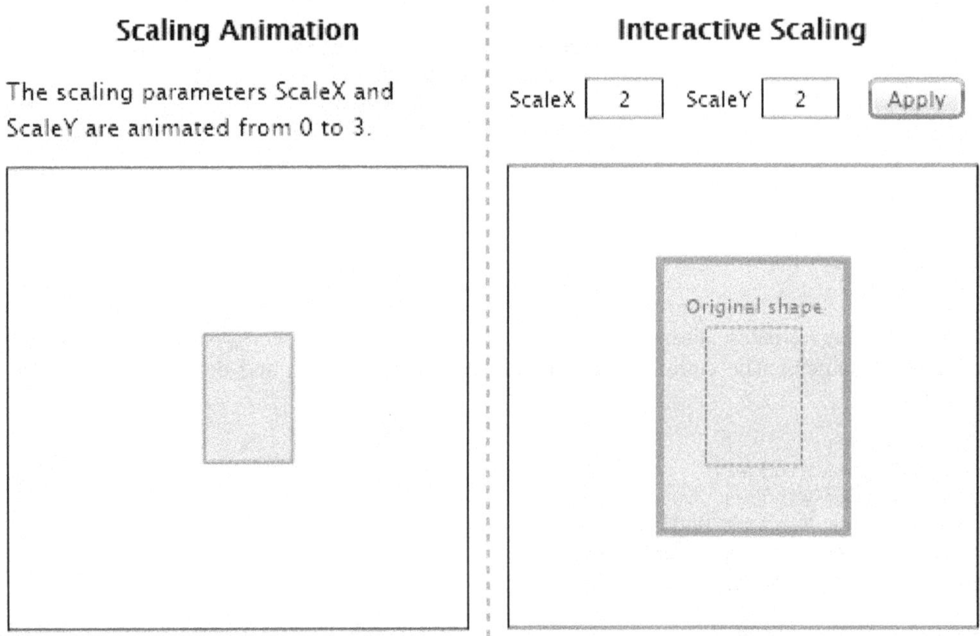

Figure 3-7 Scale transformation on Rectangle objects.

TranslateTransform Class

The TranslateTransform class enables you to move an object by setting its X and Y properties. This transform has no center properties to set because the translation effect is the same regardless of where it is centered.

Let's consider an example of a translation on Rectangle objects using the same layout as that used in the previous example. Start with a new Silverlight project and name it Example03-4. The XAML file is similar to the one used in the previous example, except for the RenderTransform property of the rectangle. To animate the translation on the rectangle, you use the following XAML snippet:

```
......
Storyboard x:Name="storyboardRect" RepeatBehavior="Forever" AutoReverse="True">
    <DoubleAnimation
             Storyboard.TargetName="rect"
             Storyboard.TargetProperty="X"
             From="-80" To="80" Duration="0:0:5"/>
    <DoubleAnimation
```

```
                Storyboard.TargetName="rect"
                Storyboard.TargetProperty="Y"
                From="-80" To="80" Duration="0:0:5"/>
</Storyboard>
......
<Rectangle Canvas.Left="100" Canvas.Top="80" Width="50" Height="70"
           Fill="LightCoral" Opacity="0.5" Stroke="Black" StrokeThickness="2">
    <Rectangle.RenderTransform>
        <TranslateTransform x:Name="rect"/>
</Rectangle.RenderTransform>
</Rectangle>
```

The animation is performed using a storyboard that animates the X and Y properties of the translation. The following XAML snippet defines the RenderTransform property for the interactive translation of the rectangle in the right pane :

```
<!-- Set interactive translation: -->
<Rectangle.RenderTransform>
    <TranslateTransform x:Name="interactiveScale"/>
</Rectangle.RenderTransform>
```

Here the X and Y properties of the translation are attached to the text fields of the corresponding TextBoxes with data binding. This allows you to interactively manipulate the translation of the rectangle by changing the text fields of the TextBoxes.

The code-behind file is also similar to the one used in the previous example, which will start the animation and deal with the button click event handler. Figure 3-8 shows a snapshot of this example.

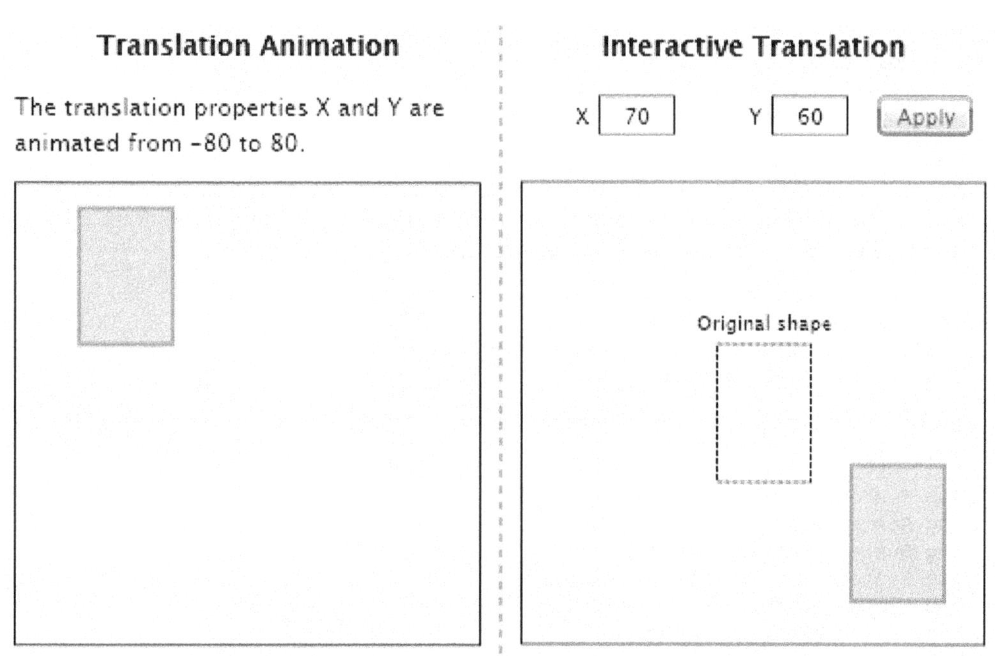

Figure 3-8 Translation transformation on rectangles.

RotateTransform Class

The RotateTransform class allows you to rotate an object by setting its Angle, CenterX, and CenterY properties. In the next example, we'll animate the rotation of a Rectangle object about its center. However, the origin of this rectangle will be moved from 0 to 180 units. For the interactive rotation, the Angle, CenterX, and CenterY properties of the transform take values directly from the user's inputs.

Start with a new Silverlight project and name it Example03-5. The XAML file is similar to the one used in the previous example, except for the RenderTransform property of the rectangle. To animate the rotation transform on the rectangle, use the following XAML snippet:

```
......
<Storyboard x:Name="storyboardRect" RepeatBehavior="Forever" AutoReverse="True">
    <DoubleAnimation
            Storyboard.TargetName="rect"
            Storyboard.TargetProperty="Angle"
            From="0" To="360" Duration="0:0:5"/>
    <DoubleAnimation
            Storyboard.TargetName="rect"
            Storyboard.TargetProperty="CenterX"
            From="-20" To="120" Duration="0:0:5"/>
    <DoubleAnimation
            Storyboard.TargetName="rect"
            Storyboard.TargetProperty="CenterY"
            From="-50" To="90" Duration="0:0:5"/>
    </Storyboard>
......
<Rectangle.RenderTransform>
    <RotateTransform x:Name="rect"/>
</Rectangle.RenderTransform>
......
```

The animation is performed using a storyboard that animates the CenterX, CenterY, and Angle properties of the rotation transform. The following XAML snippet defines the RenderTransform property for the interactive rotation transform on the rectangle in the right pane :

```
<!-- Set interactive rotation: -->
<Rectangle.RenderTransform>
    <RotateTransform x:Name="interactiveTransform"/>
</Rectangle.RenderTransform>
```

Here the Angle, CenterX, and CenterY properties will be specified by the user's input through the code-behind file:

```
using System;
using System.Windows;
using System.Windows.Controls;
using System.Windows.Media;
using System.Windows.Media.Animation;
using System.Windows.Shapes;

namespace Example03_5
{
    public partial class Page : UserControl
    {
```

```
        public Page()
        {
            InitializeComponent();
        }

        private void Page_Loaded(object sender, RoutedEventArgs e)
        {
            storyboardRect.Begin();
        }

        private void Apply_Click(object sender, RoutedEventArgs e)
        {
            interactiveTransform.CenterX = double.Parse(tbX.Text);
            interactiveTransform.CenterY = double.Parse(tbY.Text);
            interactiveTransform.Angle = double.Parse(tbAngle.Text);
        }
    }
}
```

This allows you to interactively manipulate the rotation transform on the rectangle by changing the text fields of the TextBoxes.

Figure 3-9 shows the result of running this application.

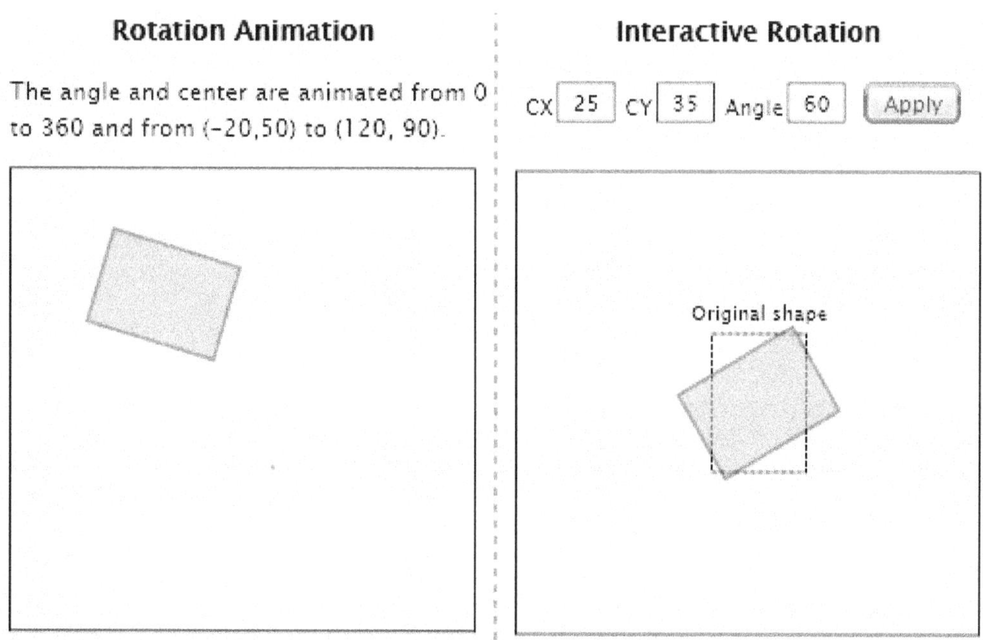

Figure 3-9 Rotation transform on rectangles.

SkewTransform Class

The SkewTransform class defines a 2D skew that stretches the coordinate space of a FrameworkElement or an UIElement object in a non-uniform manner. You can use the CenterX and CenterY properties to specify the center point for the transform, and use the AngleX and AngleY properties to specify the skew angle along the X and Y directions.

In this example, we'll animate the skew transform of a Rectangle object about its center by varying the AngleX and AngleY properties. For the interactive skew transformation, the AngleX and AngleY properties of the transform take values directly from the user's input.

Start with a new Silverlight project and name it Example03-6. The XAML file is similar to that of the previous example, except for the RenderTransform property of the rectangle. To animate the skew transform on the rectangle, use the following XAML snippet:

```
......
<Storyboard x:Name="storyboardRect" RepeatBehavior="Forever" AutoReverse="True">
    <DoubleAnimation
            Storyboard.TargetName="rectTransform"
            Storyboard.TargetProperty="AngleX"
            From="0" To="360" Duration="0:0:5"/>
    <DoubleAnimation
            Storyboard.TargetName="rectTransform"
            Storyboard.TargetProperty="AngleY"
            From="0" To="360" Duration="0:0:5"/>
</Storyboard>
......
<Rectangle.RenderTransform>
    <SkewTransform x:Name="rectTransform" CenterX="25" CenterY="35"/>
</Rectangle.RenderTransform>
......
```

The animation is performed using a storyboard that animates the AngleX and AngleY properties of the skew transform. The following XAML snippet defines the RenderTransform property for the interactive skew transform on the rectangle on the right pane :

```
<Rectangle.RenderTransform>
    <SkewTransform x:Name="interactiveTransform"/>
</Rectangle.RenderTransform>
```

Here the AngleX and AngleY properties of the skew transform are specified by the text fields of the corresponding TextBoxes. This allows you to interactively manipulate the skew transform on the rectangle by changing the text fields of the TextBoxes.

Figure 3-10 shows a snapshot of this example.

Composite Transforms

The TransformGroup class, which allows you to combine any of the above transform classes, can be applied to any UIElement or FrameworkElement object. In other words, a composite transform that consists of any number of transforms can be applied to a graphics object. The TransformGroup class derived from the Transform base class represents a combined transform that contains a collection of Transforms.

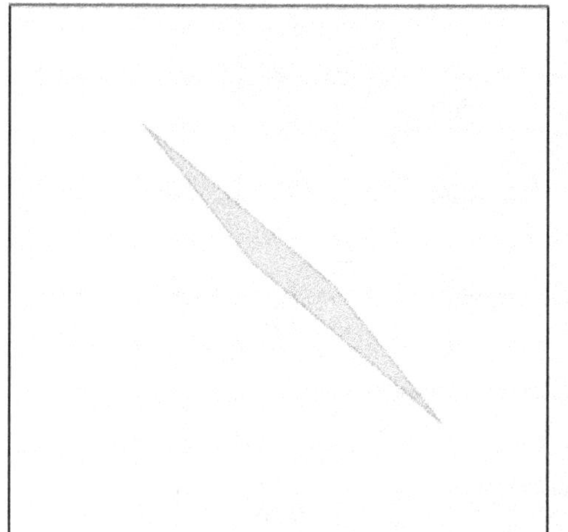

Skew Animation
The skew properties AngleX and AngleY are animated from 0 to 360.

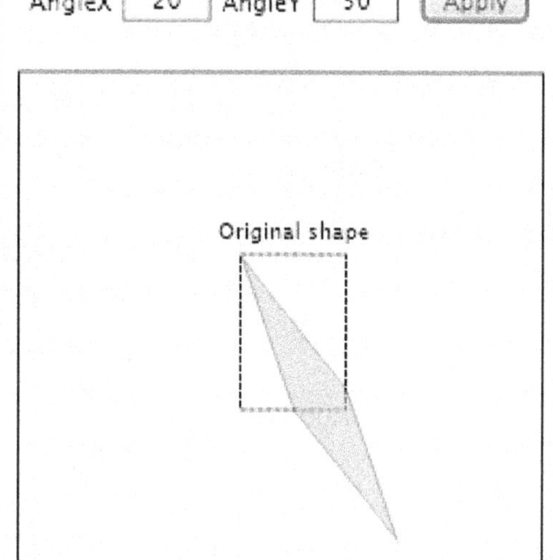

Figure 3-10 Skew transformation on rectangles.

You can represent various transforms using a simple C# code snippet. For example, to scale a rectangle 2 times in the X direction and 3 times in the Y direction, you can use a ScaleTransform object:

```
Rectangle.RenderTransformation = new ScaleTransformation(2, 3);
```

To move the rectangle 100 units in the X direction and -100 units in the Y direction, you can simply write:

```
Rectangle.RenderTransform = new TranslateTransform(100, - 100);
```

To rotate the Rectangle 45 degrees, you can create a new RotateTransform object and set the angle to 45.

```
Rectangle.RenderTransform = new RotateTransform(45);
```

To skew an element 30 degrees in the X direction and 45 degrees in the Y direction, you can use a SkewTransform:

```
Rectangle.RenderTransform = new SkewTransform(30, 45);
```

Finally, if you want to apply all of these transforms to this rectangle, you can use a TransformGroup:

```
TransformGroup tg = new TransformGroup();
tg.Children.Add(ScaleTransform(2, 3));
tg.Children.Add(TranslateTransform(100, -100));
tg.Children.Add(RotateTransform(45));
tg.Children.Add(SkewTransform(30, 45));
Rectangle.RenderTransform = tg;
```

Let's consider an example that illustrates how to use the TransformGroup class in a Silverlight application. In this example, you'll use a composite transform that contains a scale and a rotation transform. This transform is applied to a rectangle object (a square in this case) about its center. You'll animate the dependency properties for both the scale and rotation transforms.

Start with a new Silverlight project and name it Example03-7. Here, we'll only consider the animation of the combined transform. The following is the XAML file of this example:

```
<UserControl x:Class="Example03_7.Page"
    xmlns="http://schemas.microsoft.com/client/2007"
    xmlns:x="http://schemas.microsoft.com/winfx/2006/xaml"
    Height="350" Width="340" Loaded="Page_Loaded">

    <UserControl.Resources>
        <Storyboard x:Name="storyboard1" RepeatBehavior="Forever"
                    AutoReverse="True">
            <DoubleAnimation Storyboard.TargetName="scale"
                             Storyboard.TargetProperty="ScaleX"
                             From="0" To="3" Duration="0:0:5"/>
            <DoubleAnimation Storyboard.TargetName="scale"
                             Storyboard.TargetProperty="ScaleY"
                             From="0" To="3" Duration="0:0:5"/>
            <DoubleAnimation Storyboard.TargetName="rotate"
                             Storyboard.TargetProperty="Angle"
                             From="0" To="360" Duration="0:0:5"/>
        </Storyboard>
    </UserControl.Resources>

    <StackPanel Background="White">
        <TextBlock HorizontalAlignment="Center" Margin="10,10,10,0"
                   TextWrapping="Wrap" FontSize="14"
                   FontWeight="Bold" Text="Animation of Combining Transform"/>
        <Border Margin="10" BorderBrush="Black" BorderThickness="1"
                HorizontalAlignment="Left">
            <Canvas Width="340" Height="300">
                <Canvas.Clip>
                    <RectangleGeometry Rect="0,0,320,300"/>
                </Canvas.Clip>
                <Ellipse Canvas.Left="165" Canvas.Top="145" Width="10"
                         Height="10" Fill="Red"/>

                <Rectangle Canvas.Left="120" Canvas.Top="100" Width="100"
                           Height="100" Fill="LightCoral"
                           Opacity="0.5" Stroke="Black" StrokeThickness="2">
                    <Rectangle.RenderTransform>
                        <TransformGroup>
                            <ScaleTransform  x:Name="scale" CenterX="50"
                                             CenterY="50" />
                            <RotateTransform x:Name="rotate" CenterX="50"
                                             CenterY="50"/>
                        </TransformGroup>
                    </Rectangle.RenderTransform>
                </Rectangle>
            </Canvas>
        </Border>
    </StackPanel>
</UserControl>
```

Here, we specify the rectangle's RenderTransform property using a TransformGroup. Within this TransformGroup, we define two transforms: a ScaleTransform named "scale" and a RotateTransform named "rotate". Both transforms are animated using a StoryBoard defined in Resources. Within the StoryBoard, we first animate the ScaleX and ScaleY dependency properties of the ScaleTransform. Then we perform the rotation animation on the rectangle by animating the Angle property from 0 to 360 degrees.

This example produces the results shown in Figure 3-11.

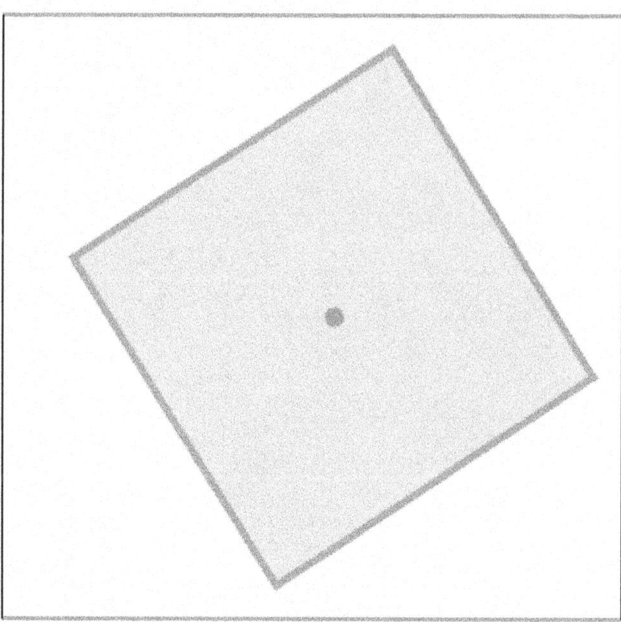

Figure 3-11 Combining transforms on a Square.

Chapter 4
Geometry and 2D Drawing

In the previous two chapters, graphics examples were created using simple shapes that derived from the Shape class. The Shape class inherits from FrameworkElement. Because Shape objects from the Shape class are elements, they can render themselves and participate in the layout system. In this sense, Shape objects are readily usable.

This chapter shows you how to create and manipulate more complex 2D graphics objects using the more powerful Path class, which can wrap complex geometry objects derived from the Geometry class. It shows you how to develop an advanced interactive 2D drawing program using the Geometry class, which allows you to add and delete, drag and move, and perform logic operations on the 2D graphics objects.

Path and Geometry Classes

In previous chapters, you learned how to create 2D graphics using simple shapes that derive from the Shape class, including Line, Rectangle, Ellipse, and Polygon. However, you haven't considered the more powerful Shape-derived class, the Path class. The Path class has the ability to draw curves and complex shapes. These curves and shapes are described using Geometry objects. To use a Path object, you create a Geometry object and use it to set the Path object's Data property. You can't draw a Geometry object directly on your screen because it is an abstract class. Instead, you need to use one of the seven derived classes, as listed below:

- LineGeometry – Represents the geometry of a straight line.
- RectangleGeometry – Represents the geometry of a 2D rectangle.
- EllipseGeometry – Represents the geometry of an ellipse.
- GeometryGroup – Represents a composite geometry, which can be added to a single path.
- CombinedGeometry – Represents a 2D geometry shape defined by the combination of two Geometry objects.
- PathGeometry – Represents a complex geometry shape that may be composed of arcs, curves, ellipses, lines, and rectangles.

- StreamGeometry – Defines a geometric shape described using StreamGeometryContext. This geometry is a read-only light-weight alternative to PathGeometry; it doesn't support data binding, animation, or modification.

The LineGeometry, RectangleGeometry, and EllipseGeometry classes describe relatively simple geometry shapes. To create more complex shapes or curves, you need to use a PathGeometry object.

There is a critical difference between the Shape class and the Geometry class. The Geometry class inherits from the Freezable class, while the Shape class inherits from FrameworkElement. Because Shape objects are elements, they can render themselves and participate in the layout system, while Geometry objects can't.

Although Shape objects are more readily usable than Geometry objects, Geometry objects are more versatile. While a Shape object is solely used to render 2D graphics, a Geometry object can be used to define the geometric region for 2D graphics, define a region for clipping, or define a region for hit testing, to name a few examples. Geometry objects can't render themselves, and must be drawn by another element, such as- a Drawing or Path element. The attributes common to shapes, such as the Fill, Stroke, and StrokeThickness properties, are attached to the Drawing or Path, which can be used to draw Geometry objects.

You can see from the above discussion that the Geometry object defines a shape, while a Path object allows you to draw the Geometry shape on your screen. In the following sections, I'll show you how to create shapes using the objects derived from the Geometry class.

Line, Rectangle, and Ellipse Geometries

The LineGeometry, RectangleGeometry, and EllipseGeometry classes correspond directly to the Line, Rectangle, and Ellipse shapes that were used in the previous chapters. For example, you can convert this XAML code, which uses the Line element

```
<Line X1="30" Y1="30" X2 ="180" Y2="30"
      Stroke="Blue" StrokeThickness="2"/>
```

into the following markup, which uses the Path element and LineGeometry:

```
<Path Stroke="Blue" StrokeThickness="2">
    <Path.Data>
        <LineGeometry StartPoint="30 30" EndPoint="180 30"/>
    </Path.Data>
</Path>
```

The only difference is that the Line shape takes X1, Y1, X2, and Y2 values, while the LineGeometry object takes StartPoint and EndPoint.

Similarly, you can convert the following code snippet:

```
<Rectangle Fill="Gray" Stroke="Blue" StrokeThickness="2"
           Width="10" Height="20"/>
```

into this RectangleGeometry:

```
<Path Fill="Gray" Stroke="Blue" StrokeThickness="2">
    <Path.Data>
        <RectangleGeometry Rect="0,0,10,20"/>
    </Path.Data>
</Path>
```

It can be seen that the Rectangle shape takes Height and Width values, while the RectangleGeometry element takes four numbers that describe the location and size of the rectangle. The first two numbers represent the X and Y coordinates where the top-left corner will be placed, while the last two numbers define the width and height of the rectangle.

You can also convert an Ellipse shape like this:

```
<Ellipse Fill="Gray" Stroke="Blue" StrokeThickness="2"
         Width="10" Height="20"/>
```

into the EllipseGeometry:

```
<Path Fill="Gray" Stroke="Blue" StrokeThickness="2">
    <Path.Data>
        <EllipseGeometry RadiuX="5" RadiusY="10" Center="5,10"/>
    </Path.Data>
</Path>
```

Notice that the two radius values are simply half of the width and height values. You can also use the Center property to offset the location of the ellipse.

It is clear from the above discussion that these simple geometries work in exactly the same way as their corresponding shapes. Geometry objects allow you to offset rectangles and ellipses, but this isn't necessary if you draw the shapes on a Canvas, which already gives you the ability to position your shapes at specific positions using the Canvas.Top and Canvas.Left properties. The real difference between the Shape and Geometry classes appears when you decide to combine more than one Geometry object in a single path, as described in the next section.

GeometryGroup Class

The simplest way to combine geometries is to use the GeometryGroup object. Here is an example that creates two circles:

```
<Path Fill="LightGray" Stroke="Blue" StrokeThickness="2">
    <Path.Data>
        <GeometryGroup FillRule="Nonzero">
            <EllipseGeometry RadiusX="50" RadiusY="50"
                             Center="120,120"/>
            <EllipseGeometry RadiusX="30" RadiusY="30"
                             Center="120,120"/>
        </GeometryGroup>
    </Path.Data>
</Path>
```

This code snippet creates an effect similar to using two Path elements, each one with an EllipseGeometry object of a different radius. By using the GeometryGroup object, you replace two elements with one, meaning you reduce the overhead of your user interface. In general, a window that uses a smaller number of elements with more complex geometries will perform faster than a window that uses a large number of elements with simple geometries. This will become significant when you create complicated computer-aided design (CAD) applications.

Let's start with a new Silverlight project and call it Example04-1. The following is the XAML code of the Page.xaml file for this example:

```
<UserControl x:Class="Example04_1.Page"
    xmlns="http://schemas.microsoft.com/client/2007"
    xmlns:x="http://schemas.microsoft.com/winfx/2006/xaml"
    Width="300" Height="150">

    <Grid x:Name="LayoutRoot" Background="White">
        <Grid.ColumnDefinitions>
            <ColumnDefinition/>
            <ColumnDefinition/>
        </Grid.ColumnDefinitions>
        <Path Fill="LightGray" Stroke="Blue" StrokeThickness="2">
            <Path.Data>
                <GeometryGroup FillRule="Nonzero">
                    <EllipseGeometry RadiusX="50" RadiusY="50" Center="70,70"/>
                    <EllipseGeometry RadiusX="30" RadiusY="30" Center="70,70"/>
                </GeometryGroup>
            </Path.Data>
        </Path>
        <Path Fill="LightGray" Stroke="Blue" StrokeThickness="2"
              Grid.Column="1">
            <Path.Data>
                <GeometryGroup FillRule="EvenOdd">
                    <EllipseGeometry RadiusX="50" RadiusY="50" Center="70,70"/>
                    <EllipseGeometry RadiusX="30" RadiusY="30" Center="70,70"/>
                </GeometryGroup>
            </Path.Data>
        </Path>
    </Grid>
</UserControl>
```

Here we create two Path objects. The GeometryGroup in each Path includes two circles with a different radius but the same center location. The main difference lies in their FillRule property: one is set to Nonzero, and the other to EvenOdd. Like the Polygon shape, the GeometryGroup also has a FillRule property that specifies which shapes to fill.

This example generates the results shown in Figure 4-1. Two solid circles are created at each different location. The left image shows the result when the FillRule of the GeometryGroup is set to Nonzero. Two solid circles with the same center location are created. If you change the FillRule property to EvenOdd, you'll obtain the results shown in the right pane. Here, you create a ring shape made up of a solid circle with a blank hole.

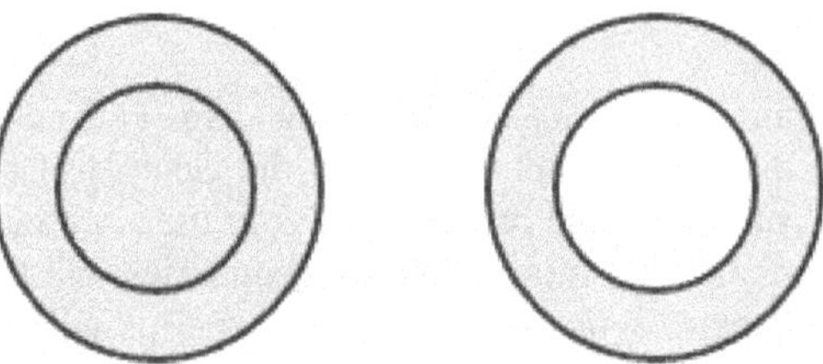

Figure 4-1 2D shapes created using GeometryGroup.

Remember that there are some drawbacks to combining geometries into a single Path element using GeometryGroup: you can't perform event handling on each of the different geometry shapes separately. Instead, the Path object will fire all of the mouse events.

I should point out that Silverlight doesn't implement the CombinedGeometry class defined in WPF. This means that you cannot perform logic operations, such as union, intersect, xor, and exclude, on shapes in Silverlight. If logic operations on shapes are required, you will need to develop your applications in WPF.

PathGeometry Class

The PathGeometry class is more powerful than the derived geometry classes discussed previously. It can be used to create any of the shapes that the other geometries can and much more. A PathGeometry object is built out of one or more PathFigure objects. Each PathFigure object is a continuous set of connected lines and curves that can be closed or open. The PathFigure object is closed if the end point of the last line in the object connects to the starting point of the first line.

The PathFigure class has four key properties, as listed below:

- StartPoint – A Point that indicates where the line or figure begins
- Segments – A collection of PathSegment objects that are used to draw the figure.
- IsClosed – If true, Silverlight adds a straight line to connect the starting and end points.
- IsFilled – If true, the area inside the figure is filled using the Path.Fill property.

Note that the PathFigure is a shape that is drawn using an unbroken line consisting of a number of segments. There are several types of segments, all of which derive from the PathSegment class. You can use different types of segments freely to build your figure. The segment classes in Silverlight are listed below:

- LineSegment – Creates a straight line between two points.
- ArcSegment – Creates an elliptical arc between two points.
- PolyLineSegment – Creates a series of straight lines.
- BezierSegment – Creates a Bezier curve between two points.
- QuadraticBezierSegment – Creates a Bezier curve that has one point instead of two.
- PolyBezierSegment – Creates a series of Bezier curves.
- PolyQuadraticBezierSegment – Creates a series of simpler quadratic Bezier curves.

The Line, Arc, and PolyLine segments may be more familiar to you than the Bezier-related segments. However, Bezier lines are one of the most important mathematical representations of curves and surfaces used in computer graphics and CAD applications. Bezier curves are polynomial curves based on a complicated mathematical representation. Fortunately, no mathematical knowledge is required in order to use the Bezier curves in Silverlight.

Lines and Polylines

It is easy to create a simple line using the LineSegment and PathGeometry classes. For example, the following XAML snippet begins at (10, 10), draws a straight line to (150, 150), and then draws a line from (150, 150) to (150, 200):

```
<Path Stroke="Black">
    <Path.Data>
        <PathGeometry>
            <PathFigure StartPoint="10,10">
                <LineSegment Point="150,150"/>
                <LineSegment Point="150,200"/>
            </PathFigure>
        </PathGeometry>
    </Path.Data>
</Path>
```

The PolyLineSegment creates a series of straight lines. You can get the same effect using multiple LineSegment objects, but a single PolyLineSegment is simpler. The following code creates a polyline:

```
<Path Stroke="Blue">
    <Path.Data>
        <PathGeometry>
            <PathFigure StartPoint="100,120">
                <PolyLineSegment
                    Points="200,120,200,220,100,170"/>
            </PathFigure>
        </PathGeometry>
    </Path.Data>
</Path>
```

Note that the number of PathFigure objects in a PathGeometry element is unlimited. This means that you can create several separate open or closed figures that are all considered part of the same path.

Arcs

An ArcSegment object is defined by its start and end points; its X- and Y-radii specified by the Size property; its X-axis rotation factor, a value indicating whether the arc should be greater than 180 degrees; and a value describing the direction in which the arc is drawn. Like the LineSegment, the ArcSegment class doesn't contain a property for the starting point of the arc: it only defines the destination point of the arc it represents. The beginning point of the arc is the current point of the PathFigure to which the ArcSegment is added.

The following markup creates an ellipse shape using two ArcSegment objects:

```
<Path Stroke="Blue">
    <Path.Data>
        <PathGeometry>
            <PathFigure StartPoint="100,50">
                <ArcSegment Point="200,50" Size="50,30"
                    SweepDirection="Counterclockwise"/>
            </PathFigure>
            <PathFigure StartPoint="100,50">
                <ArcSegment Point="200,50" Size="50,30"
                    SweepDirection="Clockwise"/>
            </PathFigure>
        </PathGeometry>
    </Path.Data>
</Path>
```

Bezier Curves

It is also easy to create a Bezier curve using the BezierSegment object. Note that a Bezier curve is defined by four points: a start point, an end point, and two control points. The BezierSegment class doesn't contain a property for the starting point of the curve; it only defines the end point. The beginning point of the curve is the current point of the PathFigure to which the BezierSegment is added.

The two control points of a cubic Bezier curve behave like magnets, attracting portions of what would otherwise be a straight line towards themselves and producing a curve. The first control point affects the beginning portion of the curve; while the second control point affects the ending portion of the curve. The curve doesn't necessarily pass through either of the control points; each control point moves its portion of the line towards itself, not through itself.

The following example shows a Bezier curve, whose two control points are animated. The X-coordinate of the first control point and the Y-coordinate of the second control point vary in the range [50, 250]. You can clearly see how the Bezier curve changes shape when the control points are animated.

Start with a new Silverlight project and name it Example04-2. Here is the markup of this example:

```
<UserControl x:Class="Example04_2.Page"
    xmlns="http://schemas.microsoft.com/client/2007"
    xmlns:x="http://schemas.microsoft.com/winfx/2006/xaml"
    Width="300" Height="300" Loaded="Page_Loaded">

    <UserControl.Resources>
        <!-- Set animation: -->
        <Storyboard x:Name="storyboard1" RepeatBehavior="Forever"
                    AutoReverse="True">
            <PointAnimation Storyboard.TargetName="bezierSegment"
                            Storyboard.TargetProperty="Point1"
                            From="50 20" To="250 20" Duration="0:0:5"/>
            <PointAnimation Storyboard.TargetName="line1"
                            Storyboard.TargetProperty="EndPoint"
                            From="50 20" To="250 20" Duration="0:0:5"/>
            <PointAnimation Storyboard.TargetName="ellipse1"
                            Storyboard.TargetProperty="Center"
                            From="50 20" To="250 20" Duration="0:0:5"/>
            <PointAnimation Storyboard.TargetName="bezierSegment"
                            Storyboard.TargetProperty="Point2"
                            From="60 50" To="60 250" Duration="0:0:5"/>
            <PointAnimation Storyboard.TargetName="line2"
                            Storyboard.TargetProperty="StartPoint"
                            From="60 50" To="60 250" Duration="0:0:5"/>
            <PointAnimation Storyboard.TargetName="ellipse2"
                            Storyboard.TargetProperty="Center"
                            From="60 50" To="60 250" Duration="0:0:5"/>
        </Storyboard>
    </UserControl.Resources>

    <Grid x:Name="LayoutRoot" Background="White">
        <Border Margin="5" BorderBrush="Black" BorderThickness="1"
                HorizontalAlignment="Left" CornerRadius="10">
            <Canvas x:Name="canvas1" Width="300" Height="270">
```

```
                <Path Stroke="Black" StrokeThickness="5">
                    <Path.Data>
                        <PathGeometry>
                            <PathFigure StartPoint="20,20">
                                <BezierSegment x:Name="bezierSegment"
                                               Point1="150,50" Point2="60,160"
                                               Point3="250,230"/>
                            </PathFigure>
                        </PathGeometry>
                    </Path.Data>
                </Path>
                <Path x:Name="path1" Fill="Red" Stroke="Red">
                    <Path.Data>
                        <GeometryGroup>
                            <LineGeometry x:Name="line1" StartPoint="20,20"
                                          EndPoint="150,50"/>
                            <EllipseGeometry x:Name="ellipse1" Center="150,50"
                                             RadiusX="5" RadiusY="5" />
                            <LineGeometry x:Name="line2" StartPoint="60,160"
                                          EndPoint="250,230"/>
                            <EllipseGeometry x:Name="ellipse2" Center="60,160"
                                             RadiusX="5" RadiusY="5" />
                        </GeometryGroup>
                    </Path.Data>
                </Path>
            </Canvas>
        </Border>
    </Grid>
</UserControl>
```

This XAML file creates a Bezier curve using BezierSegment. The two control points, Point1 and Point2, of the Bezier curve are marked specifically by two ellipse shapes. At the same time, two line segments are created to guide your eye during the animation. The first line segment connects the starting point and Point1, while the second segment connects the end point and Point2.

The animation is performed within a Storyboard element using PointAnimation, which is defined in Resources. Here, you animate not only the control points of the Bezier curve, but also the red dots (ellipses) and the guide lines. The animation is started in the code-behind file.

This example produces the result shown in Figure 4-2, where you can see how the Bezier curve changes when the control points move.

Path Mini-Language

Silverlight provides a mini-language attribute syntax for describing geometric paths. You can use this mini-language ro specify a property of type Geometry, such as the Clip property of a UIElement or the Data property of a Path element.

To understand the mini-language, you need to realize that it is simply a long string that holds a series of commands. These commands are used by Silverlight to create corresponding geometries. Each command is a single letter followed by numeric information separated by spaces or commas.

For example, in the earlier section, you created a polyline with a PathGeometry using the following XAML snippet:

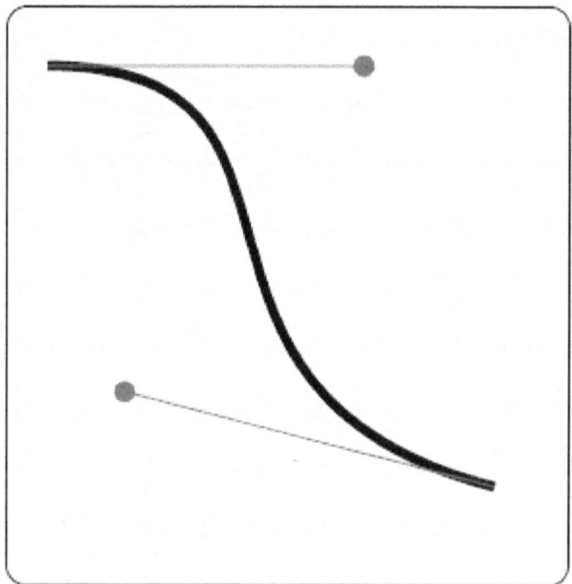

Figure 4-2 A Bezier curve.

```
<Path Stroke="Blue">
    <Path.Data>
        <PathGeometry>
            <PathFigure StartPoint="100,120">
                <PolyLineSegment
                    Points="200,120,200,220,100,170"/>
            </PathFigure>
        </PathGeometry>
    </Path.Data>
</Path>
```

You can use the path mini-language to duplicate this polyline:

```
<Path Stroke="Blue" Data="M 100 120 L 200 120 L 200 220 L 100 170"/>
```

This path uses a sequence of four commands. The first command, M, creates the PathFigure and sets the starting point to (100, 120). The following three commands (L) create line segments.

It is easy to use the mini-language to create complex geometry shapes. The mini-language uses a fairly small set of commands. For your reference, the mini-language commands are listed in Table 4-1.

Table 4-1 Commands for the Geometry Mini-Language

Name	Command	Description
Full rule	F0 or F1	Specifies geometry's FillRule property. F0 for EvenOdd, F1 for Nonzero. This command must appear at beginning of the string.
Move	M startPt	Creates a new PathFigure and sets its start point. This command must be used before any other commands

	m startPt	except for F0 or F1.
Line	L endpt l endPt	Creates a LineSegment from the current point to the specified end point.
Horizontal line	H x h x	Creates a horizontal line between the current point and the specified X-coordinate.
Vertical line	V y v y	Creates a vertical line between the current point and the specified Y-coordinate.
Cubic Bezier curve	C pt1, pt2, endPt c pt1, pt2, endPt	Creates a cubic Bezier curve between the current point and the specified end point by using the two specified control points (pt1 and pt2).
Quadratic Bezier curve	Q pt, endpt q pt, endPt	Creates a quadratic Bezier curve between the current point and the specified end point using the specified control point (pt).
Smooth cubic Bezier curve	S pt2, endpt s pt2, endPt	Creates a cubic Bezier curve between the current point and specified end point. The first control point is assumed to be the reflection of the second control point of the previous command relative to the current point.
Smooth Quadratic Bezier curve	T pt, endpoint t pt, endPoint	Creates a quadratic Bezier curve between the current point and the specified end point. The control point is assumed to be the reflection of the control point of the previous command relative to the current point.
Elliptical Arc	A size, angle, isLargeArc, Direction, endpoint a size, angle,…	Creates an elliptical arc between the current point and the specified end point. You specify the size of the ellipse, the rotation angle, and Boolean flags that set the IsLargeArc and SweepDirection properties.
Close	Z z	Ends the current figure and creates a line that connects the current point to the starting point of the figure. You don't need to use this command if you don't want to close the path.
Point	X, Y or x y	Describes the X- and Y-coordinates of a point.
Special values	Infinity -Infinity NaN	Instead of a standard numerical value, you can also use these special values. These values are case-sensitive.

The commands with uppercase letters use absolute coordinates while the commands with lowercase letters evaluate parameters relative to the previous point.

Interactive 2D Drawing

In the previous sections, we discussed Geometry, Path, and GeometryGroup. Now it is time for you to put all of them together in a real-world Silverlight application. This application allows you to draw 2D shapes using your mouse, drag and move shapes, and delete shapes interactively. It also has other features such as zooming and panning. The approach applied in this project will be useful when you develop interactive CAD-like Web applications using Silverlight.

Another point I should emphasize here is that if you develop a CAD application using WPF, you need to make necessary modifications in order for it to work in Web application using Silverlight. You can take a look at a WPF version of this project in my WPF book "Practical WPF Graphics Programming" and compare the difference between these two projects.

First I'll present all of the source code and the corresponding results, which show you what this program can do and how to use it. Next, I'll discuss the functionality of the properties and methods used in the program.

Start with a new Silverlight project and name it Example04-3. The following XAML file creates the interface and layout for the application:

```
<UserControl x:Class="Example04_3.Page"
    xmlns="http://schemas.microsoft.com/client/2007"
    xmlns:x="http://schemas.microsoft.com/winfx/2006/xaml">

    <Border BorderBrush="Gray" BorderThickness="1" Margin="2">
        <Grid x:Name="LayoutRoot" Background="White">
            <Grid.RowDefinitions>
                <RowDefinition Height="Auto"/>
                <RowDefinition/>
            </Grid.RowDefinitions>

            <StackPanel Orientation="Horizontal" Background="LightGray">
                <StackPanel Orientation="Horizontal" x:Name="toolbarPanel">
                    <StackPanel.Background>
                        <LinearGradientBrush EndPoint="0.5,1"
                                             StartPoint="0.5,0">
                            <GradientStop Color="#FFF0F0F0"/>
                            <GradientStop Color="#FF323232" Offset="1"/>
                            <GradientStop Color="#FFAAAAAA" Offset="0.638"/>
                        </LinearGradientBrush>
                    </StackPanel.Background>

                    <Canvas x:Name="newCanvas" Width="26" Height="26" Margin="2"
                            Background="#FFDDDDDD" Tag="Unchecked" Cursor="Hand"
                            MouseEnter="Toolbar_MouseEnter"
                            MouseLeave="Toolbar_MouseLeave"
                            MouseLeftButtonDown="Toolbar_MouseLeftButtonDown">
                        <Path Stroke="Blue" StrokeThickness="1" Width="20"
                              Height="20" Canvas.Left="5" Canvas.Top="3">
                            <Path.Data>
                                <GeometryGroup>
                                    <PathGeometry>
                                        <PathFigure StartPoint="0 0">
                            <PolyLineSegment Points="0,20 16 20 16,6 10,0 0,0"/>
                                        </PathFigure>
```

```
                </PathGeometry>
                <PathGeometry>
                    <PathFigure StartPoint="10 0">
                        <PolyLineSegment Points="10,6 16,6"/>
                    </PathFigure>
                </PathGeometry>
            </GeometryGroup>
        </Path.Data>
    </Path>
    <ToolTipService.ToolTip>
        <ToolTip Content="Start a new drawing"/>
    </ToolTipService.ToolTip>
</Canvas>

<Canvas Width="2" Height="20" Margin="8">
    <Line X1="0" Y1="0" X2="0" Y2="20" Stroke="Gray"
          StrokeThickness="1"/>
</Canvas>

<Canvas x:Name="squareCanvas" Width="26" Height="26"
        Margin="2" Background="#FFDDDDDD" Tag="Unchecked"
        Cursor="Hand" MouseEnter="Toolbar_MouseEnter"
        MouseLeave="Toolbar_MouseLeave"
        MouseLeftButtonDown="Toolbar_MouseLeftButtonDown">
    <Rectangle Width="20" Height="20" Stroke="Blue"
        StrokeThickness="2" Canvas.Left="3" Canvas.Top="3"/>
    <ToolTipService.ToolTip>
        <ToolTip Content="Add square"/>
    </ToolTipService.ToolTip>
</Canvas>

<Canvas x:Name="rectCanvas" Width="26" Height="26"
        Margin="2" Background="#FFDDDDDD" Cursor="Hand"
        MouseEnter="Toolbar_MouseEnter" Tag="Unchecked"
        MouseLeave="Toolbar_MouseLeave"
        MouseLeftButtonDown="Toolbar_MouseLeftButtonDown">
    <Rectangle Canvas.Top="8" Width="20" Height="12"
        Stroke="Blue" StrokeThickness="2" Canvas.Left="3"/>
    <ToolTipService.ToolTip>
        <ToolTip Content="Add rectangle"/>
    </ToolTipService.ToolTip>
</Canvas>

<Canvas x:Name="circleCanvas" Width="26" Height="26"
        Margin="2" Background="#FFDDDDDD"
        Cursor="Hand" MouseEnter="Toolbar_MouseEnter"
        Tag="Unchecked" MouseLeave="Toolbar_MouseLeave"
        MouseLeftButtonDown="Toolbar_MouseLeftButtonDown">
    <Ellipse Width="20" Height="20" Stroke="Blue"
        StrokeThickness="2" Canvas.Left="3" Canvas.Top="3"/>
    <ToolTipService.ToolTip>
        <ToolTip Content="Add circle"/>
    </ToolTipService.ToolTip>
</Canvas>
```

```
<Canvas x:Name="ellipseCanvas" Width="26" Height="26"
        Margin="2" Background="#FFDDDDDD"
        Cursor="Hand" MouseEnter="Toolbar_MouseEnter"
        Tag="Unchecked" MouseLeave="Toolbar_MouseLeave"
        MouseLeftButtonDown="Toolbar_MouseLeftButtonDown">
    <Ellipse Canvas.Top="8" Canvas.Left="3" Width="20"
        Height="12" Stroke="Blue" StrokeThickness="2"/>
    <ToolTipService.ToolTip>
        <ToolTip Content="Add ellipse"/>
    </ToolTipService.ToolTip>
</Canvas>

<Canvas Width="2" Height="20" Margin="8">
    <Line X1="0" Y1="0" X2="0" Y2="20" Stroke="Gray"
          StrokeThickness="1"/>
</Canvas>

<Canvas x:Name="selectCanvas" Width="26" Height="26"
        Margin="2" Background="#FFDDDDDD"
        Cursor="Hand" MouseEnter="Toolbar_MouseEnter"
        Tag="Unchecked" MouseLeave="Toolbar_MouseLeave"
        MouseLeftButtonDown="Toolbar_MouseLeftButtonDown">
    <Polygon Points="5 15,10 0,15 15,12 15,12,20 8,20 8,15"
             Stroke="Blue" StrokeThickness="2"
             Canvas.Left="6" Canvas.Top="3">
        <Polygon.RenderTransform>
     <RotateTransform CenterX="8" CenterY="8" Angle="45"/>
        </Polygon.RenderTransform>
    </Polygon>
    <ToolTipService.ToolTip>
        <ToolTip Content="Select/move"/>
    </ToolTipService.ToolTip>
</Canvas>

<Canvas x:Name="deleteCanvas" Width="26" Height="26"
        Margin="2" Background="#FFDDDDDD"
        Cursor="Hand" MouseEnter="Toolbar_MouseEnter"
        Tag="Unchecked" MouseLeave="Toolbar_MouseLeave"
        MouseLeftButtonDown="Toolbar_MouseLeftButtonDown">
    <ToolTipService.ToolTip>
        <ToolTip Content="Delete"/>
    </ToolTipService.ToolTip>
    <Line X1="2" Y1="2" X2="16" Y2="16" Stroke="Blue"
        StrokeThickness="3" Canvas.Left="4" Canvas.Top="5"/>
    <Line X1="2" Y1="16" X2="16" Y2="2" Stroke="Blue"
        StrokeThickness="3" Canvas.Left="4" Canvas.Top="5"/>
</Canvas>

<Canvas Width="2" Height="20" Margin="8">
    <Line X1="0" Y1="0" X2="0" Y2="20" Stroke="Gray"
        StrokeThickness="1"/>
</Canvas>

<Canvas x:Name="zoomInCanvas" Width="26" Height="26"
        Margin="2" Background="#FFDDDDDD"
```

```
        Cursor="Hand" MouseEnter="Toolbar_MouseEnter"
        Tag="Unchecked" MouseLeave="Toolbar_MouseLeave"
        MouseLeftButtonDown="Toolbar_MouseLeftButtonDown">
    <Ellipse Width="18" Height="18" Stroke="Blue"
        StrokeThickness="2" Canvas.Left="4" Canvas.Top="5"/>
    <Line X1="8" Y1="14" X2="18" Y2="14" Stroke="Blue"
        StrokeThickness="2"/>
    <Line X1="13" Y1="9" X2="13" Y2="19" Stroke="Blue"
        StrokeThickness="2"/>
    <ToolTipService.ToolTip>
        <ToolTip Content="Zoom in"/>
    </ToolTipService.ToolTip>
</Canvas>

<Canvas x:Name="zoomOutCanvas" Width="26" Height="26"
        Margin="2" Background="#FFDDDDDD"
        Cursor="Hand" MouseEnter="Toolbar_MouseEnter"
        Tag="Unchecked" MouseLeave="Toolbar_MouseLeave"
        MouseLeftButtonDown="Toolbar_MouseLeftButtonDown">
    <Ellipse Width="18" Height="18" Stroke="Blue"
        StrokeThickness="2" Canvas.Left="4" Canvas.Top="5"/>
    <Line X1="8" Y1="14" X2="18" Y2="14" Stroke="Blue"
        StrokeThickness="2"/>
    <ToolTipService.ToolTip>
        <ToolTip Content="Zoom out"/>
    </ToolTipService.ToolTip>
</Canvas>

<Canvas x:Name="originalCanvas" Width="26" Height="26"
        Margin="2" Background="#FFDDDDDD"
        Cursor="Hand" MouseEnter="Toolbar_MouseEnter"
        Tag="Unchecked" MouseLeave="Toolbar_MouseLeave"
        MouseLeftButtonDown="Toolbar_MouseLeftButtonDown">
    <Path Stroke="Blue" StrokeThickness="2" Width="20"
        Height="20" Canvas.Left="3" Canvas.Top="4">
        <Path.Data>
            <GeometryGroup>
                <RectangleGeometry Rect="0,0,20,20"/>
                <PathGeometry>
                    <PathFigure StartPoint="0 10">
                        <LineSegment Point="20 10"/>
                    </PathFigure>
                </PathGeometry>
                <PathGeometry>
                    <PathFigure StartPoint="10 0">
                        <LineSegment Point="10 20"/>
                    </PathFigure>
                </PathGeometry>
                <PathGeometry>
                    <PathFigure StartPoint="4 6">
                     <PolyLineSegment Points="0,10 4 14"/>
                    </PathFigure>
                </PathGeometry>
                <PathGeometry>
                    <PathFigure StartPoint="16 6">
```

```
                        <PolyLineSegment Points="20,10 16 14"/>
                    </PathFigure>
                </PathGeometry>
                <PathGeometry>
                    <PathFigure StartPoint="6 4">
                        <PolyLineSegment Points="10,0 14 4"/>
                    </PathFigure>
                </PathGeometry>
                <PathGeometry>
                    <PathFigure StartPoint="6 16">
                        <PolyLineSegment Points="10,20 14 16"/>
                    </PathFigure>
                </PathGeometry>
            </GeometryGroup>
        </Path.Data>
    </Path>
    <ToolTipService.ToolTip>
        <ToolTip Content="Back to original view"/>
    </ToolTipService.ToolTip>
</Canvas>

<Canvas Width="2" Height="20" Margin="8">
    <Line X1="0" Y1="0" X2="0" Y2="20" Stroke="Gray"
        StrokeThickness="1"/>
</Canvas>

<Canvas x:Name="panLeftCanvas" Width="26" Height="26"
        Margin="2" Background="#FFDDDDDD"
        Cursor="Hand" MouseEnter="Toolbar_MouseEnter"
        Tag="Unchecked" MouseLeave="Toolbar_MouseLeave"
        MouseLeftButtonDown="Toolbar_MouseLeftButtonDown">
    <Polygon Points="5 15,10 0,15 15,12 15,12,20 8,20 8,15"
             Canvas.Left="4" Stroke="Blue"
             StrokeThickness="2" Canvas.Top="8">
        <Polygon.RenderTransform>
     <RotateTransform CenterX="8" CenterY="8" Angle="270"/>
        </Polygon.RenderTransform>
    </Polygon>
    <Line X1="0" Y1="0" X2="0" Y2="20" Stroke="Blue"
        StrokeThickness="2" Canvas.Left="3" Canvas.Top="3"/>
    <ToolTipService.ToolTip>
        <ToolTip Content="Pan left"/>
    </ToolTipService.ToolTip>
</Canvas>

<Canvas x:Name="panRightCanvas" Width="26" Height="26"
        Margin="2" Background="#FFDDDDDD"
        Cursor="Hand" MouseEnter="Toolbar_MouseEnter"
        Tag="Unchecked" MouseLeave="Toolbar_MouseLeave"
        MouseLeftButtonDown="Toolbar_MouseLeftButtonDown">
    <Polygon Points="5 15,10 0,15 15,12 15,12,20 8,20 8,15"
        Stroke="Blue" StrokeThickness="2" Canvas.Top="4"
        Canvas.Left="6">
        <Polygon.RenderTransform>
      <RotateTransform CenterX="8" CenterY="8" Angle="90"/>
```

```
                </Polygon.RenderTransform>
            </Polygon>
            <Line X1="17" Y1="0" X2="17" Y2="20" Stroke="Blue"
                StrokeThickness="2" Canvas.Left="6" Canvas.Top="3"/>
            <ToolTipService.ToolTip>
                <ToolTip Content="Pan right"/>
            </ToolTipService.ToolTip>
        </Canvas>

        <Canvas x:Name="panUpCanvas" Width="26" Height="26"
                Margin="2" Background="#FFDDDDDD"
                Cursor="Hand" MouseEnter="Toolbar_MouseEnter"
                Tag="Unchecked" MouseLeave="Toolbar_MouseLeave"
                MouseLeftButtonDown="Toolbar_MouseLeftButtonDown">
            <Polygon Points="5 15,10 0,15 15,12 15,12,20 8,20 8,15"
                Stroke="Blue" StrokeThickness="2" Canvas.Top="4"
                Canvas.Left="3">
                <Polygon.RenderTransform>
             <RotateTransform CenterX="8" CenterY="8" Angle="0"/>
                </Polygon.RenderTransform>
            </Polygon>
            <Line X1="0" Y1="0" X2="20" Y2="0" Stroke="Blue"
                StrokeThickness="2" Canvas.Left="3" Canvas.Top="2"/>
            <ToolTipService.ToolTip>
                <ToolTip Content="Pan up"/>
            </ToolTipService.ToolTip>
        </Canvas>

        <Canvas x:Name="panDownCanvas" Width="26" Height="26"
                Margin="2" Background="#FFDDDDDD"
                Cursor="Hand" MouseEnter="Toolbar_MouseEnter"
                Tag="Unchecked" MouseLeave="Toolbar_MouseLeave"
                MouseLeftButtonDown="Toolbar_MouseLeftButtonDown">
            <Polygon Points="5 15,10 0,15 15,12 15,12,20 8,20 8,15"
                Stroke="Blue" StrokeThickness="2" Canvas.Top="5"
                Canvas.Left="7">
                <Polygon.RenderTransform>
              <RotateTransform CenterX="8" CenterY="8" Angle="180"/>
                </Polygon.RenderTransform>
            </Polygon>
            <Line X1="0" Y1="20" X2="20" Y2="20" Stroke="Blue"
                StrokeThickness="2" Canvas.Left="3" Canvas.Top="3"/>
            <ToolTipService.ToolTip>
                <ToolTip Content="Pan down"/>
            </ToolTipService.ToolTip>
        </Canvas>
    </StackPanel>
</StackPanel>

<ScrollViewer x:Name="scrollviewer1"
    HorizontalScrollBarVisibility="Visible"
    VerticalScrollBarVisibility="Visible" Grid.Row="1">
    <Canvas x:Name="outCanvas" Width="1500" Height="1000"
            Grid.Row="1">
        <Canvas x:Name="canvas1" Width="1500" Height="1000"
```

```
                                Background="Transparent"
                                MouseLeftButtonDown="canvas1_MouseLeftButtonDown"
                                MouseLeftButtonUp="canvas1_MouseLeftButtonUp"
                                MouseMove="canvas1_MouseMove">
                        </Canvas>
                    </Canvas>
                </ScrollViewer>
            </Grid>
        </Border>
    </UserControl>
```

Since Silverlight doesn't have a ToolBarTray, which is available in WPF, here we implement the toolbars using geometry shapes to mimic the appearance of radio buttons. You could also create a custom control for the toolbars. You will find that the direct approach used here is very simple and allows you to easily customize your toolbars whatever way you like. The toolbar buttons created here have different functionalities and can be used to add a square, rectangle, circle, or ellipse; select/move shapes; delete shapes; and zoom or pan, depending on which button is selected. Different technologies are used to create these buttons, including GeometryGroup and rotation transforms.

If you play with Silverlight, you may notice that ToolTip is hidden and can't be used directly. ToolTip can now only be added to controls through the ToolTipService. ToolTips can be set through the ToolTipService either in XAML or in code.

The drawing area is defined by a Canvas object, canvas1, where several mouse click events are involved. These events include MouseLeftButtonDown, MouseLeftButtonUp, and MouseMove, which allow you to implement interactive applications in code. More about mouse events will be discussed later in this chapter.

The drawing canvas is located inside a ScrollViewer. In WPF, there is a LayoutTransform associated with the Canvas control. You can attach the ScaleTransform to the LayoutTransform to perform the zooming effect. The scrollbar in the ScrollViewer changes appropriately as you zoom in or out. However, there is no LayoutTransform in Silverlight. You can only set the RenderTransform of the Canvas to the ScaleTransform, but the scrollbar in the ScrollViewer doesn't update to reflect the new zooming effect.

Here, I introduce a work-around. I add another Canvas called outCanvas with the same size as the drawing Canvas, and manually set its size when you perform zooming. This means everything inside the canvas1 will be affected by its RenderTransform, and the ScrollViewer will be affected by the outCanvas's size.

The code-behind file of this application is listed below:

```
using System;
using System.Windows;
using System.Windows.Browser;
using System.Collections.Generic;
using System.Windows.Input;
using System.Windows.Controls;
using System.Windows.Controls.Primitives;
using System.Windows.Media;
using System.Windows.Media.Animation;
using System.Windows.Shapes;

namespace Example04_3
{
```

```
public partial class Page : UserControl
{
    private Point startPoint = new Point();
    private Point currentPoint = new Point();
    private Rectangle rubberBand = null;
    private Thumb dragThumb;
    private double originalWidth;
    private double originalHeight;
    private Point zoomCenter = new Point();
    private double zoomFactor = 1;
    private double panLeftRightOffset = 0;
    private double panUpDownOffset = 0;
    private Path path = new Path();
    private bool isMouseCaptured = false;

    public Page()
    {
        InitializeComponent();
        AllTags_Unchecked();
        originalHeight = outCanvas.Height;
        originalWidth = outCanvas.Width;
    }

    #region Toolbar-related methods and event handlers:
    private void Toolbar_MouseEnter(object sender, MouseEventArgs e)
    {
        Canvas canvas = sender as Canvas;
        if (canvas.Tag != null)
        {
            if (canvas.Tag.ToString() != "Checked")
                canvas.Background =
                    new SolidColorBrush(Color.FromArgb(150, 221, 221, 221));
        }
    }

    private void Toolbar_MouseLeave(object sender, MouseEventArgs e)
    {
        Canvas canvas = sender as Canvas;
        if (canvas.Tag != null)
        {
            if (canvas.Tag.ToString() != "Checked")
                canvas.Background =
                    new SolidColorBrush(Color.FromArgb(0, 221, 221, 221));
        }
    }

    private void Toolbar_MouseLeftButtonDown(object sender,
            MouseButtonEventArgs e)
    {
        Canvas canvas = sender as Canvas;
        if (canvas.Tag != null)
        {
            AllTags_Unchecked();
            canvas.Tag = "Checked";
            canvas.Background =
```

```
        new SolidColorBrush(Color.FromArgb(255, 221, 221, 221));
}

if (newCanvas.Tag.ToString() == "Checked")
{
    if (HtmlPage.Window.Confirm("Do you really want to clear
        all shapes and start a new drawing?"))
    {
        canvas1.Children.Clear();
    }
    else
        return;
}
else if (zoomInCanvas.Tag.ToString() == "Checked")
{
    if (zoomFactor < 1)
        zoomFactor = 1;
    zoomFactor = zoomFactor + 0.1;
    ScaleTransform st = new ScaleTransform();
    st.ScaleX = zoomFactor;
    st.ScaleY = zoomFactor;
    canvas1.RenderTransform = st;
    outCanvas.Width = originalWidth * zoomFactor;
    outCanvas.Height = originalHeight * zoomFactor;
}
else if (zoomOutCanvas.Tag.ToString() == "Checked")
{
    zoomFactor = zoomFactor - 0.1;
    if (zoomFactor < 1)
        zoomFactor = 1;
    ScaleTransform st = new ScaleTransform();
    st.ScaleX = zoomFactor;
    st.ScaleY = zoomFactor;
    canvas1.RenderTransform = st;
    outCanvas.Width = originalWidth * zoomFactor;
    outCanvas.Height = originalHeight * zoomFactor;
}
else if (originalCanvas.Tag.ToString() == "Checked")
{
    zoomFactor = 1;
    ScaleTransform st = new ScaleTransform();
    st.ScaleX = zoomFactor;
    st.ScaleY = zoomFactor;
    canvas1.RenderTransform = st;
    outCanvas.Width = originalWidth * zoomFactor;
    outCanvas.Height = originalHeight * zoomFactor;
    scrollviewer1.ScrollToHorizontalOffset(0);
    scrollviewer1.ScrollToVerticalOffset(0);
}
else if (panLeftCanvas.Tag.ToString() == "Checked")
{
    panLeftRightOffset = panLeftRightOffset + 20;
    scrollviewer1.ScrollToHorizontalOffset(panLeftRightOffset);
}
else if (panRightCanvas.Tag.ToString() == "Checked")
```

```
    {
        panLeftRightOffset = panLeftRightOffset - 20;
        scrollviewer1.ScrollToHorizontalOffset(panLeftRightOffset);
    }
    else if (panUpCanvas.Tag.ToString() == "Checked")
    {
        panUpDownOffset = panUpDownOffset + 20;
        scrollviewer1.ScrollToVerticalOffset(panUpDownOffset);
    }
    else if (panDownCanvas.Tag.ToString() == "Checked")
    {
        panUpDownOffset = panUpDownOffset - 20;
        scrollviewer1.ScrollToVerticalOffset(panUpDownOffset);
    }
}

private void AllTags_Unchecked()
{
    foreach (Canvas can in toolbarPanel.Children)
    {
        can.Tag = "Unchecked";
        can.Background =
            new SolidColorBrush(Color.FromArgb(0, 221, 221, 221));
    }
}
#endregion

#region Draw, select, drag/move, and delete shapes:
private void canvas1_MouseLeftButtonDown(object sender,
        MouseButtonEventArgs e)
{
    if (isMouseCaptured == false)
    {
        startPoint = e.GetPosition(canvas1);
        zoomCenter = startPoint;

        if (selectCanvas.Tag.ToString() == "Checked")
        {
            if (dragThumb != null)
                canvas1.Children.Remove(dragThumb);

            if (canvas1 == e.Source)
                return;
            path = e.Source as Path;
            e.Handled = true;
            SetSelection();
        }
        else if (deleteCanvas.Tag.ToString() == "Checked")
        {
            path = e.Source as Path;
            if (path != null)
                DeletePath();
        }
        isMouseCaptured = true;
        canvas1.CaptureMouse();
```

```
        }
    }

    private void SetSelection()
    {
        if (dragThumb != null)
            canvas1.Children.Remove(dragThumb);
        if (path == null)
            return;
        AddDragThumb();
    }

    private void AddDragThumb()
    {
        dragThumb = new Thumb();
        Canvas.SetZIndex(dragThumb, 5);
        dragThumb.Height = path.Height;
        dragThumb.Width = path.Width;
        dragThumb.Cursor = Cursors.Hand;
        double side = path.Width;
        if (path.Tag != null)
        {
            if (path.Tag.ToString() == "Square" ||
                path.Tag.ToString() == "Circle")
            {
                if (path.Width > path.Height)
                    side = path.Height;
                dragThumb.Height = side;
                dragThumb.Width = side;
            }
            canvas1.Children.Add(dragThumb);
        }

        dragThumb.Opacity = 0.5;
        Canvas.SetTop(dragThumb, Canvas.GetTop(path));
        Canvas.SetLeft(dragThumb, Canvas.GetLeft(path));
        dragThumb.DragDelta +=
            new DragDeltaEventHandler(dragThumb_DragDelta);
    }

    private void dragThumb_DragDelta(object sender, DragDeltaEventArgs e)
    {
        if (path != null)
        {
            Canvas.SetLeft(path, Canvas.GetLeft(path) + e.HorizontalChange);
            Canvas.SetTop(path, Canvas.GetTop(path) + e.VerticalChange);
            Canvas.SetLeft(dragThumb, Canvas.GetLeft(dragThumb) +
                           e.HorizontalChange);
            Canvas.SetTop(dragThumb, Canvas.GetTop(dragThumb) +
                           e.VerticalChange);
        }
    }
```

```
private void DeletePath()
{
    path.Opacity = 0.5;
    if (HtmlPage.Window.Confirm("Do you really want to
                                 delete this shape?"))
    {
        canvas1.Children.Remove(path);
    }
    else
    {
        path.Opacity = 1;
        return;
    }
}

private void canvas1_MouseMove(object sender,
             System.Windows.Input.MouseEventArgs e)
{
    if (isMouseCaptured)
    {
        currentPoint = e.GetPosition(canvas1);

        double width = 0.0;
        double height = 0.0;
        double left = 0.0;
        double top = 0.0;

        if (rubberBand == null)
        {
            rubberBand = new Rectangle();
            rubberBand.Stroke =
                new SolidColorBrush(Color.FromArgb(255, 255, 100, 0));
            DoubleCollection dc = new DoubleCollection();
            Canvas.SetZIndex(rubberBand, 5);
            dc.Add(4);
            dc.Add(2);
            rubberBand.StrokeDashArray = dc;
            if (squareCanvas.Tag.ToString() == "Checked" ||
                rectCanvas.Tag.ToString() == "Checked" ||
                circleCanvas.Tag.ToString() == "Checked" ||
                ellipseCanvas.Tag.ToString() == "Checked")
            {
                canvas1.Children.Add(rubberBand);
                path = new Path();
                canvas1.Children.Add(path);
            }
        }
        width = Math.Abs(startPoint.X - currentPoint.X);
        height = Math.Abs(startPoint.Y - currentPoint.Y);
        left = Math.Min(startPoint.X, currentPoint.X);
        top = Math.Min(startPoint.Y, currentPoint.Y);

        rubberBand.Width = width;
        rubberBand.Height = height;
        Canvas.SetLeft(rubberBand, left);
```

```
            Canvas.SetTop(rubberBand, top);

            if (squareCanvas.Tag.ToString() == "Checked" ||
                rectCanvas.Tag.ToString() == "Checked" ||
                circleCanvas.Tag.ToString() == "Checked" ||
                ellipseCanvas.Tag.ToString() == "Checked")
            {
                CreateShape(path);
            }
        }
    }

    private void CreateShape(Path p)
    {
        p.Fill = new SolidColorBrush(Color.FromArgb(200, 200, 200, 200));
        p.Stroke = new SolidColorBrush(Color.FromArgb(255, 100, 100, 100));
        RectangleGeometry rg = new RectangleGeometry();
        EllipseGeometry eg = new EllipseGeometry();
        double width = Math.Abs(currentPoint.X - startPoint.X);
        double height = Math.Abs(currentPoint.Y - startPoint.Y);
        double left = Math.Min(startPoint.X, currentPoint.X);
        double top = Math.Min(startPoint.Y, currentPoint.Y);
        Canvas.SetLeft(p, left);
        Canvas.SetTop(p, top);
        p.Width = width;
        p.Height = height;
        double side = width;

        if (squareCanvas.Tag.ToString() == "Checked")
        {
            if (width > height)
                side = height;
            rg.Rect = new Rect(0, 0, side, side);
            p.Data = rg;
            p.Tag = "Square";
        }
        else if (rectCanvas.Tag.ToString() == "Checked")
        {
            rg.Rect = new Rect(0, 0, width, height);
            p.Data = rg;
            p.Tag = "Rectangle";
        }
        else if (circleCanvas.Tag.ToString() == "Checked")
        {
            if (width > height)
                side = height;
            eg.Center = new Point(side / 2, side / 2);
            eg.RadiusX = side / 2;
            eg.RadiusY = side / 2;
            p.Data = eg;
            p.Tag = "Circle";
        }

        else if (ellipseCanvas.Tag.ToString() == "Checked")
```

```
                {
                    eg.Center = new Point(width / 2, height / 2);
                    eg.RadiusX = width / 2;
                    eg.RadiusY = height / 2;
                    p.Data = eg;
                    p.Tag = "Ellipse";
                }
            }

            private void canvas1_MouseLeftButtonUp(object sender,
                         MouseButtonEventArgs e)
            {
                if (selectCanvas.Tag.ToString() == "Checked")
                    e.Handled = true;
                if (rubberBand != null)
                {
                    canvas1.Children.Remove(rubberBand);
                    rubberBand = null;
                    canvas1.ReleaseMouseCapture();
                    isMouseCaptured = false;
                }
            }
            #endregion
        }
    }
```

The above code-behind file involves several techniques, including mouse click events that allow the user to interact with the program, a rubberband for the outline of the shape to be drawn following the mouse cursor, shapes created using Geometry objects, transforms on Path and Geometry objects, etc.

Since Silverlight is merely a subset of WPF, it does not possess several WPF features. In some cases, for example, the Message Box is very useful. When a user selects a shape to be deleted, you may want him to confirm that he really wants to delete the selected shape, which requires a Message Box that allows the user to select the options. Silverlight doesn't have a MessageBox control due to the consideration of cross-browser compatiblility. However, the HtmlWindow class exposes two MessageBox-like methods called "Alert" and "Confirm", which work in the same way as the conventional MessageBox in WPF. Inside the DeletePath method of the above code listing, we use the HtmlPage.Window.Confirm method:

```
private void DeletePath()
{
    path.Opacity = 0.5;
    if (HtmlPage.Window.Confirm("Do you really want to delete this shape?"))
    {
        canvas1.Children.Remove(path);
    }
    else
    {
        path.Opacity = 1;
        return;
    }
}
```

This results in a prompt type supported by the browser window, as shown in Figure 4-3.

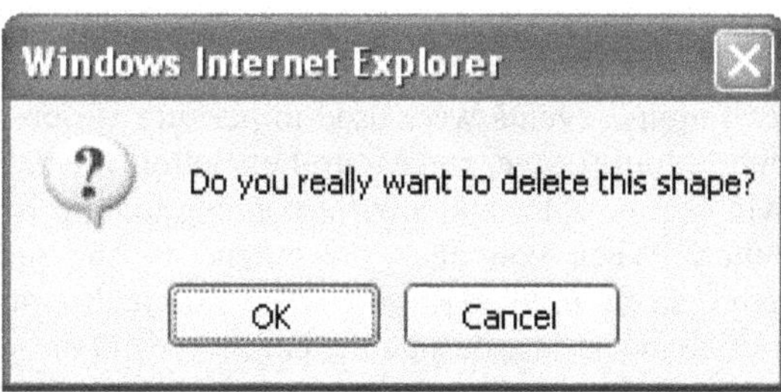

Figure 4-3 "Confirm" message displayed in the browser window.

In the following sections, I'll explain how this application works. But first I want to show you the results of this project. Figure 4-4 is a snapshot generated from this program.

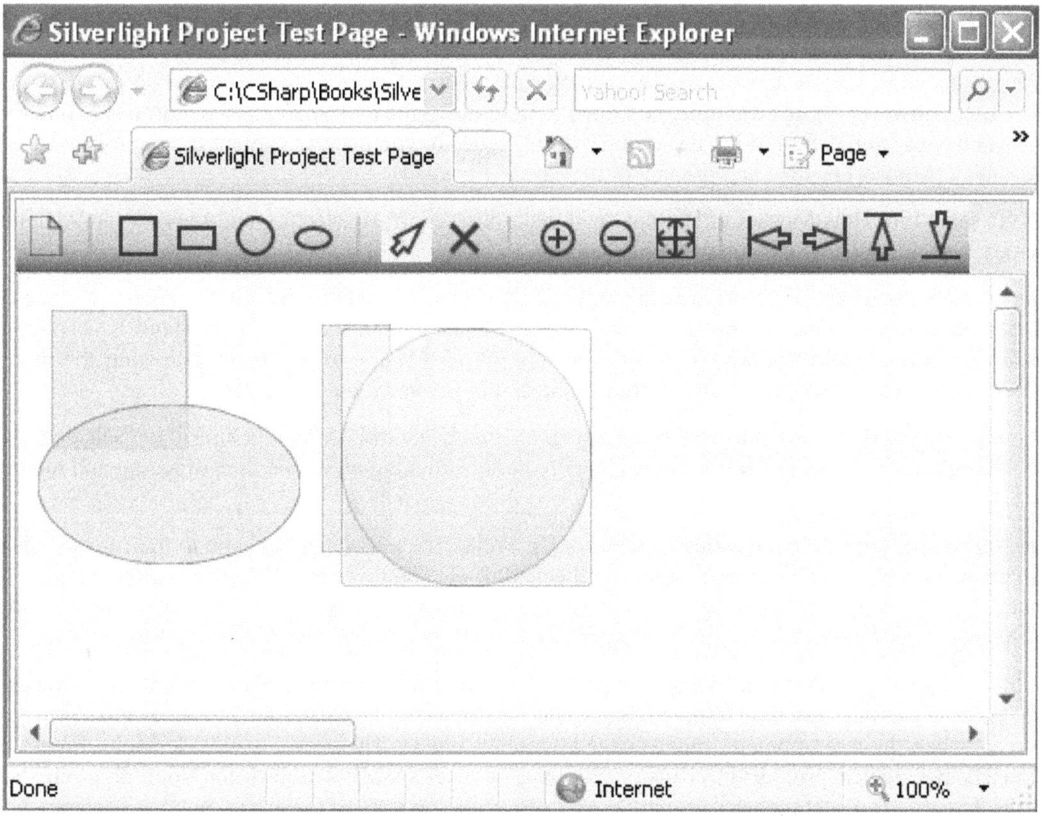

Figure 4-4 Interactive 2D drawing application in Silverlight.

You can see from this figure that the application is hosted in a browser window, and allows the user to add various shapes, including squares, rectangles, circles, and ellipses, and perform various operations on the shapes, such as dragging, moving, and deleting the shapes, as well as zooming and panning.

Mouse Events

In the above example, several mouse events were used to perform various operations for the toolbar buttons, including MouseEnter, MouseLeave, and MouseLeftButtonDown. When your mouse is over a toolbar button, the button will change color and a corresponding tool tip is displayed, which tells you the functionality of the button. When you click the buton, its Tag property will be marked as "Checked". The Tag property can be used to store custom information about the selected element. Silverlight restricts the Tag value to a string, despite the Object type in the signature. The program will use this Tag value to perform corresponding operations.

There are also several mouse events associated with the drawing Canvas, canvas1, such as LeftMouseButtomDown, LeftMouseButtonUp, and MouseMove. The mouse button events provide a MouseButtonEventArgs object. The MouseButtonEventArgs class derives from the MouseEventArgs base class. Different tasks are performed depending on which toolbar button is clicked when you press the left mouse button. First, you obtain a position (a Point object) at which the left mouse button is clicked on the canvas1 control. Then you set the mouse's Capture state. Usually, when an object receives a mouse button down event, it will receive a corresponding mouse button up event shortly thereafter. However, in this example, you need to hold down the mouse and move it around. Thus, you want to have a notification of the mouse up event. To do so, you need to capture the mouse by calling the CaptureMouse() method and passing to the canvas1 control.

At the same time, this MouseLeftButtonDown event also controls selecting and moving, and deleting shapes, depending on which button is checked.

The MouseMove event performs drawing tasks. It draws various shapes, including squares, rectangles, circles, or ellipses. When it draws a shape, a rubberband is created. This rubberband is a common feature in graphics applications. It provides an outline of a shape to be drawn following the mouse cursor, so you can visualize exactly where the shape will be drawn on your screen.

The dragging and moving are performed using a Thumb control. After clicking the "Select/Move" toolbar button, you can drag and move a shape by double clicking on it, and then dragging and moving it.

Several actions happen in the MouseLeftButtonUp event. The event adds a shape to the canvas1 if the square, rectangle, circle, or ellipse button is checked. It also removes the rubberband after creating the shape. Finally, it is responsible for terminating the moving of the shape when the Select/Move button is checked.

In this example, you use three Mouse events for canvas1. There are more mouse events in Silverlight that you can use in developing interactive graphics applications. For example, mouse events allow you to react when the mouse pointer moves over a graphics object. These events include MouseEnter and MouseLeave, which provide information about a MouseEventArgs object for your program. The MouseEventArgs object includes properties that show you the state of the mouse button. There are also many other mouse events in Silverlight that you can use in your applications. If you need more information about mouse events, you can refer to Microsoft online help or tutorial books on the topic.

Creating Shapes

In this example, the shapes are created using the path that contains either the RectangleGeometry or EllipseGeometry class. You can also create shapes directly using the Rectangle and Ellipse shapes derived from the Shape class.

Let's look at the CreateShape method. It takes a path object as its input parameter. First, you specify the Path's Fill and Stroke properties. Then you create RectangleGeometry and EllipseGeometry, and use two Point objects to set the path's location and size. One of these two points is the startPoint, recorded when the MouseLeftButtonDown event fires, and the other is the currentPoint, recorded when the MouseLeftButtonUp event fires. After some manipulation, these two points are also used to set the Rect property of the RectangleGeometry, as well as the Center and Radius of the EllipseGeometry. Pay special attention to how you draw different shapes according to which toolbar button is clicked. In this way, you can add any number of squares, rectangles, circles, or ellipses to the canvas1 control.

Dragging and Moving Shapes

This application also allows you to select, drag, and move shapes using the mouse when the Select/Move button is clicked.

In this example, the dragging and moving are performed using the Thumb control. This control applows you to drag and resize the selected shape. Here, I didn't implement the resize feature, but you can easily add this feature to the application without difficulty by following the same procedure as we did here to implement the dragging feature. In WPF, you can perform dragging and moving more easily by implementing a custom adorner. Since Silverlight doesn't includes a AdornerLayer class, we have to use the Thumb class to perform dragging and moving instead.

The dragThumb object provides an event handler implementation. When the user presses the left mose button, the dragThumb control receives a logic focus and mouse capture. The DragDelta event can be raised multiple times without limits. The event information provides a change in position, but it doesn't reposition the Thumb. You need to manually change or reposition the Thumb and the selected shape that you want to move as a result of the drag operation. The implementation of the dragging and moving process is given in the dragThumb_DragDelta event handler:

```
private void dragThumb_DragDelta(object sender, DragDeltaEventArgs e)
{
    if (path != null)
    {
        Canvas.SetLeft(path, Canvas.GetLeft(path) + e.HorizontalOffset);
        Canvas.SetTop(path, Canvas.GetTop(path) + e.VerticalOffset);
        Canvas.SetLeft(dragThumb,
                            Canvas.GetLeft(dragThumb) + e.HorizontalOffset);
        Canvas.SetTop(dragThumb, Canvas.GetTop(dragThumb) + e.VerticalOffset);
    }
}
```

It simply performs a translation transform to the selected path shape and the dragThumb using the DragDeltaEventArgs' HorizontalOffset and VerticalOffset. In practical operation, you simply click the "Select/Move" toolbar button, double click a shape that you want to drag and move, and hold down your left mouse button. The selected shape will move with your mouse pointer. You can click any white place in canvas1 to deselect the shape.

Zooming and Panning

In this example, we also add zooming and panning features. The zooming is achieved by using a ScaleTransform on the drawing canvas (canvas1) through canvas1's MouseLeftButtonDown event handler. In this way, all the graphics objects on the canvas1 get scaled accordingly. For example, the zoom-in effect can be performed using the following code snippet:

```
......
else if (zoomInCanvas.Tag.ToString() == "Checked")
{
        if (zoomFactor < 1)
            zoomFactor = 1;
        zoomFactor = zoomFactor + 0.1;
        ScaleTransform st = new ScaleTransform();
        st.ScaleX = zoomFactor;
        st.ScaleY = zoomFactor;
        canvas1.RenderTransform = st;
        outCanvas.Width = originalWidth * zoomFactor;
        outCanvas.Height = originalHeight * zoomFactor;
}
......
```

Here, we restrict the zoomFactor ≥ 1. You can alter this limitation as you like. The zoomFactor will increase by 0.1 after each mouse click on the zoom-in toolbar button. The zoomFactor is related to the ScaleTransform, which is in turn attached to the canvas1's RenderTransform. As mentioned previously, we also manually change the outCanvas's size with the same zoomFactor in order to make the ScrollViewer to work properly.

Four panning toolbar buttons allow you to pan the drawing canvas left, right, up, and down. For example, the left-panning is achieved using the following code snippet:

```
else if (panLeftCanvas.Tag.ToString() == "Checked")
{
    panLeftRightOffset = panLeftRightOffset + 20;
    scrollviewer1.ScrollToHorizontalOffset(panLeftRightOffset);
}
```

You can see that each mouse click changes the panning offset by 20 units, which is taken as the input parameters by the ScrollToHorizontalOffset method of the scrollviewer1. By changing the sign of the offset, you can pan the canvas1 left or right. Similarly, the up and down panning is performed by relating the panning offset with the ScrollToVerticalOffset method of the scrollviewer1. For user convenience, we also add a "Back to Original View" button. Clicking on this button brings canvas1 back to its original view, i.e., without zooming or panning.

Based on this example, you can develop a sophisticated 2D drawing program for various Web applications using Silverlight by adding more features. You could easily add more types of shapes, such as polygons, lines, and polylines. You could also easily add features like copy, paste, undo, edit, save, etc. to the program. In this way, you can create a desktop-like application for the Web. By now, you should begin appreciating how powerful Silverlight is!

Hit Testing in Silverlight

In the above interactive 2D drawing example, the user's interaction with the shapes is treated directly using mouse event handlers. However, Silverlight provides a more convenient HitTest method than WPF does. As you probably know, WPF provides hit-testing for visuals through the static VisualTreeHelper.HitTest method, which usually requires you to implement a HitTestCallback method to deal with the hit-testing. On the other hand, Silverlight provides a more direct HitTest method on the UIElement class. This method returns a list of elements that intersect with a Point or Rect. You can use this method to perform collision detection. In developing interactive 2D drawing applications, you can also use it to perform tasks such as dragging, moving, dropping, and deleting shapes more efficiently. In particular, when you design a complex application that contains overlapped elements, this HitTest method allow you to retrieve all of the elements (not just the topmost one) at a specified point, even the elements obscured underneath other elements. You can also find all of the elements that fall within a given area specified by Rect.

In order to use this advanced hit-testing feature, you don't need to create a callback, which is usually required in WPF. The HitTest method in Silverlight will automatically walk through your elements from top to bottom.

The following example shows how to use this new hit-testing feature in Silverlight 2.0. Start with a new Silverlight project and name it Example04-4. In this example, you'll create several rectangle shapes on a Canvas, some of which overlap each other. The program will tell you how many rectangles are hit when the user clicks a point on the rectangles.

Here is the XAML file of this example:

```
<UserControl x:Class="Example04_4.Page"
    xmlns="http://schemas.microsoft.com/client/2007"
    xmlns:x="http://schemas.microsoft.com/winfx/2006/xaml"
    Width="400" Height="300">
    <Grid x:Name="LayoutRoot" Background="White">
        <Border BorderBrush="Gray" BorderThickness="1"
                CornerRadius="10" Margin="10">
            <Canvas x:Name="canvas1"
                    MouseLeftButtonDown="OnMouseLeftButtonDown">
                <Rectangle Canvas.Left="20" Canvas.Top="20"
                           Width="100" Height="60" Stroke="Black"
                           Fill="LightBlue" Opacity="0.5"/>
                <Rectangle Canvas.Left="70" Canvas.Top="50"
                           Width="100" Height="60" Stroke="Black"
                           Fill="LightBlue" Opacity="0.5"/>
                <Rectangle Canvas.Left="150" Canvas.Top="80"
                           Width="100" Height="60" Stroke="Black"
                           Fill="LightBlue" Opacity="0.5"/>
                <Rectangle Canvas.Left="20" Canvas.Top="100"
                           Width="50" Height="50" Stroke="Black"
                           Fill="LightBlue" Opacity="0.5"/>
                <Rectangle Canvas.Left="40" Canvas.Top="60"
                           Width="50" Height="50" Stroke="Black"
                           Fill="LightBlue" Opacity="0.5"/>
                <Rectangle Canvas.Left="30" Canvas.Top="130"
                           Width="50" Height="50" Stroke="Black"
                           Fill="LightBlue" Opacity="0.5"/>
            </Canvas>
        </Border>
    </Grid>
</UserControl>
```

This XAML file adds six rectangles to the Canvas. The hit-testing is performed in code:

```
using System;
using System.Collections.Generic;
using System.Windows;
using System.Windows.Browser;
```

```
using System.Windows.Controls;
using System.Windows.Input;
using System.Windows.Media;
using System.Windows.Media.Animation;
using System.Windows.Shapes;

namespace Example04_4
{
    public partial class Page : UserControl
    {
        public Page()
        {
            InitializeComponent();
            Initialize();
        }

        private void Initialize()
        {
            foreach (Rectangle rect in canvas1.Children)
            {
                rect.Fill = new SolidColorBrush(Color.FromArgb(255, 0, 0, 255));
            }
        }

        private void OnMouseLeftButtonDown(object sender,
                     MouseButtonEventArgs e)
        {
            Initialize();
            Canvas canvas = sender as Canvas;
            int i = 0;
            foreach (UIElement element in canvas.HitTest(e.GetPosition(null)))
            {
                if (element != null)
                {
                    if (element != canvas)
                    {
                        Rectangle rect = (Rectangle)element;
                        rect.Fill = new SolidColorBrush(
                                    Color.FromArgb(255, 255, 100, 0));
                        i++;
                    }
                }
            }
            HtmlPage.Window.Alert("You hit " + i.ToString() + " rectangles.");
        }
    }
}
```

This example looks very simple. In the code-behind file, we perform the hit-testing on the Canvas, which returns all of the elements, including the Canvas itself. Here our purpose is to know how many rectangles are hit at a specified point by a mouse click. When the user clicks on the Canvas, the program starts the hit-testing process using the foreach loop. If it hits any rectangle, that rectangle will change fill color. When the process is finished, the program counts all of the rectangles that are hit. A message with the rectangle count will be displayed by a browser Alert window.

Figure 4-5 shows results of running this example.

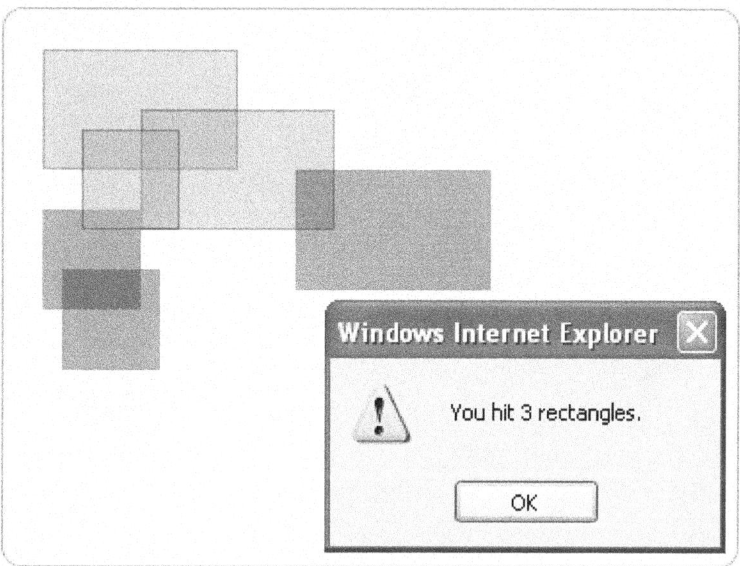

Figure 4-5 Hit Testing in Silverlight.

Chapter 5
Colors and Brushes

Almost everything visible on your computer screen is somehow related to colors and brushes. For example, a brush with a specified color is used to paint the background of a button, the foreground of text, and the fill of a shape. We have used colors and brushes throughout this book, but so far we have done most of the work with the simple SolidColorBrush object. In fact, you can use colors and brushes to paint user interface and graphics objects with anything from simple solid colors to complex sets of patterns and images. This chapter covers the color system used in Silverlight and a variety of brushes, including gradient, image, tile, and visual brushes, as well as brush transformations.

Colors

In Silverlight, a color is specified as a Color structure from the System.Windows.Media namespace. This Color structure describes a color in terms of alpha (A), red (R), green (G), and blue (B) channels. Silverlight uses a color system called sRGB, which is a standard RGB color space created coorperatively by HP and Microsoft for use on monitors, printers, and the Internet. It is designed to match typical home and office viewing conditions. sRGB has found wide applications. Software, LCD displays, digital cameras, printers, and scanners all follow the sRGB standard. For this reason, you can assume that any 8-bit image file or device interface falls in the sRGB color space.

Silverlight allows you to specify a color using sRGB. There are several ways available in Silverlight of creating colors, including:

- An ARGB color value. You specify each value as an integer in the range [0, 255].
- A predefined color name. You choose from the correspondingly named property from the System.Windows.Media.Colors class. There are 15 predefined color names in the Colors class.

Unlike WPF, Silverlight doesn't include a ColorConverter class. This means that you can't convert a color from a hex string. However, it is easy to implement a custom class that allows you to create a color from a hex string. I'll show you how to do it soon in this chapter.

System Colors

In Silverlight, as mentioned previously, a color is represented by a 32-bit structure made up of four components: A, R, G, and B, referred to as sRGB. In the sRGB system, the components' values range from 0 to 255. The alpha component of the color represents transparency, which determines how much a color is blended with the background. An alpha value of zero represents a fully transparent color, while a value of 255 in sRGB represents a fully opaque color.

The following code snippet shows two different ways of specifying a color:

```
Color color = new Color();

// Create a color from an ARGB value:
color = Color.FromArgb(100, 255, 0, 0);

// Create a color using predefined color names:
color = Colors.Red;
```

You can also use a few useful methods on any Color structure to retrieve color information. For example, you can use a predefined color name from the Colors class to obtain corresponding color information, including sRGB values.

Custom Brushes Class

You may notice that WPF has a predefined Brushes class, which allows you to specify a SolidColorBrush directly using the predefined colors. It also implements a ColorConverter class, which allows you to create a color from a hex string in code. These features are very convenient in developing rich-graphics applications, which often require color manipulations.

In this section, I'll show you how these WPF features can be easily implemented in Silverlight. Let's start with a new Silverlight project and name it Example05-1. Add a new Brushes class to the project. We will create various predefined brushes using predefined color names, and also create a brush directly from a hex string.

Here is the code listing of the Brushes class:

```
using System;
using System.Windows;
using System.Windows.Controls;
using System.Windows.Media;

namespace Example05_1
{
    public class Brushes
    {
        public static Brush FromHex(string hex)
        {
            char[] ca = hex.ToCharArray();
            if (ca.Length != 9)
                return null;
            byte a = Convert.ToByte(ca[1].ToString() + ca[2].ToString(), 16);
            byte r = Convert.ToByte(ca[3].ToString() + ca[4].ToString(), 16);
            byte g = Convert.ToByte(ca[5].ToString() + ca[6].ToString(), 16);
            byte b = Convert.ToByte(ca[7].ToString() + ca[8].ToString(), 16);
            return new SolidColorBrush(Color.FromArgb(a, r, g, b));
        }
```

```
public static Brush Red
{
    get { return new SolidColorBrush(Colors.Red); }
}

public static Brush Black
{
    get { return new SolidColorBrush(Colors.Black); }
}

public static Brush Blue
{
    get { return new SolidColorBrush(Colors.Blue); }
}

public static Brush Brown
{
    get { return new SolidColorBrush(Colors.Brown); }
}

public static Brush Cyan
{
    get { return new SolidColorBrush(Colors.Cyan); }
}

public static Brush DarkGray
{
    get { return new SolidColorBrush(Colors.DarkGray); }
}

public static Brush Gray
{
    get { return new SolidColorBrush(Colors.Gray); }
}

public static Brush Green
{
    get { return new SolidColorBrush(Colors.Green); }
}

public static Brush LightGray
{
    get { return new SolidColorBrush(Colors.LightGray); }
}

public static Brush Magenta
{
    get { return new SolidColorBrush(Colors.Magenta); }
}

public static Brush Orange
{
    get { return new SolidColorBrush(Colors.Orange); }
}
```

```
        public static Brush Purple
        {
            get { return new SolidColorBrush(Colors.Purple); }
        }

        public static Brush Transparent
        {
            get { return new SolidColorBrush(Colors.Transparent); }
        }

        public static Brush White
        {
            get { return new SolidColorBrush(Colors.White); }
        }

        public static Brush Yellow
        {
            get { return new SolidColorBrush(Colors.Yellow); }
        }
    }
}
```

Here the brushes are created using public static properties from the predefined color names. The brush from a hex string is defined using a public static method, FromHex. Inside this method, we first convert the hex string to a char array and examine whether the input hex string has the correct length. Then the corresponding sub-strings are converted to the A, R, G, B color components using the ToByte method. Finally, a SolidColorBrush object is returned, which is constructed from these color components.

It is very easy to use the predefined brush in your Silverlight applications. For example, assume that you create a Rectangle object called rect and would like to change its Fill color. You can use the following code snippet to achieve this:

```
rect.Fill = Brushes.FromHex("#33AABBCC");
Rect.Fill = Brushes.Orange;
Rect.Fill = Brushes.Transparent;
```

This is very convenient for creating a brush using the Brushes class. You can add more predefined brushes to the class.

Let's look at an example which puts all of these techniques to work. We'll implement this example in the Example05-1 project. This example allows you to select a color from a ListBox loaded with all of the predefined color names in the Colors class. When you type in the Opacity in a TextBox and select an item from the ListBox, the Fill color of a rectangle is changed accordingly.

Here is the markup of this example:

```
<UserControl x:Class="Example05_1.Page"
    xmlns="http://schemas.microsoft.com/client/2007"
    xmlns:x="http://schemas.microsoft.com/winfx/2006/xaml"
    Width="300" Height="300">
    <Grid x:Name="LayoutRoot" Background="White">
        <Border BorderBrush="Gray" BorderThickness="1"
                CornerRadius="10" Margin="10">
            <Grid>
                <Grid.ColumnDefinitions>
```

```
                    <ColumnDefinition Width="145"/>
                    <ColumnDefinition Width="145"/>
                </Grid.ColumnDefinitions>
                <StackPanel Grid.Column="0" Margin="5">
                    <TextBlock Text ="Select Color" Margin="5,5,5,0"
                               FontSize="12"/>
                    <ListBox x:Name="listBox1"
                             SelectionChanged="listBox1SelectionChanged"
                             Height="100" Margin="5"/>
                    <TextBlock Text="Show selected color:" Margin="5,5,5,0"
                               FontSize="12"/>
                    <Rectangle x:Name="rect1" Stroke="Blue" Fill="AliceBlue"
                               Height="100" Width="122" Margin="5"/>
                </StackPanel>

                <StackPanel Grid.Column="1" Margin="5">
                    <TextBlock Text="Opacity:" Margin="5,5,5,0" FontSize="12"/>
                    <TextBox x:Name="textBox" HorizontalAlignment="Left"
                             TextAlignment="Center" Text="1" Width="50"
                             Margin="5,5,5,8" FontSize="12"/>
                    <TextBlock FontWeight="Bold" Text="sRGB Information:"
                               Margin="5,5,5,2" FontSize="12"/>
                    <TextBlock Name="tbAlpha" Text="Alpha ="
                               Margin="5,0,5,2" FontSize="12"/>
                    <TextBlock Name="tbRed" Text="Red ="
                               Margin="5,0,5,2" FontSize="12"/>
                    <TextBlock Name="tbGreen" Text="Green ="
                               Margin="5,0,5,2" FontSize="12"/>
                    <TextBlock Name="tbBlue" Text="Blue ="
                               Margin="5,0,5,2" FontSize="12"/>
                    <TextBlock Name="tbRGB" Text="ARGB Hex ="
                               Margin="5,0,5,5" FontSize="12"/>
                </StackPanel>
            </Grid>
        </Border>
    </Grid>
</UserControl>
```

The corresponding code-behind file of this example is listed below:

```
using System;
using System.Windows;
using System.Windows.Controls;
using System.Windows.Media;
using System.Reflection;

namespace Example05_1
{
    public partial class Page : UserControl
    {
        private Color color;
        SolidColorBrush colorBrush = new SolidColorBrush();

        public Page()
        {
            InitializeComponent();
```

```
        Type colorsType = typeof(Colors);
        foreach (PropertyInfo property in colorsType.GetProperties())
        {
            listBox1.Items.Add(property.Name);
            color = Colors.Black;
            listBox1.SelectedIndex = 0;
            ColorInfo();
        }
    }

    public void FromString(string color)
    {
        Type colorsType = typeof(Colors);
        foreach (PropertyInfo property in colorsType.GetProperties())
        {
            listBox1.Items.Add(property.Name);
            listBox1.SelectedIndex = 0;
            ColorInfo();
        }
    }

    private void listBox1SelectionChanged(object sender, EventArgs e)
    {

        color = StringToColor(listBox1.SelectedItem.ToString());
        float opacity = Convert.ToSingle(textBox.Text);
        if (opacity > 1.0f)
            opacity = 1.0f;
        else if (opacity < 0.0f)
            opacity = 0.0f;
        color.A = (byte)(opacity * 255);
        ColorInfo();
    }

    private void ColorInfo()
    {
        rect1.Fill = new SolidColorBrush(color);
        tbAlpha.Text = "Alpha = " + color.A.ToString();
        tbRed.Text = "Red = " + color.R.ToString();
        tbGreen.Text = "Green = " + color.G.ToString();
        tbBlue.Text = "Blue = " + color.B.ToString();
        string rgbHex = string.Format("{0:X2}{1:X2}{2:X2}{3:X2}",
                        color.A, color.R, color.G, color.B);
        tbRGB.Text = "ARGB = #" + rgbHex;
    }

    public Color StringToColor(string cString)
    {
        Type cType = (typeof(Colors));
        if (cType.GetProperty(cString) != null)
        {
            object obj = cType.InvokeMember(cString,
                         BindingFlags.GetProperty, null, null, null);
            if (obj != null)
```

```
                return (Color)obj;
            }
            return Colors.Black;
        }
    }
}
```

To put all of the predefined color names from the Colors class into the ListBox, we use the following foreach loop:

```
Type colorsType = typeof(Colors);
foreach (PropertyInfo property in colorsType.GetProperties())
{
    listBox1.Items.Add(property.Name);
    ......
}
```

A using System.Reflection statement is needed to make this loop to work. You simply retrieve the PropertyInfo of the Colors class and place its name into the ListBox.

Since Silverlight doesn't contain a ColorConverter class, in order to convert a color string such as "Black" or "Red" into a Color object, we implement a StringToColor method, which also requires the System.Reflection.

Now, change the Opacity (within the range of 0 to 1) in the TextBox, and select the item from the ListBox. The rectangle's fill color will change correspondingly, and the color information will also be displayed on your screen. Figure 5-1 shows the result of running this example.

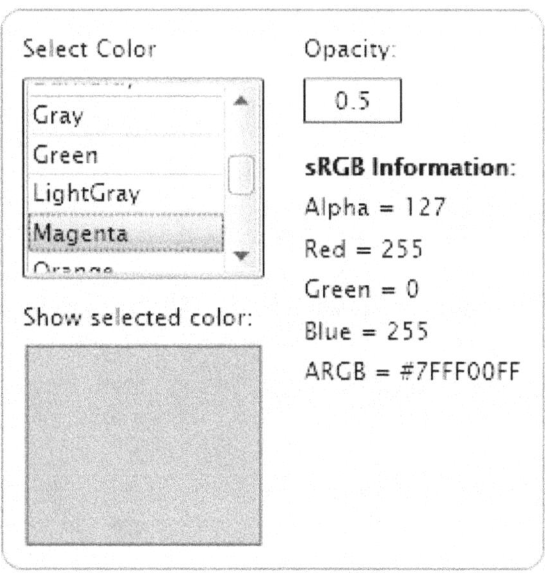

Figure 5-1 Color information in Silverlight.

Brushes

Brushes aren't new to you. You have used brushes throughout this book, but so far you have done most of your work with the simple SolidColorBrush object. However, Silverlight provides a variety of brushes that you can use to create graphically rich applications. A brush is much more than a means of applying color to pixels: it also allows you to paint with color, gradients, images, drawings, etc. A brush with gradients gives you a way to create glass effects or the illusion of depth. Painting with an ImageBrush object provides a means to stretch, tile, or fill an area with a specified bitmap.

In Silverlight, a brush paints an area with its output. Different brushes have different types of output. The following describes the different types of brushes:

- SolidColorBrush – Paints an area with a solid color. The color can have different opacities.
- LinearGradientBrush – Paints an area with a linear gradient fill, a gradually shaded fill that changes from one color to another.
- RadialGradientBrush – Paints an area with a radial gradient fill, which is similar to a linear gradient except that it radiates out in a circular pattern from a center point.
- ImageBrush – Paints an area with an image that can be stretched, scaled, or tiled.

From this list, you can see that a brush can indeed provide output other than simple solid colors. By using different brushes available in Silverlight, you can create interesting effects such as gradient, reflection, and lighting effects, among others.

In the following sections, you will explore each of these brushes and learn how to use them in your Silverlight applications.

SolidColorBrush

The most common brush, and the simplest to use, is the SolidColorBrush. This brush simply paints an area with a solid color. Please note that a brush is different from a color. A brush is an object that tells the system to paint specific pixels with a specified output defined by the brush. A SolidColorBrush paints a color in a specific area of your screen. The output of a SolidColorBrush is the color.

A SolidColorBrush can be defined by simply providing a value for its Color property. As mentioned previously, there are several ways to specify a color, including declaring ARGB values, using hexadecimal strings, and using the predefined color names in the Colors class.

Like the Colors class for colors, Silverlight also provides some handy classes for brushes. The Brushes class, for example, exposes a set of predefined brushes based on solid colors. This provides a shortcut you can use for creating common solid color brushes.

Let's consider an example. Start with a new Silverlight project and name it Example05-2. Add the Brushes class from the previous class to the current project and change its namespace from Example05-1 to Example05-2. In this example, we'll define a SolidColorBrush using different methods. We create the interface and layout using XAML and fill the color of Rectangle shapes in the code-behind file. The following is the XAML and the corresponding C# code of this example:

```
<UserControl x:Class="Example05_2.Page"
    xmlns="http://schemas.microsoft.com/client/2007"
    xmlns:x="http://schemas.microsoft.com/winfx/2006/xaml"
    Width="220" Height="290">
    <Grid x:Name="LayoutRoot" Background="White">
        <Border BorderBrush="Gray" BorderThickness="1"
                CornerRadius="10" Margin="10">
            <StackPanel Margin="10">
                <TextBlock Margin="0,0,0,5" FontSize="12">
                           From predefined brush name:</TextBlock>
                <Rectangle x:Name="rect1" Width="100" Height="30"
                           Stroke="Blue"/>
                <TextBlock Margin="0,10,0,5" FontSize="12">
                           From predefined color name:</TextBlock>
                <Rectangle x:Name="rect2" Width="100" Height="30"
                           Stroke="Blue"/>
                <TextBlock Margin="0,10,0,5" FontSize="12">
                           From ARGB value:</TextBlock>
                <Rectangle x:Name="rect3" Width="100" Height="30"
                           Stroke="Blue"/>
                <TextBlock Margin="0,10,0,5" FontSize="12">
                           From hex string:</TextBlock>
                <Rectangle x:Name="rect4" Width="100" Height="30"
                           Stroke="Blue"/>
            </StackPanel>
        </Border>
    </Grid>
</UserControl>
```

```
using System;
using System.Windows;
using System.Windows.Controls;
using System.Windows.Media;

namespace Example05_2
{
    public partial class Page : UserControl
    {
        public Page()
        {
            InitializeComponent();

            SolidColorBrush brush = new SolidColorBrush();

            // Predefined brush in Brushes Class:
            brush = (SolidColorBrush)Brushes.Red;
            rect1.Fill = brush;

            // From predefined color name in the Colors class:
            brush = new SolidColorBrush(Colors.Green);
            rect2.Fill = brush;

            // From ARGB values in the Color strutcure:
            brush = new SolidColorBrush(Color.FromArgb(100, 0, 0, 255));
            rect3.Fill = brush;
```

```
            // From a hex string:
            brush = (SolidColorBrush)Brushes.FromHex("#CBFFFFAA");
            rect4.Fill = brush;
        }
    }
}
```

In this example, you create four Rectangle shapes and specify their Fill properties using a different SolidColorBrush for each of them. Figure 5-2 shows the results of executing this sample application.

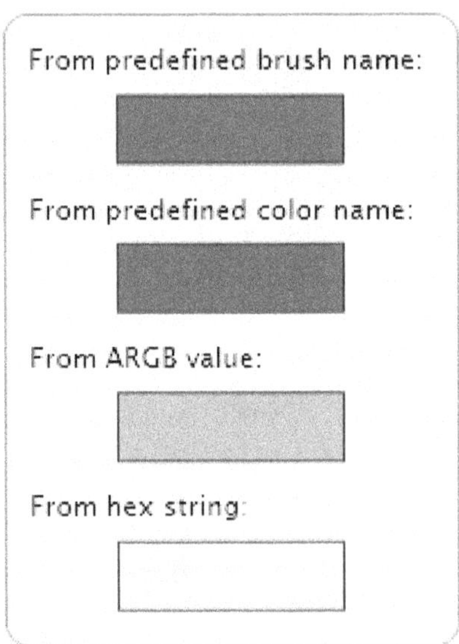

Figure 5-2 Shapes painted using SolidColorBrush.

LinearGradientBrush

The LinearGradientBrush allows you to paint an area with multiple colors, and create a blended fill effect that changes from one color to another.

The LinearGradientBrush follows a linear gradient axis. You can define the direction of the axis to obtain vertical, horizontal, or diagonal gradient effects. The gradient axis is defined by two points, StartPoint and EndPoint. These points map to a one by one matrix. For example, a StartPoint of (0, 0) and an EndPoint of (0, 1) produces a vertical gradient, while a StartPoint of (0, 0) and an EndPoint of (1, 1) generates a diagonal gradient. The StartPoint and EndPoint properties of a LinearGradientBrush let you choose the point where the first color begins to change and the point where the color change ends with the final color. Remember that the coordinates you use for the StartPoint and EndPoint aren't real coordinates. Instead, the LinearGradientBrush assigns the point (0, 0) to the top-left corner and (1, 1) to the bottom-right corner of the area you want to fill, no matter how high and wide it actually is.

Along the axis you specify a series of GradientStop objects, which are points on the axis where you want the colors to blend and transition to other colors. You can define as many GradientStop objects as you need. A GradientStop object has two properties of interest, Color and Offset. The Offset property defines a distance, ranging from 0 to 1, from the start point of the axis from which the color specified in the Color property should begin.

Now, let's look at an example using the LinearGradientBrush. Add a new WPF Window, called LinearGradientBrushExample, to the project Chapter05. Here is the markup of this example:

```
<UserControl x:Class="Example05_3.Page"
    xmlns="http://schemas.microsoft.com/client/2007"
    xmlns:x="http://schemas.microsoft.com/winfx/2006/xaml"
    Width="380" Height="410">
    <Grid x:Name="LayoutRoot" Background="White">
        <Border BorderBrush="Gray" BorderThickness="1"
                CornerRadius="10" Margin="10">
            <Grid Margin="10">
                <Grid.ColumnDefinitions>
                    <ColumnDefinition/>
                    <ColumnDefinition/>
                </Grid.ColumnDefinitions>
                <Grid.RowDefinitions>
                    <RowDefinition Height="Auto"/>
                    <RowDefinition Height="Auto"/>
                    <RowDefinition Height="Auto"/>
                </Grid.RowDefinitions>

                <StackPanel Grid.Column="0" Grid.Row="0">
                    <TextBlock Margin="5" Text="Vertical linear gradient:"
                               FontSize="12"/>
                    <Rectangle Width="100" Height="75" Stroke="Blue">
                        <Rectangle.Fill>
                            <LinearGradientBrush StartPoint="0,0"
                                                 EndPoint="1,0">
                                <GradientStop Color="Blue" Offset="0"/>
                                <GradientStop Color="Yellow" Offset="1"/>
                            </LinearGradientBrush>
                        </Rectangle.Fill>
                    </Rectangle>
                </StackPanel>

                <StackPanel Grid.Column="1" Grid.Row="0">
                    <TextBlock Margin="5" Text="Horizontal linear gradient:"
                               FontSize="12"/>
                    <Rectangle Width="100" Height="75" Stroke="Blue">
                        <Rectangle.Fill>
                            <LinearGradientBrush StartPoint="0,0"
                                                 EndPoint="0,1">
                                <GradientStop Color="Red" Offset="0"/>
                                <GradientStop Color="White" Offset="1"/>
                            </LinearGradientBrush>
                        </Rectangle.Fill>
                    </Rectangle>
                </StackPanel>

                <StackPanel Grid.Column="0" Grid.Row="1">
                    <TextBlock Margin="5,10,5,5" Text="Diagonal linear gradient
                              - with 1 Offset for White" FontSize="12"
                              TextWrapping="Wrap"/>
```

```
    <Rectangle Width="100" Height="75" Stroke="Blue">
        <Rectangle.Fill>
            <LinearGradientBrush StartPoint="0,0"
                                 EndPoint="1,1">
                <GradientStop Color="Green" Offset="0"/>
                <GradientStop Color="White" Offset="1"/>
            </LinearGradientBrush>
        </Rectangle.Fill>
    </Rectangle>
</StackPanel>

<StackPanel Grid.Column="1" Grid.Row="1">
    <TextBlock Margin="5,10,5,5" Text="Diagonal linear gradient
               - with 0.5 Offset for White" FontSize="12"
               TextWrapping="Wrap"/>
    <Rectangle Width="100" Height="75" Stroke="Blue">
        <Rectangle.Fill>
            <LinearGradientBrush StartPoint="0,0"
                                 EndPoint="1,1">
                <GradientStop Color="Green" Offset="0"/>
                <GradientStop Color="White" Offset="0.5"/>
            </LinearGradientBrush>
        </Rectangle.Fill>
    </Rectangle>
</StackPanel>

<StackPanel Grid.Column="0" Grid.Row="2">
    <TextBlock Margin="5,10,5,5" Text="Vertical linear gradient
               - multiple colors" FontSize="12"
               TextWrapping="Wrap"/>
    <Rectangle Width="100" Height="75" Stroke="Blue">
        <Rectangle.Fill>
            <LinearGradientBrush StartPoint="0,0"
                                 EndPoint="1,0">
                <GradientStop Color="Red" Offset="0.3"/>
                <GradientStop Color="Green" Offset="0.5"/>
                <GradientStop Color="Blue" Offset="0.8"/>
            </LinearGradientBrush>
        </Rectangle.Fill>
    </Rectangle>
</StackPanel>

<StackPanel Grid.Column="1" Grid.Row="2">
    <TextBlock Margin="5,10,5,5" Text="Diagonal linear gradient
               - multiple colors" FontSize="12"
               TextWrapping="Wrap"/>
    <Rectangle Width="100" Height="75" Stroke="Blue">
        <Rectangle.Fill>
            <LinearGradientBrush StartPoint="0,0"
                                 EndPoint="1,1">
                <GradientStop Color="Red" Offset="0.2"/>
                <GradientStop Color="Yellow" Offset="0.3"/>
                <GradientStop Color="Coral" Offset="0.4"/>
                <GradientStop Color="Blue" Offset="0.5"/>
                <GradientStop Color="White" Offset="0.6"/>
```

```
                                <GradientStop Color="Green" Offset="0.7"/>
                                <GradientStop Color="Purple" Offset="0.8"/>
                            </LinearGradientBrush>
                        </Rectangle.Fill>
                    </Rectangle>
                </StackPanel>
            </Grid>
        </Border>
    </Grid>
</UserControl>
```

Figure 5-3 illustrates the results of this example.

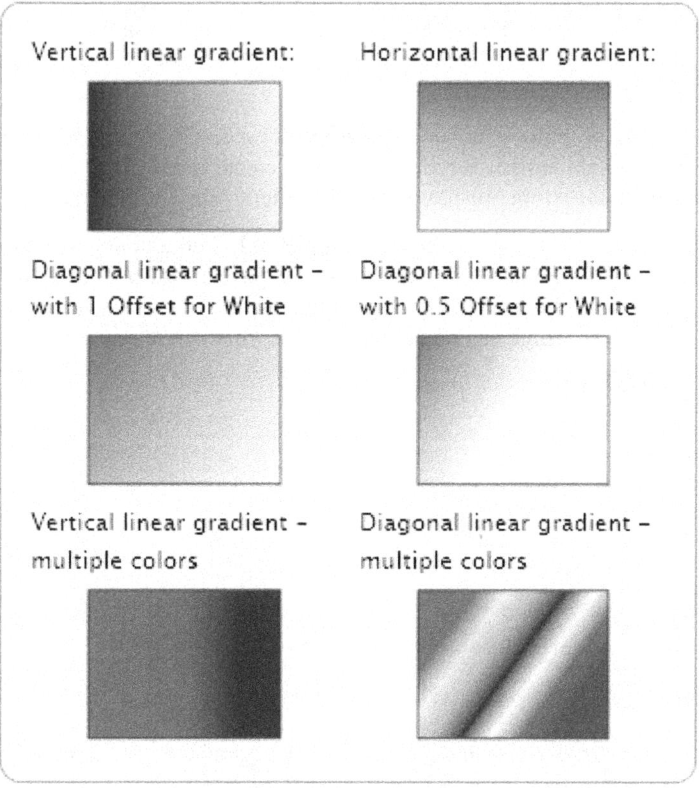

Figure 5-3 Rectangles filled with different linear gradients.

The first rectangle is filled by a LinearGradientBrush with blue and yellow along a vertical gradient axis. The second rectangle is filled by a horizontal gradient brush with red and white colors. Now look at rect3 and rect4. Both rectangles are filled by a diagonal gradient brush with green and white colors. The GradientStop for the green color has an offset of 0, which means that the green color is placed at the very beginning of the gradient. The GradientStop for the white has an offset of 1 for rect3, which places the white color at the end. For rect4, however, the offset of the GradientStop for the white color is set to 0.5, resulting in the much quicker color blend from green (in the top-left corner) to white in the middle (the point between the two corners). It can be seen from Figure 5-3 that the right side of rect4 is almost completely white. The last two rectangles, rect5 and rect6, are filled by a multi-color brush, the first along a vertical gradient axis, and the second along a diagonal gradient axis.

The LinearGradientBrush example presented here is intended to demonstrate the use of the brush's basic features in Silverlight applications. In real-world applications, you may need to create a custom colormap in order to achieve specific visual effects. In next section, I'll show you how to create custom colormaps using the LinearGradientBrush.

Custom Colormap Brush

There is no colormap class in Silverlight, but in some graphics applications, you may need custom color maps to achieve specific visual effects. These color maps are simply tables or lists of colors that are organized in some desired fashion. The UI elements, as well as the shape, surface, and image objects, can be associated with a custom color map.

In many existing CAD and software development tools, many commonly-used color maps have already been defined. Here, I'll show you how to create these colormaps using the LinearGradientBrush object.

Remember that here you simply create some predefined LinearGradientBrush objects: these objects still belong to the LinearGradientBrush type. You don't create a new type of brush itself. If you do want to create a new type of custom brush, you need to inherit from the Brush class.

Start with a new Silverlight project and name it Example05-4. Add a new ColormapBrush class to the project. In this class, you'll implement several custom colormap brushes, each with a special name. These colormaps are commonly used in graphics applications. They can be regarded as predefined LinearGradientBrush objects, which can be directly used in your Silverlight applications.

The following is the code listing of this class:

```
using System;
using System.Windows;
using System.Windows.Controls;
using System.Windows.Input;
using System.Windows.Media;

namespace Example05_4
{
    public class ColormapBrush
    {
        public static LinearGradientBrush Spring()
        {
            LinearGradientBrush brush = new LinearGradientBrush();
            GradientStop stop = new GradientStop();
            stop.Color = Color.FromArgb(255, 255, 0, 255);
            stop.Offset = 0;
            brush.GradientStops.Add(stop);
            stop = new GradientStop();
            stop.Color = Color.FromArgb(255, 255, 255, 0);
            stop.Offset = 1;
            brush.GradientStops.Add(stop);
            brush.Opacity = 1;
            brush.StartPoint = new Point(0, 0);
            brush.EndPoint = new Point(1, 0);
            return brush;
        }
```

```
public static LinearGradientBrush Summer()
{
    LinearGradientBrush brush = new LinearGradientBrush();
    GradientStop stop = new GradientStop();
    stop.Color = Color.FromArgb(255, 0, 128, 90);
    stop.Offset = 0;
    brush.GradientStops.Add(stop);
    stop = new GradientStop();
    stop.Color = Color.FromArgb(255, 255, 255, 90);
    stop.Offset = 1;
    brush.GradientStops.Add(stop);
    brush.Opacity = 1;
    brush.StartPoint = new Point(0, 0);
    brush.EndPoint = new Point(1, 0);
    return brush;
}

public static LinearGradientBrush Autumn()
{
    LinearGradientBrush brush = new LinearGradientBrush();
    GradientStop stop = new GradientStop();
    stop.Color = Color.FromArgb(255, 255, 0, 0);
    stop.Offset = 0;
    brush.GradientStops.Add(stop);
    stop = new GradientStop();
    stop.Color = Color.FromArgb(255, 255, 255, 0);
    stop.Offset = 1;
    brush.GradientStops.Add(stop);
    brush.Opacity = 1;
    brush.StartPoint = new Point(0, 0);
    brush.EndPoint = new Point(1, 0);
    return brush;
}

public static LinearGradientBrush Winter()
{
    LinearGradientBrush brush = new LinearGradientBrush();
    GradientStop stop = new GradientStop();
    stop.Color = Color.FromArgb(255, 0, 0, 255);
    stop.Offset = 0;
    brush.GradientStops.Add(stop);
    stop = new GradientStop();
    stop.Color = Color.FromArgb(255, 0, 255, 128);
    stop.Offset = 1;
    brush.GradientStops.Add(stop);
    brush.Opacity = 1;
    brush.StartPoint = new Point(0, 0);
    brush.EndPoint = new Point(1, 0);
    return brush;
}

public static LinearGradientBrush Hot()
{
    LinearGradientBrush brush = new LinearGradientBrush();
    GradientStop stop = new GradientStop();
```

```
        stop.Color = Color.FromArgb(255, 85, 0, 0);
        stop.Offset = 0;
        brush.GradientStops.Add(stop);
        stop = new GradientStop();
        stop.Color = Color.FromArgb(255, 255, 0, 0);
        stop.Offset = 0.25;
        brush.GradientStops.Add(stop);
        stop = new GradientStop();
        stop.Color = Color.FromArgb(255, 255, 85, 0);
        stop.Offset = 0.375;
        brush.GradientStops.Add(stop);
        stop = new GradientStop();
        stop.Color = Color.FromArgb(255, 255, 255, 0);
        stop.Offset = 0.625;
        brush.GradientStops.Add(stop);
        stop = new GradientStop();
        stop.Color = Color.FromArgb(255, 255, 255, 128);
        stop.Offset = 0.75;
        brush.GradientStops.Add(stop);
        stop = new GradientStop();
        stop.Color = Color.FromArgb(255, 255, 255, 255);
        stop.Offset = 1;
        brush.GradientStops.Add(stop);
        brush.Opacity = 1;
        brush.StartPoint = new Point(0, 0);
        brush.EndPoint = new Point(1, 0);
        return brush;
    }

    public static LinearGradientBrush Cool()
    {
        LinearGradientBrush brush = new LinearGradientBrush();
        GradientStop stop = new GradientStop();
        stop.Color = Color.FromArgb(255, 0, 255, 255);
        stop.Offset = 0;
        brush.GradientStops.Add(stop);
        stop = new GradientStop();
        stop.Color = Color.FromArgb(255, 255, 0, 255);
        stop.Offset = 1;
        brush.GradientStops.Add(stop);
        brush.Opacity = 1;
        brush.StartPoint = new Point(0, 0);
        brush.EndPoint = new Point(1, 0);
        return brush;
    }

    public static LinearGradientBrush Gray()
    {
        LinearGradientBrush brush = new LinearGradientBrush();
        GradientStop stop = new GradientStop();
        stop.Color = Color.FromArgb(255, 0, 0, 0);
        stop.Offset = 0;
        brush.GradientStops.Add(stop);
        stop = new GradientStop();
        stop.Color = Color.FromArgb(255, 255, 255, 255);
```

```
            stop.Offset = 1;
            brush.GradientStops.Add(stop);
            brush.Opacity = 1;
            brush.StartPoint = new Point(0, 0);
            brush.EndPoint = new Point(1, 0);
            return brush;
        }

        public static LinearGradientBrush Jet()
        {
            LinearGradientBrush brush = new LinearGradientBrush();
            GradientStop stop = new GradientStop();
            stop.Color = Color.FromArgb(255, 0, 0, 255);
            stop.Offset = 0;
            brush.GradientStops.Add(stop);
            stop = new GradientStop();
            stop.Color = Color.FromArgb(255, 0, 128, 255);
            stop.Offset = 0.143;
            brush.GradientStops.Add(stop);
            stop = new GradientStop();
            stop.Color = Color.FromArgb(255, 0, 255, 255);
            stop.Offset = 0.286;
            brush.GradientStops.Add(stop);
            stop = new GradientStop();
            stop.Color = Color.FromArgb(255, 128, 255, 128);
            stop.Offset = 0.429;
            brush.GradientStops.Add(stop);
            stop = new GradientStop();
            stop.Color = Color.FromArgb(255, 255, 255, 0);
            stop.Offset = 0.571;
            brush.GradientStops.Add(stop);
            stop = new GradientStop();
            stop.Color = Color.FromArgb(255, 255, 128, 0);
            stop.Offset = 0.714;
            brush.GradientStops.Add(stop);
            stop = new GradientStop();
            stop.Color = Color.FromArgb(255, 255, 0, 0);
            stop.Offset = 0.857;
            brush.GradientStops.Add(stop);
            stop = new GradientStop();
            stop.Color = Color.FromArgb(255, 128, 0, 0);
            stop.Offset = 1;
            brush.GradientStops.Add(stop);
            brush.Opacity = 1;
            brush.StartPoint = new Point(0, 0);
            brush.EndPoint = new Point(1, 0);
            return brush;
        }
    }
}
```

This class includes several public static methods that define different LinearGradientBrush objects. Inside each of these methods, we create a specific GradientStops collection that represents a colormap. Each method also defines three default properties: StartPoint, EndPoint, and Opacity. The default values of StartPoint = (0, 0) and EndPoint = (1, 0) define a vertical gradient brush. You can change these Point properties if you want to use a different gradient axis.

The Opacity property is used to define the alpha channel of a color. The default value of the Opacity is 1, corresponding to a completely opaque color. In this class, the color is defined using an ARGB value. The custom colormap brushes are created with different colors, each one with a different number of GradientStops and Offsets.

Now, I'll show you how to use these colormap brushes in a Silverlight application. In the following Example05-4 project, you'll first create several rectangles and fill their colors using different ColormapBrush objects. Then, you'll draw some math functions using the ColormapBrush. Here is the markup of this example:

```
<UserControl x:Class="Example05_4.Page"
    xmlns="http://schemas.microsoft.com/client/2007"
    xmlns:x="http://schemas.microsoft.com/winfx/2006/xaml"
    Width="350" Height="500">
    <Grid x:Name="LayoutRoot" Background="White">
        <Border BorderBrush="Gray" BorderThickness="1"
                CornerRadius="10" Margin="10">
            <StackPanel Margin="10">
                <TextBlock Margin="10,5,5,0" Text="Rectangles filled with
                           ColormapBrush:" FontSize="12"/>
                <Rectangle x:Name="rect1" Width="280" Height="30"
                           Stroke="Blue" Margin="0,0,0,5"/>
                <Rectangle x:Name="rect2" Width="280" Height="30"
                           Stroke="Blue" Margin="0,0,0,5"/>
                <Rectangle x:Name="rect3" Width="280" Height="30"
                           Stroke="Blue" Margin="0,0,0,5"/>
                <Rectangle x:Name="rect4" Width="280" Height="30"
                           Stroke="Blue" Margin="0,0,0,5"/>
                <Rectangle x:Name="rect5" Width="280" Height="30"
                           Stroke="Blue" Margin="0,0,0,5"/>
                <Rectangle x:Name="rect6" Width="280" Height="30"
                           Stroke="Blue" Margin="0,0,0,5"/>
                <Rectangle x:Name="rect7" Width="280" Height="30"
                           Stroke="Blue" Margin="0,0,0,5"/>
                <Rectangle x:Name="rect8" Width="280" Height="30"
                           Stroke="Blue" Margin="0,0,0,10"/>
                <TextBlock Margin="10,5,5,-5" Text="Sine and Cosine
                           curve painted using colormap:" FontSize="12"/>
                <Canvas x:Name="canvas1"/>
            </StackPanel>
        </Border>
    </Grid>
</UserControl>
```

The corresponding C# code is listed below:

```
using System;
using System.Windows;
using System.Windows.Controls;
using System.Windows.Media;
using System.Windows.Shapes;

namespace Example05_4
```

```
{
    public partial class Page : UserControl
    {
        public Page()
        {
            InitializeComponent();
            FillRectangles();
            AddMathFunction();
        }

        private void FillRectangles()
        {
            // Fill rect1 with "Spring" colormap:
            rect1.Fill = ColormapBrush.Spring();

            // Fill rect2 with "Summer" colormap:
            rect2.Fill = ColormapBrush.Summer();

            // Fill rect3 with "Autumn" colormap:
            rect3.Fill = ColormapBrush.Autumn();

            // Fill rect4 with "Winter" colormap:
            rect4.Fill = ColormapBrush.Winter();

            // Fill rect5 with "Jet" colormap:
            rect5.Fill = ColormapBrush.Jet();

            // Fill rect6 with "Gray" colormap:
            rect6.Fill = ColormapBrush.Gray();

            // Fill rect7 with "Hot" colormap:
            rect7.Fill = ColormapBrush.Hot();

            // Fill rect8 with "Cool" colormap:
            rect8.Fill = ColormapBrush.Cool();
        }

        private void AddMathFunction()
        {
            // Create a cosine curve:
            LinearGradientBrush brush = ColormapBrush.Spring();
            brush.StartPoint = new Point(0, 0);
            brush.EndPoint = new Point(0, 1);

            Polyline line1 = new Polyline();
            for (int i = 0; i < 250; i++)
            {
                double x = i;
                double y = 70 + 50 * Math.Sin(x / 4.0 / Math.PI);
                line1.Points.Add(new Point(x, y));
            }
            line1.Stroke = brush;
            line1.StrokeThickness = 5;
            Canvas.SetLeft(line1, 20);
            canvas1.Children.Add(line1);
```

```
            // Create a cosine curve:
            brush = ColormapBrush.Jet();
            brush.StartPoint = new Point(0, 1);
            brush.EndPoint = new Point(0, 0);
            line1 = new Polyline();
            for (int i = 0; i < 250; i++)
            {
                double x = i;
                double y = 70 + 50 * Math.Cos(x / 4.0 / Math.PI);
                line1.Points.Add(new Point(x, y));
            }
            line1.Stroke = brush;
            line1.StrokeThickness = 5;
            Canvas.SetLeft(line1, 20);
            canvas1.Children.Add(line1);
        }
    }
}
```

This example produces the output shown in Figure 5-4.

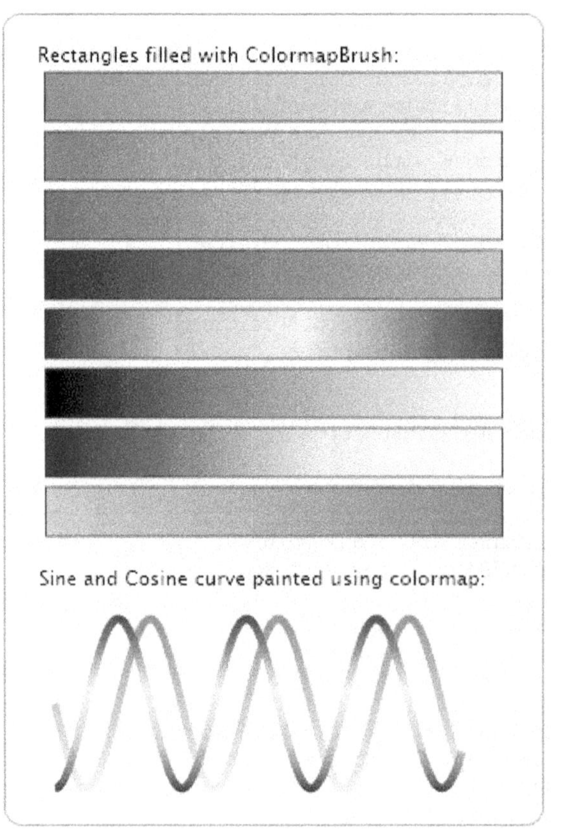

Figure 5-4 Rectangles and curves drawn using ColormapBrush objects.

Here, the default vertical colormap brush is used to paint the rectangles. You simply set the Fill property of rectangles to the corresponding method of the ColormapBrush class. For the Sine and Cosine curves, you create a new LinearGradientBrush object called brush, which is attached to a static method of the ColormapBrush. Then, you override the default properties by changing the StartPoint and EndPoint properties to define a horizontal gradient axis. You should notice that if you exchange the StartPoint and the EndPoint, you'll reverse the colormap.

Following the procedure presented here, you can easily add your own colormaps to the ColormapBrush class.

RadialGradientBrush

RadialGradientBrush works in a similar way to the LinearGradientBrush. Like the LinearGradientBrush, it takes a sequence of colors with different offsets, but differs in that it blends colors in a radial pattern. A radial gradient is defined as a circle. The axis of the RadialGradientBrush starts from the origin, which you specify using its GradientOrigin, and runs to the outer edge of the circle.

You can set the edge of the gradient circle using three properties: Center, RadiusX, and RadiusY. By default, the Center property is at (0.5, 0.5), which places the center of the circle in the middle of your fill region and in the same position as the gradient origin.

Let's take a look at an example to see how the RadialGradientBrush works. Start with a new Silverlight Project and name it Example05-5. Here is the XAML file of this example:

```
<UserControl x:Class="Example05_5.Page"
    xmlns="http://schemas.microsoft.com/client/2007"
    xmlns:x="http://schemas.microsoft.com/winfx/2006/xaml"
    Width="410" Height="340">
    <Grid x:Name="LayoutRoot" Background="White">
        <Border BorderBrush="Gray" BorderThickness="1"
                CornerRadius="10" Margin="10">
            <StackPanel>
                <StackPanel Orientation="Horizontal">
                    <StackPanel Margin="10">
                        <TextBlock Text="ellipse1" Margin="30,5,5,5"
                                   FontSize="12"/>
                        <Ellipse x:Name="ellipse1" Stroke="Blue"
                                 Width="100" Height="100" Margin="5">
                            <Ellipse.Fill>
                                <RadialGradientBrush GradientOrigin="0.5,0.5"
                                    Center="0.5,0.5" RadiusX="1" RadiusY="1">
                                    <GradientStop Color="Red" Offset="0" />
                                    <GradientStop Color="Yellow" Offset="0.3" />
                                    <GradientStop Color="Green" Offset="0.6" />
                                </RadialGradientBrush>
                            </Ellipse.Fill>
                        </Ellipse>
                    </StackPanel>

                    <StackPanel Margin="10">
                        <TextBlock Text="ellipse2" Margin="30,5,5,5"
                                   FontSize="12"/>
                        <Ellipse x:Name="ellipse2" Stroke="Blue" Width="100"
```

```
                        Height="100" Margin="5">
                    <Ellipse.Fill>
                        <RadialGradientBrush GradientOrigin="0.5,0.5"
                            Center="0,0" RadiusX="1" RadiusY="1">
                            <GradientStop Color="Red" Offset="0" />
                            <GradientStop Color="Yellow" Offset="0.3" />
                            <GradientStop Color="Green" Offset="0.6" />
                        </RadialGradientBrush>
                    </Ellipse.Fill>
                </Ellipse>
            </StackPanel>

            <StackPanel Margin="10">
                <TextBlock Text="ellipse3" Margin="30,5,5,5"
                           FontSize="12"/>
                <Ellipse x:Name="ellipse3" Stroke="Blue" Width="100"
                         Height="100" Margin="5">
                    <Ellipse.Fill>
                        <RadialGradientBrush GradientOrigin="0.5,0.5"
                           Center="0.5,0.5" RadiusX="0.5" RadiusY="0.5">
                            <GradientStop Color="Red" Offset="0" />
                            <GradientStop Color="Yellow" Offset="0.3" />
                            <GradientStop Color="Green" Offset="0.6" />
                        </RadialGradientBrush>
                    </Ellipse.Fill>
                </Ellipse>
            </StackPanel>
        </StackPanel>

        <StackPanel Orientation="Horizontal">
            <StackPanel Margin="10">
                <TextBlock Text="ellipse4" Margin="30,5,5,5"
                           FontSize="12"/>
                <Ellipse x:Name="ellipse4" Stroke="Blue" Width="100"
                         Height="100" Margin="5">
                    <Ellipse.Fill>
                        <RadialGradientBrush GradientOrigin="0.5,0.5"
                            Center="0,0" RadiusX="0.5" RadiusY="0.5">
                            <GradientStop Color="Red" Offset="0" />
                            <GradientStop Color="Yellow" Offset="0.3" />
                            <GradientStop Color="Green" Offset="0.6" />
                        </RadialGradientBrush>
                    </Ellipse.Fill>
                </Ellipse>
            </StackPanel>

            <StackPanel Margin="10">
                <TextBlock Text="ellipse5" Margin="30,5,5,5"
                           FontSize="12"/>
                <Ellipse x:Name="ellipse5" Stroke="Blue" Width="100"
                         Height="100" Margin="5">
                    <Ellipse.Fill>
                        <RadialGradientBrush GradientOrigin="0.5,0.5"
                            Center="0.5,0.5" RadiusX="1" RadiusY="0.5">
                            <GradientStop Color="Red" Offset="0" />
```

```
                        <GradientStop Color="Yellow" Offset="0.3" />
                        <GradientStop Color="Green" Offset="0.6" />
                    </RadialGradientBrush>
                </Ellipse.Fill>
            </Ellipse>
        </StackPanel>

        <StackPanel Margin="10">
            <TextBlock Text="ellipse6" Margin="30,5,5,5"
                       FontSize="12"/>
            <Ellipse x:Name="ellipse6" Stroke="Blue" Width="100"
                     Height="100" Margin="5">
                <Ellipse.Fill>
                    <RadialGradientBrush GradientOrigin="0.5,0.5"
                        Center="0.5,0.5" RadiusX="0.5" RadiusY="1">
                        <GradientStop Color="Red" Offset="0" />
                        <GradientStop Color="Yellow" Offset="0.3" />
                        <GradientStop Color="Green" Offset="0.6" />
                    </RadialGradientBrush>
                </Ellipse.Fill>
            </Ellipse>
        </StackPanel>
    </StackPanel>
</StackPanel>
</Border>
</Grid>
</UserControl>
```

This XAML file create six circles using the Ellipse shape class. The first two circles are filled using a RadialGradientBrush with a RadiusX = 1 and RadiusY = 1. The difference is that the brush for the first circle has a Center at (0.5, 0.5), which is the same as its GradientOrigin of (0.5, 0.5), while the brush for the second circle has a Center at (0, 0), which isn't lined up with its GradientOrigin of (0.5, 0.5). Ellipse3 and ellipse4 have Fill properties similar to the first two shapes, except that they have smaller RadiusX and RadiusY. The last two circles have different RadiusX and RadiusY properties, which turns the gradient into an ellipse instead of a circle.

Figure 5-5 illustrates the results of running this example.

Custom Radial Colormap Brush

Like the ColormapBrush for the custom predefined LinearGradientBrush, you can also create a ColormapRadialBrush for the predefined RadialGradientBrush. This custom defined radial brush may be useful when you want to create some special radial visual effects.

Let's start with a new Silverlight project and name it Example05-6. Add a new class, called ColormapRadialBrush, to the current project. Implement the following C# code for this class:

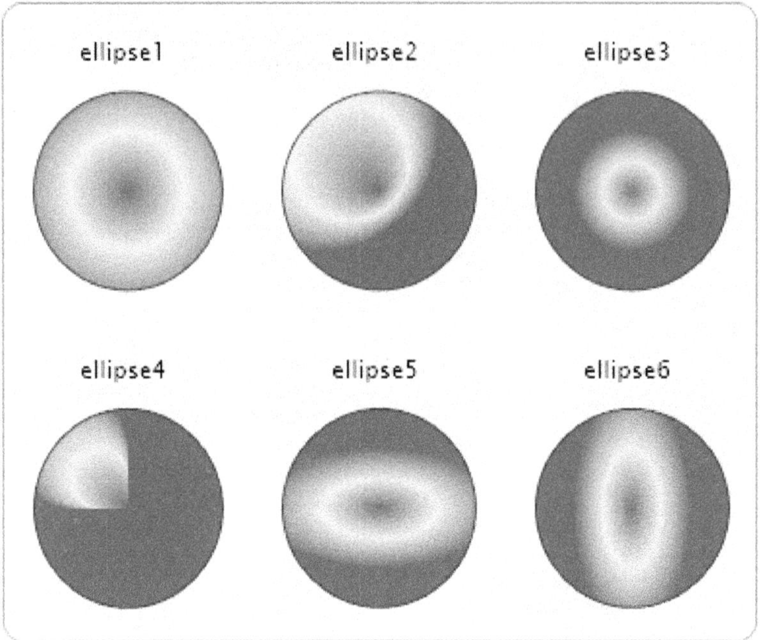

Figure 5-5 Shapes filled using RadialGradientBrush objects.

```
using System;
using System.Windows;
using System.Windows.Controls;
using System.Windows.Media;
using System.Windows.Shapes;

namespace Example05_6
{
    public class ColormapRadialBrush
    {
        public static RadialGradientBrush Spring()
        {
            RadialGradientBrush brush = new RadialGradientBrush();
            GradientStop stop = new GradientStop();
            stop.Color = Color.FromArgb(255, 255, 0, 255);
            stop.Offset = 0;
            brush.GradientStops.Add(stop);
            stop = new GradientStop();
            stop.Color = Color.FromArgb(255, 255, 255, 0);
            stop.Offset = 1;
            brush.GradientStops.Add(stop);

            brush.Center = new Point(0.5, 0.5);
            brush.GradientOrigin = new Point(0.5, 0.5);
            brush.RadiusX = 0.5;
            brush.RadiusY = 0.5;
            brush.Opacity = 1;
            return brush;
        }
```

```
public static RadialGradientBrush Summer()
{
    RadialGradientBrush brush = new RadialGradientBrush();
    GradientStop stop = new GradientStop();
    stop.Color = Color.FromArgb(255, 0, 128, 90);
    stop.Offset = 0;
    brush.GradientStops.Add(stop);
    stop = new GradientStop();
    stop.Color = Color.FromArgb(255, 255, 255, 90);
    stop.Offset = 1;
    brush.GradientStops.Add(stop);
    brush.Center = new Point(0.5, 0.5);
    brush.GradientOrigin = new Point(0.5, 0.5);
    brush.RadiusX = 0.5;
    brush.RadiusY = 0.5;
    brush.Opacity = 1;
    return brush;
}
public static RadialGradientBrush Autumn()
{
    RadialGradientBrush brush = new RadialGradientBrush();
    GradientStop stop = new GradientStop();
    stop.Color = Color.FromArgb(255, 255, 0, 0);
    stop.Offset = 0;
    brush.GradientStops.Add(stop);
    stop = new GradientStop();
    stop.Color = Color.FromArgb(255, 255, 255, 0);
    stop.Offset = 1;
    brush.GradientStops.Add(stop);
    brush.Center = new Point(0.5, 0.5);
    brush.GradientOrigin = new Point(0.5, 0.5);
    brush.RadiusX = 0.5;
    brush.RadiusY = 0.5;
    brush.Opacity = 1;
    return brush;
}
public static RadialGradientBrush Winter()
{
    RadialGradientBrush brush = new RadialGradientBrush();
    GradientStop stop = new GradientStop();
    stop.Color = Color.FromArgb(255, 0, 0, 255);
    stop.Offset = 0;
    brush.GradientStops.Add(stop);
    stop = new GradientStop();
    stop.Color = Color.FromArgb(255, 0, 255, 128);
    stop.Offset = 1;
    brush.GradientStops.Add(stop);
    brush.Center = new Point(0.5, 0.5);
    brush.GradientOrigin = new Point(0.5, 0.5);
    brush.RadiusX = 0.5;
    brush.RadiusY = 0.5;
    brush.Opacity = 1;
    return brush;
}
```

```
public static RadialGradientBrush Hot()
{
    RadialGradientBrush brush = new RadialGradientBrush();
    GradientStop stop = new GradientStop();
    stop.Color = Color.FromArgb(255, 85, 0, 0);
    stop.Offset = 0;
    brush.GradientStops.Add(stop);
    stop = new GradientStop();
    stop.Color = Color.FromArgb(255, 255, 0, 0);
    stop.Offset = 0.25;
    brush.GradientStops.Add(stop);
    stop = new GradientStop();
    stop.Color = Color.FromArgb(255, 255, 85, 0);
    stop.Offset = 0.375;
    brush.GradientStops.Add(stop);
    stop = new GradientStop();
    stop.Color = Color.FromArgb(255, 255, 255, 0);
    stop.Offset = 0.625;
    brush.GradientStops.Add(stop);
    stop = new GradientStop();
    stop.Color = Color.FromArgb(255, 255, 255, 128);
    stop.Offset = 0.75;
    brush.GradientStops.Add(stop);
    stop = new GradientStop();
    stop.Color = Color.FromArgb(255, 255, 255, 255);
    stop.Offset = 1;
    brush.GradientStops.Add(stop);
    brush.Center = new Point(0.5, 0.5);
    brush.GradientOrigin = new Point(0.5, 0.5);
    brush.RadiusX = 0.5;
    brush.RadiusY = 0.5;
    brush.Opacity = 1;
    return brush;
}

public static RadialGradientBrush Cool()
{
    RadialGradientBrush brush = new RadialGradientBrush();
    GradientStop stop = new GradientStop();
    stop.Color = Color.FromArgb(255, 0, 255, 255);
    stop.Offset = 0;
    brush.GradientStops.Add(stop);
    stop = new GradientStop();
    stop.Color = Color.FromArgb(255, 255, 0, 255);
    stop.Offset = 1;
    brush.GradientStops.Add(stop);
    brush.Center = new Point(0.5, 0.5);
    brush.GradientOrigin = new Point(0.5, 0.5);
    brush.RadiusX = 0.5;
    brush.RadiusY = 0.5;
    brush.Opacity = 1;
    return brush;
}
```

```
public static RadialGradientBrush Gray()
{
    RadialGradientBrush brush = new RadialGradientBrush();
    GradientStop stop = new GradientStop();
    stop.Color = Color.FromArgb(255, 0, 0, 0);
    stop.Offset = 0;
    brush.GradientStops.Add(stop);
    stop = new GradientStop();
    stop.Color = Color.FromArgb(255, 255, 255, 255);
    stop.Offset = 1;
    brush.GradientStops.Add(stop);
    brush.Center = new Point(0.5, 0.5);
    brush.GradientOrigin = new Point(0.5, 0.5);
    brush.RadiusX = 0.5;
    brush.RadiusY = 0.5;
    brush.Opacity = 1;
    return brush;
}

public static RadialGradientBrush Jet()
{
    RadialGradientBrush brush = new RadialGradientBrush();
    GradientStop stop = new GradientStop();
    stop.Color = Color.FromArgb(255, 0, 0, 255);
    stop.Offset = 0;
    brush.GradientStops.Add(stop);
    stop = new GradientStop();
    stop.Color = Color.FromArgb(255, 0, 128, 255);
    stop.Offset = 0.143;
    brush.GradientStops.Add(stop);
    stop = new GradientStop();
    stop.Color = Color.FromArgb(255, 0, 255, 255);
    stop.Offset = 0.286;
    brush.GradientStops.Add(stop);
    stop = new GradientStop();
    stop.Color = Color.FromArgb(255, 128, 255, 128);
    stop.Offset = 0.429;
    brush.GradientStops.Add(stop);
    stop = new GradientStop();
    stop.Color = Color.FromArgb(255, 255, 255, 0);
    stop.Offset = 0.571;
    brush.GradientStops.Add(stop);
    stop = new GradientStop();
    stop.Color = Color.FromArgb(255, 255, 128, 0);
    stop.Offset = 0.714;
    brush.GradientStops.Add(stop);
    stop = new GradientStop();
    stop.Color = Color.FromArgb(255, 255, 0, 0);
    stop.Offset = 0.857;
    brush.GradientStops.Add(stop);
    stop = new GradientStop();
    stop.Color = Color.FromArgb(255, 128, 0, 0);
    stop.Offset = 1;
    brush.GradientStops.Add(stop);
    brush.Center = new Point(0.5, 0.5);
```

```
                brush.GradientOrigin = new Point(0.5, 0.5);
                brush.RadiusX = 0.5;
                brush.RadiusY = 0.5;
                brush.Opacity = 1;
                return brush;
            }
        }
    }
```

This class includes several public static methods that define different RadialGradientBrush objects. Inside each of these methods, we create a specific GradientStops collection that represents a colormap. Each method also defines three default properties: Center, GradientOrigin, RadiusX, RadiusY, and Opacity. These properties are used to specify the corresponding properties of RadialGradientBrush. The default values of these properties remain the same as those of the RadialGradientBrush. These default properties can be overridden depending on your application's requirements. In this class, color is defined using ARGB values. The custom colormap brushes are created with different colors, each one with a different number of GradientStops and Offsets.

Now, let's consider an example that shows you how to use these radial colormap brushes in a Silverlight application. We'll implement this example in project Example05-6. In this example, you'll create several circles and specify their Fill properties using different ColormapRadialBrush objects. Here is the XAML file of this example:

```
<UserControl x:Class="Example05_6.Page"
    xmlns="http://schemas.microsoft.com/client/2007"
    xmlns:x="http://schemas.microsoft.com/winfx/2006/xaml"
    Width="450" Height="290">
    <Grid x:Name="LayoutRoot" Background="White">
        <Border Margin="10" BorderBrush="Gray"
                BorderThickness="1" CornerRadius="10">
            <Grid>
                <Grid.ColumnDefinitions>
                    <ColumnDefinition/>
                    <ColumnDefinition/>
                    <ColumnDefinition/>
                    <ColumnDefinition/>
                </Grid.ColumnDefinitions>
                <Grid.RowDefinitions>
                    <RowDefinition/>
                    <RowDefinition/>
                </Grid.RowDefinitions>

                <StackPanel Margin="2,5,2,2" Grid.Column="0" Grid.Row="0">
                    <TextBlock Text="Spring" Margin="30,0,0,0" FontSize="12"/>
                    <Ellipse x:Name="ellipse1" Stroke="Blue" Width="90"
                             Height="90" Margin="5"/>
                </StackPanel>

                <StackPanel Margin="2,5,2,2" Grid.Column="1" Grid.Row="0">
                    <TextBlock Text="Summer" Margin="30,0,0,0" FontSize="12"/>
                    <Ellipse x:Name="ellipse2" Stroke="Blue" Width="90"
                             Height="90" Margin="5"/>
                </StackPanel>

                <StackPanel Margin="2,5,2,2" Grid.Column="2" Grid.Row="0">
```

```
                <TextBlock Text="Autumn" Margin="30,0,0,0" FontSize="12"/>
                <Ellipse x:Name="ellipse3" Stroke="Blue" Width="90"
                         Height="90" Margin="5"/>
            </StackPanel>

            <StackPanel Margin="2,5,2,2" Grid.Column="3" Grid.Row="0">
                <TextBlock Text="Winter" Margin="30,0,0,0" FontSize="12"/>
                <Ellipse x:Name="ellipse4" Stroke="Blue" Width="90"
                         Height="90" Margin="5"/>
            </StackPanel>

            <StackPanel Margin="2,5,2,2" Grid.Column="0" Grid.Row="1">
                <TextBlock Text="Jet" Margin="40,0,0,0" FontSize="12"/>
                <Ellipse x:Name="ellipse5" Stroke="Blue" Width="90"
                         Height="90" Margin="5"/>
            </StackPanel>

            <StackPanel Margin="2,5,2,2" Grid.Column="1" Grid.Row="1">
                <TextBlock Text="Gray" Margin="38,0,0,0" FontSize="12"/>
                <Ellipse x:Name="ellipse6" Stroke="Blue" Width="90"
                         Height="90" Margin="5"/>
            </StackPanel>

            <StackPanel Margin="2,5,2,2" Grid.Column="2" Grid.Row="1">
                <TextBlock Text="Hot" Margin="40,0,0,0" FontSize="12"/>
                <Ellipse x:Name="ellipse7" Stroke="Blue" Width="90"
                         Height="90" Margin="5"/>
            </StackPanel>

            <StackPanel Margin="2,5,2,2" Grid.Column="3" Grid.Row="1">
                <TextBlock Text="Cool" Margin="38,0,0,0" FontSize="12"/>
                <Ellipse x:Name="ellipse8" Stroke="Blue" Width="90"
                         Height="90" Margin="5"/>
            </StackPanel>
        </Grid>
    </Border>
  </Grid>
</UserControl>
```

The corresponding code-behind file of this example is listed below:

```
using System;
using System.Windows;
using System.Windows.Controls;
using System.Windows.Media;
using System.Windows.Shapes;

namespace Example05_6
{
    public partial class Page : UserControl
    {
        public Page()
        {
            InitializeComponent();
            FillEllipses();
        }
```

```
            private void FillEllipses()
            {
                // Fill ellipse1 with "Spring" colormap:
                ellipse1.Fill = ColormapRadialBrush.Spring();

                // Fill ellipse2 with "Summer" colormap:
                ellipse2.Fill = ColormapRadialBrush.Summer();

                // Fill ellipse3 with "Autumn" colormap:
                ellipse3.Fill = ColormapRadialBrush.Autumn();

                // Fill ellipse4 with "Winter" colormap:
                ellipse4.Fill = ColormapRadialBrush.Winter();

                // Fill ellipse5 with "Jet" colormap:
                ellipse5.Fill = ColormapRadialBrush.Jet();

                // Fill ellipse6 with "Gray" colormap:
                ellipse6.Fill = ColormapRadialBrush.Gray();

                // Fill ellipse7 with "Hot" colormap:
                ellipse7.Fill = ColormapRadialBrush.Hot();

                // Fill ellipse8 with "Cool" colormap:
                ellipse8.Fill = ColormapRadialBrush.Cool();
            }
        }
    }
```

You can see from the above code that the default radial colormap brush is used to fill the circles. You simply set the Fill property of the circles to the corresponding static method in the ColormapRadialBrush. Figure 5-6 shows the results of this example.

ImageBrush

ImageBrush is used to paint an area with an ImageSource. Currently, Silverlight 2.0 only supports two image formats: png and jpg. It doesn't support the most commonly used formats such as bmp and gif. Hopefully a future version of Silverlight will support more image formats. Thus, the ImageSource can only contain png and jpg image file types. You simply specify the image you want to use by setting the ImageSource property.

The following example shows you how to specify an image to be used in the Fill property of Rectangle objects. Start with a new Silverlight project and name it Example05-7. Here is the XAML file of this example:

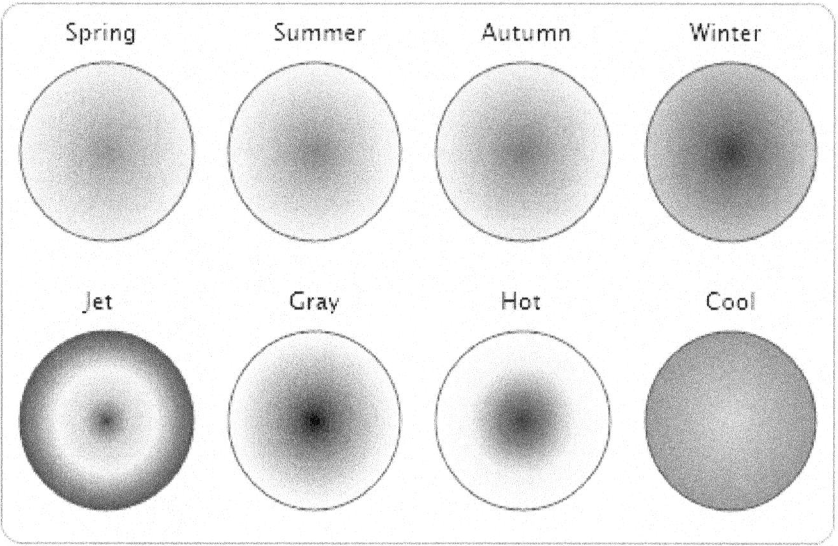

Figure 5-6 Circles painted using ColormapRadialBrush objects.

```
<UserControl x:Class="Example05_7.Page"
    xmlns="http://schemas.microsoft.com/client/2007"
    xmlns:x="http://schemas.microsoft.com/winfx/2006/xaml"
    Width="340" Height="310">
    <Grid x:Name="LayoutRoot" Background="White">
        <Border BorderBrush="Gray" BorderThickness="1"
                CornerRadius="10" Margin="10">
            <Grid>
                <Grid.ColumnDefinitions>
                    <ColumnDefinition/>
                    <ColumnDefinition/>
                </Grid.ColumnDefinitions>
                <Grid.RowDefinitions>
                    <RowDefinition/>
                    <RowDefinition/>
                </Grid.RowDefinitions>

                <StackPanel Margin="5" Grid.Column="0" Grid.Row="0">
                    <TextBlock Margin="5" Text="Stretch = None" FontSize="12"/>
                    <Rectangle Width="135" Height="100" Stroke="DarkBlue">
                        <Rectangle.Fill>
                            <ImageBrush ImageSource="ImageFile.jpg"
                                        Stretch="None"/>
                    </Rectangle.Fill>
                    </Rectangle>
                </StackPanel>

                <StackPanel Margin="5" Grid.Column="1" Grid.Row="0">
                    <TextBlock Margin="5" Text="Stretch = Fill" FontSize="12"/>
                    <Rectangle Width="135" Height="100" Stroke="DarkBlue">
                        <Rectangle.Fill>
                            <ImageBrush ImageSource="ImageFile.jpg"
                                        Stretch="Fill"/>
```

```
                    </Rectangle.Fill>
                </Rectangle>
            </StackPanel>

            <StackPanel Margin="5" Grid.Column="0" Grid.Row="1">
                <TextBlock Margin="5" Text="Stretch = Uniform"
                           FontSize="12"/>
                <Rectangle Width="135" Height="100" Stroke="DarkBlue">
                    <Rectangle.Fill>
                        <ImageBrush ImageSource="ImageFile.jpg"
                                    Stretch="Uniform"/>
                    </Rectangle.Fill>
                </Rectangle>
            </StackPanel>

            <StackPanel Margin="5" Grid.Column="1" Grid.Row="1">
                <TextBlock Margin="5" Text="Stretch = UniformToFill"
                           FontSize="12"/>
                <Rectangle Width="135" Height="100" Stroke="DarkBlue">
                    <Rectangle.Fill>
                        <ImageBrush ImageSource="ImageFile.jpg"
                                    Stretch="UniformToFill"/>
                    </Rectangle.Fill>
                </Rectangle>
            </StackPanel>
        </Grid>
    </Border>
</Grid>
</UserControl>
```

This XAML file defines four rectangles. You need to add the image file to the project by right clicking on the Solution Explorer and selecting Add – Existing Item…, and then selecting your image file. For each rectangle, the ImageBrush is used to set its Fill property. You may notice that the Stretch property of each ImageBrush is set differently to demonstrate its effect.

Figure 5-7 illustrates the results of this example. For the first rectangle, the Stretch property of the ImageBrush is set to None, which preserves the original image size and places the image at the center of the rectangle. For the second rectangle, this property is set to Fill, which is the default setting and forces the image to fill the whole area of the rectangle. For the third rectangle, the Stretch property is set to Uniform, which maintains the image's aspect ratio, but resizes the image to fit inside the rectangle's content area. For the last rectangle, the Stretch property is set to UniformToFill, which resizes the image to best-fit while preserving the original image aspect ratio. In this case, the best-fit is still much larger than the area of the rectangle, so the image gets clipped.

I should point out here that in WPF, you can obtain some special effects using ImageBrush by tiling the image across the surface of the brush, which creates a repeating pattern from the original image. You can set the TileMode property of the ImageBrush to Tile, FlipX, FlipY, or FlipXY to obtain different repeating patterns. However, Silverlight doesn't support the TileMode. This is a major limitation in Silverlight.

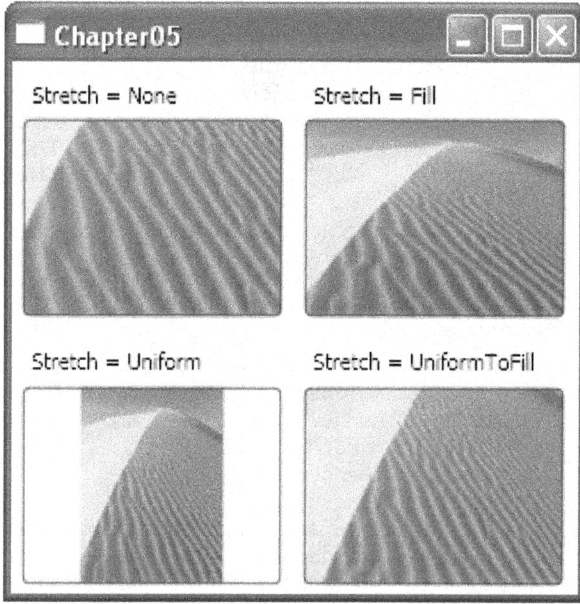

Figure 5-7 Button's background painted using ImageBrush objects.

Opacity Masks

As discussed previously, you can change a color's transparency by specifying its Opacity or by changing the color's alpha value. However, all elements in Silverlight can be modified in many different ways. The OpacityMask property can be used to make specific regions of an element transparent or partially transparent. You can use the opacity mask to create glass-like surface effects, which make an element look glossy or semi-transparent.

Although any type of Brush object can be used as an opacity mask, the gradient brush is typically used. This is because with a SolidColorBrush object, you can accomplish the same effect more easily with the Opacity property than you can with the OpacityMask. On the other hand, if used with a gradient brush that moves from a solid to transparent color,, OpacityMask can create a transparent effect that fades in over the surface of your element.

To create an opacity mask, you apply a brush to the OpacityMask property of an element or visual object. The following example shows you how to apply an opacity mask to a button control, and how to create a reflection effect by combining an opacity mask with a RenderTransform.

```
<UserControl x:Class="Example05_8.Page"
    xmlns="http://schemas.microsoft.com/client/2007"
    xmlns:x="http://schemas.microsoft.com/winfx/2006/xaml"
    Width="330" Height="370">
    <Grid x:Name="LayoutRoot" Background="White">
        <Border BorderBrush="Gray" BorderThickness="1" Margin="10">
            <StackPanel>
                <Grid Margin="5" Width="280" Height="240">
                    <Grid.Background>
                        <ImageBrush ImageSource="Flower.jpg"/>
                    </Grid.Background>
```

```
                    <Button Content="This is my button" FontSize="30"
                            Width="260" Height="100">
                        <Button.OpacityMask>
                            <LinearGradientBrush StartPoint="0 0"
                                                 EndPoint="1 0">
                                <GradientStop Offset="0" Color="#DDFFFF00" />
                                <GradientStop Offset="1" Color="#33FFFF00"/>
                            </LinearGradientBrush>
                        </Button.OpacityMask>
                    </Button>
                </Grid>
                <TextBlock Text="Text Reflection" FontSize="38"
                           FontWeight="Bold" Margin="10,0,0,0"/>
                <TextBlock Text="Text Reflection" FontSize="38"
                           FontWeight="Bold" Margin="10,30,0,0">
                    <TextBlock.RenderTransform>
                        <ScaleTransform ScaleY="-1"/>
                    </TextBlock.RenderTransform>
                    <TextBlock.OpacityMask>
                        <LinearGradientBrush StartPoint="0 0" EndPoint="0 1">
                                <GradientStop Offset="0.3" Color="#11FFFF00" />
                                <GradientStop Offset="1" Color="#AAFFFF00"/>
                            </LinearGradientBrush>
                    </TextBlock.OpacityMask>
                </TextBlock>
            </StackPanel>
        </Border>
    </Grid>
</UserControl>
```

Figure 5-8 shows the result of running this application.

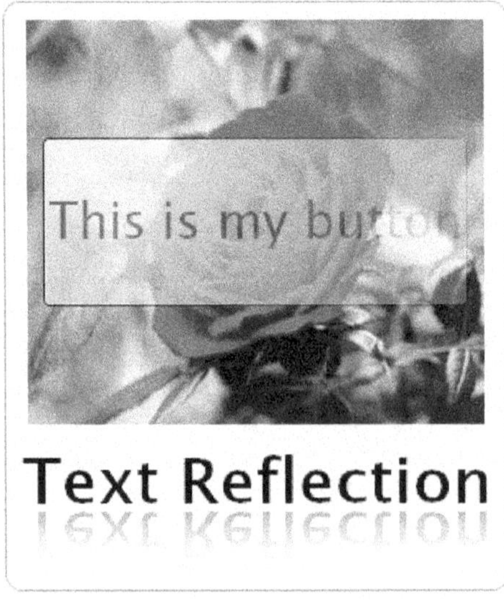

Figure 5-8 OpacityMask effects.

The button's OpacityMask property is specified by the LinearGradientBrush. The button is then placed on the top of an image background. It can be seen that by using the gradient brush as an OpacityMask that moves from a solid to a transparent color, you can create a transparent effect that fades in over the surface of your element.

In the bottom image, you reflect a TextBox using the OpacityMask property in conjunction with the RenderTransform. The LinearGradientBrush is used to fade between a completely transparent color and a partially transparent color, which makes the reflected text appear more realistic. A ScaleTransform is applied here, which flips the TextBox and makes it upside down.

Brush Transforms

In Chapter 3, we discussed object transformations. However, you can apply similar transforms to brushes. The difference between object and brush transforms is that object transformations transform the object itself, while brush transformations only affect the way the object is painted by the brush. Namely, brush transforms only change the fill pattern of the object.

The Brush class provides two transform properties, Transform and RelativeTransform. These properties allow you to rotate, scale, skew, and translate a brush's contents. When you apply a transform to a brush's Transform property and want to transform the brush contents about the center, you will need to know the size of the painted area. Suppose the painted area is 200×100. If you use a RotateTransform to rotate the brush's output 45 degrees about its center, you'd give the RotateTransform a CenterX of 100 and a CenterY of 50.

On the other hand, when you apply a transform to a brush's RelativeTransform property, that transform is applied to the brush before its output is mapped to the painted area. The following list describes the order in which a brush's contents are processed and transformed.

- First the brush's contents are processed. For a GradientBrush, this means determining the gradient area. For a TileBrush, (ImageBrush, DrawingBrush, and VisualBrush derive from the TileBush class), the ViewBox is mapped to the Viewport. This becomes the brush's output.
- Then, the brush's output is projected onto a 1 x 1 transform rectangle.
- The brush's RelativeTransform is applied, if it has one.
- The transformed output is projected onto the area to paint.
- Finally, the brush's Transform is applied, if it has one.

Because the RelativeTransform is applied while the brush's output is mapped to a 1 x 1 rectangle, the transform center and offset values appear to be relative. For example, if you use a RotateTransform to rotate the brush's output 45 degrees about its center, you would give the RotateTransform a CenterX of 0.5 and a CenterY of 0.5.

Remember that there are no effects if you apply transforms to a SolidColorBrush, because this brush always produces a solid color paint no matter if it is transformed or not.

Let's consider an example that applies the rotation transform to various brushes. You can easily apply other transforms to the brushes by following the same procedure presented in this example.

In this section, rather than create separate code examples of rotation transforms for each of the brushes, here we'll present a single example to demonstrate all of them. The coding details will then be explained in the following sections.

Here is the XAML file of the example, named BrushTransformExample:

```
<UserControl x:Class="Example05_9.Page"
    xmlns="http://schemas.microsoft.com/client/2007"
    xmlns:x="http://schemas.microsoft.com/winfx/2006/xaml"
    Width="540" Height="260">
    <Grid x:Name="LayoutRoot" Background="White">
        <Border BorderBrush="Gray" BorderThickness="1" Margin="10"
                CornerRadius="10">
            <Grid>
                <Grid.ColumnDefinitions>
                    <ColumnDefinition Width="Auto"/>
                    <ColumnDefinition Width="Auto"/>
                    <ColumnDefinition Width="Auto"/>
                    <ColumnDefinition Width="Auto"/>
                </Grid.ColumnDefinitions>
                <Grid.RowDefinitions>
                    <RowDefinition Height="Auto"/>
                    <RowDefinition Height="Auto"/>
                    <RowDefinition Height="Auto"/>
                    <RowDefinition Height="Auto"/>
                </Grid.RowDefinitions>

                <TextBlock Text="No Transform" Margin="30,5,5,0"
                           Grid.Column="1" Grid.Row="0" FontSize="12"/>
                <TextBlock Text="Relative Transform" Margin="18,5,5,0"
                           Grid.Column="2" Grid.Row="0" FontSize="12"/>
                <TextBlock Text="Transform" Margin="38,5,5,0" Grid.Column="3"
                           Grid.Row="0" FontSize="12"/>
                <TextBlock Text="LinearGradientBrush" Margin="5,25,0,5"
                           Grid.Column="0" Grid.Row="1"
                           HorizontalAlignment="Right" FontSize="12"/>
                <TextBlock Text="RadialGradientBrush" Margin="5,25,0,5"
                           Grid.Column="0" Grid.Row="2"
                           HorizontalAlignment="Right" FontSize="12"/>
                <TextBlock Text="ImageBrush" Margin="5,25,0,5" Grid.Column="0"
                           Grid.Row="3" HorizontalAlignment="Right"
                           FontSize="12"/>

                <Rectangle Width="120" Height="60" Margin="5"
                           Grid.Column="1" Grid.Row="1">
                    <Rectangle.Fill>
                        <LinearGradientBrush StartPoint="0,0" EndPoint="1,0">
                            <GradientStop Color="Gray" Offset="0.4"/>
                            <GradientStop Color="Yellow" Offset="0.5"/>
                            <GradientStop Color="Gray" Offset="0.6"/>
                        </LinearGradientBrush>
                    </Rectangle.Fill>
                </Rectangle>

                <Rectangle Width="120" Height="60" Margin="5"
                           Grid.Column="2" Grid.Row="1">
                    <Rectangle.Fill>
                        <LinearGradientBrush StartPoint="0,0" EndPoint="1,0">
                            <GradientStop Color="Gray" Offset="0.4"/>
                            <GradientStop Color="Yellow" Offset="0.5"/>
```

```
                <GradientStop Color="Gray" Offset="0.6"/>
                <LinearGradientBrush.RelativeTransform>
                    <RotateTransform CenterX="0.5"
                                     CenterY="0.5" Angle="45" />
                </LinearGradientBrush.RelativeTransform>
            </LinearGradientBrush>
        </Rectangle.Fill>
    </Rectangle>

    <Rectangle Width="120" Height="60" Margin="5"
               Grid.Column="3" Grid.Row="1">
        <Rectangle.Fill>
            <LinearGradientBrush StartPoint="0,0" EndPoint="1,0">
                <GradientStop Color="Gray" Offset="0.4"/>
                <GradientStop Color="Yellow" Offset="0.5"/>
                <GradientStop Color="Gray" Offset="0.6"/>
                <LinearGradientBrush.Transform>
                    <RotateTransform CenterX="60"
                                     CenterY="30" Angle="45" />
                </LinearGradientBrush.Transform>
            </LinearGradientBrush>
        </Rectangle.Fill>
    </Rectangle>

    <Rectangle Width="120" Height="60" Margin="5"
               Grid.Column="1" Grid.Row="2">
        <Rectangle.Fill>
            <RadialGradientBrush>
                <GradientStop Color="Gray" Offset="0.3"/>
                <GradientStop Color="Yellow" Offset="0.5"/>
                <GradientStop Color="Gray" Offset="0.7"/>
            </RadialGradientBrush>
        </Rectangle.Fill>
    </Rectangle>

    <Rectangle Width="120" Height="60" Margin="5"
               Grid.Column="2" Grid.Row="2">
        <Rectangle.Fill>
            <RadialGradientBrush>
                <GradientStop Color="Gray" Offset="0.3"/>
                <GradientStop Color="Yellow" Offset="0.5"/>
                <GradientStop Color="Gray" Offset="0.7"/>
                <RadialGradientBrush.RelativeTransform>
                    <RotateTransform CenterX="0.5"
                                     CenterY="0.5" Angle="45"/>
                </RadialGradientBrush.RelativeTransform>
            </RadialGradientBrush>
        </Rectangle.Fill>
    </Rectangle>

    <Rectangle Width="120" Height="60" Margin="5"
               Grid.Column="3" Grid.Row="2">
        <Rectangle.Fill>
            <RadialGradientBrush>
                <GradientStop Color="Gray" Offset="0.3"/>
```

```
                    <GradientStop Color="Yellow" Offset="0.5"/>
                    <GradientStop Color="Gray" Offset="0.7"/>
                    <RadialGradientBrush.Transform>
                        <RotateTransform CenterX="60"
                                         CenterY="30" Angle="45"/>
                    </RadialGradientBrush.Transform>
                </RadialGradientBrush>
            </Rectangle.Fill>
        </Rectangle>

        <Rectangle Width="120" Height="60" Margin="5"
                   Grid.Column="1" Grid.Row="3" Stroke="DarkBlue">
            <Rectangle.Fill>
                <ImageBrush ImageSource="Flower.jpg"/>
            </Rectangle.Fill>
        </Rectangle>

        <Rectangle Width="120" Height="60" Margin="5"
                   Grid.Column="2" Grid.Row="3" Stroke="DarkBlue">
            <Rectangle.Fill>
                <ImageBrush ImageSource="Flower.jpg">
                    <ImageBrush.RelativeTransform>
                        <RotateTransform CenterX="0.5"
                                         CenterY="0.5" Angle="45"/>
                    </ImageBrush.RelativeTransform>
                </ImageBrush>
            </Rectangle.Fill>
        </Rectangle>

        <Rectangle Width="120" Height="60" Margin="5"
                   Grid.Column="3" Grid.Row="3" Stroke="DarkBlue">
            <Rectangle.Fill>
                <ImageBrush ImageSource="Flower.jpg">
                    <ImageBrush.Transform>
                        <RotateTransform CenterX="60"
                                         CenterY="30" Angle="45"/>
                    </ImageBrush.Transform>
                </ImageBrush>
            </Rectangle.Fill>
        </Rectangle>
       </Grid>
    </Border>
  </Grid>
</UserControl>
```

In this example, you create several rectangle shapes that are filled using various brushes with or without transforms. This example generates the output shown in Figure 5-9.

LinearGradientBrush Transform

In this example, you create three rectangle shapes that are painted using a LinearGradientBrush. The first rectangle is filled using a LinearGradientBrush without a RotateTransform. You can see that a vertical yellow bar is at the center of the rectangle.

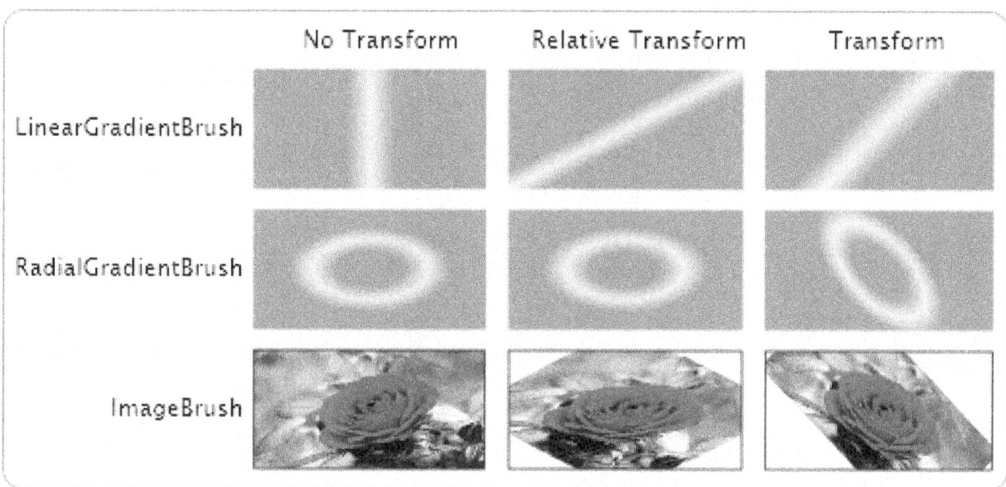

Figure 5-9 Brush Transformations.

The second rectangle is filled using a transformed LinearGradientBrush. A RotateTransform of 45 degrees is applied to the brush's RelativeTransform property. You may wonder how you obtain the result shown in Figure 5-9 for this relative transform. This can be easily understood using the definition of a brush's RelativeTransform property. Figure 5-10 shows each step of the process.

The third rectangle is painted using a LinearGradientBrush with a Transform property specified using a RotateTransform of 45 degrees. The result from this absolute transform is easy to understand: it is simply a direct rotation (45 degrees) of the original (not transformed) brush.

After understanding the difference between the RelativeTransform and Transform properties of a brush, you can easily create various interesting effects by using brushes with different transforms.

RadialGradientBrush Transform

Like the LinearGradientBrush discussed in the preceding section, the RadialGradientBrush also has two different types of transformations – Transform and RelativeTransform. In this example, the second row of rectangles is filled using different RadialGradientBrush objects. The first rectangle is painted using a brush without a rotation. Take a look at the corresponding code segment. You actually define the RadialGradientBrush to have a circular yellow ring. This circular ring becomes the ellipse seen in Figure 5-9 because you are trying to fill and fit a rectangle shape using this brush.

The fill pattern of the third rectangle in this case is obtained by directly rotating the original brush by 45 degrees. However, you might wonder why the paint pattern of the second rectangle is identical to that of the first one. Why is there no effect on the brush after it is rotated by 45 degrees relatively? The answer to this can be understood from the explanation given in Figure 5-11.

According to the process of relative transformation, the original rectangle needs to be projected onto a 1×1 transform square. In this projected space, the original ellipse pattern becomes a circular ring. The rotation should be applied to the RelativeTransform property of the brush in this projected space. Since the pattern of the brush is a ring shape, there should be no effect on the pattern when it is rotated about its center. This is why you get the same ellipse pattern as the original brush after you project the rotated brush back onto the rectangle paint area.

- Project the base tile onto the 1 x 1 transformation rectangle

- Apply the RotateTransform (45 degrees)

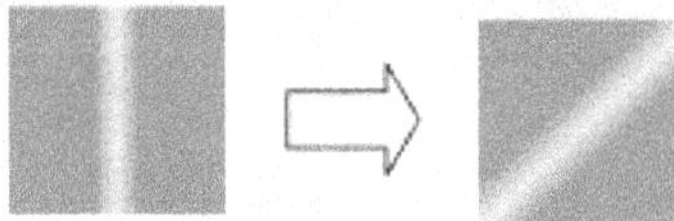

- Project the transformed base tile onto the area to paint

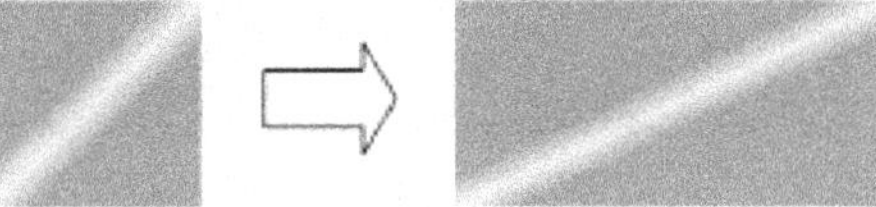

Figure 5-10 Relative rotation of a LinearGradientBrush.

- Project the base tile onto the 1 x 1 transformation rectangle

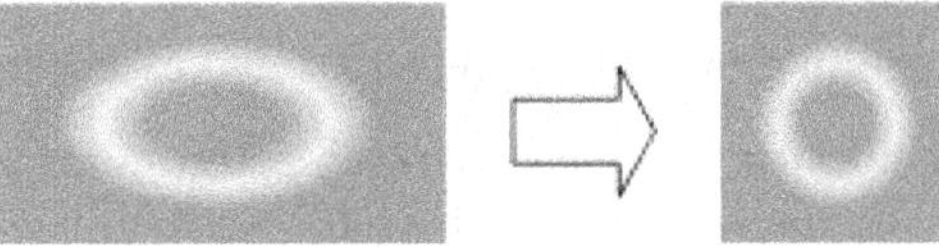

- Apply the RotateTransform (45 degrees)

- Project the transformed base tile onto the area to paint

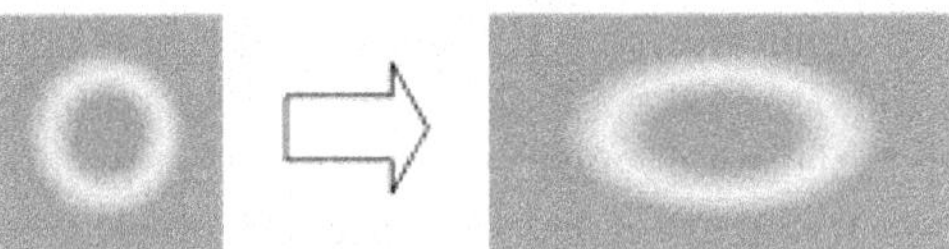

Figure 5-11 Relative rotation of a RadialGradientBrush.

ImageBrush Transform

In the third row, you fill rectangle shapes using ImageBrush. The fill image pattern using an ImageBrush with a relative rotation is different than that of a pattern using a brush with an absolute rotation. The results can be explained based on the process of the Transform and RelativeTranform properties of an ImageBrush.

Chapter 6
Animation

From the previous chapters you learned that Silverlight provides a powerful set of graphics and layout features that enable you to create attractive user interfaces and appealing graphics objects. Animation can make user interfaces and graphics even more spectacular and usable. Animation allows you to create truly dynamic Silverlight applications and make your programs more responsive and intuitive. Animation can also draw attention to important objects and guide the user through transitions to new content.

To create animations in Silverlight applications, you don't need to write your own code using timers and event handling; instead, you can directly use corresponding animation classes that Silverlight provides.

In this chapter, we'll consider the rich set of Silverlight animation classes and show how to use them in Web applications. As always, this chapter will also provide a wide range of animation examples.

Silverlight Animation Basics

Animation is an illusion that is created by quickly cycling through a series of frames, each slightly different from the last. For example, in order to create a real-time stock chart, you might follow the steps listed here:

- Create a timer.
- Check the timer at specified intervals (say, every 30 seconds) to see how much time has elapsed.
- When you check the timer, feed the lastest market stock data into your stock chart program.
- Update the stock chart with the new stock data and redraw it on your screen.

Prior to WPF and Silverlight, Web- or Window-based developers had to create and manage their own timing systems and event handling or use special custom libraries. Although this kind of timer-based animation isn't very difficult to implement, there are some issues associated with integrating it into a Windows application. For example timer-based animation usually assumes a single animation. If you want multiple animations running at the same time, you need to rewrite all of your animation code. Another issue is that the animation frame rate is fixed. If you want to change the timer interval, you might need to change your animation code too.

Silverlight includes an efficient timing system that is exposed through managed code and XAML and deeply integrated into the Silverlight and .NET framework. Silverlight animation makes it easy to animate controls and other graphical objects.

Silverlight handles all the behind-the-scenes work of managing a timing system and redrawing the screen efficiently. It provides timing classes that enable you to focus on the effects you want to create, instead of the mechanics of achieving those effects.

Property-Based Animation

The Silverlight animation system uses a different model than timer-based animation does. Basically, a Silverlight animation directly modifies the value of a dependency property over an interval of time. For example, to make a drawing of a rectangle fade out of view, you can modify its Opacity property in an animation. To make it grow or shrink, you can modify its Width and Height properties. The secret to creating the animation you want becomes determining which properties you need to modify.

For a property to have animation capabilities, it must meet the following requirements:

- It must be a dependency property.
- It must belong to a class that inherits from DependencyObject and implements the IAnimatable interface.
- There must be a compatible animation data type available.

This means that to animate a dependency property, you need to have an animation class that supports its data type. For example, the Width property of a rectangle uses the double data type. To animate it, you use the DoubleAnimation class. However, the Color property of a SolidColorBrush object uses the color structure, so it requires the ColorAnimation class. Note that Silverlight currently supports three types of animation property values: Double, Color, and Point.

There are two types of animations in Silverlight: linear interpolation animation and key frame animation. Linear interpolation animations represent animations that vary properties gradually between starting and ending values. DoubleAnimation and ColorAnimation belong to this category, and they use interpolation to smoothly change their values. On the other hand, key frame animations change property values abruptly at specified times, and are often used when changing certain data types, such as the string and reference type of objects. All key frame animation classes in Silverlight are named in the form Type Name + AnimationUsingKeyFrames; i.e., StringAnimationUsingKeyFrames and ObjectAnimationUsingKeyFrames.

Every data type supports key frame animations. However, some data types have a key frame animation class but no interpolation animation class. For example, you can animate a string using key frames, but you can't animate a string using interpolation. In other worlds, a data type that has a normal animation class that uses interpolation, such as DoubleAnimation, also has a corresponding animation type for key frame animation, such as DoubleAnimationUsingKeyFrames.

A Simple Animation Example

As you have already learned, the most common animation technique is linear interpolation. You have used this type of animation in previous chapters. Now let's use a simple example to illustrate how an animation works in Silverlight. This simple example shows how to make a rectangle move around inside a Canvas control. It uses DoubleAnimation, which is a type of animation that generates Double values, to animate the Canvas.Left and Canvas.Top properties of the rectangle.

Start with a new Silverlight project and name it Example06-1. Here is the XAML file of this example:

```
<UserControl x:Class="Example06_1.Page"
    xmlns="http://schemas.microsoft.com/client/2007"
    xmlns:x="http://schemas.microsoft.com/winfx/2006/xaml"
    Width="320" Height="270" Loaded="Page_Loaded">

    <UserControl.Resources>
        <Storyboard x:Name="storyboard1">
            <DoubleAnimation
                 Storyboard.TargetName="rect"
                 Storyboard.TargetProperty="(Canvas.Left)"
                 From="0" To="200" Duration="0:0:5"
                 AutoReverse="True" RepeatBehavior="Forever" />
            <DoubleAnimation
                 Storyboard.TargetName="rect"
                 Storyboard.TargetProperty="(Canvas.Top)"
                 From="0" To="200" Duration="0:0:5"
                 AutoReverse="True" RepeatBehavior="Forever" />
        </Storyboard>
    </UserControl.Resources>

    <Grid x:Name="LayoutRoot" Background="White">
        <Border BorderBrush="Gray" BorderThickness="1" Margin="10">
            <Canvas>
                <Rectangle x:Name="rect" Width="100" Height="50"
                           Fill="LightBlue" Stroke="DarkBlue"/>
            </Canvas>
        </Border>
    </Grid>
</UserControl>
```

The animation must be started in code:

```
using System;
using System.Windows;
using System.Windows.Controls;
using System.Windows.Media;
using System.Windows.Media.Animation;

namespace Example06_1
{
    public partial class Page : UserControl
    {
        public Page()
        {
            InitializeComponent();
        }

        private void Page_Loaded(object sender, RoutedEventArgs e)
        {
            storyboard1.Begin();
        }
```

```
        }
    }
```

You can see from this example that to apply an animation to an element in Silverlight, you create a Storyboard object, add two DoubleAnimation objects as its children, and use the TargetName and TargetProperty attached properties to specify the element (rect in this example) and property (Canvas.Left or Canvas.Right) to animate.

Then, you need to associate the Storyboard with an event that specifies when the animation begins. This can be achieved by the following steps:

- **Make the Storyboard a resource:** In Silverlight, you need to make the Storyboard into a Resource. Here you place the Storyboard inside of the UserControl object resources block so that you can easily reference the Storyboard from code and be abe to interact with it. Note that you could declare the Storyboard in any resources block that is within the same scope as the element you wish to animate. For example, you could declare it in the Canvas resources block.
- **Attach an event to an element:** There are a variety of events you can use to start an animation, including mouse related events like MouseLeftButtonDown, which fires when a user clicks on an object, or the Loaded event, which fires when an object first loads. In this example, the Loaded event is attached to the UserControl so that when the Page is first loaded, the animation will automatically start.
- **Control the animation from the event handler:** Storyboard exposes several methods that allow you to control playback of the Storyboard animation including Begin, Stop, Pause, and Resume. In this simple animation example, the Begin method is used to start the animation.

When you create a DoubleAnimation instance, there are three key properties that are required by any interpolation-based animation: the starting value (From), the ending value (To), and the time that the animation should take (Duration). In this example, you also use two more properties, AutoReverse and RepeatBehavior. These two properties control the playback and repeatability of the animation.

If you execute this sample application, you will obtain a rectangle that moves around inside the Canvas.

Instead of using the To property, you can use the By property. The By property is used to create an animation that changes a value by a set amount, rather than to a specific target. For example, you could create an animation that enlarges the rectangle's width by 50 units more than its current width, as shown here:

```
<DoubleAnimation
    Storyboard.TargetName="rect"
    Storyboard.TargetProperty="Width"
    By="50" Duration="0:0:1"
    AutoReverse="True" RepeatBehavior="Forever" />
```

This approach is necessary in this example, because you couldn't achieve the same effect using the From and To properties in XAML. In code, you can do this:

```
myDoubleAnimation.To = rect1.Width + 50;
```

However, the By value makes more sense when you create animations in XAML because the markup code doesn't provide a way to perform any calculations.

The preceding example creates the animation in XAML and starts the animation in code. As mentioned previously, you can create any Silverlight application using the code-only approach. In the next subsection, I'll show you how to create the same animation example in code ony.

Animation in Code

Rather then using XAML, you can create animations completely in procedural C# code. Start with a new Silverlight project and name it Example06-2. This example shows how to perform the same animation in the previous example. Here is the C# code of this example:

```
using System;
using System.Windows;
using System.Windows.Controls;
using System.Windows.Media;
using System.Windows.Media.Animation;
using System.Windows.Shapes;

namespace Example06_2
{
    public partial class Page : UserControl
    {
        public Page()
        {
            InitializeComponent();

            this.Width = 320;
            this.Height = 270;
            this.Loaded += new RoutedEventHandler(Page_Loaded);
        }

        void Page_Loaded(object sender, RoutedEventArgs e)
        {
            CreateRunAnimation();
        }

        public void CreateRunAnimation()
        {
            // Create drawing canvas with border:
            Border bd = new Border();
            bd.BorderBrush = new SolidColorBrush(Colors.Gray);
            bd.BorderThickness = new Thickness(1);
            bd.Margin = new Thickness(10);
            LayoutRoot.Children.Add(bd);
            Canvas canvas = new Canvas();
            bd.Child = canvas;

            // Create rectangle:
            Rectangle rect = new Rectangle();
            rect.Width = 100;
            rect.Height = 50;
            rect.Fill = new SolidColorBrush(Color.FromArgb(255, 100, 200, 255));
            rect.Stroke = new SolidColorBrush(Color.FromArgb(255, 0, 0, 150));
            canvas.Children.Add(rect);

            // Create storyboard and make it a resource:
            Storyboard storyboard1 = new Storyboard();
            this.Resources.Add("Animation", storyboard1);

            // Create two DoubleAnimations and add them to
```

```
            // storyboard as children:
            DoubleAnimation da1 = new DoubleAnimation();
            DoubleAnimation da2 = new DoubleAnimation();
            storyboard1.Children.Add(da1);
            storyboard1.Children.Add(da2);

            // Set DoubleAnimations' properties:
            Storyboard.SetTarget(da1, rect);
            Storyboard.SetTarget(da2, rect);
            Storyboard.SetTargetProperty(da1,
                                 new PropertyPath("(Canvas.Left)"));
            Storyboard.SetTargetProperty(da2, new PropertyPath("(Canvas.Top)"));
            da1.Duration = new Duration(TimeSpan.FromSeconds(5));
            da2.Duration = new Duration(TimeSpan.FromSeconds(5));
            da1.From = 0;
            da2.From = 0;
            da1.To = 200;
            da2.To = 200;
            da1.RepeatBehavior = RepeatBehavior.Forever;
            da2.RepeatBehavior = RepeatBehavior.Forever;
            da1.AutoReverse = true;
            da2.AutoReverse = true;

            // Start animation:
            storyboard1.Begin();
        }
    }
}
```

The main part of this code example is the CreateRunAnimation method. First you create the drawing canvas and the rectangle that you want to animate. Next, you create a Storyboard object, storyboard1. The key step is that you must place storyboard1 into a resources block:

```
this.Resources.Add("Animation", storyboard1);
```

Silverlight requires all animations to be declared in a resources block, regardless of whether the animations are created in XAML or in code.

The following code is used to set the animation's properties. Finally you start the animation by calling the Begin method from the Page_Loaded event hander. Running the project gives the exact results as the previous project does.

Animation and Timing Behavior

In Silverlight, an animation is a type of timeline. A timeline represents a segment of time and provides properties that allow you to specify the length of that segment, when it should start, how many times it will repeat, how fast time progresses in that segment, etc.

There are some useful members in the Timeline class, which define time-related properties used in animations, including Duration, FillBehavior, and etc. Here is a list of some properties that are often used in animations:

- BeginTime – Sets a delay time before the animation starts.
- Duration – Sets the length of time the animation runs, from start to finish, as a Duration object.

- SpeedRatio – Increases or decreases the speed of the animation. The default value is 1.
- AutoReverse – If this is set to true, the animation will play out in reverse once it is complete, returning to the original value.
- FillBehavior – Determines what happens when the animation finishes. Usually, it keeps the property fixed at the ending value (FillBehavior.HoldEnd), but you can choose to return it to its original value by setting FillBehavior.Stop.
- RepeatBehavior – Allows you to repeat an animation a specific number of times.

Since some of the timing behaviors such as Duration, RepeatBehavior, and AutoReverse play an important role in creating animations, the following sections will explain how to use them in your applications.

Duration

As mentioned previously, a timeline represents a segment of time. The length of the segment is determined by the timeline's Duration property. In the case of animations, the Duration specifies how long the animation takes to transition from its starting value to its ending value. The Duration and the TimeSpan of an animation are very similar. In the previous example, Duration is set using TimeSpan in code. This is because the Duration structure defines an implicit cast, which can convert System.TimeSpan to System.Windows.Duration as needed. That is why all of the following four statement are valid:

```
da1.Duration = TimeSpan.FromSeconds(5);
da1.Duration = new TimeSpan(0, 0, 5);
da1.Duration = new Duration(TimeSpan.FromSeconds(5));
da1.Duration = new Duration(new TimeSpan(0, 0, 5));
```

You can also specify a Duration using the special values Automatic or Forever, like this:

```
da.Duration = Duration.Automatic;
da.Duration = Duration.Forever;
```

The value Automatic simply sets the animation to a one-second duration, and Forever makes the animation infinite in length, which prevents the animation from having any effect. These values becomes useful when creating more complex animations.

Storyboard has a default duration of Automatic, which means it automatically ends when its last child animation ends. The following markup shows a storyboard whose Duration resolves in five seconds, the length of time it takes all of its child DoubleAnimation objects to complete:

```
<Storyboard>
    <DoubleAnimation
        Storyboard.TargetName="rect1"
        Storyboard.TargetProperty="Width"
        From="0" To="100" Duration="0:0:5"/>

    <DoubleAnimation
        Storyboard.TargetName="rect2"
        Storyboard.TargetProperty="Width"
        From="0" To="150" Duration="0:0:3"/>
</Storyboard>
```

You can specifically set the Duration of the Storyboard to a TimeSpan value, which forces the animation to play for a longer or shorter period than its child Timeline objects. The following code snippet sets the Duration of the storyboard to two seconds. As a result, the first DoubleAnimation stops progressing after two seconds, when it has animated the target rectangle's width to 40. The second DoubleAnimation also stops after two seconds, when it has animated rect2's width to 100.

```
<Storyboard Duration ="0:0:2">
    <DoubleAnimation
        Storyboard.TargetName="rect1"
        Storyboard.TargetProperty="Width"
        From="0" To="100" Duration="0:0:5"/>

    <DoubleAnimation
        Storyboard.TargetName="rect2"
        Storyboard.TargetProperty="Width"
        From="0" To="150" Duration="0:0:3"/>
</Storyboard>
```

RepeatBehavior

The RepeatBehavior property of a timeline controls how many times the animation repeats its duration. Using the RepeatBehavior property, you can specify how many times the timeline plays (an iteration Count) or the total length of time it should play (a repeat Duration). In either case, the animation goes through as many runs as necessary to fill the requested count or duration. By default, timelines have an iteration count of 1, which means they play once and don't repeat at all.

The following markup uses the RepeatBehavior property to make a DoubleAnimation play for 10 times by specifying the iteration count:

```
<DoubleAnimation
    Storyboard.TargetName="rect1"
    Storyboard.TargetProperty="Width"
    From="0" To="100" Duration="0:0:5"
    RepeatBehavior="10x"/>
```

You can also specify a repeat duration using the RepeatBehavior property, like this:

```
<DoubleAnimation
    Storyboard.TargetName="rect1"
    Storyboard.TargetProperty="Width"
    From="0" To="100" Duration="0:0:5"
    RepeatBehavior="0:5:30"/>
```

This makes the DoubleAnimation play for a period of 5 minutes and 30 seconds. If you set the RepeatBehavior property to Forever, the animation repeats until it is stopped interactively or by the timing system.

AutoReverse

The AutoReverse property specifies whether a timeline will play backwards at the end of each forward iteration. The following XAML snippet sets the AutoReverse property of a DoubleAnimation to true. As a result, it animates the Width property of the rectangle from zero to 100, then from 100 to zero. It plays for a total of 5 minutes.

```
<DoubleAnimation
    Storyboard.TargetName="rect1"
    Storyboard.TargetProperty="Width"
    From="0" To="100"
    Duration="0:2:30"
    AutoReverse="True"/>
```

When you use a Count value to specify the RepeatBehavior of a timeline and the AutoReverse property of that timeline is set to true, a single repetition consists of one forward iteration followed by one backward iteration.

BeginTime

The BeginTime property enables you to specify when a timeline starts. A timeline's BeginTime is relative to its parent timeline. A begin time of zero seconds means the timeline starts as soon as its parent starts. A finite value creates an offset between when the parent timeline starts playing and when the child timeline plays. By default, all timelines have a begin time of zero seconds. You may also set a timeline's begin time to null, which prevents the timeline from starting.

Note that the begin time isn't applied each time a timeline repeats due to its RepeatBehavior setting. For example, if you create a animation with a BeginTime of 5 seconds and a RepeatBehavior of Forever, there would be a 5-second delay before the animation played for the first time, but not for each successive repetition. However, if the animation's parent timeline restarts or repeats, the 5-second delay will still occur.

The BeginTime property is useful for staggering timelines. In the StoryboardInCode example, you set the BeginTime property for the second button's background animation to a 5-second delay. The following code snippet creates a storyboard that has two DoubleAnimation objects. The first animation has a Duration of 10 seconds, and the second has a Duration of 5 seconds. The BeginTime of the second DoubleAnimation is set to 10 seconds so that it begins playing after the first DoubleAnimation ends:

```
<Storyboard>
    <DoubleAnimation
        Storyboard.TargetName="rect1"
        Storyboard.TargetProperty="Width"
        From="0" To="100"
        Duration="0:0:10"
        BeginTime="0:0:0"/>

    <DoubleAnimation
        Storyboard.TargetName="rect2"
        Storyboard.TargetProperty="Width"
        From="0" To="100"
        Duration="0:0:5"
        BeginTime="0:0:10"/>
</Storyboard>
```

The other property, FillBehavior, specifies whether an animation stops or holds its last value. An animation with a FillBehavior of HoldEnd holds its output value – the property being animated retains the last value of the animation. A value of Stop causes the animation to return its original value after it ends.

Speed Controls

The Timeline class in Silverlight provides a SpeedRatio property for specifying the timeline's speed. It sets the rate, relative to its parent, at which time progresses for a timeline. Values greater than one increase the speed of the animation; values between zero and one slow it down. A value of one (the default value) indicates that the timeline progresses at the same speed as its parent. The SpeedRatio setting of a container timeline affects all of its child's Timeline objects as well.

Now, let's consider an example that shows you how to control the animation speed. Start with a new Silverlight Project and name it Example06-3. Here are the XAML file and code-behind files of this example:

```
<UserControl x:Class="Example06_3.Page"
    xmlns="http://schemas.microsoft.com/client/2007"
    xmlns:x="http://schemas.microsoft.com/winfx/2006/xaml"
    Width="450" Height="290">

    <Grid x:Name="LayoutRoot" Background="White">
        <Border BorderBrush="Gray" BorderThickness="1"
                CornerRadius="10" Margin="10">
            <StackPanel Margin="5">
                <StackPanel.Resources>
                    <Storyboard x:Name="storyboard1">
                        <DoubleAnimation
                            Storyboard.TargetName="rect1"
                            Storyboard.TargetProperty="Width"
                            From="20" To="400" Duration="0:0:10"/>

                        <DoubleAnimation
                            Storyboard.TargetName="rect2"
                            Storyboard.TargetProperty="Width"
                            From="20" To="400" Duration="0:0:10"
                            SpeedRatio="1.5"/>

                        <DoubleAnimation
                            Storyboard.TargetName="rect3"
                            Storyboard.TargetProperty="Width"
                            From="20" To="400" Duration="0:0:10"
                            SpeedRatio="0.5"/>
                    </Storyboard>
                </StackPanel.Resources>

                <TextBlock Text="Animation with a constant speed:"
                           FontSize="12"/>
                <Rectangle Name="rect1" Fill="Red" Margin="5" Width="20"
                           Height="40" HorizontalAlignment="Left" />

                <TextBlock Text="Animation with a faster speed:" FontSize="12"/>
                <Rectangle Name="rect2" Fill="Green" Margin="5" Width="20"
                           Height="40" HorizontalAlignment="Left" />

                <TextBlock Text="Animation with a slower speed:" FontSize="12"/>
                <Rectangle Name="rect3" Fill="Blue" Margin="5" Width="20"
                           Height="40" HorizontalAlignment="Left" />
```

```
                <Button Margin="5,20,0,0" HorizontalAlignment="Left"
                        Content="Start Animations" Width="100"
                        Click="Button_Click"/>
            </StackPanel>
        </Border>
    </Grid>
</UserControl>

using System;
using System.Windows;
using System.Windows.Controls;
using System.Windows.Media;
using System.Windows.Media.Animation;

namespace Example06_3
{
    public partial class Page : UserControl
    {
        public Page()
        {
            InitializeComponent();
        }

        private void Button_Click(object sender, RoutedEventArgs e)
        {
            storyboard1.Begin();
        }
    }
}
```

This XAML file creates three rectangles and a button. The Width property of the rectangles is animated using different animating speeds.

The first rectangle is animated without any speed changes for comparison. The animations for the rest of the rectangles progress with different speeds that are controlled by the SpeedRatio. Figure 6-1 illustrates the results of running this example. Click on the Start Animations button to start the animations and watch how the animations progress with different speeds.

Interactive Animations

So far, you have been using only one action of the Storyboard – the Begin method that launches the animation. However, as mentioned previously, Storyboard also has other methods which can be used to control your animations.

Here is a list of controllable storyboard actions available in Silverlight that you can use with event triggers to control a storyboard:

- Pause – Stops an animation and keeps it at its current position.
- Resume – Resumes a paused animation.
- SpeedRatio – Changes the storyboard's speed.
- SkipToFill – Advances a storyboard to the end of its fill period, if it has one.
- Stop – Stops the storyboard.

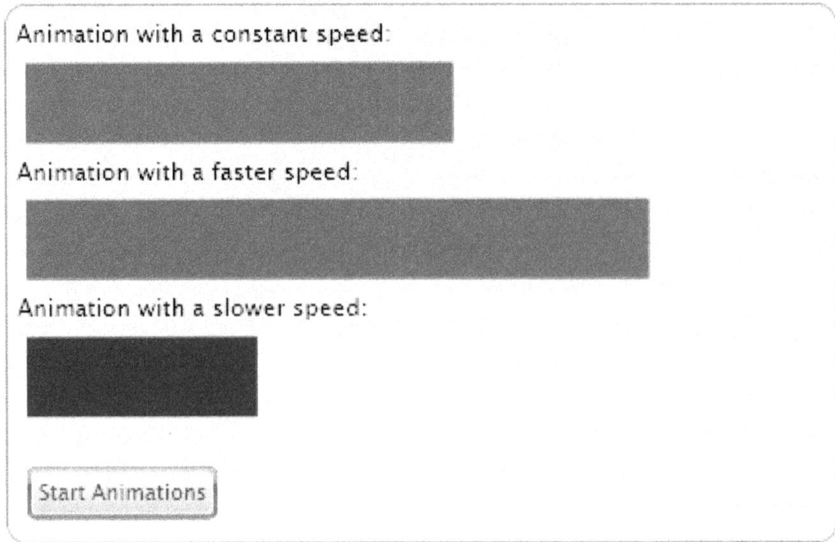

Figure 6-1 Animations with different speeds.

Let's consider an example, in which you create a circle that is painted using a RadialGradientBrush. You'll then animate the brush's RadiusX and RadiusY properties interactively. Here is the XAML file of this example:

```
<UserControl x:Class="Example06_4.Page"
    xmlns="http://schemas.microsoft.com/client/2007"
    xmlns:x="http://schemas.microsoft.com/winfx/2006/xaml"
    Width="300" Height="270">

    <UserControl.Resources>
        <Storyboard x:Name="storyboard1">
            <DoubleAnimation
               Storyboard.TargetName="ellipse"
               Storyboard.TargetProperty="(Shape.Fill).RadiusX"
               From="0" To="1" Duration="0:0:2"
               RepeatBehavior="5x"/>

            <DoubleAnimation
               Storyboard.TargetName="ellipse"
               Storyboard.TargetProperty="(Shape.Fill).RadiusY"
               From="0" To="1" Duration="0:0:2"
               RepeatBehavior="5x"/>

            <ColorAnimation
               Storyboard.TargetName="ellipse"
               Storyboard.TargetProperty=
    "(Shape.Fill).(GradientBrush.GradientStops)[2].(GradientStop.Color)"
               To="Black" Duration="0:0:2"
               RepeatBehavior="5x"/>
        </Storyboard>
    </UserControl.Resources>
```

```
    <Grid x:Name="LayoutRoot" Background="White">
        <Border BorderBrush="Gray" BorderThickness="1"
                CornerRadius="10" Margin="10">
            <StackPanel Margin="10">
                <Ellipse Name="ellipse" Width="150" Height="150">
                    <Ellipse.Fill>
                        <RadialGradientBrush>
                            <GradientStop Color="White" Offset="0"/>
                            <GradientStop Color="LightCoral" Offset="0.1"/>
                            <GradientStop Color="LightBlue" Offset="0.2"/>
                            <GradientStop Color="Red" Offset="0.3"/>
                            <GradientStop Color="Blue" Offset="0.5"/>
                            <GradientStop Color="Yellow" Offset="0.7"/>
                            <GradientStop Color="Green" Offset="0.8"/>
                            <GradientStop Color="Gold" Offset="0.9"/>
                            <GradientStop Color="Purple" Offset="1"/>
                        </RadialGradientBrush>
                    </Ellipse.Fill>
                </Ellipse>

                <StackPanel Orientation="Horizontal"
                    HorizontalAlignment="Center"
                    Margin="0,20,0,0">
                    <Button x:Name="btnBegin" Content="Begin" Width="75"
                            Height="25" Margin="2" Click="btnBegin_Click"/>
                    <Button x:Name="btnPause" Content="Pause" Width="75"
                            Height="25" Margin="2" Click="btnPause_Click"/>
                    <Button x:Name="btnResume" Content="Resume" Width="75"
                            Height="25" Margin="2" Click="btnResume_Click"/>
                </StackPanel>
                <StackPanel Orientation="Horizontal"
                            HorizontalAlignment="Center">
                    <Button x:Name="btnSkipToFill" Content="Skip To Fill"
                            Width="75" Height="25" Margin="2"
                            Click="btnSkipToFill_Click"/>
                    <Button x:Name="btnStop" Content="Stop" Width="75"
                            Height="25" Margin="2" Click="btnStop_Click"/>
                </StackPanel>
            </StackPanel>
        </Border>
    </Grid>
</UserControl>
```

The corresponding code-behind file is listed below:

```
using System;
using System.Windows;
using System.Windows.Controls;
using System.Windows.Media;
using System.Windows.Media.Animation;
using System.Windows.Shapes;

namespace Example06_4
{
    public partial class Page : UserControl
    {
```

```
        public Page()
        {
            InitializeComponent();
        }

        private void btnBegin_Click(object sender, RoutedEventArgs e)
        {
            storyboard1.Begin();
        }

        private void btnPause_Click(object sender, RoutedEventArgs e)
        {
            storyboard1.Pause();
        }

        private void btnResume_Click(object sender, RoutedEventArgs e)
        {
            storyboard1.Resume();
        }

        private void btnSkipToFill_Click(object sender, RoutedEventArgs e)
        {
            storyboard1.SkipToFill();
        }

        private void btnStop_Click(object sender, RoutedEventArgs e)
        {
            storyboard1.Stop();
        }
    }
}
```

In this example, you should pay close attention to several points. First, notice how we set the Storyboard.TargetProperty to the RadiusX (or RadiusY) property of the ellipse's fill brush using the statement:

```
Storyboard.TargetProperty="(Shape.Fill).RadiusX"
```

The Color of the GradientStop of the brush is also changed. Since the GradientStop is a collection, the color of the third GradientStop (with a LightBlue color) can be changed using the following XAML snippet:

```
<ColorAnimation
    Storyboard.TargetName="ellipse"
    Storyboard.TargetProperty=
        "(Shape.Fill).(GradientBrush.GradientStops)[2].(GradientStop.Color)"
    To="Black" Duration="0:0:2"
    RepeatBehavior="5x"/>
```

The RepeatBehavior is set to 5x, indicating that you want to repeat the original animation five times. Remember here that if you set the RepeatBehavior property to Forever, the program will throw an exception when you click the SkipToFill button, because the animation never ends and the final value is never reached.

Figure 6-2 illustrates the results of running this example.

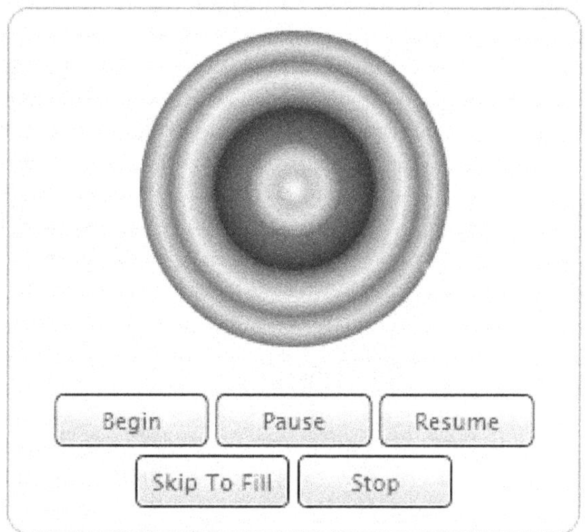

Figure 6-2 Interactive animation.

Animation and Transformation

Transformation is a powerful approach for customizing elements. When you apply transforms, you don't just change the bounds of an element. In fact, the entire visual appearance of the element can be moved by translation, enlarged or shrunk by scaling, skewed by skew transforms, or rotated by rotation transforms. For example, if you animate the rotation of a button using a RotateTransform, the entire button is rotated, including its border and its inner content.

Animating Translation

As you learned in the previous chapters, you can apply transforms to any element, even brush objects. In order to use a transform in animation, the first step is to define the transform. For example, if you want to perform a translation on a Rectangle shape, you need to specify the rectangle's RenderTransform property using the TranslateTransform:

```
<Rectangle Width="200" Height="35" Fill="Blue">
    <Rectangle.RenderTransform>
        <TranslateTransform/>
    </Rectangle.RenderTransform>
</Rectangle>
```

To animate this transformation, you need to create a Storyboard object in a resources block, which is attached to an event hander to make the rectangle translate when the mouse moves over it. For this interactive animation, the RenderTransform.X property (corresponding to the translation in the X direction) can be used as the target property.

```
    <Storyboard x:name=="storyboard1" >
<DoubleAnimation x:Name="animation1" Storyboard.TargetProperty=
    "(UIElement.RenderTransform).(TranslateTransform.X)"
    Duration="0:0:1"   From="0" To="70"/>
 </Storyboard>
```

The above XAML snippet creates a rectangle that moves 70 units in the X direction in one second. When your mouse leaves the rectangle, you can use a second Storyboard object that responds to the MouseLeave event. This animation leaves out the From property, which means it seamlessly translates the rectangle back to its original position in a snappy 0.5 seconds.

```
<Storyboard x:Name="storyboard2">
<DoubleAnimation x:Name="animation2" Storyboard.TargetProperty=
    "(UIElement.RenderTransform).(TranslateTransform.X)"
    Duration="0:0:0.5" To="0"/>
</Storyboard>
```

Let's start with a new Silverlight project and name it Exampe06-5. The following is the XAML file of this example:

```
<UserControl x:Class="Example06_5.Page"
    xmlns="http://schemas.microsoft.com/client/2007"
    xmlns:x="http://schemas.microsoft.com/winfx/2006/xaml"
    Width="320" Height="280">

    <UserControl.Resources>
        <Storyboard x:Name="storyboard1">
            <DoubleAnimation x:Name="animation1"
Storyboard.TargetProperty="(UIElement.RenderTransform).(TranslateTransform.X)"
                        Duration="0:0:1" From="0" To="70"/>
        </Storyboard>
        <Storyboard x:Name="storyboard2">
            <DoubleAnimation x:Name="animation2"
Storyboard.TargetProperty="(UIElement.RenderTransform).(TranslateTransform.X)"
                        Duration="0:0:0.5" To="0"/>
        </Storyboard>
    </UserControl.Resources>

    <Grid x:Name="LayoutRoot" Background="White">
        <Border BorderBrush="Gray" BorderThickness="1"
                CornerRadius="10" Margin="10">
            <Canvas Margin="10">
                <Rectangle x:Name="rect1" Fill="Red" Canvas.Top="0"
                           Width="200" Height="35"
                           MouseEnter="rect_MouseEnter"
                           MouseLeave="rect_MouseLeave">
                  <Rectangle.RenderTransform>
                      <TranslateTransform/>
                  </Rectangle.RenderTransform>
                </Rectangle>
                <Rectangle x:Name="rect2" Fill="Green" Canvas.Top="40"
                           Width="200" Height="35"
                           MouseEnter="rect_MouseEnter"
                           MouseLeave="rect_MouseLeave">
                    <Rectangle.RenderTransform>
                        <TranslateTransform/>
                    </Rectangle.RenderTransform>
                </Rectangle>
                <Rectangle x:Name="rect3" Fill="Blue" Canvas.Top="80"
                           Width="200" Height="35"
```

```
                    MouseEnter="rect_MouseEnter"
                    MouseLeave="rect_MouseLeave">
            <Rectangle.RenderTransform>
                <TranslateTransform/>
            </Rectangle.RenderTransform>
        </Rectangle>
        <Rectangle x:Name="rect4" Fill="Yellow" Canvas.Top="120"
                    Width="200" Height="35"
                    MouseEnter="rect_MouseEnter"
                    MouseLeave="rect_MouseLeave">
            <Rectangle.RenderTransform>
                <TranslateTransform/>
            </Rectangle.RenderTransform>
        </Rectangle>
        <Rectangle x:Name="rect5" Fill="Purple" Canvas.Top="160"
                    Width="200" Height="35"
                    MouseEnter="rect_MouseEnter"
                    MouseLeave="rect_MouseLeave">
            <Rectangle.RenderTransform>
                <TranslateTransform/>
            </Rectangle.RenderTransform>
        </Rectangle>
        <Rectangle x:Name="rect6" Fill="Gray" Canvas.Top="200"
                    Width="200" Height="35"
                    MouseEnter="rect_MouseEnter"
                    MouseLeave="rect_MouseLeave">
            <Rectangle.RenderTransform>
                <TranslateTransform/>
            </Rectangle.RenderTransform>
        </Rectangle>
    </Canvas>
  </Border>
 </Grid>
</UserControl>
```

In this example, we create two Storyboard objects, storyboard1 and storyboard2, which will be attached to the MouseEnter and MouseLeave event handlers of the rectangles respectively. Please note that we didn't specify the Storyboard.TargetName property in storyboard1 and storyboard2, because we want to dynamically change this property. We want to apply the same animation to all six of the rectangles. Dynamically changing the Storyboard.TargetName property is especially useful when you have a large number of objects that have similar animations applied to them. It is inconvenient and messy to create separate Storyboard objects for each rectangle in this example. It is a better programming practice to reuse the same Storyboard.

The following is the code-behind file of this example:

```
using System;
using System.Windows;
using System.Windows.Controls;
using System.Windows.Input;
using System.Windows.Media;
using System.Windows.Media.Animation;
using System.Windows.Shapes;

namespace Example06_5
```

```
{
    public partial class Page : UserControl
    {
        public Page()
        {
            InitializeComponent();
        }

        private void rect_MouseEnter(object sender, MouseEventArgs e)
        {
            storyboard1.Stop();
            Rectangle rect = sender as Rectangle;
            animation1.SetValue(Storyboard.TargetNameProperty, rect.Name);
            storyboard1.Begin();
        }

        private void rect_MouseLeave(object sender, MouseEventArgs e)
        {
            storyboard2.Stop();
            Rectangle rect = sender as Rectangle;
            animation2.SetValue(Storyboard.TargetNameProperty, rect.Name);
            storyboard2.Begin();
        }
    }
}
```

Inside the MouseEnter or MouseLeave event handler, we first stop the Storyboard animation, which is necessary here. If the Storyboard is running and you try to change the Storyboard.TargetName property of the animation objects programmatically, Silverlight will encounter an error. Next, you set a reference to the rectangle that was clicked by casting the sender object. The following step is to change the TargetName property of the animation to the name of the rectangle that was clicked. Finally, you call the Begin method to start the animation.

Figure 6-3 illustrates the results of running this example.

Figure 6-3 Animating Translation.

If your mouse moves over any rectangle, that rectangle will move 70 units toward right. When your mouse leaves, the rectangle will return back to its original position.

Rolling Balls

You can use an approach similar to the one used in the previous section to animate a rotation. Here I'll present a rolling ball example that shows how to create a rotation animation.

The motion of a rolling ball consists of two motions, translation and rotation. If the ball rolls without slipping, the center of the ball will move a distance of $2\pi r$ for every revolution of the ball, where r is the radius of the ball. Thus, for a rolling ball animation, you need to animate two transforms, translation and rotation. The translation and rotation must satisfy the non-slipping condition.

In this example, you create three balls. The first ball moves and rotates with a constant speed, the second ball with a faster speed, and the third one with a slower speed. Start a new Silverlight Project and name it Example06-6. Here is the XAML file of this example:

```
<UserControl x:Class="Example06_6.Page"
    xmlns="http://schemas.microsoft.com/client/2007"
    xmlns:x="http://schemas.microsoft.com/winfx/2006/xaml"
    Width="520" Height="310">

    <UserControl.Resources>
        <Storyboard x:Name="storyboard1">
            <DoubleAnimation Storyboard.TargetName="ellipse1"
                Storyboard.TargetProperty="(UIElement.RenderTransform).
                (TransformGroup.Children)[1].(TranslateTransform.X)"
                From="0" To="450" Duration="0:0:5"
                RepeatBehavior="Forever" AutoReverse="True"/>
            <DoubleAnimation x:Name="da1_rotation"
                Storyboard.TargetName="ellipse1"
                Storyboard.TargetProperty="(UIElement.RenderTransform).
                (TransformGroup.Children)[0].(RotateTransform.Angle)"
                From="0" Duration="0:0:5" RepeatBehavior="Forever"
                AutoReverse="True"/>
        </Storyboard>

        <Storyboard x:Name="storyboard2">
            <DoubleAnimation Storyboard.TargetName="ellipse2"
                Storyboard.TargetProperty="(UIElement.RenderTransform).
                (TransformGroup.Children)[1].(TranslateTransform.X)"
                From="0" To="450" Duration="0:0:5" RepeatBehavior="Forever"
                AutoReverse="True" SpeedRatio="1.5"/>
            <DoubleAnimation x:Name="da2_rotation"
                Storyboard.TargetName="ellipse2"
                Storyboard.TargetProperty="(UIElement.RenderTransform).
                (TransformGroup.Children)[0].(RotateTransform.Angle)"
                From="0" Duration="0:0:5" RepeatBehavior="Forever"
                AutoReverse="True" SpeedRatio="1.5"/>
        </Storyboard>

        <Storyboard x:Name="storyboard3">
            <DoubleAnimation Storyboard.TargetName="ellipse3"
                Storyboard.TargetProperty="(UIElement.RenderTransform).
```

```
                (TransformGroup.Children)[1].(TranslateTransform.X)"
                From="0" To="450" Duration="0:0:5" RepeatBehavior="Forever"
                AutoReverse="True" SpeedRatio="0.5"/>
            <DoubleAnimation x:Name="da3_rotation"
                Storyboard.TargetName="ellipse3"
                Storyboard.TargetProperty="(UIElement.RenderTransform).
                (TransformGroup.Children)[0].(RotateTransform.Angle)"
                From="0" Duration="0:0:5" RepeatBehavior="Forever"
                AutoReverse="True" SpeedRatio="0.5"/>
        </Storyboard>
    </UserControl.Resources>

    <Grid x:Name="LayoutRoot" Background="White">
        <Border BorderBrush="Gray" BorderThickness="1" Margin="10"
                CornerRadius="10">
            <Canvas Margin="0,10,0,0">
                <Line X1="0" Y1="62" X2="499" Y2="62" Stroke="Gray"
                      StrokeThickness="5"/>
                <Ellipse x:Name="ellipse1" Width="50" Height="50"
                         Stroke="Blue" Canvas.Top="10" Canvas.Left="0"
                         RenderTransformOrigin="0.5,0.5">
                    <Ellipse.Fill>
                        <LinearGradientBrush>
                            <GradientStop Color="Blue" Offset="0.5"/>
                            <GradientStop Color="LightBlue" Offset="0.5"/>
                        </LinearGradientBrush>
                    </Ellipse.Fill>
                    <Ellipse.RenderTransform>
                          <TransformGroup>
                                 <RotateTransform/>
                                 <TranslateTransform/>
                          </TransformGroup>
                    </Ellipse.RenderTransform>
                </Ellipse>

                <Line X1="0" Y1="132" X2="499" Y2="132" Stroke="Gray"
                      StrokeThickness="5"/>
                <Ellipse x:Name="ellipse2" Width="50" Height="50"
                         Stroke="Red" Canvas.Top="80" Canvas.Left="0"
                         RenderTransformOrigin="0.5,0.5">
                    <Ellipse.Fill>
                        <LinearGradientBrush>
                            <GradientStop Color="Red" Offset="0.5"/>
                            <GradientStop Color="LightSalmon" Offset="0.5"/>
                        </LinearGradientBrush>
                    </Ellipse.Fill>
                    <Ellipse.RenderTransform>
                        <TransformGroup>
                           <RotateTransform/>
                            <TranslateTransform/>
                        </TransformGroup>
                    </Ellipse.RenderTransform>
                </Ellipse>

                <Line X1="0" Y1="202" X2="499" Y2="202" Stroke="Gray"
```

```
                    StrokeThickness="5"/>
            <Ellipse x:Name="ellipse3" Width="50" Height="50"
                     Stroke="Green" Canvas.Top="150" Canvas.Left="0"
                     RenderTransformOrigin="0.5,0.5">
                <Ellipse.Fill>
                    <LinearGradientBrush>
                        <GradientStop Color="Green" Offset="0.5"/>
                        <GradientStop Color="LightGreen" Offset="0.5"/>
                    </LinearGradientBrush>
                </Ellipse.Fill>
                <Ellipse.RenderTransform>
                    <TransformGroup>
                        <RotateTransform/>
                        <TranslateTransform/>
                    </TransformGroup>
                </Ellipse.RenderTransform>
            </Ellipse>

            <StackPanel Orientation="Horizontal"
                        Canvas.Top="220" Margin="10">
                <Button Content="Start" Width="100" Height="25"
                        Click="Start_Click" Margin="15 0 5 0"/>
                <Button Content="Pause" Width="100" Height="25"
                        Click="Pause_Click" Margin="10 0 5 0"/>
                <Button Content="Resume" Width="100" Height="25"
                        Click="Resume_Click" Margin="10 0 5 0"/>
                <Button Content="Stop" Width="100" Height="25"
                        Click="Stop_Click" Margin="10 0 5 0"/>
            </StackPanel>
        </Canvas>
    </Border>
  </Grid>
</UserControl>
```

The following is the code-behind file of this example:

```
using System;
using System.Windows;
using System.Windows.Controls;
using System.Windows.Input;
using System.Windows.Media;
using System.Windows.Media.Animation;
using System.Windows.Shapes;

namespace Example06_6
{
    public partial class Page : UserControl
    {
        public Page()
        {
            InitializeComponent();
        }

        private void Start_Click(object sender, RoutedEventArgs e)
        {
            double nRotation = 360 * 450 / 2 / Math.PI / 25;
```

```
                // Animating ellipse1 with a constant speed:
                storyboard1.Stop();
                da1_rotation.To = nRotation;
                storyboard1.Begin();

                //Animatiing ellipse2 with a faster speed:
                storyboard2.Stop();
                da2_rotation.To = nRotation;
                storyboard2.Begin();

                // Animating ellipse3 with a slower speed:
                storyboard3.Stop();
                da3_rotation.To = nRotation;
                storyboard3.Begin();
            }

            private void Pause_Click(object sender, RoutedEventArgs e)
            {
                storyboard1.Pause();
                storyboard2.Pause();
                storyboard3.Pause();
            }

            private void Resume_Click(object sender, RoutedEventArgs e)
            {
                storyboard1.Resume();
                storyboard2.Resume();
                storyboard3.Resume();
            }

            private void Stop_Click(object sender, RoutedEventArgs e)
            {
                storyboard1.Stop();
                storyboard2.Stop();
                storyboard3.Stop();
            }
        }
    }
```

You might remember that in the Example06-3 project, we use a single Storyboard object to animate several rectangles. In this case, you need to stop the Storyboard before you dynamically change the properties of its animation objects. However, in the current example, it might not be desirable to stop an animation on one ball so that the animation can start on another ball. In fact, we want to start the animations on these three balls at the same time. Thus, you can't use the same animation object to run three separate animations at the same time, because there is only one TargetName. Therefore, we create three Storyboard objects, with each being attached to a single ball.

Each ball's RotateTransform and TranslateTransform properties are exposed in XAML, and are then used in the animations. The translation is animated from 0 to 450 in 5 seconds. For a non-slipping rolling ball, you need to calculate how many revolutions the ball goes through in the translation distance using the formula:

```
double nRotation = 360 * 450 / 2 / Math.PI / 25;
```

This gives the total degrees the ball should rotate in 5 seconds. Since it is impossible to include any mathernatical calculations in XAML, we specify the To property of the rotation animation in code.

Figure 6-4 shows the results of running this example. You can interactively control animations and examine how the SpeedRatio property affects the balls' motion.

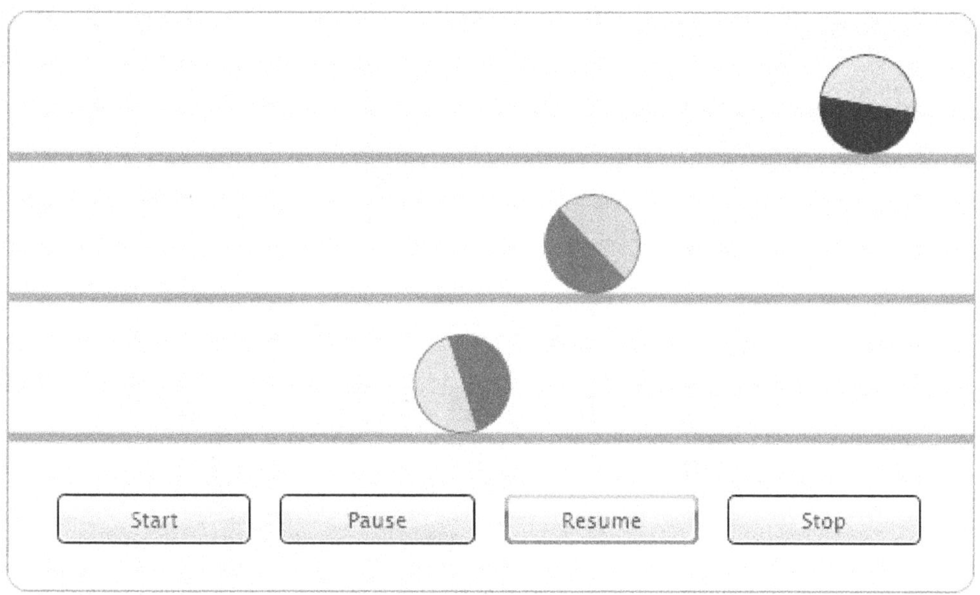

Figure 6-4 Rolling balls.

Combining Transform Animations

In Silverlight, you can easily perform composite transforms on any element using the TransformGroup, as discussed in the previous example. This can be done by simply setting the element's RenderTransform property using the TransformGroup.

Let's look at another example, named Example06-7, to illustrate how to animate composite transforms. In this example, you want to perform a combining transform, consisting of a scale, skew, and rotation, on a buttom:

```
<Button.RenderTransform>
    <TransformGroup>
        <ScaleTransform/>
        <SkewTransform/>
        <RotateTransform/>
    </TransformGroup>
</Button.RenderTransform>
```

To target this RenderTransform collection, you need to use the following path syntax:

```
RenderTransform.Children[CollectionIndex].PropertyName
```

where CollectionIndex is the index of objects in the TransformGroup. For example, if you want to animate the Angle property of the RotateTransform, you need to set the CollectionIndex = 2, as shown in the code snippet:

```
<DoubleAnimation
    Storyboard.TargetProperty="(UIElement.RenderTransform).
        (TransformGroup.Children)[2].(RotateTransform.Angle)"
    Duration="0:0:1" To="360"/>
```

Here is the XAML file of this example:

```
<UserControl x:Class="Example06_7.Page"
    xmlns="http://schemas.microsoft.com/client/2007"
    xmlns:x="http://schemas.microsoft.com/winfx/2006/xaml"
    Width="300" Height="300">

    <UserControl.Resources>
        <Storyboard x:Name="storyboard1">
            <DoubleAnimation
                Storyboard.TargetProperty="(UIElement.RenderTransform).
                (TransformGroup.Children)[0].(ScaleTransform.ScaleX)"
                Duration="0:0:1" To="1.5"/>
            <DoubleAnimation
                Storyboard.TargetProperty="(UIElement.RenderTransform).
                (TransformGroup.Children)[0].(ScaleTransform.ScaleY)"
                Duration="0:0:1" To="1.5"/>
            <DoubleAnimation
                Storyboard.TargetProperty="(UIElement.RenderTransform).
                (TransformGroup.Children)[1].(SkewTransform.AngleX)"
                Duration="0:0:1" To="30"/>
            <DoubleAnimation
                Storyboard.TargetProperty="(UIElement.RenderTransform).
                (TransformGroup.Children)[1].(SkewTransform.AngleY)"
                Duration="0:0:1" To="30"/>
            <DoubleAnimation
                Storyboard.TargetProperty="(UIElement.RenderTransform).
                (TransformGroup.Children)[2].(RotateTransform.Angle)"
                Duration="0:0:1" To="360"/>
        </Storyboard>

        <Storyboard x:Name="storyboard2">
            <DoubleAnimation
                Storyboard.TargetProperty="(UIElement.RenderTransform).
                (TransformGroup.Children)[0].(ScaleTransform.ScaleX)"
                Duration="0:0:1" To="1"/>
            <DoubleAnimation
                Storyboard.TargetProperty="(UIElement.RenderTransform).
                (TransformGroup.Children)[0].(ScaleTransform.ScaleY)"
                Duration="0:0:1" To="1"/>
            <DoubleAnimation
                Storyboard.TargetProperty="(UIElement.RenderTransform).
                (TransformGroup.Children)[1].(SkewTransform.AngleX)"
                Duration="0:0:1" To="0"/>
            <DoubleAnimation
                Storyboard.TargetProperty="(UIElement.RenderTransform).
                (TransformGroup.Children)[1].(SkewTransform.AngleY)"
```

```
                Duration="0:0:1" To="0"/>
            <DoubleAnimation
                Storyboard.TargetProperty="(UIElement.RenderTransform).
                (TransformGroup.Children)[2].(RotateTransform.Angle)"
                Duration="0:0:1" To="0"/>
        </Storyboard>
    </UserControl.Resources>

    <Grid x:Name="LayoutRoot" Background="White">
        <Border BorderBrush="Gray" BorderThickness="1"
                CornerRadius="10" Margin="10">
            <StackPanel HorizontalAlignment="Center">
                <Button Click="Button_Click" MouseEnter="Button_MouseEnter"
                        MouseLeave="Button_MouseLeave"
                        Content="Button1" Margin="10,30,10,10" Width="80"
                        Height="40" x:Name="Button1"
                        RenderTransformOrigin="0.5,0.5">
                  <Button.RenderTransform>
                        <TransformGroup>
                                <ScaleTransform/>
                                <SkewTransform/>
                                <RotateTransform/>
                        </TransformGroup>
                  </Button.RenderTransform>
                </Button>

                <Button Click="Button_Click" MouseEnter="Button_MouseEnter"
                        MouseLeave="Button_MouseLeave"
                        Content="Button2" Margin="10" Width="80" Height="40"
                        x:Name="Button2" RenderTransformOrigin="0.5,0.5">
                    <Button.RenderTransform>
                        <TransformGroup>
                            <ScaleTransform/>
                            <SkewTransform/>
                            <RotateTransform/>
                        </TransformGroup>
                    </Button.RenderTransform>
                </Button>

                <Button Click="Button_Click" MouseEnter="Button_MouseEnter"
                        MouseLeave="Button_MouseLeave"
                        Content="Button3" Margin="10" Width="80" Height="40"
                        x:Name="Button3" RenderTransformOrigin="0.5,0.5">
                    <Button.RenderTransform>
                        <TransformGroup>
                            <ScaleTransform/>
                            <SkewTransform/>
                            <RotateTransform/>
                        </TransformGroup>
                    </Button.RenderTransform>
                </Button>
                <TextBlock x:Name="myText" Text="text" Margin="5,40,5,5"/>
            </StackPanel>
        </Border>
    </Grid>
```

```
</UserControl>
```

The corresponding code-behind file is listed below:

```
using System;
using System.Windows;
using System.Windows.Controls;
using System.Windows.Input;
using System.Windows.Media;
using System.Windows.Media.Animation;
using System.Windows.Shapes;

namespace Example06_7
{
    public partial class Page : UserControl
    {
        public Page()
        {
            InitializeComponent();
        }

        private void Button_Click(object sender, RoutedEventArgs e)
        {
            Button button = sender as Button;
            myText.Text = "You are clicking on " + button.Name;

        }

        private void Button_MouseEnter(object sender, MouseEventArgs e)
        {
            storyboard1.Stop();
            Button button = sender as Button;
            Storyboard.SetTargetName(storyboard1, button.Name);
            storyboard1.Begin();
        }

        private void Button_MouseLeave(object sender, MouseEventArgs e)
        {
            storyboard2.Stop();
            Button button = sender as Button;
            Storyboard.SetTargetName(storyboard2, button.Name);
             storyboard2.Begin();
        }
    }
}
```

In this example, the button scales 1.5 times in both the X and Y directions, skews 30 degrees in both the X and Y axes, and rotates one revolution. All of these transforms are performed in one second whenever your mouse moves over the button. When the button is being transformed, it is still completely functioning – for example, you can click it and handle the Click event as normal.

To make sure the button transforms around its center, you set the RenderTransformOrigin = “0.5, 0.5”. Note that the RenderTransformOrigin property uses relative units from 0 to 1, so the point (0.5, 0.5) represents the center.

To stop the composite transforms when your mouse leaves, you starts another animation that replaces the first one. This animation seamlessly transforms the button back to its original position in one second.

The code-behind file handles the button events. Running this project produces the results shown in Figure 6-5.

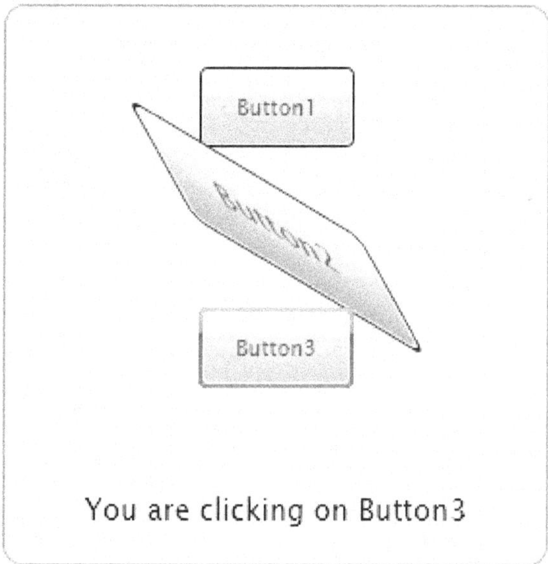

Figure 6-5 Combining transform animations.

Frame-Based Animation

The animations you have seen so far are based on the linear interpolation approach. In this section, you'll learn other types of animations, including key-frame animation and spline key frame animation.

Like the From-To-By animations based on linear interpolation, key-frame animations animate the value of a target property. A single key-frame animation can create transitions among any number of target values.

Silverlight also provides a way to create frame-based animation without using target properties. This type of animation is useful when you want to create physics-based animations or are modeling special particle effects such as fire, snow, and bubbles.

Key-Frame Animation

When you create an animation based on linear interpolation, you specify the starting and ending points. However, this approach may not enough in some situations. For example, what if you want to create an animation that has multiple segments and moves less regularly? The easiest way is to use key-frame animation.

A key-frame animation creates a transition among its target values over its Duration and can include any number of segments. Each segment represents an initial, final, or intermediate value in the animation. When you run the animation, it moves smoothly from one target value to another. To specify the animation's target values, you create key frame objects and add them to the animation's KeyFrames collection.

In addition to supporting multiple target values, some key-frame methods also support multiple interpolations. An animation's interpolation method defines how it transitions from one value to the next. There are three types of interpolations: discrete, linear, and splined.

Let's look at an example. Start with a new Silverlight project and name it Example06-8. In this example, a rectangle is painted using the LinearGradientBrush. You'll animate its GradientStop's Color property, which uses the custom color maps defined in Chapter 5. For each key frame, you specify a custom color map, such as Spring, Summer, Autumn, Winter, or Cool. The ColorAnimationUsingKeyFrames class is used to create a smooth transition from one color map to another. Here is the markup of this example:

```
<UserControl x:Class="Example06_8.Page"
    xmlns="http://schemas.microsoft.com/client/2007"
    xmlns:x="http://schemas.microsoft.com/winfx/2006/xaml"
    Width="300" Height="200" Loaded="Page_Loaded">

    <Grid x:Name="LayoutRoot" Background="White">
        <Border BorderBrush="Gray" BorderThickness="1"
                CornerRadius="10" Margin="10">
            <StackPanel Margin="15">

                <TextBlock  Name="label" TextAlignment="Center"
                            Foreground="Blue" Text="Colormap animation:"/>

                <Rectangle Name="rect" Width="200" Height="100"
                           Stroke="Blue" Margin="10">
                    <Rectangle.Fill>
                        <LinearGradientBrush StartPoint="0,0" EndPoint="1,0">
                            <GradientStop Offset="0"/>
                            <GradientStop Offset="1"/>
                        </LinearGradientBrush>
                    </Rectangle.Fill>
                </Rectangle>

                <StackPanel.Resources>
                    <Storyboard x:Name="storyboard1">
<ColorAnimationUsingKeyFrames Storyboard.TargetName="rect"
            Storyboard.TargetProperty="(Shape.Fill).
            (GradientBrush.GradientStops)[0].(GradientStop.Color)"
            RepeatBehavior="Forever">
    <LinearColorKeyFrame Value="#FF00FF" KeyTime="0:0:0" />
    <LinearColorKeyFrame Value="#00805A" KeyTime="0:0:5" />
    <LinearColorKeyFrame Value="#FF0000" KeyTime="0:0:10" />
    <LinearColorKeyFrame Value="#0000FF" KeyTime="0:0:15" />
    <LinearColorKeyFrame Value="#00FFFF" KeyTime="0:0:20" />
    <LinearColorKeyFrame Value="#FF00FF" KeyTime="0:0:25" />
</ColorAnimationUsingKeyFrames>

<ColorAnimationUsingKeyFrames Storyboard.TargetName="rect"
```

```
        Storyboard.TargetProperty="(Shape.Fill).
        (GradientBrush.GradientStops)[1].(GradientStop.Color)"
        RepeatBehavior="Forever">
    <LinearColorKeyFrame Value="#FFFF00" KeyTime="0:0:0" />
    <LinearColorKeyFrame Value="#FFFF5A" KeyTime="0:0:5" />
    <LinearColorKeyFrame Value="#FFFF00" KeyTime="0:0:10" />
    <LinearColorKeyFrame Value="#00FF08" KeyTime="0:0:15" />
    <LinearColorKeyFrame Value="#FF00FF" KeyTime="0:0:20" />
    <LinearColorKeyFrame Value="#FFFF00" KeyTime="0:0:25" />
</ColorAnimationUsingKeyFrames>
                    </Storyboard>
                </StackPanel.Resources>
            </StackPanel>
        </Border>
    </Grid>
</UserControl>
```

This example includes two key-frame animations, each one with six key frames. These key-frame animations are used to animate the color change of the LinearGradientBrush by adjusting its GradientStop's Color property. Each pair of GradientStops at a given KeyTime forms a custom colormap.

The animations in this example aren't reversible, but they do repeat. To make sure there is no jump between the final value of one iteration and the starting value of the next iteration, the animations end at the same value as their starting value. That is why you use six key frames to animate five color maps.

Figure 6-6 illustrates the results of running this example.

The above example uses a linear interpolation method. There is another type of key frame: the spline key frame. Every class that supports linear key frames also supports spline key frames.

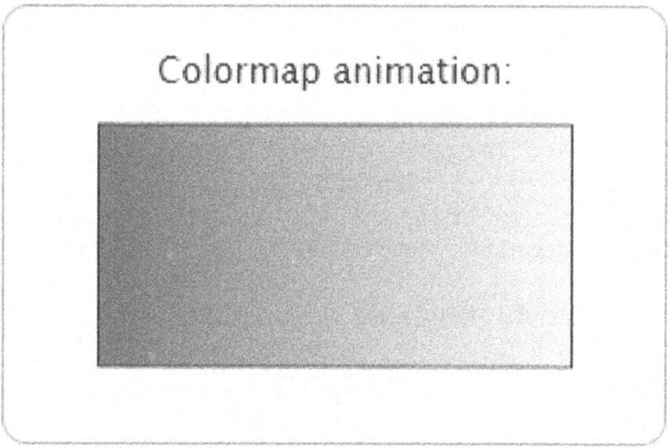

Figure 6-6 Key frame animation.

Spline Key-Frame Animation

Splined interpolation can be used to achieve more realistic timing effects. Spline key frames allow you to animate with splined interpolation. With other key frames, you specify a Value and KeyTime. With a spline key frame, you also need to specify a KeySpline. Using the KeySpline property, you define a cubic Bezier curve that affects the way interpolation is performed. This approach gives you the ability to create more seamless acceleration and deceleration. The following snippet shows a single spline key frame for the DoubleAnimationUsingKeyFrames class:

```
<SplineDoubleKeyFrame Value="20" KeyTime="0:0:5"
                      KeySpline="0,1,1,0"/>
```

You may remember from the discussion in Chapter 4 that a cubic Bezier curve is defined by a start point, an end point, and two control points. The KeySpline property of a spline key frame defines two control points of a Bezier curve that extends from (0, 0) to (1, 1). The first control point controls the curve factor of the first half of the Bezier curve, and the second control point controls the curve factor of the second half of the Bezier segment. The resulting curve describes the rate of change for that spine key frame.

Let's start with a new Silverlight project and call it Example06-9. This example demonstrates a key spline animation by comparing the motion of two balls across a Canvas. The spline key frame animation simulates the case of a ball moving along a trajectory under gravity. At the beginning, the ball moves upward with a initial velocity. Its velocity becomes zero when it reaches the highest point. After that, the ball starts free falling with an acceleration equal to the force of gravity. This process is animated approximately by two spline key frames.

Here is the XAML code of this example:

```
<UserControl x:Class="Example06_9.Page"
    xmlns="http://schemas.microsoft.com/client/2007"
    xmlns:x="http://schemas.microsoft.com/winfx/2006/xaml"
    Width="400" Height="300">

    <UserControl.Resources>
        <Storyboard x:Name="storyboard1">
            <DoubleAnimation Storyboard.TargetName="ball1"
                Storyboard.TargetProperty="(Canvas.Left)"
                To="350" Duration="0:0:5" RepeatBehavior="Forever"
                AutoReverse="True"/>

            <DoubleAnimationUsingKeyFrames Storyboard.TargetName="ball2"
                Storyboard.TargetProperty="(Canvas.Left)"
                Duration="0:0:5" RepeatBehavior="Forever"
                AutoReverse="True">
                <SplineDoubleKeyFrame Value="175" KeyTime="0:0:2.5"
                                      KeySpline="0.25,0.5,0.75,1" />
                <SplineDoubleKeyFrame Value="350" KeyTime="0:0:5"
                                      KeySpline="0.25,0.0 0.75,0.5" />
            </DoubleAnimationUsingKeyFrames>
        </Storyboard>
    </UserControl.Resources>

    <Grid x:Name="LayoutRoot" Background="White">
        <Border BorderBrush="Gray" BorderThickness="1"
                CornerRadius="10" Margin="10">
            <Canvas >
                <TextBlock Canvas.Left="10" Canvas.Top="10">
                           Ball moves in a constant speed</TextBlock>
                <Ellipse Name="ball1" Canvas.Left="0" Canvas.Top="50"
                         Width="30" Height="30">
                    <Ellipse.Fill>
```

```
                    <RadialGradientBrush>
                        <GradientStop Color="Gold" Offset="0"/>
                        <GradientStop Color="DarkGoldenrod" Offset="1"/>
                    </RadialGradientBrush>
                </Ellipse.Fill>
            </Ellipse>

            <TextBlock Canvas.Left="10" Canvas.Top="120">
                     Ball moves following spline key frames</TextBlock>
            <Ellipse Name="ball2" Canvas.Left="0" Canvas.Top="160"
                     Width="30" Height="30">
                <Ellipse.Fill>
                    <RadialGradientBrush>
                        <GradientStop Color="Gold" Offset="0"/>
                        <GradientStop Color="DarkGoldenrod" Offset="1"/>
                    </RadialGradientBrush>
                </Ellipse.Fill>
            </Ellipse>

            <StackPanel Orientation="Horizontal" Margin="5"
                        Canvas.Top="220">
                <Button x:Name="start" Content="Start" Width="80"
                        Height="25" Click="Button_Click" Margin="5"/>
                <Button x:Name="pause" Content="Pause" Width="80"
                        Height="25" Click="Button_Click" Margin="5"/>
                <Button x:Name="resume" Content="Resume" Width="80"
                        Height="25" Click="Button_Click" Margin="5"/>
                <Button x:Name="stop" Content="Stop" Width="80"
                        Height="25" Click="Button_Click" Margin="5"/>
            </StackPanel>

        </Canvas>
    </Border>
</Grid>
</UserControl>
```

In this example, the first ball moves at a constant speed. The second ball reaches a speed of zero at the end of the first spline frame (the 2.5-second mark), when the second SplineDoubleKeyFrame kicks in. Then the ball falls freely with an acceleration that is described approximately by the second spline key frame.

The corresponding code-behind file is listed below:

```
using System;
using System.Windows;
using System.Windows.Controls;
using System.Windows.Input;
using System.Windows.Media;
using System.Windows.Media.Animation;
using System.Windows.Shapes;

namespace Example06_9
{
    public partial class Page : UserControl
    {
        public Page()
```

```
            {
                InitializeComponent();
            }

            private void Button_Click(object sender, RoutedEventArgs e)
            {
                Button button = sender as Button;
                if (button.Name == "start")
                    storyboard1.Begin();
                else if (button.Name == "pause")
                    storyboard1.Pause();
                else if (button.Name == "resume")
                    storyboard1.Resume();
                else if (button.Name == "stop")
                    storyboard1.Stop();
            }
        }
    }
```

Figure 6-7 shows the results of running this application.

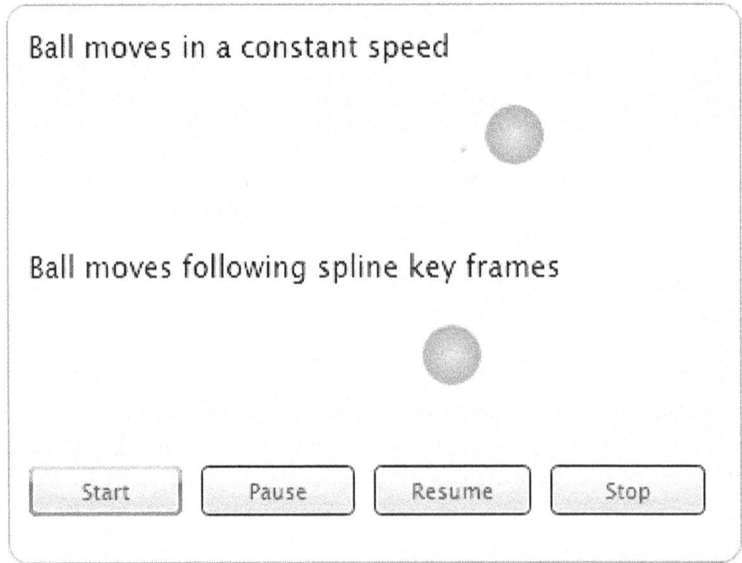

Figure 6-7 Spline key frame animation.

Path Animation

Although Silverlight provides powerful animation features, in some cases, you do need to create your own custom animations. For example, in some situations, you may need a path animation that animates an object along a geometric path. Unlike WPF, Silverlight doesn't include default Path animations. However, you can easily create your own path animations using either timer-based animation or key frame-based animation.

In the following sections, I'll show you in detail how to create path animations.

Path Animation Using Timer

It is possible to use a timer-based animation to mimic path animation in Silverlight. In a path animation, you define a geometric path. As the path animation progresses, it reads the X and Y coordinates from the path and uses this information to generate the output.

Since the timer-based animation completely bypasses the Silverlight animation system, it must be implemented in code. This method requires you to manage everything (including the frame rate) yourself.

The timer system in Silverlight that you can use in your animations is called the DispatcherTimer in the System.Windows.Threading namespace. The DispatcherTimer runs on the same thread as the user interface, and it can directly access objects on the user interface thread.

Using the DispatcherTimer is simple – you first create a DispatcherTimer object, then add the event handler dispatcherTimer_Tick to the Tick event of the DispatcherTimer object. The Interval can be set using a TimeSpan object. Finally, you call the timer's Start() method.

Let's consider an example that shows how to use a timer-based animation to simulate a path animation. Start with a new Silverlight project and name it Example06-10. In this example, you'll animate two balls moving along two ellipse paths. The following is the markup of this example:

```
<UserControl x:Class="Example06_10.Page"
    xmlns="http://schemas.microsoft.com/client/2007"
    xmlns:x="http://schemas.microsoft.com/winfx/2006/xaml"
    Width="380" Height="380" Loaded="Page_Loaded">
    <Grid x:Name="LayoutRoot" Background="White">
        <Border BorderBrush="Gray" BorderThickness="1"
                CornerRadius="10" Margin="10">
            <Canvas>
                <Path Stroke="LightBlue">
                    <Path.Data>
                        <EllipseGeometry Center="180,180"
                            RadiusX="150" RadiusY="75"/>
                    </Path.Data>
                </Path>

                <Path Stroke="LightCoral">
                    <Path.Data>
                        <EllipseGeometry Center="180,180"
                            RadiusX="75" RadiusY="150"/>
                    </Path.Data>
                </Path>

                <Path Fill="Blue">
                    <Path.Data>
                        <EllipseGeometry x:Name="ball1" Center="30,180"
                                         RadiusX="10" RadiusY="10"/>
                    </Path.Data>
                </Path>

                <Path Fill="Red">
                    <Path.Data>
                        <EllipseGeometry x:Name="ball2" Center="180,30"
                                         RadiusX="10" RadiusY="10"/>
```

```
                    </Path.Data>
                </Path>
            </Canvas>
        </Border>
    </Grid>
</UserControl>
```

Note that the two bigger ellipses in the above XAML aren't the real moving paths of the two balls, but are simply used to guide the viewer's eyes. The corresponding code-behind file is listed below:

```
using System;
using System.Windows;
using System.Windows.Controls;
using System.Windows.Threading;
using System.Windows.Input;
using System.Windows.Media;

namespace Example06_10
{
    public partial class Page : UserControl
    {
        private DispatcherTimer timer = new DispatcherTimer();
        private double time = 0;
        private double dt = 0.01;

        public Page()
        {
            InitializeComponent();
        }

        private void Page_Loaded(object sender, RoutedEventArgs e)
        {
            StartAnimation();
        }

        private void StartAnimation()
        {
            timer.Tick += new EventHandler(Timer_Tick);
            timer.Start();
        }

        private void Timer_Tick(object sender, EventArgs e)
        {
            double x = 180 + 150 * Math.Cos(2 * time);
            double y = 180 + 75 * Math.Sin(2 * time);
            ball1.Center = new Point(x, y);
            x = 180 + 75 * Math.Cos(0.5 * time);
            y = 180 + 150 * Math.Sin(0.5 * time);
            ball2.Center = new Point(x, y);
            time += dt;
        }
    }
}
```

You can see from the above code that the animation using a timer is straightforward. The StartAnimation method involves the following timer-related statements:

```
timer.Tick += new EventHandler(Timer_Tick);
timer.Start();
```

Here we add an event handler, Timer_Tick, to the timer.Tick event, and call the timer's Start method to start the animation.

All the animation-related code is implemented in the Timer_Tick event handler. Note how the time variable relates to the timer's tick event. For each tick of the timer, the time adds an additional dt (a constant time increment). The animation progresses forever with the timer's tick event. You can also interactively control the timer-based animation by using the timer's Stop method.

Inside the Timer_Tick event handler, you specify each ball's Center property using an ellipse function. The argument of this function is related to the time difference dt. Thus, as the animation progresses, each ball will move along its respective ellipse path.

Figure 6-8 illustrates the results of running this application.

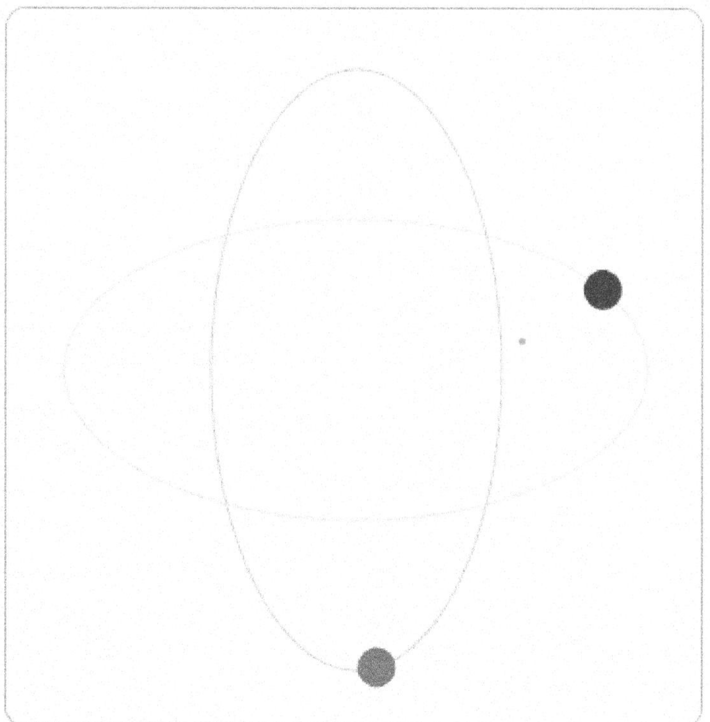

Figure 6-8 Per-frame animation.

In fact, not only can you animate an object along a simple geometric path, you can also move an object along any completed path defined by an arbitrary math function or a collection of points. The following example shows a red ball animated along a complex path described by a math function. Start with a new Silverlight object and name it Example06-11. Here is the XAML file of this example:

```
<UserControl x:Class="Example06_11.Page"
    xmlns="http://schemas.microsoft.com/client/2007"
    xmlns:x="http://schemas.microsoft.com/winfx/2006/xaml"
    Width="460" Height="460" Loaded="Page_Loaded">
```

```
        <Grid x:Name="LayoutRoot" Background="White">
            <Border BorderBrush="Gray" BorderThickness="1"
                    CornerRadius="10" Margin="10">
                <Canvas x:Name="canvas1">
                    <Path Fill="Red" Canvas.ZIndex="5">
                        <Path.Data>
                            <EllipseGeometry x:Name="ball" Center="200,200"
                                             RadiusX="5" RadiusY="5"/>
                        </Path.Data>
                    </Path>
                </Canvas>
            </Border>
        </Grid>
    </UserControl>
```

This XAML creates a red ball in the canvas1. The corresponding code-behind file is listed below:

```
using System;
using System.Windows;
using System.Windows.Threading;
using System.Windows.Controls;
using System.Windows.Input;
using System.Windows.Media;
using System.Windows.Shapes;

namespace Example06_11
{
    public partial class Page : UserControl
    {
        private DispatcherTimer timer = new DispatcherTimer();
        private double time = 0;
        private double dt = 0.005;
        public Page()
        {
            InitializeComponent();

        }

        private void Page_Loaded(object sender, RoutedEventArgs e)
        {
            Polyline pl = new Polyline();
            pl.Stroke = new SolidColorBrush(Colors.LightGray);
            pl.StrokeThickness = 1;
            canvas1.Children.Add(pl);

            for (int i = 0; i < 200; i++)
            {
                double x = 200 + 200 * Math.Cos((double)i / 50) *
                           Math.Cos((double)i / 10);
                double y = 200 + 200 * Math.Sin((double)i / 50) *
                           Math.Cos((double)i / 10);
                pl.Points.Add(new Point(x, y));
            }

            StartAnimation();
        }
```

```
        private void StartAnimation()
        {
            timer.Tick += new EventHandler(Timer_Tick);
            timer.Start();
        }

        private void Timer_Tick(object sender, EventArgs e)
        {
            double x = 200 + 200 * Math.Cos(time) * Math.Cos(5 * time);
            double y = 200 + 200 * Math.Sin(time) * Math.Cos(5 * time);
            ball.Center = new Point(x, y);
            time += dt;
        }
    }
}
```

Note that the animation path displayed on the screen is simply used to guide the viewer's eyes. The red ball moves along this path, which is described by a complicated math function inside the Timer_Tick even handler. You can animate any graphical object along any path sepecified by either a math function or a collection of points. Running this project generates the output shown in Figure 6-9.

Figure 6-9 The ball animated along a complex path.

Path Animation Using Key-Frames

It is also possible to create path animations using key-frame animation. In this case, you can reuse the rich animation feature included in Silverlight. This approach is very convenient when you want to interactively control the path animation.

Let's consider an example that shows how to create a path animation using key-frames. Start with a new Silverlight project and name it Example06-12. The XAML file of this example is very simple:

```
<UserControl x:Class="Example06_12.Page"
    xmlns="http://schemas.microsoft.com/client/2007"
    xmlns:x="http://schemas.microsoft.com/winfx/2006/xaml"
    Width="450" Height="500" Loaded="Page_Loaded">
    <Grid x:Name="LayoutRoot" Background="White">
        <Border BorderBrush="Gray" BorderThickness="1"
                CornerRadius="10" Margin="10">
            <Canvas x:Name="canvas1">
                <Path x:Name="path" Fill="Red" Canvas.ZIndex="5">
                    <Path.Data>
                        <EllipseGeometry x:Name="ball" Center="200,200"
                                 RadiusX="5" RadiusY="5"/>
                    </Path.Data>
                </Path>
                <StackPanel Orientation="Horizontal" Margin="10"
                            Canvas.Top="420" Canvas.Left="25">
                    <Button x:Name="Start" Click="Button_Click" Width="80"
                            Height="25" Content="Start" Margin="5"/>
                    <Button x:Name="Pause" Click="Button_Click" Width="80"
                            Height="25" Content="Pause" Margin="5"/>
                    <Button x:Name="Resume" Click="Button_Click" Width="80"
                            Height="25" Content="Resume" Margin="5"/>
                    <Button x:Name="Stop" Click="Button_Click" Width="80"
                            Height="25" Content="Stop" Margin="5"/>
                </StackPanel>
            </Canvas>
        </Border>
    </Grid>
</UserControl>
```

Here, we create a red ball using a path object with an EllipseGeometry. We'll animate the Center property of the ball along a spiral path. Four buttons are added to the canvas1, which allow you to interactively control the animation. The path animation based on key frames is implemented in the following code-behind file:

```
using System;
using System.Collections.Generic;
using System.Windows;
using System.Windows.Controls;
using System.Windows.Input;
using System.Windows.Media;
using System.Windows.Media.Animation;
using System.Windows.Shapes;

namespace Example06_12
{
    public partial class Page : UserControl
```

```
{
    private Storyboard sb;

    public Page()
    {
        InitializeComponent();
    }

    private void Page_Loaded(object sender, RoutedEventArgs e)
    {
        Polyline pl = new Polyline();
        pl.Stroke = new SolidColorBrush(Colors.LightGray);
        pl.StrokeThickness = 1;
        canvas1.Children.Add(pl);

        for (int i = 0; i < 700; i++)
        {
            double a = (double)(200 + i);
            double x = 200 + Math.Cos(a / 10) * Math.Exp(0.006 * a);
            double y = 200 + Math.Sin(a / 10) * Math.Exp(0.006 * a);
            pl.Points.Add(new Point(x, y));
        }

        SetAnimation();
    }

    private void SetAnimation()
    {
        sb = new Storyboard();
        this.Resources.Add("Animation", sb);

        PointAnimationUsingKeyFrames pa =
            new PointAnimationUsingKeyFrames();
        sb.Children.Add(pa);

        Storyboard.SetTarget(pa, ball);
        Storyboard.SetTargetProperty(pa, new PropertyPath("Center"));
        pa.Duration = new Duration(TimeSpan.FromSeconds(20));
        pa.RepeatBehavior = RepeatBehavior.Forever;
        pa.AutoReverse = true;

        LinearPointKeyFrame frame;
        for (int i = 0; i < 700; i++)
        {
            frame = new LinearPointKeyFrame();
            double a = (double)(200 + i);
            double x = 200 + Math.Cos(a / 10) * Math.Exp(0.006 * a);
            double y = 200 + Math.Sin(a / 10) * Math.Exp(0.006 * a);
            frame.Value = new Point(x, y);
            frame.KeyTime = TimeSpan.FromSeconds(i * 20.0 / 700);
            pa.KeyFrames.Add(frame);
        }
    }
```

```
        private void Button_Click(object sender, RoutedEventArgs e)
        {
            Button button = sender as Button;
            if (button.Name == "Start")
                sb.Begin();
            else if (button.Name == "Pause")
                sb.Pause();
            else if (button.Name == "Resume")
                sb.Resume();
            else if (button.Name == "Stop")
                sb.Stop();
        }
    }
}
```

Inside the Page_loaded event handler, we first create a spiral curve, which is used to guide the viewer's eyes. The path animation is implemented inside the SetAnimation method. We first create a Storyboard object and add it to the resources. Next, we create a PointAnimationUsingKeyFrames object and add it to the Storyboard. We then specify the TargetName, TargetProperty, Duration, RepeatBehavior, and AutoReverse properties. The key step to creating the path animation is to define the LinearPointKeyFrame using a for-loop, where 700 key frames are created using a mathematical spiral function. In this way, you can create any path animation by replacing the spiral function with your own path function, point collection, or data points from a file.

The Button_Click event handler contains the code necessary for controlling the path animation, including Start, Pause, Resume, and Stop. Running this project generates the results shown in Figure 6-10. You can click the corresponding button to interactively control the path animation.

In this chapter, we explored a variety of animation techniques in great detail. You learned how to use animations in code and how to construct and control them with XAML. Now that you've mastered the basics, you can concentrate on the art of animation – deciding which properties to animate and how to get the desired effect. This book provides many code examples on animations, which can be modified and used in your Silverlight applications.

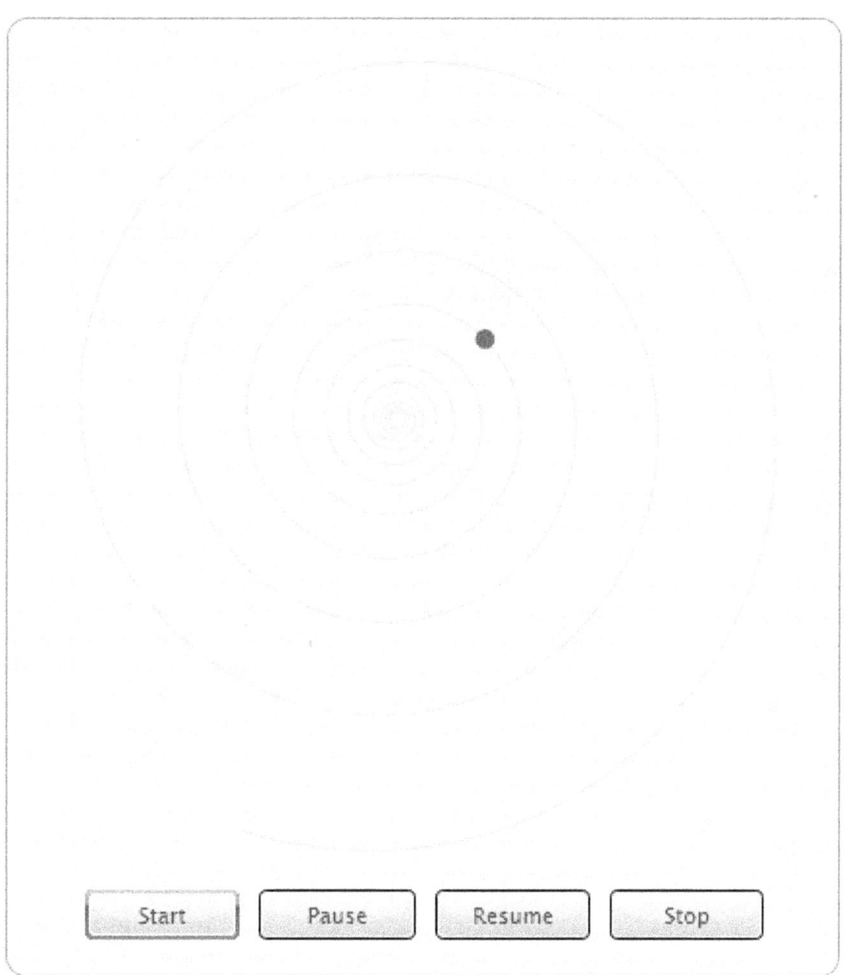

Figure 6-10 Path animation based on key frames.

Chapter 7
Physics and Games in Silverlight

If you are a game programmer, you know how to render complex game scenes on the screen. You know about game theory and how to make your games interesting and attractive. However, if your games aren't based on a solid physics foundation, they'll look and act fake. Therefore, physics plays a crucial role in game programming, because it can make your games more fun to play and more realistic.

In this chapter, you'll learn how to represent physics events and how to create simple 2D physics-based games in Silverlight. The chapter begins with ordinary differential equations (ODEs), which form a mathematical foundation for describing many physics phenomena. It then presents a variety of examples that solve different physics models using the ODE solver, including a pendulum, coupled spring system, projectile, and collision. The simulators implemented in these examples will form a starting point for developing physics-based games.

Ordinary Differiential Equations

Many physics phenomena can be described in terms of a set of ODEs. For example, if a projectile is flying through the air, it will be subject to the force of aerodynamic drag, which is a function of the object's velocity. The force acting on the projectile will vary during its flight, and the resulting equations of motion are a set of ODEs, which can't be solved analytically.

Another example is the spring-mass system. In this system, there are two forces acting on the mass: the elastic recovery force, which is proportional to the displacement of the mass; and the damping force, which is proportional to its velocity. The equations of motion describing this system are also a set of ODEs, which can't be directly solved either.

Fortunately, there are a number of techniques that can be used to solve ODEs when an analytically closed-form solution is impossible. In the next section, a technique called the Runge-Kutta method will be presented which can be used to solve the differential equations that you will encounter in your game programming. This technique has been proven to be versatile, reliable, and applicable to a wide range of applications.

Fourth-Order Runge-Kutta Method

Many techniques have been developed over the years for solving ODEs. The one presented and used in this book is called the fourth-order Runge-Kutta method. This method is one of a family of step-wise interpolation methods, indicating that from a set of initial conditions, the differential equation is solved at discrete increments of the independent variable. For the equation of motion, the independent variable is time. The fourth-order Runge-Kutta method isn't the most efficient technique available, but it is simple and reliable, and gives reasonable results as long as extremely high accuracy isn't required.

The Runge-Kutta method is designed to work on first order differential equations. It starts with an initial set of values of t (time variable) and x (position variable) from which subsequent values of x are calculated as a solution for the differential equations

$$\frac{dx}{dt} = f(x,t) \tag{7.1}$$

Here the function of f(x,t) corresponds to the velocity. Suppose that at a given time t_n, the x-position and velocity are known: x_n and f_n. You want to determine the x at a future time t_n+dt, where dt is a certain time increment. Here are the relations involved in the fourth-order Runge-Kutta method:

$$k_1 = dt \cdot f(x_n, t_n) \tag{7.2}$$

$$k_2 = dt \cdot f\left(x_n + \frac{k_1}{2}, t_n + \frac{dt}{2}\right) \tag{7.3}$$

$$k_3 = dt \cdot f\left(x_n + \frac{k_2}{2}, t_n + \frac{dt}{2}\right) \tag{7.4}$$

$$k_4 = dt \cdot f(x_n + k_3, t_n + dt) \tag{7.5}$$

$$x_{n+1} = x_n + \frac{(k_1 + 2k_2 + 2k_3 + k_4)}{6} \tag{7.6}$$

The Runge-Kutta method can be used to solve any first-order ordinary differential equation. As long as a derivative can be expressed as a function of the dependent and independent variables, this method can be used to calculate the value of the dependent variable.

Higher-Order ODEs

As mentioned preiously, the Runge-Kutta method is designed to solve first order ODEs. However, you can also use this technique to solve higher-order differential equations. The trick is to expand higher-order devivatives into a series of first-order ODEs. The Runge-Kutta method is then applied to each first-order ODE. For example, suppose you want to model a spring-mass system with damping, which can be described by the following second-order differential equations:

$$m\frac{d^2x}{dt^2} = -kx - b\frac{dx}{dt} \tag{7.7}$$

where k is the spring constant and b is the damping coefficient. Since the velocity v = dx/dt, the equation of motion for a spring-mass system in Equation (7.7) can be rewritten in terms of two first-order differential equations:

$$\begin{aligned} \frac{dv}{dt} &= -\frac{k}{m}x - \frac{b}{m}v \\ \frac{dx}{dt} &= v \end{aligned} \tag{7.8}$$

In the above equation, the derivative of v is a function of v and x, and the derivative of x is a function of v. Since the solution of v as a function of time depends on x and the solution of x as a function of time depends on v, the two equations are coupled and must be solved simultaneously using the Runge-Kutta method.

Most of the ODEs in physics are higher-order ODEs. This means that you must expand them into a series of first-order ODEs before they can be solved using the Runge-Kutta method.

ODE Solver

Now it is time to implement the ODE solver based on the fourth-order Runge-Kutta technique. The solver will be written as generally as possible so that it can be used to solve any number of coupled first-order ODEs.

For a given set of initial values t0 and x0 (here, x0 is an array for multiple coupled ODEs), an increment value dt, and an array x that stores the solution, a function f(x,t) (also an array for multiple coupled ODEs), and a number of differential equations N, you can solve ODEs through the following steps:

- Set t = t0 and x = x0.
- Repeat the subsequent tasks for i = 0, to N-1.
- Set k1 = dt * f(x, t).
- Set k2 = dt * f(x + k1/2, t + dt/2).
- Set k3 = dt * f(x + k2/2, t + dt/2).
- Set k4 = dt * f(x + k3, t + dt);
- Set x = x + (k1 + k2 + k3 + k4)/6.
- Set x0 = x.
- Set t = t + dt.

Note that to solve for multiple coupled differential equations, the Runge-Kutta variables k1 to k4 must also be arrays.

Now, start with a new Silverlight project and name it Example07-1. Add a new class, ODESolver, to the project, and change its namespace to XuMath. Here is the code listing of this class:

```
using System;
using System.Windows;

namespace XuMath
{
    public class ODESolver
    {
        public delegate double Function(double[] x, double t);

        public static double[] RungeKutta4(
            Function[] f, double[] x0, double t0, double dt)
        {
            int n = x0.Length;
            double[] k1 = new double[n];
            double[] k2 = new double[n];
            double[] k3 = new double[n];
            double[] k4 = new double[n];

            double t = t0;
            double[] x1 = new double[n];
            double[] x = x0;

            for (int i = 0; i < n; i++)
                k1[i] = dt * f[i](x, t);

            for (int i = 0; i < n; i++)
                x1[i] = x[i] + k1[i] / 2;

            for (int i = 0; i < n; i++)
                k2[i] = dt * f[i](x1, t + dt / 2);

            for (int i = 0; i < n; i++)
                x1[i] = x[i] + k2[i] / 2;

            for (int i = 0; i < n; i++)
                k3[i] = dt * f[i](x1, t + dt / 2);

            for (int i = 0; i < n; i++)
                x1[i] = x[i] + k3[i];

            for (int i = 0; i < n; i++)
                k4[i] = dt * f[i](x1, t + dt);

            for (int i = 0; i < n; i++)
                x[i] += (k1[i] + 2 * k2[i] + 2 * k3[i] + k4[i]) / 6;

            return x;
        }
    }
}
```

Notice that here, you first define a delegate function that takes a double array x and a double time variable t as its input parameters. Then you implement a static method, RungeKutta4, that returns a double array as solutions to the ODEs. This method takes a Function array f, the initial values of the array x0, the initial time t0, and the time increment dt as input parameters. You can see that the delegate function can be used simply like a normal mathematical function, and is very easy to program.

The RungeKutta4 method looks quite simple and only takes a very short code listing. However, it is very powerful in the sense that it can be used to solve first-order ODEs with any number of coupled equations. To apply the ODESolver to a specific physics problem, you simply supply the function array, initial values, and time increment. The following sections will show you how to solve physics problems using this ODE solver.

Pendulum

Let's demonstrate the usefulness of the Runge-Kutta ODE solver by applying it to the problem of a pendulum system. A pendulum is an object that is attached to a pivot point so that it can swing freely. A simple example is the gravity pendulum, which is a mass on the end of a massless string.

Equation of Motion

The equation of motion for this pendulum system can be written in the form:

$$mL\frac{d^2\theta}{dt^2} = -mg\sin\theta - bL\frac{d\theta}{dt} \tag{7.9}$$

Where m is the mass, L is the length of the string, g is the acceleration of gravity (= 9.81m/s^2), b is the damping coefficient, and θ is the swing angle. If you neglect the damping and have a very small swing angle, this equation of motion has a closed form solution. For a large swing angle and finite damping, you have to solve the equation numerically.

In order to solve this second-order differential equation using the Runge-Kutta method, you need to convert it into coupled first-order ODEs. Let dθ/dt = α. You can then rewrite Equation (7.9) in the following form:

$$\begin{aligned} \frac{d\theta}{dt} &= \alpha \\ \frac{d\alpha}{dt} &= -\frac{g}{L}\sin\theta - \frac{b}{m}\alpha \end{aligned} \tag{7.10}$$

This system consists of two coupled first-order ODEs.

Pendulum Simulator

Let's implement the pendulum simulator in the Example07-1 project. This simulator simulates the motion of a pendulum and demonstrates how to solve Equation (7.10) numerically using the Runge-Kutta method. A screenshot of the Pendulum Simulator is shown in Figure 7-1. A string with a mass hanging on one end is displayed in the right pane. In addition, there are several TextBox fields that allow the user to input the mass, string length, damping coefficient, initial angle, and initial angle velocity. A Start button begins the pendulum simulator and a Stop button stops the simulation.

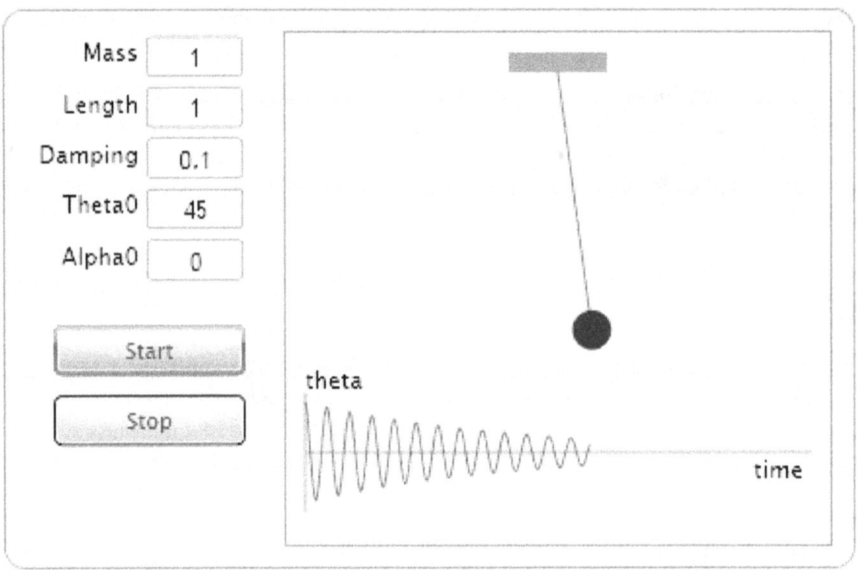

Figure 7-1 Pendulum Simulator.

The layout and user interface are implemented in the following XAML file:

```
<UserControl x:Class="Example07_1.Page"
    xmlns="http://schemas.microsoft.com/client/2007"
    xmlns:x="http://schemas.microsoft.com/winfx/2006/xaml"
    Width="460" Height="300">
    <Grid x:Name="LayoutRoot" Background="White">
        <Border BorderBrush="Gray" BorderThickness="1"
                CornerRadius="10" Margin="10">
            <StackPanel Margin="10" Orientation="Horizontal">
                <StackPanel>
                    <StackPanel Orientation="Horizontal">
                        <TextBlock Margin="5 2 2 5" FontSize="12" Width="55"
                                   TextAlignment="Right">Mass</TextBlock>
                        <TextBox Name="tbMass" Text="1" Width="50" Height="20"
                                 FontSize="12" HorizontalAlignment="Left"
                                 TextAlignment="Center" Margin="2"/>
                    </StackPanel>
                    <StackPanel Orientation="Horizontal">
                        <TextBlock Margin="5 2 2 5" FontSize="12" Width="55"
                                   TextAlignment="Right">Length</TextBlock>
                        <TextBox Name="tbLength" Text="1" Width="50" Height="20"
                                 FontSize="12" HorizontalAlignment="Left"
                                 TextAlignment="Center" Margin="2"/>
                    </StackPanel>
                    <StackPanel Orientation="Horizontal">
                        <TextBlock Margin="5 2 2 5" FontSize="12" Width="55"
                                   TextAlignment="Right">Damping</TextBlock>
                        <TextBox Name="tbDamping" Text="0.1" Width="50"
                                 Height="20" FontSize="12"
                                 HorizontalAlignment="Left"
                                 TextAlignment="Center" Margin="2"/>
```

```
                    </StackPanel>
                    <StackPanel Orientation="Horizontal">
                        <TextBlock Margin="5 2 2 5" FontSize="12" Width="55"
                                   TextAlignment="Right">Theta0</TextBlock>
                        <TextBox Name="tbTheta0" Text="45" Width="50"
                                 Height="20" FontSize="12"
                                 HorizontalAlignment="Left"
                                 TextAlignment="Center" Margin="2"/>
                    </StackPanel>
                    <StackPanel Orientation="Horizontal">
                        <TextBlock Margin="5 2 2 5" FontSize="12" Width="55"
                                   TextAlignment="Right">Alpha0</TextBlock>
                        <TextBox Name="tbAlpha0" Text="0" Width="50" Height="20"
                                 FontSize="12" HorizontalAlignment="Left"
                                 TextAlignment="Center" Margin="2"/>
                    </StackPanel>
                    <Button Click="Start_Click" Content="Start"
                            Margin="15 20,10,10" Width="100" Height="25"/>
                    <Button Click="Stop_Click" Content="Stop" Margin="15,0,10,0"
                            Width="100" Height="25"/>
                </StackPanel>

                <Border BorderBrush="Gray" BorderThickness="1"
                        Margin="10 0 0 0">
                    <Canvas x:Name="canvasLeft" Grid.Column="0"
                            Width="280" Height="280">
                        <Canvas.Clip>
                            <RectangleGeometry Rect="0 0 270 270"/>
                        </Canvas.Clip>
                        <Rectangle Fill="DarkGoldenrod" Width="50" Height="10"
                                   Canvas.Left="115" Canvas.Top="10"/>
                        <Line x:Name="line1" X1 ="140" Y1="20" X2="140"
                              Y2="150" Stroke="Red"/>
                        <Path Fill="Blue">
                            <Path.Data>
                                <EllipseGeometry x:Name="ball" RadiusX="10"
                                                 RadiusY="10" Center="140,150"/>
                            </Path.Data>
                        </Path>
                        <Line X1="10" Y1="210" X2="270" Y2="210" Stroke="Gray"/>
                        <Line X1="10" Y1="180" X2="10" Y2="240" Stroke="Gray"/>
                        <TextBlock Text="theta" FontSize="12"
                                   Canvas.Top="165" Canvas.Left="10"/>
                        <TextBlock Text="theta" FontSize="12"
                                   Canvas.Top="210" Canvas.Left="240"/>
                        <Polyline x:Name="pl" Stroke="Red"/>
                    </Canvas>
                </Border>
            </StackPanel>
        </Border>
    </Grid>
</UserControl>
```

Here, you need an animation method to display the real-time motion of the pendulum on the screen. As you learned in the previous chapter, there are two techniques available for physics-based animations: path-based key-frame animation and timer-based simulation. Either method works for the pendulum problem. Here, I'll use the timer-based animation. The following is the code-behind file of this example based on the timer-based animation:

```
using System;
using System.Windows;
using System.Windows.Threading;
using System.Windows.Controls;
using System.Windows.Input;
using System.Windows.Media;
using System.Windows.Shapes;
using XuMath;

namespace Example07_1
{
    public partial class Page : UserControl
    {
        private double PendulumMass = 1;
        private double PendulumLength = 1;
        private double DampingCoefficient = 0.5;
        private double Theta0 = 45;
        private double Alpha0 = 0;
        double[] xx = new double[2];
        private SolidColorBrush brush = new SolidColorBrush(Colors.Red);

        double time = 0;
        double dt = 0.03;
        private DispatcherTimer timer = new DispatcherTimer();

        private double xMin = 0;
        private double xMax = 50;
        private double yMin = -250;
        private double yMax = 250;

        public Page()
        {
            InitializeComponent();
            PendulumInitialize();
        }

        private void PendulumInitialize()
        {
            tbMass.Text = "1";
            tbLength.Text = "1";
            tbDamping.Text = "0.1";
            tbTheta0.Text = "45";
            tbAlpha0.Text = "0";
            line1.X2 = 140;
            line1.Y2 = 150;
            ball.Center = new Point(140, 150);
        }

        private void Start_Click(object sender, RoutedEventArgs e)
```

```
{
    PendulumMass = Double.Parse(tbMass.Text);
    PendulumLength = Double.Parse(tbLength.Text);
    DampingCoefficient = Double.Parse(tbDamping.Text);
    Theta0 = Double.Parse(tbTheta0.Text);
    Theta0 = Math.PI * Theta0 / 180;
    Alpha0 = Double.Parse(tbAlpha0.Text);
    Alpha0 = Math.PI * Alpha0 / 180;
    pl.Points.Clear();
    time = 0;
    xx = new double[2] { Theta0, Alpha0 };
    timer = new DispatcherTimer();
    timer.Tick += new EventHandler(timer_Tick);
    timer.Start();
}

private void timer_Tick(object sender, EventArgs e)
{
    // Invoke ODE solver:
    ODESolver.Function[] f = new ODESolver.Function[2] { f1, f2 };
    double[] result = ODESolver.RungeKutta4(f, xx, time, dt);

    // Display moving pendulum on screen:
    Point pt = new Point(140 + 130 * Math.Sin(result[0]),
                         20 + 130 * Math.Cos(result[0]));
    ball.Center = pt;
    line1.X2 = pt.X;
    line1.Y2 = pt.Y;

    // Display theta-time curve on screen:
    if (time < xMax)
    {
        pl.Points.Add(new Point(XNormalize(time) + 10,
                  YNormalize(180 * result[0] / Math.PI) + 70));
        pl.Stroke = brush;
    }

    // Reset the initial values for next calculation:
    xx = result;
    time += dt;

    if (time > 0 && Math.Abs(result[0]) < 0.01 &&
                    Math.Abs(result[1]) < 0.001)
    {
        timer.Stop();
    }
}

private void Stop_Click(object sender, RoutedEventArgs e)
{
    line1.X2 = 140;
    line1.Y2 = 150;
    ball.Center = new Point(140, 150);
    timer.Stop();
}
```

```
            private double f1(double[] xx, double t)
            {
                return xx[1];
            }

            private double f2(double[] xx, double t)
            {
                double m = PendulumMass;
                double L = PendulumLength;
                double g = 9.81;
                double b = DampingCoefficient;
                return -g * Math.Sin(xx[0]) / L - b * xx[1] / m;
            }

            private double XNormalize(double x)
            {
                return (x - xMin) * canvasLeft.Width / (xMax - xMin);
            }

            private double YNormalize(double y)
            {
                return canvasLeft.Height -
                       (y - yMin) * canvasLeft.Height / (yMax - yMin);
            }
        }
    }
```

Here, you first define several private members that can be changed by the user's inputs. You also define a constant time increment dt for the animation. You can control the animation speed by adjusting dt.

When the Start button is pressed, the input values for the mass, string length, damping coefficient, and initial position and velocity are obtained from the values inside their corresponding TextBox fields. At the same time, the event handler timer_Tick is fired, in which you first create a function array, then call the static RungeKutta4 method in the ODESolver class using the statements:

```
ODESolver.Function[] f = new ODESolver.Function[2] { f1, f2 };
double[] result = ODESolver.RungeKutta4(f, xx, time, dt);
```

The methods f1 and f2 represent the functions on the right-hand side of Equation (7.10). The array xx in the RungeKutta4 method represents two dependent variables, θ and α. Namely, xx[0] = θ and xx[1] = α. In this case, the result is also a double array which gives solutions to θ and α. With the animation progressing, the RungeKutta4 method gets called continuously to update the string angle and angle velocity of the pendulum.

Once the new values of angle and velocity are obtained, you update the screen that shows the moving pendulum and the swing angle as a function of time on the screen. Next, you set the current solution as the initial values for the next round simulation.

When the swing angle and angle velocity are so small that the pendulum almost doesn't swing, you can stop the animation by calling the timer's Stop method.

As you can see from this example, once the ODESolver class is written, it is a simple process to incorporate a pendulum into a game program. You can play around with the Pendulum Simulator by changing the values of the mass, damping coefficient, initial string angle, and initial angle velocity, and watch their effects on the motion of the pendulum.

Coupled-Spring System

In this section, you'll develop a spring simulator for a coupled spring system with three springs and two masses, as shown in Figure 7-2. This system is fixed at both ends. The parameters m_1 and m_2 represent masses; k_1, k_2, and k_3 are spring constants that define how stiff the springs are; and b_1, b_2, and b_3 are damping coefficients that characterize how quickly the springs' motion will stop.

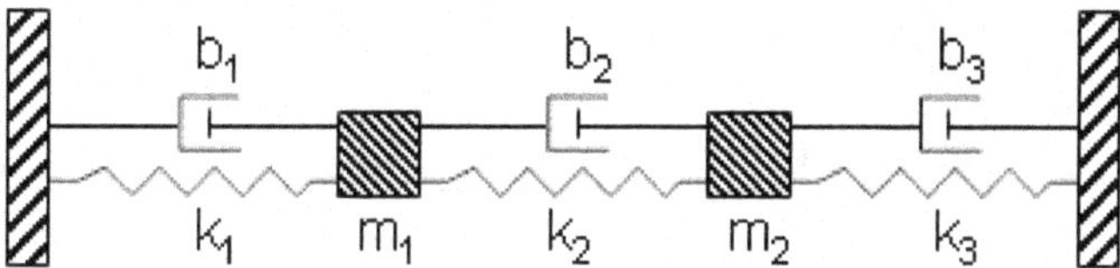

Figure 7-2 A spring-mass system.

Equations of Motion

The equations of motion for this system can be written in terms of two coupled second-order ODEs:

$$\begin{aligned} m_1 \frac{d^2 x_1}{dt^2} &= -(k_1 + k_2)x_1 + k_2 x_2 - (b_1 + b_2)\frac{dx_1}{dt} + b_2 \frac{dx_2}{dt} \\ m_2 \frac{d^2 x_2}{dt^2} &= -(k_2 + k_3)x_2 + k_2 x_1 - (b_2 + b_3)\frac{dx_2}{dt} + b_2 \frac{dx_1}{dt} \end{aligned} \tag{7.11}$$

where x_1 and x_2 are the displacements of m_1 and m_2 respectively. There are no closed-form solutions to this set of coupled differential equations. In order to solve Equation (7.11) numerically using the Runge-Kutta method, you need to first convert it into a series of first-order ODEs. This can be easily done by introducing the velocity variables $v_1 = dx_1/dt$ and $v_2 = dx_2/dt$:

$$\begin{aligned} \frac{dx_1}{dt} &= v_1 \\ \frac{dx_2}{dt} &= v_2 \\ \frac{dv_1}{dt} &= -\frac{1}{m_1}(k_1 + k_2)x_1 + \frac{k_2}{m_1}x_2 - \frac{1}{m_1}(b_1 + b_2)v_1 + \frac{b_2}{m_1}v_2 \\ \frac{dv_2}{dt} &= -\frac{1}{m_2}(k_2 + k_3)x_2 + \frac{k_2}{m_2}x_1 - \frac{1}{m_2}(b_2 + b_3)v_2 + \frac{b_2}{m_2}v_1 \end{aligned} \tag{7.12}$$

These coupled first-order ODEs are ready to be solved using the Runge-Kutta method implemented in the ODESolver class.

Coupled Spring Simulator

Now we can develop the simulator for the coupled spring system. Start with a new Silverlight project and name it Example07-2. Again, you'll create the layout and user interface for this example using XAML and perform the computation and animation in code. A sample screen shot of the layout of this example is shown in Figure 7-3.

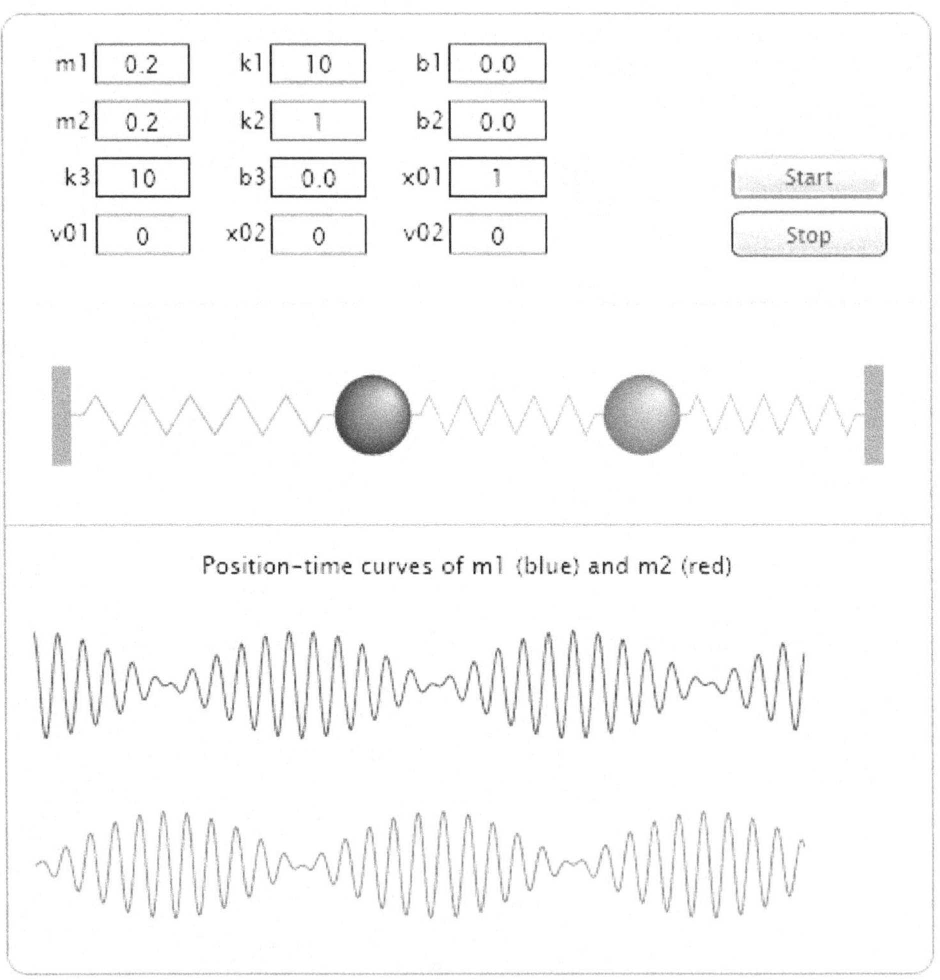

Figure 7-3 A coupled spring system.

You can see from this figure that in addition to the text fields for the masses, spring constants, and damping coefficients, there are also text fields for inputting the initial positions and velocities for m_1 and m_2. All of these parameters can be changed by the user, so this spring system simulator is very general. The bottom shows various animation results. The top image shows how the coupled spring system moves during the simulation. The positions for m_1 and m_2 as a function of time are displayed in the middle pane, from which you can clearly see how the positions for these two masses respond differently to time. The bottom image illustrates the position (x_1 vs x_2) phase diagram. If you have ever played with an oscilloscope, you have probably seen phase diagrams similar to those displayed here.

A Start button starts the simulation, a Stop button stops the simulation, and a Reset button is used to stop the simulation, return all parameters to their default values, and clear up the screen.

This layout is created using the following XAML code:

```
<UserControl x:Class="Example07_2.Page"
    xmlns="http://schemas.microsoft.com/client/2007"
    xmlns:x="http://schemas.microsoft.com/winfx/2006/xaml"
    Width="500" Height="500">
    <Grid x:Name="LayoutRoot" Background="White">
        <Border BorderBrush="Gray" BorderThickness="1"
                CornerRadius="10" Margin="10">
            <StackPanel>
                <StackPanel Orientation="Horizontal" Margin="10,10,0,0">
                    <TextBlock Text="m1" FontSize="12" Width="30"
                               TextAlignment="Right" Margin="5 5 2 5"/>
                    <TextBox x:Name="tbm1" Text="0.2" FontSize="12"
                             Width="50" Height="20"
                             TextAlignment="Center" Margin="0,0,5,0"/>
                    <TextBlock Text="k1" FontSize="12" Width="30"
                               TextAlignment="Right" Margin="5 5 2 5"/>
                    <TextBox x:Name="tbk1" Text="10" FontSize="12" Width="50"
                             Height="20" TextAlignment="Center"
                             Margin="0,0,5,0"/>
                    <TextBlock Text="b1" FontSize="12" Width="30"
                               TextAlignment="Right" Margin="5 5 2 5"/>
                    <TextBox x:Name="tbb1" Text="0.0" FontSize="12" Width="50"
                             Height="20" TextAlignment="Center"
                             Margin="0,0,5,0"/>
                </StackPanel>
                <StackPanel Orientation="Horizontal" Margin="10,0,0,0">
                    <TextBlock Text="m2" FontSize="12" Width="30"
                               TextAlignment="Right" Margin="5 5 2 5"/>
                    <TextBox x:Name="tbm2" Text="0.2" FontSize="12" Width="50"
                             Height="20" TextAlignment="Center"
                             Margin="0,0,5,0"/>
                    <TextBlock Text="k2" FontSize="12" Width="30"
                               TextAlignment="Right" Margin="5 5 2 5"/>
                    <TextBox x:Name="tbk2" Text="1" FontSize="12" Width="50"
                             Height="20" TextAlignment="Center"
                             Margin="0,0,5,0"/>
                    <TextBlock Text="b2" FontSize="12" Width="30"
                               TextAlignment="Right" Margin="5 5 2 5"/>
                    <TextBox x:Name="tbb2" Text="0.0" FontSize="12" Width="50"
                             Height="20" TextAlignment="Center"
                             Margin="0,0,5,0"/>
                </StackPanel>
                <StackPanel Orientation="Horizontal" Margin="10 0 0 0">
                    <TextBlock Text="k3" FontSize="12" Width="30"
                               TextAlignment="Right" Margin="5 5 2 5"/>
                    <TextBox x:Name="tbk3" Text="10" FontSize="12" Width="50"
```

```
                Height="20" TextAlignment="Center"
                Margin="0,0,5,0"/>
        <TextBlock Text="b3" FontSize="12" Width="30"
                  TextAlignment="Right" Margin="5 5 2 5"/>
        <TextBox x:Name="tbb3" Text="0.0" FontSize="12" Width="50"
                Height="20" TextAlignment="Center"
                Margin="0,0,5,0"/>
        <TextBlock Text="x01" FontSize="12" Width="30"
                  TextAlignment="Right" Margin="5 5 2 5"/>
        <TextBox x:Name="tbx01" Text="1" FontSize="12" Width="50"
                Height="20" TextAlignment="Center"
                Margin="0,0,5,0"/>
        <Button Content="Start" Width="80" Height="22"
               Margin="90,0,0,0" Click="Start_Click"/>
    </StackPanel>
    <StackPanel Orientation="Horizontal" Margin="10 0 0 0">
        <TextBlock Text="v01" FontSize="12" Width="30"
                  TextAlignment="Right" Margin="5 5 2 5"/>
        <TextBox x:Name="tbv01" Text="0" FontSize="12" Width="50"
                Height="20" TextAlignment="Center"
                Margin="0,0,5,0"/>
        <TextBlock Text="x02" FontSize="12" Width="30"
                  TextAlignment="Right" Margin="5 5 2 5"/>
        <TextBox x:Name="tbx02" Text="0" FontSize="12" Width="50"
                Height="20" TextAlignment="Center"
                Margin="0,0,5,0"/>
        <TextBlock Text="v02" FontSize="12" Width="30"
                  TextAlignment="Right" Margin="5 5 2 5"/>
        <TextBox x:Name="tbv02" Text="0" FontSize="12" Width="50"
                Height="20" TextAlignment="Center"
                Margin="0,0,5,0"/>
        <Button Content="Stop" Width="80" Height="22"
               Margin="90,0,0,0" Click="Stop_Click"/>
    </StackPanel>
    <Line X1="0" Y1="0" X2="500" Y2="0" Stroke="Gray"
          StrokeThickness="1" Margin="0,20,0,10"/>
    <Canvas x:Name="canvas1" Width="470" Height="90">
        <Rectangle Width="10" Height="50" Fill="DarkGoldenrod"
                  Canvas.Left="20" Canvas.Top="20"/>
        <Rectangle Width="10" Height="50" Fill="DarkGoldenrod"
                  Canvas.Left="440" Canvas.Top="20"/>
        <Canvas x:Name="spring1" Canvas.Left="30" Canvas.Top="35">
            <Polyline Stroke="Gray"
                Points="0,10 5,10 10,0 20,20 30,0 40, 20 50,0 60,20
                        70,0 80,20 90,0 100,20 105,10 110,10"/>
            <Canvas.RenderTransform>
                <ScaleTransform x:Name="scale1" CenterX="0"
                                CenterY="10"/>
            </Canvas.RenderTransform>
        </Canvas>
        <Path>
            <Path.Fill>
                <RadialGradientBrush GradientOrigin="0.75,0.25">
                    <GradientStop Color="LightBlue" Offset="0"/>
                    <GradientStop Color="Blue" Offset="1"/>
```

```
            </RadialGradientBrush>
        </Path.Fill>
        <Path.Data>
            <EllipseGeometry x:Name="mass1" RadiusX="20"
                             RadiusY="20" Center="160,45"/>
        </Path.Data>
    </Path>

    <Canvas x:Name="spring2" Canvas.Left="180" Canvas.Top="35">
        <Polyline Stroke="Gray"
            Points="0,10 5,10 10,0 20,20 30,0 40, 20 50,0 60,20
                    70,0 80,20 90,0 100,20 105,10 110,10"/>
        <Canvas.RenderTransform>
            <ScaleTransform x:Name="scale2" CenterX="0"
                            CenterY="10"/>
        </Canvas.RenderTransform>
    </Canvas>

    <Path>
        <Path.Fill>
            <RadialGradientBrush GradientOrigin="0.75,0.25">
                <GradientStop Color="Yellow" Offset="0"/>
                <GradientStop Color="Red" Offset="1"/>
            </RadialGradientBrush>
        </Path.Fill>
        <Path.Data>
            <EllipseGeometry x:Name="mass2" RadiusX="20"
                             RadiusY="20" Center="310,45"/>
        </Path.Data>
    </Path>

    <Canvas x:Name="spring3" Canvas.Left="330" Canvas.Top="35">
        <Polyline Stroke="Gray"
            Points="0,10 5,10 10,0 20,20 30,0 40, 20 50,0 60,20
                    70,0 80,20 90,0 100,20 105,10 110,10"/>
        <Canvas.RenderTransform>
            <ScaleTransform x:Name="scale3" CenterX="0"
                            CenterY="10"/>
        </Canvas.RenderTransform>
    </Canvas>

</Canvas>
<Line Stroke="Gray" StrokeThickness="1" X1="0" Y1="10"
      X2="480" Y2="10"/>
<TextBlock Text="Position-time curves of m1 (blue) and m2 (red)"
           FontSize="12" Width="450" TextAlignment="Center"
           Margin="10"/>
<Canvas x:Name="canvas2" Width="450" Height="80">
    <Canvas.Clip>
        <RectangleGeometry Rect="0 0 450 80"/>
    </Canvas.Clip>
    <Polyline x:Name="pl1" Stroke="Blue"/>
</Canvas>
<Canvas x:Name="canvas3" Width="450" Height="80"
        Margin="0 10 0 0">
```

```
                    <Canvas.Clip>
                        <RectangleGeometry Rect="0 0 450 80"/>
                    </Canvas.Clip>
                    <Polyline x:Name="pl2" Stroke="Red"/>
                </Canvas>
            </StackPanel>
        </Border>
    </Grid>
</UserControl>
```

Here, you'll also use the timer-based animation approach to display the real-time motion of the spring-mass system. The following is the corresponding C# code of this example:

```
using System;
using System.Windows;
using System.Windows.Threading;
using System.Windows.Controls;
using System.Windows.Input;
using System.Windows.Media;
using System.Windows.Shapes;
using XuMath;

namespace Example07_2
{
    public partial class Page : UserControl
    {
        private double M1;
        private double K1;
        private double B1;
        private double M2;
        private double K2;
        private double B2;
        private double K3;
        private double B3;
        private double X01;
        private double X02;
        private double V01;
        private double V02;

        private double xb1 = 3.4;
        private double xb2 = 6.6;

        private SolidColorBrush redBrush = new SolidColorBrush(Colors.Red);
        private SolidColorBrush blueBrush = new SolidColorBrush(Colors.Blue);

        double[] xx = new double[4];
        double[] result = new double[4];
        double time = 0;
        double dt = 0.01;
        private DispatcherTimer timer;

        public Page()
        {
            InitializeComponent();
            SpringsInitialize();
        }
```

```
private void SpringsInitialize()
{
    tbm1.Text = "0.2";
    tbk1.Text = "10";
    tbb1.Text = "0.0";
    tbm2.Text = "0.2";
    tbk2.Text = "1";
    tbb2.Text = "0.0";
    tbk3.Text = "10";
    tbb3.Text = "0.0";
    tbx01.Text = "1";
    tbv01.Text = "0";
    tbx02.Text = "0";
    tbv02.Text = "0";
}

private void Start_Click(object sender, RoutedEventArgs e)
{
    // Get input parameters:
    M1 = Double.Parse(tbm1.Text);
    K1 = Double.Parse(tbk1.Text);
    B1 = Double.Parse(tbb1.Text);
    M2 = Double.Parse(tbm2.Text);
    K2 = Double.Parse(tbk2.Text);
    B2 = Double.Parse(tbb2.Text);
    K3 = Double.Parse(tbk3.Text);
    B3 = Double.Parse(tbb3.Text);
    X01 = Double.Parse(tbx01.Text);
    X02 = Double.Parse(tbx02.Text);
    V01 = Double.Parse(tbv01.Text);
    V02 = Double.Parse(tbv02.Text);
    pl1.Points.Clear();
    pl2.Points.Clear();
    time = 0;
    xx = new double[4] { X01, X02, V01, V02 };
    timer = new DispatcherTimer();
    timer.Tick += new EventHandler(timer_Tick);
    timer.Start();
}

void timer_Tick(object sender, EventArgs e)
{
    // Calculate positions of m1 and m2:
    ODESolver.Function[] f =
              new ODESolver.Function[4] { f1, f2, f3, f4 };
    result = ODESolver.RungeKutta4(f, xx, time, dt);

    AnimatingSprings();
    DisplayPositions();

    xx = result;
    time += dt;
    if (time > 0 && Math.Abs(result[0]) < 0.01 &&
                    Math.Abs(result[1]) < 0.01 &&
```

```
                        Math.Abs(result[2]) < 0.005 &&
                        Math.Abs(result[2]) < 0.005)
                {
                    timer.Stop();
                }
            }

            private void AnimatingSprings()
            {
                Point pt1 = new Point(XNormalize(canvas1,
                                xb1 + result[0], 0, 10), 45);
                Point pt2 = new Point(XNormalize(canvas1,
                                xb2 + result[1], 0, 10), 45);
                mass1.Center = pt1;
                mass2.Center = pt2;

                // Animate spring1:
                scale1.ScaleX = (pt1.X - 50) / 110;

                // Animate spring2:
                Canvas.SetLeft(spring2, pt1.X + 20);
                scale2.ScaleX = (pt2.X - pt1.X - 40) / 110;

                // Animate spring3:
                Canvas.SetLeft(spring3, pt2.X + 20);
                scale3.ScaleX = (440 - pt2.X - 20) / 110;
            }

            private void DisplayPositions()
            {
                // Shaw positions of m1 and m2:

                if (time < 30)
                {
                    pl1.Points.Add(new Point(XNormalize(canvas2, time, 0, 30),
                                YNormalize(canvas2, result[0], 0, 3) - 40));
                    pl1.Stroke = blueBrush;
                    pl2.Points.Add(new Point(XNormalize(canvas3, time, 0, 30),
                                YNormalize(canvas3, result[1], 0, 3) - 40));
                    pl2.Stroke = redBrush;
                }
            }

            private void Stop_Click(object sender, RoutedEventArgs e)
            {
                SpringsInitialize();
                timer.Stop();
            }

            private double f1(double[] xx, double t)
            {
                return xx[2];
            }

            private double f2(double[] xx, double t)
```

```
        {
            return xx[3];
        }

        private double f3(double[] xx, double t)
        {
            return -(K1 + K2) * xx[0] / M1 + K2 * xx[1] / M1 -
                    (B1 + B2) * xx[2] / M1 + B2 * xx[3] / M1;
        }

        private double f4(double[] xx, double t)
        {
            return -(K2 + K3) * xx[1] / M2 + K2 * xx[0] / M2 -
                    (B2 + B3) * xx[3] / M2 + B2 * xx[2] / M2;
        }

        private double XNormalize(Canvas canvas, double x,
                                  double min, double max)
        {
            double result = (x - min) * canvas.Width / (max - min);
            return result;
        }

        private double YNormalize(Canvas canvas, double y,
                                  double min, double max)
        {
            double result = canvas.Height -
                            (y - min) * canvas.Height / (max - min);
            return result;
        }
    }
}
```

The above code seems to be very involved. However, the basic structure of the implementation is similar to that of the previous example. Most of the code deals with how to correctly display the simulation results on the screen. At the beginning, you define several private members that can be changed by the user's inputs. When the Start button is clicked, the program gets the input parameters and invokes a timer's Tick event handler to start the animation.

Inside the event handler, you call the RungeKutta4 method to solve the ODEs for this spring system with the statements:

```
ODESolver.Function[] f =
          new ODESolver.Function[4] { f1, f2, f3, f4 };
result = ODESolver.RungeKutta4(f, xx, time, dt);
```

Here you define a function array with four components which correspond to the right-hand side of Equation (7.12). The double array xx in the above statement is defined as

```
xx = new double[4] { X01, X02, V01, V02 };
```

Correspondingly, the solution should be x_1 = result[0], x_2 = result[1], v_1 = result[2], and v_2 = result[3]. You then use the solution to update the motion of the spring system and the results displayed on your screen, including the positions as a function of time.

When you animate the motion of the spring system, you should remember that you need to consider not only the two masses m_1 and m_2, but also the three springs characterized by the spring constants k_1, k_2, and k_3. The AnimatingSprings method presents the detailed procedure of how to properly animate the spring system. The position-time results shown in Figure 7-3 are produced using the DisplayPositions.

Projectiles

In this section, you'll learn how to model the flight of a projectile. You have probably worked with projectiles quite a bit in your game programming, such as bullets, golf balls, and tennis balls. Simulating projectlile motion is a straightforward application of Newtonian mechanics and kinetics in physics.

Here, we'll consider two kinds of forces acting on a projectile: gravity and aerodynamic drag force. Effects such as wind, Laminar and turbulent flows, and spin, will be neglected. We'll also create a golf game based on projectile physics.

Aerodynamic Drag Force

Aerodynamic drag is the resistance force that air exerts on a projectile traveling through it, and directly affects the trajectory of the projectile. This drag force acts in the opposite direction of the velocity of the projectile.

The aerodynamic drag force depends on the geometry of the object, the density of the air, and the square of the velocity. Drag force is usually expressed in the form:

$$F_D = \frac{1}{2} C_D \rho A v^2 \tag{7.13}$$

where F_D stands for the drag force, C_D is the drag coefficient, ρ is the density of the air, v is the velocity, and A is the characteristic body area which depends on the body geometry. For most objects, A is taken to be the frontal area. For a sphere, the frontal area would be the cross-section area; i.e., $A = \pi r^2$.

Projectile Equations of Motion

You are now ready to add aerodynamic drag force to the projectile trajectory model. For a projectile that travels in a 2D space, the total drag force in Equation (7.13) needs to be split into directional components. Because the drag force acts in the opposite direction of velocity, the X- and Y-components of the drag force will be in the same proportion relative to each other as the X- and Y-components of velocity, but their signs will be reversed. Thus, the projected drag force on the X- and Y-direction can be written in the following form:

$$\begin{aligned} F_{Dx} &= -F_D \frac{v_x}{v} \\ F_{Dy} &= -F_D \frac{v_y}{v} \end{aligned} \tag{7.14}$$

where the total magnitude of the velocity $v = \sqrt{v_x^2 + v_y^2}$. The negative signs in the above equation indicate that the drag force acts in the opposite direction of the velocity. The drag force in Equation (7.14) can be easily added to the projectile equation of motion:

$$\begin{aligned} m\frac{d^2x}{dt^2} &= -F_D\frac{v_x}{v} \\ m\frac{d^2y}{dt^2} &= -mg - F_D\frac{v_y}{v} \end{aligned} \tag{7.15}$$

There are no analytical solutions to this set of coupled differential equations. In order to solve Equation (7.15) numerically using the Runge-Kutta method, you need to first convert it into a series of first-order ODEs. This can be done easily by introducing the velocity variables v_x = dx/dt and v_y = dy/dt:

$$\begin{aligned} \frac{dx}{dt} &= v_x \\ \frac{dy}{dt} &= v_y \\ \frac{dv_x}{dt} &= -\frac{F_D v_x}{mv} \\ \frac{dv_y}{dt} &= -g - \frac{F_D v_y}{mv} \end{aligned} \tag{7.16}$$

These coupled first-order ODEs are ready to be solved using the Runge-Kutta method.

Golf Game

Let's create a simple golf game based on the projectile equations of motion described in Equation (7.16). The objective of the game is to hit a golf ball into a hole. A sample screen shot of the GolfGame is shown in Figure 7-4.

The layout and user interface consist of text fields that are used to input the initial velocity components of the golf ball. These values can be changed to adjust the trajectory of the ball. The Distance to Hole field lets you adjust the distance from the tee to the flag. The other text fields allow you to input the mass, area, drag coefficient, and the density of the air. These parameters are used to calculate the drag force acting on the golf ball.

To create such a golf game, you need to add a new WPF Window to the project Chapter07 and name it GolfGame. The layout shown in Figure 7-4 is created using the following XAML file:

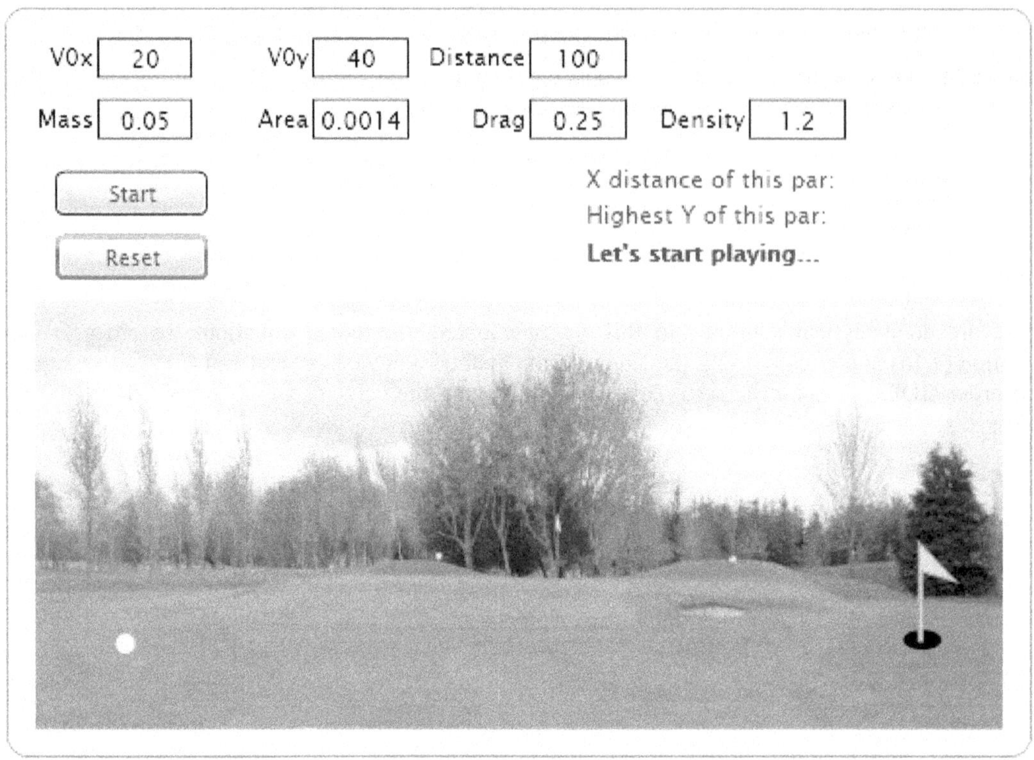

Figure 7-4 Golf game.

```
<UserControl x:Class="Example07_3.Page"
    xmlns="http://schemas.microsoft.com/client/2007"
    xmlns:x="http://schemas.microsoft.com/winfx/2006/xaml"
    Width="550" Height="395">
    <Grid x:Name="LayoutRoot" Background="White">
        <Border BorderBrush="Gray" BorderThickness="1"
                CornerRadius="10" Margin="10">
            <StackPanel Margin="5" Grid.Row="0">
                <StackPanel>
                    <StackPanel Orientation="Horizontal" Margin="5,5,5,0">
                        <TextBlock Width="30" FontSize="12"
                                   TextAlignment="Right"
                                   Margin="5 5 2 5">V0x</TextBlock>
                        <TextBox Name="tbV0x" Text="20" FontSize="12" Width="50"
                                 Height="20" TextAlignment="Center"
                                 Margin="0 0 5 0"/>
                        <TextBlock Width="50" FontSize="12"
                                   TextAlignment="Right"
                                   Margin="5 5 2 5">V0y</TextBlock>
                        <TextBox Name="tbV0y" Text="40" FontSize="12" Width="50"
                                 Height="20" TextAlignment="Center"
                                 Margin="0 0 5 0"/>
                        <TextBlock Width="50" Text="Distance" FontSize="12"
```

```
                    TextAlignment="Right" Margin="5 5 2 5"/>
            <TextBox Name="tbDistance" Text="100" FontSize="12"
                     Width="50" Height="20" TextAlignment="Center"
                     Margin="0 0 5 0"/>
        </StackPanel>
        <StackPanel Orientation="Horizontal" Margin="5,2,5,2">
            <TextBlock Width="30" FontSize="12"
                       TextAlignment="Right"
                       Margin="5 5 2 5">Mass</TextBlock>
            <TextBox Name="tbMass" Text="0.05" FontSize="12"
                     Width="50" Height="20"
                     TextAlignment="Center" Margin="0 0 5 0"/>
            <TextBlock Width="50" FontSize="12"
                       TextAlignment="Right"
                       Margin="5 5 2 5">Area</TextBlock>
            <TextBox Name="tbArea" Text="0.0014" FontSize="12"
                     Width="50" Height="20" TextAlignment="Center"
                     Margin="0 0 5 0"/>
            <TextBlock Width="50" FontSize="12"
                       TextAlignment="Right"
                       Margin="5 5 2 5">Drag</TextBlock>
            <TextBox Name="tbDrag" Text="0.25" FontSize="12"
                     Width="50" Height="20" TextAlignment="Center"
                     Margin="0 0 5 0"/>
            <TextBlock Width="50" FontSize="12"
                       TextAlignment="Right"
                       Margin="5 5 2 5">Density</TextBlock>
            <TextBox Name="tbDensity" Text="1.2" FontSize="12"
                     Width="50" Height="20" TextAlignment="Center"
                     Margin="0 0 5 0"/>
        </StackPanel>
    </StackPanel>
    <StackPanel Orientation="Horizontal">
        <StackPanel Margin="0,5,0,0" HorizontalAlignment="Left">
            <Button Name="btnStart" Click="Start_Click"
                    Content="Start" Width="80" Height="22"
                    Margin="20,5,5,5"/>
            <Button Name="btnReset" Click="Reset_Click"
                    Content="Reset" Width="80" Height="22"
                    Margin="20,5,5,5"/>
        </StackPanel>
        <StackPanel Margin="190,0,0,0" HorizontalAlignment="Left">
            <TextBlock Name="tbXMax" Foreground="DarkRed"
                       Margin="0,5,0,0" FontSize="12"
                       Text="X distance of this par:"/>
            <TextBlock Name="tbYMax" Foreground="DarkRed" Margin="0"
                       Text="Highest Y of this par:" FontSize="12"/>
            <TextBlock Name="tbResult" Foreground="DarkRed"
                       FontSize="12" FontWeight="Bold"
                       Margin="0,0,0,0"
                       Text="Let's start playing..."/>
        </StackPanel>
    </StackPanel>

    <Canvas Name="canvas1" Width="500" Height="215" Margin="5">
```

```
                    <Canvas.Background>
                        <ImageBrush ImageSource="golf01.jpg" Stretch="Fill"/>
                    </Canvas.Background>

                    <Ellipse Name="golfBall" Fill="White" Width="10" Height="10"
                             Canvas.Top="170" Canvas.Left="30"/>
                    <Ellipse Name="golfHole" Fill="Black" Width="20" Height="10"
                             Canvas.Top="170" Canvas.Left="450"/>
                    <Polygon Name="golfFlag" Canvas.Top="175" Canvas.Left="459"
                             Stroke="DarkGoldenrod" Fill="LightGray"
                             Points="0,0 0,-50 20,-30 2,-35 2,0"/>
                    <Polyline x:Name="pl"/>
                </Canvas>
            </StackPanel>
        </Border>
    </Grid>
</UserControl>
```

Note that the background of the golf court is created from an image file called golf01.jpg. The simulation and animation are performed in the corresponding code-behind file using the Runge-Kutta method and per-frame animation respectively. The following is the code-behind file of this example:

```
using System;
using System.Collections.Generic;
using System.Windows;
using System.Windows.Threading;
using System.Windows.Controls;
using System.Windows.Input;
using System.Windows.Media;
using System.Windows.Shapes;
using XuMath;

namespace Example07_3
{
    public partial class Page : UserControl
    {
        double xMin = 0;
        double yMin = 0;
        double xMax = 100;
        double yMax = 100;

        double X0 = 20;
        double Y0 = 20;
        double V0x = 10;
        double V0y = 10;
        double BallMass = 0.05;
        double BallArea = 0.0014;
        double DragCoefficient = 0.25;
        double AirDensity = 1.2;
        double DistanceToHole = 100;
        SolidColorBrush brush = new SolidColorBrush(Colors.Red);

        double[] xx = new double[4];

        DispatcherTimer timer;
        double time = 0;
```

```
double dt = 0.1;
double gravity = 9.81;
double ym = 0;

public Page()
{
    InitializeComponent();
    GolfGameInitialize();
}

private void GolfGameInitialize()
{
    tbV0x.Text = "20";
    tbV0y.Text = "40";
    tbDistance.Text = "100";
    tbMass.Text = "0.05";
    tbArea.Text = "0.0014";
    tbDrag.Text = "0.25";
    tbDensity.Text = "1.2";

    tbXMax.Text = "X distance of this par:";
    tbYMax.Text = "Highest Y of this par:";
    tbResult.Text = "Let's start playing...";
    xMin = X0 - 0.1 * DistanceToHole;
    yMin = X0 - 0.2 * DistanceToHole;
    xMax = X0 + 1.1 * DistanceToHole;
    yMax = X0 + 0.7 * DistanceToHole;
    Canvas.SetLeft(golfBall, XNormalize(X0));
    Canvas.SetTop(golfBall, YNormalize(Y0));
    Canvas.SetLeft(golfHole, XNormalize(X0 + DistanceToHole) - 10);
    Canvas.SetTop(golfHole, YNormalize(Y0) - 2);
    Canvas.SetLeft(golfFlag, XNormalize(X0 + DistanceToHole) - 2);
    Canvas.SetTop(golfFlag, YNormalize(Y0) + 4);
    pl.Points.Clear();
}

private void Start_Click(object sender, RoutedEventArgs e)
{
    timer = new DispatcherTimer();
    time = 0;
    dt = 0.1;
    pl.Points.Clear();

    // Get input parameters:
    V0x = Double.Parse(tbV0x.Text);
    V0y = Double.Parse(tbV0y.Text);
    DistanceToHole = Double.Parse(tbDistance.Text);
    BallMass = Double.Parse(tbMass.Text);
    BallArea = Double.Parse(tbArea.Text);
    DragCoefficient = Double.Parse(tbDrag.Text);
    AirDensity = Double.Parse(tbDensity.Text);

    // Set the axis limits:
    xMin = X0 - 0.1 * DistanceToHole;
    yMin = X0 - 0.2 * DistanceToHole;
```

```
        xMax = X0 + 1.1 * DistanceToHole;
        yMax = X0 + 0.7 * DistanceToHole;

        // Set the golf court:
        Canvas.SetLeft(golfHole, XNormalize(X0 + DistanceToHole) - 10);
        Canvas.SetTop(golfHole, YNormalize(Y0) - 2);
        Canvas.SetLeft(golfFlag, XNormalize(X0 + DistanceToHole) - 2);
        Canvas.SetTop(golfFlag, YNormalize(Y0) + 4);
        tbXMax.Text = "X distance of this par:";
        tbYMax.Text = "Highest Y of this par:";
        tbResult.Text = "Let's start playing...";
        xx = new double[4] { X0, Y0, V0x, V0y };

        timer.Tick += new EventHandler(timer_Tick);
        timer.Start();
    }

    private void timer_Tick(object sender, EventArgs e)
    {
        // Calculate the golf ball position:
        ODESolver.Function[] f =
                  new ODESolver.Function[4] { f1, f2, f3, f4 };
        double[] result = ODESolver.RungeKutta4(f, xx, time, dt);
        xx = result;

        double x = result[0];
        double y = result[1];

        if (y > ym)
            ym = y;

        if (y >= Y0)
        {
            Canvas.SetLeft(golfBall, XNormalize(x));
            Canvas.SetTop(golfBall, YNormalize(y));
            Point point = new Point(XNormalize(x) + 5, YNormalize(y) + 5);
            pl.Points.Add(new Point(XNormalize(x) + 5, YNormalize(y) + 5));
            pl.Stroke = brush;
        }
        if (x > X0 && y <= Y0)
        {
            double xm = Math.Round(x - X0);
            ym = Math.Round(ym - Y0);
            tbXMax.Text = "X distance of this par: " + xm.ToString() + " m";
            tbYMax.Text = "Highest Y of this par: " + ym.ToString() + " m";
            if (xm > DistanceToHole - 10 && xm < DistanceToHole + 10)
                tbResult.Text = "Congratulations! You win.";
            else
                tbResult.Text = "You missed. Try again.";
            timer.Stop();
        }
        time += dt;
    }

    private double f1(double[] xx, double t)
```

```
        {
            return xx[2];
        }

        private double f2(double[] xx, double t)
        {
            return xx[3];
        }

        private double f3(double[] xx, double t)
        {
            double A = BallArea;
            double rho = AirDensity;
            double cd = DragCoefficient;
            double m = BallMass;
            double fd = 0.5 * rho * A * cd * (xx[2] * xx[2] + xx[3] * xx[3]);
            return -fd * xx[2] / m / Math.Sqrt(xx[2] * xx[2] +
                    xx[3] * xx[3] + 1.0e-10);
        }

        private double f4(double[] xx, double t)
        {
            double A = BallArea;
            double rho = AirDensity;
            double cd = DragCoefficient;
            double m = BallMass;
            double fd = 0.5 * rho * A * cd * (xx[2] * xx[2] + xx[3] * xx[3]);
            return -gravity - fd * xx[3] / m / Math.Sqrt(xx[2] * xx[2] +
                    xx[3] * xx[3] + 1.0e-10);
        }

        private double XNormalize(double x)
        {
            double result = (x - xMin) * canvas1.Width / (xMax - xMin);
            return result;
        }

        private double YNormalize(double y)
        {
            double result = canvas1.Height -
                   (y - yMin) * canvas1.Height / (yMax - yMin);
            return result;
        }

        private void Reset_Click(object sender, RoutedEventArgs e)
        {
            GolfGameInitialize();
            pl.Stroke = new SolidColorBrush(Colors.Transparent);
        }
    }
}
```

Like the spring system discussed previously, you first define several private members that can be changed by the user's inputs. When the Start button is clicked, the values from the TextBox fields are obtained, and these values are used to initialize the ODESolver. To start the animation, the timer_Tick event handler is attached to the timer's Tick event.

Inside the event handler, you call the RungeKutta4 method to solve the ODEs for the golf ball described by Equation (7.16). Here you define a function array with four components, which correspond to the right-hand side of Equation (7.16). The double array xx in the above statement is defined as

```
xx = new double[4] { x0, y0, V0x, V0y };
```

Correspondingly, the solution should be x = result[0], y = result[1], v_x = result[2], and v_y = result[3]. You then use the solution to update the motion of the golf ball.

You can play around with the GolfGame by adjusting the variables that affect the drag force. You can see that drag effects make a big difference when it comes to the flight of a golf ball. Figure 7-4 shows the trajectory of the ball with a drag coefficient of 0.25, which is a typical value for a golf ball. In this case the golf ball travels about 100 m. If you turn off the drag effect by setting the drag coefficient to zero while using the same set of initial values, the golf ball will travel 164 m. Clearly, when it comes to projectiles such as golf balls, the drag effect must be included in the model.

Collision

An important aspect of physics modeling for games is what happens when two objects collide. Do they bounce off each other or stick to each other and travel together? If the objects do bounce off each other, which direction do they travel after the collision and at what speed do they travel? In this section, we'll consider what happens when a ball hits a wall or a flat ground.

In most ball bouncing animations, a linear collision approximation is usually used. Namely, only the vertical component of the velocity changes signs when the ball hits a wall or surface. This isn't a realistic situation. In reality, when a ball is incident obliquely on a flat surface, the ball's rebound spin, speed, and angle will generally differ from the corresponding incident values. This is much more complicated than a linear collision approximation. In this section, we'll investigate the physics of a general bouncing ball and create a general bouncing ball simulator.

Bouncing Ball Physics

The physics of a bouncing ball are characterized by the coefficient of restitution (COR) of a ball for a vertical bounce. The COR for a vertical bounce off a flat surface that remains at rest is defined as the ratio of the rebound speed to the incident speed. The horizontal COR can be defined for an oblique impact in terms of the horizontal components of the incident and rebound speeds of the contact point on the ball.

Here, our analysis of a bouncing ball is based on Garwin's model (R. Garwin, "Kinematics of an Ultraelastic rough ball", American Journal of Physics, Vol. 37, pages 88-92 (1969)). Consider a ball of mass m and radius R incident at speed V_1, angular velocity ω_1, and an angle θ_1 on a flat surface, as shown in Figure 7-5.

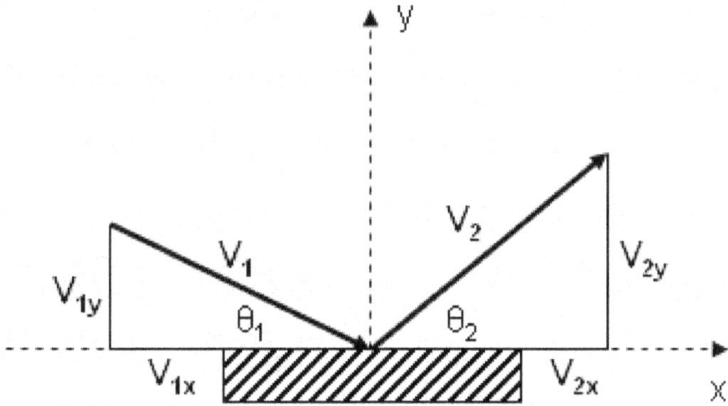

Figure 7-5 A ball is incident at velocity V_1 and angle θ_1, and rebounds at velocity V_2 and angle θ_2.

For simplicity, it is assumed that the mass of the surface is infinite and that the impact force is much larger than the gravity force during collision . In Garwin's model, the equations of motion are not needed explicitly, because the collision can be described in terms of the vertical (CORy) and horizontal (CORx) values of the COR, together with the conservation of angular momentum about the contact point. Referring to Figure 7-5, we can define

$$CORy = -\frac{V_{y2}}{V_{y1}} \tag{7.17}$$

Here, the subscripts 1 and 2 denote conditions before and after the collision, respectively. Similarly, CORx can be defined by the relation:

$$CORx = -\frac{V_{x2} - R\omega_2}{V_{x1} - R\omega_1} \tag{7.18}$$

where V_x - $R\omega$ is the net horizontal speed of a point at the bottom of the ball. Unlike CORy, CORx can be either positive or negative. If a ball is incident at a sufficiently small angle and without spin, it can slide throughout the impact without rolling and will bounce with $R\omega_2 < Vx_2$, in which case CORx < 0. A value of CORx = -1corresponds to a bounce on a frictionless surface, where $V_{x2} = V_{x1}$ and $\omega_2 = \omega_1$.

The horizontal friction force F exerts a torque FR = Id ω/dt, where I is the moment of inertia about an axis through the center of the ball, so that

$$I\frac{d\omega}{dt} + mR\frac{dV_x}{dt} = 0 \tag{7.19}$$

The conservation of angular momentum about a point at the bottom of the ball is therefore described by the relation

$$I\omega_1 + mRV_{x1} = I\omega_2 + mRV_{x2} \tag{7.20}$$

The moment of inertia of a spherical ball is given by $I = 2mR^2/5$. Equations (7.17)-(20) can be solved to show that

$$V_{x2} = \frac{[1-(2/5)CORx)]V_{x1} + (2/5)(1+CORx)R\omega_1}{1+(2/5)}$$

$$V_{y2} = -CORy\,V_{y1} \tag{7.21}$$

$$\omega_2 = \frac{(1+CORx)V_{x1} + [(2/5)-CORx]R\omega_1}{R[1+(2/5)]}$$

The above results are very interesting. If $\omega_1 = 0$ and CORx = 1, then $V_{x2} = 0.43V_{x1}$ and the corresponding spin value is $R\omega_2/V_{x2} = 10/3$. This means that the ball spins much faster than you would expect from the rolling condition $R\omega_2/V_{x2} = 1$. At the end of the collision, a ball with CORx = 1 will therefore slide backward on the surface due to the recovery of elastic energy stored in the horizontal direction. Alternatively, if $\omega_1 = 0$ and CORx = 0, then $V_{x2} = 0.71V_{x1}$ and $R\omega_2/V_{x2} = 1$, indicating that the ball rolls at the end of the duration of the impact and there is no energy recorvery or no energy stored elastically in the horizontal direction.

Because CORx is close to 1 for a superball and close to zero for a tennis ball, a superball will bounce with a smaller V_{x2} component than a tennis ball when $\omega_1 = 0$ and V_{x1} are the same for both balls. Since V_{y2} is greater for a superball (for the same V_{y1}), a superball will bounce at a steeper angle than a tennis ball. It is also easy to show that a superball with the same radius and same value of Vx1 as a tennis ball will bounce with a greater spin, by a factor of 2.38 if $\omega_1 = 0$.

Bouncing Ball Simulator

With Garwin's bouncing ball model, you can develop a realistic bouncing ball simulator that incorporates the inelastic collision, the change of horizontal speed, and the spin of the ball. The simulator is called BounceBall, and a sample screen shot is shown in Figure 7-6. The simulator consists of a ball inside a 2D 100m×100m box. The collision of the ball with the wall is described in Equation (7.21). When the ball travels inside the box (without collision), only gravity acts on the ball. If only the initial position of the ball (say x0 = 50m and y0 = 95 m) is specified and the initial velocity is set to zero (V0x = V0y = 0), the ball will drop as a free-fall object. The text fields allow you to change the mass, radius, gravity, and coefficients of restitution, as well as the initial position, velocity, and angle velocity. A Start button starts the simulation, a Stop button stops the simulation, and a Reset button stops the simulation and resets the ball and the parameters to their original position and values.

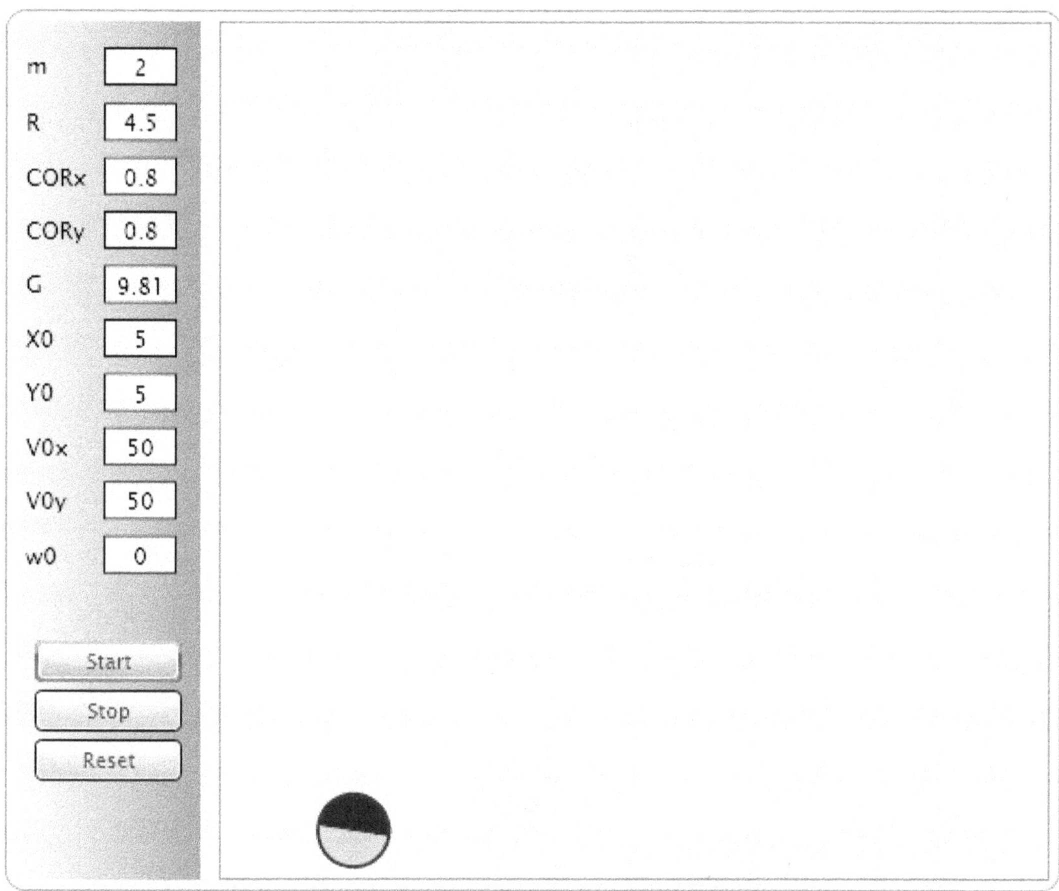

Figure 7-6 Bouncing ball simulator.

The layout of this example is created using the following XAML file:

```
<UserControl x:Class="Example07_4.Page"
    xmlns="http://schemas.microsoft.com/client/2007"
    xmlns:x="http://schemas.microsoft.com/winfx/2006/xaml"
    Width="594" Height="484">
    <Grid x:Name="LayoutRoot" Background="White">
        <Border BorderBrush="Gray" BorderThickness="1"
                CornerRadius="10" Margin="10">
            <Grid>
                <Grid.ColumnDefinitions>
                    <ColumnDefinition Width="110"/>
                    <ColumnDefinition/>
                </Grid.ColumnDefinitions>
                <StackPanel Margin="5">
                    <StackPanel.Background>
                        <LinearGradientBrush StartPoint="0 0" EndPoint="1 0">
                            <GradientStop Color="#FF888888" Offset="1"/>
                            <GradientStop Color="#FFF8F8F8" Offset="0"/>
                        </LinearGradientBrush>
                    </StackPanel.Background>
```

```
<StackPanel Orientation="Horizontal"
            VerticalAlignment="Top">
    <TextBlock Width="40" Height="20" Text="m"
               FontSize="12" Margin="5 15 2 5"/>
    <TextBox x:Name="tbM" Text="2" Width="40" Height="20"
             FontSize="12" TextAlignment="Center"
             Margin="0 10 5 2"/>
</StackPanel>
<StackPanel Orientation="Horizontal"
            VerticalAlignment="Top">
    <TextBlock Width="40" Text="R" FontSize="12"
               Margin="5 5 2 5"/>
    <TextBox x:Name="tbR" Text="4.5" Width="40" Height="20"
             FontSize="12" TextAlignment="Center"
             Margin="0 0 5 2"/>
</StackPanel>
<StackPanel Orientation="Horizontal"
            VerticalAlignment="Top">
    <TextBlock Width="40" Text="CORx" FontSize="12"
               Margin="5 5 2 5"/>
    <TextBox x:Name="tbCORx" Text="0.8" Width="40"
             Height="20" FontSize="12"
             TextAlignment="Center" Margin="0 0 5 2"/>
</StackPanel>
<StackPanel Orientation="Horizontal"
            VerticalAlignment="Top">
    <TextBlock Width="40" Text="CORy" FontSize="12"
               Margin="5 5 2 5"/>
    <TextBox x:Name="tbCORy" Text="0.8" Width="40"
             Height="20" FontSize="12"
             TextAlignment="Center" Margin="0 0 5 2"/>
</StackPanel>
<StackPanel Orientation="Horizontal"
            VerticalAlignment="Top">
    <TextBlock Width="40" Text="G" FontSize="12"
               Margin="5 5 2 5"/>
    <TextBox x:Name="tbG" Text="9.81" Width="40" Height="20"
             FontSize="12" TextAlignment="Center"
             Margin="0 0 5 2"/>
</StackPanel>
<StackPanel Orientation="Horizontal"
            VerticalAlignment="Top">
    <TextBlock Width="40" Text="X0" FontSize="12"
               Margin="5 5 2 5"/>
    <TextBox x:Name="tbX0" Text="5" Width="40" Height="20"
             FontSize="12" TextAlignment="Center"
             Margin="0 0 5 2"/>
</StackPanel>
<StackPanel Orientation="Horizontal"
            VerticalAlignment="Top">
    <TextBlock Width="40" Text="Y0" FontSize="12"
               Margin="5 5 2 5"/>
    <TextBox x:Name="tbY0" Text="5" Width="40" Height="20"
             FontSize="12" TextAlignment="Center"
             Margin="0 0 5 2"/>
```

```
    </StackPanel>
    <StackPanel Orientation="Horizontal"
                VerticalAlignment="Top">
        <TextBlock Width="40" Text="V0x" FontSize="12"
                   Margin="5 5 2 5"/>
        <TextBox x:Name="tbV0x" Text="50" Width="40" Height="20"
                 FontSize="12" TextAlignment="Center"
                 Margin="0 0 5 2"/>
    </StackPanel>
    <StackPanel Orientation="Horizontal"
                VerticalAlignment="Top">
        <TextBlock Width="40" Text="V0y" FontSize="12"
                   Margin="5 5 2 5"/>
        <TextBox x:Name="tbV0y" Text="50" Width="40" Height="20"
                 FontSize="12" TextAlignment="Center"
                 Margin="0 0 5 2"/>
    </StackPanel>
    <StackPanel Orientation="Horizontal"
                VerticalAlignment="Top">
        <TextBlock Width="40" Text="w0" FontSize="12"
                   Margin="5 5 2 5"/>
        <TextBox x:Name="tbW0" Text="0" Width="40" Height="20"
                 FontSize="12" TextAlignment="Center"
                 Margin="0 0 5 2"/>
    </StackPanel>
        <Button x:Name="Start" Click="Start_Click"
                Content="Start" Width="80" Height="22"
                Margin="2 30 2 2"/>
        <Button x:Name="Stop" Click="Stop_Click" Content="Stop"
                Width="80" Height="22" Margin="2"/>
        <Button x:Name="Reset" Click="Reset_Click"
                Content="Reset" Width="80" Height="22"
                Margin="2"/>
</StackPanel>

<Border BorderBrush="Gray" BorderThickness="1"
        Grid.Column="1" Margin="5">
    <Canvas Name="canvas1" Width="450" Height="450">
        <Canvas.Clip>
            <RectangleGeometry Rect="0 0 450 450"/>
        </Canvas.Clip>
        <Ellipse Name="ball" Canvas.Left="0" Canvas.Top="405"
                 Width="45" Height="45" Stroke="Blue"
                 StrokeThickness="2">
            <Ellipse.Fill>
                <LinearGradientBrush StartPoint="0,0"
                                     EndPoint="0,1">
                    <GradientStop Color="DarkBlue"
                                  Offset="0.5"/>
                    <GradientStop Color="LightBlue"
                                  Offset="0.5"/>
                </LinearGradientBrush>
            </Ellipse.Fill>
            <Ellipse.RenderTransform>
                <RotateTransform x:Name="ballRotate"
```

```
                                        CenterX="22.5" CenterY="22.5" Angle="0"/>
                                </Ellipse.RenderTransform>
                            </Ellipse>
                        </Canvas>
                    </Border>
                </Grid>
            </Border>
        </Grid>
    </UserControl>
```

You may notice that the ball's RenderTransform property is specified by a RotateTransform, which is responsible for the spin of the ball when it is bouncing. The simulation and animation are performed using the following code-behind file:

```
using System;
using System.Windows;
using System.Windows.Threading;
using System.Windows.Controls;
using System.Windows.Input;
using System.Windows.Media;
using System.Windows.Media.Animation;
using System.Windows.Shapes;

namespace Example07_4
{
    public partial class Page : UserControl
    {
        private double Mass;
        private double Radius;
        private double CORx;
        private double CORy;
        private double Gravity;
        private double X0;
        private double Y0;
        private double V0x;
        private double V0y;
        private double W0;

        double time = 0;
        double dt = 0.04;
        DispatcherTimer timer;
        double x = 0;
        double y = 0;
        double vx = 0;
        double vy = 0;
        double w = 0;
        double theta0 = 0;
        double theta = 0;
        double max = 100;

        public Page()
        {
            InitializeComponent();
            BallInitialize();
        }
```

```
private void BallInitialize()
{
    tbM.Text = "2";
    tbR.Text = "4.5";
    tbCORx.Text = "0.8";
    tbCORy.Text = "0.8";
    tbG.Text = "9.81";
    tbX0.Text = "5";
    tbY0.Text = "5";
    tbV0x.Text = "50";
    tbV0y.Text = "50";
    tbW0.Text = "0";

    Canvas.SetLeft(ball, 0);
    Canvas.SetTop(ball, canvas1.Height - 45);
    ball.Width = XNormalize(canvas1, 10, 0, max);
    ball.Height = canvas1.Height - YNormalize(canvas1, 10, 0, max);
}

private void SetInputParameters()
{
    Mass = Double.Parse(tbM.Text);
    Radius = Double.Parse(tbR.Text);
    CORx = Double.Parse(tbCORx.Text);
    CORy = Double.Parse(tbCORy.Text);
    Gravity = Double.Parse(tbG.Text);
    X0 = Double.Parse(tbX0.Text);
    if (X0 < Radius)
        X0 = Radius;
    Y0 = Double.Parse(tbY0.Text);
    if (Y0 < Radius)
        Y0 = Radius;
    V0x = Double.Parse(tbV0x.Text);
    V0y = Double.Parse(tbV0y.Text);
    W0 = Double.Parse(tbW0.Text);
    ball.Width = XNormalize(canvas1, 2*Radius, 0, max);
    ball.Height = canvas1.Height -
                  YNormalize(canvas1, 2*Radius, 0, max);
    Canvas.SetTop(ball, canvas1.Height - 45);
    Canvas.SetLeft(ball, 0);
}

private void Start_Click(object sender, RoutedEventArgs e)
{
    SetInputParameters();
    x = 0;
    y = 0;
    vx = 0;
    vy = 0;
    theta0 = 0;
    theta = 0;
    time = 0;
    timer = new DispatcherTimer();
    //timer.Interval = TimeSpan.FromMilliseconds(20);
    timer.Tick+=new EventHandler(timer_Tick);
```

```
        timer.Start();
    }

    private void timer_Tick(object sender, EventArgs e)
    {
        // Calculate positions and velocities of the ball for
        // the case without collision:
        x = X0 + V0x * dt;
        y = Y0 + V0y * dt - 0.5 * Gravity * dt * dt;
        theta = theta0 + 180 * W0 * dt / Math.PI;
        vx = V0x;
        if (Y0 > Radius)
            vy = V0y - Gravity * dt;
        else
            vy = V0y;
        w = W0;

        // Reset the ball's position:
        Canvas.SetLeft(ball, XNormalize(canvas1, X0 - Radius, 0, max));
        Canvas.SetTop(ball, YNormalize(canvas1, Y0 - Radius, 0, max) - 45);
        ballRotate.Angle = theta0;

        // Determine if the ball hits left or right wall:
        if ((V0x < 0 && X0 <= Radius) || (V0x > 0 && X0 >= max - Radius))
        {
            vx = -CORy * V0x;
            vy = ((1 - 2 * CORx / 5) * V0y +
                  (2 / 5) * (1 + CORx) * Radius * W0) / (1 + 2 / 5);
            w = ((1 + CORx) * V0y + (2 / 5 - CORx) *
                Radius * W0) / Radius / (1 + 2 / 5);
        }

        // Determine if the ball hits the top or bottom wall:
        if ((V0y < 0 && Y0 <= Radius) || (V0y > 0 && Y0 >= max - Radius))
        {
            vy = -CORy * V0y;
            vx = ((1 - 2 * CORx / 5) * V0x +
                  (2 / 5) * (1 + CORx) * Radius * W0) / (1 + 2 / 5);
            w = ((1 + CORx) * V0x + (2 / 5 - CORx) *
                Radius * W0) / Radius / (1 + 2 / 5);
        }

        // Reset the initial condition for next round simulation:
        X0 = x;
        Y0 = y;
        theta0 = theta;
        V0x = vx;
        V0y = vy;
        W0 = w;
        time += dt;

        // Make sure to keep the ball inside the box:
        if (time > 0 && Y0 < Radius)
            Canvas.SetTop(ball, canvas1.Height - 45);
```

```
            // Condition for stoping simulation:
            if (time > 100)
                timer.Stop();
        }

        private void Stop_Click(object sender, RoutedEventArgs e)
        {
            timer.Stop();
        }

        private void Reset_Click(object sender, RoutedEventArgs e)
        {
            BallInitialize();
            timer.Stop();
        }

        public double XNormalize(Canvas canvas, double x,
                                 double min, double max)
        {
            double result = (x - min) * canvas.Width / (max - min);
            return result;
        }

        public double YNormalize(Canvas canvas, double y,
                                 double min, double max)
        {
            double result = canvas.Height -
                           (y - min) *  canvas.Height / (max - min);
            return result;
        }
    }
}
```

The code begins with the definition of private members that can be specified by the user. When the Start button is clicked, the values from the TextBox fields are obtained, and these values are used to initialize the simulation. To start the animation, the StartAnimation event handler is attached to the timer's tick event.

Inside the event handler, you calculate the position and velocity for the ball under the influence of gravity when the ball doesn't hit to the wall. When the ball collides with the wall, its motion is determined by Equation (7.21).

Now you can play around with the bouncing ball simulator. Select a different set of input parameters and see what happens. The most interesting thing that may surprise you is that the ball will rotate (spin) at a high angular speed after collision, even if its initial angular velocity is zero.

Also, you can see the difference between a superball and a tennis ball using this simulator. Experimental data show that the coefficients of restitution are very different for superballs and tennis balls. For the superball, CORx = 0.76 and CORy = 0.86, while for the tennis ball, CORx = 0.24 and CORy = 0.79. You can perform the simulation with these two sets of parameters to examine the results. You'll find that the superball will bounce with a faster spin than the tennis ball.

Chapter 8
Charts in Silverlight

As you know, creating charts (or plots) for data visualization plays a very important role in every Windows or Web application. Using Silverlight, it is easy to add charting capabilities to Web Applications. Charts can make data easier to understand and can make reports more interesting to read. They have found widespread application in our daily life. For example, in the scientific, engineering, and mathematics communities, data and results always need to be represented graphically. You can also see stock charts in almost every news media, including the Internet, newspapers, and television.

This chapter will show you how to create real-world 2D line charts, the most basic and useful type of charts, in Silverlight. It'll also explain how to implement a custom chart control and how to reuse it in different Silverlight applications. If you want to create other specialized types of charts, such as bar, stair-step, error bars, pie, area, polar, stock, 3D surface, mesh, or contour charts, and etc., you should refer to my other book *Practcal C# Charts and Graphics*, which provides details on how to create a variety of 2D and 3D chart applications.

Simple Line Charts

The most basic and useful type of chart that you can create with Silverlight is a simple 2D line chart of numerical data. Silverlight provides a set of commands and methods that can be used to create these charts. Even the most elementary 2D chart consists of several basic elements, including lines, symbols, axes, tick markers, labels, a title, and a legend. The following list gives a quick overview of the most basic chart elements without getting into details. These elements will often be referred to in this chapter.

- Axes – a graphics object that defines a region of the chart in which the chart is drawn.
- Line – a graphics object that represents the data you have plotted.
- Text – a graphics object that is comprised of a string of characters.
- Title – the text string object that is located directly above an axis object.
- Label – the text string object associated with the axis object (X- or Y- axis).
- Legend – the text string array object that represents the colors and values of the lines.

The X-Y line chart uses two values to represent each data point. It is very useful for describing relationships between data, and is often used in the statistical analysis of data. This type of chart has wide applications in the scientific, mathmatics, engineering, and finance communities, as well as in daily life.

Creating Simple Line Charts

It is easy to create a 2D X-Y line chart in Silverlight. Let's use an example to illustrate the procedure. Start with a new Silverlight project and name it Example08-1. You'll create the user interface and layout using XAML and perform the computations and generate the data in code. The XAML file of this example is very simple:

```
<UserControl x:Class="Example08_1.Page"
    xmlns="http://schemas.microsoft.com/client/2007"
    xmlns:x="http://schemas.microsoft.com/winfx/2006/xaml"
    Width="400" Height="300">
    <Grid x:Name="LayoutRoot" Background="White">
        <Border BorderBrush="Black" BorderThickness="1"
                Margin="10" CornerRadius="10">
            <Canvas Name="chartCanvas" Width="378"  Height="278">
                <Canvas.Clip>
                    <RectangleGeometry Rect="0 0 378 278"/>
                </Canvas.Clip>
            </Canvas>
        </Border>
    </Grid>
</UserControl>
```

Here you want to create the chart on a Canvas named chartCanvas. The corresponding code-behind file that creates the line chart of this example is listed below:

```
using System;
using System.Windows;
using System.Windows.Controls;
using System.Windows.Media;
using System.Windows.Shapes;

namespace Example08_1
{
    public partial class Page : UserControl
    {
        private double xmin = 0;
        private double xmax = 6.5;
        private double ymin = -1.1;
        private double ymax = 1.1;
        private Polyline pl;

        public Page()
        {
            InitializeComponent();
            AddChart();
        }

        private void AddChart()
        {
            // Draw sine curve:
            pl = new Polyline();
```

```
            pl.Stroke = new SolidColorBrush(Colors.Black);
            for (int i = 0; i < 70; i++)
            {
                double x = i/5.0;
                double y = Math.Sin(x);
                pl.Points.Add(NormalizePoint(new Point(x, y)));
            }
            chartCanvas.Children.Add(pl);

            // Draw cosine curve:
            pl = new Polyline();
            pl.Stroke = new SolidColorBrush(Colors.Black);
            DoubleCollection dc = new DoubleCollection();
            dc.Add(4);
            dc.Add(3);
            pl.StrokeDashArray = dc;

            for (int i = 0; i < 70; i++)
            {
                double x = i / 5.0;
                double y = Math.Cos(x);
                pl.Points.Add(NormalizePoint(new Point(x, y)));
            }
            chartCanvas.Children.Add(pl);
        }

        private Point NormalizePoint(Point pt)
        {
            Point result = new Point();
            result.X = (pt.X - xmin) * chartCanvas.Width / (xmax - xmin);
            result.Y = chartCanvas.Height - (pt.Y - ymin) *
                       chartCanvas.Height / (ymax - ymin);
            return result;
        }
    }
}
```

Figure 8-1 shows the result of running this example.

How It Works

Note that the axis limits xmin, xmax, ymin, and ymax are defined in the real-world coordinate system. The Sine and Cosine functions are represented using the Polyline objects added to the chartCanvas's children collection.

A key step to creating this line chart is to transform the original data points in the world coordinate system into points in the units of device-independent pixels using the NormalizePoint method. The NormalizePoint method converts points with any unit in the world coordinate system into points with a unit of device-independent pixels in the device coordinate system.

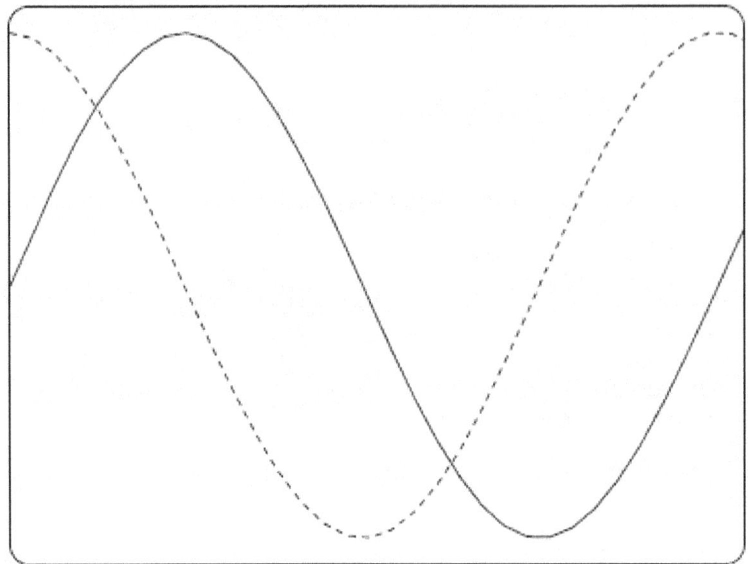

Figure 8-1 Line chart for Sine and Cosine functions.

Line Charts with Data Collection

The above example demonstrates how easy it is to create a simple 2D line chart in Silverlight, but doesn't pay much attention to the program structure. In order for the chart program to be more object-oriented and easily extended to add new features, you need to define three new classes: ChartStyle, DataCollection, and DataSeries. The ChartStyle class defines all chart layout related information. The DataCollection class holds the DataSeries objects, with each DataSeries object representing one curve on the chart. The DataSeries class holds the chart data and line styles, including the line color, thickness, dash style, etc.

Chart Style

Now, start with a new Silverlight project and name it Example08-2. Add a public class, ChartStyle, to the project. The following is the code listing of this class:

```
using System;
using System.Windows.Controls;
using System.Windows;

namespace Example08_2
{
    public class ChartStyle
    {
        public Canvas ChartCanvas { get; set; }
        public double Xmin        { get; set; }
        public double Xmax        { get; set; }
        public double Ymin        { get; set; }
        public double Ymax        { get; set; }
```

```
        public void ResizeCanvas(double width, double height)
        {
            ChartCanvas.Width = width;
            ChartCanvas.Height = height;
        }

        public Point NormalizePoint(Point pt)
        {
            if (ChartCanvas.Width.ToString() == "NaN")
                ChartCanvas.Width = 270;
            if (ChartCanvas.Height.ToString() == "NaN")
                ChartCanvas.Height = 250;
            Point result = new Point();
            result.X = (pt.X - Xmin) * ChartCanvas.Width / (Xmax - Xmin);
            result.Y = ChartCanvas.Height -
                       (pt.Y - Ymin) * ChartCanvas.Height / (Ymax - Ymin);
            return result;
        }
    }
}
```

In this class, you first create several public properties using the automatic property approach. The automatic property is a new C# feature of .NET 3.5 that provides an elegant way to make your code more concise while still retaining its flexibility of properties. This new feature allows you to avoid having to manually declare a private field and write the get/set logic. Instead, the compiler can automatically create the private field and the default get/set operations for you.

The ChartCanvas property is used to define the chart area and obtain the point conversion from the real-world coordinate system to the device independent pixels. Then, other properties are used to manipulate the chart layout, including the axis limits. You also define a ResizeCanvas method that allows the user to resize the chart canvas directly in the device coordinate system using units of device-independent pixels. Finally, you put the NormalizePoint method in this class, making the code clearer and more readable.

Data Collection

Add another public class, DataCollection, to the current project. The following is the code listing of this class:

```
using System;
using System.Windows;
using System.Collections.Generic;
using System.Windows.Controls;

namespace Example08_2
{
    public class DataCollection
    {
        private List<DataSeries> dataList;

        public DataCollection()
        {
            dataList = new List<DataSeries>();
```

```
            }

            public List<DataSeries> DataList
            {
                get { return dataList; }
                set { dataList = value; }
            }

            public void AddLines(Canvas canvas, ChartStyle cs)
            {
                int j = 0;
                foreach (DataSeries ds in DataList)
                {
                    if (ds.SeriesName == "Default Name")
                    {
                        ds.SeriesName = "DataSeries" + j.ToString();
                    }
                    ds.AddLinePattern();

                    int n = ds.LineSeries.Points.Count;
                    Point[] pts = new Point[n];
                    for (int i = 0; i < n; i++)
                    {
                        pts[i] = ds.LineSeries.Points[i];
                    }
                    ds.LineSeries.Points.Clear();

                    for (int i = 0; i < n; i++)
                    {
                        pts[i] = cs.NormalizePoint(pts[i]);
                        ds.LineSeries.Points.Add(pts[i]);
                    }
                    canvas.Children.Add(ds.LineSeries);
                    j++;
                }
            }
        }
    }
```

This class is used to hold the DataSeries objects. You begin with a member field DataSeries list and its corresponding public property DataList. The DataList property holds the DataSeries. Then you implement an AddLines method, which draws lines using the DataSeries objects in the DataCollection class. For each DataSeries, you add a line to the chart canvas using the specified line style for that DataSeries. Notice how to transform all data points from the world coordinate system to the device coordinate system using the NormalizePoint method defined in the ChartStyle class.

Please note that unlike WPF, you can't directly manipulate the point collection in the LineSeries. Here, we have to create a new point array and convert the point array from world coordinates to device coordinates, and then add this converted point array to the point collection of the LineSeries.

Data Series

Finally, you need to add the DataSeries class to the current project. The following is the code listing of this class:

```
using System;
using System.Windows;
using System.Windows.Media;
using System.Windows.Shapes;

namespace Example08_2
{
    public class DataSeries
    {
        private Polyline lineSeries = new Polyline();
        private Brush lineColor;
        private double lineThickness = 1;
        private LinePatternEnum linePattern;
        private string seriesName = "Default Name";

        public DataSeries()
        {
            LineColor = new SolidColorBrush(Colors.Black);
        }

        public Brush LineColor
        {
            get { return lineColor; }
            set { lineColor = value; }
        }

        public Polyline LineSeries
        {
            get { return lineSeries; }
            set { lineSeries = value; }
        }

        public double LineThickness
        {
            get { return lineThickness; }
            set { lineThickness = value; }
        }

        public LinePatternEnum LinePattern
        {
            get { return linePattern; }
            set { linePattern = value; }
        }

        public string SeriesName
        {
            get { return seriesName; }
            set { seriesName = value; }
        }
```

```
        public void AddLinePattern()
        {
            LineSeries.Stroke = LineColor;
            LineSeries.StrokeThickness = LineThickness;
            DoubleCollection collection;

            switch (LinePattern)
            {
                case LinePatternEnum.Dash:
                    collection = new DoubleCollection();
                    collection.Add(4);
                    collection.Add(3);
                    LineSeries.StrokeDashArray = collection;
                    break;
                case LinePatternEnum.Dot:
                    collection = new DoubleCollection();
                    collection.Add(1);
                    collection.Add(2);
                    LineSeries.StrokeDashArray = collection;
                    break;
                case LinePatternEnum.DashDot:
                    collection = new DoubleCollection();
                    collection.Add(4);
                    collection.Add(2);
                    collection.Add(1);
                    collection.Add(2);
                    LineSeries.StrokeDashArray = collection;
                    break;
                case LinePatternEnum.None:
                    LineSeries.Stroke = new SolidColorBrush(Colors.Transparent);
                    break;
            }
        }

        public enum LinePatternEnum
        {
            Solid = 1,
            Dash = 2,
            Dot = 3,
            DashDot = 4,
            None = 5
        }
    }
}
```

This class defines the Polyline object for a given DataSeries. It then defines the line style for this line object, including the line color, thickness, line pattern, and the series name. The SeriesName property will be used in creating the legend for the chart. The line pattern is defined by a public enumeration called LinePatternEnum where five line patterns are defined, including Solid (default), Dash, Dot, DashDot, and None. The None enumeration means there will be no line drawn on the chart canvas.

The line pattern is created using the AddLinePattern method. There is no need to create the solid line pattern because it is the default setting for the Polyline object. The dash or dot line pattern is created using the StrokeDashArray property of the Polyline. The invisible line (corresponding to the None type of the line pattern) is defined by setting the stroke's color to transparent.

Creating Charts

Now, you can create line charts using the ChartStyle, DataCollection, and DataSeries classes. Again, I'll use an example to illustrate how to create a line chart using these classes. Let's create Example08-2 in the project. The layout of this example is created using the following XAML file:

```
<UserControl x:Class="Example08_2.Page"
    xmlns="http://schemas.microsoft.com/client/2007"
    xmlns:x="http://schemas.microsoft.com/winfx/2006/xaml"
    Width="400" Height="300">
    <Grid x:Name="LayoutRoot" Background="White">
        <Border BorderBrush="Gray" BorderThickness="1"
                Margin="10">
            <Canvas Name="chartCanvas" Width="378" Height="278">
                <Canvas.Clip>
                    <RectangleGeometry Rect="0 0 378 278"/>
                </Canvas.Clip>
            </Canvas>
        </Border>
    </Grid>
</UserControl>
```

This markup defines a Canvas named chartCanvas, which will then be used to hold the line chart. The corresponding code-behind file of this example is listed below:

```
using System;
using System.Windows;
using System.Windows.Controls;
using System.Windows.Input;
using System.Windows.Media;
using System.Windows.Shapes;

namespace Example08_2
{
    public partial class Page : UserControl
    {
        private ChartStyle cs;
        private DataCollection dc = new DataCollection();
        private DataSeries ds = new DataSeries();

        public Page()
        {
            InitializeComponent();
            AddChart();
        }

        private void AddChart()
        {
            cs = new ChartStyle();
            cs.ChartCanvas = chartCanvas;
            cs.Xmin = 0;
            cs.Xmax = 7;
```

```
                cs.Ymin = -1.1;
                cs.Ymax = 1.1;

                // Draw Sine curve:
                ds = new DataSeries();
                ds.LineColor = new SolidColorBrush(Colors.Blue);
                ds.LineThickness = 3;
                for (int i = 0; i < 70; i++)
                {
                    double x = i / 5.0;
                    double y = Math.Sin(x);
                    ds.LineSeries.Points.Add(new Point(x, y));
                }
                dc.DataList.Add(ds);

                // Draw cosine curve:
                ds = new DataSeries();
                ds.LineColor = new SolidColorBrush(Colors.Red);
                ds.LinePattern = DataSeries.LinePatternEnum.DashDot;
                ds.LineThickness = 3;

                for (int i = 0; i < 70; i++)
                {
                    double x = i / 5.0;
                    double y = Math.Cos(x);
                    ds.LineSeries.Points.Add(new Point(x, y));
                }
                dc.DataList.Add(ds);
                dc.AddLines(chartCanvas, cs);
            }
        }
    }
```

In this class, you begin by defining instances for the ChartStyle, DataCollection, and DataSeries classes. Inside the AddChart method, you specify the axis limit properties, which were originally defined in the ChartStyle class, to meet the requirements of the current application.

Pay attention to how the DataSeries objects are added to the DataCollection class:

```
// Draw Sine curve:
ds = new DataSeries();
ds.LineColor = Brushes.Blue;
ds.LineThickness = 3;
for (int i = 0; i < 70; i++)
{
    double x = i / 5.0;
    double y = Math.Sin(x);
    ds.LineSeries.Points.Add(new Point(x, y));
}
dc.DataList.Add(ds);
```

Here you first create a new DataSeries object and define its line style, including the line color and thickness. Notice that you do not specify the line pattern for this object, so the default line pattern, Solid, is used. You then add the data points to the ds.LineSeries object's point collection. Finally, you add the data series "ds" to the DataCollection using the dc.DataList.Add method. In this way, you can add any number of DataSeries objects to the DataCollection. The AddLines method in the

DataCollection class draws curves on the chart for all the DataSeries objects contained in the DataCollection.

Figure 8-2 illustrates the results of running this example.

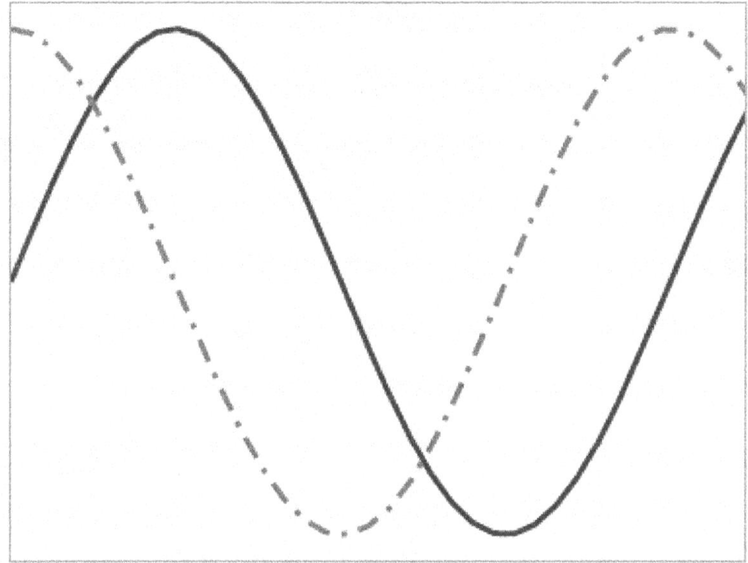

Figure 8-2 Chart for Sine and Cosine functions created using DataCollection class.

Gridlines and Labels

In the previous sections, only the lines for the Sine and Cosine functions were drawn on the chart. In this section, you will add more features to the 2D line chart, including gridlines, a title, tick markers, and labels for axes.

XAML Layout

Start with a new Silverlight project and name it Example08-3. Add the ChartStyle, DataCollection, and DataSeries classes from the previous example to the current project and change their namespace to Example08_3. You can create the chart layout using XAML, and put the title and labels for the X- and Y-axes into different cells of a Grid control. The following is the XAML file of this example:

```
<UserControl x:Class="Example08_3.Page"
    xmlns="http://schemas.microsoft.com/client/2007"
    xmlns:x="http://schemas.microsoft.com/winfx/2006/xaml"
    Width="500" Height="400">
    <Grid x:Name="LayoutRoot" Background="White">
        <Border BorderBrush="Gray" BorderThickness="1"
                CornerRadius="10" Margin="10">
            <Canvas>
                <TextBlock Margin="10" Name="tbYLabel"
                           VerticalAlignment="Center"
                           RenderTransformOrigin="0 0"
```

```
                    TextAlignment="Center" Text="Y Axis"
                    FontSize="12" FontWeight="Bold"
                    Canvas.Top="180">
                <TextBlock.RenderTransform>
                    <RotateTransform Angle="-90"/>
                </TextBlock.RenderTransform>
            </TextBlock>

            <Grid Name="grid1" Margin="10">
                <Grid.ColumnDefinitions>
                    <ColumnDefinition Width="20"/>
                    <ColumnDefinition x:Name="column1" Width="*"/>
                </Grid.ColumnDefinitions>
                <Grid.RowDefinitions>
                    <RowDefinition Height="Auto"/>
                    <RowDefinition x:Name="row1" Height="*"/>
                    <RowDefinition Height="Auto"/>
                </Grid.RowDefinitions>
                <TextBlock Margin="2" x:Name="tbTitle" Grid.Column="1"
                        Grid.Row="0" FontSize="14"
                        FontWeight="Bold" HorizontalAlignment="Stretch"
                        VerticalAlignment="Stretch"
                        TextAlignment="Center" Text="Title"/>
                <TextBlock Margin="2" x:Name="tbXLabel" Grid.Column="1"
                        Grid.Row="2" TextAlignment="Center" Text="X Axis"
                        FontSize="12" FontWeight="Bold"/>

                <Canvas Margin="2" Name="textCanvas" Width="420"
                      Height="305" Grid.Column="1" Grid.Row="1">
                    <Canvas Name="chartCanvas"/>
                </Canvas>
            </Grid>
        </Canvas>
    </Border>
  </Grid>
</UserControl>
```

Here you also create two canvas controls, textCanvas and chartCanvas. The textCanvas control is used to hold the tick mark labels, and the chartCanvas control is used to hold the chart itself. The DataCollection, DataSeries, and ChartStyle classes, which were used in the previous example, can still be used here. You can add the gridlines and labels to a new class, ChartStyleGridlines, which is inherited from the ChartStyle class.

ChartStyleGridlines Class

Add a new class, ChartStyleGridlines, to the current project. As mentioned previously, this class derives from the ChartStyle class. Here is the code listing of this class:

```
using System;
using System.Windows;
using System.Windows.Controls;
using System.Windows.Input;
using System.Windows.Media;
using System.Windows.Shapes;
```

```
namespace Example08_3
{
    public class ChartStyleGridlines : ChartStyle
    {
        private Canvas textCanvas;
        private bool isXGrid = true;
        private bool isYGrid = true;
        private Brush gridlineColor = new SolidColorBrush(Colors.LightGray);
        private GridlinePatternEnum gridlinePattern;
        private string title = "Title";
        private string xLabel = "X Label";
        private string yLabel = "Y Label";
        private double xTick = 1;
        private double yTick = 0.5;
        private double leftOffset = 20;
        private double bottomOffset = 15;
        private double rightOffset = 10;
        private Line gridline = new Line();

        public string Title
        {
            get { return title; }
            set { title = value; }
        }

        public string XLabel
        {
            get { return xLabel; }
            set { xLabel = value; }
        }

        public string YLabel
        {
            get { return yLabel; }
            set { yLabel = value; }
        }

        public GridlinePatternEnum GridlinePattern
        {
            get { return gridlinePattern; }
            set { gridlinePattern = value; }
        }

        public double XTick
        {
            get { return xTick; }
            set { xTick = value; }
        }

        public double YTick
        {
            get { return yTick; }
            set { yTick = value; }
        }
```

```
public Brush GridlineColor
{
    get { return gridlineColor; }
    set { gridlineColor = value; }
}

public Canvas TextCanvas
{
    get { return textCanvas; }
    set { textCanvas = value; }
}

public bool IsXGrid
{
    get { return isXGrid; }
    set { isXGrid = value; }
}

public bool IsYGrid
{
    get { return isYGrid; }
    set { isYGrid = value; }
}

public void AddChartStyle(TextBlock tbTitle,
    TextBlock tbXLabel, TextBlock tbYLabel)
{
    Point pt = new Point();
    Line tick = new Line();
    double offset = 0;
    double dx, dy;
    TextBlock tb = new TextBlock();
    tb.FontSize = 12;

    //  determine right offset:
    tb.Text = Xmax.ToString();
    tb.Measure(new Size(Double.PositiveInfinity,
                        Double.PositiveInfinity));
    Size size = tb.DesiredSize;
    rightOffset = size.Width / 2 + 2;

    // Determine left offset:
    for (dy = Ymin; dy <= Ymax; dy += YTick)
    {
        pt = NormalizePoint(new Point(Xmin, dy));
        tb = new TextBlock();
        tb.FontSize = 12;
        tb.Text = dy.ToString();
        tb.TextAlignment = TextAlignment.Right;
        size = new Size(tb.ActualWidth, tb.ActualHeight);
        if (offset < size.Width)
            offset = size.Width;
    }
    leftOffset = offset + 5;
```

```
ChartCanvas.Width = TextCanvas.Width - leftOffset - rightOffset;
ChartCanvas.Height =
            TextCanvas.Height - bottomOffset - size.Height / 2;
RectangleGeometry rect = new RectangleGeometry();
rect.Rect = new Rect(0, 0, ChartCanvas.Width, ChartCanvas.Height);
ChartCanvas.Clip = rect;

Canvas.SetLeft(ChartCanvas, leftOffset);
Canvas.SetTop(ChartCanvas,
       TextCanvas.Height - ChartCanvas.Height - bottomOffset);

Rectangle chartRect = new Rectangle();
chartRect.Stroke = new SolidColorBrush(Colors.Black);
chartRect.Width = ChartCanvas.Width;
chartRect.Height = ChartCanvas.Height;
ChartCanvas.Children.Add(chartRect);

// Create vertical gridlines:
if (IsYGrid == true)
{
    for (dx = Xmin + XTick; dx < Xmax;
        dx += XTick)
    {
        gridline = new Line();
        AddLinePattern();
        gridline.X1 = NormalizePoint(new Point(dx, Ymin)).X;
        gridline.Y1 = NormalizePoint(new Point(dx, Ymin)).Y;
        gridline.X2 = NormalizePoint(new Point(dx, Ymax)).X;
        gridline.Y2 = NormalizePoint(new Point(dx, Ymax)).Y;
        ChartCanvas.Children.Add(gridline);
    }
}

// Create horizontal gridlines:
if (IsXGrid == true)
{
    for (dy = Ymin + YTick; dy < Ymax;
        dy += YTick)
    {
        gridline = new Line();
        AddLinePattern();
        gridline.X1 = NormalizePoint(new Point(Xmin, dy)).X;
        gridline.Y1 = NormalizePoint(new Point(Xmin, dy)).Y;
        gridline.X2 = NormalizePoint(new Point(Xmax, dy)).X;
        gridline.Y2 = NormalizePoint(new Point(Xmax, dy)).Y;
        ChartCanvas.Children.Add(gridline);
    }
}

// Create x-axis tick marks:
for (dx = Xmin; dx <= Xmax; dx += xTick)
{
    pt = NormalizePoint(new Point(dx, Ymin));
    tick = new Line();
```

```
            tick.Stroke = new SolidColorBrush(Colors.Black);
            tick.X1 = pt.X;
            tick.Y1 = pt.Y;
            tick.X2 = pt.X;
            tick.Y2 = pt.Y - 5;
            ChartCanvas.Children.Add(tick);

            tb = new TextBlock();
            tb.FontSize = 12;
            tb.Text = dx.ToString();
            size = new Size(tb.ActualWidth, tb.ActualHeight);
            TextCanvas.Children.Add(tb);
            Canvas.SetLeft(tb, leftOffset + pt.X - size.Width / 2);
            Canvas.SetTop(tb, pt.Y + size.Height / 2);
        }

        // Create y-axis tick marks:
        for (dy = Ymin; dy <= Ymax; dy += YTick)
        {
            pt = NormalizePoint(new Point(Xmin, dy));
            tick = new Line();
            tick.Stroke = new SolidColorBrush(Colors.Black);
            tick.X1 = pt.X;
            tick.Y1 = pt.Y;
            tick.X2 = pt.X + 5;
            tick.Y2 = pt.Y;
            ChartCanvas.Children.Add(tick);

            tb = new TextBlock();
            tb.FontSize = 12;
            tb.Text = dy.ToString();
            size = new Size(tb.ActualWidth, tb.ActualHeight);
             TextCanvas.Children.Add(tb);
            Canvas.SetLeft(tb,
                   Canvas.GetLeft(ChartCanvas) - 5 - size.Width);
            Canvas.SetTop(tb, pt.Y);
        }

        // Add title and labels:
        tbTitle.Text = Title;
        tbXLabel.Text = XLabel;
        tbYLabel.Text = YLabel;
    }

    public void AddLinePattern()
    {
        gridline.Stroke = GridlineColor;
        gridline.StrokeThickness = 1;
        DoubleCollection collection;
        switch (GridlinePattern)
        {
            case GridlinePatternEnum.Dash:
                collection = new DoubleCollection();
                collection.Add(4);
                collection.Add(3);
```

```
                    gridline.StrokeDashArray = collection;
                    break;
                case GridlinePatternEnum.Dot:
                    collection = new DoubleCollection();
                    collection.Add(1);
                    collection.Add(2);
                    gridline.StrokeDashArray = collection;
                    break;
                case GridlinePatternEnum.DashDot:
                    collection = new DoubleCollection();
                    collection.Add(4);
                    collection.Add(2);
                    collection.Add(1);
                    collection.Add(2);
                    gridline.StrokeDashArray = collection;
                    break;
            }
        }

        public enum GridlinePatternEnum
        {
            Solid = 1,
            Dash = 2,
            Dot = 3,
            DashDot = 4
        }
    }
}
```

In this class, you add more member fields and corresponding properties, which are used to manipulate the chart's layout and appearance. The meaning of each field and property can be easily understood from its name. In addition, the following member fields are added to define the gridlines for your chart:

```
private bool isXGrid = true;
private bool isYGrid = true;
private Brush gridlineColor = new SolidColorBrush(Colors.LightGray);
private GridlinePatternEnum gridlinePattern;
```

These fields and corresponding properties provide a great deal of flexibility in customizing the appearance of the gridlines. The gridlinePattern field allows you to choose various line dash styles, including solid, dash, dot, dash-dot, etc. You can change the gridlines' color using the gridlineColor field. In addition, two bool fields, isXGrid and isYGrid, are defined, which allow you to turn horizontal or vertical gridlines on or off.

You then define member fields and corresponding properties for the X- and Y-labels, the title, and the ticks in order to change the labels, title, and tick marks. You can easily add more member fields to change, for example, the fonts and text color for the labels and title.

The AddChartStyle method seems quite complicated in this class; however, it is actually reasonably easy to follow. First, you define the size of the chartCanvas by considering the suitable offset relative to the textCanvas. Next, you draw gridlines with a specified color and line pattern. Please note that all of the end-points of the gridlines have been transformed from the world coordinate system to the device-independent system using the NormalizePoint method.

You then draw the tick marks for the X- and Y-axes of the chart. For each tick mark, you find the points in the device coordinate system where the tick mark joins the axes and draw a black line, 5 pixels long, from this point toward inside the chartCanvas.

The title and labels for the X- and Y-axes are attached to the corresponding TextBlock names in code. You can also create data bindings that bind the Title, Label, and YLabel properties to the corresponding TextBlock directly in the XAML file.

Testing Project

You can test the gridlines and labels using Example08-3. Open the code-behind file page.xaml.ps of the project and add the following code to it:

```
using System;
using System.Windows;
using System.Windows.Controls;
using System.Windows.Media;
using System.Windows.Shapes;

namespace Example08_3
{
    public partial class Page : UserControl
    {
        private ChartStyleGridlines cs;
        private DataCollection dc = new DataCollection();
        private DataSeries ds = new DataSeries();

        public Page()
        {
            InitializeComponent();
            AddChart();
        }

        private void AddChart()
        {
            cs = new ChartStyleGridlines();
            cs.ChartCanvas = chartCanvas;
            cs.TextCanvas = textCanvas;
            cs.Title = "Sine and Cosine Chart";
            cs.Xmin = 0;
            cs.Xmax = 7;
            cs.Ymin = -1.5;
            cs.Ymax = 1.5;
            cs.YTick = 0.5;
            cs.GridlinePattern =
                ChartStyleGridlines.GridlinePatternEnum.Dot;
            cs.GridlineColor = new SolidColorBrush(Colors.Black);
            cs.AddChartStyle(tbTitle, tbXLabel, tbYLabel);

            // Draw Sine curve:
            ds.LineColor = new SolidColorBrush(Colors.Blue);
            ds.LineThickness = 3;
            for (int i = 0; i < 70; i++)
            {
```

```
                double x = i / 5.0;
                double y = Math.Sin(x);
                ds.LineSeries.Points.Add(new Point(x, y));
            }
            dc.DataList.Add(ds);

            // Draw cosine curve:
            ds = new DataSeries();
            ds.LineColor = new SolidColorBrush(Colors.Red);
            ds.LinePattern =
                DataSeries.LinePatternEnum.DashDot;
            ds.LineThickness = 3;

            for (int i = 0; i < 70; i++)
            {
                double x = i / 5.0;
                double y = Math.Cos(x);
                ds.LineSeries.Points.Add(new Point(x, y));
            }
            dc.DataList.Add(ds);
            dc.AddLines(chartCanvas, cs);
        }
    }
}
```

This code is similar to the code used in the previous example, except that you specify the gridlines' properties.

Figure 8-3 illustrates the results of running this application.

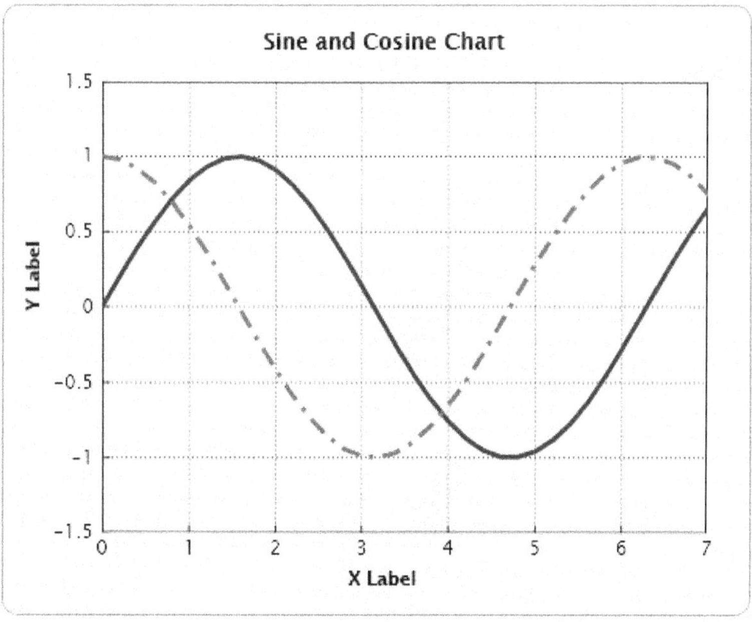

Figure 8-3 Sine and Cosine chart with gridlines and labels.

You can see that the chart has a title, labels, gridlines, and tick marks. Obviously, there is still no chart legend yet. I'll show you how to add a legend in the next section.

Legend

For a 2D line chart with multiple curves, you may want to use a legend to identify each curve plotted on your chart. The legend shows a sample of the curve type, marker symbol, color, and text label you specify for each curve.

Legend Class

Start with a new Silverlight project and name it Example08-4. Add the classes in the previous example, including ChartStyle, DataCollection, DataSeries, and ChartStyleGridlines, to the current project and change their namespaces to Example08-4. Add a new Legend class to the project. The following is the code listing of this class:

```
using System;
using System.Windows;
using System.Windows.Controls;
using System.Windows.Input;
using System.Windows.Media;
using System.Windows.Shapes;

namespace Example08_4
{
    public class Legend
    {
        private bool isLegend = false;
        private bool isBorder = true;
        private Canvas legendCanvas;

        public Legend()
        {
            legendCanvas = new Canvas();
        }

        public Canvas LegendCanvas
        {
            get { return legendCanvas; }
            set { legendCanvas = value; }
        }

        public bool IsLegend
        {
            get { return isLegend; }
            set { isLegend = value; }
        }

        public bool IsBorder
        {
            get { return isBorder; }
            set { isBorder = value; }
```

```
}

public void AddLegend(ChartStyleGridlines cs,
    DataCollection dc)
{
    TextBlock tb = new TextBlock();
    if (dc.DataList.Count < 1 || !IsLegend)
        return;
    int n = 0;
    string[] legendLabels = new string[dc.DataList.Count];
    foreach (DataSeries ds in dc.DataList)
    {
        legendLabels[n] = ds.SeriesName;
        n++;
    }

    double legendWidth = 0;
    Size size = new Size(0, 0);
    for (int i = 0; i < legendLabels.Length; i++)
    {
        tb = new TextBlock();
        tb.Text = legendLabels[i];
        tb.FontSize = 12;
        size = new Size(tb.ActualWidth,tb.ActualHeight);
        if (legendWidth < size.Width)
            legendWidth = size.Width;
    }

    legendWidth += 50;
    legendCanvas.Width = legendWidth + 5;
    double legendHeight = 21 * dc.DataList.Count;
    double sx = 6;
    double sy = 2;
    double textHeight = size.Height;
    double lineLength = 34;
    Rectangle legendRect = new Rectangle();
    legendRect.Stroke = new SolidColorBrush(Colors.Black);
    legendRect.Width = legendWidth;
    legendRect.Height = legendHeight;

    if (IsLegend && IsBorder)
        LegendCanvas.Children.Add(legendRect);

    n = 1;
    foreach (DataSeries ds in dc.DataList)
    {
        double xSymbol = sx + lineLength / 2;
        double xText = 2 * sx + lineLength;
        double yText = n * sy + (2 * n - 1) * textHeight / 2;
        Line line = new Line();
        AddLinePattern(line, ds);
        line.X1 = sx;
        line.Y1 = yText;
        line.X2 = sx + lineLength;
        line.Y2 = yText;
```

```
                LegendCanvas.Children.Add(line);

                tb = new TextBlock();
                tb.FontSize = 12;
                tb.Text = ds.SeriesName;
                LegendCanvas.Children.Add(tb);
                size = new Size(tb.ActualWidth, tb.ActualHeight);
                Canvas.SetTop(tb, yText - size.Height / 2);
                Canvas.SetLeft(tb, xText);
                n++;
            }
        }

        private void AddLinePattern(Line line, DataSeries ds)
        {
            line.Stroke = ds.LineColor;
            line.StrokeThickness = ds.LineThickness;
            DoubleCollection collection;

            switch (ds.LinePattern)
            {
                case DataSeries.LinePatternEnum.Dash:
                    collection = new DoubleCollection();
                    collection.Add(4);
                    collection.Add(3);
                    line.StrokeDashArray = collection;
                    break;
                case DataSeries.LinePatternEnum.Dot:
                    collection = new DoubleCollection();
                    collection.Add(1);
                    collection.Add(2);
                    line.StrokeDashArray = collection;
                    break;
                case DataSeries.LinePatternEnum.DashDot:
                    collection = new DoubleCollection();
                    collection.Add(4);
                    collection.Add(2);
                    collection.Add(1);
                    collection.Add(2);
                    line.StrokeDashArray = collection;
                    break;
                case DataSeries.LinePatternEnum.None:
                    line.Stroke = new SolidColorBrush(Colors.Transparent);
                    break;
            }
        }
    }
}
```

This class begins with the member fields that describe the legend behavior:

```
private bool isLegend = false;
private bool isBorder = true;
private Canvas legendCanvas;
```

The isLegend allows you to turn the legend on or off. The default setting of this field is false. Therefore, you'll need to change this default value to true if you want to display the legend on your chart. The isBorder field allows you to add (or not add) a border to the legend. The legendCanvas is used to hold the legend. You can add more member fields if you want more control over the legend. For example, you can add corresponding field members and properties to change the legend's text color, font, and background color, etc. Here I simply want to show you the basic steps of creating the legend without adding these extra features.

In this class, you place the legend on the right-hand side of the chart. You can easily move the legend to other positions in code. The AddLegend method is used to create the legend with line style, color, and text labels.

Testing Project

The layout of this example is very similar to the previous example's, except that you add a legendCanvas. Here is the XAML file of this example:

```
<UserControl x:Class="Example08_4.Page"
    xmlns="http://schemas.microsoft.com/client/2007"
    xmlns:x="http://schemas.microsoft.com/winfx/2006/xaml"
    Height="400" Width="540">
    <Grid x:Name="LayoutRoot" Background="White">
        <Border BorderBrush="Gray" BorderThickness="1"
                CornerRadius="10" Margin="10">
            <Canvas>
                <TextBlock Margin="10" Name="tbYLabel"
                           VerticalAlignment="Center"
                           RenderTransformOrigin="0 0"
                           TextAlignment="Center" Text="Y Axis" FontSize="12"
                           FontWeight="Bold" Canvas.Top="180">
                    <TextBlock.RenderTransform>
                        <RotateTransform Angle="-90"/>
                    </TextBlock.RenderTransform>
                </TextBlock>

                <Grid Name="grid1" Margin="10">
                    <Grid.ColumnDefinitions>
                        <ColumnDefinition Width="20"/>
                        <ColumnDefinition x:Name="column1" Width="*"/>
                        <ColumnDefinition Width="Auto"/>
                    </Grid.ColumnDefinitions>
                    <Grid.RowDefinitions>
                        <RowDefinition Height="Auto"/>
                        <RowDefinition x:Name="row1" Height="*"/>
                        <RowDefinition Height="Auto"/>
                    </Grid.RowDefinitions>
                    <TextBlock Margin="2" x:Name="tbTitle" Grid.Column="1"
                               Grid.Row="0" FontSize="14"
                               FontWeight="Bold" HorizontalAlignment="Stretch"
                               VerticalAlignment="Stretch"
                               TextAlignment="Center" Text="Title"/>
                    <TextBlock Margin="2" x:Name="tbXLabel" Grid.Column="1"
                               Grid.Row="2" TextAlignment="Center" Text="X Axis"
                               FontSize="12" FontWeight="Bold"/>
```

```
                    <Canvas Margin="2" Name="textCanvas" Width="380"
                            Height="305" Grid.Column="1" Grid.Row="1">
                        <Canvas Name="chartCanvas"/>
                    </Canvas>

                    <Canvas x:Name="legendCanvas" Margin="0 10 0 10"
                            Grid.Column="2" Grid.Row="1" Width="40"/>
                </Grid>
            </Canvas>
        </Border>
    </Grid>
</UserControl>
```

The corresponding code-behind file of this example is listed below:

```
using System;
using System.Windows;
using System.Windows.Controls;
using System.Windows.Media;
using System.Windows.Shapes;

namespace Example08_4
{
    public partial class Page : UserControl
    {
        private ChartStyleGridlines cs;
        private Legend lg = new Legend();
        private DataCollection dc = new DataCollection();
        private DataSeries ds = new DataSeries();

        public Page()
        {
            InitializeComponent();
            AddChart();
            lg.LegendCanvas = legendCanvas;
            lg.IsLegend = true;
            lg.IsBorder = true;
            lg.AddLegend(cs, dc);
        }

        private void AddChart()
        {
            cs = new ChartStyleGridlines();
            cs.ChartCanvas = chartCanvas;
            cs.TextCanvas = textCanvas;
            cs.Title = "Sine and Cosine Chart";
            cs.Xmin = 0;
            cs.Xmax = 7;
            cs.Ymin = -1.5;
            cs.Ymax = 1.5;
            cs.YTick = 0.5;
            cs.GridlinePattern =
                ChartStyleGridlines.GridlinePatternEnum.Dot;
            cs.GridlineColor = new SolidColorBrush(Colors.Black);
            cs.AddChartStyle(tbTitle, tbXLabel, tbYLabel);
```

```
            // Draw Sine curve:
            ds.LineColor = new SolidColorBrush(Colors.Blue);
            ds.LineThickness = 1;
            ds.SeriesName = "Sine";
            for (int i = 0; i < 70; i++)
            {
                double x = i / 5.0;
                double y = Math.Sin(x);
                ds.LineSeries.Points.Add(new Point(x, y));
            }
            dc.DataList.Add(ds);

            // Draw cosine curve:
            ds = new DataSeries();
            ds.LineColor = new SolidColorBrush(Colors.Red);
            ds.SeriesName = "Cosine";
            ds.LinePattern =
                DataSeries.LinePatternEnum.DashDot;
            ds.LineThickness = 2;
            for (int i = 0; i < 70; i++)
            {
                double x = i / 5.0;
                double y = Math.Cos(x);
                ds.LineSeries.Points.Add(new Point(x, y));
            }
            dc.DataList.Add(ds);

            // Draw sine^2 curve:
            ds = new DataSeries();
            ds.LineColor = new SolidColorBrush(Colors.Green);
            ds.SeriesName = "Sine^2";
            ds.LinePattern = DataSeries.LinePatternEnum.Dot;
            ds.LineThickness = 2;
            for (int i = 0; i < 70; i++)
            {
                double x = i / 5.0;
                double y = Math.Sin(x) * Math.Sin(x);
                ds.LineSeries.Points.Add(new Point(x, y));
            }
            dc.DataList.Add(ds);
            dc.AddLines(chartCanvas, cs);
        }
    }
}
```

Here you add one more curve to the chart for demonstration purpose. Notice that you need to specify the SeriesName property for each DataSeries because the legend uses the SeriesName as the legend labels. Otherwise, the legend will use the default SeriesName (DataSeries0, DataSeries1, DataSeries2,...) as the legend labels.

In order to have the legend on your chart, you need to call the AddLegend method. First, add a new member field to this class:

```
        private Legend lg = new Legend();
```

and set the legend's IsLegend property to true. Please note that you must place the AddLegend method after the AddChart, because the legend needs to know how many curves are on your chart.

Figure 8-4 shows the results of running this example.

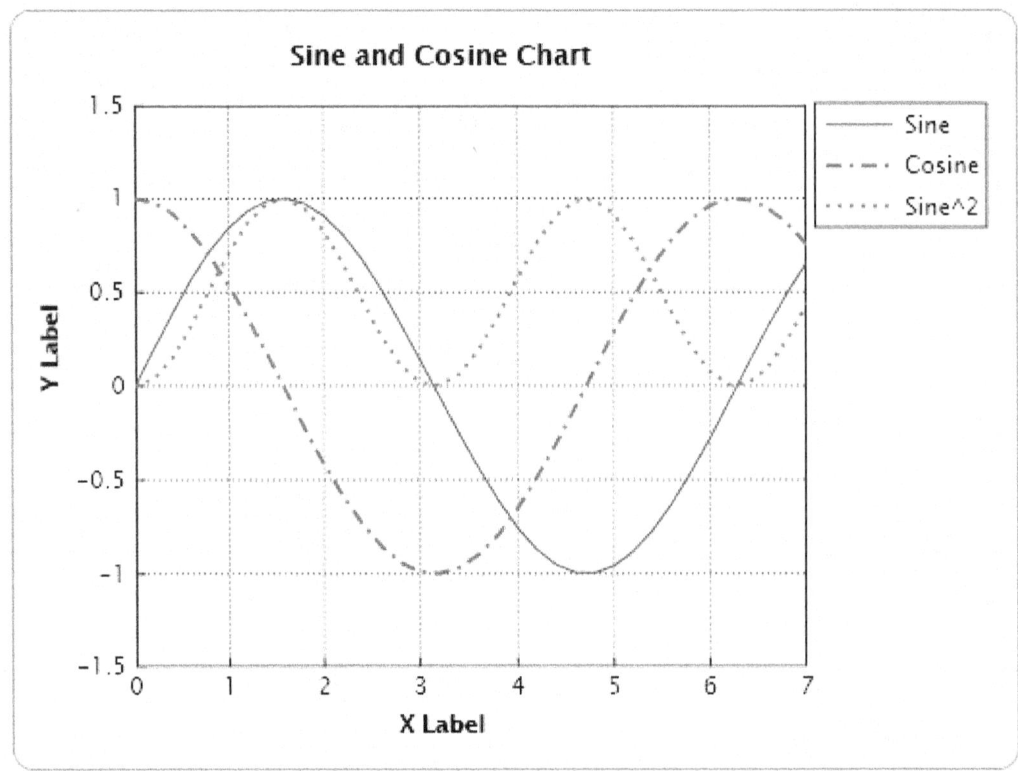

Figure 8-4 Chart with legend.

Chapter 9
3D Transformations

In the previous chapters, we discussed 2D graphics, transforms, geometry, and drawing. This chapter will explain the mathematical basics of 3D transforms, which will be used to perform operations on 3D graphics objects. Most 3D transformations are analogous to the 2D transformations described in Chapter 3. Using homogeneous coordinates and matrix representations similar to the ones used in 2D, I'll show you how to perform basic transforms, including translation, scaling, and rotation, in 3D. This chapter will also describe various projection matrices, which allow you to view 3D graphics objects on a 2D screen. As is the case with 2D, you can combine 3D basic transform matrices to represent a complicated transform with a single transform matrix.

Unlike WPF, Silverlight doesn't include a built-in 3D feature. Even the simplest 3D point object must be defined first in order to be used in Silverlight applications. In this chapter, I'll demonstrate how to create a variety of 3D transform matrices and 3D graphics objects using examples. I'll also discuss different 3D coordinate systems and show how to implement them in Silverlight.

Basic 3D Transformations

Matrix representations play an important role in transformations and operations on graphics objects. A matrix is a multi-dimensional array. This section explains the basics of 3D matrices and transformations. General 3D transforms are quite complicated. As in the case of 2D, however, you can build more useful transforms with combinations of simple basic transforms, including translation, scaling, rotation, and projection. The following sections describe these fundamental transformations. Once you understand how to use these basic 3D transformations, you can always combine them to create more general 3D transformations.

3D Point, Vector, and Matrix

As in the case of 2D, you can perform 3D matrix operations in a homogeneous coordinate system. Here, a point or vector is represented by a row matrix. In this notation, most 3D transformation matrices contain (0, 0, 0, 1) in their last column. You can use this special structure, as Silverlight did in 2D matrices, to speed up matrix operations. This approach works for most transformation matrices, except for the perspective transformation described later in this chapter, which does not contain (0, 0, 0, 1) in its last column. This means that you cannot use this method when you deal with perspective transformations. Therefore, in this book, we will instead use a standard For-loop computation method to perform matrix operations. This standard For-loop method doesn't assume that transformation matrices contain (0, 0, 0, 1) in their last column.

Let's start with a new Silverlight project, Example09-1, that shows how to define a 3D point object and matrix. Add three new classes, Point3, Vector3, and Matrix3, to the project and change their namespace to XuMath. In the Point3 class, we define a 3D point in homogeneous coordinates and perform a basic transformation on the point using a public method Transform.

Point in 3D

The following is the code listing of the Point3 class:

```
using System;

namespace XuMath
{
    public class Point3
    {
        public double X;
        public double Y;
        public double Z;
        public double W;

        public Point3()
        {
        }

        public Point3(double x, double y, double z, double w)
        {
            X = x;
            Y = y;
            Z = z;
            W = w;
        }

        // Apply a transformation to a point:
        public static Point3 Transform(Matrix3 m, Point3 pt3)
        {
            double[] result =
                m.VectorMultiply(new double[4] { pt3.X, pt3.Y, pt3.Z, pt3.W });
            Point3 pt = new Point3();
            pt.X = result[0];
            pt.Y = result[1];
            pt.Z = result[2];
            pt.W = result[3];
            return pt;
        }

        // Normalize the transformed point by its W-component:
        public static Point3 TransformNormalize(Matrix3 m, Point3 pt3)
        {
            double[] result =
                m.VectorMultiply(new double[4] { pt3.X, pt3.Y, pt3.Z, pt3.W });
```

```
            Point3 pt = new Point3();
            pt.X = result[0] / result[3];
            pt.Y = result[1] / result[3];
            pt.Z = result[2];
            pt.W = 1;
            return pt;
        }

        public static Point3 Parse(string str)
        {
            string[] astring = new string[3];
            char[] splitter = { ',' };
            astring = str.Split(splitter);
            Point3 result = new Point3();
            result.X = double.Parse(astring[0]);
            result.Y = double.Parse(astring[1]);
            result.Z = double.Parse(astring[2]);
            result.W = 1;
            return result;
        }
    }
}
```

In this class, the default W component of a 3D point in homogenous coordinates is set to 1. We first define two different constructors which can be used to create 3D point objects. We also implement three public static methods, which are used to perform the standard matrix operations on a 3D point. The TransformNormalize method returns a point that is normalized by its W-component. This is useful when we are considering perspective projection. The Parse method allows you to convert a string such as "0.5, 2, 10.7" into a Point3 object, which is useful when you want to create a 3D point from a TextBox input by the user.

Vector in 3D

The Vector3 class defines a 3D vector object and its basic math operations. Here is the code listing of this class:

```
using System;

namespace XuMath
{
    public struct Vector3
    {
        public double[] vector;

        public Vector3()
        {
            this.vector = new double[3];
            for (int i = 0; i < 3; i++)
            {
                vector[i] = 0.0;
            }
        }

        public Vector3(double[] vector)
```

```
{
    this.vector = vector;
}

#region Equals and Hashing:
public override bool Equals(object obj)
{
    return (obj is VectorR) && this.Equals((VectorR)obj);
}

public bool Equals(VectorR v)
{
    return vector == v.vector;
}

public override int GetHashCode()
{
    return vector.GetHashCode();
}

public static bool operator ==(VectorR v1, VectorR v2)
{
    return v1.Equals(v2);
}

public static bool operator !=(VectorR v1, VectorR v2)
{
    return !v1.Equals(v2);
}
#endregion

#region Definition and basics:
public double this[int n]
{
    get { return vector[n]; }
    set { vector[n] = value; }
}

public double GetNorm()
{
    double result = 0.0;
    for (int i = 0; i < 3; i++)
    {
        result += vector[i] * vector[i];
    }
    return Math.Sqrt(result);
}

public double GetNormSquare()
{
    double result = 0.0;
    for (int i = 0; i < 3; i++)
    {
        result += vector[i] * vector[i];
    }
```

```
        return result;
    }

    public void Normalize()
    {
        double norm = GetNorm();
        if (norm == 0)
        {
            return;
        }
        for (int i = 0; i < 3; i++)
        {
            vector[i] /= norm;
        }
    }

    public Vector3 GetUnitVector()
    {
        Vector3 result = new Vector3(vector);
        result.Normalize();
        return result;
    }

    #endregion

    #region Mathematical operators:
    public static Vector3 operator +(Vector3 v)
    {
        return v;
    }

    public static Vector3 operator -(Vector3 v)
    {
        double[] result = new double[v.Get3()];
        for (int i = 0; i < v.Get3(); i++)
        {
            result[i] = -v[i];
        }
        return new Vector3(result);
    }

    public static Vector3 operator +(Vector3 v1, Vector3 v2)
    {
        Vector3 result = new Vector3();
        for (int i = 0; i < 3; i++)
        {
            result[i] = v1[i] + v2[i];
        }
        return result;
    }

    public static Vector3 operator +(Vector3 v, double d)
    {
        Vector3 result = new Vector3();
        for (int i = 0; i < 3; i++)
```

```
        {
            result[i] = v[i] + d;
        }
        return result;
    }

    public static Vector3 operator +(double d, Vector3 v)
    {
        Vector3 result = new Vector3();
        for (int i = 0; i < 3; i++)
        {
            result[i] = v[i] + d;
        }
        return result;
    }

    public static Vector3 operator -(Vector3 v1, Vector3 v2)
    {
        Vector3 result = new Vector3();
        for (int i = 0; i < 3; i++)
        {
            result[i] = v1[i] - v2[i];
        }
        return result;
    }

    public static Vector3 operator -(Vector3 v, double d)
    {
        Vector3 result = new Vector3();
        for (int i = 0; i < 3; i++)
        {
            result[i] = v[i] - d;
        }
        return result;
    }

    public static Vector3 operator -(double d, Vector3 v)
    {
        Vector3 result = new Vector3();
        for (int i = 0; i < 3; i++)
        {
            result[i] = d - v[i];
        }
        return result;
    }

    public static Vector3 operator *(Vector3 v, double d)
    {
        Vector3 result = new Vector3();
        for (int i = 0; i < 3; i++)
        {
            result[i] = v[i] * d;
        }
        return result;
    }
```

```
public static Vector3 operator *(double d, Vector3 v)
{
    Vector3 result = new Vector3();
    for (int i = 0; i < 3; i++)
    {
        result[i] = d * v[i];
    }
    return result;
}

public static Vector3 operator /(Vector3 v, double d)
{
    Vector3 result = new Vector3();
    for (int i = 0; i < 3; i++)
    {
        result[i] = v[i] / d;
    }
    return result;
}

public static Vector3 operator /(double d, Vector3 v)
{
    Vector3 result = new Vector3();
    for (int i = 0; i < 3; i++)
    {
        result[i] = d / v[i];
    }
    return result;
}
#endregion;

#region Public methods:
public static double DotProduct(Vector3 v1, Vector3 v2)
{
    double result = 0.0;
    for (int i = 0; i < 3; i++)
    {
        result += v1[i] * v2[i];
    }
    return result;
}

public static Vector3 CrossProduct(Vector3 v1, Vector3 v2)
{
    Vector3 result = new Vector3(3);
    result[0] = v1[1] * v2[2] - v1[2] * v2[1];
    result[1] = v1[2] * v2[0] - v1[0] * v2[2];
    result[2] = v1[0] * v2[1] - v1[1] * v2[0];
    return result;
}

public static double TriScalarProduct(Vector3 v1,
                                      Vector3 v2, Vector3 v3)
{
```

```
            double result = v1[0] * (v2[1] * v3[2] - v2[2] * v3[1]) +
                            v1[1] * (v2[2] * v3[0] - v2[0] * v3[2]) +
                            v1[2] * (v2[0] * v3[1] - v2[1] * v3[0]);
            return result;
        }

        public static Vector3 TriVectorProduct(Vector3 v1,
                                               Vector3 v2, Vector3 v3)
        {
            return v2 * Vector3.DotProduct(v1, v3) -
                   v3 * Vector3.DotProduct(v1, v2);
        }

        #endregion;

        public override string ToString()
        {
            string s = "(";
            for (int i = 0; i < 3 - 1; i++)
            {
                s += vector[i].ToString() + ", ";
            }
            s += vector[3 - 1].ToString() + ")";
            return s;
        }

        public static Vector3 NormalVector(Point3 pt1, Point3 pt2, Point3 pt3)
        {
            Vector3 v1 = new Vector3(3);
            Vector3 v2 = new Vector3(3);
            v1[0] = pt2.X - pt1.X;
            v1[1] = pt2.Y - pt1.Y;
            v1[2] = pt2.Z - pt1.Z;
            v2[0] = pt3.X - pt2.X;
            v2[1] = pt3.Y - pt2.Y;
            v2[2] = pt3.Z - pt1.Z;

            return CrossProduct(v1, v2);
        }

        public static Vector3 Parse(string str)
        {
            string[] astring = new string[3];
            char[] splitter = { ',' };

            astring = str.Split(splitter);
            Vector3 result = new Vector3();
            result[0] = double.Parse(astring[0]);
            result[1] = double.Parse(astring[1]);
            result[2] = double.Parse(astring[2]);
            return result;
        }
    }
}
```

There are two constructors in this class. The first constructor takes no parameter and creates a vector whose elements are initialized to zero. The second constructor creates a vector to hold a given double array. In addition, we implement basic math operations for the 3D vector object.

Matrix in 3D

The Matrix3 class contains the basic matrix operations, such as matrix multiplication. The following is its code listing:

```
using System;

namespace XuMath
{
    public class Matrix3
    {
        public double[,] M = new double[4, 4];

        public Matrix3()
        {
            Identity();
        }

        public Matrix3(double m00, double m01, double m02, double m03,
                       double m10, double m11, double m12, double m13,
                       double m20, double m21, double m22, double m23,
                       double m30, double m31, double m32, double m33)
        {
            M[0, 0] = m00;
            M[0, 1] = m01;
            M[0, 2] = m02;
            M[0, 3] = m03;
            M[1, 0] = m10;
            M[1, 1] = m11;
            M[1, 2] = m12;
            M[1, 3] = m13;
            M[2, 0] = m20;
            M[2, 1] = m21;
            M[2, 2] = m22;
            M[2, 3] = m23;
            M[3, 0] = m30;
            M[3, 1] = m31;
            M[3, 2] = m32;
            M[3, 3] = m33;
        }

        // Define a Identity matrix:
        public void Identity()
        {
            for (int i = 0; i < 4; i++)
            {
                for (int j = 0; j < 4; j++)
                {
                    if (i == j)
                    {
```

```
                        M[i, j] = 1;
                    }
                    else
                    {
                        M[i, j] = 0;
                    }
                }
            }
        }

        // Multiply two matrices together:
        public static Matrix3 operator *(Matrix3 m1, Matrix3 m2)
        {
            Matrix3 result = new Matrix3();
            for (int i = 0; i < 4; i++)
            {
                for (int j = 0; j < 4; j++)
                {
                    double element = 0;
                    for (int k = 0; k < 4; k++)
                    {
                        element += m1.M[i, k] * m2.M[k, j];
                    }
                    result.M[i, j] = element;
                }
            }
            return result;
        }

        // Apply a transformation to a vector (point):
        public double[] VectorMultiply(double[] vector)
        {
            double[] result = new double[4];
            for (int i = 0; i < 4; i++)
            {
                for (int j = 0; j < 4; j++)
                {
                    result[i] += vector[j] * M[j, i];
                }
            }
            return result;
        }
    }
}
```

We'll add more public methods to the Matrix3 class in the following sections.

These three classes can be used to perform basic transformation operations for a 3D point or 3D vector object. In the next few subsections, we'll use these classes to discuss basic 3D transformations in Silverlight.

Scaling

As in the case of 2D, to scale or stretch a 3D object in the X direction, you need to multiply the X coordinates of each of the object's points by the scaling factor s_x. Similarly, you can scale an object in the Y and Z directions. In the homogenous coordinate system, a scaling transformation can be represented in the form:

$$\begin{pmatrix} x_1 & y_1 & z_1 & 1 \end{pmatrix} = \begin{pmatrix} x & y & z & 1 \end{pmatrix} \begin{pmatrix} s_x & 0 & 0 & 0 \\ 0 & s_y & 0 & 0 \\ 0 & 0 & s_z & 0 \\ 0 & 0 & 0 & 1 \end{pmatrix} = \begin{pmatrix} xs_x & ys_y & zs_z & 1 \end{pmatrix} \tag{9.1}$$

For example, suppose that you have a 3D point (1, 2, 3, 1) in the homogeneous coordinates, and you want to apply a scaling matrix to the point. This scaling matrix shrinks x and y uniformly by a factor of two, and stretches Z by a factor of three-halves. This scaling operation can easily be computed using Equation (9.1):

$$\begin{pmatrix} x_1 & y_1 & z_1 & 1 \end{pmatrix} = \begin{pmatrix} 1 & 2 & 3 & 1 \end{pmatrix} \begin{pmatrix} 0.5 & 0 & 0 & 0 \\ 0 & 0.5 & 0 & 0 \\ 0 & 0 & 1.5 & 0 \\ 0 & 0 & 0 & 1 \end{pmatrix} = \begin{pmatrix} 0.5 & 1 & 4.5 & 1 \end{pmatrix}$$

We can add a static method, Scale, to the Matrix3 class, which can be used to perform the scale transformation:

```
// Scale transform:
public static Matrix3 Scale(double sx, double sy, double sz)
{
    Matrix3 result = new Matrix3();
    result.M[0, 0] = sx;
    result.M[1, 1] = sy;
    result.M[2, 2] = sz;
    return result;
}
```

Then, you can use the following code snippet to perform the scale transformation:

```
Point3 pt = new Point3(1, 2, 3, 1);
Matrix3 m = Matrix3.Scale(0.5, 0.5, 1.5);
Point3 pt1 = Point3.Transform(m, pt);
```

Here, we first create the original point (1, 2, 3, 1), then create the scaling matrix by calling the static Scale method in the Matrix3 class. Finally, we perform a scaling operation by applying the scaling matrix to the original point. The resulting new point object after the transformation is represented by pt1 = (0.5, 1 , 4.5, 1), which gives the same result as the direct matrix computation does.

You can also perform two successive scaling transformations. For example, the first scaling matrix is the same as m1, while the second scaling matrix has scaling factors of sx = 1, sy = 0.5, and sz = 0.3. The following code snippet performs this scaling operation:

```
Point3 pt = new Point3(1, 2, 3, 1);
Matrix3 m1 = Matrix3.Scale(0.5, 0.5, 1.5);
Matrix3 m2 = Matrix3.Scale(1, 0.5, 0.3);
```

```
Point3 pt1 = Point3.Transform(m1 * m2, pt);
```

Here we calculate the two successive scaling transformations using a matrix multiplication:

```
Point3 pt1 = Point3.Transform(m1 * m2, pt);
```

This matrix multiplication has been defined as a static method in the `Matrix3` class. This code snippet produces the result (0.5, 0.5, 1.35, 1), which can be easily confirmed by direct matrix multiplication.

You can also perform reflections by using scale transforms. In the case of 2D objects, reflection across the X or Y axis is simple: you simply scale the object with a negative scaling factor. In 3D, however, you must reflect an object across a plane instead of a line. Reflecting an object across the X-Y, X-Z, and Y-Z planes is easy. Simply scale the points using -1 as one of the scale factors. For example, to reflect an object across the X-Y planes, use a scaling transformation matrix with sx = 1, sy = 1, and sz = -1.

Translation

A 2D translation matrix is easily generalized to the 3D case. To translate a point by a distance of dx in the X direction, dy in the Y direction, and dz in the Z direction, you simply multiply the point by a transform matrix in homogeneous coordinates:

$$\begin{pmatrix} x_1 & y_1 & z_1 & 1 \end{pmatrix} = \begin{pmatrix} x & y & z & 1 \end{pmatrix} \begin{pmatrix} 1 & 0 & 0 & 0 \\ 0 & 1 & 0 & 0 \\ 0 & 0 & 1 & 0 \\ dx & dy & dz & 1 \end{pmatrix} = \begin{pmatrix} x + dx & y + dy & z + dz & 1 \end{pmatrix} \tag{9.2}$$

The results of $x_1 = x + dx$, $y_1 = y + dy$, and $z_1 = z + dz$ are indeed the correct translation of a point (x, y, z, 1).

Now we can add a public static method, Translate, to the Matrix3 class, which can be used to perform the Translation transform:

```
// Translation transform:
public static Matrix3 Translate(double dx, double dy, double dz)
{
    Matrix3 result = new Matrix3();
    result.M[3, 0] = dx;
    result.M[3, 1] = dy;
    result.M[3, 2] = dz;
    return result;
}
```

For example, we can translate the original point (1, 2, 3, 1) by 2 in the X direction, 2.5 in the Y direction, and 3 in the Z direction using the following code snippet:

```
Point3 pt = new Point3(1, 2, 3, 1);
Matrix3 m = Matrix3.Translate(2, 2.5, 3);
Point3 pt1 = Point3.Transform(m, pt);
```

This gives a new point (3, 4.5, 6, 1) after the translation. You can also examine the point after two successive translations using the code snippet:

```
Point3 pt = new Point3(1, 2, 3, 1);
Matrix3 m1 = Matrix3.Translate(2, 2.5, 3);
Matrix3 m2 = Matrix3.Translate(-3, -2, -1);
Point3 pt1 = Point3.Transform(m1 * m2, pt);
```

After these two successive translations, you obtain a new point (0, 2.5, 5, 1).

Rotation and Quaternion

Rotation is one of the most commonly used transforms in 3D. 3D rotation about an arbitrary axis is also one of the most complex 3D transforms. Here, we use the quaternion notation, which can be specified either by a position Point3 object and a rotation angle or by four quaternion components in the form of (x, y, z, w).

Remember that in order to calculate the quaternion from the rotation axis vector and the rotation angle, the axis vector must be normalized. You can calculate the quaternion components from a unit rotation axis and rotation angle. Suppose that the rotation axis for a 3D rotation is denoted by a unit vector object (ax, ay, az), and the rotation angle is θ. You can find the quaternion (x, y, z, w) by using the following formula:

$$\begin{aligned} x &= ax \cdot \sin(\theta/2) \\ y &= ay \cdot \sin(\theta/2) \\ z &= az \cdot \sin(\theta/2) \\ w &= \cos(\theta/2) \end{aligned} \tag{9.3}$$

For example, if you want to rotate the original point by 45 degrees along the axis specified by a 3D vector object (1, 2, 3), the unit rotation axis can be obtained by normalizing this vector object:

$$(ax, ay\ az) = (1, 2, 3)/\sqrt{14} = (0.267, 0.535, 0.802)$$

and θ = 45 degrees. You can then easily calculate its quaternion using Equation (9.3):

$$(x, y, z, w) = (0.102, 0.205, 0.307, 0.924)$$

It can be shown that the above quaternion (x, y, z, w) is also normalized to unity. Using this quaternion, you can construct the rotation matrix:

$$\begin{pmatrix} w^2+x^2-y^2-z^2 & 2xy+2zw & 2xz-2yw & 0 \\ 2xy-2zw & w^2-x^2+y^2-z^2 & 2yz+2xw & 0 \\ 2xz+2yw & 2yz-2xw & w^2-x^2-y^2+z^2 & 0 \\ 0 & 0 & 0 & w^2+x^2+y^2+z^2 \end{pmatrix} \tag{9.4}$$

Using this information, we can create a rotation transform matrix in the Matrix3 class.

```
// Rotation transform:
public static Matrix3 Rotate(Vector3 axis, double angle)
{
    angle = angle * Math.PI / 180;
    axis = axis / axis.GetNorm();
    double x = axis[0] * Math.Sin(angle / 2);
    double y = axis[1] * Math.Sin(angle / 2);
```

```
        double z = axis[2] * Math.Sin(angle / 2);
        double w = Math.Cos(angle / 2);
        Matrix3 result = new Matrix3();
        result.M[0, 0] = w * w + x * x - y * y - z * z;
        result.M[0, 1] = 2 * x * y + 2 * z * w;
        result.M[0, 2] = 2 * x * z - 2 * y * w;
        result.M[1, 0] = 2 * x * y - 2 * z * w;
        result.M[1, 1] = w * w - x * x + y * y - z * z;
        result.M[1, 2] = 2 * y * z + 2 * x * w;
        result.M[2, 0] = 2 * x * z + 2 * y * w;
        result.M[2, 1] = 2 * y * z - 2 * x * w;
        result.M[2, 2] = w * w - x * x - y * y + z * z;
        result.M[3, 3] = w * w + x * x + y * y + z * z;
        return result;
    }
```

Let's consider an example. If you want to construct a rotation matrix by rotating 45 degrees along an axis specified by a Vector3 object (1, 2, 3), you can use the following code snippet:

```
Vector3 axis = new Vector3(new double[] { 1, 2, 3 });
Matrix3 m = Matrix3.Rotate(axis, 45);
```

which gives the following transform matrix:

$$\begin{pmatrix} 0.728 & 0.609 & -0.315 & 0 \\ -0.525 & 0.791 & 0.315 & 0 \\ 0.441 & -0.063 & 0.895 & 0 \\ 0 & 0 & 0 & 1 \end{pmatrix}.$$

Projections

Since the computer screen is two dimensional, it can't directly display 3D objects. In order to view 3D objects on a 2D screen, you have to project the objects from 3D to 2D.

The most common types of projections are called planar geometric projections. These are a distinct class of projections that maintain straight lines when mapping an object onto a viewing surface. In a planar geometric projection, a ray or projector is passed from a center of projection through the points being projected onto a planar viewing surface, called the view plane. Figure 9-1 shows the projection of a square object onto a 2D view plane.

We'll discuss two kinds of projections, Orthographic and Perspective, in the following subsections.

Orthographic Projections

Orthographic projection is a kind of parallel projection, meaning that the center of projection is located at an infinite distance from the view plane. By placing the center of projection at an infinite distance from the view plane, the projectors become parallel to the view plane. For a parallel projection, instead of specifying a center of projection, you need to specify a direction of projection. Figure 9-2 shows a parallel projection of a square object onto the view plane.

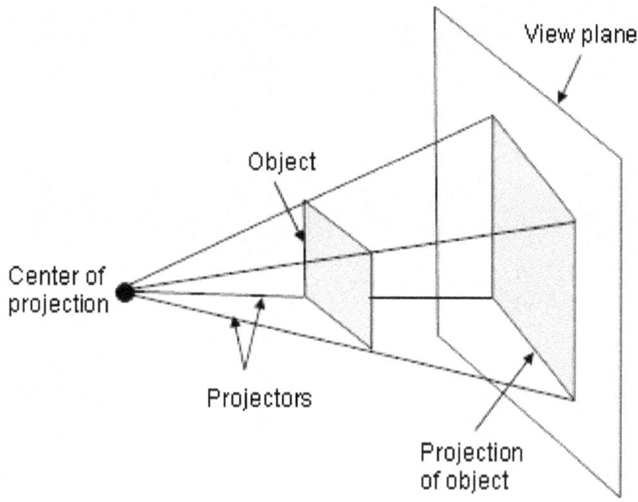

Figure 9-1 Projection of a square object from 3D to a 2D view plane.

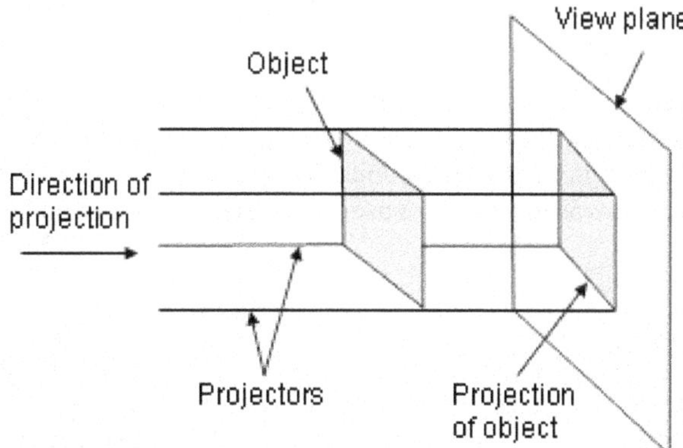

Figure 9-2 A parallel projection of a square object.

In addition to being parallel, projectors in an orthographic projection are also perpendicular to the view plane. Orthographic projections are often used in architectural and mechanical drawings. They are further categorized as either multi-view or axonometric projections, which are described below.

Multi-View Projections

A multi-view projection shows a single face of a 3D object. Common choices for viewing an object in 2D include front, side, and top view. Figure 9-3 shows a house object as well as its front, side, and top views.

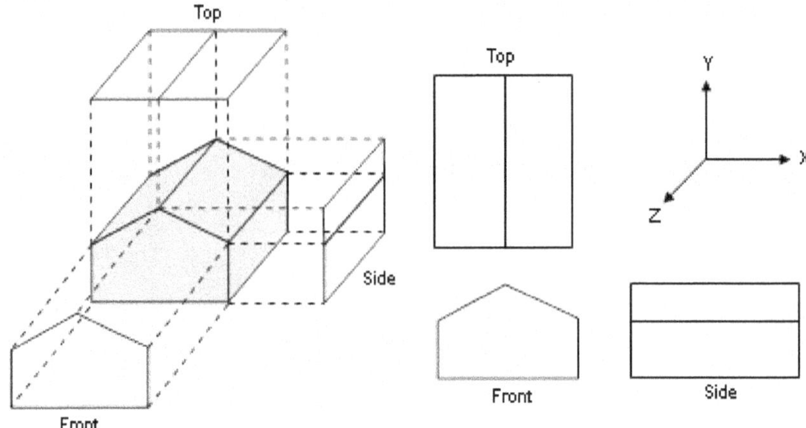

Figure 9-3 Front, side, and top views of orthographic projections.

These projections are very simple. To project a point, simply ignore the point's unneeded third coordinate. In top view, the normal of the view plane is parallel to the positive Y axis in a right-handed system, as shown in Figure 9-3. To project the top view of a 3D object, the Y coordinates are discarded and the X and Z coordinates for each point are mapped onto the view plane. By repositioning the normal of the view plane to the positive Z axis and selecting the X and Y coordinates for each point, a front view is projected onto the view plane.

Likewise, a side view can be achieved when the normal of the view plane is directed along the positive X axis, while the Y and Z coordinates of a 3D object are projected onto the view plane. These projections are often used in engineering and architectural drawings. Although they don't show the 3D aspects of an object, multi-view projections are useful because the angles and dimensions of the object are maintained.

Axonometric Projections

Multi-view projections preserve distances and angles; in other words, you can measure distances and angles directly from the projection of an object. However, it is often difficult to understand the 3D structure of an object by examining only its multi-view projections.

To make the 3D nature of an object more apparent, you can use projections that aren't parallel to the X, Y, or Z axes. This type of projection is called an axonometric orthographic projection. Unlike multi-view projections, axonometric projections allow you to place the normal of the view plane in any direction so that three adjacent faces of a "cube-like" object are visible. To avoid duplication of the views displayed by multi-view projections, the normal of the view plane is usually not placed parallel to a major axis for an axonometric view. The increased versatility of the direction of the normal of the view plane should position the view plane so that it intersects at least two of the major axes. Lines on a 3D object that are parallel in the world coordinate system are likewise projected to the view plane as parallel lines. In addition, the length of a line, or line preservation, is maintained for lines parallel to the view plane. Lines receding from the view plane maintain only their proportion and are foreshortened equally with lines along the same axes.

Axonometric projections can be further divided into three types that depend upon the number of major axes foreshortened equally. These axonometric views are defined as isometric, dimetric, or trimetric projections.

Isometric Projections:

An isometric projection is a commonly used type of axonometric projection. In this projection, all three of the major axes are foreshortened equally since the normal of the view plane makes equal angles with all three coordinate axes.

Figure 9-4 shows the isometric projection of a cube object. Isometric projection scales lines equally along each axis, which is often useful since lines along the coordinate axes can be measured and converted using the same scale.

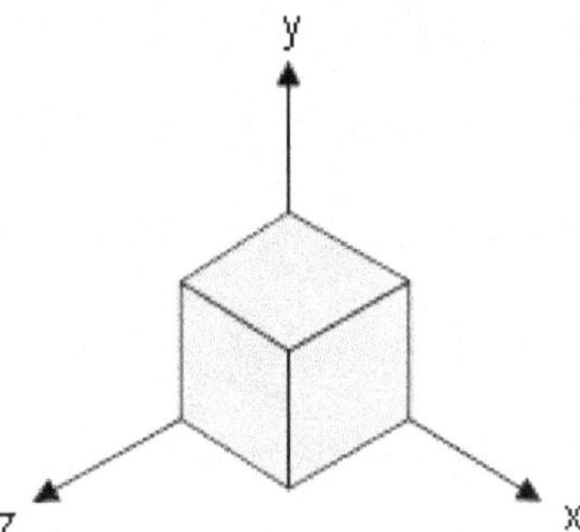

Figure 9-4 Isometric projection of a cube object.

Dimetric Projections:

Dimetric projections differ from isometric projections in the direction of the normal of the view plane. In this case, the view plane is set so that it makes equal angles with two of the coordinate axes.

Figure 9-5 shows a dimetric projection of a cube object. When the normal of the view plane is set so that the view plane is parallel to a major axis, line measurements are maintained in the projection for lines that are parallel to the chosen axis.

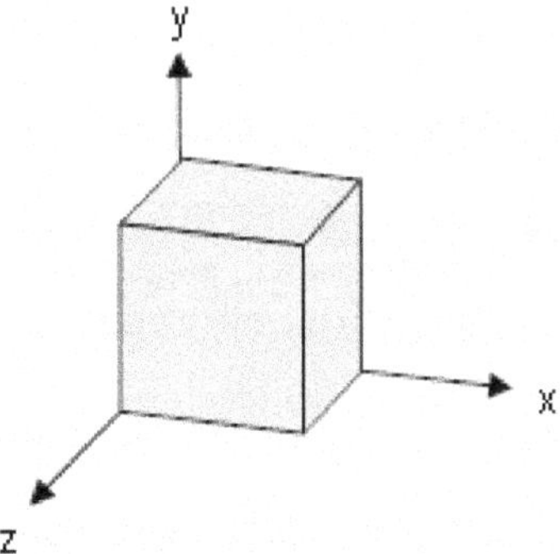

Figure 9-5 Dimetric projection of a cube object.

Trimetric Projections:

In trimetric projection, the normal of the view plane makes different angles with each coordinate axis since no two components have the same value. As with a dimetric view, a trimetric view can display different orientations when differing amounts of emphasis are placed on the faces. A potential disadvantage of trimetric projections is that measuring lines along the axes is difficult due to the difference in scaling factors.

Figure 9-6 shows a trimetric projection of a cube object. You can see how the unequal-foreshortening characteristic of theis projection affects line measurements along the different axes. While disadvantageous for maintaining measurements, a trimetric projection, with the correct orientation, can offer a realistic and natural view of an object.

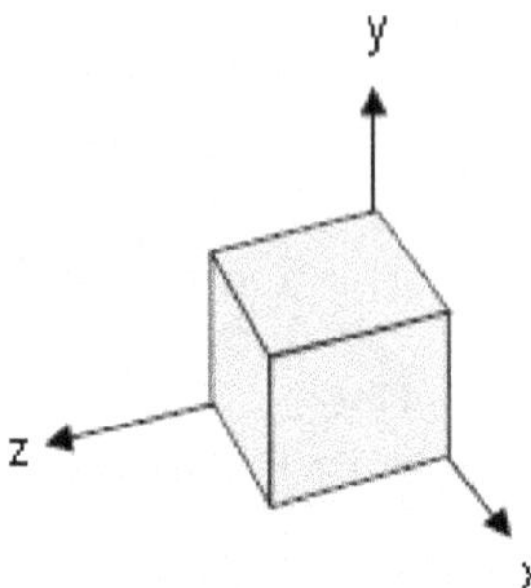

Figure 9-6 Trimetric projection of a cube object.

In addition to orthographic projections, parallel projections also include oblique projections. Oblique projections are useful because they combine the advantageous qualities of both multi-view and axonometric projections. Like axonometric projections, this type of projection emphasizes the 3D features of an object. At the same time, like multi-view projections, oblique views display the exact shape of one face. Oblique view uses parallel projectors, but the angle between the projectors and the view plane is no longer orthogonal. Because of these properties, more than one face of the object is visible in an oblique projection. We will not further discuss oblique projections in this book. For more information about these projections and their projection matrices, please refer to my other book, *Practical C# Charts and Graphics*.

Perspective Projections

In a perspective projection, objects of equal size at different distances from the view plane will be projected at different sizes, so that nearer objects will appear closer. The projectors pass from a center of projection through each point in the object to the view plane.

Figure 9-7 shows a perspective projection of two identical square objects. The square that is farther from the center of projection is projected as a smaller image on the view plane.

In comparison to parallel projections, perspective projections often provide a more natural and realistic view of a 3D object. By comparing the view plane of a perspective projection with the view as seen from the lens of a camera, the underlying principle of perspective projection is easily understood. Like the view from a camera, lines in a perspective projection not parallel to the view plane converge at a distant point (called the vanishing point) in the background. When the eye or camera is positioned close to the object, perspective foreshortening occurs, with distant objects appearing smaller in the view plane than closer objects of the same size, as shown in Figure 9-7.

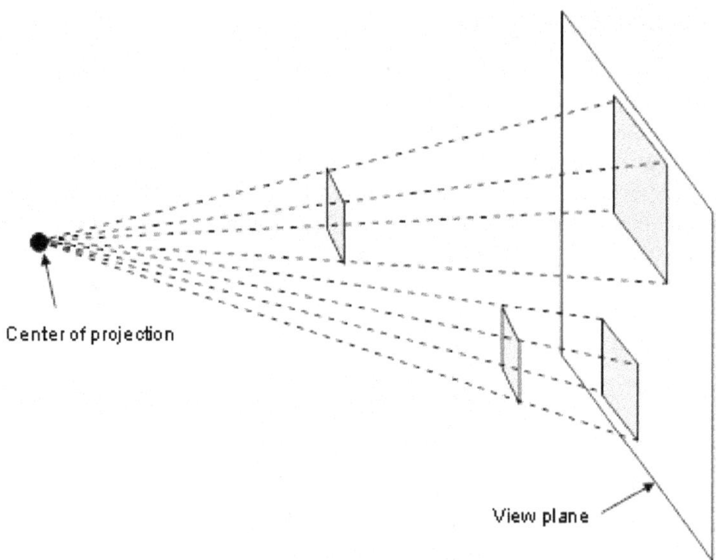

Figure 9-7 Perspective projections: objects farther from the center of projection appear smaller than closer objects.

Perspective projections can be classified by the number of vanishing points they contain. There are three types of perspective projections: one-point, two-point, and three-point perspective projections. Each type differs in the orientation of the view plane and the number of vanishing points.

One-Point Perspective Projections

In one-point perspective, lines of a 3D object along a coordinate axis converge at a single vanishing point while lines parallel to the other axes remain horizontal or vertical in the view plane. To create a one-point perspective view, the view plane is set parallel to one of the principal planes in the world coordinate system. Figure 9-8 shows a one-point perspective view of a cube. In this projection, the view plane is positioned in front of the cube and parallel to the X-Y plane.

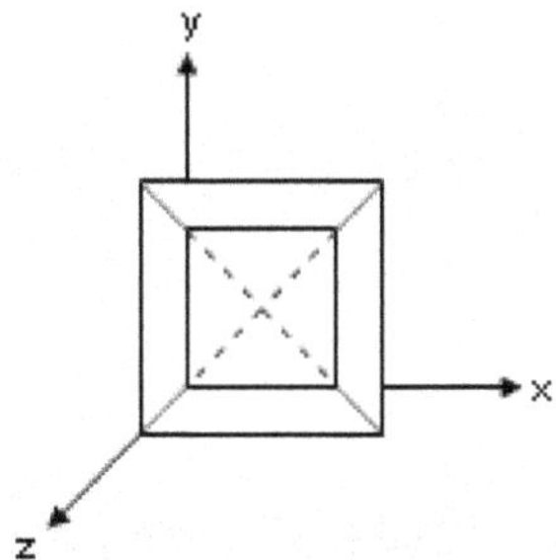

Figure 9-8 One-point perspective projection.

Two-Point Perspective Projections

Two-point perspective projects an object onto the view plane so that lines parallel to two of the major axes converge at two separate vanishing points. To create a two-point perspective projection, the view plane is set parallel to a coordinate axis rather than a plane. To satisfy this condition, the normal of the view plane should be set perpendicular to one of the major world coordinate system axes. Figure 9-9 shows a two-point perspective view of a cube. In this figure, lines parallel to the x-axis converge at a vanishing point while lines parallel to the z-axis converge at another vanishing point. Two-point perspective views often provide additional realism in comparison to other projection types; for this reason, they are commonly used in architectural, engineering, and industrial designs.

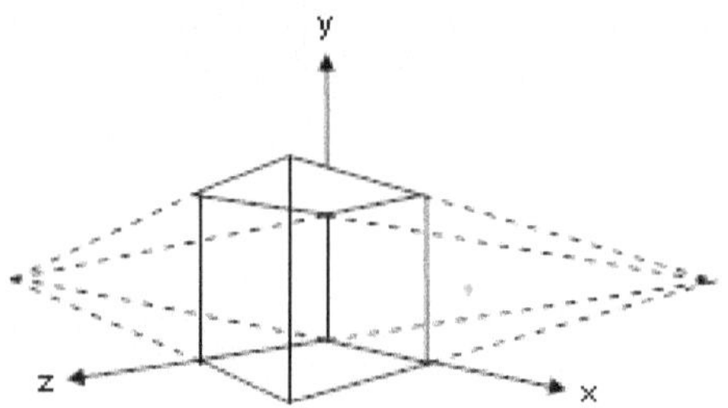

Figure 9-9 Two-point perspective projection.

Three-Point Perspective Projections

A three-point perspective projection has three vanishing points. In this case, the view plane is not parallel to any of the major axes. To position the view plane, each component of the view plane's normal is set to a non-zero value so that the view plane intersects three major axes. Three-vanishing point projection is often used by artists for highlighting features or increasing dramatic effect. Figure 9-10 shows a three-point perspective projection of a cube.

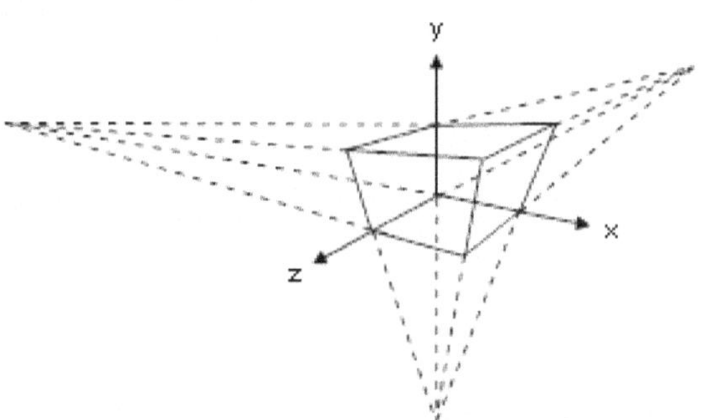

Figure 9-10 Three-point perspective projection.

Perspective Projection Matrix

Constructing a general perspective projection matrix is quite complicated. Here, we only discuss a simple case of perspective projection. This simple perspective view projects onto the X-Y plane when the center of projection lies on the Z axis. Figure 9-11 shows a point P = (x, y, z) being projected onto the point P1 = (x1, y1, z1) in the X-Y plane. The center of projection is located at (0, 0, d), where d is the distance along the Z axis. On the right of Figure 9-11 is a side view of the projection showing the Y and Z axes. The point A is the center of projection, and the point B is the point on the Z axis that has the same Z coordinates as point P.

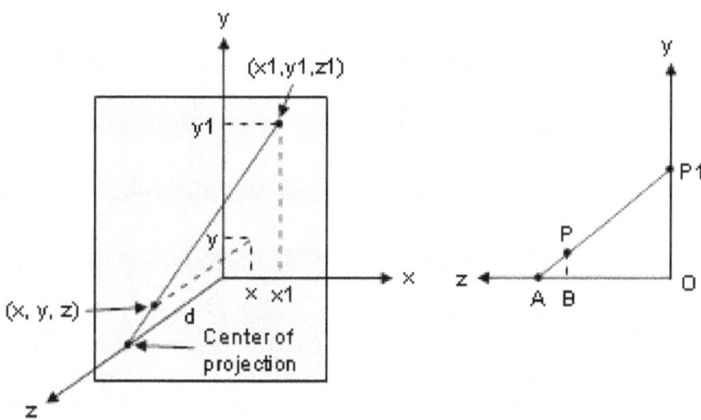

Figure 9-11 Perspective projection of a point P = (x, y, z).

From this figure, you note that AO = d, OP1 = y1, BP = y, and AB = d-z. When you solve for y1, you get y1 = d*y/(d-z). This gives the Y coordinate of the projected point P1. By examining a similar top view that shows the X and Z axes, you can find that x1 = d*x/(d-z). For the projected point on the X-Y plane, z1 should equal 0. From this information, you can construct a transform matrix for this perspective projection:

$$(x1 \quad y1 \quad z1 \quad w1) = (x \quad y \quad z \quad 1)\begin{pmatrix} 1 & 0 & 0 & 0 \\ 0 & 1 & 0 & 0 \\ 0 & 0 & 0 & -1/d \\ 0 & 0 & 0 & 1 \end{pmatrix} = (x \quad y \quad 0 \quad 1 - z/d) \tag{9.5}$$

Remember that in homogeneous coordinates, the w-component of a point represents a scaling factor. Normalizing the projected point P1 by w1, you have

$$(x1/w1 \quad y1/w1 \quad z1/w1 \quad 1) = (x/(1-z/d) \quad y/(1-z/d) \quad 0 \quad 1)$$

This agrees with the information deduced from Figure 9-11.

Projection Matrices in Silverlight

In order to dispay 3D objects on a 2D screen, a series of transforms must be performed on the 3D objects. We can use several transforms to change the 3D model coordinates into device-independent pixels. These transforms include the View transform, Projection transform, and World transform.

The World transform controls how model coordinates are transformed into world coordinates. The World transform can include translation, scaling, and rotation. The View transform controls the transition from world coordinates into camera space. It determines the camera position in the world coordinate system. The Projection transform changes the geometry of 3D objects from the camera space into the clipping space and applies perspective distortion to the objects. The clipping space refers to how the geometry is clipped to the view volume during this transformation. Finally, the geometry in the clipping space is transformed into device-independent pixels (the screen space). This transform is controlled by the Viewport settings.

Since Silverlight doesn't include 3D features, you need to implement your own classes that allow you to perform various transformations on 3D objects. However, the general forms of the View transform and Projection transform in 3D are very complicated. If you are interested in the implemention details of these general 3D features, you can read my another book *Practical WPF Graphics Programming*, which provides the mathematical basics of these transform matrices, and the procedure for constructing them from Camera and Viewport settings.

Since Silverlight applications run on the browser, in order to reduce the download file size, here we'll use a simplified approach to implement 3D features in Silverlight. We'll always assume that the projection center always lies on the positive Z axis and the projection matrix is given in Equation (9.5).

Here we want to make a little modification to Equation (9.5). Usually, when you apply the perspective transform described in Equation (9.5) to a point, you destroy its Z component information. In this case, you can't compare the point's Z coordinate to see if it lies behind or in front of the center of projection. In order to preserve the Z coordinate information, you need to modify the perspective transform matrix from Equation (9.5) to the following:

$$\begin{pmatrix} 1 & 0 & 0 & 0 \\ 0 & 1 & 0 & 0 \\ 0 & 0 & 1 & -1/d \\ 0 & 0 & 0 & 1 \end{pmatrix} \tag{9.6}$$

Here, we change the third column from (0, 0, 0, 0) to (0, 0, 1, 0) so that the Z component is not lost. Using (9.6), we can add the perspective matrix to the Matrix3 class:

```
// Perspective projection matrix:
public static Matrix3 Perspective(double d)
{
    Matrix3 result = new Matrix3();
    result.M[2, 3] = -1 / d;
    return result;
}
```

When you multiply a point with this modified perspective matrix, you need to normalize the X, Y, and Z components by the W component. This step would mess up the Z coordinate information. To preserve the Z-component information, we normalize only the X and Y components of the point. This normalization process has been implemented in the TransformNormalize method in the Point3 class. Thus, the TransformNormalize method should be used when you perform a perspective transform on a Point3 object.

The center of projection can also be regarded as the camera position. You should place the camera outside of the object that you want to view, which means that the distance d must be larger than the dimension of the object. The perspective matrix in (9.6) will reduce to an orthographic projection along the Z axis if you set a very large d value.

3D Objects in Silverlight

Using the transform and perspective matrices presented previously, we can build a Silverlight application to demonstrate how to create 3D objects. Before presenting the code example, we need to discuss one key step in creating 3D objects: the hidden surface removal technique. Here we use the simple back surface removal algorithm to perform hidden surface removal for convex solid objects.

Backface Removal

Figure 9-12 shows the geometry of a projection of a cube. The side of the cube farthest from the center of projection (or camera position) is hidden by the rest of the cube.

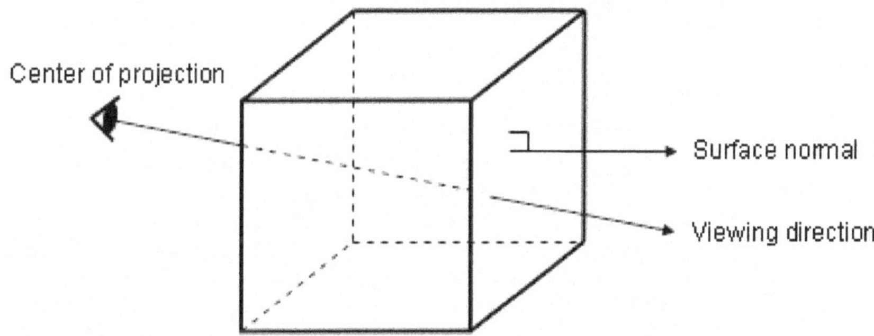

Figure 9-12 A backface is hidden from the center of projection by the cube's body.

Because this face is on the back side as seen from the center of projection, it is called a backface. Since you can't see a backface from the center of projection, you don't need to draw it on your screen. The process of identifying backfaces is called backface removal, or culling.

It can be seen from Figure 9-12 that the line from the center of projection to a backface points in more or less the same direction as a perpendicular vector pointing outwards from the face. This vector is called the surface normal.

More precisely, if the viewing direction makes an angle less than 90 degrees with a surface normal, the surface is a backface that doesn't need to be drawn. If the line and normal meet at an angle greater than 90 degrees, the surface isn't a backface and needs to be drawn on your screen.

In order to perform backface removal, first you need to compute surface normals and then determine what angle the viewing direction makes with the surface nomals. The surface normals can be computed using the NormalVector method implemented in the Vector3 class. The angle between the viewing direction and the surface normal can be determined by their dot product.

Suppose the normal vector is N and the viewing direction is V. Then the dot product of the vectors equals $|N| * |V| * \text{Cos}\theta$, where θ is the angle between these two vectors. You can use this fact to easily determine whether the viewing direction and the surface normal make an angle less or greater than 90 degrees. Since the lengths $|N|$ and $|V|$ are always positive, the dot product $N \cdot V$ is geater than zero if θ

< 90 degrees, and the dot product is less than zero if θ > 90 degrees. Thus, if the dot product is less than zero, the surface is a backface, so you don't need to draw it.

Creating a Cube in Silverlight

In this section, I'll show you how to create a simple 3D cube using a code example. The cube example will be implemented in the Example09-1 project. The following is the XAML file of this example:

```
<UserControl x:Class="Example09_1.Page"
    xmlns="http://schemas.microsoft.com/client/2007"
    xmlns:x="http://schemas.microsoft.com/winfx/2006/xaml"
    Width="450" Height="350">
    <Grid x:Name="LayoutRoot" Background="White">
        <Border BorderBrush="Gray" BorderThickness="1"
                CornerRadius="10" Margin="10">
            <StackPanel Orientation="Horizontal">
                <StackPanel Margin="5" Grid.Column="0">
                    <TextBlock Text="Camera Position" Margin="2" FontSize="12"/>
                    <TextBox Name="tbCameraPosition" Margin="2" Text="150"
                             FontSize="12" Width="70" Height="20"
                             TextAlignment="Center"/>
                    <TextBlock Text="Rotation Axis" Margin="2" FontSize="12"/>
                    <TextBox Name="tbAxis" Margin="2" Text="-1,-1,0"
                             FontSize="12" Width="70" Height="20"
                             TextAlignment="Center"/>
                    <TextBlock Text="Rotation Angle" Margin="2" FontSize="12"/>
                    <TextBox Name="tbAngle" Margin="2" Text="45" FontSize="12"
                             Width="70" Height="20" TextAlignment="Center"/>
                    <Button Margin="2,30,2,2" Click="Apply_Click"
                            Content="Apply" Width="70" Height="22"/>
                </StackPanel>
                <Border BorderBrush="Gray" BorderThickness="1" Margin="10">
                    <Canvas x:Name="canvas1" Width="300" Height="305">
                        <Canvas.Clip>
                            <RectangleGeometry Rect="0 0 300 305"/>
                        </Canvas.Clip>
                    </Canvas>
                </Border>
            </StackPanel>
        </Border>
    </Grid>
</UserControl>
```

This XAML file creates a user interface that allows you to interactively change the input parameters, such as the camera position, rotation axis, and rotation angle. The perspective matrix in (9.6) has some limitations when it comes to manipulating 3D objects. It doesn't allow you to see the other side of the object by rotating the camera because the camera is fixed at the positive Z axis. In order to change the view of the object, you need to perform a rotation transform on the object itself.

The following is the code listing of the corresponding code-behind file:

```
using System;
using System.Windows;
using System.Windows.Browser;
using System.Windows.Controls;
```

```
using System.Windows.Input;
using System.Windows.Media;
using System.Windows.Shapes;
using XuMath;

namespace Example09_1
{
    public partial class Page : UserControl
    {
        private double side = 50;
        private Point center;
        private Point3[] vertices0;
        private Point3[] vertices;
        private Face[] faces;
        private bool isVisible;

        public Page()
        {
            InitializeComponent();

            center = new Point(canvas1.Width / 2, canvas1.Height / 2);
            vertices0 = new Point3[] { new Point3(-side,-side,-side,1),
                                       new Point3( side,-side,-side,1),
                                       new Point3( side, side,-side,1),
                                       new Point3(-side, side,-side,1),
                                       new Point3(-side, side, side,1),
                                       new Point3( side, side, side,1),
                                       new Point3( side,-side, side,1),
                                       new Point3(-side,-side, side,1)};
            faces = new Face[] {new Face(0,1,2,3), new Face(4,5,6,7),
                                new Face(3,4,7,0), new Face(2,1,6,5),
                                new Face(5,4,3,2), new Face(0,7,6,1)};
            AddCube();
        }

        public void AddCube()
        {
            double cameraPosition = double.Parse(tbCameraPosition.Text);
            Vector3 rotationAxis = Vector3.Parse(tbAxis.Text);
            double rotationAnge = double.Parse(tbAngle.Text);
            Matrix3 transformMatrix =
                    Matrix3.Perspective(cameraPosition) *
                    Matrix3.Rotate(rotationAxis, rotationAnge);
            vertices = new Point3[8];
            for (int i = 0; i < vertices0.Length; i++)
                vertices[i] =
                    Point3.TransformNormalize(transformMatrix, vertices0[i]);

            canvas1.Children.Clear();
            int ii = 0;
            foreach (Face face in this.faces)
            {
                ii++;
                Point3 va = vertices[face.VertexA];
                Point3 vb = vertices[face.VertexB];
```

```
Point3 vc = vertices[face.VertexC];
Point3 vd = vertices[face.VertexD];

Vector3 normal = Vector3.NormalVector(va, vb, vc);
Vector3 viewDirection = new Vector3();
viewDirection =
    new Vector3(new double[3] { 0, 0,-cameraPosition});
double mixProduct = Vector3.DotProduct(normal, viewDirection);
isVisible = mixProduct > 0;
if (isVisible)
{
    byte red = 0;
    byte green = 0;
    byte blue = 0;
    if (ii == 1)
    {
        red = 255;
        green = 0;
        blue = 0;
    }
    else if (ii == 2)
    {
        red = 0;
        green = 255;
        blue = 0;
    }
    else if (ii == 3)
    {
        red = 0;
        green = 0;
        blue = 255;
    }
    else if (ii == 4)
    {
        red = 255;
        green = 0;
        blue = 255;
    }
    else if (ii == 5)
    {
        red = 255;
        green = 255;
        blue = 0;
    }
    else if (ii == 6)
    {
        red = 0;
        green = 255;
        blue = 255;
    }
    Polygon polygon = new Polygon();
    PointCollection collection = new PointCollection();
    collection.Add(new Point(va.X, va.Y));
    collection.Add(new Point(vb.X, vb.Y));
    collection.Add(new Point(vc.X, vc.Y));
```

```
                        collection.Add(new Point(vd.X, vd.Y));
                        polygon.Points = collection;
                        polygon.Fill =
                         new SolidColorBrush(Color.FromArgb(255, red, green, blue));
                        TranslateTransform tt = new TranslateTransform();
                        tt.X = center.X;
                        tt.Y = center.Y;
                        polygon.RenderTransform = tt;
                        canvas1.Children.Add(polygon);
                    }
                }
            }

            private void Apply_Click(object sender, RoutedEventArgs e)
            {
                AddCube();
            }
    }

        public class Face
        {
            public int VertexA, VertexB, VertexC, VertexD;
            public Face()
            {
            }

            public Face(int vertexA, int vertexB, int vertexC, int vertexD)
            {
                this.VertexA = vertexA;
                this.VertexB = vertexB;
                this.VertexC = vertexC;
                this.VertexD = vertexD;
            }
        }
    }
```

In this code-behind file, we first define eight vertices that are used to construct six faces of the cube. Here each face contains four vertices, which is different from the triangular face with 3 vertices used in WPF. The Face object is defined in the Face class.

Inside the AddCube method, we create the transformMatrix using the Perspective and Rotate matrices defined in the Matrix3 class. The parameters, camera position, rotation axis, and rotation angle are specified directly from the user's inputs. Then, we perform the transforms on the vertices that will be used to construct the cube. Next, we compute the surface normal and the dot product between the normal and the viewing direction for each face of the cube to determine which faces need to be drawn on the screen. Note how we construct the viewing direction vector (0, 0, -cameraPosition), since the cube is located at the negative Z direction relative to the center of projection (or camera position). Finally, we draw the faces in different fill colors using the Polygon shape. The translation transform on the polygon is to place the cube at the center of the drawing Canvas (canvas1).

Running this project generates the result shown in Figure 9-13. From the figure you can clearly see the foreshortening effect of the perspective projection: the farther the side of the cube is from the center of projection (or camera position) the shorter it appears on the screen.

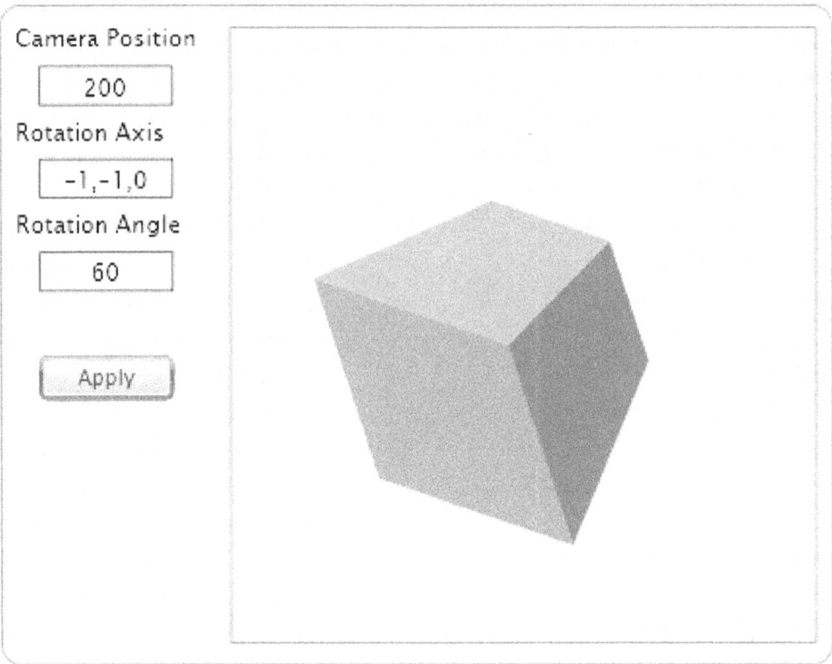

Figure 9-13 Perspective projection of a cube.

If you move the center of projection far away from the cube, the foreshortening effect of the perspective projection diminishes and eventually disappears, resulting in an orthographic projection in which the center of projection is placed at infinity from the cube. Figure 9-14 shows the result when you set the camera position at 20,000 units from the cube, which creates a result equivalent to an orthographic projection.

Object Transforms in Silverlight

In the previous section, we discussed perspective projection and the backface removal technique for convex objects. We also used a code example to demonstrate how to create a simple cube object in Silverlight based on Rotation and Perspective transformations. In fact, you can perform a variety of transformations on 3D objects in Silverlight, including scaling, translation, rotation, and combining transforms

You can also create a general 3D transform with a , which can be used to manipulate 3D objects in Silverlight. Such a matrix usually provides custom transforms that aren't provided by the basic transformations. Custom transform matrices can be multiplied to form any number of linear transforms, such as rotation and scaling, followed by translation.

By directly manipulating matrix values via the Matrix3 class, you can rotate, scale, move, and even skew a 3D object. For example, if you change the value of the element M[3, 0] to 10, you can use it to move an object 10 units along the x-axis. If you change the value in the second column of the second row to 3, you can use it to stretch an object to three times its current size in the Y direction. If you change both values at the same time, you move the object 10 units along the X-axis and stretch its dimension by a factor of 3 in the Y direction.

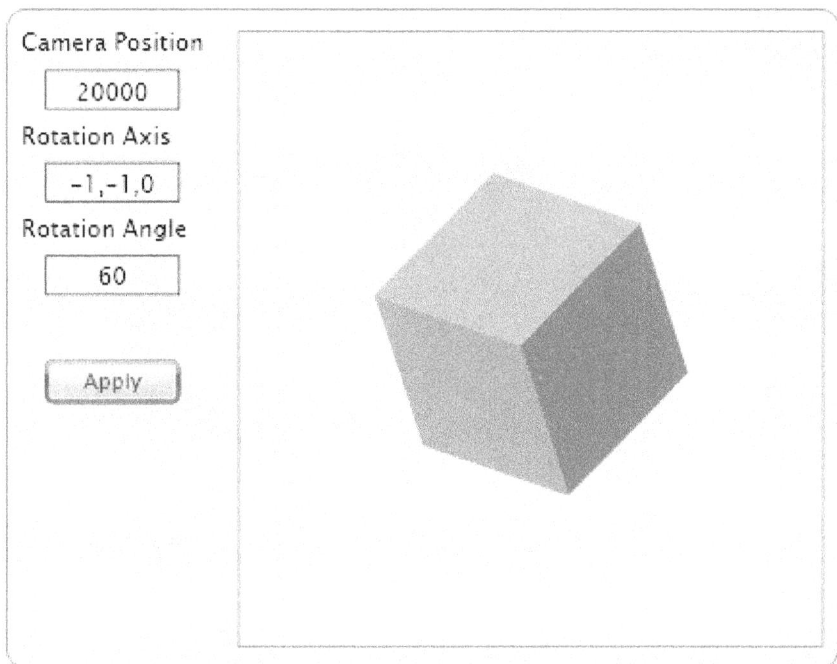

Figure 9-14 Orthographic projection of a cube.

Although a general Matrix3 transform matrix enables you to directly manipulate its elements' values, the Matrix3 class also provides several transform methods that enable you to transform an object without knowing how the underlying matrix structure is configured. For example, the Scale method enables you to construct a transform matrix by setting its s_x, s_y and s_z parameters instead of manipulating an underlying transform matrix. Likewise, the Rotate method enables you to specify a rotation transform by simply specifying the angle about a rotation axis.

In the following sections, you'll apply various transforms to the 3D cube object we used when we discussed projections.

Scale Transform

The Scale method in the Matrix3 class enables you to scale a 3D object by setting its s_x, s_y and s_z parameters. Let's look at an example. Start with a new Silverlight project and name it Example09-2. Add the Point3, Vector3, and Matrix3 classes from the previous project to the current project. The XAML file is similar to the one used in Example09-1. You can view the complete source code of the example by opening the project using Visual Studio 2008. Figure 9-15 is a screen shot from this example.

You can see from this figure that the layout is similar to the one used in the previous example, except for the changes of the parameters for the TextBlock and TextBox objects.

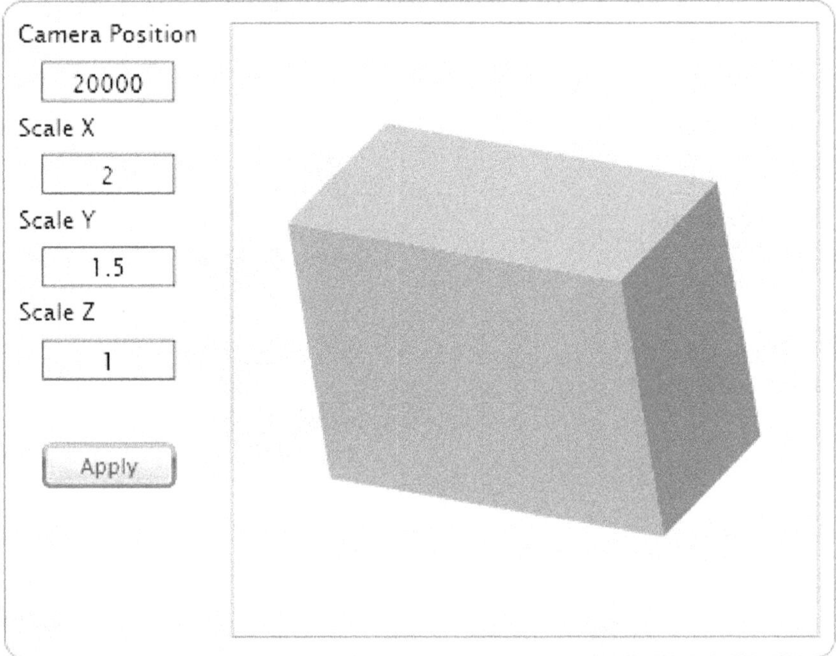

Figure 9-15 Scale transform on a cube.

The code behind file is also similar to that of Example09-1. You only need to make a small modification inside the AddCube method:

```
public void AddCube()
{
    double cameraPosition = double.Parse(tbCameraPosition.Text);
    Vector3 rotationAxis = new Vector3(new double[] { -1, -1, 0 });
    double rotationAnge = 45;
    double sx = double.Parse(tbSx.Text);
    double sy = double.Parse(tbSy.Text);
    double sz = double.Parse(tbSz.Text);
    Matrix3 transformMatrix = Matrix3.Scale(sx, sy, sz) *
                              Matrix3.Perspective(cameraPosition) *
                              Matrix3.Rotate(rotationAxis, rotationAnge);
    vertices = new Point3[8];
    for (int i = 0; i < vertices0.Length; i++)
        vertices[i] =
            Point3.TransformNormalize(transformMatrix, vertices0[i]);
… …
}
```

Here, in addition to the perspective and rotation transforms, we add a Scale transform to the transformMatrix. Without the rotation transform, you can only see the single front face of the cube, because the camera is fixed on the positive Z axis. The rotation makes the cube appear 3D on your screen. I should also point out here that the order of the matrix multiplication in the transformMatrix is important. If you exchange the order of multiplication, you might get unwanted results.

Running the project produces the result shown in Figure 9-15. Now you can change any parameter in the TextBox fields and click the Apply button to examine the scale effect on the cube.

Translate Transform

The Translate method in the Matrix3 class enables you to move a 3D object by specifying its dx, dy, and dz parameters.

Here, let's consider an example that demonstrates a translation on a cube object using a similar layout and user interface as the previous example. Start with a new Silverlight project and name it Example09-3. Add the Point3, Vector3, and Matrix3 classes from the previous example to the current project. Figure 9-16 shows a screen shot from this example.

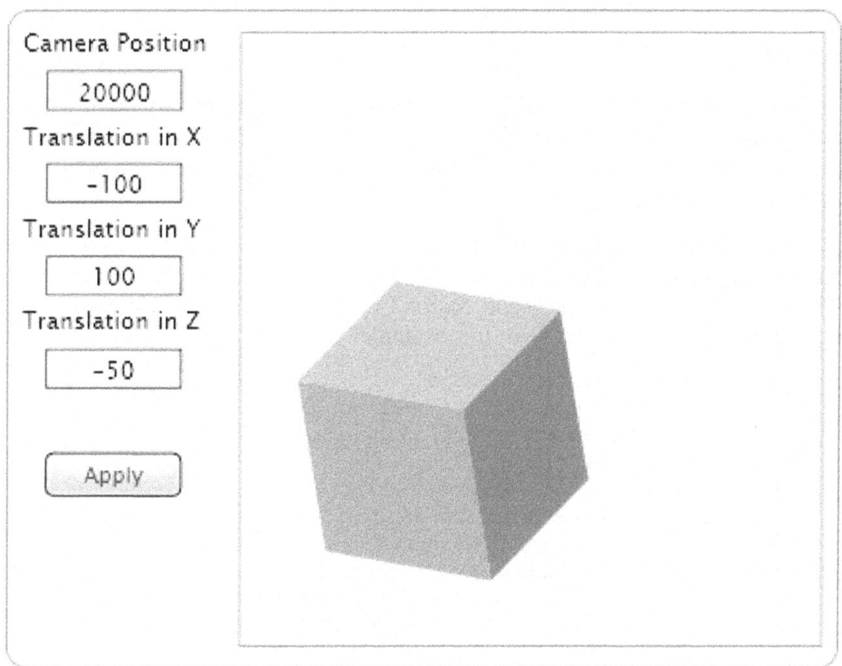

Figure 9-16 Translation on a cube.

You can see from the figure that the layout is similar to the previous scale transform example, except that you need to change the parameters for the scale transform in the TextBox fields to those for the translation transform.

The corresponding code-behind file is also similar to that of the previous example, except that you need to replace some code inside the AddCube method with the following code snippet:

```
public void AddCube()
{
    double cameraPosition = double.Parse(tbCameraPosition.Text);
    Vector3 rotationAxis = new Vector3(new double[] { -1, -1, 0 });
    double rotationAnge = 45;
    double dx = double.Parse(tbDx.Text);
    double dy = double.Parse(tbDy.Text);
    double dz = double.Parse(tbDz.Text);
    Matrix3 transformMatrix = Matrix3.Translate(dx,dy,dz) *
                              Matrix3.Perspective(cameraPosition) *
                              Matrix3.Rotate(rotationAxis, rotationAnge);
```

```
        vertices = new Point3[8];
        for (int i = 0; i < vertices0.Length; i++)
            vertices[i] =
                Point3.TransformNormalize(transformMatrix, vertices0[i]);
    ... ...
    }
```

Here, you simply replace the scale transform with a translation. Running the project produces the result shown in Figure 9-16. Now you can move the cube around your screen by playing with different translation parameters.

Matrix Transform

In the previous sections, we discussed basic 3D transforms on graphics objects. These transforms include scaling, translation, and rotation. However, if you want to perform a 3D transform that isn't provided by a basic 3D transform, such as a 3D skew transform, you can create a custom 3D transform directly using a Matrix3 object.

Here I'll use an example to illustrate how to perform 3D custom transforms on a cube object by directly manipulating the transform matrix. Start with a new Silverlight project and name it Example09-4. Add the Point3, Vector3, and Matrix3 classes from the previous class to the current project. The following is the XAML code of this example:

```
<UserControl x:Class="Example09_4.Page"
    xmlns="http://schemas.microsoft.com/client/2007"
    xmlns:x="http://schemas.microsoft.com/winfx/2006/xaml"
    Width="505" Height="350">
    <Grid x:Name="LayoutRoot" Background="White">
        <Border BorderBrush="Gray" BorderThickness="1"
                CornerRadius="10" Margin="10">
            <StackPanel Orientation="Horizontal">
                <StackPanel Margin="5" Grid.Column="0">
                    <StackPanel Orientation="Horizontal">
                        <TextBlock Text="M[0,0]" Margin="2" FontSize="12"/>
                        <TextBox Name="tbM00" Margin="2" Text="1" FontSize="12"
                                 Width="30" Height="20" TextAlignment="Center"/>
                        <TextBlock Text="M[0,1]" Margin="2" FontSize="12"/>
                        <TextBox Name="tbM01" Margin="2" Text="0" FontSize="12"
                                 Width="30" Height="20" TextAlignment="Center"/>
                    </StackPanel>
                    <StackPanel Orientation="Horizontal">
                        <TextBlock Text="M[0,2]" Margin="2" FontSize="12"/>
                        <TextBox Name="tbM02" Margin="2" Text="1.5"
                                 FontSize="12" Width="30" Height="20"
                                 TextAlignment="Center"/>
                        <TextBlock Text="M[0,3]" Margin="2" FontSize="12"/>
                        <TextBox Name="tbM03" Margin="2" Text="0" FontSize="12"
                                 Width="30" Height="20" TextAlignment="Center"/>
                    </StackPanel>
                    <StackPanel Orientation="Horizontal">
                        <TextBlock Text="M[1,0]" Margin="2" FontSize="12"/>
                        <TextBox Name="tbM10" Margin="2" Text="0" FontSize="12"
                                 Width="30" Height="20" TextAlignment="Center"/>
                        <TextBlock Text="M[1,1]" Margin="2" FontSize="12"/>
```

```
            <TextBox Name="tbM11" Margin="2" Text="1" FontSize="12"
                     Width="30" Height="20" TextAlignment="Center"/>
        </StackPanel>
        <StackPanel Orientation="Horizontal">
            <TextBlock Text="M[1,2]" Margin="2" FontSize="12"/>
            <TextBox Name="tbM12" Margin="2" Text="1.5"
                     FontSize="12" Width="30" Height="20"
                     TextAlignment="Center"/>
            <TextBlock Text="M[1,3]" Margin="2" FontSize="12"/>
            <TextBox Name="tbM13" Margin="2" Text="0" FontSize="12"
                     Width="30" Height="20" TextAlignment="Center"/>
        </StackPanel>
        <StackPanel Orientation="Horizontal">
            <TextBlock Text="M[2,0]" Margin="2" FontSize="12"/>
            <TextBox Name="tbM20" Margin="2" Text="0" FontSize="12"
                     Width="30" Height="20" TextAlignment="Center"/>
            <TextBlock Text="M[2,1]" Margin="2" FontSize="12"/>
            <TextBox Name="tbM21" Margin="2" Text="0" FontSize="12"
                     Width="30" Height="20" TextAlignment="Center"/>
        </StackPanel>
        <StackPanel Orientation="Horizontal">
            <TextBlock Text="M[2,2]" Margin="2" FontSize="12"/>
            <TextBox Name="tbM22" Margin="2" Text="1" FontSize="12"
                     Width="30" Height="20" TextAlignment="Center"/>
            <TextBlock Text="M[2,3]" Margin="2" FontSize="12"/>
            <TextBox Name="tbM23" Margin="2" Text="0" FontSize="12"
                     Width="30" Height="20" TextAlignment="Center"/>
        </StackPanel>
        <StackPanel Orientation="Horizontal">
            <TextBlock Text="M[3,0]" Margin="2" FontSize="12"/>
            <TextBox Name="tbM30" Margin="2" Text="0" FontSize="12"
                     Width="30" Height="20" TextAlignment="Center"/>
            <TextBlock Text="M[3,1]" Margin="2" FontSize="12"/>
            <TextBox Name="tbM31" Margin="2" Text="0" FontSize="12"
                     Width="30" Height="20" TextAlignment="Center"/>
        </StackPanel>
        <StackPanel Orientation="Horizontal">
            <TextBlock Text="M[3,2]" Margin="2" FontSize="12"/>
            <TextBox Name="tbM32" Margin="2" Text="0" FontSize="12"
                     Width="30" Height="20" TextAlignment="Center"/>
            <TextBlock Text="M[3,3]" Margin="2" FontSize="12"/>
            <TextBox Name="tbM33" Margin="2" Text="1" FontSize="12"
                     Width="30" Height="20" TextAlignment="Center"/>
        </StackPanel>


        <Button Margin="2,30,2,2" Click="Apply_Click"
                Content="Apply" Width="70" Height="22"/>
    </StackPanel>
    <Border BorderBrush="Gray" BorderThickness="1" Margin="10">
        <Canvas x:Name="canvas1" Width="300" Height="305">
            <Canvas.Clip>
                <RectangleGeometry Rect="0 0 300 305"/>
            </Canvas.Clip>
        </Canvas>
```

```
                </Border>
            </StackPanel>
        </Border>
    </Grid>
</UserControl>
```

This code creates the user interface shown in Figure 9-17. This layout allows you to change any element of the transform matrix.

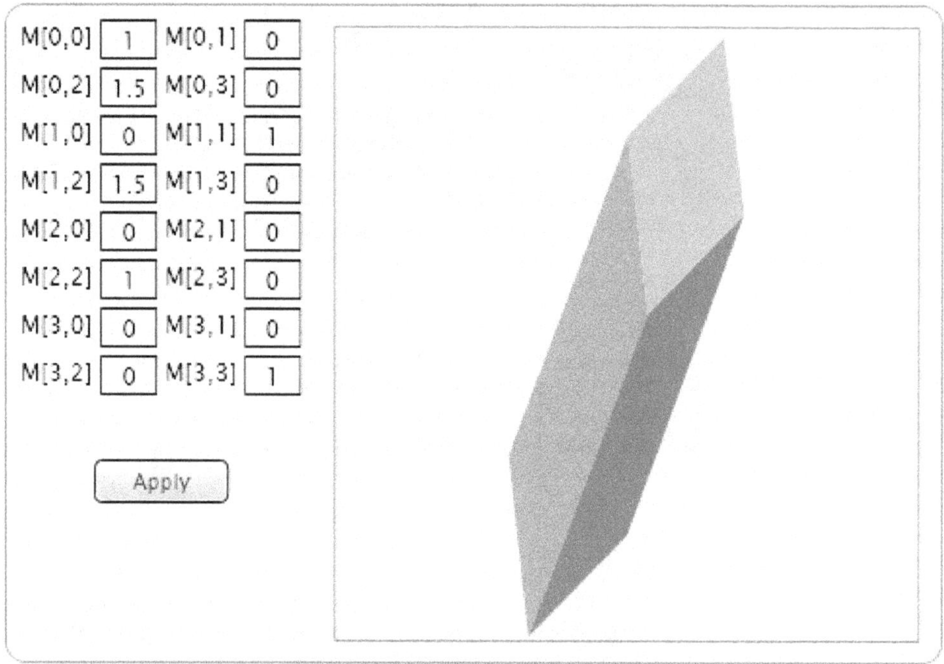

Figure 9-17 Custom transform on a cube.

The corresponding code-behind file is also similar to that of the previous example, except that you need to make changes inside the AddCube method:

```
public void AddCube()
{
    double cameraPosition = 20000;
    Vector3 rotationAxis = new Vector3(new double[] { -1, -1, 0 });
    double rotationAnge = 45;

    Matrix3 m3 = new Matrix3();
    m3.M[0,0] = Double.Parse(tbM00.Text);
    m3.M[1,0] = Double.Parse(tbM10.Text);
    m3.M[2,0] = Double.Parse(tbM20.Text);
    m3.M[3,0] = Double.Parse(tbM30.Text);
    m3.M[0,1] = Double.Parse(tbM01.Text);
    m3.M[1,1] = Double.Parse(tbM11.Text);
    m3.M[2,1] = Double.Parse(tbM21.Text);
    m3.M[3,1] = Double.Parse(tbM31.Text);
    m3.M[0,2] = Double.Parse(tbM02.Text);
```

```
        m3.M[1,2] = Double.Parse(tbM12.Text);
        m3.M[2,2] = Double.Parse(tbM22.Text);
        m3.M[3,2] = Double.Parse(tbM32.Text);
        m3.M[0,3] = Double.Parse(tbM03.Text);
        m3.M[1,3] = Double.Parse(tbM13.Text);
        m3.M[2,3] = Double.Parse(tbM23.Text);
        m3.M[3,3] = Double.Parse(tbM33.Text);

        Matrix3 transformMatrix = m3 * Matrix3.Perspective(cameraPosition) *
                                  Matrix3.Rotate(rotationAxis, rotationAnge);
        vertices = new Point3[8];
        for (int i = 0; i < vertices0.Length; i++)
            vertices[i] =
                Point3.TransformNormalize(transformMatrix, vertices0[i]);
    ... ...
    }
```

Here, we create a custom transform matrix, m3, by taking the input parameters as its elements. This matrix is then attached to the transformMatrix used to perform a custom 3D transform on the cube.

Executing this project produces the output shown in Figure 9-17. The result shown in the figure is obtained by setting the elements M[0, 2] and M[1, 2] to 1.5, resulting in a shearing effect on the cube. This 3D shearing effect has to be created using a custom transform matrix. You can use a general Matrix3 object to create any 3D transform by directly manipulating its corresponding elements.

Chapter 10
3D Objects in Silverlight

In the previous chapter, you learned the mathematical basics of 3D transformations and how these transformations are implemented in Silverlight. In this chapter, you'll learn how to create basic 3D objects in Silverlight, including 3D coordinate axes, cube, cylinder, sphere, 3D lines, and 3D surfaces.

3D Coordinate Axes

In Chapter 9, we discussed 3D transformations and projections based on three fundamental classes: Point3, Vertor3, and Matrix3. In this chapter we'll use these three classes extensively to create various 3D objects in Silverlight. For convenience, we'll put these classes into a single new file called XuMath3D.cs with the namespace XuMath3D. To this end, start with a new Silverlight project and name it Example10-1. Add a new class, XuMath3D, to the project and change its namespace to XuMath3D. The class has the following structure:

```
using System;
using System.Windows;
using System.Windows.Controls;
using System.Windows.Media;
using System.Windows.Shapes;

namespace XuMath3D
{
    public class XuMath
    {

    }

    #region Point3 class:
    public class Point3
    {
        public double X;
        public double Y;
        public double Z;
        public double W;
        ... ...
    }
```

```
        #endregion

        #region Vector3 Class:
        public class Vector3
        {
            public double[] vector;

            public Vector3()
            {
                this.vector = new double[3];
                for (int i = 0; i < 3; i++)
                {
                    vector[i] = 0.0;
                }
            }
            ... ...
        }
    #endregion

        #region Matrix3 class:
        public class Matrix3
        {
            public double[,] M = new double[4, 4];

            public Matrix3()
            {
                Identity();
            }
            ... ...
        }
        #endregion
    }
```

We'll add more classes later to this file. This single file makes it more convenient to access all of the classes in the file because you simply add a single XuMath3D.cs file to your project and add a using statement:

```
using XuMath3D;
```

Coordinates3D Class

Now, we want to add a new class, Coordinates3D, to the XuMath3D.cs file, which will include the transformations, projections, coordinate axes, and some utility methods.

```
        #region Coordinates3D class:
        public class Coordinates3D
        {
            private Canvas drawCanvas;
            private double length;
            private double xOffset = 0;
            private double yOffset = 0;
            private double xAngle = 20;
            private double yAngle = 30;
            private double zAngle = 0;
            private double cameraPosition = 20000;
```

```
private Point center;

public Coordinates3D()
{
}

public Canvas DrawCanvas
{
    get { return drawCanvas; }
    set { drawCanvas = value; }
}

public double AxisLength
{
    get { return length; }
    set { length = value; }
}

public double XOffset
{
    get { return xOffset; }
    set { xOffset = value; }
}

public double YOffset
{
    get { return yOffset; }
    set { yOffset = value; }
}

public double XAngle
{
    get { return xAngle; }
    set { xAngle = value; }
}

public double YAngle
{
    get { return yAngle; }
    set { yAngle = value; }
}

public double ZAngle
{
    get { return zAngle; }
    set { zAngle = value; }
}

public double CameraPosition
{
    get { return cameraPosition; }
    set { cameraPosition = value; }
}

public void AddCoordinateAxes()
```

```
{
    length = drawCanvas.Width / 2;
    Point3[] pt3 = new Point3[] { new Point3(0, 0, 0, 1),
                                  new Point3(length, 0, 0, 1),
                                  new Point3(0, -length, 0, 1),
                                  new Point3(0, 0, length, 1)};

    Point[] pt2 = new Point[pt3.Length];
    for (int i = 0; i < pt3.Length; i++)
        pt2[i] = Point3ToPoint(pt3[i]);

    Line line = new Line();
    line.X1 = pt2[0].X;
    line.Y1 = pt2[0].Y;
    line.X2 = pt2[1].X;
    line.Y2 = pt2[1].Y;
    line.Stroke = new SolidColorBrush(Colors.Red);
    drawCanvas.Children.Add(line);
    line = new Line();
    line.X1 = pt2[0].X;
    line.Y1 = pt2[0].Y;
    line.X2 = pt2[2].X;
    line.Y2 = pt2[2].Y;
    line.Stroke = new SolidColorBrush(Colors.Green);
    drawCanvas.Children.Add(line);
    line = new Line();
    line.X1 = pt2[0].X;
    line.Y1 = pt2[0].Y;
    line.X2 = pt2[3].X;
    line.Y2 = pt2[3].Y;
    line.Stroke = new SolidColorBrush(Colors.Blue);
    drawCanvas.Children.Add(line);
}

public Point Point3ToPoint(Point3 pt3)
{
    Point pt = new Point();
    pt3 = Point3Transform(pt3);
    pt.X = pt3.X + center.X;
    pt.Y = pt3.Y + center.Y;
    return pt;
}

public PointCollection CreatePoints(Point3 pt1, Point3 pt2,
                                    Point3 pt3, Point3 pt4)
{
    PointCollection collection = new PointCollection();
    pt1 = Point3Transform(pt1);
    pt2 = Point3Transform(pt2);
    pt3 = Point3Transform(pt3);
    pt4 = Point3Transform(pt4);
    Vector3 normal = Vector3.NormalVector(pt1, pt2, pt3);
    Vector3 viewDirection =
            new Vector3(new double[3] { 0, 0, -cameraPosition });
    double dotProduct = Vector3.DotProduct(normal, viewDirection);
```

```
            if (dotProduct > 0)
            {
                collection.Add(new Point(pt1.X + center.X, pt1.Y + center.Y));
                collection.Add(new Point(pt2.X + center.X, pt2.Y + center.Y));
                collection.Add(new Point(pt3.X + center.X, pt3.Y + center.Y));
                collection.Add(new Point(pt4.X + center.X, pt4.Y + center.Y));
            }
            return collection;
        }

        public Point3 Point3Transform(Point3 pt)
        {
            center = new Point(drawCanvas.Width / 2 + xOffset,
                                   drawCanvas.Height / 2 + yOffset);
            Vector3 rotationX = new Vector3(new double[] { -1, 0, 0 });
            Vector3 rotationY = new Vector3(new double[] { 0, -1, 0 });
            Vector3 rotationZ = new Vector3(new double[] { 0, -1, 0 });
            Matrix3 transformMatrix = Matrix3.Perspective(cameraPosition) *
                                      Matrix3.Rotate(rotationY, yAngle) *
                                      Matrix3.Rotate(rotationX, xAngle) *
                                      Matrix3.Rotate(rotationZ, zAngle);
            return Point3.TransformNormalize(transformMatrix, pt);
        }
    }
    #endregion
```

The field members and corresponding properties allow you to control the 3D coordinate axes, the location of the objects, and transformations.

- DrawCanvas property – specifies the Canvas object on which you create 3D objects.
- AxisLength property – sets the length of the coordinate axis.
- XOffset property – specifies the offset in the X-direction of the object relative to the drawing canvas's center.
- YOffset property – specifies the offset in the Y-direction of the object relative to the drawing canvas's center.
- XAngle – specifies the rotation angle around the X-axis.
- YAngle – specifies the rotation angle around the Y-axis.
- ZAngle – specifies the rotation angle around the Z-axis.
- CameraPosition property – specifies the center of projection used to construct the projection matrix and the view direction.

This class sets a simple 3D viewport (similar to the Viewport3D in WPF) that allows you to easily create 3D objects in Silverlight.

The public Point3Transform method in this class performs the perspective projection and rotation transforms on a Point3 object. Here we use three separate rotations around the X, Y, and Z axes, which will allow you to rotate objects around different coordinate axes. This method returns a transformed Point3 object.

The public method, Point3ToPoint, converts a Point3 object into a 2D Point object. This projected 2D Point can be directly used to draw objects on the screen. Inside this method, the original Point3 object is transformed into a projected 3D Point3 object using the Point3Transform method. The X and Y components of this projected Point3 object are shifted to the center of the drawing canvas and returned as the Point2 object. This method is very useful when you want to create 3D curves on the 2D screen.

The CreatePoints method is used to create a PointCollection object with four points which are used to construct a rectangular mesh. This method is very powerful when you want to create any 3D object or 3D surface with regular 4-point meshes.

The AddCoordinateAxes method allows you to add 3D coordinate Axes to the drawing canvas, which may be useful when you create 3D lines. Inside this method, the Point3 object is transformed into a 2D Point object using the Point3ToPoint method.

Creating 3D Coordinate Axes

Now we can create 3D coordinate axes using the Coordinate3D class. In the Example10-1 project, implement the following XAML code:

```
<UserControl x:Class="Example10_1.Page"
    xmlns="http://schemas.microsoft.com/client/2007"
    xmlns:x="http://schemas.microsoft.com/winfx/2006/xaml"
    Width="372" Height="322">
    <Grid x:Name="LayoutRoot" Background="White">
        <Border BorderBrush="Gray" BorderThickness="1"
                CornerRadius="10" Margin="10">
            <Canvas x:Name="canvas1" Width="350" Height="300"
                    Background="Transparent">
                <Canvas.Clip>
                    <RectangleGeometry Rect="0 0 350 300"/>
                </Canvas.Clip>
            </Canvas>
        </Border>
    </Grid>
</UserControl>
```

The corresponding code-behind file used to create coordinate axes is listed below:

```
using System;
using System.Windows;
using System.Windows.Controls;
using System.Windows.Media;
using System.Windows.Shapes;
using XuMath3D;

namespace Example10_1
{
    public partial class Page : UserControl
    {
        Coordinates3D axes;

        public Page()
        {
            InitializeComponent();

            axes = new Coordinates3D();
```

```
            axes.DrawCanvas = canvas1;
            axes.YOffset = 50;
            axes.AddCoordinateAxes();
        }
    }
}
```

Here, we simply create a Coordinates3D object, axes, and specify its DrawCanvas using the canvas1 defined in the XAML file. You can also specify the other properties such as CameraPosition and Rotation angles. Here we just move the origin of the coordinates 50 units downward relative to the center of the canvas1. Note that the default CameraPosition = 20000, which is equivalent to an orthographic projection, is used if you don't specify this property explicitly. Finally, you call the AddCoordinateAxes method to create the coordinate axes in the canvas1.

Running this project produces the result shown in Figure 10-1, where the red line corresponds to the X axis, the green line to the Y axis, and the blue line to the Z axis.

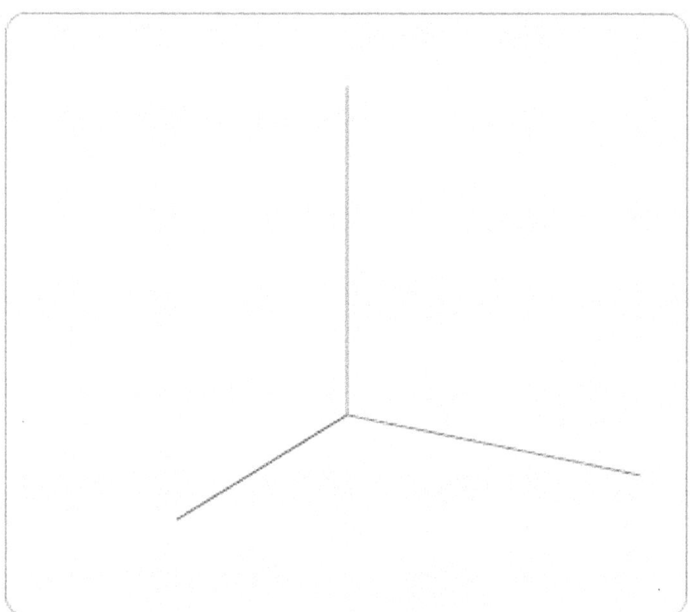

Figure 10-1 3D coordinate axes in Silverlight.

3D Line Charts

In the last section, we implemented the Coordinates3D class and demonstrated how to use it to create 3D coordinate axes in Silverlight. In this section, I'll show you how easy it is to create a 3D line chart based on this class. The 3D line chart displays a 3D plot of a set of data points. It is similar to a 2D line chart, except that an additional Z-component is used to provide data for the third dimension.

Here we will continue to use the Example10-1 project to create a 3D line chart. Add a new method AddLine3D to the page.xaml.cs file. Now the code-behind file becomes:

```
using System;
using System.Windows;
using System.Windows.Controls;
using System.Windows.Media;
using System.Windows.Shapes;
using XuMath3D;

namespace Example10_1
{
    public partial class Page : UserControl
    {
        Coordinates3D axes;

        public Page()
        {
            InitializeComponent();

            axes = new Coordinates3D();
            axes.DrawCanvas = canvas1;
            axes.YOffset = 50;
            axes.AddCoordinateAxes();

            AddLine3D();
        }

        private void AddLine3D()
        {
            Polyline pl = new Polyline();
            pl.Stroke = new SolidColorBrush(Colors.Black);
            canvas1.Children.Add(pl);
            for (int i = 0; i < 300; i++)
            {
                double t = 0.13 * i;
                double x = 130 * Math.Exp(-t / 30) * Math.Cos(t);
                double z = 130 * Math.Exp(-t / 30) * Math.Sin(t);
                double y = -4 * t;
                pl.Points.Add(axes.Point3ToPoint(new Point3(x, y, z, 1)));
            }
        }
    }
}
```

You can see how easy it is to create a 3D line chart using the Coordinates3D class. The key step is to use the point conversion method, Point3ToPoint, to create the PointCollection of the polyline. This method automatically performs various projections and transformations, and provides a 2D point collection suitable to be used to create a 2D Polyline object.

Running this project again generates the output shown in Figure 10-2.

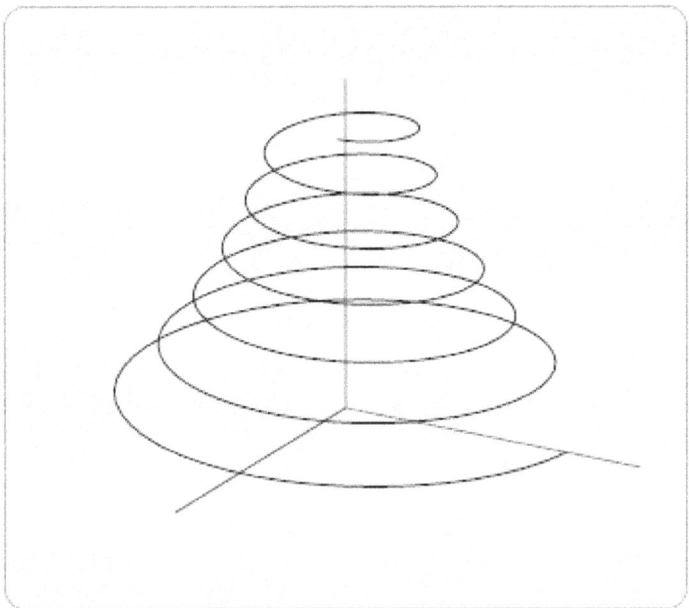

Figure 10-2 A 3D line chart in Silverlight.

Creating a Cube

In the previous chapter, we created a 3D cube object directly in the code-behind file to demonstrate various transformations in Silverlight. This approach is fine for creating a single cube object. However, it is not convenient if you want to create many cube objects on a drawing canvas or animate the cubes. In this section, we'll implement a separate Cube class that can be reused to create any number of the cubes and perform animations on the cubes.

Cube Class

Let's consider an example. Start with a new Silverlight project and name it Example10-2. Add the file, XuMath3D.cs, from the previous example to the current project, and add a new Cube class to this file:

```
#region Create a cube object:
public class Cube
{
    private double side = 50;
    private Point3 center = new Point3(0, 0, 0, 1);

    public double Side
    {
        get { return side; }
        set { side = value; }
    }

    public Point3 Center
    {
```

```
        get { return center; }
        set { center = value; }
    }

    public Cube()
    {

    }

    public void AddCube(Coordinates3D axes)
    {
        Point3[] pts = new Point3[] { new Point3(-side,-side,-side,1),
                                      new Point3( side,-side,-side,1),
                                      new Point3( side, side,-side,1),
                                      new Point3(-side, side,-side,1),
                                      new Point3(-side, side, side,1),
                                      new Point3( side, side, side,1),
                                      new Point3( side,-side, side,1),
                                      new Point3(-side,-side, side,1)};
        for (int i = 0; i < 8; i++)
            pts[i] = new Point3(pts[i].X + center.X,
                                pts[i].Y + center.Y,
                                pts[i].Z + center.Z, 1);

        Face[] faces = new Face[] {new Face(0,1,2,3), new Face(4,5,6,7),
                                   new Face(3,4,7,0), new Face(2,1,6,5),
                                   new Face(5,4,3,2), new Face(0,7,6,1)};

        int ii = 0;
        foreach (Face face in faces)
        {
            ii++;
            Point3 pt1 = pts[face.VertexA];
            Point3 pt2 = pts[face.VertexB];
            Point3 pt3 = pts[face.VertexC];
            Point3 pt4 = pts[face.VertexD];
            PointCollection collection =
                   axes.CreatePoints(pt1, pt2, pt3, pt4);
            if (collection.Count > 0)
            {
                byte red = 0;
                byte green = 0;
                byte blue = 0;
                if (ii == 1)
                {
                    red = 255;
                    green = 0;
                    blue = 0;
                }
                else if (ii == 2)
                {
                    red = 0;
                    green = 255;
                    blue = 0;
                }
```

```
                else if (ii == 3)
                {
                    red = 0;
                    green = 0;
                    blue = 255;
                }
                else if (ii == 4)
                {
                    red = 255;
                    green = 0;
                    blue = 255;
                }
                else if (ii == 5)
                {
                    red = 255;
                    green = 255;
                    blue = 0;
                }
                else if (ii == 6)
                {
                    red = 0;
                    green = 255;
                    blue = 255;
                }
                Polygon polygon = new Polygon();
                polygon.Points = collection;
                polygon.Fill =
                 new SolidColorBrush(Color.FromArgb(255, red, green, blue));
                axes.DrawCanvas.Children.Add(polygon);
            }
        }
    }
}

public class Face
{
    public int VertexA, VertexB, VertexC, VertexD;
    public Face()
    {
    }

    public Face(int vertexA, int vertexB, int vertexC, int vertexD)
    {
        this.VertexA = vertexA;
        this.VertexB = vertexB;
        this.VertexC = vertexC;
        this.VertexD = vertexD;
    }
}
#endregion
```

This class is very similar to the code used in the previous chaper, where we created the cube directly in the code-behind file. There are two public properties you can specify:

- Side property – sets the side length of the cube.
- Center property – specifies the center position of the cube. The default center position (0, 0, 0, 1) of the cube is located at the center of the drawing canvas.

The key step inside the AddCube method is creating the PointCollection object using the CreatePoints method implemented in the Coordinates3D class. The method, CreatePoints, converts four Point3 objects into a 2D PointCollection with four transformed 2D Point objects. This PointCollection object can be used to construct the polygon.

Creating Multiple Cubes

You can easily create any number of the Cube objects using the Cube class. Open the code-behind file, page.xaml.cs, of the Example10-2 project and implement the following code to it:

```
using System;
using System.Windows;
using System.Windows.Controls;
using System.Windows.Media;
using System.Windows.Shapes;
using XuMath3D;

namespace Example10_2
{
    public partial class Page : UserControl
    {
        Coordinates3D axes;

        public Page()
        {
            InitializeComponent();
            AddCube();
        }

        private void AddCube()
        {
            axes = new Coordinates3D();
            axes.DrawCanvas = canvas1;
            axes.CameraPosition = 400;
            Cube cube = new Cube();
            cube.Side = 60;
            cube.Center = new Point3(0, -20, -440, 1);
            cube.AddCube(axes);
            cube.Center = new Point3(0, -20, -200, 1);
            cube.AddCube(axes);
            cube.Center = new Point3(0, -20, 40, 1);
            cube.AddCube(axes);
        }
    }
}
```

Inside the AddCube method, we first specify properties of the Coordinates3D object axes, where the CameraPosition is set to 400, providing a perspective projection. You should see a foreshortening effect due to this perspective projection. The other properties of the axes object use their default values defined in the Coordinates3D class.

Here we create three cubes with side lengths of 60 pixels. The only difference is that their Center properties have different Z values. You can see how easy it is to create a cube on the canvas1. First, you set a simple 3D viewport using the Coordinates3D class, and then create a new Cube object. Finally, you call the AddCube method multiple times to create multiple cubes.

Running this project produces the result shown in Figure 10-3. Note that the physical dimensions of these three cubes are the same. From the figure you can clearly see the foreshortening effect of the perspective projection: the farther the cube is from the camera, the smaller it appears on the screen.

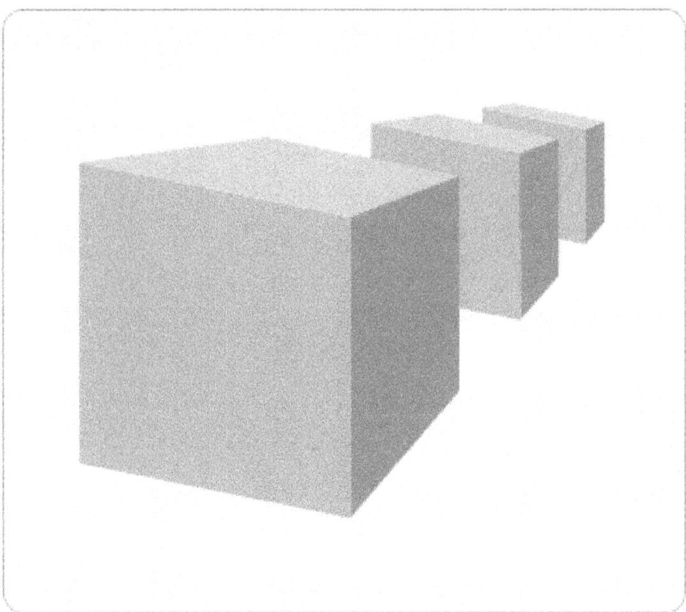

Figure 10-3 Multiple cubes in Silverlight.

Animating Cubes

In the previous section, we demonstrated how to create multiple cubes using the Cube class. In fact, you can also use this class to create cube objects and perform animations on them using the timer-based animation approach discussed in Chapter 6.

Start with a new Silverlight project and name it Example10-3. Add the XuMath3D class from the previous example to the project. Here is the XAML code of this example:

```
<UserControl x:Class="Example10_3.Page"
    xmlns="http://schemas.microsoft.com/client/2007"
    xmlns:x="http://schemas.microsoft.com/winfx/2006/xaml"
    Width="422" Height="372">
    <Grid x:Name="LayoutRoot" Background="White">
        <Border BorderBrush="Gray" BorderThickness="1"
                CornerRadius="10" Margin="10">
            <StackPanel>
```

```
                <Canvas x:Name="canvas1" Width="400"
                        Height="320" Background="Transparent">
                    <Canvas.Clip>
                        <RectangleGeometry Rect="0 0 400 350"/>
                    </Canvas.Clip>
                </Canvas>
                <StackPanel Orientation="Horizontal">
                    <Button x:Name="Start" Click="Start_Click" Content="Start"
                            Width="80" Height="22" Margin="20,0,0,0"/>
                    <Button x:Name="Stop" Click="Stop_Click" Content="Stop"
                            Width="80" Height="22" Margin="20,0,0,0"/>
                </StackPanel>
            </StackPanel>
        </Border>
    </Grid>
</UserControl>
```

The corresponding code-behind file is listed below:

```
using System;
using System.Windows;
using System.Windows.Threading;
using System.Windows.Controls;
using System.Windows.Media;
using System.Windows.Shapes;
using XuMath3D;

namespace Example10_3
{
    public partial class Page : UserControl
    {
        Coordinates3D axes1;
        Coordinates3D axes2;
        Cube cube;
        DispatcherTimer timer;
        double angle = 0;
        double delta = 1;

        public Page()
        {
            InitializeComponent();
            AddCube();
        }

        private void AddCube()
        {
            canvas1.Children.Clear();
            axes1 = new Coordinates3D();
            axes1.DrawCanvas = canvas1;
            axes1.XOffset = -100;

            axes2 = new Coordinates3D();
            axes2.DrawCanvas = canvas1;
            axes2.XOffset = 100;

            cube = new Cube();
```

```
            cube.Side = 60;
            cube.AddCube(axes1);
            cube.AddCube(axes2);
        }

        private void Start_Click(object sender, RoutedEventArgs e)
        {
            timer = new DispatcherTimer();
            axes1 = new Coordinates3D();
            axes1.DrawCanvas = canvas1;
            axes1.XOffset = -100;

            axes2 = new Coordinates3D();
            axes2.DrawCanvas = canvas1;
            axes2.XOffset = 100;
            axes2.YAngle = 0;
            axes2.ZAngle = 20;

            angle = 0;
            timer.Tick += new EventHandler(timer_Tick);
            timer.Start();
        }

        void timer_Tick(object sender, EventArgs e)
        {
            canvas1.Children.Clear();
            axes1.YAngle = angle;
            axes2.XAngle = angle;
            cube.AddCube(axes1);
            cube.AddCube(axes2);
            angle += delta;
            if (angle >= 360)
                angle = 0;
        }

        private void Stop_Click(object sender, RoutedEventArgs e)
        {
            timer.Stop();
            AddCube();
        }
    }
}
```

In this code-behind file, you create two cubes with two different Coordinate objects, axes1 and axes2. The axes1 has an Xoffset = -100, and axes2 has an Xoffset = 100. In this way, the two cubes have a 200-pixel separation between their center positions. You can also separate the two cubes by directly specifying their Center properties. However, there exists a difference when you animate the cube objects. Using the XOffset or YOffset property of the Coordinates3D object, you animate the transformation on the cubes relative to their individual centers. On the other hand, you will always animate all of the cube objects relative to a single position; i.e., the center of the drawing canvas (canvas1 in this example). Inside the Start_Click event handler, we set axes2's YAngle property to zero and its ZAngle property to 20 degrees to get a better view of the second cube when it is being animated.

For the first cube, we animate its YAngle property, which specifies a rotation around the Y axis. For the second cube, we animate its XAngle property.

A screen shot from running this project is shown in Figure 10-4. Click the Start button to start the animation.

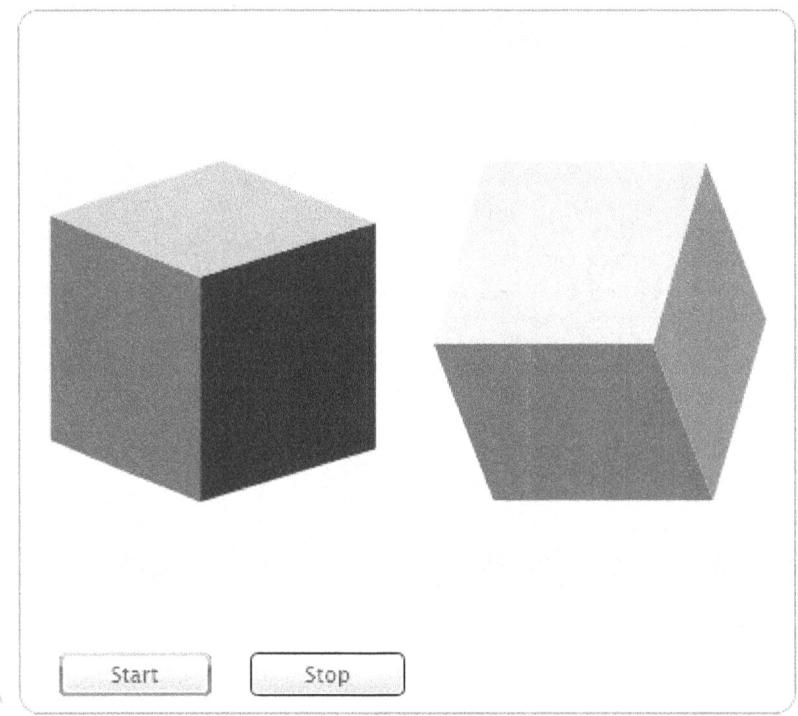

Figure 10-4 Animating cubes in Silverlight.

Creating a Sphere

In this section, you'll create a shere shape in Silverlight. To do this, you need to be familiar with the spherical coordinate system. A point in the spherical coordinate system is specified by r, θ, and φ. Here, r is the distance from the point to the origin, θ is the polar angle, and φ is the azimuthal angle in the X-Z plane from the X axis. In this notation, you also alternate the conventional Y and Z axes so that the coordinate system is consistent with the one used here. Figure 10-5 shows a point in this coordinate system.

From this figure, you can easily obtain the following relationships;

$$x = r\sin\theta\cos\varphi$$

$$y = r\cos\theta$$

$$z = -r\sin\theta\sin\varphi$$

By using the spherical coordinate system, you can easily create spherical objects in Silverlight.

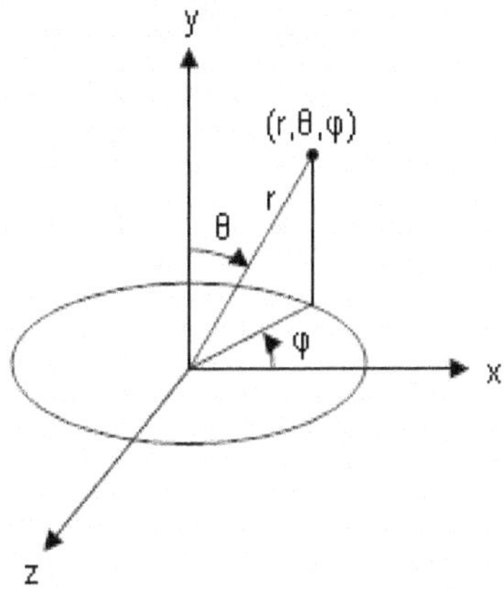

Figure 10-5 Spherical coordinate system.

Sphere Class

In order to create a sphere shape in Silverlight using these relations, you can start with the familiar concepts of longitude and latitude (sometimes called the UV-sphere method). The standard UV-sphere method is made out of u segments and v rings, as shown in Figure 10-6.

It can be seen that the u and v lines form grids on the surface of the sphere. Now it is enough to consider just one unit grid, as shown on the right of Figure 10-6. This unit grid can be regarded as a rectangular mesh. If you run over all of the grids, you generate rectangular meshes for the entire surface of the sphere.

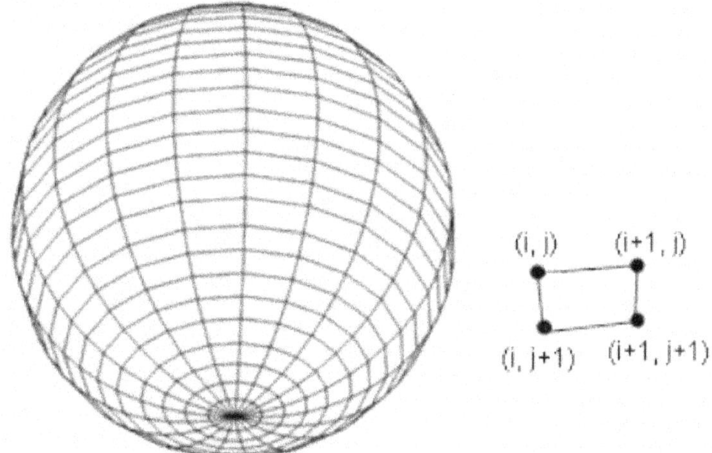

Figure 10-6 A UV-sphere model and a unit grid.

Now let's start with a new Silverlight project and name it Example10-4. Add the XuMath3D.cs file from the previous example to the current project. First add a new Sphere class to this file. Here is the code listing of this class:

```
#region Create a sphere object:
public class Sphere
{
    private double r = 50;
    private Point3 center = new Point3(0, 0, 0, 1);
    private int u = 20;
    private int v = 15;

    public Sphere()
    {
    }

    public double Radius
    {
        get { return r; }
        set { r = value; }
    }

    public Point3 Center
    {
        get { return center; }
        set { center = value; }
    }

    public int UDiv
    {
        get { return u; }
        set { u = value; }
    }

    public int VDiv
    {
        get { return v; }
        set { v = value; }
    }

    private Point3 GetPosition(double theta, double phi)
    {
        Point3 pt = new Point3();
        double snt = Math.Sin(theta * Math.PI / 180);
        double cnt = Math.Cos(theta * Math.PI / 180);
        double snp = Math.Sin(phi * Math.PI / 180);
        double cnp = Math.Cos(phi * Math.PI / 180);

        pt.X = r * snt * cnp + center.X;
        pt.Y = -r * cnt + center.Y;
        pt.Z = -r * snt * snp + center.Z;
        pt.W = 1;
        return pt;
    }
```

```
public void AddSphere(Coordinates3D axes)
{
    Point3[,] pts = new Point3[u, v];
    for (int i = 0; i < u; i++)
    {
        for (int j = 0; j < v; j++)
        {
            pts[i, j] = axes.Point3Transform(
                GetPosition(i * 180 / (u - 1), j * 360 / (v - 1)));
        }
    }

    Point offset = new Point(axes.DrawCanvas.Width / 2 +
          axes.XOffset, axes.DrawCanvas.Height / 2 + axes.YOffset);

    for (int i = 0; i < u - 1; i++)
    {
        for (int j = 0; j < v - 1; j++)
        {
            Point3 pt1 = pts[i, j];
            Point3 pt2 = pts[i + 1, j];
            Point3 pt3 = pts[i + 1, j + 1];
            Point3 pt4 = pts[i, j + 1];

            Vector3 normal = Vector3.NormalVector(pt1, pt2, pt3);
            if (i == u - 2)
                normal = Vector3.NormalVector(pt3, pt4, pt1);

            Vector3 viewDirection =
              new Vector3(new double[3] { 0, 0, -axes.CameraPosition });
            double dotProduct =
                  Vector3.DotProduct(normal, viewDirection);
            if (dotProduct > 0)
            {
                AddPolygon(axes, dotProduct,
                    new Point(pt1.X + offset.X, pt1.Y + offset.Y),
                    new Point(pt2.X + offset.X, pt2.Y + offset.Y),
                    new Point(pt3.X + offset.X, pt3.Y + offset.Y),
                    new Point(pt4.X + offset.X, pt4.Y + offset.Y));
            }
        }
    }
}


private void AddPolygon(Coordinates3D axes, double dotProduct,
                        Point pt1, Point pt2, Point pt3, Point pt4)
{
    double shade = dotProduct;
    shade /= 1024;
    int color = (int)shade;
    color += 128;
    if (color >= 255)
    {
        color = 255;
```

```
            }
            if (color < 0)
            {
                color = 0;
            }

            byte red = (byte)(color);
            byte green = (byte)(color >> 2);
            byte blue = (byte)(color >> 3);

            Polygon polygon = new Polygon();
            polygon.Points.Add(pt1);
            polygon.Points.Add(pt2);
            polygon.Points.Add(pt3);
            polygon.Points.Add(pt4);
            polygon.Fill =
                new SolidColorBrush(Color.FromArgb(255, red, green, blue));
            polygon.Stroke =
                new SolidColorBrush(Color.FromArgb(255, 200, 200, 200));
            polygon.StrokeThickness = 0.5;
            axes.DrawCanvas.Children.Add(polygon);
        }
    }
#endregion
```

In this class, you first define several field members and corresponding properties:

- Radius property – sets the radius of the sphere object.
- Center property – sets the center position of the sphere.
- UDiv property – sets the number of segments of the sphere.
- VDiv property – sets the number of rings of the sphere.

Here you construct rectangular meshes by dividing the sphere surface into segments and rings. The number of segments and rings are specified using the UDiv and VDiv properties. This class also allows you to specify the radius and position (the center location) of the sphere. The GetPosition method returns the points on a sphere surface by specifying their longitude and latitude.

Notice how you create the mesh for a unit grid inside the AddSphere method, where the four vertex points (Point3 objects) that define the unit grid are specified, and a single rectangular mesh is defined using these four vertices within two for-loops. Inside these for-loops, you also perform transformations on the original vertices using the Point3Transform method defined in the Coordinates3D class. The corresponding polygon of this rectangular mesh is created by calling the private AddPolygon method.

Inside the AddPolygon method, you first create a simple shading effect using the dot product between the surface normal and the viewing direction. You can create your own custom shading effect here if you like. This shading effect will be used to set the Fill property of the polygon. Here we also specify the Stroke property of the polygon.

Creating Multiple Spheres

You can easily create any number of Sphere objects using the Sphere class. You can test the Sphere class in the Example10-4 project. The XAML code is similar to that used in Example10-2:

```
<UserControl x:Class="Example10_4.Page"
    xmlns="http://schemas.microsoft.com/client/2007"
    xmlns:x="http://schemas.microsoft.com/winfx/2006/xaml"
    Width="372" Height="322">
    <Grid x:Name="LayoutRoot" Background="White">
        <Border BorderBrush="Gray" BorderThickness="1"
                CornerRadius="10" Margin="10">
            <Canvas x:Name="canvas1" Width="350" Height="300"
                    Background="Transparent">
                <Canvas.Clip>
                    <RectangleGeometry Rect="0 0 350 300"/>
                </Canvas.Clip>
            </Canvas>
        </Border>
    </Grid>
</UserControl>
```

The corresponding code-behind file of this example is listed below:

```
using System;
using System.Windows;
using System.Windows.Controls;
using System.Windows.Media;
using System.Windows.Shapes;
using XuMath3D;


namespace Example10_4
{
    public partial class Page : UserControl
    {
        Coordinates3D axes;

        public Page()
        {
            InitializeComponent();
            AddSphere();
        }

        private void AddSphere()
        {
            axes = new Coordinates3D();
            axes.DrawCanvas = canvas1;
            axes.CameraPosition = 600;
            Sphere sphere = new Sphere();
            sphere.Radius = 70;
            sphere.Center = new Point3(0, 0, -250, 1);
            sphere.AddSphere(axes);
            sphere.Center = new Point3(0, 0, -100, 1);
            sphere.AddSphere(axes);
            sphere.Center = new Point3(0, 0, 50, 1);
            sphere.AddSphere(axes);
        }
    }
}
```

Here you create three spheres with the same radius but at different locations. The camera position is set to 600 units, which should exhibit a perspective shortening effect.

Running this project produces the result shown in Figure 10-7.

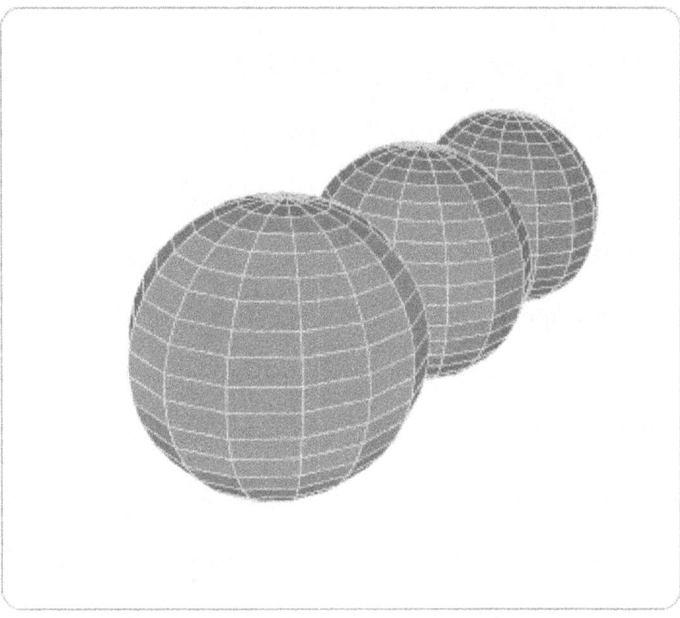

Figure 10-7 Spheres created in Silverlight.

Animating Spheres

In the previous section, we demonstrated how to create multiple spheres using the Sphere class. You can also use this class to create sphere objects and perform animations on them using the timer-based animation approach discussed in Chapter 6, as we did when we previously animated the cube objects in this chapter.

Start a new Silverlight project and name it Example10-5. Add the XuMath3D class from the previous example to the project. The XAML code of this example is exactly the same as the one used in the Example10-3 project. The code-behind file is listed below:

```
using System;
using System.Windows;
using System.Windows.Threading;
using System.Windows.Controls;
using System.Windows.Media;
using System.Windows.Shapes;
using XuMath3D;

namespace Example10_5
{
    public partial class Page : UserControl
    {
        Coordinates3D axes1;
```

```
Coordinates3D axes2;
Sphere sphere;
DispatcherTimer timer;
double angle = 0;
double delta = 2;

public Page()
{
    InitializeComponent();
    AddSphere();
}

private void AddSphere()
{
    canvas1.Children.Clear();
    axes1 = new Coordinates3D();
    axes1.DrawCanvas = canvas1;
    axes1.XOffset = -100;
    axes1.CameraPosition = 300;

    axes2 = new Coordinates3D();
    axes2.DrawCanvas = canvas1;
    axes2.XOffset = 100;
    axes2.CameraPosition = 300;

    sphere = new Sphere();
    sphere.Radius = 50;
    sphere.UDiv = 10;
    sphere.VDiv = 10;
    sphere.AddSphere(axes1);
    sphere.AddSphere(axes2);
}

private void Start_Click(object sender, RoutedEventArgs e)
{
    timer = new DispatcherTimer();
    timer.Interval = TimeSpan.FromMilliseconds(10);
    axes1 = new Coordinates3D();
    axes1.DrawCanvas = canvas1;
    axes1.XOffset = -100;
    axes1.CameraPosition = 300;

    axes2 = new Coordinates3D();
    axes2.DrawCanvas = canvas1;
    axes2.XOffset = 100;
    axes2.YAngle = 0;
    axes2.ZAngle = 20;
    axes2.CameraPosition = 300;

    angle = 0;
    timer.Tick += new EventHandler(timer_Tick);
    timer.Start();
}

void timer_Tick(object sender, EventArgs e)
```

```
            {
                canvas1.Children.Clear();
                axes1.YAngle = angle;
                axes2.XAngle = angle;
                sphere.AddSphere(axes1);
                sphere.AddSphere(axes2);
                angle += delta;
                if (angle >= 360)
                    angle = 0;
            }

            private void Stop_Click(object sender, RoutedEventArgs e)
            {
                timer.Stop();
                AddSphere();
            }
        }
    }
```

In this class, you create two spheres with different Coordinate objects, axes1 and axes2. The axes1 has an Xoffset = -100, and axes2 has an Xoffset = 100. In this way, the two spheres have a 200-pixel separation between their center positions.

Inside the Start_Click event handler, you set axes2's YAngle property to zero and its ZAngle property to 20 degrees to get a better view of the second sphere when it is being animated.

For the first sphere, you animate its YAngle property to specify rotation around the Y axis. For the second sphere, you animate its XAngle property.

A screen shot from running this project is shown in Figure 10-8. You can click the Start or Stop button to control the animation.

Creating a Cylinder

In this section, I'll show you how to create cylinder objects in Silverlight. Here, we'll create a cylinder that allows you to specify its radius and height.

As you probably know, in a cylindrical coordinate system, a point is specified by three parameters, r, θ, and y, which are a bit different from the conventional definition of the system using r, θ, and z. The notation we use here is only for convenience because the computer screen can always be described using the X-Y plane. Here, r is the distance of a projected point on the X-Z plane from the origin, and θ is the azimuthal angle.

Figure 10-9 shows a point in the cylindrical coordinate system. From this figure you have:

$$x = r\cos\theta$$

$$z = -r\sin\theta$$

$$y = y$$

By using the cylindrical coordinate system, you can easily create cylindrical objects in Silverlight.

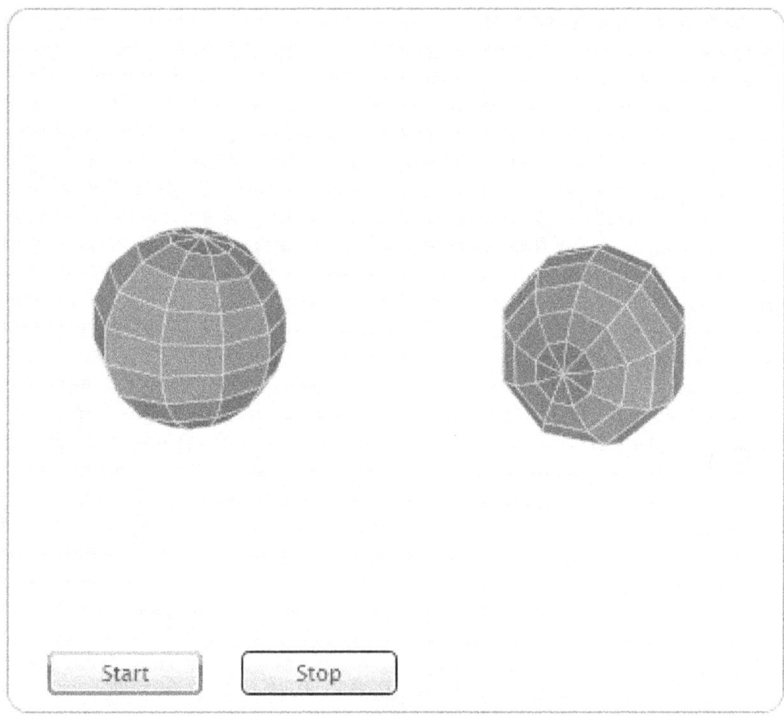

Figure 10-8 Animating spheres in Silverlight.

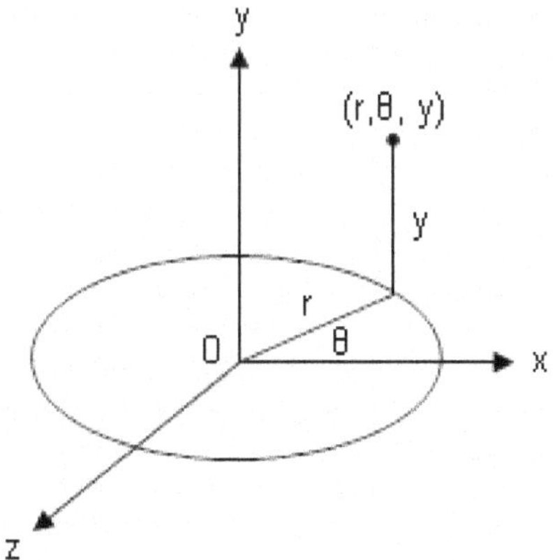

Figure 10-9 Cylindrical coordinate system.

Cylinder Class

In order to create a cylinder in Silverlight using the above relationships, we first need to make slices on the surface of the cylinder. As shown in Figure 10-10, the cylinder surface is divided into n slices, and a unit cell is formed by the i-th and i+1-th slice lines. You can see that each unit contains six vertices and three surfaces, which need to be meshed. Furthermore, the outer surface can be represented using a rectangular mesh, while both the top and bottom surface can be represented by triangular meshes.

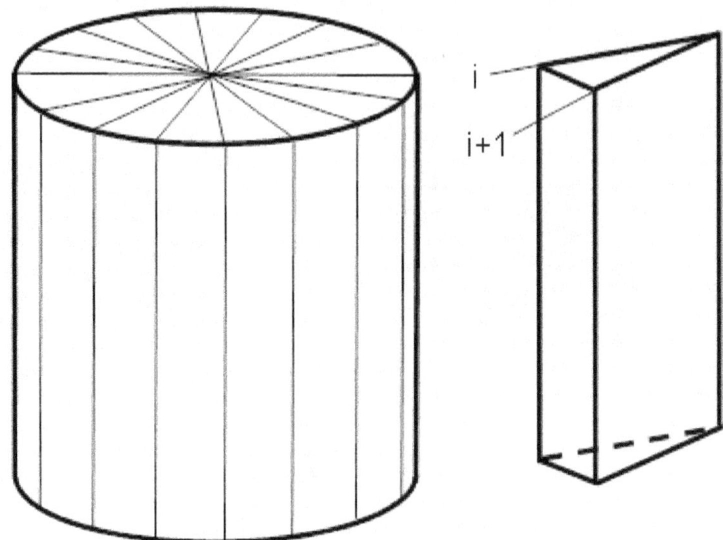

Figure 10-10 A cylinder and a unit cell.

With this background information, now it is time to consider an example in which we create cylinder objects in Silverlight. Start with a new Silverlight project and name it Example10-5. Add the XuMath3D class from the previous example to the current project. Add a new Cylinder class to the XuMath3D.cs file. Here is the code listing of this class:

```
#region Create a cylinder object:
public class Cylinder
{
    private double radius = 50;
    private double height = 100;
    private Point3 center = new Point3(0, 0, 0, 1);
    private int nDiv = 15;

    public Cylinder()
    {
    }

    public double Radius
    {
        get { return radius; }
        set { radius = value; }
    }

    public double Height
    {
        get { return height; }
        set { height = value; }
```

```
}

public Point3 Center
{
    get { return center; }
    set { center = value; }
}

public int NDiv
{
    get { return nDiv; }
    set { nDiv = value; }
}

private Point3 GetPosition(double r, double theta, double y)
{
    Point3 pt = new Point3();
    double sn = Math.Sin(theta * Math.PI / 180);
    double cn = Math.Cos(theta * Math.PI / 180);

    pt.X = r * cn + center.X;
    pt.Y = -y + center.Y;
    pt.Z = -r * sn + center.Z;
    pt.W = 1;
    return pt;
}

public void AddCylinder(Coordinates3D axes)
{
    double h = height / 2;
    Point3[,] pts = new Point3[nDiv, 4];

    for (int i = 0; i < nDiv; i++)
    {
        pts[i, 0] = axes.Point3Transform(
                         GetPosition(radius, i * 360 / (nDiv - 1), h));
        pts[i, 1] = axes.Point3Transform(
                         GetPosition(radius, i * 360 / (nDiv - 1), -h));
        pts[i, 2] = axes.Point3Transform(
                         GetPosition(0, i * 360 / (nDiv - 1), -h));
        pts[i, 3] = axes.Point3Transform(
                         GetPosition(0, i * 360 / (nDiv - 1), h));
    }

    Vector3 normal = new Vector3();
    Vector3 viewDirection =
          new Vector3(new double[3] { 0, 0, -axes.CameraPosition });

    for (int i = 0; i < nDiv - 1; i++)
    {
        // Top surface:
        Point3 pt1 = pts[i, 0];
        Point3 pt2 = pts[i + 1, 0];
        Point3 pt3 = pts[i + 1, 3];
        normal = Vector3.NormalVector(pt1, pt2, pt3);
```

```
            double dotProduct = Vector3.DotProduct(normal, viewDirection);
            Point offset = new Point(axes.DrawCanvas.Width / 2 +
                  axes.XOffset, axes.DrawCanvas.Height / 2 + axes.YOffset);
            if (dotProduct > 0)
            {
                AddPolygon(axes, dotProduct,
                           new Point(pt1.X + offset.X, pt1.Y + offset.Y),
                           new Point(pt2.X + offset.X, pt2.Y + offset.Y),
                           new Point(pt3.X + offset.X, pt3.Y + offset.Y),
                           new Point(pt3.X + offset.X, pt3.Y + offset.Y));
            }

            // Bottom surface:
            pt1 = pts[i + 1, 1];
            pt2 = pts[i, 1];
            pt3 = pts[i, 2];
            normal = Vector3.NormalVector(pt1, pt2, pt3);
            dotProduct = Vector3.DotProduct(normal, viewDirection);

            if (dotProduct > 0)
            {
                AddPolygon(axes, dotProduct,
                           new Point(pt1.X + offset.X, pt1.Y + offset.Y),
                           new Point(pt2.X + offset.X, pt2.Y + offset.Y),
                           new Point(pt3.X + offset.X, pt3.Y + offset.Y),
                           new Point(pt3.X + offset.X, pt3.Y + offset.Y));
            }

            // Outer surface:
            pt1 = pts[i, 0];
            pt2 = pts[i, 1];
            pt3 = pts[i + 1, 1];
            Point3 pt4 = pts[i + 1, 0];
            normal = Vector3.NormalVector(pt1, pt2, pt3);
            dotProduct = Vector3.DotProduct(normal, viewDirection);

            if (dotProduct > 0)
            {
                AddPolygon(axes, dotProduct,
                           new Point(pt1.X + offset.X, pt1.Y + offset.Y),
                           new Point(pt2.X + offset.X, pt2.Y + offset.Y),
                           new Point(pt3.X + offset.X, pt3.Y + offset.Y),
                           new Point(pt4.X + offset.X, pt4.Y + offset.Y));
            }
        }
    }

    private void AddPolygon(Coordinates3D axes, double dotProduct,
                            Point pt1, Point pt2, Point pt3, Point pt4)
    {
        double shade = dotProduct;
        shade /= 1024;
        int color = (int)shade;
        color += 128;
        if (color >= 255)
```

```
            {
                color = 255;
            }
            if (color < 0)
            {
                color = 0;
            }

            byte red = (byte)(color);
            byte green = (byte)(color >> 2);
            byte blue = (byte)(color >> 3);

            Polygon polygon = new Polygon();
            if (pt3 != pt4)
            {
                polygon.Points.Add(pt1);
                polygon.Points.Add(pt2);
                polygon.Points.Add(pt3);
                polygon.Points.Add(pt4);
            }
            else if (pt3 == pt4)
            {
                polygon.Points.Add(pt1);
                polygon.Points.Add(pt2);
                polygon.Points.Add(pt3);
            }

            polygon.Fill =
                new SolidColorBrush(Color.FromArgb(255, red, green, blue));
            polygon.Stroke =
                new SolidColorBrush(Color.FromArgb(255, 200, 200, 200));
            polygon.StrokeThickness = 0.5;
            axes.DrawCanvas.Children.Add(polygon);
        }
    }
#endregion
```

In this class, we first define several field members and their corresponding public properties:

- Radius property – sets the radius of the cylinder.
- Height property – sets the height of the cylinder.
- Center property – sets the center position of the cylinder.
- NDiv property – sets the number of slices used to mesh the cylinder surface.

The GetPosition method creates a point on the cylinder surface using the cylindrical coordinates. Inside the AddCylinder method, we construct six vertices for a unit cell (see Figure 10-10), then perform the mesh process for the three surfaces of this unit cell, including the top, bottom, and outer surfaces. The meshes for these surfaces are generated separately by calling the private AddPolygon method in this class.

Inside the AddPolygon method, you first create a simple shading effect using the dot product between the surface normal and the viewing direction. You can create your own custom shading effect here if you like. This shading effect will be used to set the Fill property of the polygon. Here we also specify the Stroke property of the polygon.

Creating Multiple Cylinders

You can easily create any number of cylinder objects using the Cylinder class. You can test the Cyinder class in the Example10-6 project. The XAML code is similar to that used in Example10-2. The code-behind file is listed below:

```
using System;
using System.Windows;
using System.Windows.Controls;
using System.Windows.Media;
using System.Windows.Shapes;
using XuMath3D;


namespace Example10_6
{
    public partial class Page : UserControl
    {
        Coordinates3D axes;

        public Page()
        {
            InitializeComponent();
            AddCylinder();
        }

        private void AddCylinder()
        {
            axes = new Coordinates3D();
            axes.DrawCanvas = canvas1;
            axes.CameraPosition = 500;
            Cylinder cylinder = new Cylinder();
            cylinder.NDiv = 30;
            cylinder.Center = new Point3(0, 0, -250, 1);
            cylinder.AddCylinder(axes);
            cylinder.Center = new Point3(0, 0, -100, 1);
            cylinder.AddCylinder(axes);
            cylinder.Center = new Point3(0, 0, 50, 1);
            cylinder.AddCylinder(axes);
        }
    }
}
```

Here you create three cylinders with the same physical dimensions but at different locations. The camera position is set to 500 units, which should create a perspective shortening effect.

Figure 10-11 shows the results of running this application.

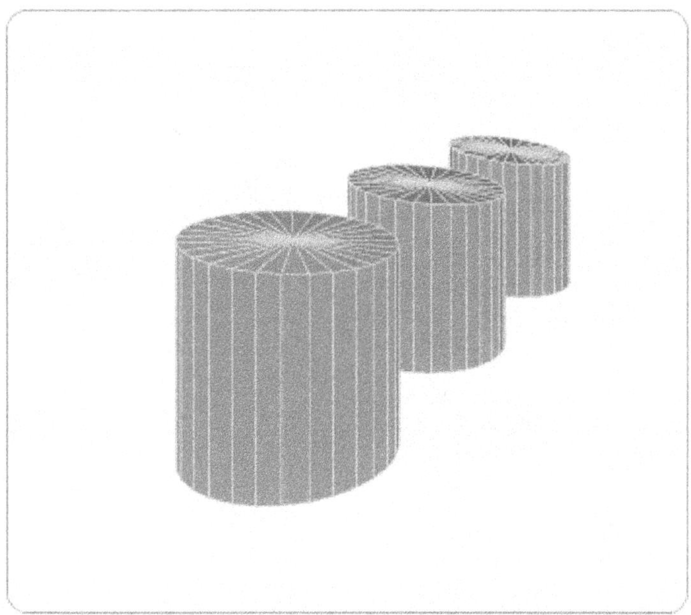

Figure 10-11 Cylinders created in Silverlight.

Animating Cylinders

In the previous section, we demonstrated how to create multiple cylinders using the Cylinder class. You can also use this class to create cylinder objects and perform animations on them using the timer-based animation approach discussed in Chapter 6, as we previously did when we animated the cube and sphere objects in this chapter.

Start with a new Silverlight project and name it Example10-7. Add the XuMath3D class from the previous example to the project. The XAML code of this example is exactly the same as that in the Example10-3 project. The code-behind file is listed below:

```
using System;
using System.Windows;
using System.Windows.Threading;
using System.Windows.Controls;
using System.Windows.Media;
using System.Windows.Shapes;
using XuMath3D;

namespace Example10_7
{
    public partial class Page : UserControl
    {
        Coordinates3D axes1;
        Coordinates3D axes2;
        Cylinder cylinder;
        DispatcherTimer timer;
        double angle = 0;
        double delta = 2;
```

```
public Page()
{
    InitializeComponent();
    AddCylinder();
}

private void AddCylinder()
{
    canvas1.Children.Clear();
    axes1 = new Coordinates3D();
    axes1.DrawCanvas = canvas1;
    axes1.XOffset = -100;

    axes2 = new Coordinates3D();
    axes2.DrawCanvas = canvas1;
    axes2.XOffset = 100;

    cylinder = new Cylinder();
    cylinder.Radius = 50;
    cylinder.NDiv = 10;
    cylinder.AddCylinder(axes1);
    cylinder.AddCylinder(axes2);
}

private void Start_Click(object sender, RoutedEventArgs e)
{
    timer = new DispatcherTimer();
    timer.Interval = TimeSpan.FromMilliseconds(10);
    axes1 = new Coordinates3D();
    axes1.DrawCanvas = canvas1;
    axes1.XOffset = -100;

    axes2 = new Coordinates3D();
    axes2.DrawCanvas = canvas1;
    axes2.XOffset = 100;
    axes2.YAngle = 0;
    axes2.ZAngle = 20;

    angle = 0;
    timer.Tick += new EventHandler(timer_Tick);
    timer.Start();
}

void timer_Tick(object sender, EventArgs e)
{
    canvas1.Children.Clear();
    axes1.YAngle = angle;
    axes2.XAngle = angle;
    cylinder.AddCylinder(axes1);
    cylinder.AddCylinder(axes2);
    angle += delta;
    if (angle >= 360)
        angle = 0;
}
```

```
            private void Stop_Click(object sender, RoutedEventArgs e)
            {
                timer.Stop();
                AddCylinder();
            }
        }
    }
```

In this class, you create two cylinders with different Coordinate objects, axes1 and axes2. The axes1 has an Xoffset = -100 and axes2 has an Xoffset = 100. In this way, the two cylinders have a 200-pixel separation between their center positions.

Inside the Start_Click event handler, you set axes2's YAngle property to zero and its ZAngle property to 20 degrees to get a better view of the second cylinder when it is being animated.

For the first cylinder, you animate its YAngle property to specify a rotation around the Y axis. For the second one, you animate its XAngle property.

A screen shot from running this project is shown in Figure 10-12. You can click the Start or Stop button to control the animation.

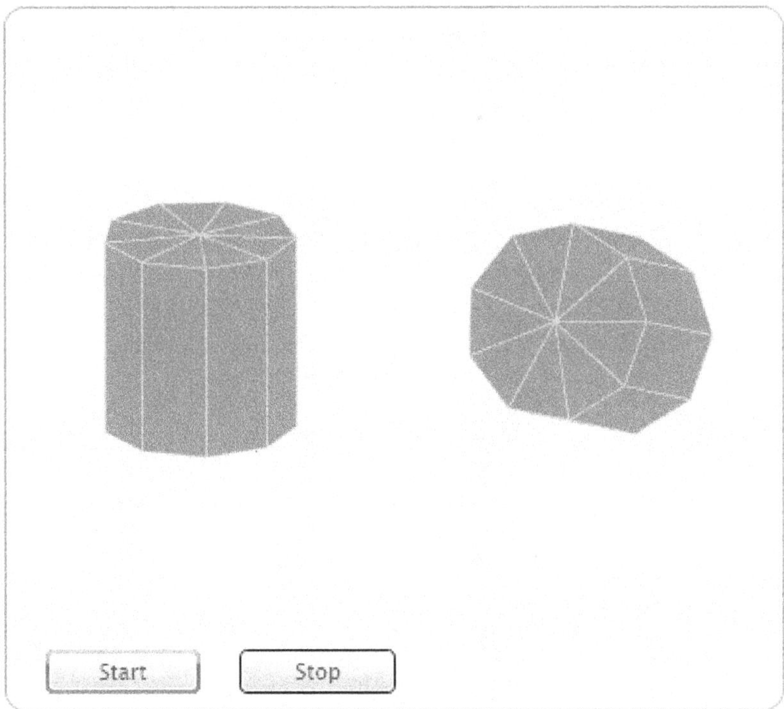

Figure 10-12 Animating cylinders in Silverlight.

Creating 3D Surfaces

This section will show you how to create 3D surfaces in Silverlight. Surfaces play an important role in various applications such as computer graphics, virtual reality, computer games, and 3D data visualizations. The section begins by describing data structures and the algorithms used to manipulate and display simple surfaces. Using this technique, you can create a variety of simple surfaces, including surfaces containing random data.

Mathematically, a surface draws a Z function on a surface for each X and Y coordinate in a region of interest. For each X and Y value, a simple surface can have at most one Z value. Complex surfaces can have multiple Z values for each pair of X and Y values, and are out of the scope of this book. If you are interested in creating complex surfaces, you can read my other book, *Practical WPF Graphics Programming*, where you can find a detailed procedure for creating a variety of complex surfaces.

The coordinate system in here is oriented so that the Y axis is viewed in the "up" direction. Thus, we'll consider surfaces defined by functions that return a Y value (instead of a Z value) for each X and Z coordinate in a region of interest. To translate a function from a system that gives Z as a function of X and Y, simply reverse the roles of the Y and Z axis.

You can define a simple surface by the Y-coordinates of points above a rectangular grid in the X-Z plane. The surface is formed by joining adjacent points using straight lines. Simple surfaces are useful for visualizing 2D data arrays (matrices) that are too large to display in numerical form, and for graphing functions of two variables.

Surface Class

The simplest way to store surface data is to use a 2D array. For each point (X, Z) in the region defined for the surface, the (X, Z) entry in the array gives the Y coordinate of the corresponding point on the surface.

Creating simple surfaces is easy. Let's start with a new Silverlight project and name it Example10-8. Add the class, XuMath3D, from the previous example to the current project. Add a new class called Surface to the XuMath3D.cs file. Here is the code listing of this class:

```
#region Create a 3D simple surface:
public class Surface
{
    public delegate Point3 Function(double x, double z);

    private double xmin = -3;
    private double xmax = 3;
    private double ymin = -8;
    private double ymax = 8;
    private double zmin = -3;
    private double zmax = 3;
    private int nx = 30;
    private int nz = 30;
    private Color lineColor = Colors.Black;
    private Color fillColor = Colors.White;
    private Point3 center = new Point3();
    private bool isHiddenLine = false;

    public bool IsHiddenLine
```

```
{
    get { return isHiddenLine; }
    set { isHiddenLine = value; }
}

public Color LineColor
{
    get { return lineColor; }
    set { lineColor = value; }
}

public Color FillColor
{
    get { return fillColor; }
    set { fillColor = value; }
}

public double Xmin
{
    get { return xmin; }
    set { xmin = value; }
}

public double Xmax
{
    get { return xmax; }
    set { xmax = value; }
}

public double Ymin
{
    get { return ymin; }
    set { ymin = value; }
}

public double Ymax
{
    get { return ymax; }
    set { ymax = value; }
}

public double Zmin
{
    get { return zmin; }
    set { zmin = value; }
}

public double Zmax
{
    get { return zmax; }
    set { zmax = value; }
}

public int Nx
{
```

```
        get { return nx; }
        set { nx = value; }
    }

    public int Nz
    {
        get { return nz; }
        set { nz = value; }
    }

    public Point3 Center
    {
        get { return center; }
        set { center = value; }
    }

    public void AddSurface(Coordinates3D axes, Function f)
    {
        double dx = (Xmax - Xmin) / Nx;
        double dz = (Zmax - Zmin) / Nz;
        if (Nx < 2 || Nz < 2)
            return;

        Point3[,] pts = new Point3[Nx, Nz];
        for (int i = 0; i < Nx; i++)
        {
            double x = Xmin + i * dx;
            for (int j = 0; j < Nz; j++)
            {
                double z = Zmin + j * dz;
                pts[i, j] = f(x, z);
                pts[i, j] = new Point3(pts[i, j].X + center.X,
                                       pts[i, j].Y + center.Y,
                                       pts[i, j].Z + center.Z, 1);
                pts[i, j] = GetNormalize(pts[i, j], axes, Xmin, Xmax,
                                         Ymin, Ymax, Zmin, Zmax);
            }
        }

        Point3[] p = new Point3[4];
        for (int i = 0; i < Nx - 1; i++)
        {
            for (int j = 0; j < Nz - 1; j++)
            {
                p[0] = pts[i, j];
                p[1] = pts[i, j + 1];
                p[2] = pts[i + 1, j + 1];
                p[3] = pts[i + 1, j];
                PointCollection collection =
                                axes.CreatePoints(p[0], p[1], p[2], p[3]);

                Polygon polygon = new Polygon();
                polygon.Stroke = new SolidColorBrush(lineColor);
                polygon.Fill = new SolidColorBrush(Colors.Transparent);
                polygon.Points = collection;
```

```
                //Create polygon face:
                if (IsHiddenLine == false)
                {
                    polygon.Fill = new SolidColorBrush(fillColor);
                }
                axes.DrawCanvas.Children.Add(polygon);
            }
        }
    }

    private Point3 GetNormalize(Point3 pt, Coordinates3D axes, double xmin,
            double xmax, double ymin, double ymax, double zmin, double zmax)
    {
        double xlength = 0.7 * axes.DrawCanvas.Width;
        double ylength = 0.7 * axes.DrawCanvas.Height;
        pt.X = -xlength + xlength * (pt.X - xmin) / (xmax - xmin);
        pt.Y = ylength - ylength * (pt.Y - ymin) / (ymax - ymin);
        pt.Z = -xlength + xlength * (pt.Z - zmin) / (zmax - zmin);
        pt.W = 1;
        return pt;
    }
}
#endregion
```

First, you define a public delegate function that allows users to import their own functions or data, which will be used to draw the surface. Then, you define several fields and their corresponding public properties. The Nx and Nz properties define the 2D data grid in the X-Z plane. The bool property, IsHiddenLine, is used to control whether the hidden lines appear on your surface. The default value is false for IsHiddenLine (without hidden lines). The axis limit parameters let you specify the X, Y, and Z value regions of your surface function in the real-world coordinate system.

Inside the AddSurface method, you first populate a 2D point array with the delegate function f(x, z) on the 2D data grid, then normalize the data of this array into a proper region in the drawing canvas by calling the GetNormalize method. Next, you define a rectangular mesh using four adjacent vertex points, then convert these vertex points into a 2D PointCollection object by calling the CreatePoints method in the Coordinates3D class. Next, you specify the Points property of the polygon using this PointCollection object and create the polygon in the drawing canvas. The entire surface will be created when you run over all the grid points.

Creating Simple Surfaces

Here, I'll show you how to create some simple surfaces using the Surface class presented in the previous section. Here is the XAML code of this example:

```
<UserControl x:Class="Example10_8.Page"
    xmlns="http://schemas.microsoft.com/client/2007"
    xmlns:x="http://schemas.microsoft.com/winfx/2006/xaml"
    Width="372" Height="322">
    <Grid x:Name="LayoutRoot" Background="White">
        <Border BorderBrush="Gray" BorderThickness="1"
                CornerRadius="10" Margin="10">
            <Canvas x:Name="canvas1" Width="350" Height="300"
                    Background="Transparent">
```

```
                <Canvas.Clip>
                    <RectangleGeometry Rect="0 0 350 300"/>
                </Canvas.Clip>
            </Canvas>
        </Border>
    </Grid>
</UserControl>
```

A simple surface is created in the code-behind file:

```
using System;
using System.Windows;
using System.Windows.Controls;
using System.Windows.Media;
using System.Windows.Shapes;
using XuMath3D;

namespace Example10_8
{
    public partial class Page : UserControl
    {
        private Coordinates3D axes;
        private Surface surface;
        public Page()
        {
            InitializeComponent();
            AddSinc();
        }

        private void AddSinc()
        {
            axes = new Coordinates3D();
            axes.DrawCanvas = canvas1;
            axes.YAngle = 45;
            surface = new Surface();
            surface.IsHiddenLine = true;
            surface.Xmin = -8;
            surface.Xmax = 8;
            surface.Zmin = -8;
            surface.Zmax = 8;
            surface.Ymin = -1;
            surface.Ymax = 1;
            surface.AddSurface(axes, Sinc);
        }

        private Point3 Sinc(double x, double z)
        {
            double r = Math.Sqrt(x * x + z * z) + 0.00001;
            double y = Math.Sin(r) / r;
            return new Point3(x, y, z, 1);
        }

    }
}
```

Here, you first create a Coordinates3D and a Surface instance, axes and surface, and then specify the properties of the axes and surface. Next, you define a Sinc function, which is called directly by the AddSurface method in the Surface class. Inside the AddSinc method, you also specify the data range of interest.

Figure 10-13 shows the results of running this application. Here, two surfaces, one with hidden lines and the other without hidden lines, are created by specifying a different IsHiddenLine property.

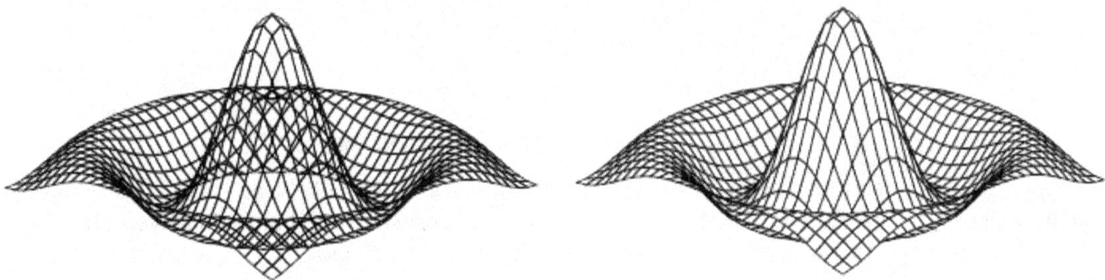

Figure 10-13 Simple surfaces with (left) and without (right) hidden lines.

You can also easily create a variety of surfaces using other functions or data from data files. For example, you can create a peak surface using the following Peaks function:

```
private void AddPeaks()
{
    canvas1.Children.Clear();
    axes = new Coordinates3D();
    axes.DrawCanvas = canvas1;
    axes.YAngle = 45;
    surface = new Surface();
    surface.Nx = 20;
    surface.Nz = 20;
    surface.Xmin = -3;
    surface.Xmax = 3;
    surface.Zmin = -3;
    surface.Zmax = 3;
    surface.Ymin = -8;
    surface.Ymax = 8;
    surface.AddSurface(axes, Peaks);
}

private Point3 Peaks(double x, double z)
{
    double y = 3 * Math.Pow((1 - x), 2) *
        Math.Exp(-x * x - (z + 1) * (z + 1)) -
        10 * (0.2 * x - Math.Pow(x, 3) -
        Math.Pow(z, 5)) * Math.Exp(-x * x - z * z) -
        1 / 3 * Math.Exp(-(x + 1) * (x + 1) - z * z);
    return new Point3(x, y, z, 1);
}
```

This function produces the surface shown in Figure 10-14.

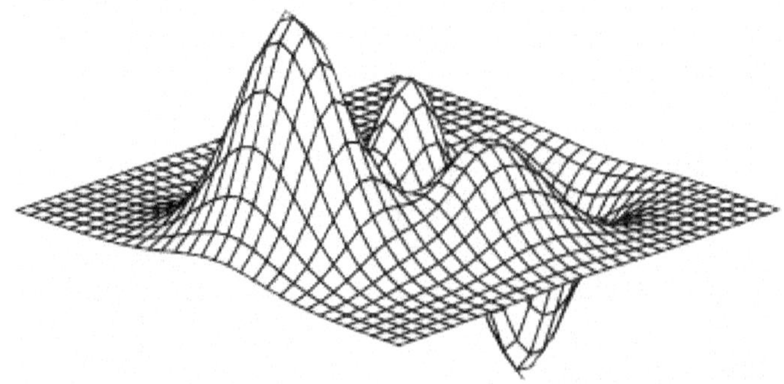

Figure 10-14 Peak surface in Silverlight.

In this chapter, you learned how to create various 3D shapes in Silverlight. You can add more custom shape classes to the XuMath3D.cs file to build your own custom 3D shape library in Silverlight. If you want to learn more about 3D models, you can read my other book, *Practical WPF Graphics Programming*.

The surfaces presented here still lack many of the useful features found in professional surface plots, such as colormaps with the Y data values, 3D axis labels, tick marks, color bars, etc. If you are interested in creating professional 3D surface charts, you can read my other book, *Practical C# Charts and Graphics*.

Chapter 11
Silverlight Built-in Controls

Silverlight 2 implements over 30 basic built-in controls that you can use in developing your Silverlight applications. In this chapter, you'll take a quick tour of the basic Silverlight built-in controls, including the layout controls such as Grid, StackPanel, and Canvas, and the most commonly-used controls in Web applications, such as TextBlock, TextBox, and Button. Although Web developers have been using these controls for years, this chapter provides some details about how to implement them in Silverlight applications.

Layout Controls

Silverlight supports a flexible layout management system that enables developers and designers to easily coordinate how controls are positioned within a UI surface. This layout system supports both a fixed position model where controls are positioned using explicit coordinates, as well as a more dynamic position model where layouts and controls can be automatically sized as the browser resizes.

In Silverlight applications, you can use layout panels to coordinate the position and resizing of the controls contained within them. Silverlight includes three of the most commonly used layout panels: Grid, StackPanel, and Canvas. In this section, you'll see how these layout panels work, and you'll begin using them in Silverlight applications.

StackPanel

The StackPanel control is one of the simplest layout panels. It supports the positioning of its children controls in either row or column layouts. It is typically used when you want to arrange a small subsection of the UI on your page.

For example, we could use the StackPanel to vertically arrange four buttons on the page using the XAML markup below:

```
<UserControl x:Class="Example11_1.Page"
   xmlns="http://schemas.microsoft.com/client/2007"
   xmlns:x="http://schemas.microsoft.com/winfx/2006/xaml"
   Width="400" Height="200">
   <Grid x:Name="LayoutRoot" Background="White">
       <StackPanel>
```

```
            <Button Content="Button 1"/>
            <Button Content="Button 2"/>
            <Button Content="Button 3"/>
            <Button Content="Button 4"/>
        </StackPanel>
    </Grid>
</UserControl>
```

This code creates the result shown in Figure 11-1.

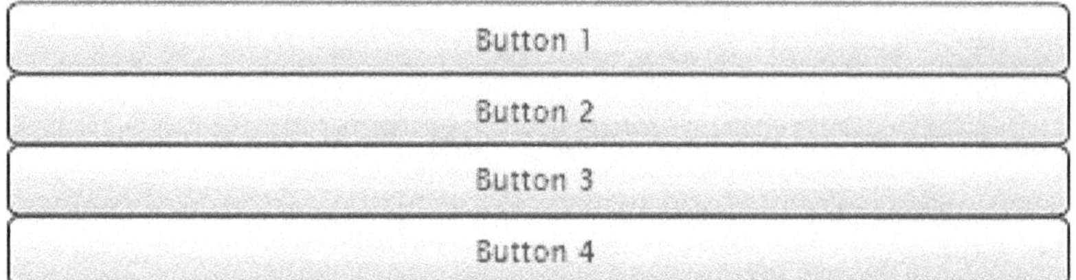

Figure 11-1 StackPanel in action.

By default, the StackPanel positions its children controls vertically, making each one as tall as is necessary to display its content. In this example, the TextBlock and buttons are sized just large enough to accommodate the text inside. All of the children controls are stretched to the full width of the StackPanel, which is the width of the page. If you increase the page's width, the StackPanel widens as well, and the buttons stretch themselves to fit.

The StackPanel can also be used to arrange elements horizontally by setting the Orientation property:

```
<StackPanel Orientation="Horizontal">
```

Now, the children controls are given the minimum width necessary to fit their text, and are stretched to the full height of the page, as shown in Figure 11-2.

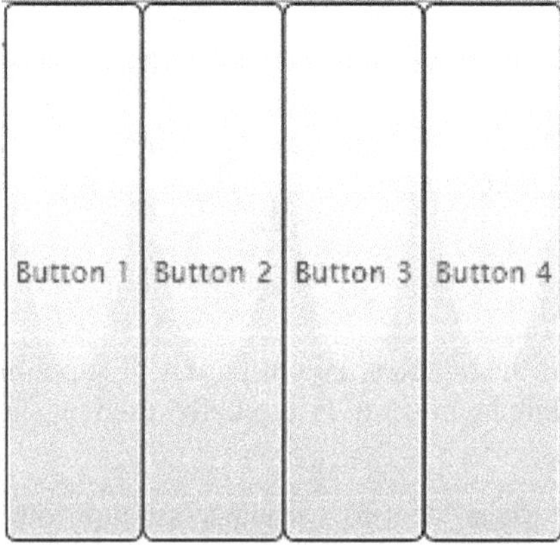

Figure 11-2 StackPanel with horizontal orientation.

Clearly, the layouts shown in Figure 11-1 or Figure 11-2 don't provide the flexibility that real applications need. Fortunately, you can fine-tune the way the StackPanel works by specifying its layout properties, such as Margin, Width, Height, etc. The margin property adds a bit space around a control and has separate components for the top, bottom, left, and right edges. The Width and Height properties explicitly set the size of a control.

Let's consider an example that shows you how to nest the StackPanel controls. Start with a new Silverlight project and name it Example11-1. Here is XAML of this example:

```
<UserControl x:Class="Example11_1.Page"
    xmlns="http://schemas.microsoft.com/client/2007"
    xmlns:x="http://schemas.microsoft.com/winfx/2006/xaml"
    Width="480" Height="180">
    <Grid x:Name="LayoutRoot" Background="White" ShowGridLines="True">
        <StackPanel Orientation="Horizontal" Margin="10">
            <StackPanel>
                <Button Content="Button 1" Width="80" Height="30" Margin="5"/>
                <Button Content="Button 2" Width="80" Height="30" Margin="5"/>
                <Button Content="Button 3" Width="80" Height="30" Margin="5"/>
                <Button Content="Button 4" Width="80" Height="30" Margin="5"/>
            </StackPanel>
            <Button Content="Button 5" Width="80" Height="30" Margin="5"/>
            <Button Content="Button 6" Width="80" Height="30" Margin="5"/>
            <Button Content="Button 7" Width="80" Height="30" Margin="5"/>
            <Button Content="Button 8" Width="80" Height="30" Margin="5"/>
        </StackPanel>
    </Grid>
</UserControl>
```

Here we nest a StackPanel with a VerticalAlignment (default) within another StackPanel with a HorizontalAlignment. The horizontally-aligned StackPanel has five direct children, a StackPanel and four Buttons, while the inner StackPanel has four Buttons as its own children elements. The size and Margin properties of all Buttons are explicitly specified.

Figure 11-3 shows the result of running this example.

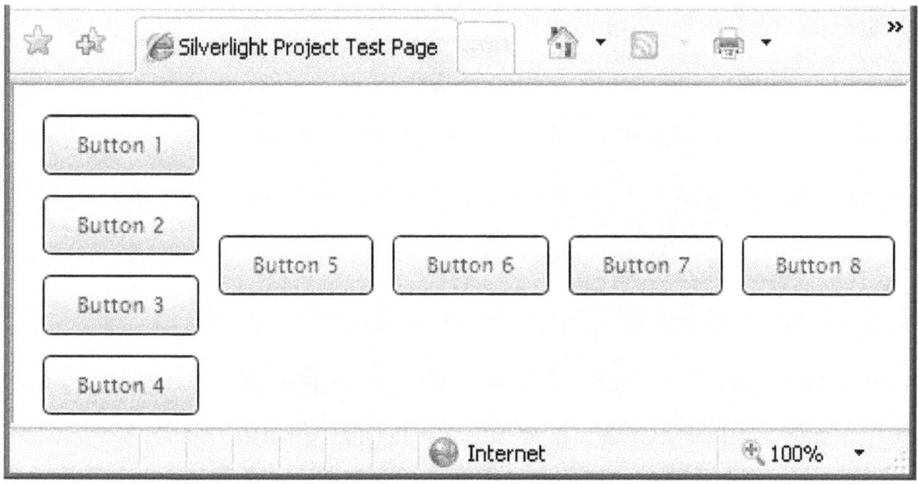

Figure 11-3 Nested StackPanel controls in Silverlight.

By default, the StackPanel automatically arranges the children elements at the center of the page. You can control this behavior by specifying the StackPanel's VerticalAlignment or HorizontalAlignment property. The HorizontalAlignment property determines how the StackPanel's children are positioned when there is extra horizontal space available. You can choose Center, Left, Right, or Stretch. Similarly, the VerticalAlignment property determines how its children are positioned inside the panel when there is extra vertical space available. You can choose Center, Top, Bottom, or Stretch.

Grid

The Grid control is the most flexible layout panel in Silverlight. Much of what you can accomplish with the other layout panels is also possible with the Grid. It is also an ideal tool for dividing your page into smaller regions that you can manage with other panels. In fact, the Grid panel is so useful that when you create a new XAML document for a page in Visual Studio 2008, it automatically adds the Grid tags as the LayoutRoot panel.

The Grid supports the arrangement of controls in multi-row and multi-column layouts. You can create a Grid layout in two steps. First, you specify the number of columns and rows in the Grid; then you assign the appropriate row and column to each contained element.

The Grid panel is conceptually similar to an HTML Table element, but unlike an HTML Table, you don't embed controls within column and row elements. Instead, you specify a Grid's Row and Column definitions using Grid.RowDefinitions and Grid.ColumnDefinitions. You can then use the XAML "Attached Property" syntax on controls contained within the grid to indicate which Grid row and column they should be populated within.

Let's consider an example that shows how to create a Grid layout that has three rows and three columns, and then place four buttons within it. Start with a new Silverlight project and name it Example11-2. Here is XAML of this example:

```
<UserControl x:Class="Example11_2.Page"
    xmlns="http://schemas.microsoft.com/client/2007"
    xmlns:x="http://schemas.microsoft.com/winfx/2006/xaml"
    Width="300" Height="200">
    <Grid x:Name="LayoutRoot" Background="White" ShowGridLines="True">
        <Grid.ColumnDefinitions>
            <ColumnDefinition/>
            <ColumnDefinition/>
            <ColumnDefinition/>
        </Grid.ColumnDefinitions>
        <Grid.RowDefinitions>
            <RowDefinition/>
            <RowDefinition/>
            <RowDefinition/>
        </Grid.RowDefinitions>
        <Button Content="Button 1" Width="80" Height="30"
                Margin="5" Grid.Column="1" Grid.Row="0"/>
        <Button Content="Button 2" Width="80" Height="30"
                Margin="5" Grid.Column="2" Grid.Row="1"/>
        <Button Content="Button 3" Width="80" Height="30"
                Margin="5" Grid.Column="0" Grid.Row="1"/>
        <Button Content="Button 4" Width="80" Height="30"
                Margin="5" Grid.Column="1" Grid.Row="2"/>
    </Grid>
```

```
</UserControl>
```

Figure 11-4 shows the results of running this application. Notice that the ShowGridLines property is set to true so that you can see the separation among cells.

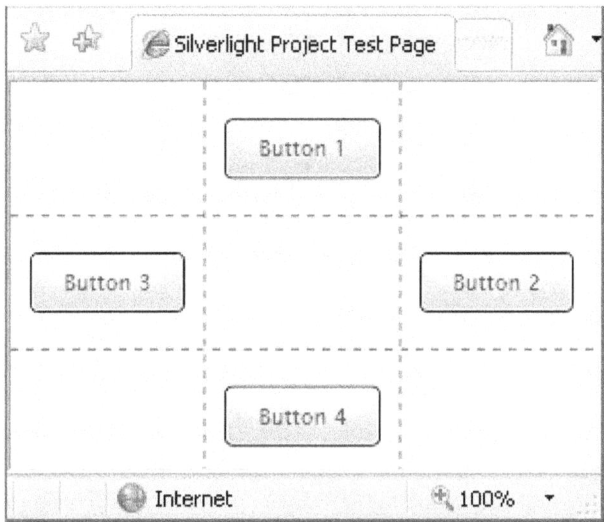

Figure 11-4 Grid layout in Silverlight.

As shown in this example, you don't need to supply any information in a RowDefinition or ColumnDefinition element. If you leave them empty as shown here, the Grid will share the available page space evently between all rows and columns. Each cell in the Grid created using the above code will be exactly the same size, depending on the size of your page.

Note that each button must be placed into its cell explicitly. You can leave certain cells blank. There exists one exception. If you don't specify the Grid.Row or GridColumn property, the Grid assumes that it is 0. Thus, you leave both attributes off of a control to place it in the first cell of the Grid.

Another point is that the Grid fits controls into predefined rows and columns. This is different than the StackPanel layout, which creates implicit rows or columns as it lays out its children elements. If you want to create a Grid with more than one row and column, you must define the rows and columns explicitly using RowDefinition and ColumnDefinition objects.

In addition to supporting automatic stretching according to the available page space, the Grid's RowDefinition and ColumnDefinition controls also support absolute sizing. For Example:

```
<ColumnDefinition Width="100"/>
<RowDefinition Heoght="50"/>
```

In this case, the column has a fixed width of 100 units and the row has a fixed height of 50 units.

The Grid's RowDefinition and ColumnDefinition elements also support an AutoSizing mode:

```
<ColumnDefinition Width="Auto"/>
<RowDefinition Heoght="Auto"/>
```

which automatically size the Column or Row based on the size of the content contained within it.

The Grid's Row and ColumnDefinitions also support a feature called "Proportional Sizing". This feature enables the size of a Grid's Rows and Columns to be spaced proportionally relative to each other. For example, you could have the second row grow at 2x the rate of the first one.

You'll find that the Grid provides much more flexibility. It will probably be the most common layout panel control you'll use in developing your Silverlight applications.

Canvas

The Canvas panel is a basic layout panel that supports positioning controls contained within it using explicit coordinates. It is a very useful layout tool when you need a drawing surface, such as for charting, interactive drawings, and CAD-like applications. Since the Canvas doesn't include any complex layout logic to optimize the sizing preference of its children elements, it is also the most lightweight of the layout panels.

You position elements in a Canvas by specifying the attached properties, which allow you to specify a control's position relative to its immediate parent Canvas control's Left and Top coordinates. Canvas.Left sets the number of units between the left edge of your control and the left edge of the Canvas. Canvas.Top sets the number of units between the top of your control and the top of the Canvas.

You can size the elements that are added to the Canvas panel explicitly using their Width and Height properties. This is more common when using the Canvas than it is with other panels because the Canvas has no layout logic of its own. If you don't set the Width and Height properties, the element on the Canvas will reach its desired size – in other words, it will grow just large enough to fit its content.

Here, I'll use an example to demonstrate how to place Buttons on the Canvas. Start with a new Silverlight project and name it Example11-3. This example uses the following XAML:

```
<UserControl x:Class="Example11_3.Page"
    xmlns="http://schemas.microsoft.com/client/2007"
    xmlns:x="http://schemas.microsoft.com/winfx/2006/xaml">
    <Grid x:Name="LayoutRoot" Background="White">
        <Canvas Background="LightBlue">
            <Button Canvas.Left="50" Canvas.Top="20"
                    Content="Button 1, (50, 20)"/>
            <Button Canvas.Left="200" Canvas.Top="40"
                    Content="Button 2, (200, 40)"/>
            <Button Canvas.Left="60" Canvas.Top="60" Canvas.ZIndex="1"
                    Height="100" Content="Button 3, (60, 60)"/>
            <Button Canvas.Left="120" Canvas.Top="120"
                    Height="100" Content="Button 4, (120, 130)"/>
            <Button Canvas.Left="180" Canvas.Top="180"
                    Height="100" Content="Button 5, (180, 180)"/>
        </Canvas>
    </Grid>
</UserControl>
```

This application generates the result shown in Figure 11-5.

Here we add five Buttons to the Canvas by explicitly specifying their coordidnates with the attached properties Canvas.Left and Canvas.Top. We also set the Height property to 100 units for the last three Buttons.

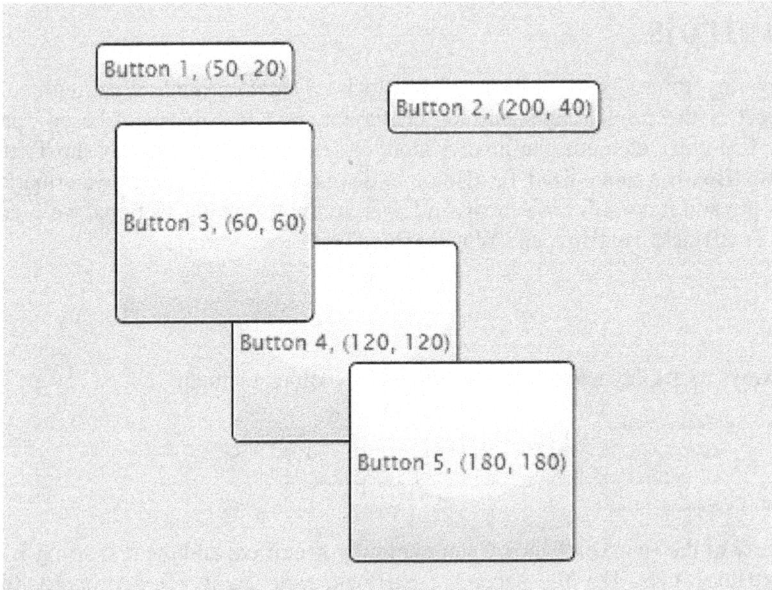

Figure 11-5 Explicitly positioned Buttons in a Canvas.

One thing you might have noticed in this example is that we don't explicitly set the size for the top-level control. This causes it to behave differently when you resize the page. If you set fixed Width and Height properties for the top-level control, your Silverlight application will always remain that fixed size. Expand the broswer when you are viewing a Silverlight application with a fixed size and this becomes apparent. If you remove the Width and Height attributes on the root control as you do in this example, your Silverlight application will then automatically expand or shrink to fill the page.

Note that even though the Canvas stretches to fill the available space when you resize the broswer, none of the Buttons on the Canvas move or change size. They are fixed relative to the origin of their parent Canvas.

If you have overlapping elements, you can set the attached Canvas.ZIndex property to control how they are layered. By default, all the elements you add to the Canvas have the same ZIndex = 0. When elements have the same ZIndex, they are displayed on your screen in the same order as they exist in Canvas.Children collection, which is based on the order that they are defined in XAML. Elements declared later in XAML, such as Button 5, are displayed on top of elements that are declared earlier, such as Button 4.

However, you can promote any element to a higher level by increasing its ZIndex. That is because higher ZIndex elements always appear over lower ZIndex elements, such as Button 3, whose ZIndex is set to 1 so that it is layered on the top of Button4.

The actual value you use for the ZIndex property has no meaning. What is important is how the ZIndex value of one element compares to the ZIndex value of another. You can set the ZIndex using any positive or negative integer.

Text Controls

Silverlight includes three Text controls: TextBlock, TextBox, and WatermarkedTextBox. The TextBlock object is the primary element for displaying text in Silverlight-based applications. The TextBox is the text-entry element that always stores a text string provided by the Text property. The WatermarkedTextBox is a specialized TextBox that displays a customizable "watermark" whenever its contents are empty and it doesn't have the main focus. In the following sections, we'll consider the key features of the TextBlock, TextBox, and WatermarkedTextBox controls.

TextBlock

There are two ways to display a text string using the TextBlock element:

```
<StackPanel>
    <TextBlock>Hello, Silverlight!</TextBlock>
    <TextBlock Text="Hello, Silverlight!"/>
</StackPanel>
```

The Text property of the first TextBlock is not explicitly specified, and the text string is directly placed inside the TextBlock tags. For the second TextBlock, you set its Text property to a text string explicitly. Both TextBlocks display the same result on your screen.

There are several font-related properties you can specify when you define a TextBlock object:

- FontFamily – represents a set of typefaces that share the same family name, such as "Arial".
- FontSize – Specifies a positive value as the desired font size in pixels. The default value is 14.666 pixels, which is exactly 11 points.
- FontStyle – specifies whether the font style is normal or italic.
- FontWeight – Describes the relative weight of a font, in terms of the lightness or heaviness of the strokes.

Currently, Silverlight supports only nine types of fonts for text elements, including Arial, Arial Black, Comic Sans MS, Courier New, Georgia, Lucida Sans Unicode, Times New Roman, Trebuchet MS, and Verdana. If you need additional fonts, you can use the SetFontSource method to add downloaded font content to the existing collection of the fonts for a TextBlock object.

Another useful property of the TextBlock is the TextWrapping property, which indicates how text should wrap in a TextBlock. The TextWrapping enumeration defines two values, NoWrap and Wrap. NoWrap means no line wrapping is performed. Wrap means that line breaking will occur if the line overflows beyond the available block width.

The TextBlock also allows you to use Run and LineBreak objects. The Run object is a text element that represents a discrete section of text. The LineBreak object represents an explicit new line in a TextBlock.

Let's start with a new Silverlight project and name it Example11-4. From this example, you'll learn how to specify a variety of attributes for TextBlock elements. The output of this example is shown in Figure 11-6.

Different Fonts:

Text Font - Arial

Text Font - Arial Black

Text Font - Comic Sans MS

Text Font - Courier New

Text Font - Georgia

Text Font – Lucida Sans Unicode

Text Font - Times New Roman

Text Font - Trebuchet MS

Text Font - Verdana

Test Run and LineBreak Objects:

This is Arial with default fontsize

Courier New: 24

Times New Roman Italic: 18

Verdana Bold 14

Test TextWrapping:

Without text wrapping: Avery Johnson was

With text wrapping: Avery Johnson was dismissed as coach of the Dallas Mavericks the day after a disappointing season.

Figure 11-6 TextBlocks with various attributes.

The results of this example can be generated using the XAML below:

```
<UserControl x:Class="Example11_4.Page"
    xmlns="http://schemas.microsoft.com/client/2007"
    xmlns:x="http://schemas.microsoft.com/winfx/2006/xaml"
    Width="400" Height="600">
    <Grid x:Name="LayoutRoot" Background="White">
        <StackPanel Margin="10">
            <TextBlock Text="Different Fonts:" FontFamily="Verdana"
                       FontSize="20" FontStyle="Italic"
                       FontWeight="ExtraBlack" Foreground="Red"
```

```
             Margin="0,5,2,2"/>
 <TextBlock Text="Text Font - Arial" FontFamily="Arial"
            FontSize="20" Foreground="DarkBlue" Margin="20,2,2,2"/>
 <TextBlock Text="Text Font - Arial Black" FontFamily="Arial Black"
            FontSize="20" Foreground="DarkBlue" Margin="20,2,2,2"/>
 <TextBlock Text="Text Font - Comic Sans MS"
            FontFamily="Comic Sans MS" FontSize="20"
            Foreground="Brown" Margin="20,2,2,2"/>
 <TextBlock Text="Text Font - Courier New" FontFamily="Courier New"
            FontSize="20" Foreground="DarkGreen" Margin="20,2,2,2"/>
 <TextBlock Text="Text Font - Georgia" FontFamily="Georgia"
            FontSize="20" Foreground="#FF008888" Margin="20,2,2,2"/>
 <TextBlock Text="Text Font - Lucida Sans Unicode"
            FontFamily="Lucida Sans Unicode" FontSize="20"
            Margin="20,2,2,2"/>
 <TextBlock Text="Text Font - Times New Roman"
            FontFamily="Times New Roman" FontSize="20"
            Margin="20,2,2,2"/>
 <TextBlock Text="Text Font - Trebuchet MS"
            FontFamily="Trebuchet MS" FontSize="20"
            Foreground="#FF000066" Margin="20,2,2,2"/>
 <TextBlock Text="Text Font - Verdana" FontFamily="Verdana"
            FontSize="20" Foreground="DarkGoldenrod"
            Margin="20,2,2,2"/>

 <TextBlock Text="Test Run and LineBreak Objects:"
            FontFamily="Verdana" FontSize="20" FontStyle="Italic"
            FontWeight="ExtraBlack" Foreground="Red"
            Margin="0,10,2,2"/>
<TextBlock FontFamily="Arial" Width="400"
           Text="This is Arial with default fontsize"
           Margin="20,2,2,2">
    <LineBreak/>
    <Run Foreground="Maroon" FontFamily="Courier New" FontSize="24"
         Text="Courier New: 24"/>
    <LineBreak/>
    <Run Foreground="Teal" FontFamily="Times New Roman" FontSize="18"
         FontStyle="Italic" Text="Times New Roman Italic: 18"/>
    <LineBreak/>
    <Run Foreground="SteelBlue" FontFamily="Verdana" FontSize="14"
         FontWeight="Bold" Text="Verdana Bold 14"/>
</TextBlock>

<TextBlock Text="Test TextWrapping:" FontFamily="Verdana"
           FontSize="20" FontStyle="Italic"
           FontWeight="ExtraBlack" Foreground="Red"
           Margin="0,10,2,2"/>
<!-- TextBlock with no text wrapping -->
<TextBlock Width="300" TextWrapping="NoWrap" Margin="20,2,2,2"
           HorizontalAlignment="Left">
     Without text wrapping: Avery Johnson was dismissed as coach of
     the Dallas Mavericks the day after a disappointing season.
</TextBlock>
<!-- TextBlock with text wrapping -->
<TextBlock Width="300" TextWrapping="Wrap" Margin="20,2,2,2"
```

```
                        HorizontalAlignment="Left">
                With text wrapping: Avery Johnson was dismissed as coach of the
                Dallas Mavericks the day after a disappointing season.
            </TextBlock>
        </StackPanel>
    </Grid>
</UserControl>
```

Note that the TextBlock object has two important read-only properties, ActualHeight and ActualWidth, which specify the rendered height and width of the TextBlock. These properties can differ from the Height and Width properties of the TextBlock. Setting the TextWrapping property affects the ActualHeight and ActualWidth values of the TextBlock. Sometimes, you may find that part of the text string is cut off at the right edge of the TextBlock, which is because the ActualWidth is different from the Width property. In this case, you need to adjust the ActualWidth value to display the entire text string.

TextBox

The TextBox element is the text-entry control in Silverlight. The TextBox aways stores a string. Many properties available to the TextBlock, such as font-related properties and TextWrapping, are also available to the TextBox.

Usually, the TextBox control stores a single line of text. However, there are many cases when you'll want to create a multiline text box for dealing with a block of content. In this case, you simply set the TextWrapping property to Wrap. Wrap always breaks at the edge of the control.

In order to actually see the entire text string in a TextBox, the TextBox must be sized correctly. If the TextBox doesn't have enough room, part of the text may disappear, even though you can still view it by moving your mouse cursor.

Sometimes, you'll create a text box purely for the purpose of displaying text. In this case, set the IsReadOnly property to true to prevent editing by the user.

Text selection is an important feature of the TextBox. You can select text in the TextBox by clicking and dragging with the mouse or by holding down the Shift key while you move through the text with the arrow keys. You can aso use the standard keys to perform- various operations, such as copying using Ctrl + C and pasting using Ctrl + V.

The TextBox in Silverlight also allows you to determine or change the currently selected text programmatically using the SelectionStart, SelectionLength, and SelectedText properties. SelectionStart identifies the zero-based position where the selection begins. For example, if you set this property to 5, the first selected character is the 6th character in the TextBox. The SelectionLength property indicates the total number of selected characters. Finally, the SelectedText property allows you to quickly examine or change the selected text in the TextBox. You can react to the selection being changed using the SelectionChanged event handler.

Another limitation of the TextBox is that it doesn't have scroll bars. For a multiline TextBox, it is inconvenient to navigate using the Up and Down arrows through a 1000-line TextBox. You can work around this limitation by combining the TextBox with a ScrollViewer control. I'll show you how to implement such a TextBox with a scrollbar feature using the ScrollViewer control.

Start with a new Silverlight project and name it Example11-5. Here is the XAML of this example:

```
<UserControl x:Class="Example11_5.Page"
    xmlns="http://schemas.microsoft.com/client/2007"
    xmlns:x="http://schemas.microsoft.com/winfx/2006/xaml"
    Width="500" Height="300">
    <Grid x:Name="LayoutRoot" Background="White">
        <Grid Margin="5">
            <Grid.RowDefinitions>
                <RowDefinition Height="2*"></RowDefinition>
                <RowDefinition Height="*"></RowDefinition>
            </Grid.RowDefinitions>
                <ScrollViewer VerticalScrollBarVisibility="Auto">
                <TextBox x:Name="textBox" AcceptsReturn="True"
                         SelectionChanged="text_SelectionChanged" Padding="10"
                         Background="#FFDDDDFF" Foreground="#FF000066"
                         TextWrapping="Wrap" Width="400">
                    <TextBox.Text>
                        "Avery Johnson was dismissed as coach of the Dallas
Mavericks the day after a disappointing season ended with a first-round playoff
exit in New Orleans. Incredible highs and heartbreaking lows marked the tenure
of Johnson, who leaves as the most successful coach in franchise history by many
measures. Avery Johnson was dismissed as coach of the Dallas Mavericks the day
after a disappointing season ended with a first-round playoff exit in New
Orleans. Incredible highs and heartbreaking lows marked the tenure of Johnson,
who leaves as the most successful coach in franchise history by many measures.

Johnson became the eighth coach in team history on March 19, 2005 and posted a
record of 194-70 (.735) during the regular season. He led the Mavs to the
playoffs four consecutive years, including a trip to the 2006 NBA Finals. His
postseason record of 23-24 (.489) included 12 losses in the last 15 games."
                    </TextBox.Text>
                </TextBox>
                </ScrollViewer>
                <ScrollViewer Foreground="Blue" Grid.Row="1" Margin="0,10,0,5"
                              VerticalScrollBarVisibility="Auto">
                <StackPanel>
                    <TextBlock x:Name="textTitle" Text="Current selection:"
                               Foreground="Red" Padding="10 10 10 0"/>
                    <TextBlock x:Name="textSelection" TextWrapping="Wrap"
                               Padding="10 0 10 10"/>
                </StackPanel>
            </ScrollViewer>
        </Grid>
    </Grid>
</UserControl>
```

Here, we specify several attributes for the TextBox, including the Foreground, Background color, and the AcceptsReturn. We also set the SelectionChanged to the text_SelectionChanged event handler, which allows you to deal with the selected text programmatically.

We also add a ScrollViewer to the TextBox and set its VerticalScrollBarVisibility property to Auto. In this case, when the text string needs more vertical space than the available vertical space in the TextBox, a vertical scrollbar will be added to the TextBox, allowing you to view text by moving the scroll bar.

We also add two TextBlock controls to another ScrollViewer, which are used to display the selected text from the TextBox.

The corresponding code-behind file is listed below:

```
using System;
using System.Windows;
using System.Windows.Controls;
using System.Windows.Input;
using System.Windows.Media;

namespace Example11_5
{
    public partial class Page : UserControl
    {
        public Page()
        {
            InitializeComponent();
        }

        private void text_SelectionChanged(object sender, RoutedEventArgs e)
        {
            if (textSelection == null)
                return;

            textTitle.Text = "Current selection: " +
                             String.Format("charaters start: {0},
                                            String length: {1}".
                                            textBox.SelectionStart,
                                            textBox.SelectionLength);
            textSelection.Text = textBox.SelectedText;
        }
    }
}
```

Inside the text_SelectionChanged event handler, the Text property of the TextBlock named textTitle is specified by the start character and string length of the selected text from the TextBox. The TextBlock named textSelection is used to display the content of the selected text.

Running this application produces the result shown Figure 11-7.

WatermarkedTextBox

The WatermarkedTextBox is a specialized TextBox control. The properties and features discussed for the TextBox in the previous section are also applicable to the WatermarkedTextBox. The watermark in the WatermarkedTextBox is typically text that indicates the purpose of the TextBox. For example, a text box might display the text "Username" until the user enters a username.

A watermark does not have to be a text string. Any object that derives from UIElement can be used. For example, an empty WatermarkedTextBox might display an image or a TextBlock with customized properties.

For example, the following code snippet creates a TextBox with a simple text watermark:

```
<WatermarkedTextBox Watermark="Watermark test" Height="30" Width="200"/>
```

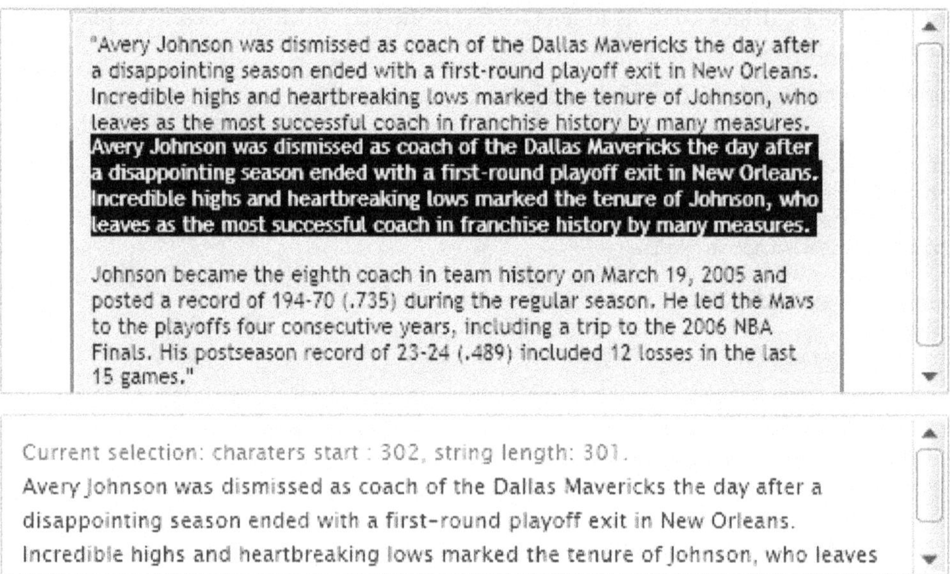

Figure 11-7 Selecting text in a TextBox.

The following code creates a custom watermark, in which a UIElement object (the Button) serves as a watermark:

```
<WatermarkedTextBox Height="50" Width="300">
    <WatermarkedTextBox.Watermark>
        <Button Height="40" Width="260" Content="Button as a watermark" />
    </WatermarkedTextBox.Watermark>
</WatermarkedTextBox>
```

Please note that the above code only works for the Silverlight 2 Beta 1, and the WatermarkedTextBox control has been removed in Silverlight 2 Beta 2. This is due to the fact that the Watermark property will be added to the TextBox control in a future version of Silverlight. Therefore, it does not make sense to have a separate WatermarkedTextBox control.

Button Controls

Silverlight incudes three types of button controls: the standard Button, the CheckBox, and the RadioButton. Every type of button includes only a few members. They define the Click event and add support for commands, which allow you to develop interactive Silverlight applications. The Buttons also have a ClickMode property that determines when a button fires its Click event in response to mouse actions. The default value is ClickMode.Release, which means the Click event fires when the mouse is clicked and released. However, you can also choose to fire the Click event mouse when the mouse button is first pressed (ClickMode.Press) or whenever the mouse moves over the button and pauses there (ClickMode.Hover).

Button

The Button represents the standard push button. Silverlight also implements variations of the Button, including the RepeatButton and the ToggleButton. The RepeatButton fires Click events continuously, as long as the button is held down. The standard button fires only one Click event per user click. The ToggleButton represents a button that has two states, pushed or unpushed. When you click a ToggleButton, it stays in its pushed state until you click it again to release it. This is sometimes described as sticky click behavior.

Both the RepeatButton and ToggleButton are defined in the System.Window.Controls.primitive namespace, which indicates they are not often used on their own. Instead, they are used to build more complex controls by composition, or extended with features through inheritance. For example, you can use the RepeatButton to build a higher-level ScrollBar control. The RepeatButton forms the arrow buttons at the ends of the scroll bar – scrolling continues as long as you hold the arrow down. Similarly, the ToggleButton is used to derive the more useful CheckBox and RadioButton.

Of course, you can also use both the RepeatButton and the ToggleButton directly in your Silverlight applications. The ToggleButton is useful when you create a custom ToolBar control.

Here I'll use an example to show you how to create various buttons. Start with a new Silverlight application and name it Example11-6. Here is the XAML of this example:

```
<UserControl x:Class="Example11_6.Page"
    xmlns="http://schemas.microsoft.com/client/2007"
    xmlns:x="http://schemas.microsoft.com/winfx/2006/xaml"
    Width="500" Height="230">
    <Grid x:Name="LayoutRoot" Background="White">
        <StackPanel Orientation="Horizontal" Margin="10">
            <StackPanel>
                <TextBlock Text="Buttons:" Margin="5"/>
                <Button Content="Default Button" Click="Button_Click"
                        Width="100" Height="30" Margin="5"/>
                <Button Content="Red Button" Click="Button_Click"
                        Background="Red" Width="100" Height="30" Margin="5"/>
                <Button Content="Green Button" Click="Button_Click"
                        Background="Green" Width="100" Height="30" Margin="5"/>
                <Button Content="Blue Button" Click="Button_Click"
                        Background="Blue" Width="100" Height="30" Margin="5"/>
            </StackPanel>

            <StackPanel Margin="20 0 0 0">
                <TextBlock Text="RepeatButtons:" Margin="5"/>
                <RepeatButton Content="Default RepeatButton"
                              Click="Button_Click"
                        Width="150" Height="30" Margin="5"/>
                <RepeatButton Content="Red RepeatButton" Click="Button_Click"
                        Background="Red" Width="150" Height="30" Margin="5"/>
                <RepeatButton Content="Green RepeatButton" Click="Button_Click"
                        Background="Green" Width="150" Height="30" Margin="5"/>
                <RepeatButton Content="Blue RepeatButton" Click="Button_Click"
                        Background="Blue" Width="150" Height="30" Margin="5"/>
            </StackPanel>

            <StackPanel Margin="20 0 0 0">
                <TextBlock Text="ToggleButtons:" Margin="5"/>
```

```
                <ToggleButton Content="Default ToggleButton"
                              Click="Button_Click"
                        Width="150" Height="30" Margin="5"/>
                <ToggleButton Content="Red ToggleButton" Click="Button_Click"
                        Background="Red" Width="150" Height="30" Margin="5"/>
                <ToggleButton Content="Green ToggleButton" Click="Button_Click"
                        Background="Green" Width="150" Height="30" Margin="5"/>
                <ToggleButton Content="Blue ToggleButton" Click="Button_Click"
                        Background="Blue" Width="150" Height="30" Margin="5"/>
            </StackPanel>
        </StackPanel>
    </Grid>
</UserControl>
```

Here we create various Buttons, RepeatButtons, and ToggleButtons with different Background colors. The Click action for all of the buttons is handled by a single Button_Click event in the code-behind file:

```
using System;
using System.Windows;
using System.Windows.Browser;
using System.Windows.Controls.Primitives;
using System.Windows.Controls;
using System.Windows.Input;
using System.Windows.Media;

namespace Example11_6
{
    public partial class Page : UserControl
    {
        public Page()
        {
            InitializeComponent();
        }

        private void Button_Click(object sender, RoutedEventArgs e)
        {
            UIElement element = sender as UIElement;

            if(element.GetType().ToString() == "System.Windows.Controls.Button")
                HtmlPage.Window.Alert("You are clicking the " +
                         ((Button)element).Content.ToString());
            else if (element.GetType().ToString() ==
                         "System.Windows.Controls.Primitives.RepeatButton")
                HtmlPage.Window.Alert("You are clicking the " +
                         ((RepeatButton)element).Content.ToString());
            else if (element.GetType().ToString() ==
                         "System.Windows.Controls.Primitives.ToggleButton")
                HtmlPage.Window.Alert("You are clicking the " +
                         ((ToggleButton)element).Content.ToString());
        }
    }
}
```

Figure 11-8 shows the results of running this application. When you click any button, a message box will appear to indicate which button is being clicked.

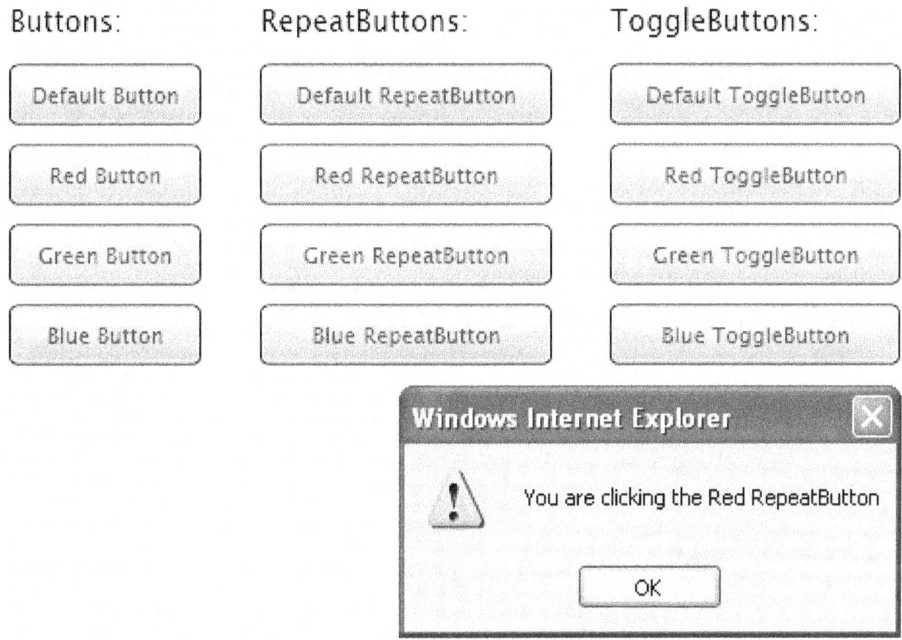

Figure 11-8 Various buttons in Silverlight.

CheckBox

The CheckBox control is a different sort of button which derives from the ToggleButton. This means that it can be switched on or off by the user. Switching the CheckBox on means placing a checkmark on it.

The CheckBox has an important property, IsChecked, which is a nullable Boolean. This property can be set to True, False, or Null. Obviously, True represents a checked box, while False represents an empty one. The Null value is a little trickier because it represents an indeterminate state, which is displayed as a shaded box. This state is used to represent values that haven't been set. For example, if you have a CheckBox that allows you to change the font size in a text application, and the current selection includes text with different font sizes, you might set the check box to Null to show an indeterminate state.

In order to assign a Null value in Silverlight, you need to use the Null markup extension as shown in the following code snippet:

```
<CheckBox Content="My check box" IsChecked="{x:Null}"/>
```

The CheckBox also defines three events that fire when the CheckBox enters specific states: Checked, UnChecked, and Indeterminate. In most cases, it is more convenient to consolidate this logic into one event handler using the Click event handler of the CheckBox.

RadioButton

Like the CheckBox, the RadioButton also uses the IsChecked property and the same Checked, UnChecked, and indeterminate events. In addition, the RadioButton adds another property called GroupName, which allows you to control how the RadioButtons are placed into groups.

Usually, radio buttons are grouped by their container. For example, if you place three RadioButton controls in a single StackPanel, they form a group from which you can select just one of the three. On the other hand, if you place a combination of radio buttons in two separate StackPanel controls, you have two independent groups in your application.

The GroupName propery allows you to override this default behavior. You can use it to create more than one group in the same container or to create a single group that spans multiple containers.

Let's consider an example that shows how to create CheckBox and RadioButton objects. Start with a new Silverlight application and name it Example11-7. Here is XAML of this example:

```
<UserControl x:Class="Example11_7.Page"
    xmlns="http://schemas.microsoft.com/client/2007"
    xmlns:x="http://schemas.microsoft.com/winfx/2006/xaml"
    Width="400" Height="300">
    <Grid x:Name="LayoutRoot" Background="White">
        <StackPanel Orientation="Horizontal" Margin="10">
            <StackPanel>
                <CheckBox Content="Default CheckBox" Click="CheckBox_Click"
                          IsChecked="{x:Null}" IsThreeState="True"/>
                <CheckBox Content="Red CheckBox" Click="CheckBox_Click"
                          IsChecked="True" IsThreeState="True"
                          Background="Red"/>
                <CheckBox Content="Green CheckBox" Click="CheckBox_Click"
                          IsChecked="False" IsThreeState="True"
                          Background="Green"/>
                <CheckBox Content="Blue CheckBox" Click="CheckBox_Click"
                          IsChecked="False" IsThreeState="True"
                          Background="Blue"/>
                <RadioButton Content="Default RadioButton: Group 1"
                             Click="RadioButton_Click" IsChecked="True"
                             Margin="0 20 0 0"/>
                <RadioButton Content="Red RadioButton: Group 1"
                             Click="RadioButton_Click" IsChecked="False"
                             Background="Red"/>
                <RadioButton Content="Green RadioButton: Group 1"
                             Click="RadioButton_Click" IsChecked="False"
                             Background="Green"/>
                <RadioButton Content="Blue RadioButton: Group 2"
                             GroupName="Group2" Click="RadioButton_Click"
                             IsChecked="True" Background="Green"/>
            </StackPanel>
            <StackPanel Margin="20 125 0 0">
                <RadioButton Content="Default RadioButton: Group 2"
                             GroupName="Group2" Click="RadioButton_Click"
                             IsChecked="False"/>
                <RadioButton Content="Red RadioButton: Group 3"
                             Click="RadioButton_Click" IsChecked="True"
                             Background="Red"/>
```

```
                <RadioButton Content="Green RadioButton: Group 3"
                             Click="RadioButton_Click" IsChecked="False"
                             Background="Green"/>
                <RadioButton Content="Blue RadioButton: Group 3"
                             Click="RadioButton_Click" IsChecked="False"
                             Background="Green"/>
            </StackPanel>
        </StackPanel>
    </Grid>
</UserControl>
```

Here, we first create several CheckBox objects with different background colors. Then we create eight radio buttons, which are held in two StackPanel containers. These radio buttons are divided into three groups. The radio buttons in Group 2 belong to two different containers.

The Click events are handled in the code-behind file:

```
using System;
using System.Windows;
using System.Windows.Browser;
using System.Windows.Controls;
using System.Windows.Media;

namespace Example11_7
{
    public partial class Page : UserControl
    {
        public Page()
        {
            InitializeComponent();
        }

        private void CheckBox_Click(object sender, RoutedEventArgs e)
        {
            CheckBox box = sender as CheckBox;
            HtmlPage.Window.Alert("You are clicking the " +
                                  box.Content.ToString());
        }

        private void RadioButton_Click(object sender, RoutedEventArgs e)
        {
            RadioButton button = sender as RadioButton;
            HtmlPage.Window.Alert("You are clicking the " +
                                  button.Content.ToString());
        }
    }
}
```

Figure 11-9 shows the results of running this application. Click the radio-buttons in different groups and examine how they react.

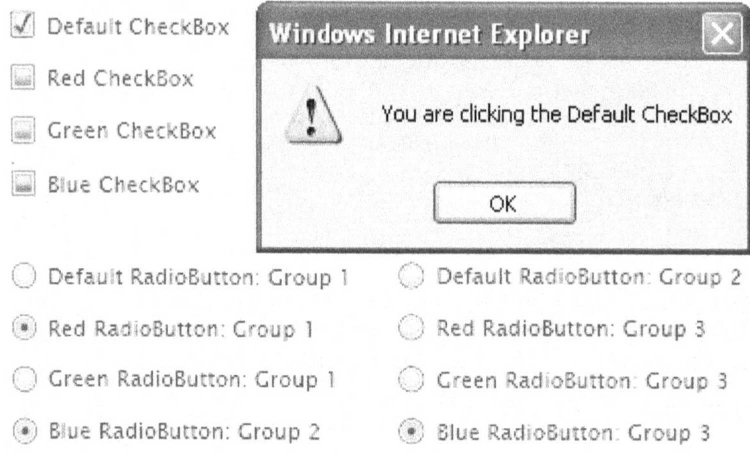

Figure 11-9 CheckBoxes and RadioButtons in Silverlight.

ToolTip

Silverlight includes a ToolTip control that creates a pop-up window to display information about an element in your applications.

In Silverlight Beta 2, ToolTip is hidden and can't be used directly. Unlike in Beta 1, you can't simply set the ToolTip property of your controls. Instead, ToolTip can only be added to controls through the ToolTipService. In addition, the ToolTipService API in Beta 2 has been cut back. The following public properties and methods that were available in Beta 1 have been removed from the ToolTipService:

- BetweenShowDelayProperty
- InitialShowDelayProperty
- ShowDurationProperty
- GetBetweenShowDelay
- GetInitialShowDelay
- GetShowDuration
- SetBetweenShowDelay
- SetInitialShowDelay
- GetToolTip
- SetShowDuration

All of the above properties and methods are no longer available in Beta 2.

ToolTip must now be specified through the ToolTipService, either in XAML or in code. For example, you can use a ToolTip to provide the name of a Button:

```
<Button Content="Button" ToolTipService.ToolTip="Button with a simple tooltip"/>
<Button Content="Button">
<ToolTipService.ToolTip>
```

```
        <TextBlock Text=="Button with a TextBlock"/>
    </ToolTipService.ToolTip>
    </Button>
```

When your mouse moves over this button, the text "Button with a simple tooltip" appears in a pop-up window.

The content of a ToolTip control can vary from a simple text string to more complex content, such as a StackPanel with embedded text and images. In this case, you need to break the ToolTip property out into a separate element. Here is an example code snippet that sets the ToolTip property of a button using a more complex StackPanel container:

```
<Button Content="Button with an image tooltip.">
    <ToolTipService.ToolTip>
        <StackPanel Margin="10">
            <TextBlock Margin="3" Text="Image tooltip - cool!"/>
            <Image Source="smiley.jpg"/>
         </StackPanel>
    </ToolTipService.ToolTip>
</Button>
```

In this case, Silverlight implicitly creates a ToolTip object. The difference is that here the ToolTip object contains a StackPanel rather than a simple text string.

Note that the content of a ToolTip can't receive focus, so please don't put user-interface controls in the ToolTip object. For example, if you place a button in the ToolTip, the button will appear, but will not be clickable.

Here I'll show you how to create various tooltips for different elements, including Buttons and TextBoxes.

Start with a new Silverlight project and name it Example11-8. Here is XAML of this example:

```
<UserControl x:Class="Example11_8.Page"
    xmlns="http://schemas.microsoft.com/client/2007"
    xmlns:x="http://schemas.microsoft.com/winfx/2006/xaml"
    Width="400" Height="600">
    <Grid x:Name="LayoutRoot" Background="White">
        <StackPanel Margin="10" HorizontalAlignment="Left">
            <TextBlock Text="Simple tooltip using Tooltip class:" FontSize="16"
                       Margin="10 10 0 0" FontWeight="Bold"/>
            <Button Content="Button with a simple tooltip"
                    ToolTipService.ToolTip="Button with a simple tooltip"
                    Width="200" Height="50" HorizontalAlignment="Left"
                    Margin="30 10 0 10"/>
            <CheckBox Content="CheckBox with a simple tooltip"
                      ToolTipService.ToolTip="CheckBox with tooltip"
                      IsChecked="True" HorizontalAlignment="Left"
                      Margin="30 0 0 0"/>
            <RadioButton Content="RadioButton with a simple tooltip"
                         ToolTipService.ToolTip="RadioButton with tooltip"
                         IsChecked="True" HorizontalAlignment="Left"
                         Margin="30 0 0 0"/>

            <TextBlock Text="Simple tooltip using ToolTipService class:"
                       FontSize="16" Margin="10 10 0 0" FontWeight="Bold"/>
```

```
            <!-- TextBlock and TextBox have to use ToolTipService: -->
            <TextBlock Text="TextBlock with a simple tooltip" FontSize="12"
                       Margin="30 0 0 10">
                <ToolTipService.ToolTip >
                    <ToolTip Content="TextBlock with a simple tooltip"/>
                </ToolTipService.ToolTip>
            </TextBlock>
            <TextBox Text="TextBox with a simple tooltip" FontSize="12"
                     Width="200" HorizontalAlignment="Left" Margin="30 0 0 10">
                <ToolTipService.ToolTip >
                    <ToolTip Content="TextBox with a simple tooltip"/>
                </ToolTipService.ToolTip>
            </TextBox>

            <!-- A button with an image tooltip: -->
            <Button Content="Button with an image tooltip." Height="50"
                    Width="250" HorizontalAlignment="Left" Margin="30 10 0 0">
                <ToolTipService.ToolTip>
                    <StackPanel Margin="10">
                        <TextBlock Margin="3"
                             Text="This button with an image tooltip - cool!"
                             FontSize="14" Foreground="Red"/>
                        <Image Source="smiley.jpg"/>
                    </StackPanel>
                </ToolTipService.ToolTip>
            </Button>
            <Image Source="smiley.jpg" Visibility="Collapsed"/>
        </StackPanel>
    </Grid>
</UserControl>
```

Figure 11-10 shows the results. You can hover over the various controls and examine how the ToolTips work.

Note that there is a bug in the ToolTip with an image. In order to display the image tooltip, you have to create a dummy Image object outside the ToolTip with the same Source as the image used in the ToolTip:

```
<Image Source="smiley.jpg" Visibility="Collapsed"/>
```

Here, the Visibility property is set to Collapsed, indicating that the image is invisible. Hopefully, Silverlight will fix this bug in its next release.

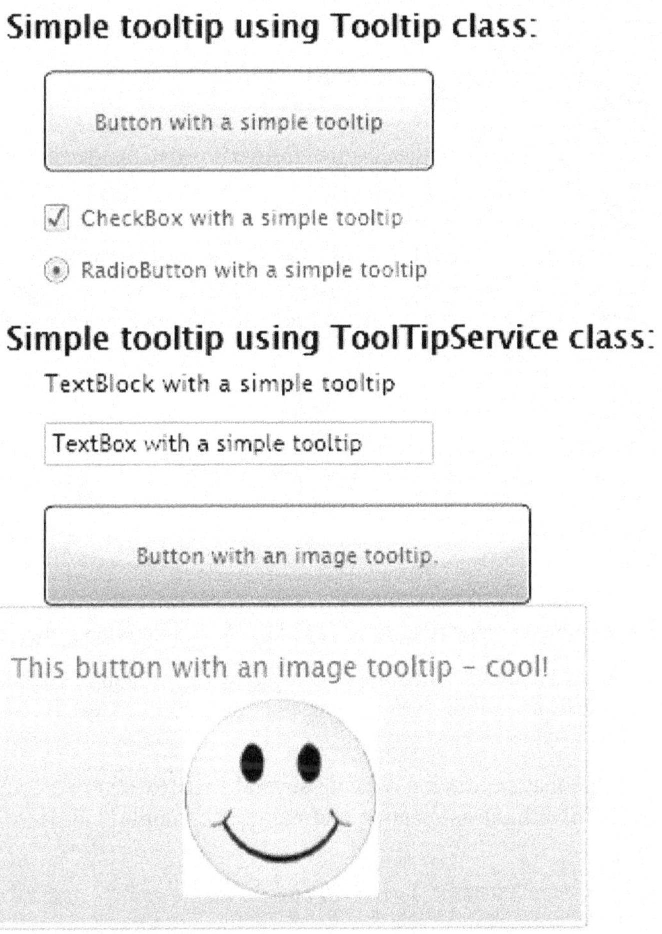

Simple tooltip using Tooltip class:

Button with a simple tooltip

CheckBox with a simple tooltip

RadioButton with a simple tooltip

Simple tooltip using ToolTipService class:

TextBlock with a simple tooltip

TextBox with a simple tooltip

Button with an image tooltip.

This button with an image tooltip - cool!

Figure 11-10 Tooltip demonstration in Silverlight.

ListBox and DataGrid Controls

Silverlight includes two important controls, ListBox and DataGrid, that wrap a collection of items.

ListBox

The ListBox control represents the common list with variable length lists that allow the user to select an item. It also allows multiple selection if you set the SelectionMode property to Multiple or Extended.

To add items to the ListBox, you can nest ListBoxItem elements inside the ListBox element. Since the ListBoxItem is a content-based element, you can add any UIElement objects to it.

```
<ListBox Margin="5">
    <ListBoxItem Content="Item1"/>
    <ListBoxItem>
        <Button Content="Button 1"/>
    </ListBoxItem>
    <ListBoxItem>
        <CheckBox Content="CheckBox 1" IsChecked="True"/>
    </ListBoxItem>
</ListBox>
```

You can see that the ListBox stores each nested object in its Items collection. The ListBox is very powerful at creating the ListBoxItem objects it needs implicitly. You can place your object directly inside the ListBox element. The following code snippet uses nested StackPanel objects to combine text and image content:

```
<ListBox>
    <ListBoxItem>
        <StackPanel Orientation="Horizontal" Margin="5">
            <Image Source="smiley.jpg"/>
            <TextBlock Text="This is my image"/>
        </StackPanel>
    </ListBoxItem>
</ListBox>-->
```

Here, the StackPanel becomes the item that is wrapped by the ListBoxItem object.

The ability to nest arbitrary elements inside the ListBoxItem allows you to create a variety of list-based controls without needing to use other classes. For example, you can easily create a ListBox with a check box to every item.

Let's consider an example that creates a page with several ListBox controls configured in a variety of ways. Start with a new Silverlight application and name it Example11-9. Here is the XAML of this example:

```
<UserControl x:Class="Example11_9.Page"
    xmlns="http://schemas.microsoft.com/client/2007"
    xmlns:x="http://schemas.microsoft.com/winfx/2006/xaml"
    Width="600" Height="300" >
    <Grid x:Name="LayoutRoot" Background="White">
        <StackPanel Orientation="Horizontal">
            <StackPanel>
                <TextBlock Text="This listbox contains various elements"
                           FontSize="12" Margin="5"/>
                <ListBox x:Name="listBox1" Margin="5 0 5 5">
                    <ListBoxItem Content="Item 1 "/>
                    <Button Content="Button 1"/>
                    <CheckBox Content="CheckBox 1" IsChecked="True"/>
                    <ListBoxItem>
                        <StackPanel Orientation="Horizontal" Margin="5">
                            <Image Source="smiley.jpg"/>
                            <TextBlock Text=" This is my image"
                                       VerticalAlignment="Center"/>
                    </StackPanel>
                    </ListBoxItem>
                </ListBox>
            </StackPanel>
```

```
        <StackPanel>
            <TextBlock Text="This listbox includes a checkbox list"
                       FontSize="12" Margin="10 5 5 5"/>
            <ListBox x:Name="listBox2" Margin="10 0 5 5"
                     SelectionChanged="listBox2_SelectionChanged" >
                <CheckBox Content="CheckBox 1" Click="CheckBox_Click"
                          ClickMode=="Press"/>
                <CheckBox Content="CheckBox 2" Click="CheckBox_Click"
                          ClickMode=="Press" />
                <CheckBox Content="CheckBox 3" Click="CheckBox_Click"
                          ClickMode=="Press" />
            </ListBox>
            <Button Margin="10,10,5,0" Click="Button_Click"
                    Content="Examine Checked Items"/>
            <TextBlock Text="Current selection:" FontSize="12"
                       Margin="10 5 5 5"/>
            <TextBlock  Name="textSelection" TextWrapping="Wrap"
                        FontSize="12" Margin="10 5 5 5"/>
        </StackPanel>
    </StackPanel>
  </Grid>
</UserControl>
```

This XAML code creates two ListBox objects, listBox1 and listBox2. The listBox1 contains various UIElement objects, while the listBox2 contains a CheckBox list. Here, you can also examine how the CheckBox list works. The SelectionChanged and Click events of the CheckBox objects are handled in the code-behind file:

```
using System;
using System.Windows;
using System.Windows.Controls;
using System.Windows.Input;
using System.Windows.Media;

namespace Example11_9
{
    public partial class Page : UserControl
    {
        public Page()
        {
            InitializeComponent();
        }

        private void listBox2_SelectionChanged(object sender,
                     SelectionChangedEventArgs e)
        {
            if (listBox2.SelectedItem == null)
                return;
            textSelection.Text = string.Format(
                "Selected item at position {0}. \r\nChecked state is {1}.",
                listBox2.SelectedIndex,
                ((CheckBox)listBox2.SelectedItem).IsChecked);
        }

        private void Button_Click(object sender, RoutedEventArgs e)
```

```
            {
                string text = "";
                foreach (CheckBox box in listBox2.Items)
                {
                    if (box.IsChecked == true)
                    {
                        text = text + box.Content.ToString() + " is checked.\r\n";
                    }
                }
                textSelection.Text = text;
            }

            private void CheckBox_Click(object sender, RoutedEventArgs e)
            {
                CheckBox box = sender as CheckBox;
                textSelection.Text = string.Format(
                    "Selected item at position {0}. \r\nChecked state is {1}.",
                listBox2.SelectedIndex, box.IsChecked);
            }
        }
    }
```

The Button Click events loop through the collection of items to determine which CheckBox objects are checked.

Figure 11-11 shows the result of running this application.

Note that there is an issue with Silverlight where it incorrectly fires the ListBox's GotFocus event twice instead of once, which interferes with the ListBox's selection logic and causes problems associated with some controls in the ListBox, such as CheckBox and TextBox. In this example, we demonstrate a workaround by changing the ClickMode property of the CheckBox from the default of Release to Press.

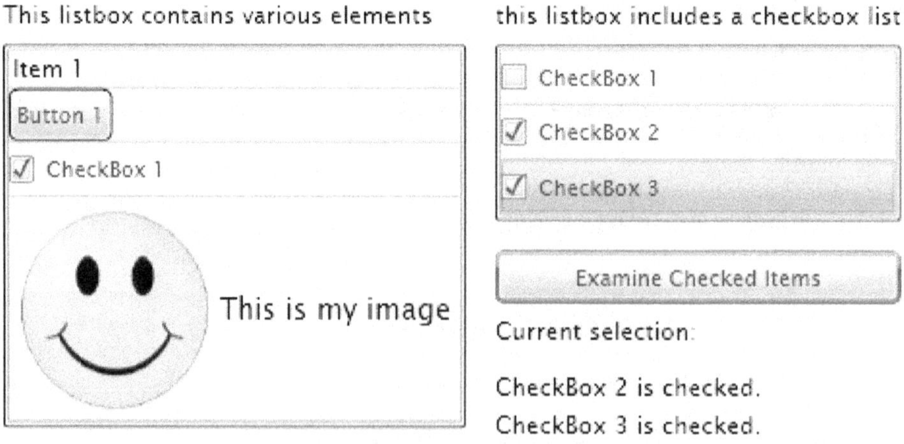

Figure 11-11 ListBox controls in Silverlight.

DataGrid

Silverlight 2 includes a new DataGrid control that provides a flexible way to display a collection of data in rows and columns. The built-in column types include a text box column, a check box column, and a template column for hosting custom content. The built-in row type includes a drop-down details section that you can use to display additional content below the cell values.

To fill data in the DataGrid, set the ItemsSource property to an IEnumerable implementation. Each row in the grid is bound to an object in the data source, and each column in the grid is bound to a property of the data object.

By default, the DataGrid control generates columns automatically when you set the ItemsSource property. The generated columns are of type DataGridCheckBoxColumn for bound Boolean (and nullable Boolean) properties, and of type DataGridTextBoxColumn for all other properties. If a property doesn't have a String or numeric value type, the generated text box columns are read-only and display the data object's ToString value.

You can prevent automatic column generation by setting the AutoGenerateColumns property to false. This is useful if you want to create and configure all columns explicitly. Alternatively, you can let the grid generate columns, but handle the AutoGeneratingColumn event to customize columns after creation. To rearrange the display order of the columns, you can set the DisplayIndex property for individual columns.

Regardless of whether you generate columns, you can use the DataGrid.Columns collection to programmatically add, insert, remove, and change any columns in the control at run time. Alternatively, you can specify columns in XAML, in which case you must set AutoGenerateColumns to false. Creating your own columns enables you to use additional column types, such as the DataGridTemplateColumn type or custom column types. The DataGridTemplateColumn type provides an easy way to create a simple custom column. The CellTemplate and CellEditingTemplate properties enable you to specify content templates for both display and editing modes.

To customize DataGrid behavior, you can handle events for selection change, cell editing, and data entry errors. The DataGrid also exposes several events for row recycling that you can handle to further customize rows.

The DataGrid control supports common table formatting options, such as alternating row backgrounds and the ability to show or hide headers, grid lines, and scroll bars. Additionally, the control provides several style and template properties that you can use to completely change the appearance of the control and its rows, columns, cells, and row or column headers.

In the following, I'll show you how to create a simple DataGrid application using an example. Start with a new Silverlight application and name it Example11-10. Since the DataGrid is an extended control in Silverlight, you need to add it to the reference of your application before using it. To do this, just find the DataGrid control on the Toolbox and drag it into the root layout Grid named "LayoutRoot", as shown in Figure 11-12. This processs has several consequences behind the scenes:

- It automatically adds a reference in your application to System.Windows.Controls.Data.
- It adds an xmlns called "my" to the root UserControl, which specifies that the DataGrid is System.Windows.Controls.Data assembly. You can change the xmlns name "my" to any other name you like, such as "data" or "local".
- It also adds an interface of the DataGrid as a child of its parent container Grid called LayoutRoot.

Next, we need to fill in some data in the DataGrid. In Silverlight, the data is more commonly set in the code-behind file, which is what we'll do in this example. Here is the XAML of this example:

```
<UserControl xmlns:my="clr-namespace:System.Windows.Controls;
                        assembly=System.Windows.Controls.Data"
    x:Class="Example11_10.Page"
    xmlns="http://schemas.microsoft.com/winfx/2006/xaml/presentation"
    xmlns:x="http://schemas.microsoft.com/winfx/2006/xaml"
    Width="500" Height="300">
    <Grid x:Name="LayoutRoot" Background="White">
        <my:DataGrid x:Name="dataGrid" AutoGenerateColumns="True"
                     Margin="10" RowBackground="LightSteelBlue"
                     AlternatingRowBackground="Azure"/>
    </Grid>
</UserControl>
```

Figure 11-12 Add a DataGrid control to a Silverlight Application.

Here, we set AutoGenerateColumns to true. Note that columns are only generated when the ItemsSource property is being set or changed, so if you change the value of AutoGenerateColumns after the DataGrid already has an ItemsSource specified, no columns will be generated until the next time the ItemsSource property is changed. We also set different colors for alternating rows using the AlternatingRowBackground property.

The data is filled in the code-behind file shown below:

```
using System;
using System.Collections.Generic;
using System.Windows;
using System.Windows.Controls;
using System.Windows.Input;
using System.Windows.Media;

namespace Example11_10
{
    public partial class Page : UserControl
    {
        public Page()
        {
```

```
            InitializeComponent();
            List<Customer> source = new List<Customer>();

            for (int i = 0; i < 40; i++)
            {
                Customer customer = new Customer();
                string phoneNumber = "";
                if (i < 10)
                    phoneNumber = "123-456-780" + i.ToString();
                else if (i >= 0)
                    phoneNumber = "123-456-78" + i.ToString();
                customer = new Customer()
                {
                    FirstName = "First name " + i.ToString(),
                    LastName = "Last name " + i.ToString(),
                    PhoneNumber = phoneNumber,
                    Availability = (i % 2 == 0)
                };
                source.Add(customer);
            }

            dataGrid.ItemsSource = source;
        }
    }

    public class Customer
    {
        public string FirstName { get; set; }
        public string LastName { get; set; }
        public string PhoneNumber { get; set; }
        public bool Availability { get; set; }
    }
}
```

Here, you first add a new Customer class that includes several public properties to bind to the DataGrid. The new .NET feature of Automatic properties is used to define this class. Then, you create a Customer collection named source in the page.xaml.cs class and bind it to the ItemsSource of the dataGrid control. Figure 11-13 shows the result of running this project.

Other Common Controls

Silverlight 2 also includes several other controls, including HyperlinkButton, Calendar, DatePicker, Image, and MediaElement, etc. These controls are very useful when you develop RIA Web applications. In this section, we will briefly discuss these controls and show how to use them using a code example.

HyperlinkButton

The HyperlinkButton represents a button control that displays a hyperlink. When clicked, the HyperlinkButton allows users to navigate to a Web page within the same Web application or a Web page external from the current application. The destination URI is specified with the NavigateUri property. You can specify a window or frame within the destination Web page using the TargetName property.

FirstName	LastName	PhoneNumber	Availability
First name 0	Last name 0	123-456-7800	✓
First name 1	Last name 1	123-456-7801	
First name 2	Last name 2	123-456-7802	✓
First name 3	Last name 3	123-456-7803	
First name 4	Last name 4	123-456-7804	✓
First name 5	Last name 5	123-456-7805	
First name 6	Last name 6	123-456-7806	✓
First name 7	Last name 7	123-456-7807	
First name 8	Last name 8	123-456-7808	✓
First name 9	Last name 9	123-456-7809	
First name 10	Last name 10	123-456-7810	✓

Figure 11-13 DataGrid in Silverlight.

The target specified in the HyperlinkButton should be a standard HTML target. The following lists some target names and describes the results when used in the HyperlinkButton control:

- _blank – loads the linked document into a new blank window.
- _media – loads the linked document into a new blank window.
- _parent – loads the page into the window in which the link was clicked (the active window).
- _search – loads the linked document into a new blank window.
- _self – loads the page into the window in which the link was clicked (the active window).
- _top – loads the page into the window in which the link was clicked (the active window).
- “” – loads the page into the window in which the link was clicked (the active window).

For example, clicking the following HyperlinkButton will navigate to my home page:

```
<HyperlinkButton Content="Click here to go to Dr. Xu's home page."
    NavigateUri="http://www.drxudotnet.com" TargetName="_blank"/>
```

Calendar and DatePicker

The Calendar control provides a graphical UI for the user to select a date. It displays dates one month at a time, and provides the ability to scroll from month to month or switch to a yearly view.

The Calendar control allows you to control the range of displayable and selectable dates, or to disable the selection of dates in the past. It also provides style and template properties that you can use to customize the appearance of the control or its selection indicator.

The DatePicker control allows a user to select a date by either typing it into a TextBox or by using a drop-down Calendar.

The DatePicker shares many properties with the Calendar, so you can control the range of displayable or selectable dates on a DatePicker and its drop-down Calendar at the same time. DatePicker also provides events for detecting the appearance or disappearance of the Calendar.

Let's consider an example that demonstrates how to use the Calendar and DatePicker controls. Start with a new Silverlight application and name it Example11-11. Here is the XAML of this example:

```
<UserControl xmlns:my="clr-namespace:System.Windows.Controls;
                       assembly=System.Windows.Controls.Extended"
    x:Class="Example11_11.Page"
    xmlns="http://schemas.microsoft.com/client/2007"
    xmlns:x="http://schemas.microsoft.com/winfx/2006/xaml"
    Width="250" Height="400">
    <Grid x:Name="LayoutRoot1" Background="White">
        <StackPanel Margin="20">
            <TextBlock Text="Calendar demonstration" FontSize="12"
                       FontWeight="Bold" Margin="0 0 0 5"/>
            <TextBox x:Name="textBox1" IsReadOnly="True"
                     Text="Display selected date" Width="200"
                     HorizontalAlignment="Left" Margin="0 0 0 10"/>
            <my:Calendar x:Name="calendar1"
                SelectedDatesChanged="calendar1_SelectedDatesChanged"
                HorizontalAlignment="Left"/>

            <TextBlock Text="DatePicker demonstration" FontSize="12"
                FontWeight="Bold" Margin="0 20 0 5"/>
            <my:DatePicker x:Name="datePicker1" Margin="0 0 0 10"/>
            <my:DatePicker x:Name="datePicker2" SelectedDateFormat="Long"/>
        </StackPanel>
    </Grid>
</UserControl>
```

Note that the Calendar and DatePicker controls are in System.Windows.Controls.Extended.dll, so you need to add the corresponding reference to the xml namespace in order to use these controls. Here, you create a Calendar object and a TextBox used to display the selected date from the Calendar. Then you create two DatePicker objects, one to display the date in Short (default) format and the other to display the date in Long format. You use the DataSelected event to bind the selected date from the Calendar to the Text property of the WatermarkedTextBox object, which is achieved in the code-behind file:

```
using System;
using System.Windows;
using System.Windows.Controls;
using System.Windows.Input;
using System.Windows.Media;

namespace Example11_11
{
    public partial class Page : UserControl
    {
        public Page()
        {
            InitializeComponent();
        }
```

```
        private void calendar1_SelectedDatesChanged(object sender,
                        SelectionChangedEventArgs e)
        {
            textBox1.Text = calendar1.SelectedDate.ToString();
        }
    }
}
```

Figure 11-14 shows the result of running this project.

Figure 11-14 Calendar and DatePicker in Silverlight.

Image

To create an image in Silverlight, you can use an Image object. The following code snippet shows how to create an image using the Image control:

```
<Image source = "flower.jpg"/>
```

Here, the Source property is used to specify the location of the image you want to display. If you don't set the Width and Height properties of an Image as in the above code snippet, it will display with the natural dimensions of the image specified by the Source property. Setting the Height and Width creates a containing rectangular area that the image is displayed in.

You can also specify how the image fills this containing area by using the Stretch property. The Stretch property accepts the following values, which the Stretch enumeration defines:

- None: The image does not stretch to fill the output dimensions.

- Uniform: The image is scaled to fit the output dimensions. However, the aspect ratio of the content is preserved. This is the default value.
- UniformToFill: The image is scaled so that it completely fills the output area but preserves its original aspect ratio.
- Fill: The image is scaled to fit the output dimensions. Because the content's height and width are scaled independently, the original aspect ratio of the image might not be preserved. That is, the image might be distorted to completely fill the output area.

The following example shows how the Stretch property affects the image. Start with a new Silverlight project and name it Exampel11-12. Here is the XAML of this example:

```
<UserControl x:Class="Example11_12.Page"
    xmlns="http://schemas.microsoft.com/client/2007"
    xmlns:x="http://schemas.microsoft.com/winfx/2006/xaml"
    Width="400" Height="300">
    <Grid x:Name="LayoutRoot" Background="White" ShowGridLines="True">
        <Grid.ColumnDefinitions>
            <ColumnDefinition/>
            <ColumnDefinition/>
        </Grid.ColumnDefinitions>
        <Grid.RowDefinitions>
            <RowDefinition/>
            <RowDefinition/>
        </Grid.RowDefinitions>

        <StackPanel Margin="5" Grid.Column="0" Grid.Row="0">
            <TextBlock Margin="5" Text="Stretch = None" FontSize="12"/>
            <Border BorderBrush="DarkBlue" BorderThickness="1"
                    Width="100" Height="100">
                <Image Source="Sunset.jpg" Height="100" Width="100"
                       Stretch="None"/>
            </Border>
        </StackPanel>

        <StackPanel Margin="5" Grid.Column="1" Grid.Row="0">
            <TextBlock Margin="5" Text="Stretch = Fill" FontSize="12"/>
            <Border BorderBrush="DarkBlue" BorderThickness="1"
                    Width="100" Height="100">
                <Image Source="Sunset.jpg" Height="100" Width="100"
                       Stretch="Fill"/>
            </Border>
        </StackPanel>

        <StackPanel Margin="5" Grid.Column="0" Grid.Row="1">
            <TextBlock Margin="5" Text="Stretch = Uniform" FontSize="12"/>
            <Border BorderBrush="DarkBlue" BorderThickness="1"
                    Width="100" Height="100">
                <Image Source="Sunset.jpg" Height="100" Width="100"
                       Stretch="Uniform"/>
            </Border>
        </StackPanel>

        <StackPanel Margin="5" Grid.Column="1" Grid.Row="1">
            <TextBlock Margin="5" Text="Stretch = UniformToFill" FontSize="12"/>
```

```
            <Border BorderBrush="DarkBlue" BorderThickness="1"
                    Width="100" Height="100">
                <Image Source="Sunset.jpg" Height="100" Width="100"
                       Stretch="UniformToFill"/>
            </Border>
        </StackPanel>
    </Grid>
</UserControl>
```

Figure 11-15 illustrates the results of running this example. For the first image, the Stretch property is set to None, which preserves the original image size. The displayed image is only a portion of the original image. For the second image, the Stretch property is set to Fill, which forces the image to fill the specified image size: 100 x 100 pixels. For the third image, the Stretch property is set to Uniform, which maintains the image aspect ratio, but resizes the image to fit the specified image size. For the last image, the Stretch property is set to UniformToFill, which resizes the image to best-fit while preserving the original aspect ratio. In this case, the best-fit is still much larger than the specified image size, so the image gets clipped.

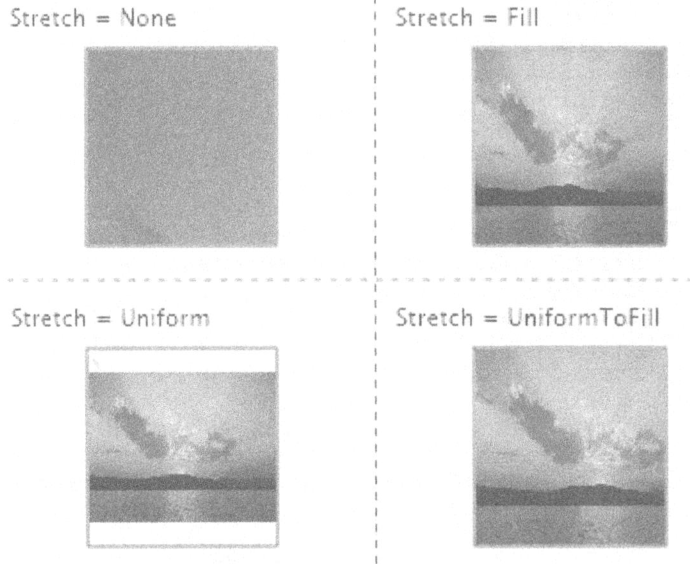

Figure 11-15 Images in Silverlight.

Note that currently, the Image in Silverlight supports only two image formats, .jpg and .png. You therefore need to convert your image file into one of these two supported file formats before setting the Source of your Image object.

MediaElement

The MediaElement is a Silverlight control. Like all other elements, the MediaElement can be placed directly in your user interface. If you use the MediaElement to play audio, this fact isn't important, but if you use it for video, you place it where the video window should appear.

Adding media to a page is as simple as adding a MediaElement to your markup and providing a Uniform Resource Identifier (URI) to the media to play. The following example creates a

MediaElement and sets its Source property to the URI of a video file. The MediaElement begins playing when the page loads.

```
<MediaElement Source="myMedia.wmv"/>
```

The MediaElement object can play Windows Media Video (WMV), Windows Media Audio (WMA), and MP3 files.

The MediaElement provides several media-specific properties. The following list describes a few of these properties.

- AutoPlay – Specifies whether the MediaElement should begin playing automatically. The default value is True.
- IsMuted – Specifies whether the MediaElement is silenced. A value of True mutes the MediaElement. The default value is False.
- Stretch – Specifies how video is stretched to fill the MediaElement object. Possible values are None, Uniform, UniformToFill, and Fill. The default is Fill.
- Volume – Specifies the volume of the MediaElement object's audio as a value from 0 to 1, with 1 being the loudest. The default value is 0.5.

In addition to its media-specific properties, MediaElement also has all the properties of a UIElement, such as Opacity and Clip.

You can also interactively control media playback by using the Play, Pause, and Stop methods of a MediaElement object. The following example defines a MediaElement object and several buttons for controlling media playback. Start with a new Silverlight project and name it Example11-13. Here is the XAML of this example:

```
<UserControl x:Class="Example11_13.Page"
    xmlns="http://schemas.microsoft.com/client/2007"
    xmlns:x="http://schemas.microsoft.com/winfx/2006/xaml"
    Width="400" Height="300">
    <Grid x:Name="LayoutRoot" Background="White">
        <StackPanel Margin="10">
            <MediaElement x:Name="media" Source="RollingBalls.wmv" Margin="10"/>
            <StackPanel Orientation="Horizontal">

                <!-- Stops media playback: -->
                <Button Content="Stop" Click="Button_Click" Background="Red"
                        Width="60" Height="30" Margin="10,5"/>

                <!-- Pauses media playback: -->
                <Button Content="Pause" Click="Button_Click" Background="Orange"
                        Width="60" Height="30" Margin="10,5"/>

                <!-- Starts media playback: -->
                <Button Content="Play" Click="Button_Click" Background="Green"
                        Width="60" Height="30" Margin="10,5"/>
            </StackPanel>
        </StackPanel>
    </Grid>
</UserControl>
```

The interactive control is achieved in the code-behind file:

```
using System;
using System.Windows;
using System.Windows.Controls;
using System.Windows.Media;

namespace Example11_13
{
    public partial class Page : UserControl
    {
        public Page()
        {
            InitializeComponent();
        }

        private void Button_Click(object sender, RoutedEventArgs e)
        {
            Button button = sender as Button;
            if (button.Content.ToString() == "Stop")
                media.Stop();
            else if (button.Content.ToString() == "Pause")
                media.Pause();
            else if (button.Content.ToString() == "Play")
                media.Play();
        }
    }
}
```

Running this project generates the result shown in Figure 11-16. You can interactively control the video playback by clicking the corresponding Stop, Pause, and Play buttons.

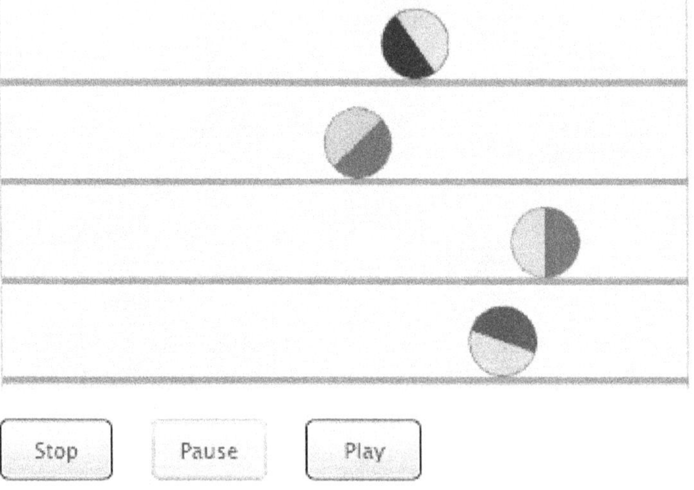

Figure 11-16 Interactive MediaElement in Silverlight.

Ink Control

Another exciting control in Silverlight is the InkPresenter, which provides a drawing surface for displaying ink strokes. InkPresenter derives from the Canvas, and behaves similarly in some aspects. The primary purpose of the InkPresenter control is to allow stylus input directly from the user. The stylus is a penlike input device used in tablet PCs. However, the InkPresenter works with the mouse in the same way as it works with the stylus. Thus, a user can still draw lines and manipulate elements on the drawing surface of the InkPresenter using a mouse.

The strokes collection in the InkPresenter holds System.Windows.Ink.Stroke objects, which represent graphical input that the user draws on the drawing surface of the InkPresenter. Each line or curve that the user draws becomes a separate Stroke object.

Let use an example to illustrate how to use this Ink control. Start with a new Silverlight project and name it Example11-14. In this example, the user will be allowed to set the Stroke attributes, including thickness, color, and outline color. Here is the XAML file of this example:

```
<UserControl x:Class="Example11_14.Page"
    xmlns="http://schemas.microsoft.com/winfx/2006/xaml/presentation"
    xmlns:x="http://schemas.microsoft.com/winfx/2006/xaml"
    Width="400" Height="400">
    <Grid x:Name="LayoutRoot" Background="White">
        <Grid.ColumnDefinitions>
            <ColumnDefinition/>
            <ColumnDefinition/>
            <ColumnDefinition/>
        </Grid.ColumnDefinitions>
        <Grid.RowDefinitions>
            <RowDefinition Height="40*"/>
            <RowDefinition Height="81*"/>
        </Grid.RowDefinitions>

        <StackPanel>
            <TextBlock Text="Pen Thickness" Margin="5 5 5 0"
                       HorizontalAlignment="Center"/>
            <ListBox x:Name="listBox1" Height="100" Margin="5 0 5 0"/>
        </StackPanel>
        <StackPanel Grid.Column="1">
            <TextBlock Text="Pen Color" Margin="5 5 5 0"
                       HorizontalAlignment="Center"/>
            <ListBox x:Name="listBox2" Height="100" Margin="5 0 5 0"/>
        </StackPanel>
        <StackPanel Grid.Column="2">
            <TextBlock Text="Outline Color" Margin="5 5 5 0"
                       HorizontalAlignment="Center"/>
            <ListBox x:Name="listBox3" Height="100" Margin="5 0 5 0"/>
        </StackPanel>
        <InkPresenter x:Name="myInk" Grid.Row="1" Grid.ColumnSpan="3"
                      Cursor="Stylus" Background="LightGray" Margin="5 0 5 5"
                      MouseLeftButtonDown="myInk_MouseLeftButtonDown"
                      MouseMove="myInk_MouseMove"
                      MouseLeftButtonUp="myInk_MouseLeftButtonUp"/>
    </Grid>
</UserControl>
```

Here, we create three ListBox controls, which hold the stroke thickness, stroke color, and stroke outline color, respectively. By selecting different items from these list boxes, the user can change the stroke's attributes. We also add an InkPresenter control to the project. The event handlers MouseLeftButtonDown, MouseMove, and MouseLeftButtonUp will be used to handle the user's drawing events in the code-behind file:

```
using System;
using System.Collections.Generic;
using System.Windows;
using System.Windows.Input;
using System.Windows.Controls;
using System.Windows.Media;
using System.Windows.Shapes;
using System.Windows.Ink;
using System.Reflection;

namespace Example11_14
{
    public partial class Page : UserControl
    {
        private Stroke pen;
        private Color penColor;
        private Color outlineColor;
        private double penThickness;

        public Page()
        {
            InitializeComponent();

            //Initialize list boxes:
            for (int i = 1; i < 15; i++)
            {
                listBox1.Items.Add(i);
            }

            Type colorsType = typeof(Colors);
            foreach (PropertyInfo property in colorsType.GetProperties())
            {
                listBox2.Items.Add(property.Name);
                listBox3.Items.Add(property.Name);
                penColor = Colors.Black;
                listBox2.SelectedIndex = 0;
                listBox3.SelectedIndex = 0;
            }

        }

        private void myInk_MouseLeftButtonDown(object sender,
                MouseButtonEventArgs e)
        {
            // capture mouse and create a pen:
            myInk.CaptureMouse();
            pen = new Stroke();
            myInk.Strokes.Add(pen);
```

```
            // set the desired pen attributes:
            penColor = StringToColor(listBox2.SelectedItem.ToString());
            outlineColor = StringToColor(listBox3.SelectedItem.ToString());
            pen.DrawingAttributes.Color = penColor;
            pen.DrawingAttributes.OutlineColor = outlineColor;
            if (listBox1.SelectedItem == null)
                penThickness = 1;
            else
                penThickness = double.Parse(listBox1.SelectedItem.ToString());
            pen.DrawingAttributes.Width = penThickness;
            pen.DrawingAttributes.Height = penThickness;

            // add the stylus points:
            pen.StylusPoints.Add(e.StylusDevice.GetStylusPoints(myInk));
        }

        private void myInk_MouseMove(object sender, MouseEventArgs e)
        {
            if (pen != null)
            {
                // add the stylus points
                pen.StylusPoints.Add(e.StylusDevice.GetStylusPoints(myInk));
            }
        }

        private void myInk_MouseLeftButtonUp(object sender,
                MouseButtonEventArgs e)
        {
            if (pen != null)
            {
                // add the stylus points
                pen.StylusPoints.Add(e.StylusDevice.GetStylusPoints(myInk));
            }

            // release mouse capture and we are done
            myInk.ReleaseMouseCapture();
            pen = null;
        }

        // Convert string to color:
        public Color StringToColor(string cString)
        {
            Type cType = (typeof(Colors));
            if (cType.GetProperty(cString) != null)
            {
                object obj = cType.InvokeMember(cString,
                             BindingFlags.GetProperty, null, null, null);
                if (obj != null)
                    return (Color)obj;
            }
            return Colors.Black;
        }
    }
}
```

Note that in order to access the Stroke object, we add a using statement at the beginning:

```
using System.Windows.Ink;
```

Next, we populate listBox2 and listBox3 with color name items, using a method similar to that used in Chapter 5. Inside the MouseLeftButtonDown event handler, we specify the stroke's attributes – thickness, color, and outline color – using items selected from the corresponding list boxes. Then we add the stylus points collection to the stroke object. We also use the MouseCapture mode to collect the stylus points from the mouse's movement.

Running this project produces the result shown in Figure 11-17. First, you select the pen thickness, pen color, and pen outline color from the corresponding list boxes; then you can draw on the drawing surface of the InkPresenter control.

Figure 11-17 Ink control in Silverlight.

MultiScaleImage Control and Deep Zoom

The MultiScaleImage control is a new element added to Silverlight 2. It enables you to open a multi-resolution image that can be scaled and repositioned for detailed viewing, which gives you a new and unique way of managing images in your Silverlight applications. Based on this control, you can implement an exciting DeepZoom effect, which allows you to arrange images so that you can zoom in and out easily.

The best way to create the DeepZoom effect in a Silverlight application is to use the DeepZoom composer tool, which can be downloaded from the Microsoft Download Center. Here, I'll show you how to build a simple DeepZoom application using an example.

Now start with the Microsoft DeepZoom Composer Preview 1 and create a new project called Example11-15. Now you can see the composer tool shown in Figure 11-18.

The DeepZoom Composer tool follows a simple workflow of Import – Compose – Export. First, you select the Import tab and select Add Image to import images. You can add as many images as you want. You can see from Figure 11-18 that I have added nine images to the project.

Figure 11-18 DeepZoom Composer.

The next step is to Compose by clicking the Compose tab, which allows you to place images on the design surface and then zoom in and out. For example, if you look at Figure 11-18, you'll see where I've placed nine images and zoomed out to fit the entire design area.

In this simple example, we have zoomed out all of the nine images at the same scale. The tool allows you to build far more complex applications with different zooming in or out ratios. We are now ready to go to the third step, exporting the composed images, as shown in Figure 11-18.

There are several options you can specify before export. First, you need to give the project a name and export it to a specified location. Next, you need to specify the Image type. The Image Formats are straightforward, with only two selections, JPEG and PNG. The tool also allows you to export composed images as a composition or a collection.

The composition option generates a single high-resolutions image. In this case, you arrange all of your images on the design surface, and during export, flatten everything into a large image before breaking them up into the various tiles. However, if you want to do more with your images, such as programmatically move individual images around or filter your images, you need to export your composed images as a collection.

With collections, instead of flattening your entire composition into a single image before generating your image tree, you actually generate an image tree for each image in your application. This is equivalent to generating a single high-resolution image for each image you use, which allows you to control each image individually while still retaining the layered zooming and fading effects – the DeepZoom effects. Note that the composition application usually runs faster than the collection application. In our simple example, we export the images as a composition.

Finally, you can select the output type as either Export Images or Export Images and Silverlight Project. If you select the former option, the composer tool only generates the composed images, and you need to manually integrate the exported images into your Silverlight applications. On the other hand, if you select the latter option, the composer tool automatically creates both the composed images and the Silverlight project for you. I prefer the latter option because you don't need to do anything on your part to create the DeepZoom effect.

Click the OK button, and DeepZoom Composer creates the images and Silverlight project. You can open the Silverlight project using Visual Studio 2008 with Silverlight 2 Beta 2 installed. In our example, the project solution file called DeepZoomProject.sln is located in the directory ~\Example11-15\source images\OutputSdi\mydeepzoom. Now the Solution Explorer in Visual Studio 2008 will look something like Figure 11-19.

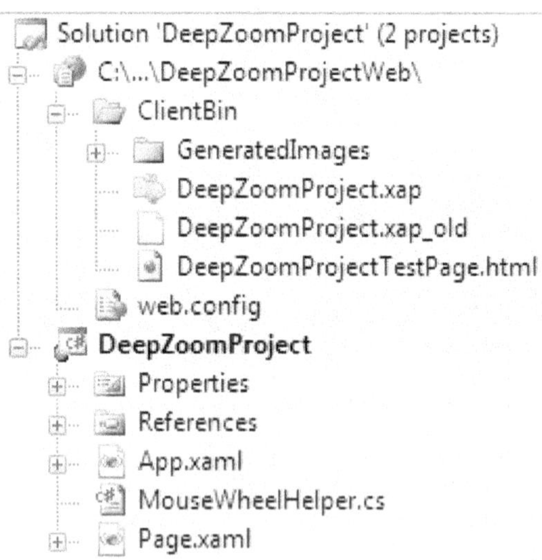

Figure 11-19 File structure of the DeepZoom project.

From this file structure you can see that DeepZoom Composer has used the option of Add a new Web to the solution for hosting the control, instead of the option of using an HTML test page to host Silverlight within the project that we have used for all of the other examples throughout of this book.

In order to run this Web application, you need to specify a proper Web server or set up the IIS service on your local machine. Otherwise, you will get a blank page when you run the project. Note that even if you don't have a Web server or the IIS on your local machine, there is still a workaround allowing you to test your DeepZoom project. In this case, Visual Studio 2008 tries to create a TestPage.html in the ~\mydeepzoom\DeepZoomProject\Bin\Debug (or Release depending on which mode you select) directory. Just copy the directory ~\mydeepzoom\DeepZoomProjectWeb\ClientBin\GeneratedImages to the Debug (or Release) directory. Press F5 to run the project again, and it should work.

You can view the XAML of the project:

```
<UserControl x:Class="DeepZoomProject.Page"
    xmlns="http://schemas.microsoft.com/winfx/2006/xaml/presentation"
    xmlns:x="http://schemas.microsoft.com/winfx/2006/xaml"
    Width="1024" Height="768">
    <Grid x:Name="LayoutRoot" Background="#FFFFFFFF">
        <Border BorderThickness="1,1,1,1" Margin="10,10,10,10"
                   BorderBrush="#FF9F9F9F">
           <MultiScaleImage x:Name="msi" MinHeight="480" MinWidth="640"
                                Height="768" Width="1024"/>
        </Border>
    </Grid>
</UserControl>
```

This XAML adds a MultiScaleImage control named msi to the project. The image source and the mouse event handlers are specified in code-behind. The code-behind file generated by the DeepZoom Composer for this project is listed below:

```
using System;
using System.Collections.Generic;
using System.Linq;
using System.Net;
using System.Windows;
using System.Windows.Controls;
using System.Windows.Documents;
using System.Windows.Input;
using System.Windows.Media;
using System.Windows.Media.Animation;
using System.Windows.Shapes;

namespace DeepZoomProject
{
    public partial class Page : UserControl
    {
        //
        // Based on prior work done by Lutz Gerhard, Peter Blois,
        // and Scott Hanselman
        //
        Point lastMousePos = new Point();

        double _zoom = 1;
        bool mouseButtonPressed = false;
        bool mouseIsDragging = false;
        Point dragOffset;
        Point currentPosition;

        public double ZoomFactor
        {
            get { return _zoom; }
            set { _zoom = value; }
        }
```

```
public Page()
{
    InitializeComponent();

    //
    // We are setting the source here because of an issue that
    // exists in Blend 2.5 when the Source is set via XAML
    //
    this.msi.Source = new DeepZoomImageTileSource(new
         Uri("GeneratedImages/dzc_output.xml", UriKind.Relative));

    //
    // Firing an event when the MultiScaleImage is Loaded
    //
    this.msi.Loaded += new RoutedEventHandler(msi_Loaded);

    //
    // Firing an event when all of the images have been Loaded
    //
    this.msi.ImageOpenSucceeded +=
         new RoutedEventHandler(msi_ImageOpenSucceeded);

    //
    // Handling all of the mouse and keyboard functionality
    //
    this.MouseMove += delegate(object sender, MouseEventArgs e)
    {
        if (mouseButtonPressed)
        {
            mouseIsDragging = true;
        }
        this.lastMousePos = e.GetPosition(this.msi);
    };

    this.MouseLeftButtonDown +=
         delegate(object sender, MouseButtonEventArgs e)
    {
        mouseButtonPressed = true;
        mouseIsDragging = false;
        dragOffset = e.GetPosition(this);
        currentPosition = msi.ViewportOrigin;
    };

    this.msi.MouseLeave += delegate(object sender, MouseEventArgs e)
    {
        mouseIsDragging = false;
    };

    this.MouseLeftButtonUp +=
         delegate(object sender, MouseButtonEventArgs e)
    {
        mouseButtonPressed = false;
        if (mouseIsDragging == false)
        {
```

```
            bool shiftDown = (Keyboard.Modifiers & ModifierKeys.Shift)
                             == ModifierKeys.Shift;

            ZoomFactor = 2.0;
            if (shiftDown) ZoomFactor = 0.5;
            Zoom(ZoomFactor, this.lastMousePos);
        }
        mouseIsDragging = false;
    };

    this.MouseMove += delegate(object sender, MouseEventArgs e)
    {
        if (mouseIsDragging)
        {
            Point newOrigin = new Point();
            newOrigin.X = currentPosition.X -
                          (((e.GetPosition(msi).X - dragOffset.X) /
                          msi.ActualWidth) * msi.ViewportWidth);
            newOrigin.Y = currentPosition.Y -
                          (((e.GetPosition(msi).Y - dragOffset.Y) /
                          msi.ActualHeight) * msi.ViewportWidth);
            msi.ViewportOrigin = newOrigin;
        }
    };

    new MouseWheelHelper(this).Moved +=
         delegate(object sender, MouseWheelEventArgs e)
    {
        e.Handled = true;
        if (e.Delta > 0)
            ZoomFactor = 1.2;
        else
            ZoomFactor = .80;

        Zoom(ZoomFactor, this.lastMousePos);
    };
}

void msi_ImageOpenSucceeded(object sender, RoutedEventArgs e)
{
    //If collection, this gets you a list of all of the
    //MultiScaleSubImages
    //
    //foreach (MultiScaleSubImage subImage in msi.SubImages)
    //{
    //    // Do something
    //}
}

void msi_Loaded(object sender, RoutedEventArgs e)
{
    Zoom(.5, new Point(this.ActualWidth / 2, this.ActualHeight / 2));
}

public void Zoom(double zoom, Point pointToZoom)
```

```
            {
                Point logicalPoint = this.msi.ElementToLogicalPoint(pointToZoom);
                this.msi.ZoomAboutLogicalPoint(zoom, logicalPoint.X,
                                                     logicalPoint.Y);
            }

            /*
             *  Sample event handlerrs tied to the Click of event of various buttons
             *  for showing all images, zooming in, and zooming out!
             *
            private void ShowAllClick(object sender, RoutedEventArgs e)
            {
                this.msi.ViewportOrigin = new Point(0, 0);
                this.msi.ViewportWidth = 1;
                ZoomFactor = 1;
            }

            private void zoomInClick(object sender, RoutedEventArgs e)
            {
                Zoom(1.2, new Point(this.ActualWidth / 2, this.ActualHeight / 2));
            }

            private void zoomOutClick(object sender, RoutedEventArgs e)
            {
                Zoom(.8, new Point(this.ActualWidth / 2, this.ActualHeight / 2));
            }
             * */
        }
    }
```

You can see from the above code that the MultiScaleImage is just like the other controls in Silverlight in that it can declare functions used to handle events. To pan around and zoom in or out on the image, you will use the mouse events MouseLeftButtonDown, MouseLeftButtonUp, MouseMove, and MouseWheelEvent in a similar manner in order to drag, drop, and zoom in on any control. DeepZoom Composer has already implemented these handlers for you.

Now you can run the project by pressing F5. The output is shown in Figure 11-20. You can pan and deep zoom the images on your screen with your mouse.

If you want to customize your deep zoom project, you can modify the XAML or code-behind file directly within Visual Studio. For example, you can change the size of the images and add a TextBox to the project by modifying the original XAML according to the following:

```
<UserControl x:Class="DeepZoomProject.Page"
    xmlns="http://schemas.microsoft.com/winfx/2006/xaml/presentation"
    xmlns:x="http://schemas.microsoft.com/winfx/2006/xaml"
    Width="400" Height="450">
    <Grid x:Name="LayoutRoot" Background="#FFFFFFFF">
        <StackPanel>
            <TextBlock Text="This my DeepZoom project" Margin="10,10,10,0"/>
               <Border BorderThickness="1,1,1,1" Margin="10,10,10,10"
                       BorderBrush="#FF9F9F9F">
                      <MultiScaleImage x:Name="msi" MinHeight="100"
                          MinWidth="100" Height="400" Width="400"/>
            </Border>
        </StackPanel>
```

```
    </Grid>
</UserControl>
```

Re-running the project produces the result shown in Figure 11-21.

Figure 11-20 Output from the DeepZoom project.

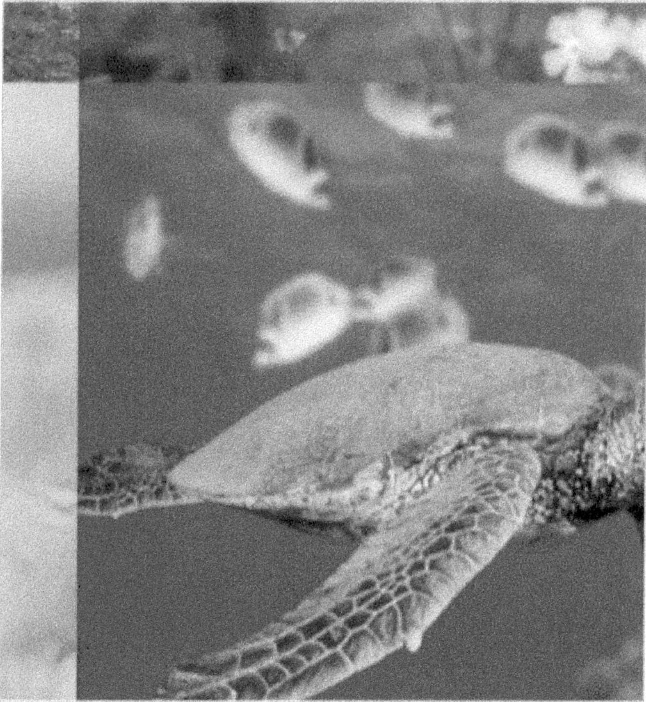

Figure 11-21 Result from the Customized DeepZoom project.

Chapter 12
Styles, Templates, and Data Binding

In the previous chapter you learned about Silverlight's basic built-in controls, which use their default visual appearances. Silverlight also enables you to easily create an application with has a unique look and feel to distinguish it from other applications. By using styles and templates, you have a great amount of flexibility with the appearance of your application. You can make slight changes to your application's appearance, such as changing the color of the controls and elements to something other than their default values, or more drastic changes, such as changing the shape of your buttons. The two classes that assist you in specifying the appearance of your application are Style and ControlTemplate. You use a Style to set property values; then, when you apply the style to multiple instances of a control, each control uses the property value that you set in the style. If you want to change the appearance of a control beyond setting its properties, you can create a ControlTemplate. A ControlTemplate defines the appearance and visual behavior of a control. Any element that inherits from FrameworkElement can have a style applied to it. Elements that inherit from the control have a ControlTemplate.

Data binding is a connection between the UI and a business object or other data provider. It allows you to create bindings that take information from the properties of any object. Silverlight includes ListBox and DataGrid controls that can handle entire collections of information and allow you to navigate through them. However, these ItemsControl objects will become more powerful and useful if the data binding is implemented behind the scenes.

Styles

A style in Silverlight is a collection of property values that can be applied to a control. The Silverlight style system plays a similar role to the cascading style sheet (CSS) standard in HTML documents. Like CSS, Silverlight styles allow you to set properties once and apply the style to multiple controls, which gives the controls a uniform appearance. When you apply a style to a control, you can still locally set properties on the control, and the property value that is set locally takes precedence over the property value set by the style.

You can define a style that wraps all the properties you want to set in the Resources. The best place to define the styles is within the Application.Resources tag in the App.xaml file of your application. This allows you to reuse the styles across all of the pages and controls in the entire project.

The following code snippet defines a style for a Button control:

```
</Application.Resources>
    <Style TargetType="Button" x:Key="ButtonStyle">
        <Setter Property="Width" Value="250"/>
        <Setter Property="Margin" Value="20 10 0 0"/>
        <Setter Property="HorizontalAlignment" Value="Left"/>
        <Setter Property="FontSize" Value="20"/>
        <Setter Property="Foreground" Value="Brown"/>
    </Style>
</Application.Resources>
```

This markup creates a style for a Button control. It holds a Setter collection with five Setter objects, one for each property that you want to set. Each Setter object names the property that it acts on and the value that it applies to that property. This style object has a key name, ButtonStyle, so you can refer to this key name when you apply the style to Button controls in your application.

Every Silverlight element can use a single style (or no style). The style applies to an element through the element's Style property. You can use the following code snippet to configure a button to use the style you created previously:

```
<Button Content="Customized Button" Style="{StaticResource ButtonStyle}"/>
```

Of course, you can also set a style programatically. The following code sets a style to a Button control named myButton:

```
myButton.Style = (Style)Application.Current.Resources["ButtonStyle"];
```

The Silverlight style system adds many benefits. It not only allows you to create groups of settings that are clearly related, but also streamlines your code by making it easier to apply these settings. You can apply a style without worrying about which properties it sets. In the previous example, five properties of the Button were organized into a stye named ButtonStyle. If you later decide that you need change some of the properties, you can change the values of the corresponding Setters. All the buttons that use the style automatically acquire the new style settings.

A Simple Style Example

Let's consider an example that shows how to use styles in a Silverlight application. This example creates three styles: one for a TextBlock, one for a TextBox, and one for a Button. Each style is applied to three instances of a control to create a uniform appearance for each TextBlock, TextBox, and Button. Start with a new Silverlight project and name it Example12-1. Here is the XAML of the Styles defined in the App.xaml file:

```
<Application xmlns="http://schemas.microsoft.com/client/2007"
             xmlns:x="http://schemas.microsoft.com/winfx/2006/xaml"
             x:Class="Example12_1.App">
    <Application.Resources>
        <Style TargetType="TextBlock" x:Key="TextBlockStyle">
            <Setter Property="Width" Value="120"/>
            <Setter Property="Foreground" Value="DarkBlue"/>
            <Setter Property="FontSize" Value="14"/>
            <Setter Property="FontWeight" Value="Bold"/>
            <Setter Property="TextAlignment" Value="Right"/>
            <Setter Property="VerticalAlignment" Value="Center"/>
        </Style>

        <Style TargetType="TextBox" x:Key="TextBoxStyle">
```

```
            <Setter Property="Width" Value="150"/>
            <Setter Property="Height" Value="25"/>
            <Setter Property="Margin" Value="4"/>
            <Setter Property="Background" Value="LightGray"/>
            <Setter Property="FontSize" Value="14"/>
        </Style>

        <Style TargetType="Button" x:Key="ButtonStyle">
            <Setter Property="Width" Value="250"/>
            <Setter Property="Margin" Value="20 10 0 0"/>
            <Setter Property="HorizontalAlignment" Value="Left"/>
            <Setter Property="FontSize" Value="20"/>
            <Setter Property="Foreground" Value="Brown"/>
        </Style>
    </Application.Resources>
</Application>
```

Here, you define three styles: TextBlockStyle, TextBoxStyle, and ButtonStyle. These styles can be used in your application, as shown in the page.xaml file of this example:

```
<UserControl x:Class="Example12_1.Page"
    xmlns="http://schemas.microsoft.com/client/2007"
    xmlns:x="http://schemas.microsoft.com/winfx/2006/xaml"
    Width="400" Height="300">

    <Grid x:Name="LayoutRoot" Background="White">
        <StackPanel x:Name="stackPanel1" Margin="10">
            <StackPanel Orientation="Horizontal">
                <TextBlock Style="{StaticResource TextBlockStyle}"
                           Text="First Name:"/>
                <TextBox Style="{StaticResource TextBoxStyle}"/>
            </StackPanel>
            <StackPanel Orientation="Horizontal">
                <TextBlock Style="{StaticResource TextBlockStyle}"
                           Text="Last Name:"/>
                <TextBox Style="{StaticResource TextBoxStyle}"/>
            </StackPanel>
            <StackPanel Orientation="Horizontal">
                <TextBlock Style="{StaticResource TextBlockStyle}"
                           Text="Phone Number:"/>
                <TextBox Style="{StaticResource TextBoxStyle}"/>
            </StackPanel>

            <Button Content="Customized Button 1"
                    Style="{StaticResource ButtonStyle}"/>
            <Button Content="Customized Button 2"
                    Style="{StaticResource ButtonStyle}"/>
        </StackPanel>
    </Grid>
</UserControl>
```

We also add a third Button and set its style programmatically in the code-behind file:

```
using System;
using System.Windows;
using System.Windows.Controls;
using System.Windows.Media;
```

```
namespace Example12_1
{
    public partial class Page : UserControl
    {
        public Page()
        {
            InitializeComponent();
            Button button = new Button();
            stackPanel1.Children.Add(button);
            button.Content = "Customized Button 3";
            button.Style = (Style)Application.Current.Resources["ButtonStyle"];
        }
    }
}
```

Figure 12-1 shows the result of running this application.

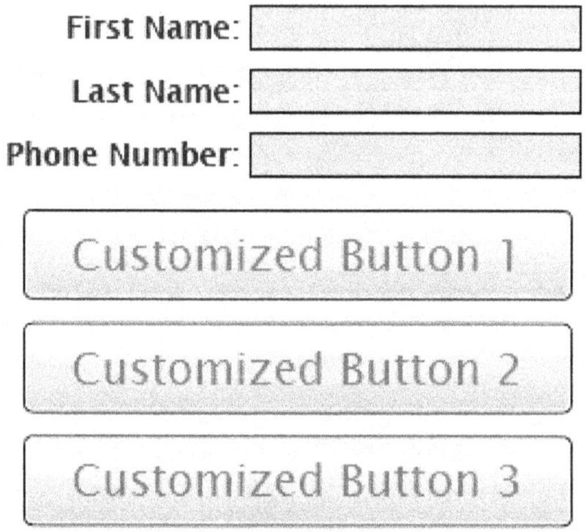

Figure 12-1 Styles in Silverlight.

Control Styles

To define a style, you may wonder which properties you can add to a style. There are two ways to do this that you may find useful. When you define a control in XAML, you can use Intellisense to reveal all of its properties that can be added to your style. The other approach is to consult the properties listing of the online or local Silverlight help document. The help document lists all of the default styles used for the built-in controls. If you are not sure which properties you can modify using styles, please read the "Control Styles and Templates" section of the Silverlight document for details.

The following code snippet shows the default styles for the Button control, a list taken directly from the Silverlight help document. To customize these styles, add the following XAML to your project, add an x:Key attribute to the Style element, and reference the style as shown in the example presented in the previous section.

```
<Style TargetType="Button" x:Key="ButtonStyle">
    <Setter Property="IsEnabled" Value="true" />
    <Setter Property="IsTabStop" Value="true" />
    <Setter Property="Background" Value="#FF003255" />
    <Setter Property="Foreground" Value="#FF313131" />
    <Setter Property="MinWidth" Value="5" />
    <Setter Property="MinHeight" Value="5" />
    <Setter Property="Margin" Value="0" />
    <Setter Property="HorizontalContentAlignment" Value="Center" />
    <Setter Property="VerticalContentAlignment" Value="Center" />
    <Setter Property="Cursor" Value="Arrow" />
    <Setter Property="TextAlignment" Value="Left" />
<Setter Property="TextWrapping" Value="NoWrap" />
    <Setter Property="FontSize" Value="11" />

<!-- Cannot currently parse FontFamily type in XAML
     so it's being set in code -->
    <!-- <Setter Property="FontFamily" Value="Trebuchet MS" /> -->
<!-- Cannot currently parse FontWeight type in XAML
     so it's being set in code -->
<!-- <Setter Property="FontWeight" Value="Bold" /> -->
</Style>
```

You can see that most properties of the Button control can be modified by changing their default values. However, some properties, such as the FontFamily and FontWeight, can't be set using styles in the current version of Silverlight. We hope that these properties will be available in the Style in the next release. In order to modify the FontFamily and FontWeight of a Button, you need to use in-line styles in XAML like below:

```
<Button Content="myButton" FontFamily="Times New Roman" FontWeight="Bold"/>
```

To change styles for the other controls in Silverlight, simply open the default Styles for the controls that you want to modify from the Silverlight document, as we did here for the Button; add the modified Styles to your application; and then reference the Styles when you create controls.

Once you have set styles for your controls, you are still free to override any attribute of any style for any individual control. For example, you set the Style property of a Button control using the ButtonStyle defined above, but you can still change its FontSize and Cursor properties in-line:

```
<Button Content="myButton" Style="{StaticResource ButtonStyle}"
        FontSize="30" Cursor="Hand"/>
```

Here the defined Button uses the Style but overrides the two properties FontSize and Cursor. The result is just what you want: application of the rest of the style, but with these two properties overridden, for the Button.

Here, you see how styles allow you to define named sets of property values and easily apply them to the appropriate element. Styles are a key scheme that support many other Silverlight features. For example, styles give you a way to apply new control templates to a range of controls; use different formatting depending on the current system themes; dynamically reskin your application; and enhance elements with automatic animations. You'll learn about control templates in next section.

Control Templates

In the previous sections, you learned how to modify characteristics of the appreance of the controls in your applications using styles. However, there is a limit to how much of the appearance of your control you can modify using styles. Sometimes you may want to customize the controls in your application beyond what their setting properties allow you to do. For example, you might want the buttons in your application to be shaped differently than the default rectangle. When you replace the appearance of an existing control without changing its functionality, you change the control's skin.

In Silverlight, the skin of a control is defined by its ControlTemplate. Because you create a ControlTemplate in XAML, you can change a control's appearance without writing any code. The Control class has a public Template property that can be set by application developers. The Templates allow any control to start out without its default specific appearance and to have its appearance entirely dictated by a design you supply.

Every control in Silverlight has a default template, which gives it the default appearance you are used to. When you create a new template for a control, you redefine its visual structure and visual behavior. This means that in a new template, you don't impose a template on top of the skin of the control. Instead, you simply replace the default template with your own.

Creating Control Templates

In this section, you'll build a simple custom Button control and learn how the control template works. As you know, the basic Button control uses its default settings to draw its rectangle shape and border. To apply a custom control template, you simply set the Template property of your control. Although you can define an in-line template, this approach rarely makes sense, because you will always want to reuse your template to skin multiple instances of the same control in your application. To this end, you need to define your control template as a resource and refer to it using a StaticResource reference, as shown below:

```
<Button Template="{StaticResource ButtonTemplate}"/>
```

This approach not only makes it easier to create a whole host of customized buttons, but also gives you the flexibility to modify your control template later without disrupting the rest of your application's user interface.

You can place the ButtonTemplate resource in the Resource collection of the containing page or the Application.Resources in the App.xaml file. Here is the basic outline for the control template:

```
<ControlTemplate TargetType="Button" x:Key="ButtonTemplate">
… …
</ControlTemplate>
```

You can see that the control template sets the TargetType property to explicitly indicate that it is designed for buttons.

Let's consider a code example that shows how to apply a template to a Button control. Start with a new Silverlight project and name it Example12-2. Here is the XAML of this example:

```
<UserControl x:Class="Example12_2.Page"
    xmlns="http://schemas.microsoft.com/client/2007"
    xmlns:x="http://schemas.microsoft.com/winfx/2006/xaml"
    Width="400" Height="300">
```

```
    <UserControl.Resources>
        <ControlTemplate TargetType="Button" x:Key="ButtonTemplate">
            <Grid>
                <Rectangle Stroke="Red" StrokeThickness="5" RadiusX="50"
                           RadiusY="50" Width="200" Height="150">
                    <Rectangle.Fill>
                        <LinearGradientBrush StartPoint="0 0" EndPoint="1 0">
                            <GradientStop Offset="0.2" Color="LightBlue"/>
                            <GradientStop Offset="0.8" Color="DarkBlue"/>
                        </LinearGradientBrush>
                    </Rectangle.Fill>
                </Rectangle>

                <TextBlock Text="My Button" Foreground="Yellow" FontSize="30"
                           HorizontalAlignment="Center"
                           VerticalAlignment="Center"/>
            </Grid>
        </ControlTemplate>
    </UserControl.Resources>

    <Grid x:Name="LayoutRoot" Background="White">
        <StackPanel>
            <Button Template="{StaticResource ButtonTemplate}"
                    Content="My Template Button" Width="300" Height="200"
                    Click="Button_Click" Margin="10"/>
            <TextBlock x:Name="textBlock" Text="Please click the button"
                       TextAlignment="Center" Margin="10"/>
        </StackPanel>
    </Grid>
</UserControl>
```

Here the ControlTemplate named ButtonTemplate is placed in the root UserControl.Resources. The default Rectangle shape is replaced by a new round-corner rectangle filled with a gradient brush and with a TextBlock inside it. You then create a Button control that references this template resource.

This button also has a Click event, which is handled in the code-behind file:

```
using System;
using System.Windows;
using System.Windows.Controls;
using System.Windows.Input;
using System.Windows.Media;

namespace Example12_2
{
    public partial class Page : UserControl
    {
        public Page()
        {
            InitializeComponent();
        }

        int i = 0;
        private void Button_Click(object sender, RoutedEventArgs e)
        {
```

```
                i++;
                textBlock.Text = "Button is Clicked " + i.ToString() + " times.";
            }
        }
    }
```

Running this application generates the result shown in Figure 12-2.

Figure 12-2 A Button with a control template.

Template Bindings

You may notice that the Button created using the ButtonTemplate in the previous section has some limitations. For example, the size and content of the button can't be modified. It always displays "My Button" and always has the same size, regardless of the values of Width, Height, and Content that are specified in-line. This is because the size of the Button and the Content displayed within it are hard-coded.

Fortunately, Silverlight has a tool that is designed exactly for this purpose: template binding. You can use a {TemplateBinding ControlProperty} markup extension syntax inside your control template to bind it to properties of the control. This allows your template to adapt as properties are set on the Control by the user.

Let's consider a new example that is similar to the previous example, but with TemplateBinding. Start with a new Silverlight project and name it Example12-3. Here is the XAML of this example:

```
<UserControl x:Class="Example12_3.Page"
    xmlns="http://schemas.microsoft.com/client/2007"
    xmlns:x="http://schemas.microsoft.com/winfx/2006/xaml"
    Width="400" Height="300">

    <UserControl.Resources>
        <ControlTemplate TargetType="Button" x:Key="ButtonTemplate">
            <Grid>
                <Rectangle Stroke="Red" StrokeThickness="5"
                           RadiusX="50" RadiusY="50"
                           Width="{TemplateBinding Width}"
                           Height="{TemplateBinding Height}">
                    <Rectangle.Fill>
```

```
                        <LinearGradientBrush StartPoint="0 0" EndPoint="1 0">
                            <GradientStop Offset="0.2" Color="LightBlue"/>
                            <GradientStop Offset="0.8" Color="DarkBlue"/>
                        </LinearGradientBrush>
                    </Rectangle.Fill>
                </Rectangle>

                <ContentPresenter Content="{TemplateBinding Content}"
                                  FontFamily="{TemplateBinding FontFamily}"
                                  FontSize="{TemplateBinding FontSize}"
                                  Foreground="{TemplateBinding Foreground}"
                                  HorizontalAlignment="Center"
                                  VerticalAlignment="Center"/>

            </Grid>
        </ControlTemplate>
    </UserControl.Resources>

     <Grid x:Name="LayoutRoot" Background="White">
        <StackPanel>
            <StackPanel Orientation="Horizontal">
                <Button Template="{StaticResource ButtonTemplate}"
                        Content="Button 1" Width="100" Height="100"
                        Click="Button_Click" Margin="10"
                        FontFamily="Times New Roman" FontSize="20"
                        Foreground="White"/>
                <Button Template="{StaticResource ButtonTemplate}"
                        Content="Button 2" Width="200" Height="100"
                        Click="Button_Click" Margin="10"
                        FontFamily="Times New Roman" FontSize="30"
                        Foreground="White"/>
                <Button Template="{StaticResource ButtonTemplate}"
                        Content="Button 3" Width="200" Height="200"
                        Click="Button_Click" Margin="10"
                        FontFamily="Times New Roman" FontSize="40"
                        Foreground="White"/>
            </StackPanel>
            <TextBlock x:Name="textBlock" Text="Please click a button"
                       TextAlignment="Center" Margin="10"/>
        </StackPanel>
    </Grid>
</UserControl>
```

Notice that you use the ContentPresenter object to replace the TextBlock in the ButtonTemplate. The ContentPresenter enables the button to display not just text strings, but any custom content as well.

We then use the ButtonTemplate on three buttons with different sizes. The click events of these three buttons are handled in the code-behind file:

```
using System;
using System.Windows;
using System.Windows.Controls;
using System.Windows.Input;
using System.Windows.Media;

namespace Example12_3
```

```
{
    public partial class Page : UserControl
    {
        public Page()
        {
            InitializeComponent();
        }

        int i1 = 0, i2 = 0, i3 = 0;
        private void Button_Click(object sender, RoutedEventArgs e)
        {
            Button button = sender as Button;
            if (button.Content.ToString() == "Button 1")
            {
                i1++;
                textBlock.Text = button.Content.ToString() +
                                 " is Clicked " + i1.ToString() + " times.";
            }
            else if (button.Content.ToString() == "Button 2")
            {
                i2++;
                textBlock.Text = button.Content.ToString() +
                                 " is Clicked " + i2.ToString() + " times.";
            }
            else if (button.Content.ToString() == "Button 3")
            {
                i3++;
                textBlock.Text = button.Content.ToString() +
                                 " is Clicked " + i3.ToString() + " times.";
            }
        }
    }
}
```

Figure 12-3 shows the results of running this application.

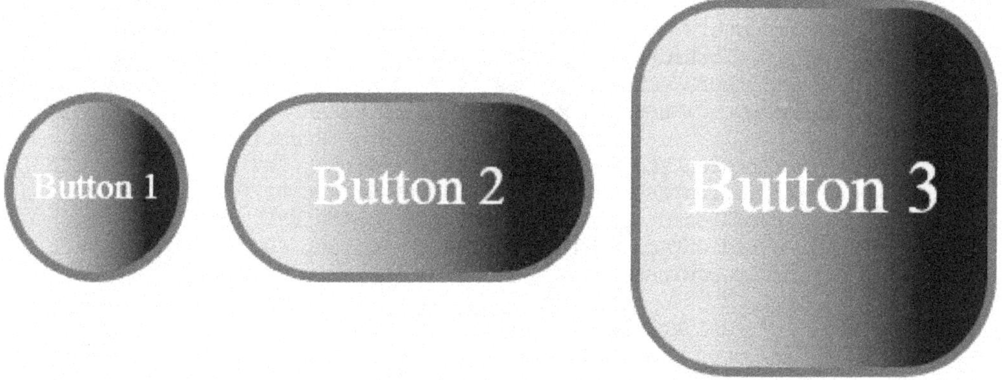

Button 2 is Clicked 7 times.

Figure 12-3 Buttons with control templates.

Note that template binding is similar to the ordinary data binding (which will be discussed later in this chapter), but is lighter weight because it is specifically designed for use in control templates. It only supports one-way data binding. If you run into a situation where template binding won't work, you can use a general data binding instead. For example, the rectangle in the above ButtonTemplate has RadiusX and RadiusY properties, which can't be set using TemplateBinding objects. You have to use data binding to set these properties. These properties in the example are hard-coded, and can't be changed in-line.

Default Templates

As in the case of default styles, evey control has a default control template. The Silverlight help document lists all of the default control templates used for the built-in controls. If you are not sure which template bindings are needed, please read the "Control Styles and Templates" section of the Silverlight document for details.

The following code snippet shows the default control template for the Button control, which is taken directly from the Silverlight help document.

```
<ControlTemplate TargetType="Button">
    <Grid x:Name="RootElement">
        <Grid.Resources>
            <!-- Visual constants used by the template -->
            <Color x:Key="LinearBevelLightStartColor">#FCFFFFFF</Color>
            <Color x:Key="LinearBevelLightEndColor">#F4FFFFFF</Color>
            <Color x:Key="LinearBevelDarkStartColor">#E0FFFFFF</Color>
            <Color x:Key="LinearBevelDarkEndColor">#B2FFFFFF</Color>
            <Color x:Key="MouseOverLinearBevelDarkEndColor">#7FFFFFFF</Color>
            <Color x:Key="HoverLinearBevelLightStartColor">#FCFFFFFF</Color>
            <Color x:Key="HoverLinearBevelLightEndColor">#EAFFFFFF</Color>
            <Color x:Key="HoverLinearBevelDarkStartColor">#D8FFFFFF</Color>
            <Color x:Key="HoverLinearBevelDarkEndColor">#4CFFFFFF</Color>
            <Color x:Key="CurvedBevelFillStartColor">#B3FFFFFF</Color>
```

```
        <Color x:Key="CurvedBevelFillEndColor">#3CFFFFFF</Color>
        <SolidColorBrush x:Key="BorderBrush" Color="#FF000000" />
        <SolidColorBrush x:Key="AccentBrush" Color="#FFFFFFFF" />
        <SolidColorBrush x:Key="DisabledBrush" Color="#A5FFFFFF" />
        <LinearGradientBrush x:Key="FocusedStrokeBrush"
                             StartPoint="0.5,0" EndPoint="0.5,1">
            <GradientStop Color="#B2FFFFFF" Offset="0" />
            <GradientStop Color="#51FFFFFF" Offset="1" />
            <GradientStop Color="#66FFFFFF" Offset="0.325" />
            <GradientStop Color="#1EFFFFFF" Offset="0.325" />
        </LinearGradientBrush>

        <!-- Visual states of the template -->
        <Storyboard x:Key="Normal State" />
        <Storyboard x:Key="MouseOver State">
            <ColorAnimation Duration="0:0:0.2"
                Storyboard.TargetName="LinearBevelDarkEnd"
                Storyboard.TargetProperty="Color"
                To="{StaticResource MouseOverLinearBevelDarkEndColor}" />
        </Storyboard>
        <Storyboard x:Key="Pressed State">
            <DoubleAnimation Duration="0:0:0.1"
                Storyboard.TargetName="LinearBevelLightEnd"
                Storyboard.TargetProperty="Offset" To=".2" />
            <ColorAnimation Duration="0:0:0.1"
                Storyboard.TargetName="LinearBevelLightStart"
                Storyboard.TargetProperty="Color"
                To="{StaticResource HoverLinearBevelLightEndColor}" />
            <ColorAnimation Duration="0:0:0.1"
                Storyboard.TargetName="LinearBevelLightEnd"
                Storyboard.TargetProperty="Color"
                To="{StaticResource HoverLinearBevelLightEndColor}" />
            <ColorAnimation Duration="0:0:0.1"
                Storyboard.TargetName="LinearBevelDarkStart"
                Storyboard.TargetProperty="Color"
                To="{StaticResource HoverLinearBevelDarkStartColor}" />
            <ColorAnimation Duration="0:0:0.1"
                Storyboard.TargetName="LinearBevelDarkEnd"
                Storyboard.TargetProperty="Color"
                To="{StaticResource HoverLinearBevelDarkEndColor}" />
            <DoubleAnimation Duration="0:0:0.1"
                Storyboard.TargetName="DownStroke"
                Storyboard.TargetProperty="Opacity" To="1" />
            <DoubleAnimation Duration="0:0:0.1"
                Storyboard.TargetName="FocusVisualElement"
                Storyboard.TargetProperty="Opacity" To="0" />
        </Storyboard>
        <Storyboard x:Key="Disabled State">
            <DoubleAnimation Duration="0:0:0"
                Storyboard.TargetName="Disabled"
                Storyboard.TargetProperty="Opacity" To="1" />
        </Storyboard>
    </Grid.Resources>

    <Rectangle x:Name="Background" RadiusX="4" RadiusY="4"
```

```
    Fill="{TemplateBinding Background}" />
<Rectangle x:Name="BackgroundGradient" RadiusX="4" RadiusY="4"
    StrokeThickness="1" Stroke="{StaticResource BorderBrush}">
    <Rectangle.Fill>
        <LinearGradientBrush StartPoint="0.7,0" EndPoint="0.7,1">
            <GradientStop x:Name="LinearBevelLightStart"
                Color="{StaticResource LinearBevelLightStartColor}"
                Offset="0" />
            <GradientStop x:Name="LinearBevelLightEnd"
                Color="{StaticResource LinearBevelLightEndColor}"
                Offset="0.35" />
            <GradientStop x:Name="LinearBevelDarkStart"
                Color="{StaticResource LinearBevelDarkStartColor}"
                Offset="0.35" />
            <GradientStop x:Name="LinearBevelDarkEnd"
                Color="{StaticResource LinearBevelDarkEndColor}"
                Offset="1" />
        </LinearGradientBrush>
    </Rectangle.Fill>
</Rectangle>
<Grid x:Name="CurvedBevelScale" Margin="2">
    <Grid.RowDefinitions>
        <RowDefinition Height="7*" />
        <RowDefinition Height="3*" />
    </Grid.RowDefinitions>
    <Path x:Name="CurvedBevel" Stretch="Fill" Margin="3,0,3,0"
        Data="F1 M 0,0.02 V 0.15 C 0.15,0.22 0.30,0.25 0.50,0.26 C
              0.70,0.26 0.85,0.22 1,0.15 V 0.02 L 0.97,0 H 0.02 L
              0,0.02 Z">
        <Path.Fill>
            <LinearGradientBrush StartPoint="0.5,0" EndPoint="0.5,1">
                <GradientStop x:Name="CurvedBevelFillStart"
                    Color="{StaticResource CurvedBevelFillStartColor}"
                    Offset="0" />
                <GradientStop x:Name="CurvedBevelFillEnd"
                    Color="{StaticResource CurvedBevelFillEndColor}"
                    Offset="1" />
            </LinearGradient and Brush>
        </Path.Fill>
    </Path>
</Grid>
<Rectangle x:Name="Accent" RadiusX="3" RadiusY="3" Margin="1"
    Stroke="{StaticResource AccentBrush}" StrokeThickness="1" />
<Grid x:Name="FocusVisualElement" Visibility="Collapsed">
   <Rectangle RadiusX="3" RadiusY="3" Margin="2"
       Stroke="{StaticResource AccentBrush}" StrokeThickness="1" />
    <Rectangle RadiusX="3" RadiusY="3"
        Stroke="{TemplateBinding Background}" StrokeThickness="2" />
    <Rectangle RadiusX="3" RadiusY="3"
        Stroke="{StaticResource FocusedStrokeBrush}"
        StrokeThickness="2" />
</Grid>
<Grid x:Name="DownStroke" Opacity="0">
    <Rectangle Stroke="{TemplateBinding Background}" RadiusX="3"
        RadiusY="3" StrokeThickness="1" Opacity="0.05"
```

```
                Margin="1,2,1,1" />
            <Rectangle Stroke="{TemplateBinding Background}" RadiusX="3"
                RadiusY="3" StrokeThickness="1" Opacity="0.05"
                Margin="1,1.75,1,1" />
            <Rectangle Stroke="{TemplateBinding Background}" RadiusX="3"
                RadiusY="3" StrokeThickness="1" Opacity="0.05"
                Margin="1,1.5,1,1" />
            <Rectangle Stroke="{TemplateBinding Background}" RadiusX="3"
                RadiusY="3" StrokeThickness="1" Opacity="0.05"
                Margin="1,1.25,1,1" />
            <Rectangle Stroke="{TemplateBinding Background}" RadiusX="3"
                RadiusY="3" StrokeThickness="1" Opacity="1" Margin="1" />
            <Rectangle RadiusX="4" RadiusY="4" StrokeThickness="1"  Margin="1">
                <Rectangle.Stroke>
                    <LinearGradientBrush EndPoint="0.5,1" StartPoint="0.5,0">
                        <GradientStop Color="#A5FFFFFF" Offset="0" />
                        <GradientStop Color="#FFFFFFFF" Offset="1" />
                    </LinearGradientBrush>
                </Rectangle.Stroke>
            </Rectangle>
        </Grid>

        <ContentPresenter
            Content="{TemplateBinding Content}"
            ContentTemplate="{TemplateBinding ContentTemplate}"
            FontFamily="{TemplateBinding FontFamily}"
            FontSize="{TemplateBinding FontSize}"
            FontStretch="{TemplateBinding FontStretch}"
            FontStyle="{TemplateBinding FontStyle}"
            FontWeight="{TemplateBinding FontWeight}"
            Foreground="{TemplateBinding Foreground}"
            HorizontalContentAlignment="{TemplateBinding
                                        HorizontalContentAlignment}"
            Padding="{TemplateBinding Padding}"
            TextAlignment="{TemplateBinding TextAlignment}"
            TextDecorations="{TemplateBinding TextDecorations}"
            TextWrapping="{TemplateBinding TextWrapping}"
            VerticalContentAlignment="{TemplateBinding
                                      VerticalContentAlignment}"
            Margin="4,5,4,4" />

        <Rectangle x:Name="Disabled" RadiusX="4" RadiusY="4"
            Fill="{StaticResource DisabledBrush}" Opacity="0"
            IsHitTestVisible="false" />
    </Grid>
</ControlTemplate>
```

By examining the default control template, you can anticipate which template bindings are needed. If you look at the default control template for the Button control, you'll find that it uses a template binding exactly the same way as our custom ButtonTemplate defined in the Example12-3 project does. You'll also find that the default button template includes a few more template bindings that are not used in our ButtonTemplate, such as Background and TextWrapping. This means that if you set these properties on the Button in Example12-3, they'll have no effect on the ButtonTemplate.

In many situations, leaving out some template bindings isn't an issue. In fact, you don't need to bind a property if you don't plan to use it or don't want it to change your template.

Data Binding

Data binding is a relationship that tells Silverlight to extract some information from a source object and use it to set a property in a target object.

Data-binding assists with the separation of the User Interface level from the other layers of your application. This separation of responsibility is further reinforced by decoupling the UI target from its source through the the use of a Binding object. For example, rich client applications often use two-way data binding, which adds the ability to push information from the user interface back to other layers of your application. Since many Web applications need to deal with data at least some of the time, data binding plays an important role in Silverlight applications.

There are three possible binding modes in Silverlight:

- OneTime binding – sets the target; then the binding is completed. This is great for displaying data that rarely or never changes.
- OneWay binding – sets the target and keeps it up to date as the source changes. This is great for displaying data that the user is not permitted to change.
- TwoWay binding – sets the target and keeps the target up to date as the source changes, and keeps the source up to date as the user changes the target or changes something else in the application that will cause your application to change the source.

Element-To-Element Binding

Unlike WPF, Silverlight doesn't support direct element-to-element binding. For example, the following code snippet is valid in WPF:

```
<Slider x:Name="slider1" Minimum="1" Maximum="40" Value="20" Margin="5"/>
<TextBlock x:Name="textBlock" Text="My simple text"
           FontSize="{Binding ElementName=slider1, path=Value}"/>
```

Here the FontSize property of the TextBlock is directly bound to the Value of the slider1. This will not work in Silverlight because direct element-to-element binding is not allowed in Silverlight. In the current version of Silverlight, only CLR object to UI target binding is possible.

If you really want element-to-element binding in your Silverlight application, you can achieve it in code. The following code example will demonstrate how to perform element-to-element bindings in code. Start with a new Silverlight project and name it Example12-4. Here is XAML of this example:

```
<UserControl x:Class="Example12_4.Page"
    xmlns="http://schemas.microsoft.com/client/2007"
    xmlns:x="http://schemas.microsoft.com/winfx/2006/xaml"
    Width="400" Height="300" Loaded="UserControl_Loaded">
    <StackPanel x:Name="LayoutRoot" Background="White">
        <TextBox x:Name="textBox1" TextChanged="textBox_TextChanged"
                 Margin="5"/>
        <TextBox x:Name="textBox2" TextChanged="textBox_TextChanged"
                 Margin="5"/>
        <TextBlock x:Name="textBlock" Text="My simple text" Margin="5"/>
```

```
        <Slider x:Name="slider1" Minimum="1" Maximum="40" Margin="5"
                Value="20"/>
    </StackPanel>
</UserControl>
```

Here, you create two TextBoxes, a TextBlock, and a Slider. You want to perform a two-way binding between the two text boxes, textBox1 and textBox2, meaning that the text in the other TextBox will change correspondingly when you change the text in one of the TextBoxes. At the same time, the FontSize of the two TextBoxes and the TextBlock is bound to the Value property of the Slider. All these bindings are accomplished using the event handlers textbox_TextChanged and slider1_ValueChanged in code:

```
using System;
using System.Windows;
using System.Windows.Controls;
using System.Windows.Media;

namespace Example12_4
{
    public partial class Page : UserControl
    {
        public Page()
        {
            InitializeComponent();
        }

        private void UserControl_Loaded(object sender, RoutedEventArgs e)
        {
            slider1.ValueChanged += new
                RoutedPropertyChangedEventHandler<double>(slider1_ValueChanged);
        }

        private void textBox_TextChanged(object sender, TextChangedEventArgs e)
        {
            TextBox textBox = sender as TextBox;
            if(textBox.Name=="textBox1")
                textBox2.Text=textBox1.Text;
            else if(textBox.Name=="textBox2")
                textBox1.Text=textBox2.Text;
        }

        private void slider1_ValueChanged(object sender,
                     RoutedPropertyChangedEventArgs<double> e)
        {
            textBox1.FontSize = slider1.Value;
            textBox2.FontSize = slider1.Value;
            textBlock.FontSize = slider1.Value;
        }
    }
}
```

Figure 12-4 shows the result of running this application. If you enter any text in one of the TextBoxes, the same text appears in the other TextBox immediately. If you move the thumb of the slider1, the font size of all of the text will change immediately. Thus, in this way, you achieve element-to-element binding in Silverlight.

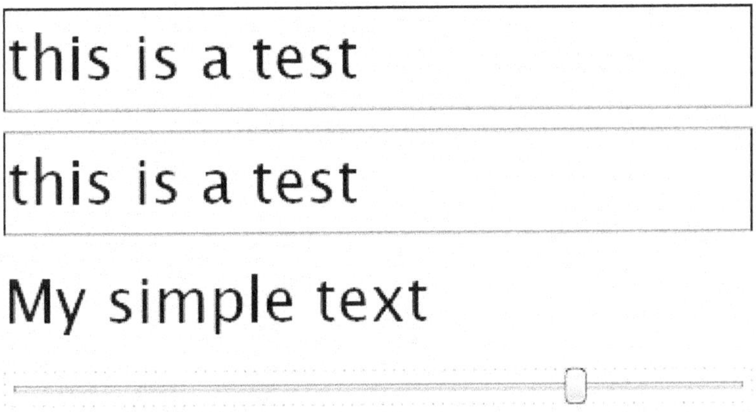

this is a test

this is a test

My simple text

Figure 12-4 Element-to-element bindings in Silverlight.

You can also chain data bindings. For example, you could create a data binding for the TextBBlock.FontSize property that links to the TextBox.Text property, which contains a binding expression that links to the Slider.Value property. In this case, when the user moves the slider thumb to a new position, the value flows from the Slider to the TextBox and then from the TextBox to the TextBlock. At the same time, the font size of the TextBlock can also be set by typing a font size into the TextBox. All the controls are synchronized so that if you type a new number in the text box, the font size of the text block is adjusted and the slider thumb is moved to the corresponding position.

Let's use a code example to accomplish this data binding. Start with a new Sliverlight application and name it Example12-5. Here is the XAML of this example:

```
<UserControl x:Class="Example12_5.Page"
    xmlns="http://schemas.microsoft.com/client/2007"
    xmlns:x="http://schemas.microsoft.com/winfx/2006/xaml"
    Width="300" Height="300" Loaded="UserControl_Loaded">
    <Grid x:Name="LayoutRoot" Background="White">
        <StackPanel>
            <TextBlock x:Name="textBlock" Text="My Text" Margin="10"/>
            <StackPanel Orientation="Horizontal">
                <TextBlock Text="Exact Font Size" Margin="10" FontSize="12"/>
                <TextBox x:Name="textBox" Text="20" TextAlignment="Center"
                         FontSize="12" Width="100" Height="22"
                         TextChanged="textBox_TextChanged"/>
            </StackPanel>
            <Slider x:Name="slider1" Minimum="1" Maximum="40" Value="20"
                    Margin="10"/>
        </StackPanel>
    </Grid>
</UserControl>
```

Again, here we'll use the textbox_TextChanged and slider1_ValueChanged events to perform the data binding in the code-behind file:

```
using System;
using System.Windows;
using System.Windows.Controls;
using System.Windows.Media;
```

```
namespace Example12_5
{
    public partial class Page : UserControl
    {
        public Page()
        {
            InitializeComponent();
        }

        private void UserControl_Loaded(object sender, RoutedEventArgs e)
        {
            slider1.ValueChanged += new
                RoutedPropertyChangedEventHandler<double>(slider1_ValueChanged);

        }

        private void slider1_ValueChanged(object sender,
                     RoutedPropertyChangedEventArgs<double> e)
        {
            textBox.Text = Math.Round(slider1.Value, 0).ToString();
        }

        private void textBox_TextChanged(object sender, TextChangedEventArgs e)
        {
            if (textBox.Text != "")
            {
                textBlock.FontSize = double.Parse(textBox.Text);
                slider1.Value = double.Parse(textBox.Text);
            }
        }
    }
}
```

You can see that you set a two-way binding between slider1 and textbox so that values travel both ways. This project generates the output of Figure 12-5. Now, whenever the TextBlock.FontSize property changes when the slider is dragged, the current value is inserted into the text box. Even better, you can edit the value in the text box to apply a specific font size.

My Text

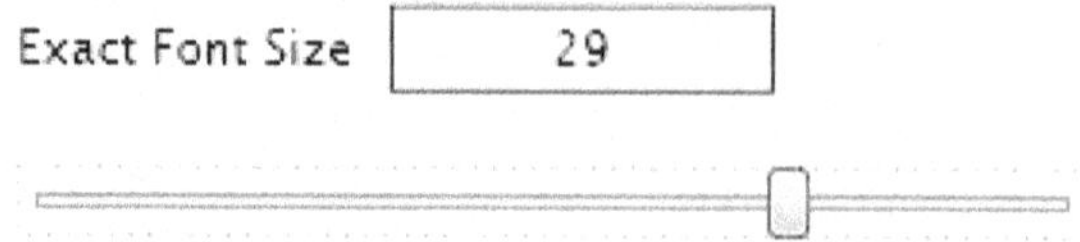

Figure 12-5 Chain binding in Silverlight.

Binding to Non-Element Objects

In the previous section, you learned how to use code to add bindings that link two elements. But in data-driven applications, it is more common to create binding expressions that draw their data from a nonvisual object. The information you want to display must be stored in public properties, and the target of the binding can be any public property of virtually any CLR object. There are two restrictions: the first is that the target must be a FrameworkElement, which inherits directly from UIElement and is an ancestor to all the visual UI elements. The other restriction is that the property you assign as the target must be a Dependency Property.

When you bind to an object that isn't an element, you need to use the DataContext property. The DataContext property is very useful if you need to bind several properties of the same object to different elements because you can set the DataContext property of a higher-level container control rather than setting it directly on the target element.

Let's consider an example that shows how to use the DataContext property. Start with a Silverlight Application and name it Example12-6. Add to the project a class named Customer.cs, which will represent the business layer. You want to have your business object participate in one-way or two-way binding with the Elements in your UI layer. To do so, it must implement the INotifyPropertyChanged interface, which requires a single event named PropertyChanged. You must then fire the PropertyChanged event whenever a property changes and indicate which property has changed by supplying the property name as a string. It is up to you to raise this event when a property changes, but you don't need to define a separate event for each property.

Here is the code listing of your Customer class:

```
using System;
using System.ComponentModel;
using System.Windows;
using System.Windows.Controls;
using System.Windows.Media;

namespace Example12_6
{
    public class Customer : INotifyPropertyChanged
    {
        private string lastName;
        private string firstName;
        private string phoneNumber;
        private bool isAvailabe;

        public event PropertyChangedEventHandler PropertyChanged;

        public string LastName
        {
            get { return lastName; }
            set
            {
                lastName = value;
                NotifyPropertyChanged("LastName");
            }
        }

        public string FirstName
        {
            get { return firstName; }
            set
            {
                firstName = value;
```

```
                NotifyPropertyChanged("FirstName");
            }
        }

        public string PhoneNumber
        {
            get { return phoneNumber; }
            set
            {
                phoneNumber = value;
                NotifyPropertyChanged("PhoneNumber");
            }
        }

        public bool IsAvailable
        {
            get { return isAvailabe; }
            set
            {
                isAvailabe = value;
                NotifyPropertyChanged("IsAvailable");
            }
        }

        public void NotifyPropertyChanged(string propertyName)
        {
            if (PropertyChanged != null)
            {
                PropertyChanged(this,
                    new PropertyChangedEventArgs(propertyName));
            }
        }
    }
}
```

Here, you split the creation of the PropertyChangedEventArgs call into a separate public method named NotifyPropertyChanged so that you can use it for more than one property in the Customer class.

Now, you can perform data binding to elements in your UI layer using the Customer object. The UI is created using XAML like below:

```
<UserControl x:Class="Example12_6.Page"
    xmlns="http://schemas.microsoft.com/client/2007"
    xmlns:x="http://schemas.microsoft.com/winfx/2006/xaml"
    Width="400" Height="230" Loaded="UserControl_Loaded">
    <Grid x:Name="LayoutRoot" Background="White">
        <Grid.ColumnDefinitions>
            <ColumnDefinition Width="1*"/>
            <ColumnDefinition Width="2*"/>
        </Grid.ColumnDefinitions>
        <Grid.RowDefinitions>
            <RowDefinition/>
            <RowDefinition/>
            <RowDefinition/>
            <RowDefinition/>
            <RowDefinition/>
```

```
        </Grid.RowDefinitions>

        <TextBlock Margin="10" Text="Last Name:" HorizontalAlignment="Right"/>
        <TextBox x:Name="textLastName" Margin="5" Text="{Binding LastName}"
                 Grid.Column="1" Height="25" TextAlignment="Center"/>
        <TextBlock Margin="10" Text="First Name:" Grid.Row="1"
                   HorizontalAlignment="Right"/>
        <TextBox x:Name="textFirstName" Margin="5" Text="{Binding FirstName}"
                 Grid.Column="1" Grid.Row="1" Height="25"
                 TextAlignment="Center"/>
        <TextBlock Margin="10" Text="Phone Number:" Grid.Row="2"
                   HorizontalAlignment="Right"/>
        <TextBox x:Name="textPhoneNumber" Margin="5"
                 Text="{Binding PhoneNumber}" Grid.Column="1" Grid.Row="2"
                 Height="25" TextAlignment="Center"/>
        <TextBlock Margin="10" Text="Availability:" Grid.Row="3"
                   HorizontalAlignment="Right"/>
        <CheckBox x:Name="checkAvailibility" Margin="5"
                  IsChecked="{Binding IsAvailable}" Content="Available"
                  Grid.Column="1" Grid.Row="3" Height="25"
                  TextAlignment="Center"/>
        <Button Content="Check Change" Click="Button_Click" Grid.Column="1"
                Grid.Row="4" Width="100" Height="25" HorizontalAlignment="Left"
                Margin="10"/>
    </Grid>
</UserControl>
```

Here, you use three text boxes to display the information, LastName, FirstName, and PhoneNumber, and a check box to display the Availability information. Here, you assign these elements to their corresponding binding objects. For example:

```
<TextBox x:Name="textLastName" Margin="5" Text="{Binding LastName}"
         Grid.Column="1" Height="25" TextAlignment="Center"/>
```

where the Text property of the TextBox named textLastName is bound to the LastName property of the Customer object.

The Button control is used to demonstrate how the data binding source can be changed at runtime.

The DataContext property of the elements is set in the code-behind file:

```
using System;
using System.Windows;
using System.Windows.Controls;
using System.Windows.Media;

namespace Example12_6
{
    public partial class Page : UserControl
    {
        Customer customer;

        public Page()
        {
            InitializeComponent();
        }
```

```
        private void UserControl_Loaded(object sender, RoutedEventArgs e)
        {
            customer = new Customer();
            customer.LastName = "Xu";
            customer.FirstName = "Jack";
            customer.PhoneNumber = "123-456-7890";
            customer.IsAvailable = true;
            LayoutRoot.DataContext = customer;
        }

        private void Button_Click(object sender, RoutedEventArgs e)
        {
            if (customer.LastName == "Xu")
            {
                customer.LastName = "Barkley";
                customer.FirstName = "Charles";
                customer.PhoneNumber = "098-765-4321";
                customer.IsAvailable = false;
            }
            else
            {
                customer.LastName = "Xu";
                customer.FirstName = "Jack";
                customer.PhoneNumber = "123-456-7890";
                customer.IsAvailable = true;
            }
        }
    }
}
```

In this class, you create a customer object and assign the LastName, FirstName, PhoneNumber, and IsAvailable properties to it. Finally, you set the DataContext property of the parent container control of the elements using the customer object.

Instead of setting the DataContext property of the container, you can get the same result by specifying the DataContext property of the individual element like below:

```
textLastName.DataContext = customer;
textFirstName.DataContext = customer;
textPhoneNumber.DataContext = customer;
checkAvailibility.DataContext = customer;
```

In addition, you implement the Button's Click event handler to change the data source of the Customer object.

Running the application generates the result shown in Figure 12-6. Note that when the customer's properties change by clicking the "Check Change" button, the UI elements are updated automatically by responding to the click event.

Last Name: Barkley

First Name: Charles

Phone Number: 098-765-4321

Availability: Available

Check Change

Figure 12-6 Data binding to a custom object.

Binding to Object Collection

As shown in the previous section, binding to a single custom object is quite straightforward. But things become more interesting when you need to bind to a collection of objects. In Silverlight, the classes that derive from ItemsControl have the ability to show an entire list of items. Data binding possibilities include the ListBox and DataGrid.

Although Silverlight only provides two built-in ItemsControl objects, these two controls allow you to show your data in a virtually unlimited number of ways. This is because both the ListBox and DataGrid controls support data templates, which allow you to control exactly how items are displayed.

In the following, you'll implement a Silverlight application that shows a list of books using a DataGrid control. A screen shot which displays a book list is shown in Figure 12-7. Each item in the list includes the thumbnail image of the book, the book title, and the author. When you click a book, detailed information about the book will be displayed, including the subtitle, publish date, ISBN number, book description, and an image of the front cover of the book.

In order to create this example, you need to customize the default DataGrid, which involves several techniques you have learned, such as the ControlTemplate, DataTemplate, and data binding. You also need to build your data access logic. You can populate the DataGrid object by retrieving the list of books from a database or from a Web server through Silverlight's built-in networking API, which enables Silverlight clients to call remote REST, SOAP/WS, or XML HTTP services. Since this book concentrates on user interfaces and graphics, details about the Web services and networking API are beyond the scope of this book. You can refer to Silverlight's help documents and other books on the topic.

In this example, you'll use an XML file to populate the DataGrid object. LINQ to XML provides a quick and straightforward way to extract XML data from a separate file, Web location, or application resource and make it available to the elements in your application.

Start with a new Silverlight application and name it Example12-7. Right-click the References in the Solution Explorer and select Add Reference... From the Add Reference window, select System.Xml.Linq and System.Windows.Controls.Data. Add a new XML file called BookList.xml and three book image files to the project.

Here is a portion of the BookList.xml file used in this example:

```
<?xml version="1.0" encoding="utf-8" ?>
<books>
  <book>
      <title>Practical WPF Graphics Programming</title>
      <author>by Dr. Jack Xu</author>
      <subtitle>Advanced .NET Graphics Development with the Windows Presentation
               Foundation</subtitle>
      <publishdate>November, 2007</publishdate>
      <isbn10>0979372518</isbn10>
      <isbn13>978-0979372513</isbn13>
      <img contentType="image.jpg" src="homeWPF.jpg"/>
      <link>wpf_link</link>
      <description>This book emphasizes practical usefulness for your real-world
graphics applications and tries to explain WPF graphics concepts based on code
examples. This in-depth book on graphics programming in WPF contains over 120
ready-to-run code examples that provide you with everything you need to know to
add advanced graphics to your applications. From basic 2D shapes to complex
interactive 3D models, this book clearly explains every step it takes to build a
variety of WPF graphics applications using code examples. You'll learn how to
use WPF to create impressive graphic effects and high-fidelity user
interfaces.</description>
</book>
… …
</books>
```

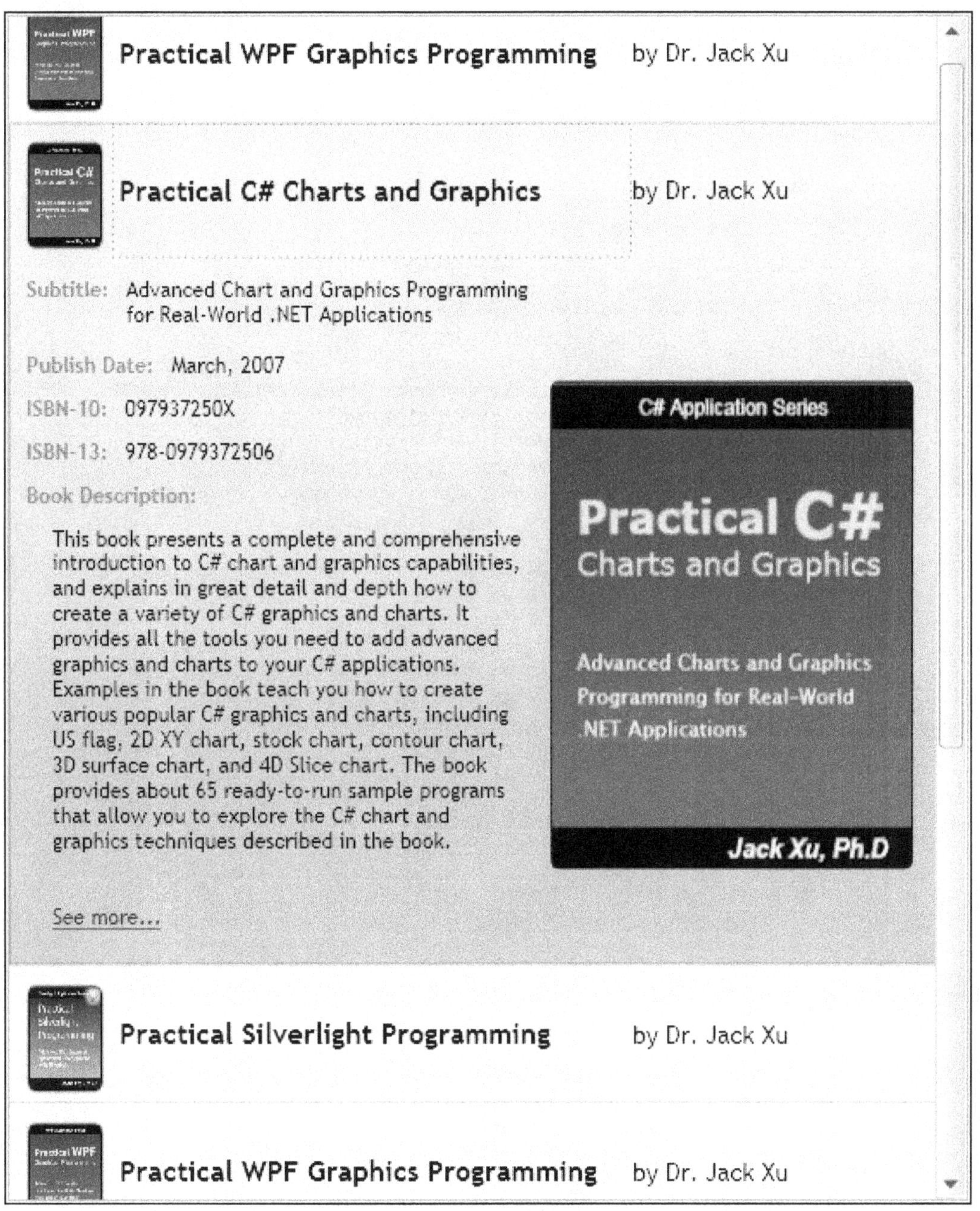

Figure 12-7 A list of books.

The above XML file wraps the entire document in a top-level <books> element and places each <book> in a separate book element. The individual properties for each book are provided as nested elements. These properties include title, author, ISBN, book description, etc. You can add any number of <book> items to this file.

The following is the XAML file of this example:

```
<UserControl xmlns:data="clr-namespace:System.Windows.Controls;
                         assembly=System.Windows.Controls.Data"
    x:Class="Example12_7.Page"
    xmlns="http://schemas.microsoft.com/winfx/2006/xaml/presentation"
    xmlns:x="http://schemas.microsoft.com/winfx/2006/xaml"
    Width="580" Height="825" Loaded="UserControl_Loaded">

<Grid x:Name="LayoutRoot" Width="850" Height="680" Background="White"
      HorizontalAlignment="Left" VerticalAlignment="Top">
        <data:DataGrid x:Name="results" RowHeight="75" IsReadOnly="True"
                       Width="560" Margin="10" Grid.Column="0" Grid.Row="0"
                       RowBackground="#99FAFAFA"
                       AlternatingRowBackground="#55FAFAFA"
                       HeadersVisibility="None" GridlinesVisibility="Horizontal"
                       VerticalScrollBarVisibility="Auto"
                       HorizontalScrollBarVisibility="Hidden"
                       RowDetailsVisibilityMode="VisibleWhenSelected"
                       SelectionMode="Single" HorizontalAlignment="Left">
            <data:DataGrid.Columns>
                <data:DataGridTemplateColumn Width="60">
                    <data:DataGridTemplateColumn.CellTemplate>
                        <DataTemplate>
                            <Border CornerRadius="5" BorderThickness="1"
                                    Margin="10,10,5,5" BorderBrush="DarkGray"
                                    Background="Black">
                                <Image Source="{Binding ImageUri}"
                                       Stretch="Fill" Margin="1"/>
                            </Border>
                        </DataTemplate>
                    </data:DataGridTemplateColumn.CellTemplate>
                </data:DataGridTemplateColumn>
                <data:DataGridTextColumn DisplayMemberBinding="{Binding Title}"
                                         FontSize="16" FontWeight="Bold"
                                         Width="300"/>
                <data:DataGridTextColumn DisplayMemberBinding="{Binding Author}"
                                         FontSize="14" Width="300"/>
            </data:DataGrid.Columns>

            <data:DataGrid.RowDetailsTemplate>
                <DataTemplate>
                    <Grid x:Name="detailGrid" Margin="5,5,5,0"
                          Background="Transparent">
                        <Grid.ColumnDefinitions>
                            <ColumnDefinition Width="Auto"/>
                            <ColumnDefinition Width="Auto"/>
                        </Grid.ColumnDefinitions>

                        <Grid.RowDefinitions>
                            <RowDefinition Height="Auto"/>
                            <RowDefinition Height="10" />
                        </Grid.RowDefinitions>

                        <StackPanel>
                            <StackPanel Orientation="Horizontal">
```

```
    <TextBlock Text="Subtitle:" Foreground="#666666"
               Margin="5,5,5,0"
               FontFamily="Trebuchet MS"
               FontSize="12" FontWeight="Bold"/>
    <TextBlock Text="{Binding Subtitle}"
               Margin="5,5,5,0"
               FontFamily="Trebuchet MS"
               FontSize="12" TextWrapping="Wrap"
               Width="230"/>
</StackPanel>
<StackPanel Orientation="Horizontal">
    <TextBlock Text="Publish Date:"
               Foreground="#666666" Margin="5,0,5,0"
               FontFamily="Trebuchet MS"
               FontSize="12" FontWeight="Bold"/>
    <TextBlock Text="{Binding PublishDate}"
               Margin="5,0,5,5"
               FontFamily="Trebuchet MS"
               FontSize="12"/>
</StackPanel>
<StackPanel Orientation="Horizontal">
    <TextBlock Text="ISBN-10:" Foreground="#666666"
               Margin="5,5,5,0"
               FontFamily="Trebuchet MS"
               FontSize="12" FontWeight="Bold"/>
    <TextBlock Text="{Binding ISBN10}"
               Margin="5,5,5,5"
               FontFamily="Trebuchet MS"
               FontSize="12"/>
</StackPanel>
<StackPanel Orientation="Horizontal">
    <TextBlock Text="ISBN-13:" Foreground="#666666"
               Margin="5,5,5,0"
               FontFamily="Trebuchet MS"
               FontSize="12" FontWeight="Bold"/>
    <TextBlock Text="{Binding ISBN13}"
               Margin="5,5,5,5"
               FontFamily="Trebuchet MS"
               FontSize="12"/>
</StackPanel>

<TextBlock Text="Book Description:"
           Foreground="#666666" Margin="5,5,5,0"
           FontFamily="Trebuchet MS" FontSize="12"
           FontWeight="Bold"/>
<TextBlock Text="{Binding Description}"
           TextWrapping="Wrap" Margin="20,10,5,0"
           FontFamily="Trebuchet MS" FontSize="12"
           Width="250" HorizontalAlignment="Left"/>
<TextBlock x:Name="linkMore" Text="See more..."
           Margin="20,0,0,10"
           FontFamily="Trebuchet MS" FontSize="12"
           HorizontalAlignment="Left"
           MouseLeftButtonDown="LinkMore_MouseDown"
           MouseEnter="LinkMore_MouseEnter"
```

```
                                        MouseLeave="LinkMore_MouseLeave"
                                        Foreground="Blue" Cursor="Hand"
                                        Tag="{Binding LinkMore}"
                                        TextDecorations="Underline"/>
                        </StackPanel>

                        <Border Grid.Column="1" Height="270" Width="210"
                                CornerRadius="5" BorderThickness="0"
                                Margin="10,20,20,0" BorderBrush="DarkGray"
                                Background="Black" VerticalAlignment="Center">
                            <Image Source="{Binding BigImageUri}" Stretch="Fill"
                                   Margin="1" Width="210" Height="270"/>
                        </Border>
                    </Grid>
                </DataTemplate>
            </data:DataGrid.RowDetailsTemplate>
        </data:DataGrid>
    </Grid>
</UserControl>
```

In this XAML file, you first need to add the following namespace and assembly:

```
xmlns:data="clr-namespace:System.Windows.Controls;
            assembly=System.Windows.Controls.Data"
```

This allows you to use the DataGrid control in XAML. Then you create the book thumbnail image, title, and author. Note that to place the thumbnail image of the book, you need to use the DataTemplate within the DataGridTemplateColumn.CellTemplate to define how a bound data object should be displayed in a specified cell of the DataGrid control. A data template is just a block of XAML markup and can include any combination of elements. It should also include one or more data binding expressions that retrieve the information to be displayed.

Next, you define another DataTemplate inside the RowDetailsTemplate tag to set a variety of data bindings to corresponding properties. This DataTemplate allows you to display the detailed information about the selected book, including the ISBN, book description, and the front cover image of the book.

When the DataGrid object is bound to the collection of <books>, a single row is created for each book. The data bindings are automatically established by the DataTemplate objects shown earlier, which extract the information of the book from the BookList.xml file and display it in the corresponding row of the DataGrid control.

Our next step is to parse and convert the information in the BookList.xml file into MySource objects that you can manipulate and databind your controls against.

You can do this by implementing a MySource class, which defines properties that map to the XML content from the BookList.xml file. You can append this class directly to the code behind file Page.xaml.cs:

```
public class MySource
{
    public BitmapImage ImageUri { get; set; }
    public BitmapImage BigImageUri { get; set; }
    public string Title { get; set; }
    public string Author { get; set; }
    public string Subtitle { get; set; }
```

```
        public string ISBN10 { get; set; }
        public string ISBN13 { get; set; }
        public string Description { get; set; }
        public string PublishDate { get; set; }
        public string Comment { get; set; }
        public string LinkMore { get; set; }
    }
```

Here you use the new C# automatic properties feature. Next, you can use LINQ and LINQ to XML to easily parse the XML document and translate it into a sequence of MySource objects in the code behind file:

```
using System;
using System.Linq;
using System.Xml.Linq;
using System.Windows;
using System.Windows.Browser;
using System.Windows.Controls;
using System.Windows.Input;
using System.Windows.Media;
using System.Windows.Media.Imaging;

namespace Example12_7
{
    public partial class Page : UserControl
    {
        public Page()
        {
            InitializeComponent();
        }


        private void UserControl_Loaded(object sender, RoutedEventArgs e)
        {
            DisplayBooks();
        }

        private void DisplayBooks()
        {
            XDocument xmlBooks = XDocument.Load("BookList.xml");
            var books = from book in xmlBooks.Descendants("book")
                        where book.Element("title") != null
                        select new MySource
                        {
                            Title = (string)book.Element("title"),
                            Author = (string)book.Element("author"),
                            Subtitle = (string)book.Element("subtitle"),
                            PublishDate = (string)book.Element("publishdate"),
                            ISBN10 = (string)book.Element("isbn10"),
                            ISBN13 = (string)book.Element("isbn13"),
                            Description = (string)book.Element("description"),
ImageUri = new BitmapImage(new
           Uri((string)book.Element("img").Attribute("src"), UriKind.Relative)),
BigImageUri = new BitmapImage(new
           Uri((string)book.Element("img").Attribute("src"), UriKind.Relative)),
                            LinkMore = (string)book.Element("link")
```

```
                };
            results.ItemsSource = books;
        }

        private void LinkMore_MouseEnter(object sender, MouseEventArgs e)
        {
            TextBlock text = sender as TextBlock;
            if (text.Name == "linkMore")
                text.Foreground =
                    new SolidColorBrush(Color.FromArgb(255, 200, 0, 0));
        }

        private void LinkMore_MouseLeave(object sender, MouseEventArgs e)
        {
            TextBlock text = sender as TextBlock;
            if (text.Name == "linkMore")
                text.Foreground =
                    new SolidColorBrush(Color.FromArgb(255, 0, 0, 255));
        }

        private void LinkMore_MouseDown(object sender, MouseButtonEventArgs e)
        {
            TextBlock text = sender as TextBlock;
            if (text.Tag.ToString() == "wpf_link")
HtmlPage.Window.Navigate(new Uri("http://www.drxudotnet.com/wpf_index.html",
                              UriKind.Absolute));
            else if (text.Tag.ToString() == "csharp_link")
HtmlPage.Window.Navigate(new Uri("http://www.drxudotnet.com/csharp_index.html",
                              UriKind.Absolute));
            else if (text.Tag.ToString() == "sl_link")
HtmlPage.Window.Navigate(new
        Uri("http://www.drxudotnet.com/silverlight_index.html",
UriKind.Absolute));
        }
    }
}
```

Note how we load the XML file using the XDocument object and parse its contents to the MySource objects using the LINQ to XML command. The key step here is to bind the ItemSource property of the DataGrid named results to the sequence of book information from the BookList.xml file:

```
results.ItemsSource = books;
```

This statement establishes various data bindings defined in the XAML file automatically.

You may also notice that the TextBlock with a text string "See more…" is defined as a hyperlink control. You can also directly use a HyperlinkButton for the same purpose.

Now, you can obtain the result shown in Figure 12-7 from running this application.

Chapter 13
Expression Blend

In the previous chapters, you built a variety of user interfaces and Silverlight applications directly using XAML markup and C# code. This approach is very useful for explaining Silverlight code and programming concepts and creating simple Web applications.

However, to create complex Silverlight applications in a more productive way, you may rather use a design tool named Expression Blend to generate the XAML that you need. The Expression Blend is a full-featured design tool used for designing layouts and user interfaces, creating animations, and adding interactivity to your WPF or Silverlight Applications. This chapter will present an overview of the Expression Blend and how to use it to build Silverlight applications.

Expression Blend Overview

Microsoft Expression Blend is a new design tool for creating highly-interactive user interfaces for WPF and Silverlight applications. With Expression Blend, you can design and create the UI of an application without worrying about the logic of the application. Once the UI is completed with Expression Blend, you can pass the UI to Visual Studio 2008 to implement the event handlers and business logic of the application.

In this book, the latest Expression Blend 2.5 June 2008 Preview is used. You can download the public preview from the Microsoft Expression website:

```
www.microsoft.com/expression
```

Workspace

With the Blend 2.5 Preview installed, you should see the New Project dialog shown in Figure 13-1 when you start a new project with Expression Blend. This dialog launches by default and presents a list of available project types you can use to get started. Currently, there are four templates you can choose from:

- WPF Application – creates a WPF application using Expression Blend.
- WPF Control Library – creates a WPF control library using Expression Blend.
- Silverlight 1 Site – creates a Silverlight 1 application using Expression Blend.

- Silverlight 2 Application – creates a Silverlight 2 application using Expression Blend.

You should select the last option, Silverlight 2 Application, to create a Silverlight 2 application, as shown in Figure 13-1.

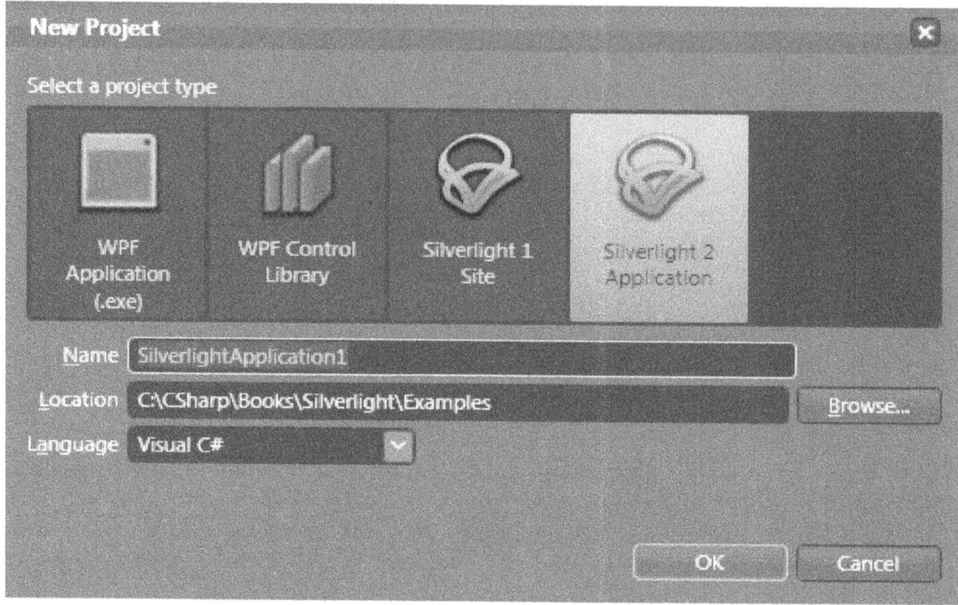

Figure 13-1 New Project dialog window.

Enter a name for your application and click the OK button to create a new solution file and Silverlight application project. This brings up a new Design Workspace with various panels labeled as shown in Figure 13-2.

Expression Blend has two workspaces, a Design Workspace (Figure 13-2) and an Animation Workspace. The Animation Workspace rearranges various panels and places the interaction panel at the bottom of the page so that it has a bigger area of focus. You can switch to the Animation Workspace by selecting Window – Active Workspace – Animation Workspace. You can also switch between workspaces by simply pressing F6. Figure 13-3 shows Expression Blend in the Animation Workspace view.

File Structure

Expression Blend includes a full "What You See Is What You Get" (WYSIWYG) designer for WPF and Silverlight applications. When you open Silverlight pages and controls, you can switch the design area to be in design view, a XAML source view, or a split-view that shows both the design view and the XAML source view at the same time.

You can see from the upper right hand corner that the solution, project, and other files generated by Expression Blend are compatible and identical to the files created by Visual Studio 2008 (see Figure 13-4). In fact, you can open development environments on the same files simultaneously and they will both work. There is no need for exporting/importing between these two IDEs.

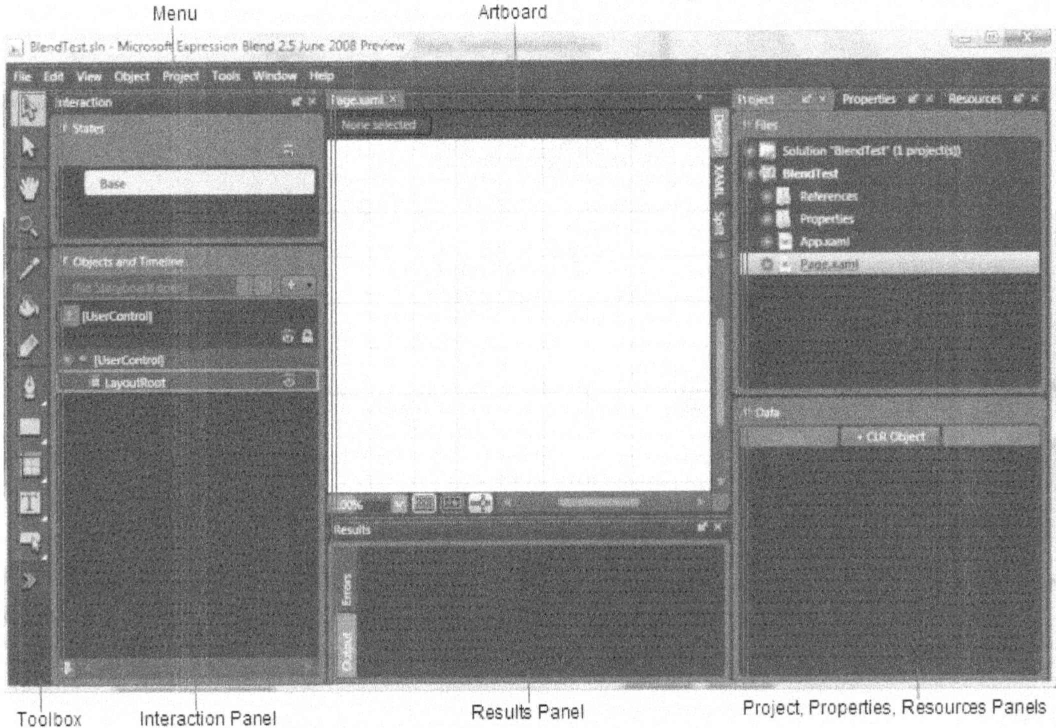

Figure 13-2 Design Workspace in Expression Blend.

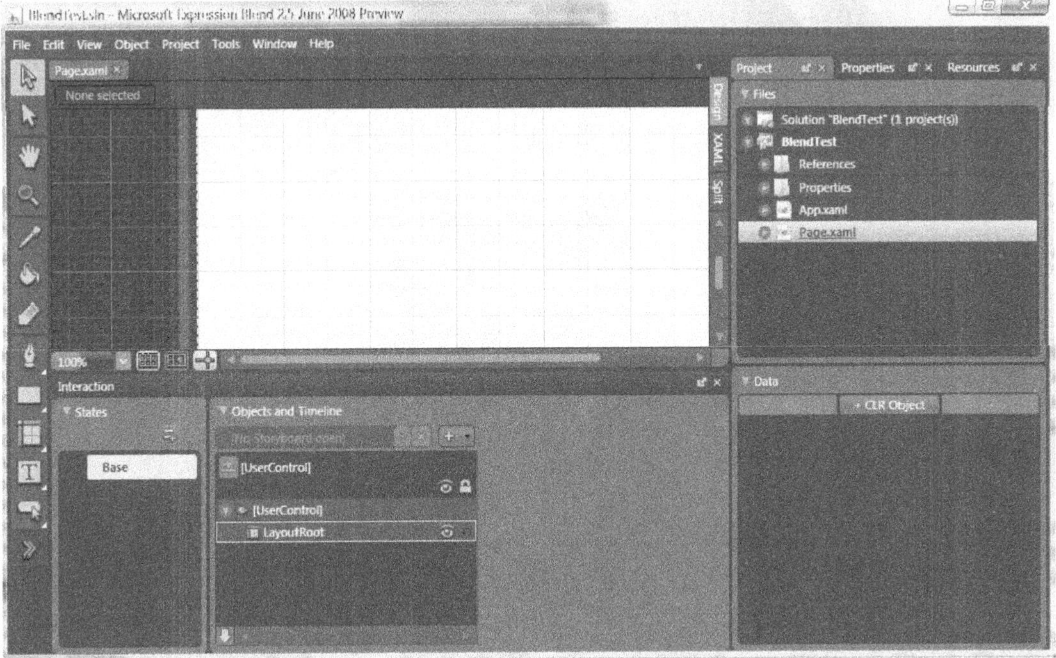

Figure 13-3 Animation Workspace in Expression Blend.

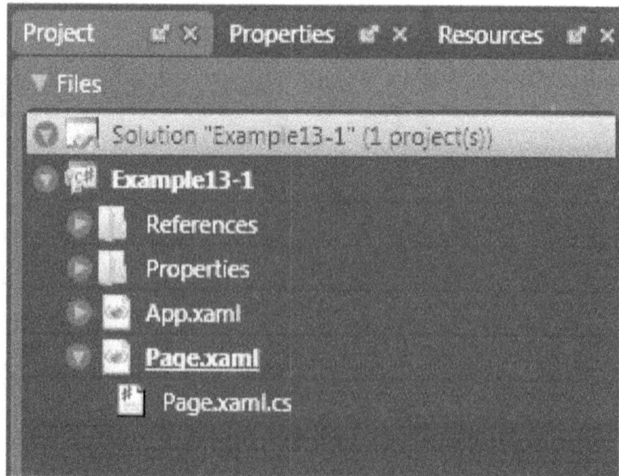

Figure 13-4 File structure in Expression Blend.

Toolbox

The Workspace in Expression Blend consists of all the visual interface elements, including the artboard, Toolbox, workspace configurations, authoring views, and menus. Expression Blend has the ability to zoom in or out of the entire workspace. You can scale the workspace to a desired size without losing any quality within the visual interface. You can zoom out to fit more information on your computer screen or zoom in for better readability.

Now, we take a look at the upper left hand corner of the Expression Blend, which contains the Interactive Panel and the Toolbar. Expression Blend has a slightly different Toolbox than Visual Studio 2008. The Toolbox enables you to create and manipulate objects within your application. There are several special icons on the Toolbox. Many of these icons have a small mark in the lower right hand corner, meaning they can be expanded to find related tools, such as the icon for layout controls (Grid, Stack,Canvas, Border, and ScrollViewer) and text controls (TextBox and TextBlock). Figure 13-5 shows the expanding Shape tool to display the shapes of Rectangle, Ellipse, and Line.

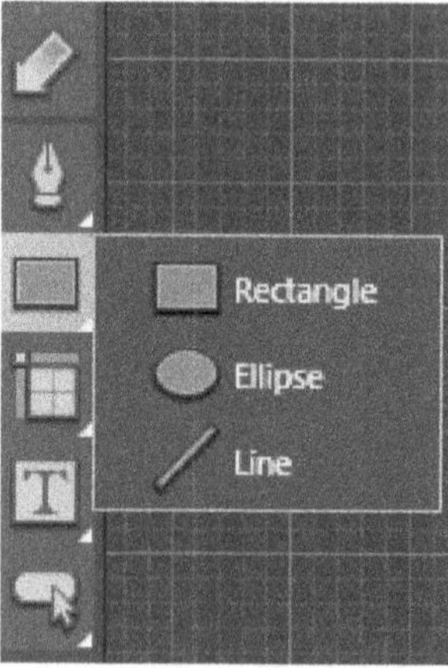

Figure 13-5 Expanding the Shape tool in the Toolbox.

Clicking on the final ">>" icon on the Toolbox brings up the Asset Library, which allows you to access all of the controls, including any user controls, custom controls, or third party controls, if the "Show All" check box on the upper right hand corner is checked, as shown in Figure 13-6. Note that from within the Asset Library you can also search for the control you need, and by clicking on the Details radio button you can determine which class a control is in. Once you select a control from the Toolbox, you can click and drag it onto the design area.

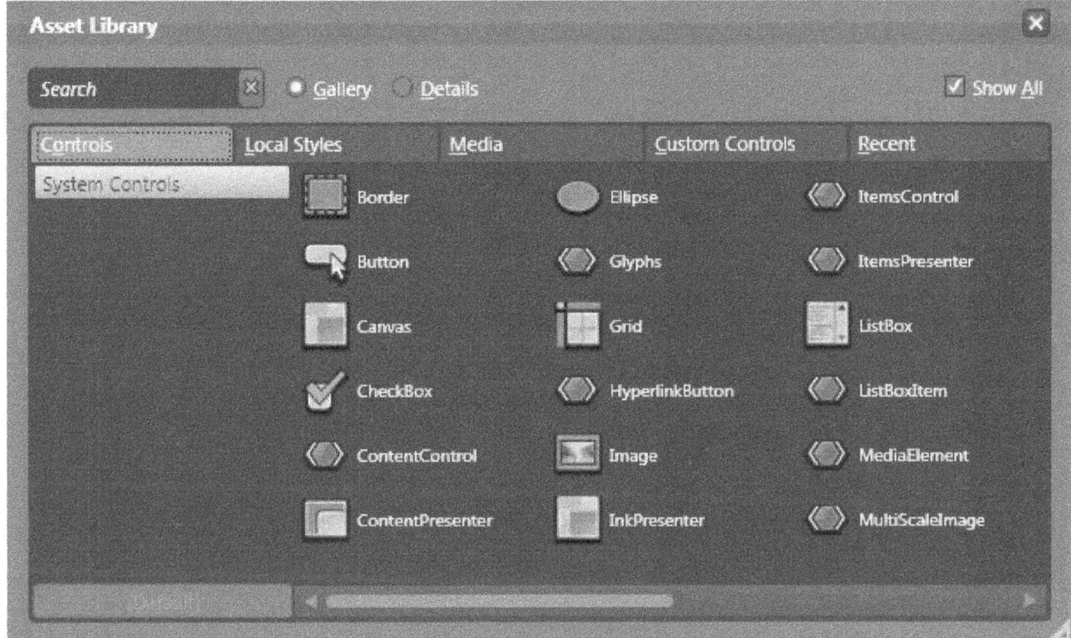

Figure 13-6 Asset library.

Artboard and Interaction Panel

The Artboard is also called the design surface, which is the main panel in Expression Blend. The design surface is where you can draw and manipulate all the objects, either visually or by amending their underlying XAML code directly.

On the right side of Artboard, there are three tabs. The Design tab gives you the pure design surface; the XAML tab provides you the XAML editing window; and the Split tab gives you a split window – one half in design view and the other half in XAML view. Figure 13-7 shows Artboard in split view.

In design view, you can use the Zoom feature: when you are working on complex interfaces, you can zoom in for a detailed view and zoom out for an overview.

As shown in Figure 13-2, the Interaction panel is located just to the right of the Toolbox. You can use the Interaction panel to view all of the objects on your design surface, including their hierarchy when you use more than one container objects. You can also use it to select objects to modify. Sometimes, it is impossible to select a specific object directly on the design surface because objects can be placed off screen or behind orther objects. You can also use the Interaction panel to create and modfify animation timelines.

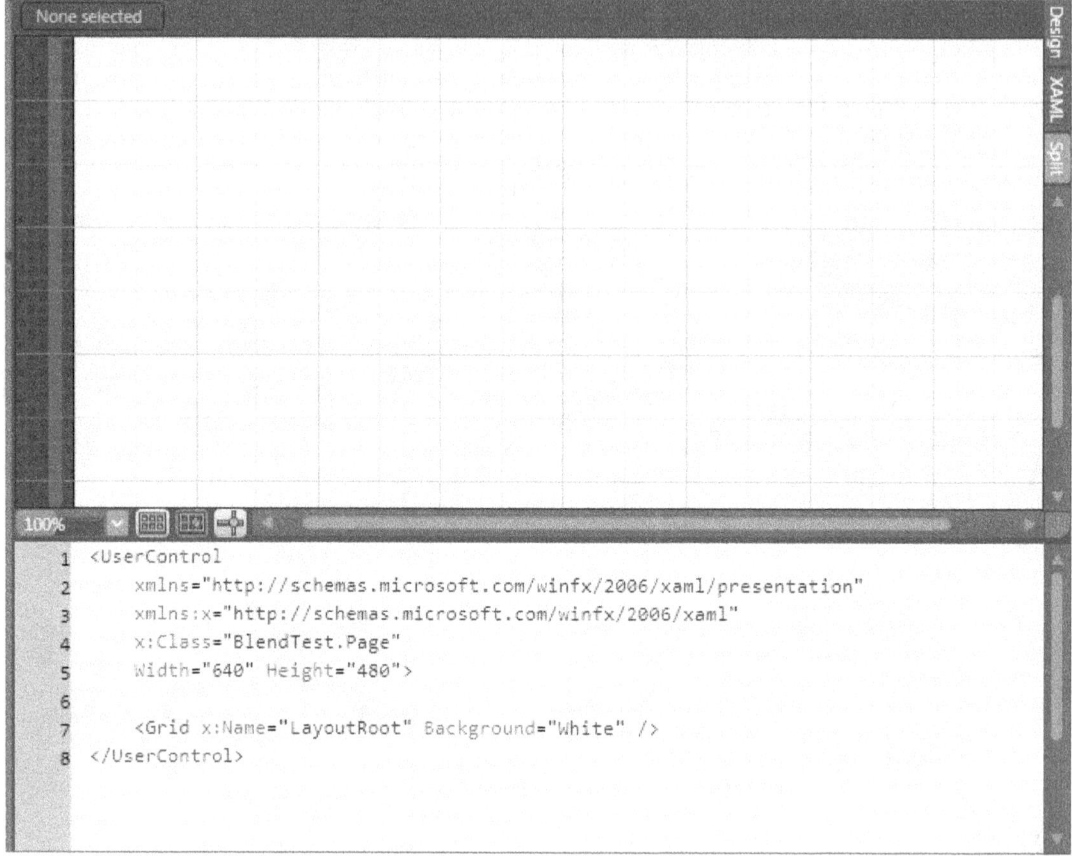

Figure 13-7 Artboard in split view.

Properties Panel

Figure 13-8 shows the Properties panel, which is used to manage all the visual aspects of a specific object. Since XAML elements have many configurable properties, this panel provides useful shortcuts to access and modify these properties.

You can see from Figure 13-8 that this Properties panel is divided into several categories, which allow you to access to the following visual aspects of controls:

- Brushes – Allow you to set the fill, stroke, and opacity mask properties for your control.
- Appearance – Allows you to set appearance properties for your object. Note that these properties will change based on the object being considered.
- Layout – Allows you to specify the various layout options for your project, such as Width, Height, and Alignment properties.
- Common Properties – This option is not easy to use, depending on the objects that you are considering. For example, if you are editing a control, a common property will be its tab index, but if you are editing a shape object, the tab index will not be available.

Figure 13-8 Properties panel in Expression Blend.

- Transform – Allows you to change the RenderTransform of your project, which defines how your object can be manipulated by the rendering system.
- Miscellaneous – You can edit properties that aren't available on any of the other classifications. For example, if you are editing a Rectangle shape, you can change its Clip and RenderTransform Origin properties here.

Note that these category panels are further subdivided. Many of them have an arrow at the bottom of the panel that can be used to expand and contract the properties view.

The Properties panel also includes a Search feature, which allows you to search for a particular property that you want to edit.

Using Expression Blend

In this section, I'll show you how to build two simple Silverlight applications using Expression Blend. In the first example, we animate the rotation and Width properties of a rectangle. We will complete this entire project using Expression Blend.

The second example shows you how to use Expression Blend to make a dynamic navigation menu, much like the one at the top of the Silverlight.net Website. When your mouse hovers over the title, the title text will light up and the corresponding content text will appear below the title. When you click on the navigation item, you will be directed to the corresponding Web page. I'll create the user interface in Expression Blend, and implement the event handlers in Visual Studio 2008, since I want to take full advantage of the advanced intellisense feature found only in Visual Studio (Expression Blend lacks this feature).

Rectangle Animation

Let's start with a simple example of a rectangle animation. Start with Expression Blend, open the New Project dialog box to create a Silverlight 2 application, and name it Example13-1. Expression Blend will create a new project which includes everything you need for a Silverlight application.

Creating the Rectangle Shape

Here, I'll provide you with detailed step to show how Expression Blend works. First, we need to create the Rectangle shape. In the ToolBox, click the Rectangle control. On the Artboard or design surface, draw the rectangle by dragging from any point on the design surface to define the width and height of the rectangle. Notice that as you draw the shape, its width and height appear on the screen. You can also set the Width and Height properties of the rectangle from the Layout category of the Properties panel. Here, we set the Width = 200 and Height = 100 units.

Next, we want to set the Stroke and Fill properties of the rectangle. Under the Brushes category in the Properties panel, click Stroke, then click the Solid color brush tab, since we want to use the SolidColorBrush object to set the Stroke property. Now you can define the brush by picking a blue color.

Then we want to use a linear gradient brush to specify the Fill properties of the rectangle. Under the Brushes in the Properties panel, click Fill, then click the Gradient brush tab. You can add more gradient stops by clicking on the colorbar located at the bottom of the Color Editor, as shown in Figure 13-9. You can see that five gradient stops are specified. At this step, you can set any color you like for each gradient stop.

You can also visually perform various transformations on the brush using the Brush Transform tool in the Toolbox. This tool lets you move, rotate, skew, or resize the gradient brush. The following is the procedure we use to transform our gradient brush:

Figure 13-9 Set brush for the Fill property of the rectangle.

- Select the rectangle we just created.
- In the Toolbox, click the Brush transform tool.
- In the Properties panel, under Brushes, click Fill, because we want to transform the gradient brush defined for the Fill property of the rectangle.
- On the design surface, you can move the brush by dragging anywhere inside the rectangle or by dragging the gradient arrow. You can also rotate the brush by putting your mouse pointer outside either end of the gradient arrow and dragging when your pointer changes to a rotation handler.

Figure 13-10 shows the result after the brush transformation. The gradient arrow in the figure is used to perform the transform on the brush.

Figure 13-10 The transformed linear gradient brush.

Creating Animation

So far, we have created a nice, gradient-filled rectangle. Next, we want to animate this rectangle. Switch to the Animation Workspace by pressing F6. In the Objects and Timeline section, click the "+" button to create a new timeline. A timeline is a sequence of animations that you can apply to objects in a project.

The Create Storyboard Resource dialog will appear. Here we will use the default name of Storyboard1 and click OK.

Select the rectangle and click the Record Keyframe button to insert a keyframe, as shown in Figure 13-11. A keyframe is just a marker on the timeline that indicates when a property change occurs. The yellow line indicates the time in the sequence of animation. The default time is set to zero seconds.

Figure 13-11 Insert keyframe in a timeline.

Drag the top of the yellow line and place it at 2. Click the Record Keyframe button again. This indicates that the duration of animation is set to two seconds. Click on the properties panel and select the Layout category. Change the value of the Width property to 100. This will change the rectangle's width from its original 200 units to 100 units.

Next, click on the Rotate tab in the Transform category. Enter 360 for the Angle value. This will rotate the rectangle by 360 degrees.

You can preview the animation by clicking the Play button in the Objects and Timeline section.

You can also configure your animation timeline to loop once (default), more than once, or endlessly. To achieve this:

- In the Objects view, expand the notes under the rectangle that contain the animation that you want to loop. In our case, the Width property and the Angle child property of the rectangle contain the animation timeline that can be looped, as shown in Figure 13-12.
- Right click the Angle and the click Edit Repeat Count. The Edit Repeat dialog appears.
- Set the animation to loop infinitely by clicking the Set to Forever button.
- Click Ok. The gray timeline bar extends to reflect the new duration of the animation.
- Repeat the above steps for the Width property.

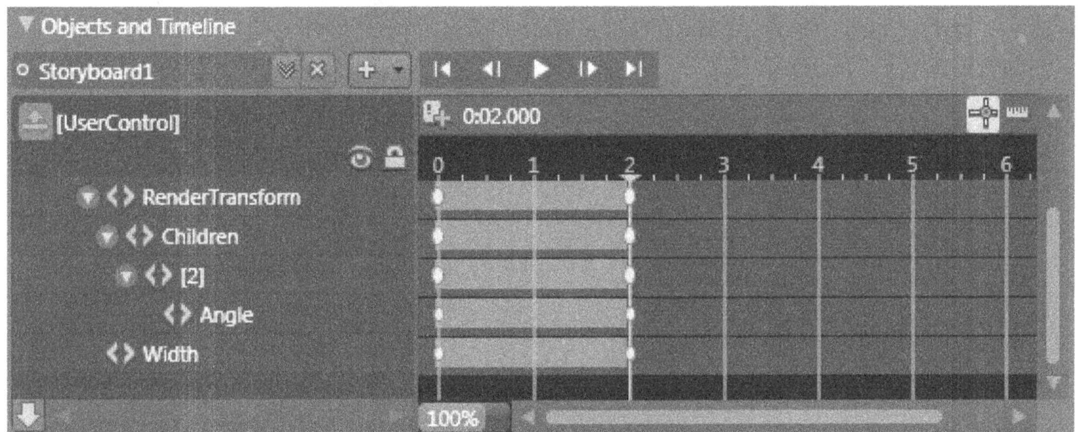

Figure 13-12 Configure timeline loop.

Event Handling

Even though the animation can be previewed in Expression Blend, it doesn't work when you try to run the project by pressing F5. As mentioned previously in Chapter 1, unlike WPF, the Silverlight application doesn't support event triggers. The animation you just created for the rectangle only means that you have set a animation resource that can be used in your code-behind file.

To make the animation work, you need to add an event handler. You can visually add the event handler in Expression Blend. Here we want to add a Loaded event to the main page.

In the Interaction panel, select the main UserControl. In the Properties panel, click the Events button to bring up the Events panel shown in Figure 13-13. You can see that in the Events panel, you can set various event handlers, including mouse and key events.

In the Loaded field, enter Page_Loaded and hit the return key. The Page_Loaded handler is added to your project and the code-behind file should be automatically opened in Visual Studio 2008. You should find that Expression Blend has created an empty Page_Loaded event handler in the code-behind file.

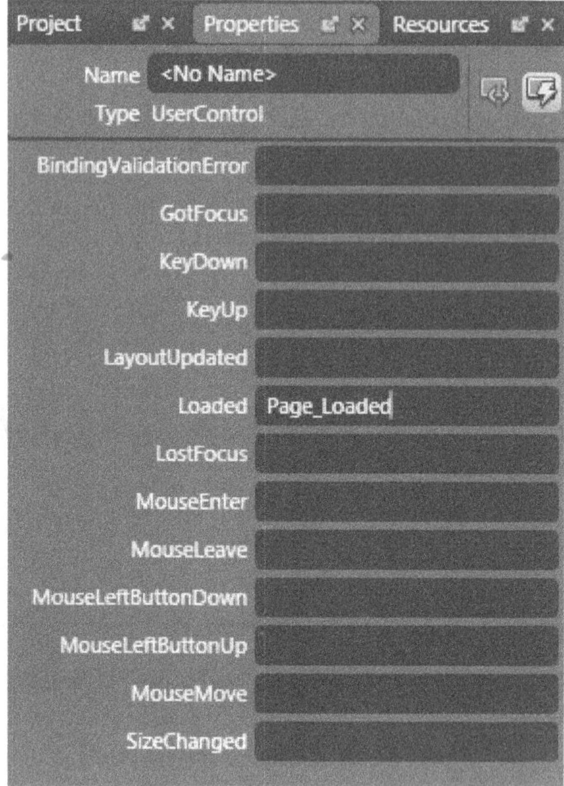

Figure 13-13 Events panel in Expression Blend.

Now open the XAML file generated by Expression Blend:

```
<UserControl
    xmlns="http://schemas.microsoft.com/winfx/2006/xaml/presentation"
    xmlns:x="http://schemas.microsoft.com/winfx/2006/xaml"
    x:Class="Example13_1.Page"
    Width="640" Height="480" Loaded="Page_Loaded">

    <UserControl.Resources>
        <Storyboard x:Name="Storyboard1">
            <DoubleAnimationUsingKeyFrames
                Storyboard.TargetName="rectangle"
                Storyboard.TargetProperty=
                    "(UIElement.RenderTransform).(TransformGroup.Children)[2].
                    (RotateTransform.Angle)" BeginTime="00:00:00"
                     RepeatBehavior="Forever">

                <SplineDoubleKeyFrame KeyTime="00:00:00" Value="0"/>
                <SplineDoubleKeyFrame KeyTime="00:00:02" Value="360"/>
            </DoubleAnimationUsingKeyFrames>
            <DoubleAnimationUsingKeyFrames Storyboard.TargetName="rectangle"
                Storyboard.TargetProperty="(FrameworkElement.Width)"
                BeginTime="00:00:00" RepeatBehavior="Forever">
                <SplineDoubleKeyFrame KeyTime="00:00:00" Value="200"/>
```

```
            <SplineDoubleKeyFrame KeyTime="00:00:02" Value="100"/>
        </DoubleAnimationUsingKeyFrames>
    </Storyboard>
</UserControl.Resources>

<Grid x:Name="LayoutRoot" Background="White" >
    <Rectangle HorizontalAlignment="Stretch" Margin="182,136,241,235"
        VerticalAlignment="Stretch" Stroke="#FF0000FF" x:Name="rectangle"
        RenderTransformOrigin="0.5,0.5" Width="200" Height="100">
        <Rectangle.RenderTransform>
            <TransformGroup>
                <ScaleTransform/>
                <SkewTransform/>
                <RotateTransform/>
                <TranslateTransform/>
            </TransformGroup>
        </Rectangle.RenderTransform>
        <Rectangle.Fill>
            <LinearGradientBrush
                EndPoint="0.981000006198883,0.962000012397766"
                StartPoint="0.0270000007003546,0.0260000005364418">
                <GradientStop Color="#FF000000"/>
                <GradientStop Color="#FFFFFF00" Offset="1"/>
                <GradientStop Color="#FFFF0014" Offset="0.268"/>
                <GradientStop Color="#FF00FF00" Offset="0.567"/>
                <GradientStop Color="#FF0000FF" Offset="0.795"/>
            </LinearGradientBrush>
        </Rectangle.Fill>
    </Rectangle>
</Grid>
</UserControl>
```

You can see that the Page_Loaded event is indeed added to the main UserControl. The corresponding code-behind file of this example is listed below:

```
using System;
using System.Windows;
using System.Windows.Controls;
using System.Windows.Documents;
using System.Windows.Ink;
using System.Windows.Input;
using System.Windows.Media;
using System.Windows.Media.Animation;
using System.Windows.Shapes;

namespace Example13_1
{
    public partial class Page : UserControl
    {
        public Page()
        {
            // Required to initialize variables
            InitializeComponent();
        }

        private void Page_Loaded(object sender, RoutedEventArgs e)
```

```
            {

            }
        }
    }
```

Now you need manually add the following one line code to the Page_Loaded event handler:

```
Storyboard1.Begin();
```

which will start the animation when you run the project.

Now, pressing F5 will produce an animated rectangle, as shown in Figure 13-14.

Figure 13-14 Animated rectangle created in Expreesion Blend.

Dynamic Menu

This example shows you how to create a dynamic navigation menu bar much like the one at the top of the Silverlight.net Website. When your mouse is over the title, the title text will light up and the corresponding content text will appear below the title. When you click on a navigation item, you will be directed to the corresponding webpage. I'll create the user interface in Expression Blend, and implement the event handlers in Visual Studio 2008, since we want to take full advantage of the advanced intellisense feature found only in Visual Studio (Expression Blend lacks this feature).

I will only provide an outline of creating this example because I already gave the detailed steps in the previous example. Start with a new Silverlight 2 project in Expression Blend and name it Example13-2. Create a navigation menu that visually resembles Figure 13-15.

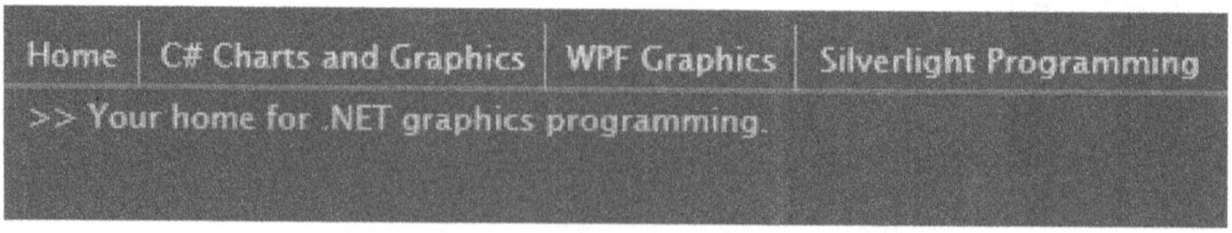

Figure 13-15 UI created in Expression Blend.

Here you first add a Canvas control to the LayoutRoot. Then you add the various TextBox controls and draw several path lines.

Next, you can visually add the various mouse event handlers for navigation items. For example, we add the mouse events MouseEnter, MouseLeave, and MouseLeftButtonDown to the Home item, as shown in Figure 13-16. Repeat adding the mouse events to the other navigation items.

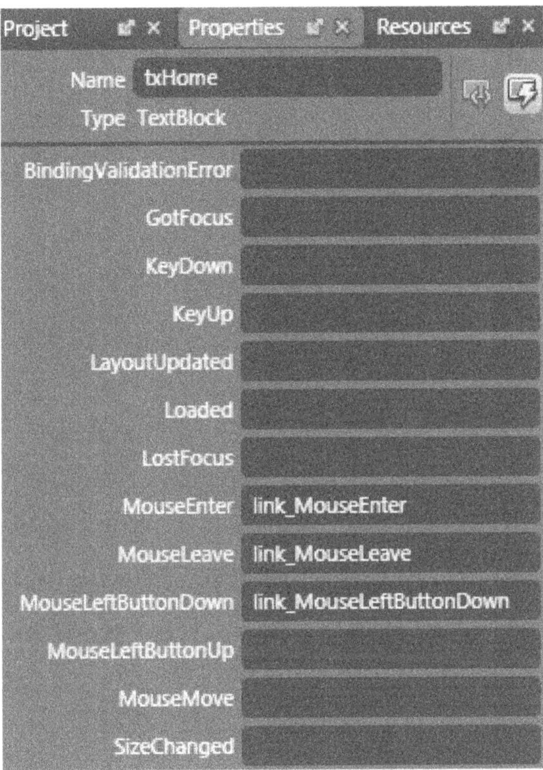

Figure 13-16 Set mouse events for Home item.

Next we need to create an animation for navigation items and the text contents. For a navigation item, we can simply change its text opacity property to highlight the text when your mouse hovers over it. For the text content, we can animate its Translate property. For the details, you can view the XAML and the code-behind file. Here is the XAML of this example:

```
<UserControl
    xmlns="http://schemas.microsoft.com/client/2007"
    xmlns:x="http://schemas.microsoft.com/winfx/2006/xaml"
    x:Class="Example13_2.Page"
    Width="500" Height="100" Loaded="UserControl_Loaded">
    <UserControl.Resources>
        <Storyboard x:Name="txContentStoryboard">
            <DoubleAnimationUsingKeyFrames BeginTime="00:00:00"
                Storyboard.TargetName="txContent" Storyboard.TargetProperty=
                    "(UIElement.RenderTransform).(TransformGroup.Children)[3].
                    (TranslateTransform.X)">
                <SplineDoubleKeyFrame KeyTime="00:00:00" Value="50"/>
                <SplineDoubleKeyFrame KeyTime="00:00:01" Value="0"/>
```

```
            </DoubleAnimationUsingKeyFrames>
            <ColorAnimationUsingKeyFrames BeginTime="00:00:00"
                Storyboard.TargetName="txContent" Storyboard.TargetProperty=
                    "(TextBlock.Foreground).(SolidColorBrush.Color)">
                <SplineColorKeyFrame KeyTime="00:00:00" Value="#00A4A1A1"/>
                <SplineColorKeyFrame KeyTime="00:00:01" Value="#FFA4A1A1"/>
            </ColorAnimationUsingKeyFrames>
        </Storyboard>
        <Storyboard x:Name="txEnterStoryboard">
            <ColorAnimationUsingKeyFrames BeginTime="00:00:00"
                Storyboard.TargetProperty=
                "(TextBlock.Foreground).(SolidColorBrush.Color)">
                <SplineColorKeyFrame KeyTime="00:00:00" Value="#66FFFFFF"/>
                <SplineColorKeyFrame KeyTime="00:00:01" Value="#FFFFFFFF"/>
            </ColorAnimationUsingKeyFrames>
        </Storyboard>
        <Storyboard x:Name="txLeaveStoryboard">
            <ColorAnimationUsingKeyFrames BeginTime="00:00:00"
               Storyboard.TargetProperty=
                   "(TextBlock.Foreground).(SolidColorBrush.Color)">
                <SplineColorKeyFrame KeyTime="00:00:00" Value="#FFFFFFFF"/>
                <SplineColorKeyFrame KeyTime="00:00:01" Value="#66FFFFFF"/>
            </ColorAnimationUsingKeyFrames>
        </Storyboard>
    </UserControl.Resources>

    <Grid x:Name="LayoutRoot" Background="#FF323232" Margin="20,10,20,10">
        <Canvas x:Name="myCanvas">
            <Path HorizontalAlignment="Stretch" Margin="0,30,0,0"
                  VerticalAlignment="Stretch" Data="M0,0 L460,0"
                  Fill="#FFB7B4B4" Stretch="Fill" Stroke="#FFB9B9B9"
                  StrokeThickness="0.5" x:Name="path1"/>
            <TextBlock x:Name="txHome" Text="Home" TextWrapping="Wrap"
                       Margin="10,10,5,5" Foreground="#66FFFFFF" FontSize="12"
                       MouseEnter="link_MouseEnter" MouseLeave="link_MouseLeave"
                       MouseLeftButtonDown="link_MouseLeftButtonDown"/>
               <Path Canvas.Left="52" Canvas.Top="6" Data="M0,0 L0,24"
                     Fill="#FFB7B4B4" Stretch="Fill" Stroke="#FFB9B9B9"
                     StrokeThickness="0.5" x:Name="path2"/>
               <TextBlock Canvas.Left="50" x:Name="txCsharp"
                          Text="C# Charts and Graphics" TextWrapping="Wrap"
                          Foreground="#66FFFFFF" Margin="10,10,5,5"
                          FontSize="12" MouseEnter="link_MouseEnter"
                          MouseLeave="link_MouseLeave"
                          MouseLeftButtonDown="link_MouseLeftButtonDown"/>
            <Path Canvas.Left="205" Canvas.Top="6" Data="M0,0 L0,24"
                  Fill="#FFB7B4B4" Stretch="Fill" Stroke="#FFB9B9B9"
                  StrokeThickness="0.5" Margin="0,0,0,0" x:Name="path3"/>
            <TextBlock Canvas.Left="203" x:Name="txWPF" Text="WPF Graphics"
                       TextWrapping="Wrap" Foreground="#66FFFFFF"
                       Margin="10,10,5,5" FontSize="12"
                       MouseEnter="link_MouseEnter" MouseLeave="link_MouseLeave"
                       MouseLeftButtonDown="link_MouseLeftButtonDown"/>
            <Path Canvas.Left="298" Canvas.Top="6" Data="M0,0 L0,24"
                  Fill="#FFB7B4B4" Stretch="Fill" Stroke="#FFB9B9B9"
```

```
                StrokeThickness="0.5" Margin="0,0,0,0" x:Name="path4"/>
            <TextBlock Canvas.Left="297" x:Name="txSilverlight"
                       Text="Silverlight Programming" TextWrapping="Wrap"
                       Foreground="#66FFFFFF" Margin="10,10,5,5"
                       FontSize="12" MouseEnter="link_MouseEnter"
                       MouseLeave="link_MouseLeave"
                       MouseLeftButtonDown="link_MouseLeftButtonDown"/>

            <TextBlock Canvas.Left="0" Canvas.Top="22" x:Name="txContent"
                       Text="&gt;&gt; Your home for .NET graphics programming."
                       TextWrapping="Wrap" Foreground="#FFA4A1A1"
                       Margin="10,10,5,5" FontSize="12"
                       RenderTransformOrigin="0.5,0.5">
                <TextBlock.RenderTransform>
                    <TransformGroup>
                        <ScaleTransform/>
                        <SkewTransform/>
                        <RotateTransform/>
                        <TranslateTransform/>
                    </TransformGroup>
                </TextBlock.RenderTransform>
            </TextBlock>
        </Canvas>
    </Grid>
</UserControl>
```

In the above XAML, we have manually removed the TargetName property from the animation timelines, TxEnterStoryboard and TxLeaveStoryboard, because we want to apply these same animations to each of the navigation items. We'll dynamically change the TargetName property in code for these animations.

The following lists the code-behind file of this example:

```
using System;
using System.Windows;
using System.Windows.Browser;
using System.Windows.Controls;
using System.Windows.Documents;
using System.Windows.Ink;
using System.Windows.Input;
using System.Windows.Media;
using System.Windows.Media.Animation;
using System.Windows.Shapes;

namespace Example13_2
{
    public partial class Page : UserControl
    {
        public Page()
        {
            // Required to initialize variables
            InitializeComponent();
        }

        private void UserControl_Loaded(object sender, RoutedEventArgs e)
        {
```

```
        }

        private void link_MouseEnter(object sender, MouseEventArgs e)
        {
            SetDefaultLinkText();
            TextBlock tx = sender as TextBlock;
            tx.Opacity = 1;

            if (tx.Name == "txHome")
                txContent.Text = ">> Your home for .NET graphics programming.";
            else if (tx.Name == "txCsharp")
                txContent.Text = ">> More about the book
                                 'Practical C# Charts and Graphics'...";
            else if (tx.Name == "txWPF")
                txContent.Text = ">> More about the book
                                 'Practical WPF Graphics Programming'...";
            else if (tx.Name == "txSilverlight")
                txContent.Text = ">> More about the book
                                 'Practical Silverlight Programming'...";

            txEnterStoryboard.SetValue(Storyboard.TargetNameProperty, tx.Name);
            txEnterStoryboard.Begin();
            txContentStoryboard.Begin();
        }

        private void link_MouseLeave(object sender, MouseEventArgs e)
        {
            TextBlock tx = sender as TextBlock;
            //if (tx.Name != linkClickString)
            tx.Opacity = 0.4;
            txLeaveStoryboard.SetValue(Storyboard.TargetNameProperty, tx.Name);
            txLeaveStoryboard.Begin();
        }

        private void link_MouseLeftButtonDown(object sender,
                MouseButtonEventArgs e)
        {
            SetDefaultLinkText();
            TextBlock tx = sender as TextBlock;
            tx.Opacity = 1;
            tx.Cursor = Cursors.Arrow;

            if (tx.Name == "txHome")
                HtmlPage.Window.Navigate(new Uri("http://www.drxudotnet.com",
                                                 UriKind.Absolute));
            else if (tx.Name == "txCsharp")
                HtmlPage.Window.Navigate(new
                    Uri("http://www.drxudotnet.com/csharp_index.html",
                        UriKind.Absolute));
            else if (tx.Name == "txWPF")
                HtmlPage.Window.Navigate(new
                    Uri("http://www.drxudotnet.com/wpf_index.html",
                        UriKind.Absolute));
            else if (tx.Name == "txSilverlight")
```

```
                HtmlPage.Window.Navigate(new
                    Uri("http://www.drxudotnet.com/silverlight_index.html",
                        UriKind.Absolute));
            }

            private void SetDefaultLinkText()
            {
                txHome.Opacity = 0.4;
                txHome.Cursor = Cursors.Hand;
                txCsharp.Opacity = 0.4;
                txCsharp.Cursor = Cursors.Hand;
                txWPF.Opacity = 0.4;
                txWPF.Cursor = Cursors.Hand;
                txSilverlight.Opacity = 0.4;
                txSilverlight.Cursor = Cursors.Hand;
            }
        }
    }
```

Here, the event handlers are implemented in Visual Studio 2008.

Running this project by pressing F5 in Expression Blend or Visual Studio 2008 creates a dynamic navigation menu, as shown in Figure 13-17.

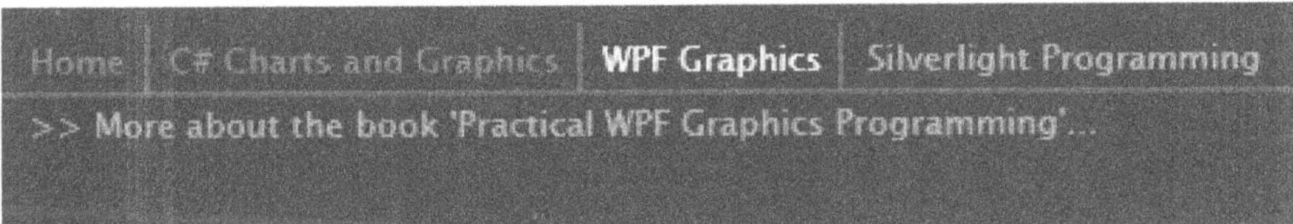

Figure 13-17 Dynamic menu created in Expreesion Blend.

Chapter 14
Custom Controls

In the previous chapters, we directly implemented the XAML and code-behind files for various Silverlight applications. For simple projects, this approach works well. However, if you want to reuse the same code in multiple Web applications, you should avoid using this direct method. Silverlight provides a powerful means, the user control, to solve this problem.

The custom user controls in Silverlight are just like the default controls such as Button or TextBox. Typically, the controls you design can encapsulate UI functionality and can be reused in multiple Silverlight applications. These custom controls can reduce the amount of code you have to type, as well as make it easier for you to change the implementation. There is no reason to duplicate code in your applications, as this leaves a lot of room for bugs, making it a good programming practice to create functionalities specific to the user control in the control's source code, which can reduce code duplication and modularize your code.

You can implement new custom controls by deriving a class from one of the existing Control classes that can be either a Control base class or a common Control like a Button or TextBox. Aternatively, you can create a reusable User Control, which makes it easy to use a XAML markup file to compose the control's user interface.

The simplest way to create a custom control is to create a UserControl object. UserControl consists of modules of XAML and C# code that you can reuse throughout your application. It simply represents a simple form of custom control through the aggregation of existing controls and code. If you want your resusable custom units of UI to be shared aross multiple Silverlight applications, you need to build Silverlight class library assemblies.

In this chapter, I'll show you how to create a Booklist control using three different approaches. The first two methods focus on building a Booklist custom user control using either Visual Studio 2008 or Expression Blend. The third approach concentrates on implementing a Booklist class library, which can be shared across multiple Silverlight applications.

Creating a User Control Using Visual Studio

In this section, I'll use an example to demonstrate how to build a user control using Visual Studio 2008.

Start with a new Silverlight project using Visual Studio 2008 and name the project Example14-1. Now you need to add a user control to the project by following these steps: right-click on the project in the

Solution Explorer, and select Add – New Item…, bringing up the Add New Item window. In this window, select the Silverlight User Control template and name your new control BooklistControl, as shown in Figure 14-1.

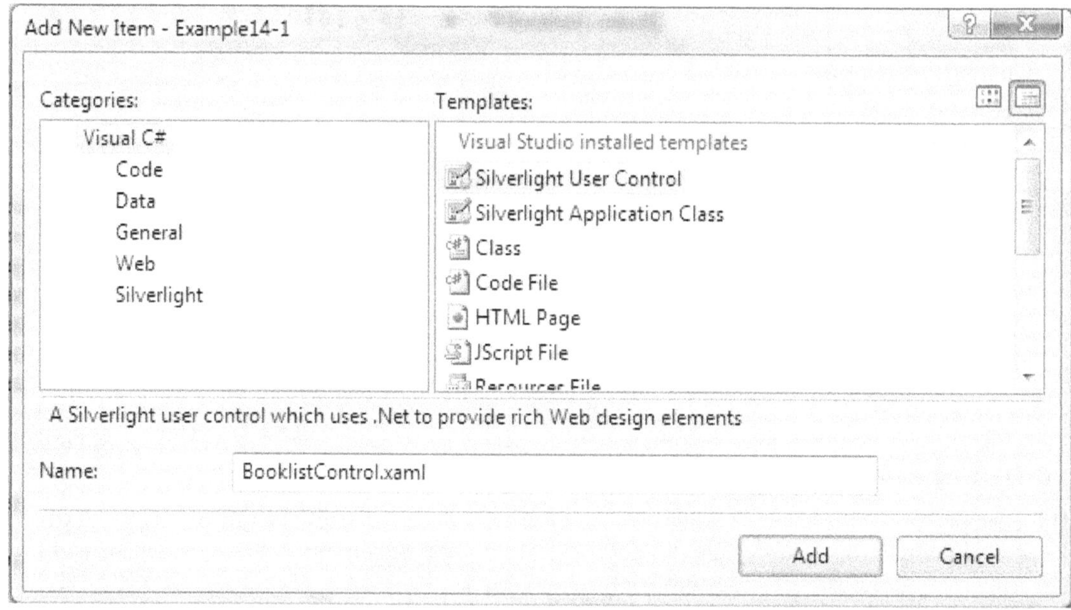

Figure 14-1 Add New Item window.

After the above steps, two files, BooklistControl.xaml and BoolistControl.xaml.cs, are immediately added to your project.

Implementing the User Control

Now, it is time to implement the Booklist user control. Open the BooklistControl.xaml file:

```
<UserControl x:Class="Example14_1.BooklistControl"
    xmlns="http://schemas.microsoft.com/winfx/2006/xaml/presentation"
    xmlns:x="http://schemas.microsoft.com/winfx/2006/xaml">
    Width="400" Height="300">
    <Grid x:Name="LayoutRoot" Background="White">

    </Grid>
</UserControl>
```

This XAML is basically the same as Page.xaml, except the class name has been changed to protect the innocent namespace. You can now implement the user interface and layout of the BooklistControl in this XAML file. Here is the XAML you need for the Booklist user control:

```
<UserControl x:Class="Example14_1.BooklistControl"
    xmlns="http://schemas.microsoft.com/winfx/2006/xaml/presentation"
    xmlns:x="http://schemas.microsoft.com/winfx/2006/xaml">

    <Border BorderBrush="Black" BorderThickness="1" Margin="5,5,5,0">
        <Grid x:Name="BooklistGrid" Background="LightGray">
```

```
        <Grid.ColumnDefinitions>
            <ColumnDefinition Width="10" />
            <ColumnDefinition Width="auto" />
            <ColumnDefinition Width="10" />
            <ColumnDefinition Width="auto"/>
            <ColumnDefinition Width="10" />
        </Grid.ColumnDefinitions>
        <Grid.RowDefinitions>
            <RowDefinition Height="10" />
            <RowDefinition Height="auto" />
            <RowDefinition Height="auto" />
            <RowDefinition Height="auto" />
            <RowDefinition Height="auto" />
            <RowDefinition Height="auto" />
            <RowDefinition Height="auto" />
            <RowDefinition Height="10" />
        </Grid.RowDefinitions>

        <TextBlock Text="Book Image: " Grid.Row="1" Grid.Column="1"
                   Foreground="Blue" FontSize="12"/>
        <Image x:Name="bookImage" Stretch="Fill" Width="80" Height="100"
               Margin="1" Grid.Row="1" Grid.Column="3"
               HorizontalAlignment="Left"/>
        <TextBlock Text="Title: " Grid.Row="2" Grid.Column="1"
                   Foreground="Blue" FontSize="12"/>
        <TextBlock x:Name="bookTitle" Grid.Row="2" Grid.Column="3"
                   Width="350" TextWrapping="Wrap" FontWeight="Bold"/>
        <TextBlock Text="Subtitle: " Grid.Row="3" Grid.Column="1"
                   Foreground="Blue" FontSize="12"/>
        <TextBlock x:Name="bookSubtitle" Grid.Row="3" Grid.Column="3"
                   Width="350" TextWrapping="Wrap" FontSize="12"/>
        <TextBlock Text="Author: " Grid.Row="4" Grid.Column="1"
                   Foreground="Blue" FontSize="12"/>
        <TextBlock x:Name="bookAuthor" Grid.Row="4" Grid.Column="3"
                   Width="350" TextWrapping="Wrap"/>
        <TextBlock Text="ISBN: " Grid.Row="5" Grid.Column="1"
                   Foreground="Blue" FontSize="12"/>
        <TextBlock x:Name="bookISBN" Grid.Row="5" Grid.Column="3"
                   Width="350" TextWrapping="Wrap"/>
        <TextBlock Text="Publish Date: " Grid.Row="6" Grid.Column="1"
                   Foreground="Blue" FontSize="12"/>
        <TextBlock x:Name="bookPublishDate" Grid.Row="6" Grid.Column="3"
                   Width="350" TextWrapping="Wrap"/>
    </Grid>
  </Border>
</UserControl>
```

This BooklistControl contains several items, book cover image, title, subtitle, author, ISBN, and publish date. You need to design a public interface so that the BooklistControl can be exposed to the outside world. In other words, it is time to create the properties, methods, and events that the control consumer (the application that uses your control) will rely on to interact with your Booklist control.

In order to support Silverlight features such as data binding, styles, and animation, the properties of your user control should always register as dependency properties.

The first step in creating a dependency property is to define a static field for it, with the word Property added to the end of the property name. Now add the following dependency properties to the code-behind file, BooklistControl.xaml.cs:

```
using System;
using System.Windows;
using System.Windows.Controls;
using System.Windows.Media;
using System.Windows.Media.Imaging;

namespace Example14_1
{
    public partial class BooklistControl : UserControl
    {
        public BooklistControl()
        {
            InitializeComponent();

            Loaded += new RoutedEventHandler(Page_Loaded);
        }

        void Page_Loaded(object sender, RoutedEventArgs e)
        {
            bookImage.Source = ImageUri;
            bookTitle.Text = Title;
            bookSubtitle.Text = Subtitle;
            bookAuthor.Text = Author;
            bookISBN.Text = ISBN;
            bookPublishDate.Text = PublishDate;
        }

        public static readonly DependencyProperty ImageUriProperty =
            DependencyProperty.Register("ImageUri", typeof(BitmapImage),
            typeof(BooklistControl),
            new PropertyMetadata(new PropertyChangedCallback(ImageUriChanged)));

        public BitmapImage ImageUri
        {
            get { return (BitmapImage)GetValue(ImageUriProperty); }
            set { SetValue(ImageUriProperty, value); }
        }

        private static void ImageUriChanged(DependencyObject sender,
                DependencyPropertyChangedEventArgs e)
        {
            BooklistControl control = sender as BooklistControl;
            control.ImageUri = (BitmapImage)e.NewValue;
        }

        public static readonly DependencyProperty TitleProperty =
            DependencyProperty.Register("Title", typeof(string),
            typeof(BooklistControl),
            new PropertyMetadata(new PropertyChangedCallback(StringChanged)));

        public string Title
```

```
{
    get { return (string)GetValue(TitleProperty); }
    set { SetValue(TitleProperty, value); }
}

public static readonly DependencyProperty SubtitleProperty =
   DependencyProperty.Register("Subtitle", typeof(string),
   typeof(BooklistControl),
   new PropertyMetadata(new PropertyChangedCallback(StringChanged)));

public string Subtitle
{
    get { return (string)GetValue(SubtitleProperty); }
    set { SetValue(SubtitleProperty, value); }
}

public static readonly DependencyProperty AuthorProperty =
   DependencyProperty.Register("Author", typeof(string),
   typeof(BooklistControl),
   new PropertyMetadata(new PropertyChangedCallback(StringChanged)));

public string Author
{
    get { return (string)GetValue(AuthorProperty); }
    set { SetValue(AuthorProperty, value); }
}

public static readonly DependencyProperty ISBNProperty =
   DependencyProperty.Register("ISBN", typeof(string),
   typeof(BooklistControl),
   new PropertyMetadata(new PropertyChangedCallback(StringChanged)));

public string ISBN
{
    get { return (string)GetValue(ISBNProperty); }
    set { SetValue(ISBNProperty, value); }
}

public static readonly DependencyProperty PublishDateProperty =
   DependencyProperty.Register("PublishDate", typeof(string),
   typeof(BooklistControl),
   new PropertyMetadata(new PropertyChangedCallback(StringChanged)));

public string PublishDate
{
    get { return (string)GetValue(PublishDateProperty); }
    set { SetValue(PublishDateProperty, value); }
}

private static void StringChanged(DependencyObject sender,
        DependencyPropertyChangedEventArgs e)
{
    BooklistControl control = sender as BooklistControl;
    if (e.Property == TitleProperty)
        control.Title = (string)e.NewValue;
```

```
                else if (e.Property == SubtitleProperty)
                    control.Subtitle = (string)e.NewValue;
                else if (e.Property == AuthorProperty)
                    control.Author = (string)e.NewValue;
                else if (e.Property == ISBNProperty)
                    control.ISBN = (string)e.NewValue;
                else if (e.Property == PublishDateProperty)
                    control.PublishDate = (string)e.NewValue;
            }
        }
    }
```

After defining the dependency properties, you add standard property wrappers to the properties to make them easier to access and useable in XAML. Note that the property wrappers should not contain any logic, because properties may be set and retrieved directly using the SetValue and GetValues methods of the base DependencyObject class. For example, the property synchronization logic in this control is implemented using callbacks through the PropertyMetaData method. These callbacks fire when the property changes through the property wrapper or a direct SetValue call.

The property change callbacks are responsible for keeping the property values consistent with coppresponding dependency properties. Whenever the property values are changed, the corresponding dependency properties are adjusted accordingly. In this example, there are two kinds of property change callbacks, ImageUriChanged and StringChanged.

The statements inside the Page_Loaded method are also required for data binding.

```
bookImage.Source = ImageUri;
bookTitle.Text = Title;
bookSubtitle.Text = Subtitle;
bookAuthor.Text = Author;
bookISBN.Text = ISBN;
bookPublishDate.Text = PublishDate;
```

Instead setting data binding in code, you can also set the data binding in XAML.

Testing the User Control

In the above section, you completed the user control implementation. Now you can test the control in a real-world Silverlight application.

Open the Page.xaml file. At the top of this file add a namespace for your control with a prefix of your choosing (local will be used in this example):

```
xmlns:local="clr-namespace:Example14_1;assembly=Example14-1"
```

Then you can reuse the BooklistControl just like a built-in control in Silverlight. Here we add three BooklistControls to the test page:

```
<UserControl x:Class="Example14_1.Page"
    xmlns="http://schemas.microsoft.com/winfx/2006/xaml/presentation"
    xmlns:x="http://schemas.microsoft.com/winfx/2006/xaml"
    xmlns:local="clr-namespace:Example14_1;assembly=Example14-1"
    Width="480" Height="500">
    <Grid x:Name="LayoutRoot" Background="White">
        <ScrollViewer>
            <StackPanel>
```

```
                <local:BooklistControl ImageUri="csharp.jpg"
                       Title="Practical C# Charts and Graphics"
                       Subtitle="Advanced Chart and Graphics Programming for
                                 Real-World .NET Applications"
                       Author="Jack Xu" ISBN="978-0-9793725-0-6"
                       PublishDate="March, 2007"/>

                <local:BooklistControl ImageUri="wpf.jpg"
                       Title = "Practical WPF Graphics Programming"
                       Subtitle = "Advanced .NET Graphics Development with
                                   the Windows Presentation Foundation"
                       Author = "Jack Xu" ISBN = "978-0-9793725-1-3"
                       PublishDate = "Nov. 2007"/>

                <local:BooklistControl ImageUri="silverlight.jpg"
                       Title="Practical Silverlight Programming"
                       Subtitle="Advanced  Graphics and User Interface
                                 Development With Silverlight 2.0"
                       Author="Jack Xu" ISBN="978-0-9793725-2-0"
                       PublishDate="August, 2008"/>
            </StackPanel>
        </ScrollViewer>
    </Grid>
</UserControl>
```

You also need to add three book cover pictures to the project.

Pressing F5 to run the application produces the result shown in Figure 14-2.

Creating a User Control Using Expression Blend

As shown in the previous section, Silverlight enables developers to easily encapsulate part of their UI into a reusable use control. This approach works great when you know in advance that you need to encapsulate UI in a user control.

However, you don't always know if you want to encapsulate some UI functionality as a user control until after you've already started defining it on a parent page or control. For example, you may simply be working on a book list UI for a specific book in Expression Blend. You may begin by creating some UI to encapsulate the book information.

Let's start with a new Silverlight project in Expression Blend and name it Example14-2. Lay out a book list UI similar to the one used in the previous example on the design surface, as shown in Figure 14-3.

After carefully laying it all out, you may realize that you want to use the exact same UI for other books. At this moment, you may want to create a reusable book list user control so that you can avoid copying and pasting the same piece of code over and over again.

Title: **Practical C# Charts and Graphics**
Subtitle: Advanced Chart and Graphics Programming for Real-World .NET Applications
Author: Jack Xu
ISBN: 978-0-9793725-0-6
Publish Date: March, 2007

Book Image:
Title: **Practical WPF Graphics Programming**
Subtitle: Advanced .NET Graphics Development with the Windows Presentation Foundation
Author: Jack Xu
ISBN: 978-0-9793725-1-3
Publish Date: Nov. 2007

Book Image:

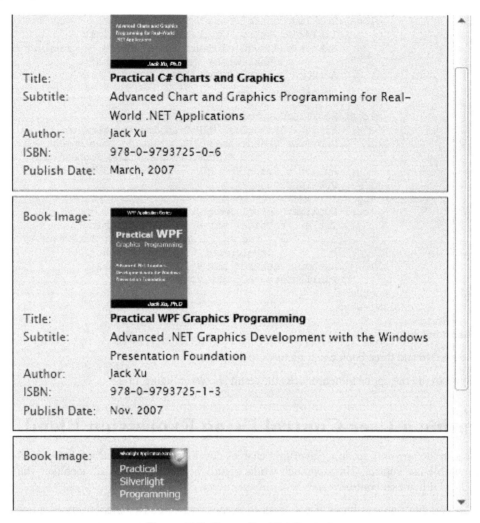

Figure 14-2 Reuse Booklist Controls.

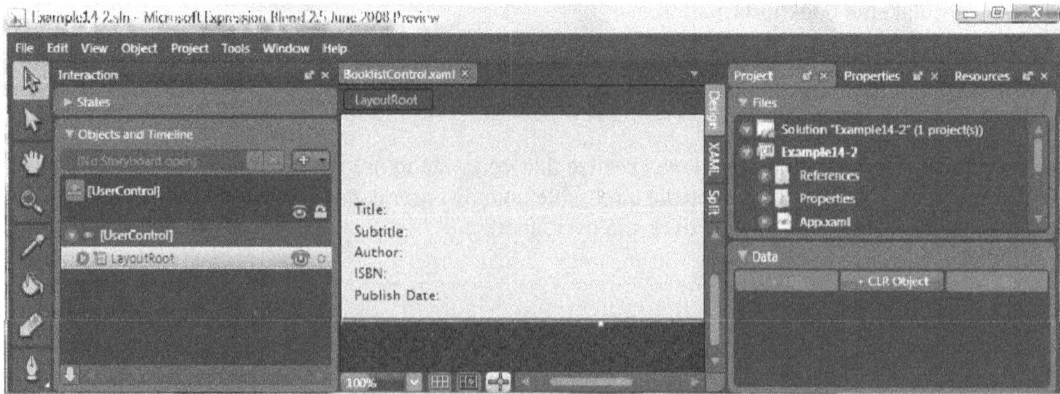

Figure 14-3 Book list UI in Expression Blend.

Making a User Control

Expression Blend provides a shortcut that lets you select the controls you want to encapsulate as a user control in the design surface, and then right click and choose the "Make Control..." option, as shown in Figure 14-4. This brings up a prompt window that asks for the name of the new user control you are creating. Enter BooklistControl in the name field and click the OK button. This will cause Expression Blend to create a new user control that encapsulates the content you selected.

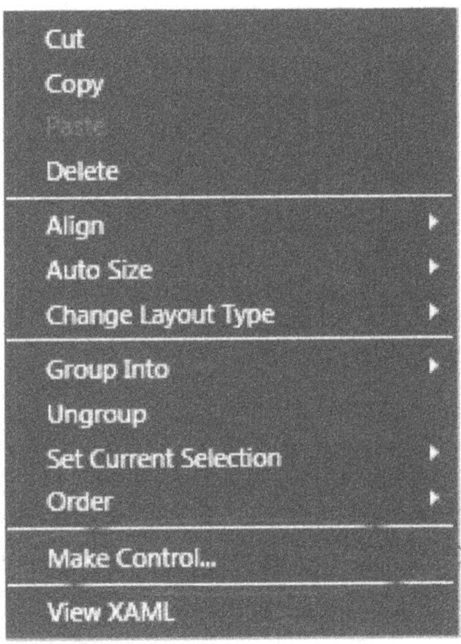

Figure 14-4 Make user control option in Expression Blend.

When you re-build the project and go back to the original page, you'll see the same UI as before, except now the book list UI is encapsulated inside the BooklistControl. This can be seen clearly when you open the Page.xaml file:

```
<UserControl
    xmlns="http://schemas.microsoft.com/winfx/2006/xaml/presentation"
    xmlns:x="http://schemas.microsoft.com/winfx/2006/xaml"
    x:Class="Example14_2.Page" xmlns:Example14_2="clr-namespace:Example14_2">

     <Example14_2:BooklistControl Height="216.197" Width="462.314"/>
</UserControl>
```

Here, Expression Blend automatically performs several tasks for you. It add a namespace and a BooklistControl to the Page.xaml. It also implements the corresponding code for the user control, which can be viewed by opening BooklistControl.xaml.

```
<UserControl
    xmlns="http://schemas.microsoft.com/winfx/2006/xaml/presentation"
    xmlns:x="http://schemas.microsoft.com/winfx/2006/xaml"
    xmlns:d="http://schemas.microsoft.com/expression/blend/2008"
    xmlns:mc="http://schemas.openxmlformats.org/markup-compatibility/2006"
    mc:Ignorable="d"
    x:Class="Example14_2.BooklistControl"
```

```
    d:DesignWidth="462.314" d:DesignHeight="216.197">

    <Grid x:Name="LayoutRoot" Background="White" >
        <Border BorderBrush="Black" BorderThickness="1" Margin="0,0,0,0">
            <Grid x:Name="BooklistGrid" Background="LightGray">
                <Grid.ColumnDefinitions>
                    <ColumnDefinition Width="10" />
                    <ColumnDefinition Width="auto" />
                    <ColumnDefinition Width="10" />
                    <ColumnDefinition Width="auto"/>
                    <ColumnDefinition Width="10" />
                </Grid.ColumnDefinitions>
                <Grid.RowDefinitions>
                    <RowDefinition Height="10" />
                    <RowDefinition Height="auto" />
                    <RowDefinition Height="auto" />
                    <RowDefinition Height="auto" />
                    <RowDefinition Height="auto" />
                    <RowDefinition Height="auto" />
                    <RowDefinition Height="auto" />
                    <RowDefinition Height="10" />
                </Grid.RowDefinitions>

                <TextBlock Text="Book Image: " Grid.Row="1" Grid.Column="1"
                           Foreground="Blue" FontSize="12"/>
                <Image x:Name="bookImage" Stretch="Fill" Width="80" Height="100"
                       Margin="1" Grid.Row="1" Grid.Column="3"
                       HorizontalAlignment="Left"/>
                <TextBlock Text="Title: " Grid.Row="2" Grid.Column="1"
                           Foreground="Blue" FontSize="12"/>
                <TextBlock x:Name="bookTitle" Grid.Row="2" Grid.Column="3"
                           Width="350" TextWrapping="Wrap" FontWeight="Bold"/>
                <TextBlock Text="Subtitle: " Grid.Row="3" Grid.Column="1"
                           Foreground="Blue" FontSize="12"/>
                <TextBlock x:Name="bookSubtitle" Grid.Row="3" Grid.Column="3"
                           Width="350" TextWrapping="Wrap" FontSize="12"/>
                <TextBlock Text="Author: " Grid.Row="4" Grid.Column="1"
                           Foreground="Blue" FontSize="12"/>
                <TextBlock x:Name="bookAuthor" Grid.Row="4" Grid.Column="3"
                           Width="350" TextWrapping="Wrap"/>
                <TextBlock Text="ISBN: " Grid.Row="5" Grid.Column="1"
                           Foreground="Blue" FontSize="12"/>
                <TextBlock x:Name="bookISBN" Grid.Row="5" Grid.Column="3"
                           Width="350" TextWrapping="Wrap"/>
                <TextBlock Text="Publish Date: " Grid.Row="6" Grid.Column="1"
                           Foreground="Blue" FontSize="12"/>
                <TextBlock x:Name="bookPublishDate" Grid.Row="6" Grid.Column="3"
                           Width="350" TextWrapping="Wrap"/>
            </Grid>
        </Border>
    </Grid>
</UserControl>
```

This XAML is almost identical to that generated by Expression Blend when you originally create the UI and layout for the book list in the main page.

Data Binding

In the above section, Expreesion Blend created a Booklist user control that encapsulates the Booklist UI. Now you can reuse the control to create as many booklists as you want. Here, we'll create three booklist controls by modifying the Page.xaml file to the following:

```
<UserControl
    xmlns="http://schemas.microsoft.com/winfx/2006/xaml/presentation"
    xmlns:x="http://schemas.microsoft.com/winfx/2006/xaml"
    x:Class="Example14_2.Page" xmlns:Example14_2="clr-namespace:Example14_2"
    Width="470">

    <ScrollViewer>
        <StackPanel>
            <Example14_2:BooklistControl x:Name="csharpControl"/>
            <Example14_2:BooklistControl x:Name="wpfControl" />
            <Example14_2:BooklistControl x:Name="silverlightControl" />
        </StackPanel>
    </ScrollViewer>
</UserControl>
```

Now we need to create a Booklist data model class that allows you to establish corresponding data binding between the UI and the information about the book. You can add this class, named Booklist, to the bottom of the code-behind file of Page.xaml.cs. Here I present the entire code listing for your reference:

```
using System;
using System.Windows;
using System.Windows.Controls;
using System.Windows.Media;
using System.Windows.Media.Imaging;

namespace Example14_2
{
    public partial class Page : UserControl
    {
        // Define Booklist data models:
        private Booklist csharpBooklist;
        private Booklist wpfBooklist;
        private Booklist silverlightBooklist;

        public Page()
        {
            // Required to initialize variables
            InitializeComponent();
            BooklistBinding();
        }

        private void BooklistBinding()
        {
            // Create three Booklist objects:
            csharpBooklist = new Booklist()
            {
                ImageUri = new BitmapImage(new Uri("csharp.jpg",
                                           UriKind.Relative)),
```

```
                Title = "Practical C# Charts and Graphics",
                SubTitle = "Advanced Chart and Graphics Programming for
                            Real-World .NET Applications",
                Author = "Jack Xu",
                ISBN = "978-0-9793725-0-6",
                PublishDate = "March, 2007"
            };

            wpfBooklist = new Booklist()
            {
                ImageUri = new BitmapImage(new Uri("wpf.jpg",
                                           UriKind.Relative)),
                Title = "Practical WPF Graphics Programming",
                SubTitle = "Advanced .NET Graphics Development with the
                            Windows Presentation Foundation",
                Author = "Jack Xu",
                ISBN = "978-0-9793725-1-3",
                PublishDate = "Nov. 2007"
            };

            silverlightBooklist = new Booklist()
            {
                ImageUri = new BitmapImage(new Uri("silverlight.jpg",
                                           UriKind.Relative)),
                Title = "Practical Silverlight Programming",
                SubTitle = "Advanced  Graphics and User Interface
                            Development With Silverlight 2.0",
                Author = "Jack Xu",
                ISBN = "978-0-9793725-2-0",
                PublishDate = "August, 2008"
            };

            // Bind Booklist objects to BooklistControls:
            csharpControl.DataContext = csharpBooklist;
            wpfControl.DataContext = wpfBooklist;
            silverlightControl.DataContext = silverlightBooklist;
        }
    }

    public class Booklist
    {
        public BitmapImage ImageUri {get; set;}
        public string Title { get; set; }
        public string SubTitle { get; set; }
        public string Author { get; set; }
        public string ISBN { get; set; }
        public string PublishDate { get; set; }
    }
}
```

Here, we create the Booklist class using the new automatic properties language feature. Then, within the code-behind file of Page.xaml.cs, you can instantiate any number of Booklist objects. In this example, we create three Booklist objects, which represent my books about C#, WPF, and Silverlight, respectively. We then programmatically bind the Booklist objects to BooklistControls on the page.

You can do that by setting the DataContext property on each BooklistControl to the appropriate book list data model, as listed in the BooklistBinding method:

```
// Bind Booklist objects to BooklistControls:
csharpControl.DataContext = csharpBooklist;
wpfControl.DataContext = wpfBooklist;
silverlightControl.DataContext = silverlightBooklist;
```

The last step is to add Binding statements within the BooklistControl.xaml file, which will set up data binding between the corresponding properties (Source and Text) of the Image and TextBlock controls within the user control and the properties on the Booklist data model objects:

```
<Image x:Name="bookImage" Stretch="Fill" Width="80" Height="100" Margin="1"
       Grid.Row="1" Grid.Column="3" HorizontalAlignment="Left"
       Source="{Binding ImageUri}"/>
<TextBlock x:Name="bookTitle" Grid.Row="2" Grid.Column="3" Width="350"
           TextWrapping="Wrap" FontWeight="Bold" Text="{Binding Title}"/>
<TextBlock x:Name="bookSubtitle" Grid.Row="3" Grid.Column="3" Width="350"
           TextWrapping="Wrap" FontSize="12" Text="{Binding SubTitle}"/>
<TextBlock x:Name="bookAuthor" Grid.Row="4" Grid.Column="3" Width="350"
           TextWrapping="Wrap" Text="{Binding Author}"/>
<TextBlock x:Name="bookISBN" Grid.Row="5" Grid.Column="3" Width="350"
           TextWrapping="Wrap" Text="{Binding ISBN}"/>
<TextBlock x:Name="bookPublishDate" Grid.Row="6" Grid.Column="3" Width="350"
           TextWrapping="Wrap" Text="{Binding PublishDate}"/>
```

If you press F5 to run the project, you'll obtain the exact same result shown in Figure 14-2.

Creating a Silverlight Class Library

As mentioned previously, custom user controls can only be reused within a single Silverlight application. While this single application assembly model may suffice for some applications, Silverlight also allows you to create additional class libraries (DLLs). The reasons for implementing library assemblies in Silverlight include:

- Enabling developers to build reusable, factored units of UI and functionality that can be shared across multiple Silverlight applications.
- Allowing third-party control developers to package, distribute, and sell custom controls.
- Factoring an application's UI and code using a combination of in-package and on-demand files to improve initial application download and startup times and overall perceived performance.

In this section, we will create a Silverlight class library for the same booklist application, which was dicussed previously in Examples 14-1 and 14-2.

Silverlight Class Library Example

Start with Visual Studio 2008 and create a new project to bring up the New Project window. In this case, instead of selecting Silverlight Application, you will need to select Silverlight Class Library, and name it Example14-3, as shown in Figure 14-5.

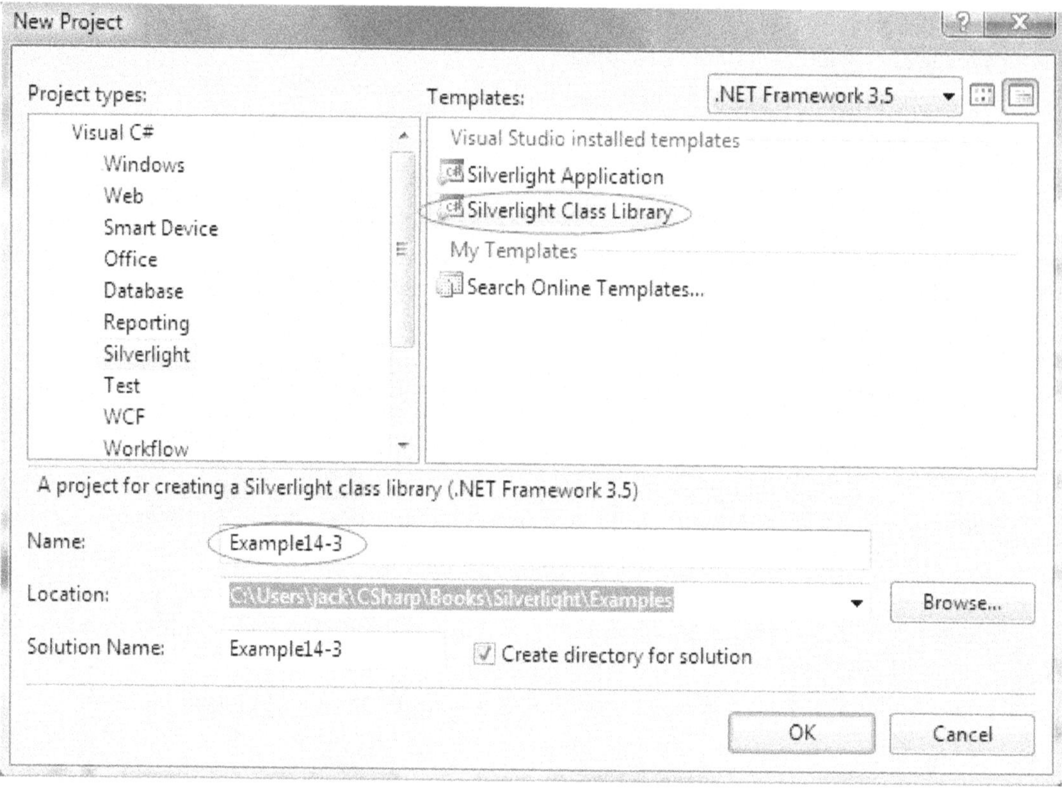

Figure 14-5 New Project window in Visual Studio 2008.

Rename Class1.cs Booklist.cs in Solution Explorer and enable Visual Studio 2008 to change the Class1 class's name reference in the project.

The next step is to add a generic.xaml file to the project, which will hold the default UI styles for the controls (such as the TextBlock and Image controls in our booklist example) in this Control Library. Right click the project in Solution Explorer, Select Add – New Items… In the Add New Item window, select Text File and name it generic.xaml, as shown in Figure 14-6.

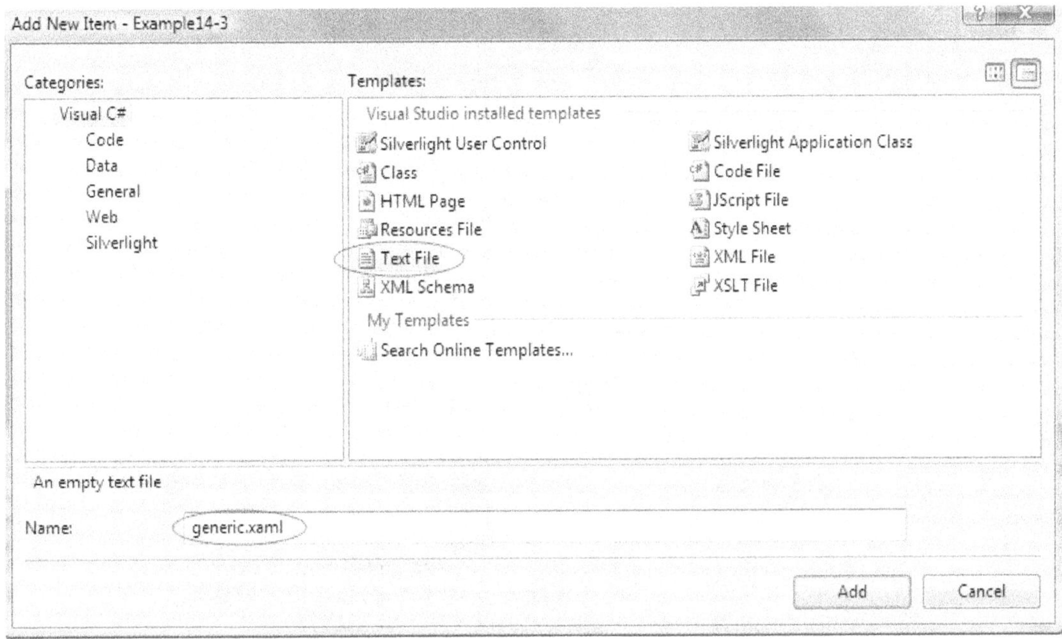

Figure 14-6 Add a generic.xaml file to the project.

Implementing Class Library

First, we need to add default UI styles to the generic.xaml file. Here is the XAML code of generic.xaml:

```
<ResourceDictionary
    xmlns="http://schemas.microsoft.com/winfx/2006/xaml/presentation"
    xmlns:x="http://schemas.microsoft.com/winfx/2006/xaml"
    xmlns:local="clr-namespace:Example14_3;assembly=Example14-3">

    <Style TargetType="local:Booklist">

        <Setter Property="Template">
            <Setter.Value>
                <ControlTemplate TargetType="local:Booklist">

                    <Grid x:Name="RootElement" Background="White" Margin="5">
                        <Border BorderBrush="Black" BorderThickness="1"
                                Margin="0,0,0,0">
                            <Grid x:Name="BooklistGrid" Background="LightGray">
                                <Grid.ColumnDefinitions>
                                    <ColumnDefinition Width="10" />
                                    <ColumnDefinition Width="auto" />
                                    <ColumnDefinition Width="10" />
                                    <ColumnDefinition Width="auto"/>
                                    <ColumnDefinition Width="10" />
                                </Grid.ColumnDefinitions>
                                <Grid.RowDefinitions>
                                    <RowDefinition Height="10" />
```

```
                                    <RowDefinition Height="auto" />
                                    <RowDefinition Height="auto" />
                                    <RowDefinition Height="auto" />
                                    <RowDefinition Height="auto" />
                                    <RowDefinition Height="auto" />
                                    <RowDefinition Height="auto" />
                                    <RowDefinition Height="10" />
                                </Grid.RowDefinitions>

        <TextBlock Text="Book Image: " Grid.Row="1" Grid.Column="1"
                   Foreground="Blue" FontSize="12"/>
        <Image x:Name="bookImage" Stretch="Fill" Width="80" Height="100"
               Margin="1" Grid.Row="1" Grid.Column="3"
               HorizontalAlignment="Left"/>
        <TextBlock Text="Title: " Grid.Row="2" Grid.Column="1"
                   Foreground="Blue" FontSize="12"/>
        <TextBlock x:Name="bookTitle" Grid.Row="2" Grid.Column="3" Width="350"
                   TextWrapping="Wrap" FontWeight="Bold"/>
        <TextBlock Text="Subtitle: " Grid.Row="3" Grid.Column="1"
                   Foreground="Blue" FontSize="12"/>
        <TextBlock x:Name="bookSubtitle" Grid.Row="3" Grid.Column="3"
                   Width="350" TextWrapping="Wrap" FontSize="12"/>
        <TextBlock Text="Author: " Grid.Row="4" Grid.Column="1"
                   Foreground="Blue" FontSize="12"/>
        <TextBlock x:Name="bookAuthor" Grid.Row="4" Grid.Column="3"
                   Width="350" TextWrapping="Wrap"/>
        <TextBlock Text="ISBN: " Grid.Row="5" Grid.Column="1"
                   Foreground="Blue" FontSize="12"/>
        <TextBlock x:Name="bookISBN" Grid.Row="5" Grid.Column="3"
                   Width="350" TextWrapping="Wrap"/>
        <TextBlock Text="Publish Date: " Grid.Row="6" Grid.Column="1"
                   Foreground="Blue" FontSize="12"/>
        <TextBlock x:Name="bookPublishDate" Grid.Row="6" Grid.Column="3"
                   Width="350" TextWrapping="Wrap"/>
                                  </Grid>
                          </Border>
                      </Grid>

                  </ControlTemplate>
              </Setter.Value>
          </Setter>
      </Style>

  </ResourceDictionary>
```

Here, we create a ResourceDictionary and add a reference to the xml namespace:

```
xmlns:local="clr-namespace:Example14_3;assembly=Example14-3">
```

We then add the Style tags to define the style for our control. Within the Style tag's TargetType, we specify the target control (Booklist in our example). We also need to assign the TargetType for the ControlTemplate property with Booklist as well.

With a Style, you can define the full appearance of a control, including a Storyboard for visual state transitions. The user interface of the current Booklist control simply includes an Image and several TextBlock controls, which are held by a Grid panel. This part of the code is almost identical to that used in the previous two examples, Example14-1 and Example14-2. You can copy the code from Example14-2 and paste it here.

Like we did in Example14-1, you need to define the corresponding dependency properties of the control library in order to expose them to outside world. You should implement these dependency properties and logic in Booklist.cs. Here is the code listing of this file:

```
using System;
using System.Windows;
using System.Windows.Controls;
using System.Windows.Media;
using System.Windows.Media.Imaging;

namespace Example14_3
{
    public class Booklist : Control
    {
        public Booklist()
        {
            this.DefaultStyleKey = typeof(Booklist);
            Loaded += new RoutedEventHandler(Page_Loaded);
        }

        void Page_Loaded(object sender, RoutedEventArgs e)
        {
            Image bookImage = GetTemplateChild("bookImage") as Image;
            TextBlock bookTitle = GetTemplateChild("bookTitle") as TextBlock;
            TextBlock bookSubtitle =
                      GetTemplateChild("bookSubtitle") as TextBlock;
            TextBlock bookAuthor = GetTemplateChild("bookAuthor") as TextBlock;
            TextBlock bookISBN = GetTemplateChild("bookISBN") as TextBlock;
            TextBlock bookPublishDate =
                      GetTemplateChild("bookPublishDate") as TextBlock;

            bookImage.Source = ImageUri;
            bookTitle.Text = Title;
            bookSubtitle.Text = Subtitle;
            bookAuthor.Text = Author;
            bookISBN.Text = ISBN;
            bookPublishDate.Text = PublishDate;
        }

        public static readonly DependencyProperty ImageUriProperty =
           DependencyProperty.Register("ImageUri",
               typeof(BitmapImage), typeof(Booklist),
            new PropertyMetadata(new PropertyChangedCallback(ImageUriChanged)));

        public BitmapImage ImageUri
        {
            get { return (BitmapImage)GetValue(ImageUriProperty); }
            set { SetValue(ImageUriProperty, value); }
        }

        private static void ImageUriChanged(DependencyObject sender,
                DependencyPropertyChangedEventArgs e)
```

```
{
    Booklist control = sender as Booklist;
    control.ImageUri = (BitmapImage)e.NewValue;
}

public static readonly DependencyProperty TitleProperty =
    DependencyProperty.Register("Title",
        typeof(string), typeof(Booklist),
    new PropertyMetadata(new PropertyChangedCallback(StringChanged)));

public string Title
{
    get { return (string)GetValue(TitleProperty); }
    set { SetValue(TitleProperty, value); }
}

public static readonly DependencyProperty SubtitleProperty =
   DependencyProperty.Register("Subtitle",
       typeof(string), typeof(Booklist),
   new PropertyMetadata(new PropertyChangedCallback(StringChanged)));

public string Subtitle
{
    get { return (string)GetValue(SubtitleProperty); }
    set { SetValue(SubtitleProperty, value); }
}

public static readonly DependencyProperty AuthorProperty =
   DependencyProperty.Register("Author",
       typeof(string), typeof(Booklist),
   new PropertyMetadata(new PropertyChangedCallback(StringChanged)));

public string Author
{
    get { return (string)GetValue(AuthorProperty); }
    set { SetValue(AuthorProperty, value); }
}

public static readonly DependencyProperty ISBNProperty =
   DependencyProperty.Register("ISBN", typeof(string), typeof(Booklist),
   new PropertyMetadata(new PropertyChangedCallback(StringChanged)));

public string ISBN
{
    get { return (string)GetValue(ISBNProperty); }
    set { SetValue(ISBNProperty, value); }
}

public static readonly DependencyProperty PublishDateProperty =
   DependencyProperty.Register("PublishDate",
       typeof(string), typeof(Booklist),
   new PropertyMetadata(new PropertyChangedCallback(StringChanged)));

public string PublishDate
{
```

```
            get { return (string)GetValue(PublishDateProperty); }
            set { SetValue(PublishDateProperty, value); }
        }

        private static void StringChanged(DependencyObject sender,
                DependencyPropertyChangedEventArgs e)
        {
            Booklist control = sender as Booklist;
            if (e.Property == TitleProperty)
                control.Title = (string)e.NewValue;
            else if (e.Property == SubtitleProperty)
                control.Subtitle = (string)e.NewValue;
            else if (e.Property == AuthorProperty)
                control.Author = (string)e.NewValue;
            else if (e.Property == ISBNProperty)
                control.ISBN = (string)e.NewValue;
            else if (e.Property == PublishDateProperty)
                control.PublishDate = (string)e.NewValue;
        }
    }
}
```

You can see from the above code that the Booklist class inherits from the Control base class. This base class can be changed according to your application's requirements. For example, it can be a UserControl or even a Button control. The definition for the dependency properties of the control library is identical to that used in the code-behind file of Example14-1. The only difference is that you can't directly reference the control names defined in generic.xaml. You have to use the GetTemplateChild method to retrieve the corresponding controls, as we did inside the Page_loaded handler:

```
Image bookImage = GetTemplateChild("bookImage") as Image;
TextBlock bookTitle = GetTemplateChild("bookTitle") as TextBlock;
TextBlock bookSubtitle = GetTemplateChild("bookSubtitle") as TextBlock;
TextBlock bookAuthor = GetTemplateChild("bookAuthor") as TextBlock;
TextBlock bookISBN = GetTemplateChild("bookISBN") as TextBlock;
TextBlock bookPublishDate =
          GetTemplateChild("bookPublishDate") as TextBlock;
```

Then you can bind dependency properties to the corresponding controls:

```
bookImage.Source = ImageUri;
bookTitle.Text = Title;
bookSubtitle.Text = Subtitle;
bookAuthor.Text = Author;
bookISBN.Text = ISBN;
bookPublishDate.Text = PublishDate;
```

I should point out here that you can establish data bindings directly using TemplateBinding in generic.xaml. However, I found that while the TemplateBinding works fine for the TextBlock controls, it doesn't work for the Image control. That is why I use the above step for data binding.

Now we have finished the implementation of our Booklist class library. Press F5 to build the project. If everything is fine at this point, the control library is ready for use in different Silverlight applications.

Testing Booklist Library

To test the Booklist class library created in the last section, we need to create a Silverlight Application project. In Solution Explorer, right click the Solution's node, select Add – New Project… to bring up the Add New Project window. Select the Silverlight Application template and name it TestBooklist. Make the TestBooklist project your Startup Project by right-clicking the Project's node and selecting Set as Startup Project.

In order to use the Booklist control library in our TestBooklist application, we need to add a reference to the Control Library project. Right-click the References node under the TestBooklist project and select Add Reference… to bring up the Add Reference dialog window. Click the Project tab, select the Example4-3 project (the assembly name for our Booklist library), and hit OK.

You can now use the Booklist library within the page. First, you need to add an xml namespace definition to the UserControl tag.

```
xmlns:local="clr-namespace:Example14_3;assembly=Example14-3"
```

Then the Booklist library can be used as a standard Silverlight control. Here is the XAML of this test project:

```
<UserControl x:Class="TestBooklist.Page"
    xmlns="http://schemas.microsoft.com/winfx/2006/xaml/presentation"
    xmlns:x="http://schemas.microsoft.com/winfx/2006/xaml"
    xmlns:local="clr-namespace:Example14_3;assembly=Example14-3"
    Width="480" Height="500">
    <Grid x:Name="LayoutRoot" Background="White">
        <ScrollViewer>
            <StackPanel>
                <local:Booklist
                       ImageUri="csharp.jpg"
                       Title="Practical C# Charts and Graphics"
                       Subtitle="Advanced Chart and Graphics Programming for
                                 Real-World .NET Applications"
                       Author="Jack Xu" ISBN="978-0-9793725-0-6"
                       PublishDate="March, 2007"/>

                <local:Booklist
                       ImageUri="wpf.jpg"
                       Title = "Practical WPF Graphics Programming"
                       Subtitle = "Advanced .NET Graphics Development with
                                   the Windows Presentation Foundation"
                       Author = "Jack Xu" ISBN = "978-0-9793725-1-3"
                       PublishDate = "Nov. 2007"/>

                <local:Booklist
                       ImageUri="silverlight.jpg"
                       Title="Practical Silverlight Programming"
                       Subtitle="Advanced  Graphics and User Interface
                                 Development With Silverlight 2.0"
                       Author="Jack Xu" ISBN="978-0-9793725-2-0"
                       PublishDate="August, 2008"/>
            </StackPanel>
        </ScrollViewer>
    </Grid>
</UserControl>
```

Of course, you will need to add three book cover images to the project.

Press F5 to run the application. The result will be the same as that shown in Figure 14-2.

In this chapter, we created a booklist control using three different approaches. You learned the detailed procedure for custom control and class library development in Silverlight. You should now know how to create your own custom controls for your real-world Silverlight applications.

Index

Also Available from Dr. Jack Xu:

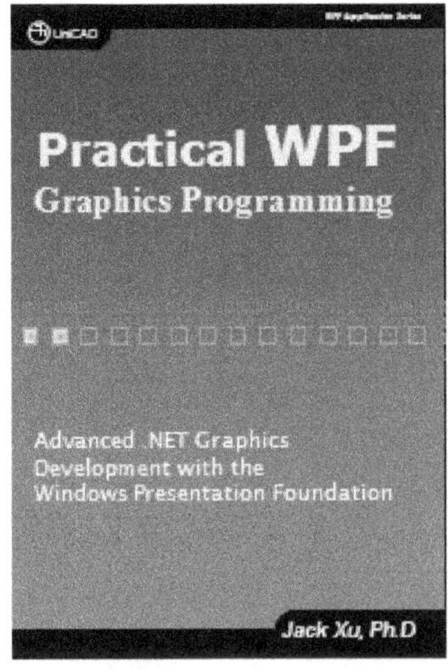

Programming expert Jack Xu provides you with everything you need to add advanced graphics to your applications in this in-depth introduction to graphics programming with the Windows Presentation Foundation (WPF). From basic 2D shapes to complex interactive 3D models, Dr. Xu clearly explains every step it takes to build a variety of WPF graphics applications using code examples. You'll learn how to use WPF to create impressive graphics effects and high-fidelity user interfaces. This book includes:

- An overview of WPF graphics capabilities and the mathematical basics of computer graphics.
- Step-by-step procedures to create a variety of 2D and 3D custom geometries and shapes with complete ready-to-run XAML and C# code for each application.
- Powerful 2D chart applications and user controls that can be directly used in your WPF applications or can be easily modified to create your own sophisticated chart packages.
- Detailed procedures of how to create various 3D surfaces in WPF using rectangular meshes.
- An introduction to building physics-based models, games, and fractals.
- Advanced color, lighting, and shading effects for 3D graphics objects.
- Direct interaction with graphics models, including animation, transformations, hit-testing, and mouse events.

For details, see www.drxudotnet.com

Also Available from Dr. Jack Xu:

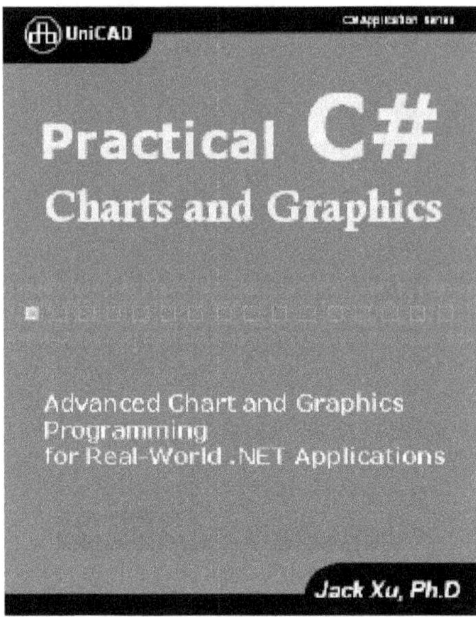

www.ingramcontent.com/pod-product-compliance
Lightning Source LLC
Chambersburg PA
CBHW080135060326
40689CB00018B/3793

* 9 7 8 0 9 7 9 3 7 2 5 2 0 *